THE
GLASS
CANDLESTICK
BOOK

VOLUME 2
FOSTORIA TO JEFFERSON

Identification and Value Guide

Tom Felt and
Elaine & Rich Stoer

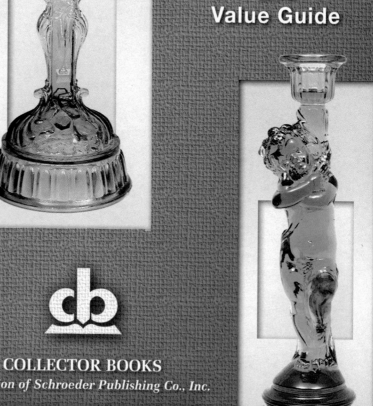

db

COLLECTOR BOOKS
A Division of Schroeder Publishing Co., Inc.

Front cover: Heisey No. 142 Cascade in sahara (top right), Fostoria No. 1103 Queen Anne Lustre in green with crystal candle cup and bobeche, Fostoria No. 2694 Arlington duo candlestick in milk glass, Imperial No. 320/2 Double Scroll candlestick in green ice, Indiana No. 373 two-light candlestick in crystal (center), Heisey No. 134 Trident two-light candlestick in alexandrite, Hazel Atlas Florentine No. 2 candlestick in yellow, and Fostoria No. 2535 candlestick in ruby.

Back cover: Imperial No. 5033 Cathay candle servant in crystal satin, Indiana No. 305 two-light candlestick in milk glass, Indiana/Tiara No. 10345 Sandwich tall candlestick in Chantilly green, Gillinder No. 4 handled chamberstick in custard, Gillinder No. 7 crucifix candlestick in amethyst, Imperial No. 43790 candleholder in caramel slag, Heisey No. 111 Cherub in moongleam, and Jeannette No. 3423 Eagle candleholder in blue iridescent.

Cover design by Beth Summers
Book design by Terri Hunter

COLLECTOR BOOKS
P.O. Box 3009
Paducah, Kentucky 42002-3009
www.collectorbooks.com

Copyright © 2003 Tom Felt and Elaine & Rich Stoer

Searching For A Publisher?

We are always looking for people knowledgeable within their fields. If you feel that there is a real need for a book on your collectible subject and have a large comprehensive collection, contact Collector Books.

The current values in this book should be used only as a guide. They are not intended to set prices, which vary from one section of the country to another. Auction prices as well as dealer prices vary greatly and are affected by condition as well as demand. Neither the authors nor the publisher assumes responsibility for any losses that might be incurred as a result of consulting this guide.

CONTENTS

INTRODUCTION

Almost every manufacturer of glassware included at least one candlestick among their offerings to the public — and for most companies, candlesticks were a staple, offered in a bewildering variety of shapes and sizes. This volume is the second in a series that will attempt to present a comprehensive sampling of these candlesticks. It is, of course, impossible to include every candlestick ever made — in some instances because there just hasn't been enough research done on some of these companies, while in other cases we were not able to photograph or find original catalog representations suitable for publication. We also made a decision to omit most candelabra (using as a rough definition those items that have removable arms, bobeches, and candle cups), only including such items when it seemed to us that they had particular importance or interest to collectors of candlesticks. Similarly, we have omitted votive candleholders, tea lights, and most other holders requiring non-standard candles.

Our focus has primarily been on American-made candlesticks. We will also include information on foreign reproductions whenever this information is available to us.

The arrangement of the book follows a standard format. Companies are listed alphabetically and are prefaced with a brief history. When possible, we show you examples of trademarks or labels used by the company. The listings for the candlesticks are presented chronologically, though sometimes this involves guesswork on our part. When possible, we show a photograph of each candlestick. If a photograph is not available, we provide a picture from an advertisement or company catalog. The accompanying text includes as much information as is available, including pattern numbers, names, dimensions, and dates of production, when known. Listings of colors and decorations, such as etchings and cuttings, have either been verified through research or the authors' personal knowledge, but necessarily are incomplete and should not be assumed to be comprehensive.

Many companies made candlesticks that closely resemble those made by other manufacturers. Whenever possible we have included additional pictures of the "lookalikes," but have set them apart in purple shaded boxes.

We have also tried to avoid making identifications that cannot be supported by current research. On a few occasions, however, we have found the temptation to do so irresistible. When this happens, our conclusions will also be set apart in a purple shaded box, not to be taken as gospel, but just as a reasonably informed guess. As we continue to uncover new information for previous volumes, we will share it with you.

In addition to a standard index, a visual index will also be found at the rear of this volume. It presents all of the candlesticks in the book in such a way that you can quickly browse through them to tentatively identify a candlestick, when you do not know its manufacturer.

The authors welcome comments from readers. You can write us in care of the publisher or e-mail us directly at tomfelt@bigfoot.com or rstoer@worldnet.att.net.

PRICING

Our approach to pricing is to assign a range for each listing. Rarer items will generally have a broader range than the less volatile commonplace ones. Prices shown are always for each piece. Since pairs are often more desirable than singles, you may be able to lean toward the high end of the range for each candleholder that is part of a pair.

We've spent several years compiling sales data from eBay and other auctions as well as from antique dealers and private collectors in an attempt to provide realistic values for each piece shown. Despite this effort, we've not been able to gather any direct pricing information for several of the thousands of items shown in these volumes. Some of these we've attempted to price based on information from items of similar age, quality, and design. Others we don't feel that we can price with any degree of accuracy and have omitted their pricing information altogether.

In some cases our research has led us to figures that differ greatly from those published by other authors. When we vary from the "norm" in this manner it is based on good data or we wouldn't take such a stand. Like most authors, we are not attempting to set prices, but only to reflect what our own research has shown. As always, the final price is an issue to be settled between the buyer and seller.

All prices listed in this book are for items in excellent or mint condition. Chips, cracks, stains, scratches, worn paint, etc. all affect an item's value, often greatly (some scratches to the bottom of a piece are to be expected and will have no bearing on the value). The value of very old (nineteenth century) and very rare pieces is less affected by minor imperfections, but items that are more commonplace may be virtually un-saleable if damaged. We do not mean to discourage the purchase of an item just because it is flawed. Several of the pieces in our collection are less-than-perfect and we still enjoy them immensely. Simply remember to adjust its value accordingly when buying (or selling) a damaged piece.

An item's desirability (and thereby its value) is based on scarcity, design, quality, and condition. The following are some additional guidelines as to what is desirable in today's market. Keep in mind that these are generalities and will not apply in all cases:

1) If an item is available in color, the colored version will generally sell for more than the crystal.
   a) The most desirable colors are ruby and cobalt, sometimes bringing a price ten times that of the same piece in crystal. Dark amber is the least desirable, and often brings about the same price as crystal. Other colors fall somewhere in between.
   b) Items made from fusing two pieces of different colored glass together, such as those made by Boston & Sandwich, Fenton, and Heisey, are often worth far more than single color items of the same type.
2) Items with etched patterns (usually on the base) are worth more than plain ones.
3) Nice or elaborate wheel cuttings add value. Very simple ones add little or nothing.
4) Nice hand painted designs add value (note the word "nice").
5) Items with heavy bands of gold trim are often worth less than the same item without.
6) Items with (factory) bobeches and prisms are worth more than the same piece without.
   a) Colored or etched bobeches can greatly add to the value of the item.
   b) Large, colored, or otherwise unusual prisms will generally add value.

SIZES

Sizes listed are taken from actual examples when available, otherwise they are taken from manufacturers' catalogs. Catalog sizes are often inaccurate and change for the same item from one catalog to another. Therefore our sizes will often not match the manufacturers catalog's size. The items themselves also vary from one to another; i.e., bases are often formed by hand while the piece is still warm. The more the base is "flared," the shorter the candleholder will be and the wider the base will be, causing both dimensions to be different from the same piece with a slightly different shaped base. Size differences of ± ¼" or more from those listed are not unusual.

ACKNOWLEDGMENTS

This book could not have been written without the assistance of many people. Among them, we would like to express our special gratitude to Walt Adams, Mary Arrojo, Shirley Bolman, Tom and Neila Bredehoft, Bill Burke, Frank Chiarenza, Harry and Neda Freed, Bob and Helen Jones, Vicki Meehan (Heisey Collectors of America), Linda Polen, Gary Schneider, Dean Six, and Harold and Mildred Willey.

FOSTORIA GLASS COMPANY, Fostoria, Ohio (1887 – 1891); Moundsville, West Virginia (1891 – 1986).

This firm was organized by a group of investors from Wheeling, West Virginia, at a time when the promise of cheap natural gas was luring many new companies to the Fostoria, Ohio, area. However, the gas supplies proved to be short-lived, so in 1891 they moved to Moundsville, West Virginia, where coal (from which the hotter burning gas needed for glass production could be produced) was abundant. Initial production was limited to pressed glass, but after the move to Moundsville, they also began manufacturing high-quality blown stemware. In 1909, the company elected W.A.B. Dalzell as president and general manager, a position he held until his death in 1928. It was under his stewardship that Fostoria firmly established itself as an industry leader, when between 1924 and 1926 they introduced several new patterns in attractive colors, including the first all-glass dinnerware set. In order to promote their expanded lines they embarked on one of the industry's first national advertising campaigns. Sustained advertising in popular women's magazines made Fostoria a household word by the end of the decade. In 1928, Calvin B. Roe became president and guided the company through the depression years with still more innovative marketing techniques. These included having Fostoria's salespeople set up in-store displays and instruct each retailer's personnel on how to market their glassware to housewives and brides-to-be. W.A.B. Dalzell's son, William F. Dalzell, served as president from 1945 to 1958, and it was during this time that Fostoria's business reached its peak. In 1950, they made over eight million pieces of glass and employed nearly 1000 people, making them one of the largest manufacturers of handmade glassware in the United States. In 1965, they bought the Morgantown Glassware Guild, which continued to operate under its own name but with Fostoria management until 1971. Fostoria continued to prosper for several years, but by May of 1982, rising production costs, foreign competition, and an aging plant forced them to cease the manufacture of pressed glass. They survived the next year by producing leaded crystal, and in 1983 were purchased by the Lancaster Colony Corporation. Limited pressed glass production resumed, but the company's fate had been sealed, and in 1986 the Moundsville factory closed its doors forever. The Fostoria brand name is still owned by Lancaster Colony and can be found on items produced by the Indiana Glass Co. (another subsidiary of Lancaster Colony) and on other pieces, some of them imported.

THE ABANDONED FOSTORIA FACTORY, MOUNDSVILLE, OHIO. TAKEN JULY, 2002.

Fostoria's many attractive designs were a large part of their long success. The cubist American pattern was introduced in 1915, and remained in continuous production from its inception until the factory closed. In fact, it's still being made by Lancaster Colony and is probably the single most successful pattern in the history of glassmaking. Another early pattern that survived until the end was Queen Anne (which began as Cascade and evolved into Colony and then Maypole).

Besides these early examples, the next four decades would see a plethora of stylish and popular designs emanate from Fostoria's remarkable designer, George Sakier (1897 – 1988). From the twenties to the fifties, he designed many of their most popular patterns. His role in Fostoria's success cannot be overstated. In a long career as artist and industrial designer, Sakier exhibited at many major art museums, designed for the 1933 and 1939 World's Fairs, served as art director for *Harper's Bazaar*, and designed furniture, bathroom fixtures, product labels, and even clothing. His association with Fostoria began in 1929 and continued until the factory closed, with the artist submitting designs from his home base (initially New York and later Paris). These included a majority of the candlesticks made between 1929 and 1986. In later years, he also designed candlesticks for Venini & Co. in Murano, Italy.

Colors

Fostoria's earliest colors were opal (milk glass, with some opalescence, 1897 to ca. 1915) and emerald (1898). Other early colors are known (opaque blue and green) that may have been experimental.

EARLY COLORS – 1924 THROUGH EARLY 1960S

amber	dark and light (light amber is almost a peach color)	1922 – 1941
amethyst	medium purple	1948 – 1961
aqua milk glass	opaque light blue	1957 – 1959
azure	light blue	1928 – 1932
azure tint	light blue, sometimes tending toward green	1936 – 1943
bittersweet	bright orange	1960 – 1962
blue	rich, medium blue	1924 – 1927
blue opalescent	blue with white highlights	1959 – 1970
burgundy	deep amethyst	1933 – 1941
canary	yellow-green (the actual color varied a lot)	1923 – 1925
Caribee blue	opalescent blue	1954 – 1957
coral sand	opalescent pink	1954 – 1957
ebony	black	1924 – 1942 and 1953 – 1963
empire green	rich, dark green	1933 – 1941 and 1948 – 1951
gold tint	yellow, very similar to the earlier topaz	1937 – 1943
green	medium green	1922 – 1941
green opalescent	green with white highlights	1959 – 1970
milk glass	opaque white	1953 – 1965
opal	crystal with white (opalescent) highlights	1959 – 1970
opaque jadite	jade (rare color)	1930s
orchid	lavender (not as rich as the later wistaria)	1926 – 1929
peach milk glass	opaque pink	1957 – 1959
pink opalescent	pink with white highlights	1959 – 1970
regal blue	dark or cobalt blue	1933 – 1941
rose	pink (sometimes called dawn)	1928 – 1941
ruby	red (originally called oriental ruby)	1934 – 1942
topaz	yellow	1929 – 1938
wistaria	light purple (lavender) that changes hue with lighting	1931 – 1938
yellow opalescent	yellow with white highlights	1959 – 1962

Other colors mentioned in early advertisements include mulberry pink (1922), amethyst (1922), turquoise (1922), champagne (1929 — probably an early name for topaz), spruce green (1951 – 1952), cinnamon (1951 – 1952 — possibly another name for amethyst), chartreuse (1951), spruce (1951), bitter green (1952 – 1953), dawn (1953), dusk (1953), honey (1953 – 1954), lime (1953 – 1954), tokay (1953 – 1954), firelight (1954), smoke (1955 – 1957), turquoise (1955), fawn (1958), harvest yellow (1958), mint green (1958), and sky blue (1958).

Fostoria referred to their transparent pink as both rose and dawn. This confusion seemed to be mostly in their advertisements as their catalogs generally referenced it as rose. Both names refer to the same color, so we'll use rose for consistency.

Two other colors underwent somewhat confusing changes in the 1930s. Fostoria's original yellow, introduced in 1929, was called topaz. In 1937, topaz was replaced with gold tint. It is unclear if the formula changed at all, but there seems to be little or no difference in the color. Advertisements in 1937 emphasized the appropriateness of the color for Fostoria's "golden jubilee," their fiftieth year of production. (It may be our imagination, but gold tint appears to be slightly greener.)

A change to another color's name has been virtually ignored by most books on Fostoria, perhaps because both the new name and the new color are so similar to the old. In 1936, azure tint was advertised as a brand new color. While it's possible that this was simply a re-introduction of azure (since there seems to be a gap in azure production after 1932), it was at about this time that Fostoria seemed to have trouble controlling the color, and many (but not all) pieces made after 1936 exhibit a green/blue tint not seen in the earlier azure. For that reason, we suspect that some change in the formula may have taken place at that time. Since most collectors find the pure blue more attractive, values of pieces with the green shading will be worth somewhat less than the stated price. Azure tint can be found on Baroque, Flame, and other patterns introduced between 1936 and 1943. Both azure tint and gold tint were discontinued in 1943.

LATE COLORS — AFTER 1960:

amber		1950s – 1980s
bittersweet	orange/yellow (amberina)	1960 – 1962
brown		1960s, 1972 – 1986
blue	various shades	1960s, 1977 – 1980s
cobalt blue	both medium and dark	1972 – 1980
copper blue	bright medium blue	1964 – 1973
crystal mist	satin finish	1980 – 1982
dark blue		1977 – 1986
fern green	Morgantown's moss green	1967 – 1968
gold yellow		1960 – 1965
gray		1973 – 1986
gray mist	transparent smokey color	1962 – 1971
green	various shades	1950s – 1980s
lavender	not as vivid as wistaria	1962 – 1970
light blue		1982 – 1986
nut brown	Imperial color	1985 – 1986
olive green		1963 – 1986
Mayan blue	Morgantown's peacock blue	1967 – 1968
moss green		1960
peach	pale pink	1980 – 1986
peach mist	pale pink, satin finish	1980 – 1982
pink		1957 – 1986
royal blue	cobalt blue	1961 – 1965
ruby		1960s – 1970s, 1981 – 1986
sun gold		1985
tangerine	Morgantown's gypsy fire	1967 – 1968
teal blue		1960
teal green		1964 – 1970
ultra blue	dark blue (Imperial color)	1985 – 1986
yellow		1960 – 1970s, 1982 – 1983

Other colors mentioned in advertisements include green mist (1968), lemon twist (1968), pink lady (1968), flamingo orange (1968), onyx (1970), terra (1970), nutmeg (1970), plum (1971), snow (1973), sunrise (1973), midnight blue (1973), apple green (1974), antique blue (1975), black pearl (1968 – 1973), lemon twist (1972 – 1973), flaming orange (1972 – 1973), plum (1972 – 1974), apple green (1974 – 1975), blue mist (1980), and rust (1980).

Some of these colors are just changes of name and not necessarily new colors. In other cases, the same name was used for significantly different shades; e.g., cobalt blue was used both to describe a medium blue made in the 1970s and a deeper, true cobalt.

FINISHES

mother-of-pearl (light iridescence)	1924 – 1927
onyx lustre: mother-of-pearl (light iridescence) on ebony	1924 – 1927

Note: Other iridescent finishes were used by Fostoria in the early 1920s and later. Onyx lustre is sometimes called taffeta lustre by collectors. Onyx lustre was Fostoria's name. Fostoria's iridescence (mother-of-pearl) is easily removed! A good scrubbing of your $500.00+ pair of onyx lustre candlesticks may turn them into a nice pair of $35.00 black ones. Examine iridescent pieces carefully when shopping, and be wary of items with labels plastered on the iridescent surface. If you find this, have the seller remove the label before you buy. We are not aware of anyone else's iridescent finish exhibiting this problem.

Satin finishes were also used on many colors, beginning in 1934 with silver mist (crystal satin). Many other mist colors were offered over the years.

ETCHINGS

Many early candleholders were etched with floral designs that had no names or had only letter identifiers. Beginning in the 1920s, etchings were given names along with the numbers. The most popular of these seem to be June, Navarre, and Versailles. As such, these patterns often command the highest prices. Other popular patterns include Chintz, Corsage, Mayflower, Meadow Rose, Vesper, and Royal.

MISCELLANEOUS

By cross-referencing color, etching/cutting, and item manufacturing dates, you can narrow the date of manufacture of a particular candleholder to the point where they overlap. Consult the books listed in the bibliography to assist you in identifying etchings, cuttings, and other decorations.

Throughout their history, Fostoria had their own way of spelling bobeche (as bobache). When we use it in quotations, the quote is accurate.

LABELS AND LOGOS

The brown and white Fostoria label was used circa 1924 – 1957.

The red, white, and blue label was used from 1957 to 1986.

A round red, white, and blue label was used on items sold in Fostoria's outlet stores, and is found on items manufactured by Indiana in the years since Fostoria closed, including pieces that are not made from Fostoria molds. More recently, pieces imported from Europe will also be found with a rectangular Fostoria label.

LOGO, CA. 1913 – 1923

LABEL, 1924 – 1957

LABEL, 1957 – 1986

LABEL USED IN OUTLET STORES AND ON NON-FOSTORIA PIECES

No. 112 Cascade candlestick. Later became part of the Queen Anne line. 8¾" high (sometimes listed in catalogs as 9" high) with a 4¾" base. Circa 1889 – 1924. Made in crystal. Some early catalogs show the swirls reversed (i.e., clockwise on the base rather than counter-clockwise), but this was probably just an accident in the printing. An early catalog shows a No. 183 peg with spring socket designed to fit this candlestick, converting it to an oil lamp. Also available with a removable bobeche and prisms. This same shape was used as the base for the No. 4 lustre on the following page, as well as for a series of multiple-light candelabra and a banquet lamp. Although this candlestick is a match for the Colony line, it was never officially part of it since it was discontinued years before Colony was introduced. $30.00 – 35.00.

FO-1. NO. 112 CASCADE CANDLESTICK (LATER BECAME PART OF THE QUEEN ANNE LINE)

CASCADE COMPARISON

The Cascade pattern was reported by David Dalzell, president of Fostoria from 1968 to 1982, to be a direct copy of a Baccarat pattern (also copied by McKee). FO-1a provides a comparison of the candlesticks produced by the three companies, from left to right:

1) Baccarat (France). This candlestick was being made in the 1990s and might still be in production. It has a solid base, which makes it very heavy. The glass is of excellent quality and is mold marked "Baccarat" on the rim and marked again on the bottom with an acid etched Baccarat logo: "Baccarat (France)."

FO-1A: A COMPARISON OF SWIRL CANDLESTICKS, FROM LEFT TO RIGHT: BACCARAT (FRANCE), TWO VERSIONS; FOSTORIA'S NO. 112; McKEE "RAY"

2) This is an earlier version of the candlestick to its left. This one is in canary, but they were also made in crystal. Although smaller than the Fostoria, it is almost identical in shape, and we believe that Baccarat also made this candlestick in a larger size, very close to Fostoria's No. 112. This Baccarat is mold marked beneath the base with the word "Depose," which in this usage means roughly the same as "Registered." Some similar examples have been marked with "Depose Baccarat," while others have not been marked at all. An unmarked version of this candlestick in the same size would take an experienced eye to tell apart from the Fostoria, but don't worry too much about getting fooled, because the Baccarat candlesticks generally sell for quite a bit more than the Fostoria ones.

3) Fostoria's No. 112 candlestick.

4) McKee "Ray." Made in both milk glass, as shown, and crystal. Note the difference in the tops. This same candlestick was later made by the Kemple Glass Works, but Kemple added three small "nub" feet beneath the base.

FO-2. No. 4 LUSTRE CANDLESTICK

No. 4 lustre candlestick. Shown in early catalogs as part of the Cascade pattern. 9⅜" high with a 4¾" round base. Circa 1889 – 1924. Became part of the Colony line from 1938 to 1944. Made in crystal, with a fixed bobeche and ten prisms. Other candlesticks that were part of (or associated with) the Colony line are FO-15 (p. 14), FO-24 (p. 17), FO-123 through FO-125 (p. 46-47), and FO-137 (p. 50). Crystal: $40.00 – 50.00.

No. 5 handled candleholder. Shown in an early advertisement with other pieces from the Cascade pattern. 2½" high with a 3¼" base. Circa 1889 – 1904. Made in crystal. $35.00 – 45.00.

FO-3. No. 5
HANDLED
CANDLEHOLDER

No. 6 ribboned candleholder. Shown in an early advertisement with other pieces from the Cascade pattern. 3½" high and 4¼" across. Circa 1889 – 1904. Made in crystal, this candleholder was advertised as being available with "assorted colored ribbon" woven through the base. (See FO-4a.) A report in the *American Pottery and Glass Review*, November 14, 1899, referred to this piece as "The Vester, one of those attractive little pieces which catch the eye at first glance… so made that bright ribbons are run through the plate of the candlestick in many different colors, orange, blue, pink and red." The shape is very similar to a socket and bobeche from one of Fostoria's candelabra, but molded in a single piece and with the ribbon threaded through the holes intended for prism wires. Crystal: $35.00 – 50.00.

FO-4. No. 6 RIBBONED CANDLE-
HOLDER, FROM 1904 CATALOG

FO-4A. A VERY EARLY AD FROM DECEMBER 26, 1889, SHOWING (L TO R) THE No. 3 BANQUET CANDELABRA, No. 6 RIBBONED CANDLEHOLDER, No. 2 FOUR LIGHT CANDELABRA, AND No. 5 HANDLED CANDLEHOLDER

No. 140 Virginia handled candleholder. Unknown size. Circa 1888 – 1904. Crystal. $35.00 – 45.00.

FO-5. No. 140
VIRGINIA HANDLED
CANDLEHOLDER,
FROM 1904 CATALOG

Handled candleholder. 2½" high by 5¾" across. Is this Fostoria? The candle cup certainly bears a resemblance to the No. 140 handled candleholder on the previous page, but it differs in other respects — the swirls on the socket are reversed and the pattern on the base is completely different, as is the series of scallops on the base. It could be Hobbs, McKee, U.S. Glass, or any of the other early pattern glass companies — or it could be Fostoria. If anyone recognizes this pattern, please let us know.

FO-5B. CLOSE-UP OF PATTERN ON BASE OF UNKNOWN HANDLED CANDLEHOLDER

FO-5A. UNKNOWN HANDLED CANDLEHOLDER

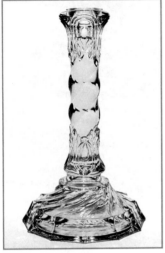

FO-6. No. 17 CANDLESTICK

No. 17 candlestick. 8¾" high with a 5¼" base. Circa 1892 – 1904. Crystal: $45.00 – 55.00.

FO-7. No. 18 CANDLESTICK FROM A 1904 CATALOG

No. 18 candlestick. Unknown size. Circa 1892 – 1904. Crystal: $45.00 – 55.00.

FO-8. No. 19 SAUCER CANDLE-HOLDER, FROM 1904 CATALOG

No. 19 saucer candleholder. Unknown size. Handled chamber stick. Circa 1892 – 1904. This is probably the piece referred to in the April 9, 1891, issue of the *American Pottery and Glass Reporter* as part of "a cheap line of glass boat candlesticks." Crystal. $35.00 – 45.00.

FO-9. No. 737
CANDLESTICK

No. 737 candlestick. 8½" high with a 3⅞" base. Circa 1898 – 1905. Made in crystal, this candleholder has six sides, a beaded top rim, and a deep-pressed floral design. $55.00 – 65.00.

FO-10. No. 543
CANDLESTICK
IN OPAL

No. 543 candlestick. 5⅞" high with a 3¾" square base. Circa 1900 – 1901. Offered in opal with Decoration No. 1 (green and gold or pink and gold on the raised portions) or Decoration No. 2 (same colors with a floral decal on the center of the panels). The example shown has very faint remains of the gold decoration on the top rim. $22.00 – 30.00.

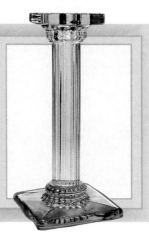

FO-11. No. 1064
CANDLESTICK

No. 1064 candlestick. 8" high with a 3¾" square base. Circa 1901 – 1925. Made in crystal. Came with a cut and polished base with a pontil (early examples also had a cut and polished top). A report in the *Crockery and Glass Journal*, September 19, 1901, mentioned this as a new candlestick with "a fluted Corinthian column." $60.00 – 75.00.

Note: This same report in the *Crockery and Glass Journal* also mentions a "regular square-sided stick" as new, a description that does not seem to match any of the candlesticks appearing in catalogs from the 1901 period.

FO-12. No. 1081
CANDLESTICK

No. 1081 candlestick. 8¼" high with a 4¼" hexagonal base. Circa 1902 – 1928. Made in crystal. Available with cutting No. 56. This candlestick was also used as the base for a Colonial Princess Lamp, with a font, chimney, and globe added. $25.00 – 35.00. Add 50 – 80% for cutting.

No. 1192 candlestick. 10½" high with a 5" three-toed base. Circa 1902 – 1906. Known only in crystal. This massive candlestick (two pounds in weight) with its religious symbols was probably made primarily for use by churches. It is very similar to a candlestick made by the U.S. Glass Company. (See FO-13a for a comparison.) Shown on the left is Fostoria's No. 1192. On the right is U.S. Glass's No. 101 candlestick (circa 1898 and possibly made earlier by Gillinder). A close comparison of catalog pictures reveals that there are differences in the design so minor that they might be assumed to be artist's errors, except that they can actually be found in the glass pieces when side by side. However, it is not necessary to search for these variances since the most notable difference is that the Fostoria version is made in one piece whereas the U.S. Glass version is made in two pieces, joined at the top of the base with a wafer. The U.S. Glass candlestick is known only in milk glass, but was probably made in crystal also. Crystal: $85.00 – 95.00.

FO-13. No. 1192
CANDLESTICK

FO-13A. COMPARISON OF FOSTORIA'S
No. 1192 CANDLESTICK IN CRYSTAL
AND U. S. GLASS COMPANY'S No. 101
CANDLESTICK IN OPAL

FO-14. No. 1103
CANDLESTICK

No. 1103 candlestick. This is the candlestick version of the lustres in FO-15 below, at least one of which became part of the Queen Anne pattern. 9¼" high with a 4¾" base (listed as 9½" high). Circa 1903 – 1928. Made in crystal. When introduced, these candlesticks were described by the *Crockery and Glass Journal*, September 24, 1903, as having "a cascade effect, the glass being twisted from base to top in a pleasing fashion." This candlestick was used as the base of the Diana Princess Lamp, with the addition of a fount, globe, and chimney. $50.00 – 65.00.

FO-15. No. 1103
QUEEN ANNE
LUSTRE, 14½"
HIGH, WITH
GREEN BASE

No. 1103 Queen Anne lustre, 14½" high, circa 1903 – 1928 and 1934 – 1942; No. 1103 Queen Anne lustres, 19½" high and 22½" high, circa 1903 – 1928. The 14½" size was made with the base cast in crystal, green, amber, or blue, all with crystal candle cups and bobeches. These colored versions were offered between 1926 and 1927. The two taller sizes were made in crystal only. The 14½" size was re-introduced in crystal as part of the Colony line in 1934. There were also a series of No. 1103 pedestals (11", 15", and 19") made using this base. Other candlesticks that were part of (or associated with) the Colony line are FO-2 (p. 10), FO-24 (p. 17), FO-123 through FO-125 (p. 46-47), and FO-137 (p. 50). For a later Queen Anne candlestick, see FO-73 (p. 31). 14½" crystal: $150.00 – 200.00; amber: $250.00 – 300.00; blue, green: $300.00 – 400.00. 19½" crystal: $200.00 – 250.00. 22½" crystal: $300.00 – 400.00.

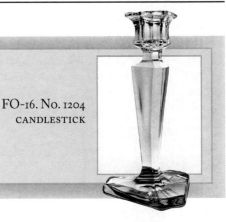

FO-16. No. 1204
CANDLESTICK

No. 1204 candlestick. 8" high with a 4" triangular base and a triangular stem (listed as a 8½" high in a 1924 catalog). Circa 1905 – 1928 and again in 1982 as No. CA 10/325. Made in crystal. The base and/or top can be found cut and polished. Found with the "D" etching or the No. 73 cutting. $35.00 – 40.00. Add 50 – 80% for etched, 20 – 40% for cut.

FO-17. No. 1205
CANDLESTICK

No. 1205 candlestick. 8" high with a 4" hexagonal base. Circa 1905 – 1925. Made in crystal. Available with a cut top and bottom with a ground pontil. $35.00 – 40.00.

FO-18. No. 1218
CANDLESTICK

No. 1218 candlestick. 7⅝" high with a 3¾" square base (listed as 8" high in catalogs). Circa 1905 – 1928. The base and sometimes the top can be found cut and polished. Made in crystal and can be found with No. 72, 320, and 345 cuttings as well as "A" and "E" etchings. Also made with silver deposit as No. 3218. Crystal: $30.00 – 40.00. Add 40 – 80% for etched, 20 – 40% for cut.

FO-19. No. 19
CANDLESTICKS
IN 12" AND 15"
HEIGHTS

No. 19 candlestick, 12" high with a 4¼" square base. Circa 1905 – 1924. Also made in 10" and 15" heights, with these sizes apparently only produced for a few years. 7" and 18" heights have also been reported, but we have been unable to verify these. Made in crystal. A reported example in wistaria is probably sun-purpled. Available unfinished or with a cut top and bottom. These were alternatively offered as shelf supports, with some catalogs listing them as "candle columns." An earlier candleholder also used this number (see FO-8). Westmoreland's 9½" No. 1000 candlestick is very similar, but with a base that appears to be more rectangular than square. 10": $40.00 – 50.00. 12": $60.00 – 75.00. 15": $80.00 – 100.00.

Note: The following report appears in the *Crockery and Glass Journal,* April 9, 1908: "One of the specialties shown by the Fostoria Glass Co. is a glass toilet set of nine pieces, including ewer and basin, soap and brush holder, mug, puff-box, tumblers and candlestick. The set is of the twist-pillar pattern, and calculated to appeal to summer cottagers particularly. It is really a very desirable adjunct of the simple life, and ought to meet with a liberal sale." We have been unable to identify this candlestick.

FO-20. No. 1453 CANDLESTICK, FROM CATALOG

No. 1453 candlestick. 11" high. Circa 1909 – 1925. Made in crystal. Available cut top and bottom. Available with etching "F." $40.00 – 50.00. Add 50 – 80% for etched.

FO-21. No. 1485 CANDLESTICK, 8⅛" HIGH, WITH "B" ETCHING

No. 1485 colonial candlestick, 8⅛" high with a 4" base, circa 1906 – 1928 and 1933 – 1938; No. 1485 colonial candlesticks, 9½" high and 11½" high, circa 1906 – 1925. Made in crystal, dark blue, and green. Available etched with No. 144, 145, 159, 160, 321, or etching "B," or with silver deposit overlay as No. 3485. Also offered with the top and bottom cut and polished. The 8" size was reissued in 1933 as a base for the No. 2279 candleholder with peg bobeche and prisms. Crystal, 8": $35.00 – 40.00; 9½": $45.00 – 55.00; 11½": $55.00 – 65.00. Add 50 – 80% for etched. Add 100 – 150% for color.

FO-22. No. 1490 CANDLE-STICK, 8¼" HIGH, WITH "C-2" ETCHING

No. 1490 candlestick. 8¼" high with a 4" square base, circa 1906 – 1928; and 15" high, circa 1924 – 1927. Made in crystal and offered with eight different cuttings, silver deposit decoration, or as a 13½" candle lamp "With Shade and Candle all ready to light." (The latter consisted of the candlestick, a peg lamp base, a chimney, and a shade that fit over the chimney. The same pieces could be used with any candlestick and were advertised as a safety feature, since the flame of the candle could not come into contact with the shade.) The 8" size can be found with the "A" or "C-2" etchings, the No. 161 or 162 cuttings, and the following decorations: No. 12 Dresden (black enamel and gold), 17 Daisy (enamel with gold band), 19 Blue Border (enamel decoration), or 20 Black Border (enamel and gold decoration). The 15" size was also offered etched. May be found with the top and bottom cut smooth with a ground pontil. 8": $35.00 – 40.00. 15": $80.00 – 100.00. 8" candle lamp with shade: $125.00 – 150.00. Add 50 – 80% for etched.

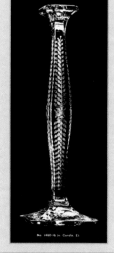

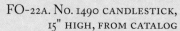

FO-22A. No. 1490 CANDLESTICK, 15" HIGH, FROM CATALOG

No. 1513 candleholder. Called Florence in some reference books. 3" high with a 4¼" saucer base. Circa 1907 – 1925. Made in crystal. Offered both with and without a handle. The handled version must have been more popular, since we have never seen one without the handle. The top of the candle cup is cut and polished. $30.00 – 35.00.

FO-23. No. 1513 CANDLEHOLDER

No. 161 candlestick. 7¼" high with a 4" base. Originally made circa 1907 – 1925 and then reissued as part of the Colony line as No. 2412 (later No. 2412/323) from 1937 – 1972. In the 1920s, Colonial Candle Company of Cape Cod offered these candlesticks with the base and candle cup decorated in solid colors (old blue, rose, and yellow). Made in crystal. Other candlesticks that were part of (or associated with) the Colony line are FO-2 (p. 10), FO-15 (p. 14), FO-123 through FO-125 (p. 46-47) and FO-137 (p. 50). $35.00 – 40.00.

FO-24. No. 161 CANDLESTICK

No. 1612 Christmas candlestick. 5" high. Circa 1909 – 1925. Known only in crystal. The designation as a "Christmas candlestick" appeared routinely in most of Fostoria's catalogs, though what makes this candlestick especially suitable for Christmas isn't clear. $35.00 – 40.00.

FO-25. No. 1612 CHRISTMAS CANDLESTICK, FROM CATALOG

No. 1639 candlestick. 8" high. Circa 1909 – 1928. Made in crystal. A 1909 catalog shows this candleholder offered as a 13½" candle lamp. "With Spearhead Prisms, Shade, and Candle all ready to light." (The latter consisted of the candlestick, a peg lamp base, a chimney, and a shade that fit over the chimney. The same pieces could be used with any candlestick and were advertised as a safety feature, since the flame of the candle could not come into contact with the shade.) Available with the "D" etching. Crystal: $40.00 – 45.00. Candle lamp w/shade and prisms: $150.00 – 200.00. Add 50 – 80% for etched.

FO-26. No. 1639 CANDLE-STICK, WITH "D" ETCHING

No. 1640 candlestick. 8¼" high with a 4¼" base. Circa 1909 – 1925. Made in crystal. This was also offered as No. 1640 lustre with candle peg and 6" prisms (FO-27a). The prisms were reportedly also made by Fostoria, contrary to the usual practice of American companies to import their prisms from Bohemia. Available unfinished or with the top and/or bottom cut smooth, with a ground pontil. $35.00 – 40.00. With peg/prisms $65.00 – 75.00.

FO-27. No. 1640
CANDLESTICK

FO-27A. No. 1640 11½"
LUSTRE, FROM CATALOG

FO-28. No. 1642
CANDLESTICK,
FROM CATALOG

No. 1642 candlestick. 8" high. Circa 1909 – 1925. Made in crystal. Available unfinished or with the top and/or bottom cut smooth, with a ground pontil. $35.00 – 40.00.

FO-29. No. 1643
CANDLESTICK,
FROM CATALOG

No. 1643 candlestick. 9" high. Circa 1909 – 1921. Available unfinished or with the top and/or bottom cut smooth, with a ground pontil. Made in crystal. $35.00 – 40.00.

FO-30. No. 1666
HANDLED
CHAMBER STICK

No. 1666 handled chamber stick. 2½" high with a diameter of 5". Circa 1909 – 1925. The top will be cut and polished. Made in crystal. $22.00 – 27.00.

No. 21 lustre candlestick. 12½" high with a 5½" base. Circa 1909 – 1925, reissued 1934 – 1936. Made in crystal. The same base was used for the No. 21 Princess lamp, with the addition of a fount, chimney, and glass shade. Lustre: $80.00 – 100.00.

FO-31. No. 21 LUSTRE CANDLE-STICK, FROM CATALOG

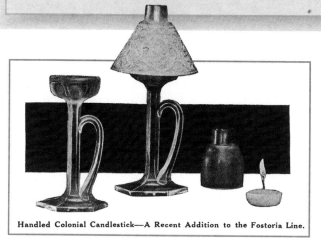

Handled Colonial Candlestick—A Recent Addition to the Fostoria Line.

FO-32A. ADVERTISEMENT FROM *THE POTTERY, GLASS & BRASS SALESMAN*, DECEMBER 21, 1911, SHOWING THE ASSEMBLED HANDLED COLONIAL CANDLESTICK AND ITS COMPONENTS

Handled colonial candlestick or candle lamp. Unknown pattern number. 8⅛" high with a 3⅞" hexagonal base. Circa 1911 – 1912. This colonial candle lamp was designed by Phillip Ebeling. Patent D42,389 was filed January 19, 1912, and was approved on April 9, 1912. There is no candleholder element since it was intended to be used with the small round candle, chimney, and shade, as seen in FO-032a. Crystal: $60.00 – 75.00.

FO-32. HANDLED COLONIAL CANDLESTICK

No. 1856 candlestick. 8⅛" high with a 4" cut and polished base. Circa 1912 – 1928. Available with cutting No. 163 or deep etched as seen in the accompanying photograph. A somewhat similar candlestick was made by Heisey as No. 68 (See HE-25 on p. 109.) Crystal: $35.00 – 40.00. Add 50 – 80% for etched, 20 – 40% for cut.

FO-33. No. 1856 CANDLESTICK WITH ETCHING

IS THIS FOSTORIA?

This candlestick looks identical to Fostoria's No. 1856 except for the scrollwork on the stem and candle cup. It has a polished pontil just like some other Fostoria candlesticks of the same era, and the glass quality is consistent with Fostoria's, but at this point we just don't know.

FO-33A. UNKNOWN CANDLESTICK, SIMILAR TO FOSTORIA'S No. 1856 EXCEPT FOR MOLDED SCROLL PATTERN

**FO-34. No. 1962
TROPHY HANDLED
CANDLESTICK**

No. 1962 trophy handled candlestick. 9½" high with a 4½" base. Circa 1914 – 1928. Made in crystal. Available with an unnamed deep etching or with hand painted floral decorations. This is a handled version of the No. 1963 candlestick below. $50.00 – 55.00. Add 20 – 30% for h/p decoration in good condition. Add 50 – 80% for deep etched.

**FO-35. No. 1963
CANDLESTICK,
ETCHED**

No. 1963 candlestick. 9" high. Circa 1914 – 1928. Paden City and New Martinsville made a very similar candlestick (as No. 115 and No. 10 – 21, respectively), but theirs were usually in color, and Fostoria only made these in crystal. The New Martinsville and Paden City versions are believed to have used the same mold (and the same workers, but that's a tale for volume three), so they can only be told apart by color, if at all. All were offered with cuttings, but only Fostoria offered the unnamed etching shown here. Central also made this candlestick as No. T1376½. Plain: $30.00 – 35.00. Add 50 – 80% for deep etched.

**FO-36. No. 1964
CANDLESTICK**

No. 1964 candlestick. 9⅜" high with a 4¼" base. Circa 1914 – 1928. Made in crystal. Available with an unnamed deep etching. Central also made this candlestick as No. T1376. $40.00 – 45.00. Add 50 – 80% for deep etched.

**FO-37. No. 1965
CANDLESTICK**

No. 1965 candlestick. 8" high with a 3⅞" base. Circa 1914 – 1928. Made in crystal. Available with an unnamed deep etching and the No. 164 cutting. $40.00 – 45.00. Add 50 – 80% for deep etched. Add 20 – 30% for cut.

No. 2056 American candlestick. 7¼" high. Circa 1915 – 1926. First of a long line of candlesticks in the ever-popular American pattern, designed by Phillip Ebeling. Known in crystal and blue. Originally sold as part of a boudoir set with tray, quart jug, tumbler, and match box (replaced in 1925 with an oval ash tray with match stand). Known to collectors as the "Eiffel Tower" candlestick. This shape was also used for an electric lamp in two sizes (7" and 8¼") with a cord hole drilled in place of the candle cup. For other candleholders in the American pattern, see FO-42 (p. 22), FO-95 (p. 38), FO-118 through FO-120 (p. 45), FO-131 (p. 48), and FO-221 (p. 71). Crystal: $100.00 – 125.00. Blue: $400.00 – market.

FO-38. No. 2056 AMERICAN CANDLESTICK, FROM CATALOG

No. 2063 chamber stick. 2¼" high with 4½" base. Circa 1916 – 1927. Originally made in crystal, beginning in 1924 they were also made in amber, blue, and green. This is very similar to Heisey's No. 150 Banded Flute saucer foot candlestick (HE-17 on p. 106), but the Heisey candlestick has three small bands encircling the upper candle cup and has the handle attached more inboard. Also, Heisey's Banded Flute is larger (5") in circumference and was made in crystal only. (See FO-39a for a comparison of the two.) Crystal: $22.00 – 28.00. Amber, green: $30.00 – 40.00. Blue: $40.00 – 50.00.

FO-39. No. 2063 CHAMBER STICK IN AMBER

FO-39A. COMPARISON OF FOSTORIA'S No. 2063 CHAMBER STICK IN GREEN AND HEISEY'S No. 150 BANDED FLUTE SAUCER FOOT CANDLESTICK IN CRYSTAL

No. 2080 candlestick. 6⅜" high with a 3¾" base. Circa 1916 – 1926. Known only in crystal. In the 1920s, Colonial Candle Company of Cape Cod offered these candlesticks with a floral decoration on the top of the column. $20.00 – 30.00.

FO-40. No. 2080 CANDLESTICK

No. 2108 candlestick. 8½" high. Circa 1916 – 1921. Made in crystal and applied colors. $35.00 – 45.00. Add 10 – 20% for colored finish.

(From the collection of Helen and Bob Jones.)

FO-41. No. 2108 CANDLESTICK IN CRYSTAL WITH APPLIED YELLOW COLOR

FO-42.
No. 2056½
AMERICAN
CANDLESTICK

No. 2056½ American candlestick. 7¼" high with a 3⅜" square base. Circa 1922 – 1944. Made in crystal; rare in ruby. After Fostoria's closing this candleholder continued to be made by Dalzell Viking (under the Fostoria label) and more recently has been reissued by Smith. Glass quality is the only way we know to tell the old from the reissues. The American pattern was also very popular in England where it was sold as the Georgian line by the National Glass Company, Ltd. (not to be confused with the National Glass Company in the United States). This candlestick was one of the pieces advertised in a London trade journal in 1925. For other candleholders in the American pattern, see FO-38 (p. 21), FO-95 (p. 38), FO-118 through FO-120 (p. 45), FO-131 (p. 48), and FO-221 (p. 71). Old crystal: $50.00 – 65.00. New crystal: $20.00 – 25.00. Ruby: $325.00 – market.

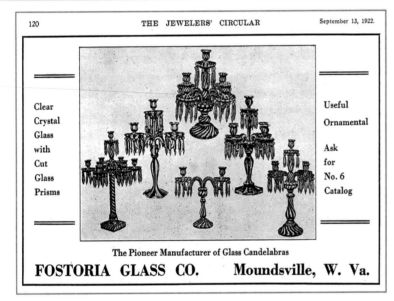

FO-43. 1922 ADVERTISEMENT SHOWING (L TO R) NO. 3 BANQUET CANDELABRA, NO. 24 FOUR-LIGHT CANDELABRA, NO. 15 TWO-LIGHT CANDELABRA, NO. 13 FIVE-LIGHT CANDELABRA, NO. 17 FIVE-LIGHT CANDELABRA, AND NO 7 FIVE-LIGHT CANDELABRA

The accompanying picture is a reprint of an advertisement from the September 13th, 1922 issue of *The Jewelers' Circular* showing a few of Fostoria's many candelabra. Although we stated in volume one that we will not attempt to cover elaborate candelabra in this series, they were too large a part of Fostoria's early history to ignore completely. Although this ad is from 1922, most of the items shown here date back to Fostoria's very beginnings and sadly, all would be gone in just a few years (although the No. 24 [second from left] would be one of two reissued in 1959). A rough pricing estimate for Fostoria's early candelabra is $100.00 – 125.00 per candle cup. The 1959 reissues of No. 24 and No. 25 (not shown) would be $80.00 – 100.00 per candle cup.

No. 2244 candlestick. Made in two sizes, 6" and 8" high. Circa 1922 – 1928. Made in crystal and offered deep etched, cut, or with many decorations including: No. 9 Newport (coin gold band), 12 Dresden (black enamel and gold), 17 Daisy (enamel with gold band), 21 (enamel and gold), 22 (blue and gold or rose and gold), 31 Laurel (encrusted gold), 32 Regent (encrusted gold), and 36 Poinsetta [sic] (encrusted gold and blue). Cutting No. 165 was also offered. 6": $30.00 – 35.00. 8": $35.00 – 40.00. Add 50 – 80% for deep etched. Add 10 – 30% for cut or enameled.

FO-44. NO. 2244 CANDLESTICKS, 6" AND 8", WITH DEEP ETCHING, FROM CATALOG

No. 2245 candlestick. Made in two sizes, 6⅛" high with a 4" base and 8¼" high with a 4¼" base. Circa 1922 – 1928. Made in amber, canary, rose, blue, green, and crystal. Can be found deep etched or with other decorations including: No. 12 Dresden (black enamel and gold), 17 Daisy (enamel with gold band), 19 Blue Border (enamel decoration), 20 Black Border (enamel and gold decoration), 21 (enamel and gold), 22 (blue and gold or rose and gold), 29 Empress (encrusted gold), 31 Laurel (encrusted gold), 32 Regent (encrusted gold), 36 Poinsetta [sic] (encrusted gold and blue), and 39 Royal (encrusted gold). 6⅛", crystal: $15.00 – 20.00; amber, green, rose: $22.00 – 30.00; blue, canary: $30.00 – 40.00. 8¼", crystal: $18.00 – 22.00; amber, green, rose: $25.00 – 35.00; blue, canary: $35.00 – 45.00. Add 100 – 150% for deep etched. Add 10 – 15% for enameled.

FO-45. No. 2245 CANDLESTICKS, 6⅛" IN CANARY AND 8¼" IN BLUE

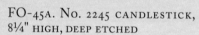

FO-45A. No. 2245 CANDLESTICK, 8¼" HIGH, DEEP ETCHED

No. 2246 candlestick. 8¼" high with a 4⅛" base and a 1¾" square top. Circa 1922 – 1928. Available deep etched or with the No. 23 black & gold enamel decoration. Crystal: $30.00 – 35.00. Add 40 – 60% for deep etched. Add 10 – 15% for decorated.

FO-46. No. 2246 CANDLE- STICK, DEEP ETCHED

No. 2247 candlestick. 8½" high. Circa 1922 – 1925. Made in crystal. In recent years, Mikasa has offered a similar candlestick, made in Austria in crystal and various colored stains, 8" high with a 3" diameter base. (See FO-47a.) $30.00 – 35.00.

FO-47. No. 2247 CANDLESTICK, FROM 1924 CATALOG

FO-47A. MIKASA CANDLESTICKS IN BLUE AND RED STAIN

FO-48. No. 2279 CANDLE-
HOLDER AND BOBACHE
COMBINED, FROM 1924
CATALOG

No. 2279 candleholder and bobache [sic] combined. 4½" in diameter. Circa 1922 – 1924. This was made for use on any tall candleholder to convert it to a lustre with six prisms. Available in crystal. A design patent was filed December 21, 1922, but wasn't approved until January 24, 1924, as D63,854. The designer was given as Calvin B. Roe, who was vice president of the company at the time. $20.00 – 25.00 without prisms.

FO-49. No. 1842
CANDLESTICK,
FROM 1924
CATALOG

No. 1842 candlestick. 8½" high. Circa 1923 – 1925. The early pattern number suggests that this candlestick may actually date as early as 1912, but it does not appear in the early catalogs available to us, so if it is an early candlestick it may only have been produced intermittently. Made in crystal. $30.00 – 35.00.

FO-50. No. 2268
CANDLESTICK, FROM
1924 CATALOG, DEEP
ETCHED

No. 2268 candlestick. 6" high. Circa 1923 – 1926. Available with an unnamed deep etching. Crystal: $30.00 – 35.00. Add 50 – 80% for deep etched.

No. 2269 candlestick. 6" high with a 4" base. Circa 1924 – 1928. Made in crystal, amber, blue, canary, ebony, green, and onyx luster (a mother-of-pearl iridescence on black). Available deep etched or with the following decorations: No. 25 Vase and Scroll, 36 Poinsetta [sic] (encrusted gold and blue), 37 (encrusted gold), 39 Royal (encrusted gold), 44 Rivera (cutting with encrusted gold), 52 Pasadena (gold or silver band on ebony), and 53 (orange band on ebony). Crystal: $22.00 – 28.00. Amber, green, ebony: $25.00 – 38.00. Canary, blue: $35.00 – 50.00. Onyx lustre: $250.00 – market. Add 40 – 70% for deep etched. Add 10 – 15% for decorated.

FO-51. No. 2269 CANDLESTICKS
IN BLUE AND CANARY

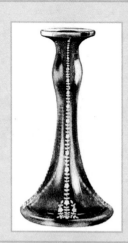

No. 2275 candlestick. Made in two sizes: 7" high with a 4" base; 9½" high (listed as 9" in catalog). Circa 1924 – 1928. Made in amber, crystal, blue, canary, ebony, and green. Was also available deep etched and with the No. 37 encrusted gold decoration. 7", crystal: $22.00 – 28.00; amber, green, ebony: $25.00 – 38.00; canary, blue: $35.00 – 50.00. 9¼", crystal: $28.00 – 35.00; amber, green, ebony: $35.00 – $45.00; canary, blue: $50.00 – 65.00. Add 40 – 60% for deep etched.

FO-52A. No. 2275 CANDLESTICK, 9½", FROM 1924 CATALOG, DEEP ETCHED

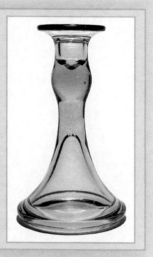

FO-52. No. 2275 CANDLESTICK, 7" IN AMBER

No. 2297 candlestick. 7" high with a 4½" round base that rests on three feet. Circa 1924 – 1928. Made in amber, crystal, blue, green, ebony, and canary. Can be found wheel-cut or with the following decorations: No. 39 Royal (encrusted gold), 52 Pasadena (gold or silver band on ebony), or 53 (orange band on ebony). A very similar candlestick in a shorter size with an oval base was made as No. 2299 (see FO-55 below). Crystal, amber $25.00 – $35.00. Blue, green, ebony: $35.00 – 45.00. Canary: $40.00 – 55.00. Add 5 – 10% for cutting or decoration.

FO-53. No. 2297 CANDLESTICKS IN GREEN AND AMBER

No. 2298 St. Clair candlestick. 3⅜" high with a 2⅛" x 2¾" rectangular base. Circa 1924 – 1927. Made in amber, crystal, ebony, blue, green, and canary, also came etched with No. 288 Cupid brocade or with the following decorations: No. 25 Vase and Scroll, 57 Waveland (white gold on ebon), or 67 Poinsetta [sic] (decoration on ebony). These were sometimes sold with the No. 2298 clock. Crystal, amber: $18.00 – 26.00. Blue, green, ebony: $30.00 – 35.00. Canary: $40.00 – 65.00. Add 100 – 200% for examples with Cupid brocade etch. Add 10 – 20% for other decorations.

FO-54. No. 2298 ST. CLAIR CANDLESTICKS IN EBONY AND BLUE

No. 2299 St. Alexis candlestick. 5" high with a 3" x 4⅛" oval base. Circa 1924 – 1927. Made in amber (light and dark), crystal, blue, green, ebony, and canary. Sometimes sold with the No. 2297 clock. Known with the following decorations: No. 52 Pasadena (gold or silver band on ebony), 53 (orange band on ebony), 57 Waveland (white gold on ebony), 69 Saturn (plain colored bands). A very similar candlestick in a taller size with a round base was made as No. 2297 (see FO-53 above). Crystal, amber: $18.00 – 25.00. Blue, green, ebony: $30.00 – 35.00. Canary: $40.00 – 50.00. Add 5 – 10% for Nugget (gold on ebony).

FO-55. No. 2299 ST. ALEXIS CANDLE-STICKS IN BLUE, CANARY AND DARK AMBER

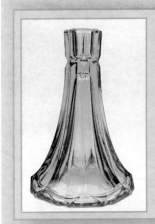

No. 2311 candlestick. 6⅜" high with a 4⅜" base. Circa 1924 – 1927. Made in crystal, amber, blue, green and canary. Also sold with a peg candleholder/bobeche and eight 4" prisms as the No. 2311 9" lustre. Crystal, amber: $35.00 – 40.00. Blue, green: $40.00 – 50.00. Canary: $50.00 – 60.00. Add 50% to the above prices for a crystal peg insert. Add 100% if the insert is the same color as the candlestick.

FO-56. No. 2311
CANDLESTICK IN CANARY

FO-56A. No. 2311 LUSTRE
IN GREEN WITH MATCHING
PEG BOBECHE AND RARE 4"
GREEN PRISMS

FO-57. No. 2324 3" CANDLESTICKS, GREEN
WITH CUPID BROCADE ETCH AND BLUE
WITH GRAPE BROCADE ETCH

No. 2324 candlestick, five sizes: 2" high with 4½" base, circa 1926 – 1932; 3" high with 4½" base, circa 1924 – 1953 and 1981 – 1982; 6" high with 4¾" base, circa 1926 – 1935 and 1981 – 1982; 9" high with 5" base, circa 1924 – 1930; 12" high, circa 1924 – 1928. Also No. 2324½ candlestick, 3" high, circa 1924 – 1926.

The 3" size (which varies from 2⅞" to 3⅜") was usually advertised as being 4" high. A No. 2324½ candlestick, 3" high with a 1½" candle opening for an oversized candle was shown in 1924, but must have been short-lived, since it was discontinued by 1926. The initial colors for all sizes were amber, blue, canary, crystal, ebony, and green. In 1926, orchid was added for all but the 12" size. By 1928, rose was also available. Onyx lustre and mother-of-pearl are known only in the 3" size and must have been made between 1925 and 1927. The 3" and 6" sizes were reissued in crystal in 1981 – 1982. Their numbers at that time were No. CA 11/314 and No. CA 11/319 respectively. The latter was also available in light blue.

There were three patents that applied to this candlestick, all designed by William H. Magee. D68,057 (for the head only) was filed June 20, 1925, and approved August. 25, 1925. D69,844 (for the 2" size) was filed January 11, 1926, and approved April 6, 1926. D71,656 (for the 4" size) was filed January 11, 1926, and approved December 14, 1926. Several other companies made very similar candleholders. See CB-44b, p. 61, and CB-58b & c, p. 66 in volume one of this series for a comparison of similar styles.

FO-57A. No. 2324 3" CANDLE-
STICK IN ONYX LUSTRE
(SCARCE TO RARE)

Etchings include: No. 273 Royal, 274 Seville, 275 Vesper, 276 Beverly, 287 Grape Brocade, 288 Cupid Brocade, 289 Paradise Brocade, 334 Colonial Mirror, 335 Willow, 336 Plymouth, 337 Sampler, 340 Buttercup, 341 Romance. Known cuttings and carvings consist of: No. 12 Morning Glory, 184 Arbor, 186 Thelma, 188 Berry, 192 Kingsley, 197 Chatteris, 705 Barcelona, 743 Heraldry, 797 Daphne, 815 Holly. Other decorations include: No. 30 Azalea (gold decoration on green), 46 (fired on colors with gold bands), 49 Coronada (white and yellow gold encrusted Royal etching), 52 Pasadena (gold or silver band on ebony), 53 (orange band on ebony), 55 (tinted bands), 56 Antique (colors on crystal), 57 Waveland (white gold on ebony), 58 Amherst (white gold on etching No. 274 Seville), 66 Hammered Silver, 67 Poinsetta [sic] (decoration on ebony), 69 Saturn, 70

FO-57B. No. 2324 CANDLESTICKS, 2" IN EBONY, 3" IN MOTHER OF PEARL,
6" IN BLUE, AND 9" IN DARK AMBER

Arlington, 604 Club Design B (ebony with single gold lines), 609 Lines (silver on ebony), and with gold band and platinum band decorations. This was also a very popular blank for use by other decorating companies.

2", crystal: $8.00 – 10.00; amber: $12.00 – 15.00; blue, green, orchid: $15.00 – 20.00. 3", crystal: $10.00 – 12.50; amber: $12.00 – 15.00; blue, ebony, green, orchid, rose, mother-of-pearl: $15.00 – 20.00; canary: $25.00 – 30.00; onyx lustre: $200.00 to market. 6", crystal: $15.00 – 20.00; amber: $20.00 – 25.00; blue, green, orchid: $35.00 – 45.00. 9", crystal: $20.00 – 25.00, amber: $25.00 – 30.00, blue, green, orchid: $45.00 – 60.00. 12", crystal: $25.00 – 30.00; amber: $40.00 – 55.00; blue, green: $50.00 – 75.00. The brocade etchings (No. 287 Grape, 288 Cupid, and 289 Paradise) are by far the most in-demand and will increase the values listed by 200 – 400%. Other etchings add between 100 – 150%. Morning Glory is the sought-after cutting/carving and will add 100 – 200% to the values listed. Other cuttings add 20 – 50%. Nice decorations in good condition add 10 – 20%. Worn decorations, or those unattractive to today's collectors, can actually hurt the value of the item.

FO-57c. No. 2324 12" CANDLESTICK, FROM 1924 CATALOG, ETCHED

IS THIS FOSTORIA?

It's a candle arm peg insert that converts a single light candleholder to a two light. It's 3" high with a 5¼" spread. We believe it to be a Fostoria piece but have never been able to confirm it. We know it in amber and green, both of which are good matches to Fostoria's renderings of those colors.

FO-58. UNKNOWN CANDLE-ARM INSERT IN AMBER. POSSIBLY FOSTORIA

No. 2333 candlestick. Made in two sizes: 7½" high (listed as 8") with a 4⅞" base; 11" high. Circa 1924 – 1928. The 7½" size was made in amber, canary, crystal, blue, and green. The 11" size was available in amber and crystal only. 7½", crystal: $25.00 – 30.00; amber: $35.00 – 45.00; blue, green: $55.00 – 75.00; canary: $75.00 – 95.00. 11", crystal: $40.00 – 50.00; amber: $70.00 – 80.00.

FO-59. No. 2333 7½" CANDLESTICK IN BLUE

No. 2352 lily candleholder. Height varies from 5½" to 6", depending on the shape of the leaf. 4" round base. Circa 1927 – 1928. Made in amber, blue, crystal, green and orchid. Crystal: $25.00 – 30.00. Amber: $35.00 – 40.00. Blue, green, orchid: $40.00 – 60.00.

FO-60. No. 2352 LILY CANDLEHOLDER IN ORCHID

27

FO-61. No. 2362 3½" CANDLESTICKS IN BLUE, ORCHID, AND GREEN WITH PARADISE BROCADE ETCHING

No. 2362 candlestick. Made in two sizes: 3⅛" high with a 4⅝" base; and 9" high with a 5" base. Circa 1926 – 1929. Designed by William H. Magee, with patent D70,021 filed February 25, 1926, and approved April 27, 1926. Made in amber, blue, crystal, green, and orchid. The 9" version is difficult to find. The 3¼" version is known with two brocade etchings, No. 287 Grape and 289 Paradise, and one cutting, No. 186 Thelma. Two other decorations are also known: No. 69 Saturn and 70 Arlington. 3¼", crystal: $15.00 – 20.00; amber: $20.00 – 25.00; blue, green, orchid: $35.00 – 45.00. 9", crystal: $20.00 – 25.00; amber: $25.00 – 30.00; blue, green, orchid: $45.00 – 60.00. Add 200 – 400% for a brocade etching. Cuttings and decorations add 10 – 20%.

FO-61A. No. 2362 9" CANDLESTICK IN AMBER

FO-62. No. 2372 CANDLEBLOCK IN BLUE WITH SPIRAL OPTIC DESIGN

No. 2372 candleblock. 1½" high with a 4¼" base. Circa 1927 – 1929. Available plain or with spiral optic design. Made in amber, azure, blue, crystal, green, rose, and orchid. According to one catalog, a patent for this candleblock design was applied for, but we have been unable to uncover any evidence that it was granted. Can be found with two brocade etchings, No. 287 Grape and 289 Paradise, or with the No. 185 Arvida cutting. Cambridge made a similar candlestick around the same time as No. 632. (See CB-62 on p. 67 of volume one of this series.) Like the Fostoria candleholder, it also nests directly on its rolled-down rim. Another similar rolled-edge candleholder made by Imperial as No. 718R (see IM-25 on p. 185) differs by having a 2½" diameter foot. Crystal: $10.00 – 12.50. Amber: $15.00 – 20.00. Blue, green, orchid: $25.00 – 30.00. Add 200 – 400% for a brocade etching. Cuttings and decorations add 10 – 20%.

FO-63. No. 2375 FAIRFAX CANDLEHOLDER IN IRIDESCENT ROSE WITH No. 290 OAK LEAF BROCADE ETCHING

No. 2375 Fairfax candleholder. 3" – 3⅜" high with a 4½" – 4¾" base. Circa 1927 – 1960. Made in amber, azure, crystal, ebony, gold tint, green, orchid, rose, and topaz. This candleholder was very similar to Fostoria's No. 2324 (see FO-57 on p. 26), except that the ring around the bottom of the candle cup is hexagonal on the No. 2375 and round on the No. 2324. A similar style was also made by the Diamond Glass-ware Company (see DI-6 on p.133 of volume one of this series for a photo). Available with two cuttings, No. 192 Kingsley and 194 Orleans, and many etchings, including: No. 72 Oakwood, 73 Palm Leaf, 277 Vernon, 278 Versailles, 279 June, 280 Trojan, 282 Acanthus, 283 Kashmir, 284 New Garland, 285 Minuet, 290 Oak Leaf, 309 Legion, 310 Fuchsia, and 312 Mayday. Crystal: $10.00 – 12.50. Amber: $12.00 – 15.00. Azure, ebony, green, orchid, rose: $15.00 – 20.00. Add 200 – 400% for a brocade etching, 100 – 150% for other etchings, and 10 – 30% for cuttings.

No. 2375½ Fairfax candleholder. 2⅜" high with a 4" base. 4¾" across the top. Circa 1927 – 1932. Made in amber, azure, crystal, green, rose, topaz, and orchid. Available with several popular plate etchings, including No. 277 Vernon, 278 Versailles, 279 June, 280 Trojan, 282 Acanthus, 283 Kashmir, and two brocade etchings, No. 290 Oak Leaf and 72 Oakwood. These mushroom shaped, footed candleholders made an attractive console set when sold with the 12" No. 2375½ centerpiece and 3¾" No. 2309 flower block. Crystal: $12.00 – 15.00. Amber: $18.00 – 22.00. Green, rose, topaz: $25.00 – 30.00. Azure, orchid: $30.00 – 35.00. Add 200 – 400% for a brocade etching and 100 – 150% for other etchings.

FO-64. No. 2375½ Fairfax candleholders in azure with No. 278 Versailles etching and topaz with No. 279 June etching

No. 2383 trindle candleholder. 4" high with a 4¾" base. Circa 1927 – 1939. Made in amber, azure, crystal, ebony, green, rose, and topaz. Available with the No. 73 Palm Leaf brocade etching and two decorations: No. 506 Viennese (gold decoration on ebony) and 608 Block (silver on ebony). Crystal: $20.00 – 25.00. Amber: $30.00 – 35.00. Ebony, green, rose, topaz: $35.00 – 40.00. Azure $45.00 – 50.00.

FO-65. No. 2383 trindle candleholders in azure and topaz

No. 2384 candlestick. 9" high. Circa 1927. Made in crystal, amber, blue, ebony, and green. This appears to be a molded design, but is described as a "Grape Stem decoration" in *Fostoria Tableware, 1924 – 1943* by Milbra Long & Emily Seate. At least four versions of this decoration were offered on this candleholder: No. 61 (white gold on crystal), 62 (white and yellow gold on crystal), 63 (yellow gold on green), and 64 (gold? on amber, blue or ebony). $50.00 – 65.00. Add 20 – 30% for decorated.

FO-66. No. 2384 Grape Stem candlestick in crystal

No. 2390 candleholder. 3⅛" high with a 4¾" base. Circa 1927 – 1929. Made in amber, azure, green, orchid, and rose. Amber: $15.00 – 20.00. Green, rose: $20.00 – 30.00. Azure, orchid: $25.00 – 35.00.

FO-67. No. 2390 candleholder in amber

FO-68. No. 2393 CANDLEHOLDERS IN AZURE AND AMBER

No. 2393 candleholder. 2¼" high with a 4" base. 5" across. Circa 1928 – 1930. Made in amber, azure, green and rose. Crimped, with a spiral optic. Amber $15.00 – 20.00. Green, rose: $20.00 – 30.00. Azure: $25.00 – 35.00.

FO-69. No. 2394 CANDLEHOLDERS IN ROSE WITH No. 279 JUNE ETCHING, BURGUNDY, AND GREEN WITH No. 278 VERSAILLES ETCHING

No. 2394 footed candleholder. 1¾" high. 4¾" across rim. Circa 1928 – 1940. Made in amber, azure, burgundy, crystal, empire green, light green, orchid, regal blue, rose, topaz (gold tint), and wistaria. Designed by William H. Magee. Design patent D76,880 was filed August 3, 1928, and approved November 29, 1928. Offered with many different etchings, including: No. 72 Oakwood, 73 Palm Leaf, 277 Vernon, 278 Versailles, 279 June, 280 Trojan, 281 Verona, 282 Acanthus, 283 Kashmir, 284 New Garland, 285 Minuet, 286 Manor, and 290 Oak Leaf. Cuttings include: No. 188 Berry, 194 Orleans, 196 Lattice, 197 Chatteris, 198 Warwick, and 704 Royal Garden. Other known decorations are No. 30 Azalea (gold decoration on green), 73 Palm Leaf (mother-of-pearl iridescence and gold on brocade etching No. 291), and 502 Firenze (gold edge on plate etching No. 281 Verona). Somewhat similar candleholders were made by a number of other companies. Cambridge's No. 1155 and 1156 three-footed candlesticks (CB-76 on p. 71 of volume 1 of this series) are the most dissimilar, because they have a figured design in the bowl. Fenton's No. 848 (or No. 1234) candleholder has small peg feet and was made with both six and nine "petals" – the scallops being much more defined so that the bowl resembles a lotus (FN-16 on p. 183 of volume 1 of this series). McKee made a three-footed candlestick as part of their No. 156 Octagon Edge pattern, which suggests that it ought to have an eight-sided bowl; however, in the catalog drawing it appears to be almost round and has feet very similar to those on the Fostoria candleholder. Since the catalog page mentions that the pattern has an optic, this may mean that the candlestick will have an eight-paneled optic. We hope to be able to offer more definitive information about this candlestick in volume three. Finally, the Liberty Works made a very similar candleholder in 1930, which will also appear in volume three — but with distinctive feet in the shape of curlicues and with three broad ribs in the bowl. (Compare the narrow ribs on the Fostoria candleholder.) Crystal $9.00 – 12.00. Amber: $10.00 – 12.50. Green, rose, topaz: $15.00 – 22.00. Azure, burgundy, empire green, royal blue, orchid: $20.00 – 27.50. Wistaria: $35.00 – 40.00. Add 200 – 400% for a brocade etching, 100 – 200% for other etchings, and 20 – 40% for cuttings.

FO-69A. No. 2394 CANDLEHOLDER IN EMPIRE GREEN WITH GOLD DECORATION

FO-70. No. 2395 CANDLEHOLDER IN GREEN

No. 2395 candleholder. 3⅜" high with a 4½" base. Circa 1929 – 1932. Made in amber, azure, crystal, ebony, green, rose, and topaz. Offered with the following etchings: No. 278 Versailles, 279 June, 280 Trojan, and 290 Oak Leaf. The No. 502 Firenze decoration (gold edge on plate etching No. 281 Verona) was also available. Amber: $20.00 – 25.00. Ebony, green, topaz and rose: $25.00 – 30.00. Azure $30.00 – 35.00. Add 200 – 400% for a brocade etching, 100 – 150% for other etchings.

No. 2395½ candleholder. 5" high with a 3½" x 4¼" oval base. Sometimes known as Palm Leaf. A trade journal report in 1929 referred to this as the Grecian pattern. Circa 1929 – 1939. Made in amber, azure, crystal, ebony, green, topaz, and rose. Available etchings were: No. 73 Palm Leaf, 278 Versailles, 279 June, 280 Trojan, 282 Acanthus, 283 Kashmir, and 310 Fuchsia. The No. 194 Orleans cutting and No. 501 Fern (gold edge on ebony) and 610 Triangle (silver on ebony) decorations were also available. Crystal: $15.00 – 20.00. Amber: $25.00 – 30.00. Ebony, green, topaz and rose: $30.00 – 35.00. Azure $35.00 – 40.00. Add 200 – 300% for a brocade etching, 100 – 150% for other etchings, and 10 – 30% for cuttings.

FO-71. No. 2395½ CANDLE-HOLDER IN EBONY, WITH FERN ETCH

No. 2402 candleholder. 1¾" high with a 4½" diameter. Circa 1929 – 1939 in all colors listed below; reissued in ebony from 1953 to 1957. Also made in amber, azure, green, rose and topaz. Designed by George Sakier and probably among his earliest work for the company. All colors: $18.00 – 25.00.

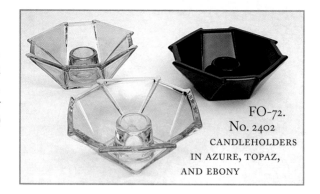

FO-72. No. 2402 CANDLEHOLDERS IN AZURE, TOPAZ, AND EBONY

No. 2412 Queen Anne candlestick. 9" high with a 4⅝" base. Circa 1927 – 1929 in amber, blue, crystal and green. Candlesticks and candelabra of this twist design were a part of Fostoria's line since its earliest days. Individual items came and went, but the basic design survived until the factory closed in 1986. At this point the line was called Queen Anne. Later it would be known as Colony, though by that time this particular candlestick had been discontinued. It was returned to production in 1981 – 1982 as part of the Maypole Giftware line. Colors of that time were peach (pink), light blue, and yellow. The item number at that time was CA 10/326. Crystal was made again in 1982. For earlier candleholders in the Queen Anne pattern, see FO-14 and FO-15 (p. 14). Crystal: $30.00 – 35.00. Amber: $35.00 – 50.00. Blue, green: $70.00 – 90.00. All 1980s colors: $40.00 – 50.00.

FO-73. No. 2412 QUEEN ANNE candlestick. THIS IS A 1981 RE-ISSUE IN PEACH (PINK) AS PART OF THE MAYPOLE GIFTWARE LINE

No. 2415 combination bowl. 3½" high with a 7" x 12¾" diameter. Circa 1929 – 1932. Made in amber, azure, ebony, rose, and topaz and offered with the following etchings: No. 280 Trojan, 290 Oak Leaf, 501 Fern (gold edge on ebony), and 502 Firenze (gold edge on etching No. 281 Verona). Amber: $45.00 – 60.00. Azure, ebony, rose, topaz: $60.00 – 80.00. Add 75 – 150% for etched.

FO-74. No. 2415 COMBINATION BOWL IN AMBER

FO-75. No. 2425 CANDLEHOLDER IN GREEN

No. 2425 candleholder. 2⅜" high with a 3¾" base. Circa 1928 – 1932. Made in amber, azure, crystal, ebony, green, rose, and topaz. Amber, crystal: $20.00 – 25.00. Azure, ebony, green, rose, topaz: $30.00 – 40.00.

FO-76. No. 2430 DIADEM 1½" CANDLE-HOLDER *(computer composite showing approximate shape)*

No. 2430 Diadem candleholder. 1½" high. Circa 1930? We have no catalog or other information on this candleholder. The only one of these we've ever seen is in the Fostoria Glass Museum, Moundsville, West Virginia. It looks like a small nut dish with a candle receptacle added. The Diadem pattern was designed by George Sakier. Ebony: $30.00 – 35.00.

FO-77. No. 2430 DIADEM 10" CANDLESTICK IN TOPAZ WITH No. 332 MAYFLOWER ETCHING

No. 2430 Diadem candlestick. 10" high with a 4⅝" base. Circa 1930 – 1932. Known in amber, azure, crystal, ebony, green, rose, and topaz. It was offered with the No. 284 New Garland and 285 Minuet etchings, and the No. 704 Royal Garden cutting. Other decorations were No. 505 Cockatoo (gold on ebony) and 608 Block (silver on ebony). The Diadem pattern was design by George Sakier. Crystal: $40.00 – 50.00. All other colors: $75.00 – 100.00. Add 40 – 80% for etched. Add 20 – 40% for cut. Fostoria offered many advertising aids over the years, intended to be given out to customers. One such was *The Glass of Fashion* by Helen Ufford, brought out in 1931. In discussing the use of candles, she made the following points (all punctuation, including ellipses, as they appear in the original):

Candles: Our dinner tables… formal or informal… ceremonious or casual… should be candle-lighted. The friendly glow of candlelight gives to our tables a glamour that we can capture in no other way. For the arrangement of the candles, we must keep very active our sense of proportion and balance. Candles of natural wax are good always… really best… for either the formal or the informal setting. Sometimes, however, we use gay colored candles, to carry out a special decorative scheme, or a festive idea. For our formal tables, usually tall candlesticks, of glass or silver, single containers or candelabra… or our informal tables, shorter candles at a height where the candles "smile" at us, not "stare" at us.

This discussion was accompanied by the illustration seen on FO-77a, which featured an informal dinner setting with four of the No. 2430 Diadem candlesticks.

FO-77A. ORIGINAL ILLUSTRATION FROM *THE GLASS OF FASHION* (1931), SHOWING AN INFORMAL DINNER SETTING, INCLUDING No. 2430 DIADEM CANDLESTICKS

FO-78. No. 2430 DIADEM 2⅛" CANDLEHOLDER IN EBONY

No. 2430 Diadem candleholder. 2⅛" high with a 4¼" base. Circa 1938 – 1942 in crystal and 1954 – 1958 in ebony. This seems to have been a late addition to the Diadem pattern, after most of the colored pieces had been discontinued. It was offered with the No. 332 Mayflower etching, 515 Richelieu decoration, 616 St. Regis cut and encrusted gold band, and the 771 Federal, 772 Tulip, 774 Gothic, and 775 Kimberley cuttings. The Diadem pattern was designed by George Sakier. Crystal: $20.00 – 25.00. Ebony: $25.00 – 30.00. Add 40 – 80% for etched. Add 20 – 40% for cut.

No. 2433 candlestick. 2⅞" with a 4" base and a rim diameter of 4¾". Called Three Stem in a November 1930 trade journal report and sometimes known as Twenty-Four Thirty-Three today. Circa 1930 – 1932. Made with a crystal foot and an azure, rose, topaz, or wistaria bowl, or a crystal bowl with an amber, ebony, or green foot. Also available in all crystal. Offered with No. 284 New Garland, 285 Minuet, 286 Manor, and 308 Wildflower etchings and with the No. 704 Royal Garden cutting. This was a George Sakier design. It was patented as D85,065, filed January 21, 1931, and approved September 8, 1931. Eugene Stahl was listed on the patent application as designer, though we know from Sakier's sketch books that he actually created this pattern. We haven't been able to determine Stahl's position at the factory, but he may have signed the patent application in Sakier's absence as an officer of the company. A January 1932 price list mentions a 4" candlestick in this pattern, and a September 1932 price list includes an 8" candlestick – neither of these size candlesticks are known, and are probably errors in the listings. Crystal $25.00 – 30.00. Amber, azure, green, ebony, rose, topaz: $45.00 – 60.00. Wistaria: $65.00 – 85.00. Add 40 – 80% for etched. Add 30 – 40% for cut.

FO-79. No. 2433 CANDLESTICK IN TOPAZ WITH CRYSTAL FOOT, WITH No. 332 MAYFLOWER ETCHING

No. 2436 lustre. 8¾" high with a 4½" base. Circa 1930 – 1940. Made in amber, crystal, ebony, green, rose, topaz, and wistaria. All have turned down crystal "fixed" bobeches with 8 prisms. Crystal: $65.00 – 85.00. Amber, ebony, green, rose, topaz: $125.00 – 150.00. Wistaria: $200.00 – market.

FO-80. No. 2436 LUSTRE IN EBONY WITH CRYSTAL TOP

No. 2443 candlestick. 3½" high with a 4½" base. Circa 1931 – 1939. Made in amber, azure, crystal (plain and silver mist), ebony, green, rose, topaz, ruby, and wistaria. Available with No. 286 Manor or 308 Wildflower etchings. Crystal, crystal satin: $15.00 – 20.00. Azure, ebony, green, topaz, rose: $25.00 – 30.00. Wistaria: $35.00 – 40.00. Ruby: $45.00 – 50.00. Add 40 – 80% for etched.

FO-81. No. 2443 CANDLESTICK IN AZURE

No. 2446 candleholder. Called Lifesaver by collectors. 5⅝" high with a 4" base. Circa 1931 – 1935. Made in amber, azure, crystal, ebony, green, rose, and topaz. This was another design by George Sakier. A "Primer of Modern Design" appearing in *Arts and Decoration*, November 1933, was illustrated with designs of George Sakier, with this piece shown as an example of "geometric modern." Crystal: $25.00 – 30.00. Amber, ebony, green, rose, topaz: $40.00 – 50.00. Azure: $50.00 – 60.00.

FO-82. No. 2446 LIFESAVER CANDLE-HOLDERS IN GREEN, EBONY, AND TOPAZ

FO-83. No. 2447 DUO CANDLESTICK
IN WISTARIA

No. 2447 duo candlestick. 5" with a 4⅝" base. Circa 1931 – 1939. Made in amber, crystal, ebony, green, rose, ruby, topaz, wistaria. Available with No. 308 Wildflower etching and two decorations: No. 505 Cockatoo (gold on ebony) and 507 Nugget (gold on ebony). Cuttings included 704 Royal Garden and 751 Heirloom. Designed by George Sakier. A "Primer of Modern Design" appearing in *Arts and Decoration*, November 1933, was illustrated with designs of George Sakier, with this piece shown as an example of "geometric modern." Crystal: $15.00 – 20.00. Amber, ebony, green, rose and topaz: $30.00 – 40.00. Ruby, wistaria: $65.00 – 90.00. Add 40 – 80% for etched. Add 20 – 50% for cut.

FO-84.
No. 2449
HERMITAGE
CANDLESTICK
IN TOPAZ

No. 2449 Hermitage candlestick. 5¾" high with a 3½" base. Circa 1931 – 1939, made in amber, azure, crystal, ebony, green, topaz (gold tint), and wistaria. From 1974 through 1979, this candleholder was reissued as Lexington in brown, olive green, and yellow. Brown, crystal, olive green: $15.00 – 20.00. Azure, ebony, gold tint, green, topaz, yellow: $20.00 – 25.00. Wistaria: $40.00 – 50.00.

FO-85. No.
2453 LUSTRE
IN TOPAZ

No. 2453 lustre. 7⅝" high with a 3⅝" base. Circa 1931 – 1940 (reissued in crystal and ebony, 1953 – 1957). This lustre candleholder has a fixed bobeche with eight prisms. Made in amber, crystal, ebony, green, topaz, and wistaria. Crystal: $40.00 – 55.00. Amber, ebony, green, topaz: $90.00 – 100.00. Wistaria: $125.00 – market.

FO-86.
No. 2455
CANDLESTICK
IN TOPAZ

No. 2455 candlestick. 6" high with a 3½" round, three-footed base. Circa 1931 – 1932. Reportedly made in amber, crystal, ebony, green, and topaz. The bowl in the pattern has a narrow optic. A limited production line, difficult to find in any color. $35.00 – 45.00.

No. 2466 candleholder. 2⅝" high with a 4" base. Circa 1931 – 1933. Made in amber, crystal, ebony, green, and topaz. This candleholder was advertised in groups of four as companions to the Fostoria "plateau" center-piece for floating short-stemmed flowers, a set designed by George Sakier. It was advertised as "fresh from Paris" (where Sakier lived) and "such a relief from those tall center-pieces that force your guests to play hide-and-seek all through dinner." Crystal: $13.00 – 18.00. Colors: $20.00 – 25.00.

FO-87. No. 2466 CANDLE-HOLDER IN EBONY

Two-light candelabra. 10¼" high with a 5¼" hexagonal base and an 11½" spread. This rare topaz candleholder never made it to production and is the only one known to collectors. We can't be sure of the date it was manufactured but we assume it to have been in the early thirties. We base this assumption on overall design and the fact that the motif between the arms matches the stopper on the No. 4020 decanter, which was made from 1930 to 1932. It was probably intended to be sold with bobeches and prisms and is on display at the Fostoria Glass Museum in Moundsville, Ohio. Our thanks go to Mary Arrojo and the rest of the museum staff for allowing us to photograph it. Unable to price.

FO-88. TWO-LIGHT CANDE-LABRA (SAMPLE ONLY, NEVER MANUFAC-TURED)

No. 2470 candlestick. Known as Twenty-Four Seventy. 5¾" high with a 3⅛" square base. Circa 1931 – 1938. Available with a topaz or rose bowl on a crystal stem or a crystal bowl on an amber, green, or wistaria stem. Solid crystal was also available. Offered etched with No. 309 Legion, 310 Fuchsia, 311 Florentine, or 313 Morning Glory. Cuttings included No. 709 York and 711 Inverness. Crystal: $30.00 – 40.00. Amber/crystal, Rose/crystal, Topaz/crystal: $40.00 – 60.00. Green/crystal: $60.00 – 80.00. Wistaria/crystal: $100.00 – 130.00. Add 40 – 60% for etched.

FO-89. No. 2470 CANDLE-STICK IN ROSE WITH A CRYSTAL STEM

No. 2470½ candlestick. Known as Twenty-Four Seventy. 5½" high with a 3⅛" round four-footed base. Circa 1932 – 1945. Made in amber, burgundy, crystal, green, empire green, regal blue, rose, ruby, topaz (gold tint), and wistaria. Many etchings and cuttings were offered. The etchings included No. 286 Manor, 310 Fuchsia, 311 Florentine, 313 Morning Glory, 315 Chateau, 316 Midnight Rose, 318 Springtime and 323 Rambler. Cuttings consisted of No. 707 Staunton, 708 Nairn, 713 Eaton, 714 Oxford, 715 Carlisle, 716 Canterbury, 717 Marlboro, 718 Doncaster, 719 Lancaster, 720 Nottingham, 721 Buckingham, 722½ Leicester, 722 Wellington, and 723 Westminster. Crystal: $16.00 – 20.00. Amber: $18.00 – 25.00. Green, rose, topaz: $25.00 – 35.00. Burgundy, empire green, regal blue, ruby: $45.00 – 60.00. Wistaria: $65.00 – 80.00. Add 40 – 80% for etched or cut.

FO-90. No. 2470½ CANDLE-STICK IN AMBER

FO-91.
No. 2472 DUO
CANDLESTICK
IN AMBER

No. 2472 duo candlestick. 5" high with a 4⅞" base and an 8¼" spread. Circa 1932 – 1958. Re-issued in crystal in 1982 as No. CA 10/332. Originally made in amber, crystal (plain or silver mist), ebony, green, rose, and topaz. Available with the following etchings: No. 315 Chateau, 316 Midnight Rose, 323 Rambler, 326 Arcady, and 327 Navarre. Cuttings consisted of: No. 713 Eaton, 717 Marlboro, 741 Watercress, 752 Evangeline, 754 Cavendish, 758 Bordeaux, 759 Weylin, 761 Melba, and 762 Cumberland. Designed by George Sakier. Crystal: $20.00 – $22.00. All colors: $45.00 – $60.00. Add 40 – 80% for etched or cut.

FO-92.
No. 2481
CANDLESTICK
IN GREEN

No. 2481 candlestick. 5⅞" high with a 3¾" base. Circa 1932 – 1938. Made in amber, crystal, ebony, green, rose, and topaz (gold tint). This candleholder is not easy to find. Available etchings consist of: No. 315 Chateau, 316 Midnight Rose, and 318 Springtime. Cuttings include: No. 713 Eaton, 715 Carlisle, and 749 Celebrity. Crystal: $35.00 – 40.00. All colors: $40.00 – $50.00. Add 40 – 80% for etched or cut.

FO-93. No. 2482 TRINDLE CANDLESTICK
IN CRYSTAL WITH No. 316
MIDNIGHT ROSE ETCHING

No. 2482 trindle candlestick. Also listed as No. 2482/336, No. 2482/337 (with a center bobeche and prisms), and No. 2482/338 (with bobeches and prisms on both arms). 6⅞" high with a 5" base and an 8⅜" arm spread. Circa 1932 – 1973. Made in amber, crystal, ebony, green, rose, and topaz. The design was by George Sakier. When etched, the decoration appears on the shield beneath the center candle cup as well as the base, making the etched versions particularly attractive. Etchings include: No. 315 Chateau, 316 Midnight Rose, 318 Springtime, 323 Rambler, 326 Arcady, and 327 Navarre. Cuttings include: No. 714 Oxford, 716 Canterbury, 717 Marlboro, and 752 Evangeline. Crystal: $35.00 – 40.00. Crystal with Navarre etching: $90.00 – 120.00. All colors: $50.00 – 70.00. Add 40 – 80% for other etchings or cuttings.

No. 2484 duo candlestick/candelabra. 8" high with a 5¾" base and an 8" arm spread (10" with bobeches). Circa 1932 – 1978. Known in crystal (plain and Silver Mist), azure, and topaz. It was shown as new in the October 1932 issue of *House & Garden* and must have been an instant success, since by March of 1933 it was being touted as "the largest selling candelabra ever produced by Fostoria." The release of this candlestick/candelabra preceded the No. 2496 Baroque line by four years. Although it officially become part of that pattern when it was introduced, this candlestick and a few other items with the No. 2484 designation retained their original pattern number throughout the years. Designed by George Sakier. Patent No. D91,685 was filed on December 19, 1933, and approved on March 6, 1934. For other candleholders that were part of (or associated with) the Baroque pattern, see FO-98 through FO-100 (p. 39), FO-108 through FO-110 (p. 41-42), and FO-158 (p. 55). Crystal: $40.00 – 50.00. Topaz: $80.00 – 90.00. Azure: $90.00 – 110.00. Add for bobeches/prisms: $40.00 – 50.00.

FO-94. No. 2484 DUO CANDELABRA IN TOPAZ (LATER PART OF BAROQUE LINE)

FO-94A. FOSTORIA No. 2484 DUO CANDELABRA

LOOKALIKES

Two other companies made candlesticks that at first glance can be confused with Fostoria's No. 2484. FO-94b shows a candlestick believed to be made by the Indiana Glass Company. (See IN-63 on p. 255 for further information.) The candlestick shown in FO-94c is even more similar in appearance. This one has been attributed to the Paden City Glass Manufacturing Company, but we have been unable to confirm this.

FO-94C. TWO-LIGHT CANDLESTICK, POSSIBLY MADE BY PADEN CITY GLASS MFG. COMPANY

FO-94B. TWO-LIGHT CANDLESTICK, BELIEVED TO BE MADE BY INDIANA GLASS COMPANY

FO-95.
No. 2056/319
AMERICAN
CANDLESTICK

No. 2056/319 American candlestick. Later listed as No. AM 01/319. 6¼" high with a 3⅝" octagonal base. Circa 1933 – 1982. Made in crystal. The older versions have a slightly fatter stem and are more impressive than the ones produced in the later years. For other candleholders in the American pattern, see FO-38 (p. 21), FO-42 (p. 22), FO-118 through FO-120 (p. 45), FO-131 (p. 48), and FO-221 (p. 71). $25.00 – 30.00.

IS THIS FOSTORIA'S AMERICAN?

It has been identified as such by some collectors, but we doubt it. We believe it to be of English or other Western European origin. It's often claimed to be a rare piece of Fostoria American, but isn't even really all that rare. They are seen occasionally on eBay, usually from sellers in the U.K. Some pieces in the American pattern were made for the English market only, so that is a possibility in this case. Known only in crystal. $100.00 – 125.00.

FO-96. UNKNOWN CANDLESTICK OFTEN ATTRIBUTED TO FOSTORIA'S AMERICAN PATTERN

FO-97. No. 4024
CANDLEHOLDER
IN BURGUNDY
WITH CRYSTAL
FOOT

No. 4024 candleholder. 5⅝" high with a 2⅞" base. Circa 1933 – 1939. Made in crystal (available plain or with a silver mist [frosted] foot), burgundy, empire green, and regal blue (all colors with a crystal foot). The only etching offered was No. 322 Nectar, but many cuttings were available, including: No. 726 Meteor, 727 National, 728 Embassy, 729 Rocket, 730 Whirlpool, 731 Celestial, 732 Seaweed, 733 Marquette, 734 Planet, 735 Shooting Stars, 736 Directoire, 737 Quinfoil, 739 Rock Garden, 740 Rondeau, and 741 Watercress. Crystal: $25.00 – 30.00. All colors: $45.00 – 60.00.

No. 2484 trindle candlestick/candelabra. 9⅛" high with a 6¼" base and a 10½" arm spread (12½" with bobeches). Circa 1933 – 1982. Known in azure tint, crystal, and probably also made in gold tint. This was the three light version of the candlestick/candelabra shown in FO-94 and followed its introduction by only a few months. See FO-94 for more on the inclusion of the No. 2484 items into the later No. 2496 Baroque line. Designed by George Sakier. Patent No. D91,688 was filed on January 2, 1933, and approved on March 6, 1934. For other candleholders that were part of (or associated with) the Baroque pattern, see FO-94 (p. 37), FO-99 and FO-100 (below), FO-108 through FO-110 (p. 41-42), and FO-158 (p. 55). Crystal: $50.00 – 60.00. Azure tint: $100.00 – 120.00. Add for bobeches/prisms: $60.00 – 75.00.

FO-98. No. 2484 TRINDLE CANDLE-STICK (LATER PART OF BAROQUE LINE)

No. 2496 trindle candlestick. 5⅝" high with a 5⅛" base and an 8¼" arm spread. Circa 1933 – 1958. This was the first item to have the number that would be associated with the bulk of the Baroque line, but it would still be another three years before that name was used for the pattern. Made in amber, azure tint, burgundy, crystal (plain and Silver Mist), empire green, green, gold tint, regal blue, and ruby. Etchings included No. 323 Rambler, 326 Arcady, 327 Navarre, 328 Meadow Rose and 338 Chintz. Available cuttings were No. 741 Watercress, 760 Wheat, and 767 Beacon. The Silver City Glass Company also decorated this candlestick with sterling overlay and 24 carat gold. Designed by George Sakier. Patent No. D91,687 was filed December 19, 1933, and approved March 6, 1934. For other candleholders that were part of (or associated with) the Baroque pattern, see FO-94

FO-99. No. 2496 TRINDLE CANDLESTICKS IN TOPAZ AND AMBER (LATER PART OF BAROQUE LINE)

(p. 37), FO-98 (above), FO-100 (below), FO-108 through FO-110 (p. 41-42), and FO-158 (p. 55). Crystal: $20.00 – 25.00. Crystal with Navarre etching: $60.00 – 75.00. Amber, gold tint: $65.00 – 80.00. Azure tint: $75.00 – 90.00. Burgundy, green: $125.00 – 150.00. Empire green, Regal blue, ruby: $150.00 – 175.00. Add 40 – 80% for cuttings or etchings other than Navarre.

No. 2484 lustre. 7¾" high with a 4¼" base. Circa 1934 – 1978. The design includes a fixed bobeche with eight prisms. Known in azure tint, crystal, and gold tint. Became part of the No. 2496 Baroque line in 1936, but retained its original pattern number. Designed by George Sakier. Patent No. D94,442 was filed on November 10, 1934, and approved January 29, 1935. For other candleholders that were part of (or associated with) the Baroque pattern, see FO-94 (p. 37), FO-98 and FO-99 (above), FO- 108 through FO-110 (p. 41-42), and FO-158 (p. 55). Crystal: $40.00 – 50.00. Gold tint: $60.00 – 70.00. Azure tint: $75.00 – 90.00.

FO-100. No. 2484 LUSTRE (LATER PART OF BAROQUE LINE)

FO-101. No. 2510
SUNRAY 3"
CANDLESTICK

No. 2510 Sunray candlestick (sometimes also listed as Sun-Ray). 3" high with a 4⅜" base. Circa 1935 – 1943. Made in crystal and crystal "Glacier" (with Silver Mist ribs). Designed by George Sakier. Crystal: $20.00 – 22.50.

FO-102. No.
2510 SUNRAY
5½" CANDLE-
STICK, FROM
CATALOG

No. 2510 Sunray candlestick (sometimes also listed as Sun-Ray). 5½" high. Circa 1935 – 1943. Made in crystal and crystal "Glacier" (with Silver Mist ribs). Designed by George Sakier. The Silver City Glass Company is known to have decorated this candlestick with non-tarnish silver overlay. Crystal: $25.00 – 35.00.

FO-103.
No. 2510
SUNRAY DUO
CANDELABRA

No. 2510 Sunray duo candlestick/candelabra (sometimes also listed as Sun-Ray). 6⅜" high with a 4⅝" round base and a 7" arm spread (8" with bobeches). Circa 1935 – 1943. Made in crystal and crystal "Glacier" (with Silver Mist ribs). Made with at least one etching, No. 328 Meadow Rose. It was also offered as a two-light candelabra using two No. 2527 bobeches and 16 prisms. Designed by George Sakier. The Silver City Glass Company is known to have decorated this candlestick with non-tarnish silver overlay. Crystal (plain): $30.00 – 40.00; with Meadow Rose etching: $60.00 – 80.00. Add for bobeches/prisms: $40.00 – 50.00.

FO-104. No.
2527 NOCTURNE
DUO
CANDELABRA

No. 2527 Nocturne duo candlestick/candelabra. 8½" high with a 5" round base and a 6" arm spread (7" with bobeches). Circa 1935 – 1944. Made in crystal and also offered as a candelabra with two No. 2527 bobeches and 16 prisms. The only etching we're aware of for this candlestick is No. 325 Corsage, but there were several cuttings, including: No. 751 Heirloom, 756 Bouquet, 757 Society, and 776 Laurel. Designed by George Sakier. Crystal $45.00 – 55.00. Corsage etch: $60.00 – 75.00. Add 20 – 30% for cut. Add for bobeches/prisms: $40.00 – 50.00.

No. 2533 duo candlestick. 6⅛" high with a 5¼" round base and a 6½" arm spread. Circa 1935 – 1944. Made in crystal. Known with the No. 324 Daisy etching and the following cuttings: No. 747 Fantasy, 748 Allegro, 755 Palmetto. Crystal: $35.00 – 40.00. With Daisy etching: $50.00 – 60.00. Add 20 – 40% for cutting.

FO-105.
No. 2533 DUO
CANDLESTICK

No. 2535 candlestick. 5⅝" high with a 4½" round base. Circa 1935 – 1944. Made in burgundy, crystal (plain or Silver Mist), empire green, regal blue, and ruby. Offered with two etchings, No. 324 Daisy and 325 Corsage, and two cuttings, No. 745 Ivy and 746 Gossamer. Crystal: $20.00 – 25.00. Burgundy, empire green, regal blue, ruby: $65.00 – 80.00. Add 40 – 60% for etched, 20 – 40% for cut.

FO-106. No.
2535 CANDLE-
STICKS IN
REGAL BLUE,
EMPIRE GREEN,
AND RUBY

No. 4113 candlestick. 5⅝" high (listed as 6") with a 3¼" base. Circa 1936 – 1944. This is a blown candleholder made in burgundy, crystal, empire green, and regal blue. Crystal $25.00 – 35.00. Burgundy: $40.00 – 50.00. Empire green, regal blue: $55.00 – 65.00.

FO-107. No. 4113
CANDLESTICK IN
BURGUNDY

No. 2496 Baroque candlestick. 5¾" high with a 4⅛" base. Circa 1936 – 1958. Made in azure tint, gold tint, and crystal. Etchings included: No. 325 Corsage, 326 Arcady, 327 Navarre, 328 Meadow Rose, 329 Lido, 331 Shirley, 338 Chintz, and decoration No. 514 Gold Lace. Available cuttings were: No. 760 Wheat, 763 Cyrene, 767 Beacon, 771 Federal, and 772 Tulip. The Silver City Glass Company also decorated this candlestick with sterling overlay and 24 carat gold. Designed by George Sakier. Design patent No. D103,058 was filed November 7, 1936, and approved February 2, 1937. For other candleholders that were part of (or associated with) the Baroque pattern, see FO-94 (p. 37), FO-98 through FO-100 (p. 39), FO-109 and FO-110 (following page), and FO-158 (p. 55). Crystal: $18.00 – 22.50. Crystal with Navarre etching: $40.00 – 50.00. Gold tint: $35.00 – 45.00. Azure tint: $50.00 – 60.00. Add 30 – 60% for other etchings or cuttings.

FO-108.
No. 2496
BAROQUE
CANDLESTICK
IN GOLD TINT

No. 2496 Baroque duo candlestick. 4½" high with a 4⅝" base and an 8" arm spread. Circa 1936 – 1965. Made in azure tint, crystal (plain and Silver Mist), and gold tint. Available etchings were: No. 326 Arcady, 327 Navarre, 328 Meadow Rose, 329 Lido, 331 Shirley, 332 Mayflower, 338 Chintz, and decoration No. 514 Gold Lace. Cuttings were No. 760 Wheat and 767 Beacon. Designed by George Sakier. For other candleholders that were part of (or associated with) the Baroque pattern, see FO-94 (p. 37), FO-98 through FO-100 (p. 39), FO-108 (preceding page), FO-110 (below), and FO-158 (p. 55). Crystal: $15.00 – 20.00. Crystal with Navarre etching: $45.00 – 55.00. Gold tint: $40.00 – 50.00. Azure tint: $50.00 – 60.00. Add 30 – 60% for other etchings or cuttings.

FO-109. No. 2496 BAROQUE DUO CANDLESTICK IN AZURE TINT

FO-109A. TWO-LIGHT CANDLESTICK, MADE IN BOHEMIA. BAROQUE LOOKALIKE

BOHEMIAN LOOKALIKE

The candlestick in FO-109a is of recent vintage. It is 4¼" high with an oblong base (5" by 3⅞") and an 8" arm spread. It is 24% lead crystal and is made in Czechoslovakia. The label is similar to one used by the Jihlava Glassworks of Antoninuv Dul. Although it differs in some respects from the Fostoria candlestick, especially in the addition of the oblong, ribbed base, the arms and candle cups are obviously based upon George Sakier's original design.

FO-110. No. 2496 BAROQUE CANDLESTICK WITH 22 CARAT GOLD FLANDERS DECORATION BY SILVER CITY GLASS COMPANY

No. 2496 Baroque low candlestick. 3⅞" high with a 4⅜" base. Circa 1936 – 1965. Made in azure tint, crystal, and gold tint. Crystal was re-issued 1974 – 1979. Also known in experimental opaque red slag, a color not placed in production. Offered with the following etchings: No. 327 Navarre, 328 Meadow Rose, 329 Lido, 331 Shirley, and 338 Chintz. Cuttings were 760 Wheat and 767 Beacon. Also decorated by the Silver City Glass Company in non-tarnish sterling and 22 carat gold. Designed by George Sakier. Design patent D103,058 was filed November 7, 1936, and approved February 2, 1937. For other candleholders that were part of (or associated with) the Baroque pattern, see FO-94 (p. 37), FO-98 through FO-100 (p. 39), FO-108 and FO-109 (above), and FO-158 (p. 55). Crystal: $10.00 – 15.00. Gold tint: $25.00 – 30.00. Azure tint: $30.00 – 40.00. Crystal with Navarre etching: $40.00 – 50.00. Add 30 – 60% for other etchings or cuttings. *(From the collection of Linda Polen.)*

ANOTHER LOOKALIKE

FO-110a shows a very similar candleholder, but with a patterned dome base and a leaf-edged candle cup. We don't believe that it is Fostoria but have no information as to who made it. Perhaps it is also a Czechoslovakian copy, like the two-light in FO-109a above.

FO-110A. BAROQUE LOOKALIKE FROM UNKNOWN MANUFACTURER

No. 2545 Flame candleblock. 1⅜" high with a 4" rayed hexagonal base. Circa 1936 – 1958. Made in azure tint, crystal, ebony, and gold tint. Also sold as a candle lamp using a No. 26 lamp chimney & base. (The chimney was available plain or with the No. 5 Colonial carving.) Designed by George Sakier. This candleblock can be easily confused with Heisey's No. 1469 Ridgeleigh pattern, which was initially issued a year earlier, in 1935. An illustration of this is found in a photograph in the archives of the Heisey Collectors of America showing a display of Heisey glassware in a department store. The glassware is clearly labeled Ridgeleigh — and in the midst of all of the other pieces, some salesperson has helpfully placed a pair of Flame candleblocks. Crystal $15.00 – 20.00. Azure tint, ebony, gold tint: $30.00 – 40.00. Add for No. 26 chimney/base: $60.00 – 65.00.

FO-111A. No. 2545 FLAME CANDLEBLOCK IN AZURE TINT WITH NO. 26 HURRICANE LAMP INSERT

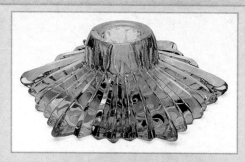

FO-111. No. 2545 FLAME CANDLEBLOCK IN AZURE TINT

No. 2545 Flame candlestick. 4½" high with a 4" round base. Circa 1936 – 1958. Made in azure tint, crystal, and gold tint. Offered etched with No. 331 Shirley, 332 Mayflower, and decoration No. 514 Italian Lace (Gold Lace) all-over etching with gold edge. Designed by George Sakier. Crystal $20.00 – 25.00. Azure tint, gold tint: $35.00 – 45.00. Add 40 – 80% for etched.

FO-112. No. 2545 FLAME CANDLESTICK WITH NO. 332 MAYFLOWER ETCHING

No. 2545 Flame lustre. 7½" high with a 4⅜" round base. Circa 1936 – 1942. Made in azure tint, crystal, and gold tint. Offered with four etchings: No. 327 Navarre, 329 Lido, 331 Shirley, and 332 Mayflower. This candleholder has a fixed bobeche with eight prisms, and was designed by George Sakier. Crystal $35.00 – 45.00. Azure tint, gold tint: $70.00 – 80.00. Add 40 – 80% for etched.

FO-113. No. 2545 FLAME LUSTRE

FO-114. No. 2545 FLAME DUO CANDLESTICK
IN GOLD TINT

No. 2545 Flame duo candlestick/candelabra. 6⅞" high with a 5½" round base and a 10" arm spread. Circa 1936 – 1958. Made in azure tint, crystal, and gold tint. Offered as a two-light candelabra using two No. 2524 bobeches and twelve "B" prisms. Several etchings were available, including: No. 325 Corsage, 327 Navarre, 328 Meadow Rose, 329 Lido, 331 Shirley, 332 Mayflower, and decoration No. 514 Italian Lace (Gold Lace) all-over etching with gold edge. Four cuttings were also offered: No. 760 Wheat, 766 Ripple, 767 Beacon, and 768 Bridal Shower. Designed by George Sakier. Design patent No. D103,057 was filed November 7, 1937, and approved February 2, 1937. Crystal: $40.00 – 50.00. Crystal with Navarre etching: $80.00 – 90.00. Azure tint, gold tint: $70.00 – 90.00. Add 30 – 70% for other etchings or cuttings. Add $50.00 – 60.00 for bobeches with prisms.

FO-115.
No. 2546 DUO
CANDLESTICK

No. 2546 duo candlestick/candelabra. This was a companion piece to the four-light Quadrangle candlestick shown below. 4¾" high with a 4⅛" x 5½" octagonal base and a 7" arm spread. Circa 1936 – 1944. Known in crystal and azure tint, and probably also made in gold tint. Also offered as a candelabra using two No. 2546 square bobeches and fourteen "B" prisms. Crystal: $50.00 – 60.00. Azure tint: $65.00 – 80.00. With bobeches and prisms: $170.00 – 215.00.

FO-116. No. 2546
QUADRANGLE
CANDLESTICK IN
AZURE TINT

No. 2546 Quadrangle candlestick/candelabra. 4⅞" high with a 4⅞" square base and a 7" arm spread. Circa 1936 – 1939. Made in azure tint and crystal. Designed by Findley Williams. Patent No. D103,060 was filed November 11, 1936, and approved February 2, 1937. Crystal: $65.00 – 80.00. Azure tint: $100.00 – 125.00. With bobeches and prisms: $320.00 – 425.00.

FO-117. No. 2547
TRINDLE
CANDLESTICK IN
GOLD TINT

No. 2547 trindle candlestick. 5" high with 3" x 5⅞" base and a 7" arm spread. Circa 1937 – 1939. Known in azure tint, crystal, and gold tint. Crystal: $60.00 – 80.00. Azure tint, gold tint: $90.00 – 120.00.

No. 2056 American duo candlestick/candelabra. 6½" high with a 4½" round base and an 8¼" arm spread (9" with bobeches). Circa 1936 – 1958. Made in crystal only. Also available with two No. 2527 bobeches and 16 prisms. For other candleholders in the American pattern, see FO-38 (p. 21), FO-42 (p. 22), FO-95 (p. 38), FO-119 and FO-120 (below), FO-131 (p. 48), and FO-221 (p. 71). $100.00 – 125.00. With bobeches and prisms: $180.00 – 225.00.

FO-118. No. 2056 AMERICAN DUO CANDLESTICK

FO-118A. No. 2056 AMERICAN DUO CANDELABRA

No. 2056 American candleholder. Later listed as No. 2056/314 and AM 01/314. 3" high with a 4½" round base. Circa 1937 – 1982. Made in crystal. Reissued by Dalzell Viking and — possibly — Indiana Glass Company in the 1980s – 1990s in cobalt, amber, crystal, and pink. These reissues may have a round red, white, and blue Fostoria label (see FO-119a), but the glass quality is very poor. This was also offered by Fostoria as a candlelamp, complete with No. 26 peg insert and globe. For other candleholders in the American pattern, see FO-38 (p. 21), FO-42 (p. 22), FO-95 (p. 38), FO-119 (above), FO-120 (below), FO-131 (p. 48), and FO-221 (p. 71). Crystal: $12.00 – 15.00. Cobalt, pink: $20.00 – 25.00. Amber: $30.00 – 50.00. Add for No. 26 chimney/base: $60.00 – $65.00. Add another $10.00 – 15.00 for votive candlelamp insert.

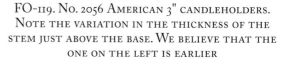

FO-119. No. 2056 AMERICAN 3" CANDLEHOLDERS. NOTE THE VARIATION IN THE THICKNESS OF THE STEM JUST ABOVE THE BASE. WE BELIEVE THAT THE ONE ON THE LEFT IS EARLIER

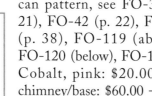

FO-119A. LATE REISSUE OF No. 2056 AMERICAN 3" CANDLEHOLDER IN COBALT (PROBABLY DALZELL VIKING)

No. 2056½ American duo candlestick. Also listed as No. 2056½/331 and AM 01/331. 4½" high with a 4⅝" round base and an 8½" arm spread. Circa 1937 – 1982. Made in crystal. For other candleholders in the American pattern, see FO-38 (p. 21), FO-42 (p. 22), FO-95 (p. 38), FO-118 and FO-119 (above), FO-131 (p. 48), and FO- 221 (p. 71). $25.00 – 35.00.

FO-120. No 2056½ AMERICAN DUO CANDLESTICK

FO-121.
No. 2550 SPOOL
CANDLEBLOCK
IN GOLD TINT

No. 2550 Spool candleblock. 2¼" high with a 2¾" diameter. Circa 1937 – 1943. Made in crystal, azure tint, gold tint. Crystal: $10.00 – 12.00. Azure tint, gold tint: $18.00 – 22.50.

FO-122. No. 2550½ SPOOL CAN-
DLEHOLDER IN CRYSTAL

No. 2550½ Spool candleholder. 2⅝" high with a 4¼" scalloped base. Circa 1938 – 1943. Made in azure tint, crystal, and gold tint. This candleholder was also available as a No. 2550 candle lamp, with a No. 26 peg and chimney. A very similar candleholder was made by L. E. Smith as No. 305. Besides the slight differences in shape (see FO-122a for a comparison), the Fostoria base sits flat while the Smith base rests on the tips of the scallops, leaving gaps. Crystal: $8.00 – 12.00. Azure tint, gold tint: $18.00 – 22.50. Add for No. 26 chimney/base: $60.00 – 65.00.

FO-122A. COMPARISON OF FOSTORIA'S No.
2550½ SPOOL CANDLEHOLDER (LEFT) WITH L.
E. SMITH'S No. 305 IN BLACK (RIGHT)

FO-123. No. 2412
COLONY DUO CAN-
DLESTICK

No. 2412 Colony duo candlestick. Later known as No. 2412/332. 6¼" high with a 4⅝" base and an 8¼" arm spread. Circa 1938 – 1965. Made in crystal, this was one of the many candlesticks offered in the Colony pattern, and is sometimes referred to as the "spearhead" candleholder. This design was by George Sakier. Also available as a two light candelabrum using two No. 2412 bobeches and eight "B" prisms. Other candlesticks that were part of (or associated with) the Colony line are FO-2 (p. 10), FO- 15 (p. 14), FO-24 (p. 17), FO-124 (below), and FO-125 (following page), and FO-137 (p. 50). $30.00 – 35.00. With bobeches/prisms: $70.00 – 90.00.

FO-124. No.
2412 COLONY
LUSTRE, FROM
CATALOG

No. 2412 Colony lustre. 7½" high. Circa 1938 – 1959. Made in crystal, this candleholder has a fixed bobeche with eight "U Drop" prisms. Other candlesticks that were part of (or associated with) the Colony line are FO-2 (p. 10), FO-15 (p. 14), FO-24 (p. 17), FO-123 (above), FO-125 (following page), and FO-137 (p. 50). $60.00 – 75.00.

No. 2412½ Colony lustre. 6" high with a 3½ " base. Circa 1938 – 1942. Made in crystal, with a fixed bobeche and three prisms. Other candlesticks that were part of (or associated with) the Colony line are FO-2 (p. 10), FO-15 (p. 14), FO-24 (p. 17), FO-123 and FO-124 (preceding page), and FO-137 (p. 50). $40.00 – 45.00.

FO-125. No. 2412½ COLONY LUSTRE

No. 2560 Coronet candlestick. 4⅜" high with a 4¼" round base. Circa 1938 – 1943 and 1950 – 1959. Made in crystal and offered etched with No. 332 Mayflower, 333 Willowmere, or decoration No. 515 Richelieu. Available cuttings were No. 774 Gothic, 775 Kimberley, and 785 Cynthia. $20.00 – 25.00. Add 40 – 80% for etched or cut.

FO-126. No. 2560 CORONET CANDLESTICK WITH NO. 332 MAYFLOWER ETCHING

No. 2560 Coronet duo candlestick. 5" high with a 5" round base and a 9⅛" arm spread. Circa 1938 – 1943 and 1950 – 1962. Made in crystal. Available etched with No. 332 Mayflower, 333 Willowmere, or decoration No. 515 Richelieu. Also offered cut with: No. 774 Gothic, 775 Kimberley, or 785 Cynthia. Tiffin made a similar candlestick at around the same period, but as can be seen in FO-127a, there are significant differences. $25.00 – 35.00. Add 40 – 80% for etched or cut.

FO-127. No. 2560 CORONET DUO CANDLESTICK WITH NO. 332 MAYFLOWER ETCHING

FO-127A. TIFFIN CANDLESTICK, SIMILAR IN DESIGN TO FOSTORIA'S NO. 2560

FO-128. No. 2560½
CORONET CANDLE-
STICK WITH NO. 333
WILLOWMERE
ETCHING

No. 2560½ Coronet candlestick. 3⅞" high with a 4¼" round base. Circa 1938 – 1957. Made in crystal and available with the No. 332 Mayflower or 333 Willowmere etchings. Also available with the No. 785 Cynthia cutting. $20.00 – 25.00. Add 40 – 80% for etched or cut.

FO-129. No.
2563 VIKING
CANDLESTICK

No. 2563 Viking candlestick. 4⅝" high with a 4⅛" round base. Circa 1939 – 1943. Made in crystal and offered with at least one cutting, No. 799 Mulberry. $40.00 – 50.00. Add 40 – 80% for cut.

IS THIS FOSTORIA?

Candlestick. 3½" high with a 4" round base. Is this Fostoria? We don't know, but the glass quality and design features don't rule it out. One of the authors purchased a pair of these, complete with Fostoria's No. 26 peg inserts and globes. Of course, those will fit candleholders from most manufacturers, so cannot be taken as proof one way or the other. At this point, attribution to Fostoria is just an intriguing possibility.

FO-130. UNKNOWN CANDLESTICK. POSSIBLY FOSTORIA

FO-131. No.
2056 AMERICAN
HURRICANE
LAMP, FROM
ADVERTISEMENT

No. 2056 American hurricane lamp base. 3" high with a 4¾" diameter. Circa 1939 – 1943 and 1953 – 1958. Made in crystal. For other candleholders in the American pattern, see FO-38 (p. 21), FO-42 (p. 22), FO-95 (p. 38), FO-118 through FO-120 (p. 45), and FO-221 (p. 71). Base only: $75.00 – 90.00.

In 1939, Fostoria introduced four elaborate new etchings, collectively known as "Master Etchings." Their individual pattern names were No. 334 Colonial Mirror, 335 Willow, 336 Plymouth, and 337 Sampler. Two candleholders were advertised with these etchings, No. 2324 and the No. 2574 Raleigh shown below. By 1943 all four were discontinued. FO-132a shows a close-up of Plymouth, probably most attractive of the Master Etchings series.

No. 2574 Raleigh candlestick. 4⅛" high with a 4⅝" round base. Circa 1939 – 1944. Made in crystal. Offered etched with No. 334 Colonial Mirror, 335 Willow, 336 Plymouth, or 337 Sampler. Cuttings included No. 776 Laurel and 787 Pilgrim. $15.00 – 20.00. With Plymouth etching: $40.00 – 50.00. Other etchings or cuttings, add 40 – 80% to price of plain.

FO-132. No. 2574 Raleigh candlestick with Plymouth master etching

FO-132A. Close-up of Plymouth master etching

No. 2574 Raleigh duo candlestick. 5¼" high with a 5" base and an 8½" arm spread. Circa 1939 – 1965. Made in crystal and available with the No. 337 Sampler etching or the No. 792 Wentworth or 826 Minuet cuttings (do not confuse with the No. 285 Minuet etching). $35.00 – 45.00. Add 30 – 60% for etched or cut.

FO-133. No. 2574 Raleigh duo candlestick with No. 826 Minuet cutting

No. 2424 Kent candlestick. 3¼" high with a 3¼" hexagonal base. Circa 1939 – 1943 and reissued as No. CA 12/314 in 1982. Made in crystal. Available with the No. 13 Brocade carving or No. 797 Daphne cutting. $15.00 – 20.00. Add 30 – 50% for cut.

FO-134. No. 2424 Kent candlestick

No. 2424 Kent duo candlestick. 4¾" high with a 3⅞" hexagonal base and a 6" arm spread. Circa 1940 – 1943. Made in crystal. $20.00 – 25.00.

FO-135. No. 2424 Kent duo candlestick

49

FO-136. No. 6023 SONATA DUO
CANDLESTICK WITH No. 12
MORNING GLORY CARVING

No. 6023 Sonata duo candlestick. Also listed as No. 332. 5¼"
high with a 4¾" round base and a 6" arm spread. Circa 1940 –
1963. Made in crystal and available with the following etchings:
No. 338 Chintz, 339 Rosemary, 340 Buttercup, and 341
Romance. Also offered with carvings No. 12 Morning Glory
and 46 Cornucopia, and with several cuttings: No. 743 Heraldry,
798 Christine, 800 Selma, 804 Salon, 805 Aloha, 806 Cadence,
807 Coventry, 814 Christiana, 815 Holly, 816 Gadroon, and 817
Mount Vernon. Listed as part of the Sonata line and "for use
with any plain bowls." Plain: $20.00 – 25.00. With Chintz, Cor-
nucopia, Morning Glory, or Romance: $45.00 – 55.00. Add 40
– 60% to plain for other etchings or cuttings.

FO-137.
No. 2412
COLONY
CANDLESTICK

No. 2412 Colony candlestick. 3¼" high with a 4½" base.
Circa 1940 – 1966 in crystal. Reissued 1981 – 1982 in crystal, peach, yellow, and light blue as part of the Maypole Giftware line. At that time the line number was No. 2412/323.
In 1982, it was changed to No. CA 10/314. Other candlesticks that were part of (or associated with) the Colony line
are FO-2 (p. 10), FO-15 (p. 14), FO-24 (p. 17), and FO-
123 through FO-125 (p. 46-47). Crystal: $10.00 – 15.00.
Blue, peach, and yellow: $35.00 – 45.00.

FO-138. No.
2592 MYRIAD
CANDLESTICK

No. 2592 Myriad candlestick. 3½" high with a 3½"
round base. Circa 1941 – 1944, in crystal only. Probably designed by George Sakier, since the rest of the
pattern was created by him. $25.00 – 35.00.

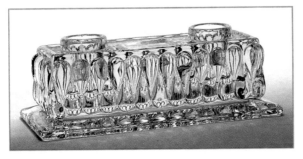

FO-139. No. 2592
MYRIAD DUO
CANDLESTICK

No. 2592 Myriad duo candlestick. 2¼"
high with a 6½" long rectangular base.
Circa 1942 – 1944. Made in crystal.
Designed by George Sakier. $40.00 –
60.00.

No. 2594 candlestick. Known as Plume. 5¾" high with a 4¼" round base. Circa 1941 – 1957. Made in crystal and offered with No. 340 Buttercup or 341 Romance etchings. Designed by George Sakier. Plain: $18.00 – 22.50. Buttercup: $25.00 – 30.00. Romance: $30.00 – 35.00.

FO-140. No. 2594 PLUME CANDLESTICK

No. 2594 trindle candlestick. Known as Plume. 7¾" high with a 5⅜" round base and a 6¾" arm spread. Circa 1941 – 1957. Made in crystal and offered with No. 284 New Garland, 340 Buttercup, and 341 Romance etchings. Designed by George Sakier. Plain: $40.00 – 45.00. New Garland, Buttercup: $50.00 – 60.00. Romance: $65.00 – 75.00.

FO-141. No. 2594 PLUME TRINDLE CANDLESTICK

No. 2596 candlestick. 4¾" high with a 4⅛" round base. Circa 1940 – 1943. Made in crystal and offered etched with No. 341 Romance or 12 Morning Glory, and the 47 Stars and Bars carving. Also available cut with No. 807 Coventry or 819 Greek Key. Plain: $20.00 – 25.00. Romance: $35.00 – 45.00. Stars and Bars: $60.00 – 70.00. Morning Glory: $40.00 – 50.00. Coventry, Greek Key: $30.00 – 40.00.

FO-142. No. 2596 CANDLESTICK

No. 2598 duo candlestick. 8" high with a 5" round base and a 7" arm spread. Circa 1940 – 1943. Made in crystal and designed by George Sakier. $50.00 – 70.00.

FO-143. No. 2598 DUO CANDLESTICK

FO-144. No. 2600 ACANTHUS TRINDLE CANDLESTICK

No. 2600 Acanthus trindle candlestick/candelabra. Advertised as part of the Regency Ensemble. 10" high with a 4⅛" base and a 9" arm spread (10" with bobeches). Circa 1940 – 1943. Made in crystal. Also offered as a three-light candelabra using three No. 2545 bobeches and 18 prisms. $90.00 – 120.00. With bobeches and prisms: $180.00 – 240.00.

FO-145. No. 2601 LYRE DUO CANDLESTICK

No. 2601 Lyre duo candlestick. Advertised as part of the Regency Ensemble. 8" high with a 5" base and a 5¾" arm spread. Circa 1940 – 1948. Made in crystal. Designed by George Sakier. $45.00 – 65.00.

FO-146. No. 2620 WISTAR CANDLESTICK, FROM CATALOG

No. 2620 Wistar candlestick. 4" high. Circa 1942 – 1943. Made in crystal. Some pieces in the pattern were reissued in 1954 in white, aqua, and peach milk glass, but this candlestick does not appear to have been among them. The design consists of ivy leaves around a ribbed stem with a circle of stars beneath the socket. $20.00 – 25.00.

No. 2630 Century candlestick. Later listed as No. 2630/316 and CE 01/316. 4⅜" high with a 4¼" round base. Circa 1949 – 1982. Known in crystal and pink (probably peach, from 1982). Available etched with No. 342 Bouquet, 343 Heather, 344 Camellia, 345 Starflower, Crystal Print 6 (Lacy Leaf), and Crystal Print 7 (Milkweed). Made available as well with cutting No. 933 Bridal Wreath. The Silver City Glass Company also offered this blank with non-tarnish sterling and 22 carat gold decorations. Crystal: $13.00 – 17.50. Pink: $75.00 – 100.00. Add 20 – 40% for etched or cut.

FO-147. No. 2630 CENTURY CANDLESTICK WITH No. 343 HEATHER CUTTING

FO-147A. No. 2630 CENTURY CANDLESTICK IN PINK (PEACH)

No. 2630 Century duo candlestick. Later listed as No. 2630/331. 6¾" high with a 5½" round base and a 6⅛" arm spread. Circa 1949 – 1980. Made in crystal and available etched with No. 342 Bouquet, 343 Heather, 344 Camellia, 345 Starflower, Crystal Print 6 (Lacy Leaf), and Crystal Print 7 (Milkweed). Also available with cutting No. 933 Bridal Wreath. $25.00 – 30.00. Add 20 – 40% for etched or cut.

FO-148. No. 2630 CENTURY DUO CANDLE-STICK WITH NO. 343 HEATHER CUTTING

No. 2630 Century trindle candlestick. Later listed as No. 2630/336. 7¾" high with a 5½" round base and a 7½" arm spread. Circa 1949 – 1980. Made in crystal and available etched with No. 342 Bouquet, 343 Heather, 344 Camellia, and 345 Starflower, or cutting No. 823 Sprite. $35.00 – 45.00. Add 20 – 40% for etched or cut.

FO-149. No. 2630 CENTURY TRINDLE CANDLESTICK WITH UNKNOWN CUTTING

Plume candlestick. Unknown size. Designed by George Sakier. Patent No. D153,038 was filed May 11, 1948, and approved on March 8, 1949. We have never seen one, nor even a catalog picture, so it is possible that this candlestick was never produced.

FO-150. PLUME CANDLESTICK (ORIGINAL PATENT DRAWING)

No. 2636 Plume candlestick. 9⅝" high with a 5⅛" round base. Circa 1949 – 1958. Made in crystal. Designed by George Sakier. Patent No. D153,037 was filed May 4, 1948, and approved March 8, 1949. $45.00 – 60.00.

FO-151. No. 2636 PLUME CANDLESTICK

FO-152. No. 2636
PLUME DUO
CANDLESTICK

No. 2636 Plume duo candlestick. 9¾" high with a 6¼" round base and a 10" arm spread. Circa 1949 – 1958. Made in crystal. Designed by George Sakier. Patent No. D159,756 was filed December 28, 1949, and approved August 15, 1950. $75.00 – 95.00.

FO-153. No. 2638 CONTOUR CANDLEHOLDERS
IN CRYSTAL AND EBONY

No. 2638 Contour candleholder. 4½" high and 5¾" long. Circa 1949 – 1965. Made in crystal and ebony. In a January 1968 list of new goods, this candleholder was included as No. 2739/316, part of the "Roulette line," which never appeared in any price list and may have only been made on a trial basis. A second candleholder was added to the Contour line in 1953. (See FO-160 on p. 56.) Crystal: $17.50 – 22.50. Ebony $25.00 – 35.00.

FO-154. No. 2639
DUO CANDLESTICK

No. 2639 duo candlestick. 9¾" high with a 5⅜" x 4¼" oval base and a 5⅝" arm spread. Circa 1949 – 1957. Made in crystal. The pattern features three ivy leaves as a center panel. Designed by George Sakier. Patent No. D159,757 was filed December 28, 1949, and approved August 15, 1950. $75.00 – 85.00.

FO-155. No. 2640 GARDEN CENTER (NOTE ORIGINAL BROWN AND WHITE LABEL)

No. 2640 Garden Center. 7" high when assembled. Circa 1949 – 1963. Made in crystal, this set consists of six individual arms that fit into a 5" diameter flower block. It is often found with the matching No. 2640 14" lily pond bowl. Candle-block w/six arms: $140.00 – 160.00. Complete with lily pond underplate: $210.00 – 240.00.

Unknown number and size, but probably about 8" high. Circa 1949 – 1950. Made in crystal. Designed by George Sakier. This candlestick was included in an exhibition of Fostoria at the Metropolitan Museum of Art and pictured in *U.S. Industrial Design 1949 – 1950.* Unable to price. *(Artist's rendition.)*

FO-156. UNKNOWN CANDLESTICK, DESIGNED BY GEORGE SAKIER

No. 2652 trindle candlestick. 5¾" high with a 3" x 9" long rectangular base. Circa 1951 – 1957. Made in crystal. $75.00 – 95.00.

FO-157. No. 2652 TRINDLE CANDLESTICK

No. 2653 trindle candlestick. Circa 1951 – 1955. Made in crystal. Although apparently never considered officially to be part of the No. 2496 Baroque pattern, a report in the *Jewelers' Circular – Keystone,* June 1951, showed these candlesticks as part of a console set, describing them as a "match" for the accompanying Baroque floral bowl. 6¼" high with a 9" long rectangular base. For other candleholders that were part of (or associated with) the Baroque pattern, see FO-94 (p. 37), FO-98 through FO-100 (p. 39), and FO-108 through FO-110 (p. 41-42). $75.00 – 95.00.

FO-158. No. 2653 TRINDLE CANDLESTICK, FROM CATALOG

No. 2655 four-light candlestick/candelabra. 11⅜" high. Circa 1951 – 1955. Made only in crystal, this was also available as a four-light candelabra using either three No. 2545 bobeches and 18 prisms or four bobeches and 24 prisms. $125.00 – 150.00. With three bobeches/prisms: $215.00 – 260.00. With four bobeches/prisms: $245.00 – 300.00.

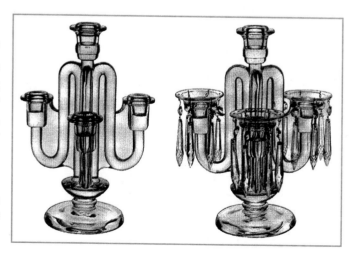

FO-159. No. 2655 4 LIGHT CANDLESTICK AND CANDELABRA, FROM CATALOG

No. 2666 Contour flora candle. 2¼" high with a 6" diameter base. Circa 1953 – 1965. Made in crystal and ebony. Also offered with two etchings, No. 346 Thistle and Crystal Print 2 (Skyflower) and the following cuttings: No. 834 Nosegay, 835 Pine, 836 Ingrid, 837 Wheat, 839 Plume, 840 Circlet, 841 Spray, 842 Regal, and 843 Crest. For an earlier candleholder in the Contour pattern, see FO-153 on p. 54. Crystal: $15.00 – 20.00. Crystal w/Pine cutting: $30.00 – 35.00. Ebony: $25.00 – 30.00. Other etchings or cuttings: Add 40 – 80% to the price of plain.

FO-160. No. 2666 Contour flora candle in ebony

FO-161. No. 2667 Capri candleblock

No. 2667 Capri candleblock. 2½" high, with a 2½" x 2½" base. Circa 1953 – 1960. Made in crystal and ebony. Crystal: $20.00 – 25.00. Ebony: $25.00 – 30.00.

FO-162. No. 2667 Capri candlestick, from catalog

No. 2667 Capri candlestick. 6" high. Circa 1953 – 1958. Made in crystal and ebony. Crystal: $25.00 – 30.00. Ebony: $30.00 – 35.00.

FO-163. No. 2668/313 candlestick

No. 2668/313 candlestick. Also offered as a No. 2668/459 hurricane lamp with a glass shade. 2½" high with a 3⅝" diameter body. Circa 1953 – 1964. Made in crystal and ebony. Crystal: $15.00 – 20.00. Ebony: $22.00 – 27.50. Add $30.00 for hurricane globe.

FO-164. No. 2620/314 Betsy Ross candlestick in aqua

No. 2620/314 Betsy Ross candlestick. 3" high with a 4¾" diameter. It was also available as a No. 314 hurricane lamp with a chimney. Circa 1954 – 1965. Made in aqua, peach, and white milk glass. The pattern is known with the No. 523 Fruit and Flowers enamel decoration. In the 1940s, the same line in crystal was called Wistar. There was a candlestick included, but it was different from this one (see FO-146 on p. 52). $12.00 – 15.00. With Fruits and Flowers decoration: $18.00 – 22.50. Complete with chimney: $35.00 – 45.00.

No. 2685 Seascape candleholder. 1⅞" high. 4½" diameter. Circa 1954 – 1957. Made in caribee blue, coral sand, and crystal. All have an opalescent edge. Can be found with the No. 347 Vintage etching. Crystal, coral sand: $20.00 – 30.00. Caribee blue: $25.00 – 35.00. Add 10 – 20% for etched.

FO-165. No. 2685 SEASCAPE CANDLEHOLDER IN CARIBEE BLUE

No. 2183 candleholder. 2¾" high. 4½" across the top. Circa 1955 – 1958. Made in milk glass. Also sold with a chimney as a hurricane lamp. $15.00 – 20.00. Complete with chimney: $40.00 – 45.00.

FO-166. No. 2183 CANDLE-HOLDERS IN MILK GLASS

No. 2675/312 Randolph candleholder. 1⅝" high and 4" in diameter. Circa 1955 – 1965. Made in white, peach, and aqua milk glass. White: $12.00 – 15.00. Aqua, peach: $15.00 – 22.50.

FO-167. No. 2675/312 RAN-DOLPH CANDLE-HOLDER IN AQUA

No. 2675/319 Randolph candlestick. 6½" high with a 4½" base. Circa 1955 – 1965. Made in white, peach, and aqua milk glass. White: $20.00 – 25.00. Aqua, peach: $25.00 – 30.00.

FO-168. No. 2675/319 RANDOLPH CANDLESTICKS IN PEACH, AQUA, AND MILK GLASS

No. 2675/460 Randolph hurricane lamp base. Listed as No. 2675/459 hurricane lamp, when complete with No. 2675/461 chimney. 3⅜" high (14¾" with shade) with a 4⅜" round base and a 6¼" diameter top. Circa 1956 – 1965. Made in white milk glass. Base only: $30.00 – 40.00. Complete with chimney: $60.00 – 80.00.

FO-169. No 2675/460 RANDOLPH HURRICANE LAMP BASES IN MILK GLASS

FO-170. No. 2694 ARLINGTON DUO CANDLESTICK IN MILK GLASS

No. 2694 Arlington duo candlestick. 5¼" high with a 4⅜" round base and an 8½" arm spread. Circa 1957 – 1959. Milk glass only. $40.00 – 50.00.

FO-171. No. 2702 CANDLE-HOLDERS IN THREE SIZES (CRYSTAL WITH BRASS TOPS)

No. 2702 candleholders. Reversed, these can be used as vases. Made in three sizes: 6¾" high with a 2" vase opening, 8" high with a 2⅜" vase opening, and 9½" high with a 2⅞" vase opening. Circa 1956 – 1962. Made in crystal with brass tops. The swirl pattern is molded on the interior of the vases. The tops are permanently affixed and cannot be unscrewed. 6¾": $25.00 – 30.00, 8": $30.00 – 35.00. 9½": $35.00 – 40.00. Note: prices will be less if brass finish is worn or pitted.

FO-172. No. 2708 CANDLEHOLDER (CRYSTAL WITH BRASS FITTING)

No. 2708 candleholder. 8" high with a 3" diameter base and 3¾" across the top. Circa 1957 – 1962. Made in crystal with a brass fitting connecting the top and bottom sections. The pieces can be unscrewed. Reversed, this candlestick could be used as a vase, but was not listed in catalogs as a vase. $30.00 – 35.00. Note: price will be less if brass finish is worn or pitted. *(From the collection of Helen and Bob Jones.)*

FO-173. No. 2708 DUO CANDLEHOLDER, FROM CATALOG (CRYSTAL WITH BRASS FITTING)

No. 2708 duo candleholder. 10" high with a 3" diameter base. Circa 1957 – 1961. Made in crystal with a brass fitting connecting the candleholder arm to the base. $40.00 – 50.00. Note: price will be less if brass finish is worn or pitted.

Coronation candleholder. Made in two sizes: 6" high and 8" high. Unknown number. Circa 1957, in crystal. $30.00 – 35.00.
(Artist's rendition.)

FO-174.
CORONATION
CANDLEHOLDER

No. 2712/311 Berry flora-candle. 2⁵⁄₁₆" high with a 2½" base and a top diameter of 4½". Circa 1958 – 1965. Known in milk glass, amber, and blue. Since this pattern was created especially to be made in milk glass, the transparent colors may be a later re-issue. Milk glass: $20.00 – 25.00. Amber: $10.00 – 12.00. Blue: $15.00 – 20.00.

FO-175. No.
2712/311 BERRY
FLORA-CANDLE IN
AMBER

No. 2713/311 Vintage leaf candleholder. 1¾" high and 8⅜" long. Circa 1958 – 1965. This leaf shaped candleholder with detailed veining and an open handle was made only in milk glass: $25.00 – 30.00.

FO-176. No.
2713/311 VINTAGE
LEAF CANDLE-
HOLDERS IN
MILK GLASS

No. 2713/315 Vintage candleholder. 4⅛" high with a 3½" hexagonal base. Circa 1958 – 1965. Made in milk glass with a grape pattern on the side panels. $20.00 – 25.00.

FO-177. No.
2713/315 VINTAGE
CANDLEHOLDER
IN MILK GLASS

No. 2722/364 Table Charms trindle candle arm. Circa 1959 – 1965. Three different components are used to make a set. The core component is the No. 2722/334 three-branch arm. The other pieces consist of a combination of No. 2722/312 vases and No. 2722/364 flora-candle/snack bowls. Made in crystal, pink opalescent, and yellow opalescent. The most common configuration was one arm, one vase, and three flora-candles, but as the accompanying advertisement states, "The 'add-a-part' feature means sale after sale, because one combination suggests more and bigger arrangements." The pricing is for the basic configuration, but others should be similar. Crystal: $75.00 – 90.00. Pink opalescent: $125.00 – 150.00. Yellow opalescent: $175.00 – 200.00.

FO-178. JULY 1959 ADVERTISEMENT FOR No. 2722/364 TABLE CHARMS FROM *CHINA, GLASS AND TABLEWARES*

FO-179. No. 1515/311 HEIRLOOM CANDLEVASE IN BLUE OPALESCENT

No. 1515/311 Heirloom candlevase. 8" – 10" high (heights vary according to the way the candle is "pulled") with a 3⅝" base. Circa 1959 – 1961. Made in bittersweet, blue opalescent, crystal opalescent, green opalescent, pink opalescent, and yellow opalescent. Yellow opalescent: $80.00 – 120.00. All other colors: $35.00 – 50.00.

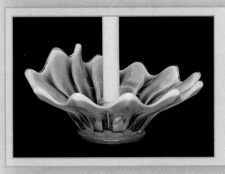

FO-180. No. 2183/311 HEIRLOOM FLORA CANDLE IN YELLOW OPALESCENT

No. 2183/311 Heirloom flora candle. 3" high and 7" in diameter. Since this is a free-form piece, these sizes will vary substantially. Circa 1959 – 1962. Made in bittersweet, blue opalescent, crystal opalescent, green opalescent, pink opalescent, and yellow opalescent. Bittersweet, yellow opalescent: $45.00 – 65.00. All other colors: $30.00 – 40.00.

No. 2726/311 Heirloom candleholder. 3" – 3¼" high with a 2¼" base. Circa 1959 – 1970. Made in crystal, blue, green, pink, and yellow, all with opalescent edges, and in ruby and bittersweet (orange) with crystal edges. Yellow opalescent: $60.00 – 75.00. All other colors: $35.00 – 45.00.

FO-181. No. 2726/311 HEIRLOOM CANDLEHOLDERS (L TO R) IN GREEN OPALESCENT, RUBY, BLUE OPALESCENT, PINK OPALESCENT, CRYSTAL OPALESCENT, AND BITTERSWEET

No. 2730/319 Heirloom candle-vase. 6" high with a 3¾" base. Circa 1960 – 1962. Made in crystal, blue, green, pink, and yellow, all with opalescent edges, and in bittersweet (orange with crystal edges). This candleholder is reversible, and when turned upside down, fits over a peg in a No. 2730/254 12" bowl to form an epergne vase. Yellow opalescent: $175.00 – 225.00. Other colors: $45.00 – 60.00.

FO-182. No. 2730/319 HEIRLOOM CANDLE-VASE IN GREEN OPALESCENT

No. 1372/316 Coin candleholder. 4⅝" high with a 3½" hexagonal base. Circa 1960 – 1982. Made in amber, blue, crystal, olive green, dark emerald green, and ruby, all with frosted coins. Pieces in the pattern without frosted coins are recent reissues by Dalzell Viking and/or Indiana Glass Company for Lancaster Colony. This pattern was inspired by the original U.S. Coin pattern made by the United States Glass Company in 1892 which featured reproductions of actual coins. That pattern was discontinued after only a few months, when the Department of the Treasury deemed the practice to be illegal. The six "coins" on the base of the Fostoria candlestick do not depict actual coins, but feature alternately the Liberty Bell and a colonial head, with the date 1887 (chosen to commemorate the founding of Fostoria). Other pieces in the pattern also have coins with the torch of Liberty or an eagle. A special edition of the pattern, including the low candlestick, was made for Avon sales representatives from 1961 to 1977 with

FO-183. No. 1372/316 COIN CANDLEHOLDERS IN BLUE AND AMBER. NOTE THE DIFFERENCE IN THE SOCKETS. THE STYLE ON THE LEFT IS THE OLDER OF THE TWO

Avon motif coins (the Avon insignia, a lady with a rose, a door knocker, and a globe showing the Western Hemisphere) and the date of Avon's founding, 1886. A Canadian version is also known, made for Canada's centennial in 1967. The Canadian coins feature a wild cat walking, a howling wolf, a Canada goose flying with wings down, and a bird flying with wings spread. Each has the word "CANADA" and the dates, "1867 – 1967." Two different style tops were offered on the Fostoria candlestick (see the accompanying photograph), with the scalloped version dating from 1960 – 1973 and the one with the flat panels from 1974 to 1982. A taller candlestick was added to the pattern later. (See FO-201 on p. 66.) In the late 1970s, A.A. Importing also sold a low coin glass candlestick in crystal with the coins circling the column, different enough that it should cause no confusion with the Fostoria original. Crystal, amber, olive green: $15.00 – 25.00. Blue, dark green, ruby: $35.00 – 45.00.

FO-184. No. 2742/311 Sculpture candleholder in gray mist

No. 2742/311 Sculpture candleholder. 3½" high with a 2¾" four-footed base. Circa 1961 – 1972. Made in crystal and gray mist. A second candleholder was added to the Sculpture line in 1963. (See FO-187 below.) $15.00 – 20.00.

FO-185. No. 2749/314 Windsor Crown candleholder (drawing from catalog)

No. 2749/314 Windsor Crown candleholder. 3½" high. Circa 1962 – 1965. Made in crystal, gold, and royal blue. There was one other candleholder in the unusual Crown collection: the Luxembourg Crown (FO-192 on the following page). Crystal: $25.00 – 30.00. Gold, royal blue: $40.00 – 50.00.

FO-186. No. 2752/314 Facets candleholder in gold

No. 2752/314 Facets candleholder. 3½" high with a 2½" base. Circa 1962 – 1965. Made in crystal, gold, and pink. All colors: $15.00 – 20.00.

FO-187. No. 2757/313 Sculpture candle twist (drawing from catalog)

No. 2757/313 Sculpture candle twist. 2" high. Circa 1963 – 1971. Made in crystal and in gray mist. For an earlier candleholder in the Sculpture pattern, see FO-184 on the top of this page. $10.00 – 12.00.

FO-188. No. 2761/467 lustre

No. 2761/467 lustre. 10½" high with a 4⅝" base. Has an attached bobeche with eight 5" flat prisms. Circa 1963 – 1973. Crystal. $75.00 – 95.00.

No. 2762/333 candelabra. 12" high two-light with No. 2762 bobeches and eight 4" flat prisms. Circa 1963 – 1969. Crystal. $125.00 – 150.00.

FO-189. No. 2762/333 CANDELABRA (DRAWING FROM CATALOG)

FO-189A. No. 2762/333 AND No. 2765/337 CANDELABRA FROM *THE JEWELERS' CIRCULAR-KEYSTONE*, JUNE 1963

No. 2765/337 candelabra. 11¼" high three-light with No. 2765 bobeches and ten 4" flat prisms. Circa 1963 – 1969. Crystal. $150.00 – 175.00.

FO-190. No. 2765/337 CANDELABRA (DRAWING FROM CATALOG)

No. 2763/327 candlestick, 9¼" high; No. 2763/459 hurricane, 13½" high with No. 2763 5" shade; No. 2767/459 hurricane, 17½" high with No. 2767 9" shade; No. 2767/467 lustre with No. 2769 bobeche and ten 4" flat prisms; and No. 2767/468 hurricane lustre with bobeche, ten flat prisms, and No. 2767 shade. All have a 5¼" round base. Circa 1963 – 1974. Reissued as No. CA10/327 candle lamp with a blown shade, 1981 – 1982. Made in crystal. Trade journal reports emphasize the versatility of this candleholder, since it can be used with three sizes of candle, ranging from a standard taper to a 2½" diameter candle. Designed by George Sakier. No. 2763/327: $70.00 – 85.00. No. 2763/459, 2767/459: $80.00 – 95.00. No. 2767/467: $110.00 – 125.00. No. 2767/459: $120.00 – 135.00.

FO-191. No. 2763/327 CANDLESTICK

No. 2766/311 Luxembourg Crown trindle candle bowl. 4¾" high and 7½" in diameter. Circa 1963 – 1965. Made in crystal, gold, royal blue, and ruby. Intended to hold both candles and flowers. There was one other candleholder in the unusual Crown collection: the Windsor Crown (FO-185 on the preceding page). Crystal $45.00 – 55.00. Colors $60.00 – 70.00.

FO-192. No. 2766/311 LUXEMBOURG CROWN TRINDLE CANDLE BOWL

FO-193. No. 2768/337 TRINDLE CANDLESTICK

No. 2768/337 trindle candlestick/candelabra. Listed in 1982 as No. CA 12/337. 12" high three-light with a 5¼" hexagonal base and a 12" arm spread (14" with bobeches). Circa 1963 – 1982. Crystal. $80.00 – 100.00. With three No. 2765 bobeches and 30 4" flat prisms: $170.00 – 220.00.

FO-194. No. 2771/311 CANDLEHOLDER AND No. 2771/310 HURRICANE (DRAWINGS FROM CATALOG)

No. 2771/310 hurricane. Also available as No. 2771/311 candleholder. Dimensions unknown. Made 1964 only. The catalog indicates they were available in colors, but does not specify which ones, so any of the colors from this time period are possible. $25.00 – 30.00. With chimney: $35.00 – 40.00.

FO-195. No. 2772/311 CANDLEHOLDER AND No. 2772/310 HURRICANE (DRAWINGS FROM CATALOG)

No. 2772/310 hurricane. Also available as No. 2772/311 candleholder. Dimensions unknown. Made 1964 only. The catalog indicates they were available in colors, but does not specify which ones, so any of the colors from this time period are possible. $25.00 – 30.00. With chimney: $35.00 – 40.00.

No. 2777/327 Rebecca candlestick. Also referred to in some advertisements as Rebecca-at-the-Well. 9⅞" high with a 5" base. Circa 1964 – 1970. Made in copper blue, crystal, and olive green, all with a silver mist (frosted) finish. This was an accurate reproduction of an early Bakewell, Pears design circa 1850, showing a woman carrying an urn on her shoulder. Made for the Henry Ford Museum Collection and marked HFM in the folds of the skirt, just above the base on the figure's left side. A matching compote was also made. All colors: $60.00 – 80.00.

FO-196. No. 2777/327 REBECCA CANDLESTICKS IN OLIVE MIST AND COPPER BLUE MIST. THE INSERT SHOWS WHERE THE INITIALS HFM ARE LOCATED

No. 2776/327 Sandwich candlestick. Later listed as No. CA 11/327. 9" high with a 4" hexagonal base. Circa 1965 – 1977 and 1979 – 1981. Originally made for the Henry Ford Museum Collection in crystal, copper blue, and olive green. These colors will be marked HFM just below the bottom ring on the stem. Late colors included cobalt blue, crystal, ebony, and ruby in plain or satin finish. These will not be marked. Also known in teal green, reportedly made by Lancaster Colony (Indiana Glass Company) in the 1990s. As the name suggests, this is a reproduction of a candlestick originally made by the Boston and Sandwich Glass Company (see BS-22 on p. 41 of volume 1 in this series). The original candlestick would have been made in two pieces, connected by a wafer, while the reproduction is molded as a single piece. Crystal: $15.00 – 20.00. Olive green, teal: $25.00 – $30.00. Cobalt, copper blue, ebony, ruby: $35.00 – 45.00.

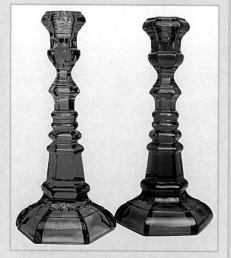

FO-197. No. 2776/327 SANDWICH CANDLESTICKS IN COPPER BLUE AND RUBY

LOOKALIKE

Another facsimile of the same Sandwich candlestick made by an unknown manufacturer can be seen in the accompanying photograph (FO-197a). It is very similar to Fostoria's No. 2776/327 but close inspection will reveal several differences. The unknown candlestick has a much deeper socket opening, a hollow stem (whereas the Fostoria candlestick is solid), and a slightly different shape to the candle cup. It also has a more pronounced pseudo wafer and sharper corners. These are often sold as being made by the New England Glass Company, but we don't believe they have enough age to be New England glass. We know them in three colors: black, canary, and medium blue, all of which are usually seen with a satin finish. These characteristics suggest that the Tiffin factory of the United States Glass Company may have been the manufacturer, but we have no evidence that Tiffin ever made a candleholder such as this. Additional information will be presented on this candlestick in volume three.

FO-197A. FOSTORIA NO. 2776/327 IN OLIVE GREEN AND UNKNOWN LOOK-ALIKE IN CANARY SATIN

No. 2782/315 candleholder. 3½" high. Also made as a No. 2782/459 hurricane (12¼" high with chimney). Circa 1964 – 1974. Made in crystal. All of the trade journals reports pictured the hurricane lamp with a thicker than normal candle. $15.00 – 20.00. With chimney: $25.00 – 30.00.

FO-198. No. 2782/459 HURRICANE FROM AN AD IN *CHINA, GLASS & TABLEWARES*, DECEMBER 1964

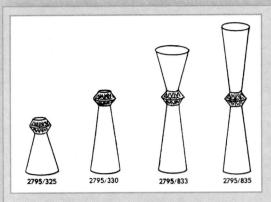

FO-199. GROUPING OF NO. 2795 SHANTUNG CANDLEHOLDERS AND CANDLE/VASES (DRAWINGS FROM CATALOG)

No. 2795/325 Shantung candleholder, 8" high; No. 2795/330 Shantung candleholder, 12" high; No. 2795/833 Shantung candle/vase, 18" high; and No. 2795/835 Shantung candle/vase, 22" high. Circa 1967 – 1968. The candleholders were made in a combination of crystal and either fern green, Mayan blue, or tangerine as part of the Group International Collection. The candle/vases were made in combinations of fern green with tangerine or Mayan blue with fern green. These were made after Fostoria bought the Morgantown Glass Works and used Morgantown colors. (Fern green was Morgantown's moss green, tangerine was their gypsy fire, and Mayan blue their peacock blue). Like the Coventry pieces below, these probably combine blown tops and bottoms in color from Morgantown with pressed crystal "knobs" from Fostoria. No. 325: $35.00 – 45.00. No. 330: $45.00 – 55.00. No. 833: $65.00 – 80.00. No. 835: $75.00 – 90.00.

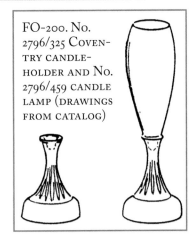

FO-200. No. 2796/325 COVENTRY CANDLEHOLDER AND No. 2796/459 CANDLE LAMP (DRAWINGS FROM CATALOG)

No. 2796/325 Coventry candleholder, 8" high; and No. 2796/459 Coventry candle lamp, 19" high. Circa 1967 – 1968. Made in fern green, Mayan blue, and tangerine, all with crystal standards as part of the Group International Collection. These were made after Fostoria bought the Morgantown Glass Works and the Morgantown factory produced the blown colored pieces to unite with the Fostoria-made pressed crystal pieces. (Fern green was Morgantown's moss green, tangerine was their gypsy fire, and Mayan blue their peacock blue). No. 325: $45.00 – 50.00. No. 459: $125.00 – 150.00.

FO-201. No. 1372/326 COIN CANDLEHOLDER IN RUBY

No. 1372/326 Coin candleholder. 8" high with a 3⅜" base. Circa 1968 – 1982. Originally made in amber, crystal, olive green, and ruby. This pattern was inspired by the original U.S. Coin pattern made by the United States Glass Company in 1892, which featured reproductions of actual coins, and was discontinued a few months later when the Department of the Treasury deemed this to be illegal. The three "coins" on the Fostoria candlestick do not depict actual coins, but feature the Liberty Bell, a torch, and an eagle with the date 1887 (chosen to commemorate the founding of Fostoria). Other pieces in the pattern also have coins with a colonial head. See FO-183 (p. 61) for an earlier candlestick in the same pattern. Some pieces in the pattern have been reissued in recent years by Lancaster Colony, but there are no reports of the candlestick being included among them. Crystal, amber, olive green: $30.00 – 45.00. Ruby: $45.00 – 65.00.

FO-202. No. 2808/318 CARIBBEAN CANDLEHOLDER (DRAWING FROM CATALOG)

No. 2808/318 Caribbean footed candleholder. 5½" high. Circa 1969 – 1970. Made in crystal and steel gray. $15.00 – 20.00.

No. 2816/325 Sierra candle pedestal. Made in crystal and known with the No. 921 Sierra Ice cutting. Circa 1969 – 1970. Note the difference between the photograph in FO-203a (from the November 1969 issue of *China, Glass & Tablewares*) and the catalog drawing in FO-203. $25.00 – 30.00.

FO-203. No. 2816/325 SIERRA CANDLE PEDESTAL (DRAWING FROM CATALOG)

FO-203A. No. 2816/325 SIERRA CANDLE PEDESTAL FROM *CHINA, GLASS & TABLEWARES*, NOVEMBER 1969. (NOTE DIFFERENCE IN SHAPE OF CANDLE PEDESTAL)

No. 2842/311 Serendipity candleblock. 1½" high, approximately 4" x 4½". Circa 1972 – 1974. Made in crystal and listed as an "individual candleholder." Trade journal reports described this unusual pattern as having a "Scandinavian flavor." For other candleholders in the Serendipity line, see FO-205 below and FO-208 on the following page. $12.00 – 16.00.

FO-204. No. 2842/311 SERENDIPITY CANDLEBLOCKS

No. 2842/327 Serendipity candleblock. 9½" wide. Circa 1972 – 1974. Made in crystal. Holds a large candle. For other candleholders in the Serendipity line, see FO-204 above and FO-208 on the following page. $15.00 – $20.00.

FO-205. No. 2842/327 SERENDIPITY CANDLEBLOCK (DRAWING FROM 1973 CATALOG)

FO-205A. SELECTION OF SERENDIPITY GIFT ITEMS (WITH A "SCANDINAVIAN FLAVOR") FROM *CHINA, GLASS & TABLEWARES*, DECEMBER 1972

No. 2844/311 Sea Shells flora candlestick. 2¾" high with a 7" diameter. Circa 1971 – 1973. Made in copper blue, crystal, and green. All colors: $20.00 – 30.00.

FO-206. No. 2844/311 SEA SHELLS FLORA CANDLESTICK IN GREEN

No. 2844/317 Sea Shells flared candlestick. 3½" high. Circa 1971 – 1973. Made in crystal, copper blue, and green. This was made from the same mold as the No. 2844/311 flora candlestick above, with the edge flared. All colors: $15.00 – 25.00.

FO-207. No. 2844/317 SEA SHELLS FLARED CANDLESTICK (DRAWING FROM 1972 CATALOG)

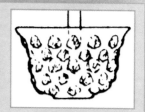

No. 2866/313 Serendipity candleblock, 2" high; No. 2866/315 Serendipity candleblock, 4" high; and No. 2866/319 Serendipity candleblock, 6" high. Circa 1973 – 1974. Made in crystal. Blenko made a similar set of candleblocks from 1987 to the present, in 2", 3", and 4" heights. (See BL-42 on p. 33 of volume one of this series.) For other candleholders in the Serendipity line, see FO-204 and FO-205 on the previous page. All sizes: $8.00 – 14.00.

FO-208. GROUPING OF No. 2866 SERENDIPITY CANDLEBLOCK (DRAWINGS FROM CATALOG)

FO-209. No. 2521/327 BIRD CANDLEHOLDER (DRAWING FROM 1974 CATALOG)

No. 2521/327 bird candleholder. Also listed as No. LE 06/327. Part of the Centennial II Collection. 1½" high. Circa 1974 – 1979 in lead crystal; made again as No. CA15/312 in ruby from 1981 to 1982. Some of the Centennial II pieces were reissued using old molds from the early 1900s, but we have found no evidence that this was the case with the bird candleholder. $12.00 – 18.00.

FO-210. No. 2864/327 CANDLEHOLDER (DRAWING FROM 1974 CATALOG)

No. 2864/327 candleholder (called candle "B"). Also listed as No. LE 05/327. Part of the Centennial II Collection. 2½" diameter. Circa 1974 – 1981. Made in lead crystal. Some of the Centennial II pieces were reissued using old molds from the early 1900s, but we have found no evidence that this was the case with this candleholder. $5.00 – 8.00.

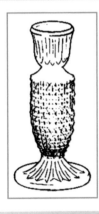

FO-211. No. 2883/319 CANDLESTICK (DRAWING FROM 1974 CATALOG)

No. 2883/319 candlestick. Also listed as No. LE 04/319. Part of the Centennial II Collection. 6" high. Circa 1974 – 1981. Made in lead crystal. Some of the Centennial II pieces were reissued using old molds from the early 1900s, but we have found no evidence that this was the case with this candlestick. $13.00 – 18.00.

FO-212. No. 2921/317 WOODLAND CANDLESTICKS IN GREEN, FROM CATALOG

No. 2921/317 Woodland candlestick. 5" high. Circa 1977 – 1978. Made in blue, brown, crystal, and green. All colors: $10.00 – 14.00.

No. FL 03/317 Flame flora candleholder. 4" high. Circa 1977 – 1980. Made in crystal, brown, and green. All colors: $6.00 – 10.00.

FO-213. No. FL 03/317 FLAME FLORA CANDLEHOLDERS AND FL 03/757 VASE IN BROWN, FROM CATALOG

No. FL 05/756 Flame flora candleholder/vase. 6" high. Circa 1977 – 1980. Made in crystal, brown, and green. This candleholder can be use as a vase when turned upside-down. All colors: $8.00 – 12.00.

FO-214. No. FL 05/756 FLAME FLORA CANDLE-HOLDER/VASE IN GREEN

No. GL 06/313 Glacier stackable candleholder. Also listed as No. GL 07/313 and GL 08/313, depending on the color. 1¾" high and 2½" across. Circa 1977 – 1980. Made in crystal (No. GL 06/313), brown (No. GL 08/313), and green (No. GL 07/313). Described as "stackable," because they could be stacked to create multiple-height candlesticks, as well as when not in use. All colors: $6.00 – 8.00.

FO-215. No. GL 07/313 GLACIER STACKABLE CANDLEHOLDER IN GREEN

Heart & Diamond convertible candlestick. 7⅛" high. Made especially for Avon in crystal only. Circa 1978 – 1981. Placed in one direction, it holds a taper candle. When turned over, it serves as a votive candleholder or a vase. $10.00 – 12.00.

FO-216. HEART & DIAMOND CONVERTIBLE CANDLESTICK (MADE FOR AVON)

FO-217. CAPE COD 2⅜" CANDLEHOLDER IN RUBY (MADE FOR AVON)

Cape Cod candleholder. 2⅜" high with a 3¼" base. Made in ruby especially for Avon. Circa 1978 – 1983. $5.00 – 8.00.

FO-218. CAPE COD 8⅝" CANDLEHOLDER/PERFUME BOTTLE IN RUBY (MADE FOR AVON)

Cape Cod candleholder/perfume bottle. 8⅝" high with a 3⅛" base. Made in ruby especially for Avon. Circa 1978 – 1983. The base is hollow and came filled with 5 oz. of "Charisma" cologne. The removable socket served as a stopper. Part of Avon's "1876 Cape Cod Collection." According to the box "…its name commemorates both the spirit of [the] 1876 Philadelphia Centennial, which celebrated the 100th anniversary of the Declaration of Independence, and the area where Sandwich glass originated." $8.00 – 10.00.

FO-219. CAPE COD 10¼" HURRICANE LAMP IN RUBY (MADE FOR AVON)

Cape Cod hurricane lamp. 10¼" high with a base that is 4½" high and 4½" across. Made especially for Avon in ruby with a crystal globe. Circa 1978 – 1983. Very similar to the candleholder in FO-217, but with a broad rim added to hold the globe. Marked "AVON" on the underside of the base. $10.00 – 12.00.

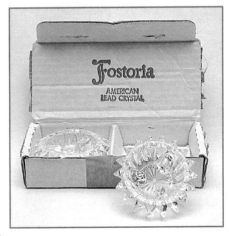

FO-220. No. ST 06/327 CANDLEHOLDERS IN ORIGINAL BOX

No. ST 06/327 candleholder. 1" high and 3⅛" in diameter. Circa 1979 – 1981. Made in lead crystal. These were sold boxed in pairs with a card on the care of Fostoria crystal. $15.00 – 20.00.

No. AM 01/311 American chamber candleholder. 2" high and 4½" across. Circa 1980 – 1982. This was the last candleholder to be added to the No. 2056 American pattern. For other candleholders in the American pattern, see FO-38 (p. 21), FO-42 (p. 22), FO-95 (p. 38), FO-118 through FO-120 (p. 45), and FO-131 (p. 48). $35.00 – 50.00.

FO-221. No. AM 01/311 AMERICAN CHAMBER CANDLEHOLDER

No. 315 Holly candlestick. 4½" high. Circa 1981 – 1982. Made in ruby and possibly in crystal and dark green. After Fostoria went out of business, Indiana Glass continued making some pieces in this pattern in the late 1980s, including the candlestick. $35.00 – 45.00.

FO-222. HOLLY AND RUBY GIFTWARE ASSORTMENT, FROM 1982 CATALOG

No. 318 Lotus Giftware low candlestick, 5½" high; and No. 323 Lotus Giftware high candlestick, 7½" high. Circa 1981 – 1982. Made in crystal with an ebony, crystal mist, or peach mist base. The accompanying catalog reprint also shows the same color combinations on the No. 789 bud vases. All color combinations, No. 318: $35.00 – 45.00. No. 323: $45.00 – 55.00.

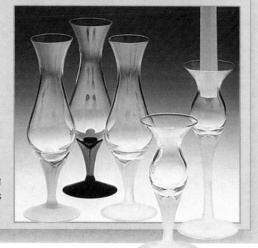

FO-223. LOTUS GIFTWARE VASES AND CANDLESTICKS IN PEACH MIST, EBONY, AND CRYSTAL MIST, FROM 1982 CATALOG

Duchess candlestick. 8¼" high with a 4¼" base. Made as No. 10009 (later, No. 009) in horizon blue from 1982 to 1984 and then as No. 292 in cobalt blue from 1984 to 1986. Produced for Tiara Exclusives from an old Indiana Glass Company mold (the No. 4 Wedgewood design candlestick, circa 1918 – 1929; see IN-2 on p. 236). We understand that the reason Tiara (which was owned by Lancaster Colony, parent company of Indiana as well) had Fostoria make these was because Indiana was solely involved in the manufacture of machine made glass and could no longer produce hand pressed items like these. Fenton also made some of the Tiara items for the same reason. $20.00 – 25.00.

FO-224. No. 292 DUCHESS CANDLESTICKS IN COBALT BLUE, FROM TIARA EXCLUSIVES FALL 1984 CATALOG

FO-225.
No. CA 12/323
CANDLESTICK, FROM
1982 CATALOG

No. CA 12/323 candlestick. 7" high. Circa 1982. Made in crystal. This was included as part of the "Handcrafted Candlestick Collection" in the 1982 catalog, with the others all earlier candlesticks that were reissued that year. This one also looks like it could certainly be from an earlier period, but if so, we have been unable to document it. $20.00 – 30.00.

FO-226. No.
HE 03/313
HERITAGE
CANDLEHOLDER,
FROM 1984
CATALOG

No. HE 03/313 Heritage candleholder. Unknown size. Circa 1983 – 1986. Made in crystal. $4.00 – 6.00.

FO-227. No.
V103/319 VIRGINIA
CANDLEHOLDERS IN
LIGHT BLUE AND
DARK BLUE

No. V 103/319 Virginia candleholder. 6" high with a 4" base. Circa 1983 – 1986. Made in crystal, brown, dark blue, gray, green, light blue, peach, and ruby. This candleholder is unusual in that it is nine sided. It was also available as No. 466 globe hurricane and as No. 469 chimney hurricane. All colors: $10.00 – 15.00. With peg insert and hurricane shades: $25.00 – 35.00.

FO-228. CANDLESTICKS
FROM FOSTORIA'S CRYS-
TAL AND GOLD GIFT-
WARE LINE, FROM *CHINA,*
GLASS & TABLEWARES,
MAY 1984

Unknown pattern number. 6" high. Circa 1984. Made in crystal. This was part of the crystal and gold giftware line, advertised in the May 1984 issue of *China, Glass & Tablewares.* $25.00 – 30.00.

FO-229.
No. 079
VENETIAN
CANDLE-
HOLDER
(MADE FOR
TIARA
EXCLUSIVES)

No. 078 Venetian candleholder, 5½" high with a 4" base, circa 1984 – 1986; and No. 079 Venetian candleholder, 7⅜" high with a 4½" base, circa 1984 – 1986. This was an original design made for Tiara Exclusives by Fostoria in 24% lead crystal. Also offered as No. 046 as a candlelamp (or hurricane lamp). The molds were moved to the Indiana Glass Company, who continued production of the taller size from 1987 to 1998 in non-lead crystal, plain and with satin highlights, cranberry stain on the base, or ruby stain overall. (See IN-110 on p. 267.) The small size was also made by Indiana in black. (See IN-111 on p. 267.) $25.00 – $30.00.

No. 341 Old Williamsburg candlestick. 7" high with a 3¾" base. Circa 1985 – 1986. Made in crystal, nut brown, and ultra blue. This is a reissue of a candlestick originally made by Heisey as No. 2 from 1903 to 1957 (see HE-2 on p. 98) and then by Imperial from 1958 to 1982 (see IM-137 on p. 217). Although the colors made by Fostoria are all ones that were originally offered by Imperial, the latter did not made this candlestick in ultra blue. Also, Imperial's reissues of the candlestick in nut brown had ground bottoms, whereas the Fostoria versions are probably unfinished on the bottoms. Early Imperial crystal candlesticks are also ground on the bottom, so it is only their later crystal candlesticks that probably cannot be distinguished from the Fostoria versions. The original Heisey candlesticks have a ground bottom with a polished punty and will be of finer quality crystal. The mold is still in the possession of Lancaster Colony Corporation, Fostoria's parent company. $30.00 – 35.00.

FO-230. No. 341 CANDLESTICK, FROM NEW PRODUCT BROCHURE. (FROM HEISEY MOLD)

No. 32 Old Williamsburg handled candlestick. 5½" high with a 2⅞" base. Circa 1984 – 1985. Made in crystal, and possibly also nut brown and ultra blue. This is a reissue of a candlestick originally made by Heisey from 1910 to 1922 (see HE-20 on p. 107) and then by Imperial from 1980 – 1981 (see IM-177 on p. 228). The mold is still in the possession of Lancaster Colony Corporation, Fostoria's parent company. $20.00 – 30.00.

FO-231. No. 32 HANDLED CANDLESTICK, FROM NEW PRODUCT BROCHURE. (FROM HEISEY MOLD)

FO-232. TRANSITION CANDLEHOLDER, FROM NEW PRODUCT BROCHURE

Transition candleholder. Unknown size with a square base. Circa 1985 – 1986. Made in lead crystal. Some of the other pieces in the pattern bear a strong resemblance to Cambridge Square. $8.00 – 12.00.

No. 318 Celestial candleholder. 1¼" high with a 5¼" diameter. Circa 1985 – 1986. Made in crystal, blue, or sun gold with iridescent finish. This was a reissue of a candleholder originally made by the Federal Glass Company as No. S-500 in Gem-Tone (crystal with purple and marigold iridescence), limelight (avocado green), and other colors. (See FD-8 on p. 174 of volume 1 of this series.) The mold is currently in the possession of the Indiana Glass Company, who reissued it in 1997 as the base for the No. 12011 Celestial candlelamp, with nubs added to hold a hurricane globe in place. (See IN- 114 on p. 268.) All colors $6.00 – 10.00.

FO-233. No. 318 CELESTIAL CANDLEHOLDER IN BLUE. (FROM FEDERAL MOLD)

FO-234. No. 830 CANDLE-DISH MADE EXCLUSIVELY FOR PRINCESS HOUSE

No. 830 candle-dish. 1¾" high and 6¼" in diameter. Circa 1980s. Made exclusively for Princess House in lead crystal. Holds three slim taper candles. $8.00 – 10.00.

FRY (H. C.) GLASS COMPANY, Rochester, Pennsylvania (1902 – 1933). Founded

by Henry C. Fry as the Rochester Glass Company, within months of its opening advertisements appeared stating that "To avoid conflictions in the similarity of names of other Glass Companies using the name of 'Rochester,' the Rochester Glass Company will hereafter be known as the H. C. Fry Glass Company." The reference was to, among others, the Rochester Tumbler Company, which had also been founded by Henry C. Fry many years previous. It had become the Rochester Tumbler Works of the National Glass Company around 1900. Although this factory had burned at around the time that Fry had begun construction of his new factory, it was in the process of being rebuilt in 1902.

During his tenure at the National Glass Company, Fry had been elected its first president, but had resigned in 1901 and immediately begun construction of his new factory. Its specialty, like that of the earlier company, was initially the production of pressed and blown tumblers. However, the blanks produced by the new factory quickly gained a reputation for unsurpassed quality and were widely bought by other decorating firms, so the line was expanded to include a full range of table ware. At the same time, the output of Fry's own cutting department was attracting notice. Just months after the factory opened, they exhibited what was described as, at 31" high, "Probably the largest vase ever manufactured." The account in the *China, Glass and Pottery Review* from October 1902 went on to state that "Aside from its mammoth size, it is one of the most perfect pieces of cut glass, so experts say, that has ever been produced in this country." In 1905, they surpassed even this effort with a huge punch bowl exhibited at the Lewis and Clark Exposition in Portland, Oregon. The entire set stood five feet high and was valued at $5,000.

Some cut glass continued to be made on into the 1920s. However, as this market diminished, the company began moving in other directions. A major innovation in 1915 was the introduction of oven ware, initially in clear crystal, followed in 1921 by pearl, or opalescent, oven glass. The next development in 1922 was the announcement of a new art glass line in Foval, which utilized the pearl coloring with jade green or Delft blue trim on shapes suitable for the jewelry store trade. Other transparent colors and a wider variety of stemware and tableware followed in the later 1920s.

Financial difficulties resulted in the company going into receivership in 1925, while remaining in operation. They were reorganized in 1929. Despite the optimism expressed at this time, the company only managed to stay in operation for a few years longer, finally closing in 1933.

FRY LOGO

COLORS

Pearl (opalescent white) was introduced in 1921, followed by Foval in 1922. A contraction of Fry OVenglass Art Line, Foval was offered in all pearl, or with Delft blue, jade green, or rose trim. The same colors were also used for festooning (applied loops) on pearl. Delft blue, jade green, or rose were also used occasionally as solid colors or with pearl festooning. A trade journal report from August 1922 also mentions a combination of pearl and golden glow yellow, though we have found no additional documentation for this. Golden glow was mentioned again in 1925 as new, in this case referring to Fry's transparent amber. Emerald was also being offered by this time. Seagreen is mentioned in a trade journal report from 1927, probably the light green also made by Fry. By 1928, rose, royal blue, and amber were also in production, with ebony and gold (light amber) being made by 1929. Azure blue (a light blue) probably also dates from this same period. Late colors include fuchsia (a deep amethyst), made around 1930, and cobalt blue, made in 1931. (The latter, reported by Hazel Marie Weatherman, may be a continuation of the earlier royal blue.)

FR-1. CANDLESTICK, PROBABLY CUT FROM NO. 4525 BLANK. ADVERTISEMENT FROM *Crockery and Glass Journal*, OCTOBER 1, 1903

Candlestick. Dimensions unknown. This was the earliest candlestick advertised by Fry in the October 1, 1903 issue of the *Crockery and Glass Journal*. This probably was cut using the same blank as the No. 4525 Colonial candlestick shown on the following page from an undated catalog. Since Fry also sold blanks to other companies, this same shape can be found in the Lackawanna Cut Glass Company's catalog as their No. 2081 candlestick with the Seneca cutting and in T. B. Clark and Company's 1905 catalog as their No. 364 candlestick with the Hague cutting. $150.00 – 175.00.

No. 4525 Colonial candlestick. Made in two sizes, 8" and 10". This candlestick appears in an undated catalog. Other pieces on the same catalog page were advertised in 1906, but of course may have been introduced earlier. $150.00 – 175.00.

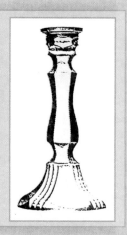

FR-2. No. 4525 COLONIAL CANDLESTICK, FROM CATALOG

No. 4525 candlestick. Made in two sizes, 8" and 10". This candlestick is from a catalog of blanks for use by other decorating companies, circa 1902 – 1905, and could be the blank used for the two preceding cut versions. The pattern number is the same as the No. 4525 Colonial candlestick immediately above. If this is the case, it is remarkable how much the shape was modified by being cut. However, note the repetition of another pattern number for both FR-5 below and FR-7 on the following page, which are clearly not from the same blanks, so it appears that we cannot rely on the pattern number alone to make a connection. (Not priced, since it is unlikely that uncut blanks will turn up in today's market.)

FR-3. No. 4525 CANDLESTICK, FROM CATALOG OF BLANKS FOR USE BY DECORATING COMPANIES

No. 4527 candlestick. 10" high. This candlestick is from a catalog of blanks for use by other decorating companies, circa 1902 – 1905. (Not priced, since it is unlikely that uncut blanks will turn up in today's market.)

FR-4. No. 4527 CANDLESTICK, FROM CATALOG OF BLANKS FOR USE BY DECORATING COMPANIES

No. 4528 candlestick. 10" high. This candlestick is from a catalog of blanks for use by other decorating companies, circa 1902 – 1905. Note that this same pattern number was used for a completely different candlestick (FR-7 on the following page). (Not priced, since it is unlikely that uncut blanks will turn up in today's market.)

FR-5. No. 4528 CANDLESTICK, FROM CATALOG OF BLANKS FOR USE BY DECORATING COMPANIES

FR-6. No. 4529 CANDLESTICK, FROM CATALOG OF BLANKS FOR USE BY DECORATING COMPANIES

No. 4529 candlestick. 10" high. This candlestick is from a catalog of blanks for use by other decorating companies, circa 1902 – 1905. (Not priced, since it is unlikely that uncut blanks will turn up in today's market.)

FR-7. No. 4528 COLONIAL CANDLESTICK, FROM CATALOG

No. 4528 Colonial candlestick. 5" high. This candlestick appears in a catalog on a page with other pieces advertised in 1906, as well as in one that is probably later, circa 1909. The size and shape are intriguingly similar to Heisey's 5" No. 5 candlestick (see HE-5a on p. 101), which was originally made in 1904. Since many of Heisey's early colonial candlesticks were copies of cut glass originals, it raises the suggestion that Fry's candlestick may have come out before 1904 and that it served as an inspiration for Heisey's version. $100.00 – 125.00.

No. 4530 Colonial candlestick. 8" high with a 4" square base. Offered both plain or notched, as seen in the accompanying photograph. Also offered with the Daisy cutting seen in FR-8a, from an undated catalog, probably ca. 1909. An earlier catalog page, which includes other items advertised in 1906, shows the notched version only. $150.00 – 175.00.

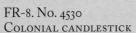

FR-8. No. 4530 COLONIAL CANDLESTICK

FR-8A. No. 4530 COLONIAL CANDLESTICK WITH DAISY CUTTING, FROM CATALOG

No. 4531 Colonial candlestick. Made in two sizes, 8" and 10". The example shown is 8⅛" high with a 4" hexagonal base. Production dates are unknown, but it appears in both of the undated catalogs mentioned above. The page that may date to 1906, since it contains other items advertised that year, shows the 8" size only; the later page, probably ca. 1909, shows both sizes. 8": $150.00 – 175.00. 10": $175.00 – 200.00.

FR-9. No. 4531 COLONIAL 8" CANDLESTICK

Foval candlestick. Made in four sizes: 10" high with a 4" diameter base; 12" with a 4⅜" diameter base; 14" and 17" with a 4⅝" diameter base. Various pattern numbers appear in catalogs: No. 1101, described as "all white" (probably all pearl with crystal threading); No.1102, all Delft (FR-10c, considered very rare); No. 1103, in pearl with jade or Delft buttons and threading (FR-10); or No. 1105, in pearl with only the buttons in jade or Delft (FR-10a). These candlesticks were among the first items advertised when Foval was introduced in 1922. We don't know how long production continued. The candlesticks are also known to have been decorated with silver overlay by the Rockwell Company of Meriden, Connecticut. This candlestick has been reproduced. (See FR-11 and FR-12 below.) 10" or 12", pearl with Delft or jade trim: $175.00 – 250.00. All Delft, other sizes: Unable to price.

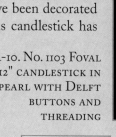

FR-10. No. 1103 Foval 12" candlestick in pearl with Delft buttons and threading

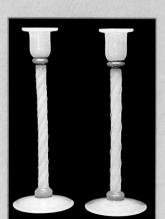

FR-10A. No. 1105 Foval 12" candlesticks in pearl with jade and Delft buttons

FR-10B. No. 1103 Foval 12" candlestick in pearl with jade buttons and threading and 17" size in pearl with Delft threading and buttons.
(From the collection of Bill Burke)

FR-10C. No. 1102 Foval 12" candlestick in Delft (very rare)

REPRODUCTIONS

Foval fake. Although often found signed with the Fry logo in a shield, this is a relatively recent reproduction, origin unknown. Research indicates that real Foval was rarely, if ever, signed. Also, the shape and colors are different.

FR-11. Foval fake

FR-12. Foval fake

Foval fake. 10¾" high with a 3⅞" diameter foot. Although often found signed with the Fry logo in a shield, this is another relatively recent reproduction, origin unknown. Research indicates that real Foval was rarely, if ever, signed. Also, the shape is different and the color of the threading a brighter blue than Delft.

Unknown Candlestick, Signed Fry

FR-13. Unknown candlestick, with fake Fry signature

Unknown candlestick. 10" high with a 4¾" diameter base. Acid-etched "Fry" on the bottom, but the jury is out as to who the actual manufacturer is. Although obviously of high quality, knowledgeable researchers feel it is too ornate to be a typical Fry design. As summed up in the H. C. Fry Glass Society's *The Collector's Encyclopedia of Fry Glassware,* "The simple, almost plain form of the Pearl Art Glass produced by Fry is possibly the strongest aid in its identification. The beauty was in the glass itself, and therefore, when compared with similar types of glass from other companies, it is almost conspicuous in the absence of unnecessary gaudery." Research also indicates that Foval was sold with paper labels and only rarely, if ever, signed. So who made this candlestick? Pending positive identification as the product of some other company, it remains an unknown, but with a strong presumption that someone added the fraudulent Fry signature to an older piece of glassware.

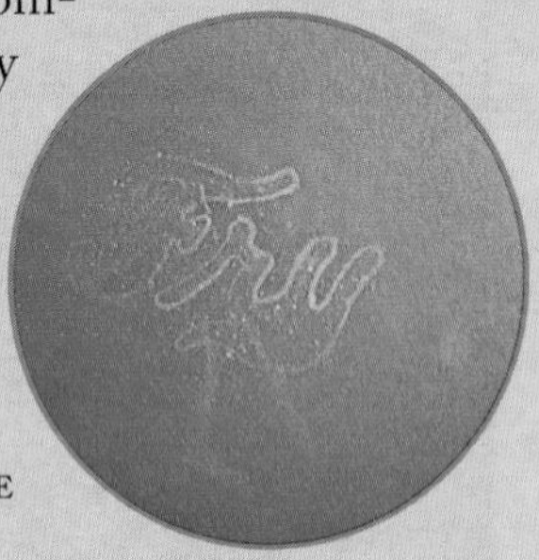

FR-13A. Close-up of fake Fry signature

Foval candlestick. 12" high with a 4½" to 5" diameter bell bottom base. Production dates unknown, but probably mid- to late-1920s. Seen here in pearl with jade festooning, jade with pearl festooning, and rose, the rarest Foval color. This candlestick was often used for a lamp base (as seen in FR-14b), with a hollow stem and a notch cut in the base to allow egress for the electric cord. The festooned ware is sometimes referred to as Radioware, because of the resemblance of the loops to radio waves, still a new phenomenon in the 1920s. $200.00 – market.

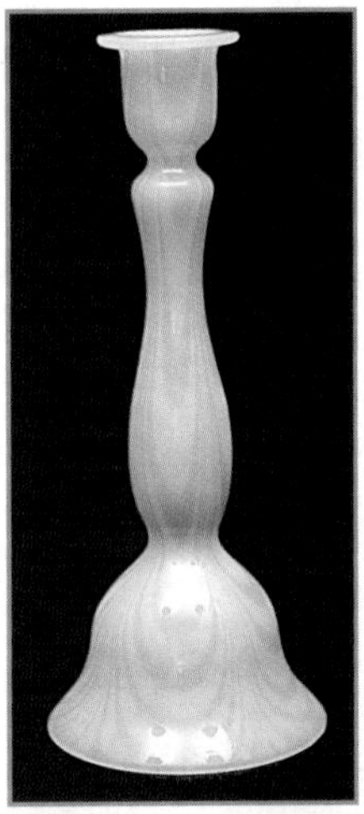

FR-14. Foval Radioware candlestick in pearl with jade festooning

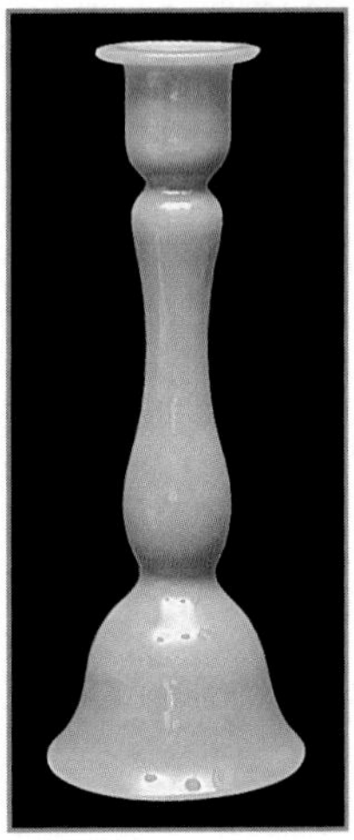

FR-14A. Foval Radioware candlestick in rose (rare)

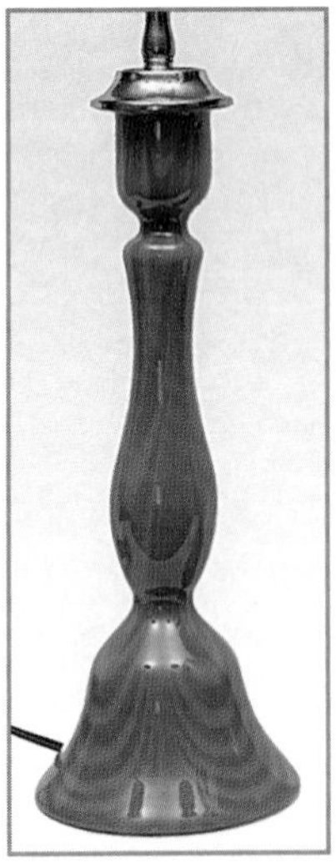

FR-14B. Foval Radioware lamp base in jade with pearl festooning

FR-15. Foval candlestick in pearl with stippled finish and jade trim

Foval candlestick. 10⅝" high with a 4¼" diameter base. Production dates unknown, but probably mid- to late-1920s. The example shown is in pearl Foval with jade trim, with a stippled finish. Both the treatment and the candlestick are considered very rare. The stem has a hole that goes all the way through to the base. Unable to price.

Foval candlestick. 10" high with a 4¾" diameter base. Production dates unknown, but probably mid- to late-1920s. Very unusual example of an all jade piece, shown with silver overlay. Unable to price.

FR-16. FOVAL CANDLESTICK IN JADE WITH SILVER OVERLAY DECORATION

ARE THESE FRY?

Candlestick. 12" high with a 4½" diameter round foot. It this Fry? We have no documentation for this style candlestick having been made by Fry, but its color matches Fry's emerald and its quality is consonant with theirs. Knowledgeable collectors believe there is a possibility that it is Fry, while other equally knowledgeable researchers have attributed it to Morgantown. Whoever made it, it is a beautiful candlestick. $100.00 – 125.00.

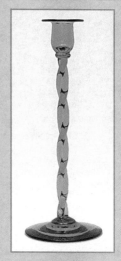

FR-17. CANDLESTICK IN GREEN, POSSIBLY FRY OR MORGANTOWN

FR-18. THREADED CANDLESTICK, POSSIBLY FRY OR STEUBEN

Candlestick. 5¼" high with a 4⅝" diameter base. Also known with the top turned down and the base not as deeply cupped as the example seen here. Fry introduced a line of threaded (or reeded) glass in 1928, including some pieces with random bubbles. However, another company that also made glassware with both these treatments is Steuben – while the absence of documentation from either of these companies for this style candlestick has led to its being attributed by knowledgeable researchers as both Fry and Steuben, the preponderance of current evidence points more to Steuben. Whoever made it, it is a wonderful example of freehand work. $150.00 – 200.00. *(From the collection of Bill Burke.)*

Candlestick. 3" high with a 5" diameter round, saucer foot. Introduced in 1928 and probably in production until the factory closed in 1933. Made both with a plain foot and diamond optic. Known in crystal, emerald, rose, royal blue, amber, azure blue, ebony, and fuchsia, with a wide variety of decorative treatments, as can be seen in the accompanying photographs. A distinctive feature of this candlestick is the way the foot is turned up to form a saucer. All colors: $20.00 – 25.00. Add 25 – 40% for decoration.

FR-19. Candlesticks in crystal with various decorations. (Note diamond optic on two of the bases)

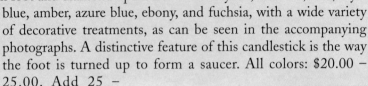

FR-19A. Candlesticks in crystal and amber with gold trim

FR-19B. Candlesticks in crystal with enamel decoration and green

FR-19C. Candlesticks in pink with various decorations. (Note diamond optic on first base)

FR-19D. Candlesticks in light blue. (Note diamond optic on first base)

FR-19E. Candlesticks in cobalt, amethyst, and ebony

Candlestick, petal foot and swirl connector. 4" high with a 3¾" diameter eight-scalloped base. A number of pieces are known with this style foot and swirl connector and are probably part of a line that was reported as new in 1929, after the company's emergence from receivership and subsequent reorganization. The new line combined crystal with emerald, royal blue, gold (light amber), and ebony. Production probably continued until the factory closed in 1933. One of the ebony examples in the accompanying photographs is decorated with silver overlay and is marked "sterling." All colors: $75.00 – 100.00. Add 50 – 75% for silver overlay.

FR-20. Candlesticks in ebony with petal foot and crystal swirl connector (one with sterling silver overlay decoration)

FR-20A. Candlesticks in amber, cobalt, and green with petal foot and crystal swirl connector

GENERAL HOUSEWARES CORPORATION, Stamford, Connecticut.

Importer of a general line of housewares, including saucepans, BBQ cooking implements, and cutlery. During the 1980s they marketed a line of glass candlesticks that were reproductions of Boston and Sandwich designs from the mid-1800s. We believe that they were imported from Taiwan and were sold through various department stores, gift shops and candle shops. In January of 2000 GHC was acquired by Corning Consumer Products, who began marketing their product lines under the "World Kitchen" umbrella.

These candleholders are often marked on the base with the GHC logo (which consists of the initials GHC under what looks to be a roof) but unmarked versions, apparently from the same molds, are also known. It is not clear at this time if these were imported by GHC or someone else. Known colors are crystal (plain and satin finish), amber, medium blue, light blue, and moss green.

Dolphin candlestick. 10½" high with a 3⅝" square base. Circa 1980s. This is a copy of a dolphin candlestick made famous by the Boston and Sandwich Glass Company during the mid-1800s. An original can be seen in BS-14 on p. 39, volume one of this series. These have nice detail and color but the glass quality is poor. They photograph better than they look in person. So far as we know, this style is always marked with the GHC logo on the base. (See GH-1a.) Known colors are crystal and medium blue. Crystal: $20.00 – 25.00. Blue: $35.00 – 45.00.

GH-1. DOLPHIN
CANDLESTICK IN BLUE

GH-1A. CLOSE-UP OF GHC LOGO ON CANDLESTICK BASE

Doric Column candlestick. 9" high with a 3⅝" square base. Circa 1980s. Can be found marked or unmarked. Unmarked examples were still being imported well into the 1990s but we don't know if GHC was the importer. Like all of GHC's known candlesticks, this is a copy of a Boston and Sandwich candlestick. These can be distinguished from the originals by the solid stem (column) on the GHC copies. The Boston & Sandwich versions have a hollow stem and a wafer joined socket. Several original examples can be seen in BS-19, p. 40 in volume one of this series. Colors include moss green, blue, crystal, and crystal with a satin finish. Crystal (plain or satin), moss green: $15.00 – 20.00. Blue: $25.00 – 30.00.

GH-2. DORIC
COLUMN
CANDLESTICK
IN CRYSTAL
SATIN

Petal & Loop candlestick. 6⅝" high with a 4¼" base. Circa 1980s. A copy of a Boston and Sandwich design known to collectors as Petal & Loop. These vary from the originals in that they have six loops on the base where the originals have seven. They are also molded in one piece whereas the originals had the socket attached to the base with a semi-molten wafer of glass. For more information on the original see BS-8 on p. 37 of volume one in the series. These have been found marked and unmarked. Known colors are amber, light blue, and crystal. Crystal, amber: $12.00 – 16.00. Blue: $20.00 – 25.00.

GH-3.
PETAL & LOOP
CANDLESTICK IN
DARK AMBER

GIBSON GLASS, Milton, West Virginia (1982 to the present). Charles Gibson, a veteran glass

blower who had worked first for the Bischoff Glass Company and then for the Blenko Glass Company, originally started Gibson Glass in 1976 to manufacture paperweights. This initial effort only lasted for about a year, but he reopened the shop in 1982. Paperweights remain a key part of his output, as well as handcrafted marbles, but he also produces a wide variety of mold-blown pieces, including cruets, figurines, vases, perfume bottles, Christmas ornaments, etc. Every piece is either made by Charles Gibson or produced under his direct supervision. His son, Philip Gibson, is also a glassblower and John Desmeules makes many of the paperweights. Each item is marked with the Gibson name and the date of manufacture, except in those rare instances when the design of the item makes it impossible to do so.

Production by this firm is varied, but quantities are very limited. The glass is made using cullet from other companies, such as Fenton, so the colors produced at any given time depend on what is available. Vaseline is especially popular with collectors, with other colors including amethyst, blue, cobalt, crystal, green, ruby, and tangerine. Many items are offered plain and with a choice of finishes, including opalescent, carnival, and crackled. The candlesticks shown below are examples of Gibson's paperweight production. We know of at least one other blown candlestick that was made by him, and certainly others are possible.

GB-1. HANDLED PAPERWEIGHT CANDLEHOLDER, DATED 1984

Handled paperweight candleholder. 3" high. Dated 1984. The design consists of five red flowers against a green "leafy" background, with controlled bubbles in the center of each flower and between the leaves. $35.00 – 50.00.

GB-2. HANDLED PAPERWEIGHT CANDLEHOLDER, DATED 2000

Handled paperweight candleholder. 2⅞" high. Dated 2000. Although made sixteen years later, this is the same basic design as the paperweight above. In this one, each of the flowers is a different pastel color: green, pink, blue, white, and yellow. Note the difference in the way in which the handle was applied. This same style of paperweight candleholder has also been made by others, including the various Saint Clair shops, by Joe Rice, and by Prestige Art Glass. (See volume 3 of this series.) $30.00 – 40.00.

GB-3. HANDLED PAPERWEIGHT CANDLEHOLDER, DATED 2000

Handled paperweight candleholder. 3" high. Dated 2000. Another example of a Gibson candleholder showing a different style decoration. $30.00 – 40.00.

GILLINDER & SONS, INC., 135 Oxford St., Philadelphia, Pennsylvania (1867 – 1930), and
GILLINDER BROTHERS (now Gillinder Glass), Port Jervis, New York (1912 – present).

Established by William T. Gillinder in 1861 as the Franklin Flint Glass Works, the company originally manufactured lamp chimneys and hand-blown glassware. In 1863, Edwin Bennett joined the firm, forming Gillinder and Bennett. It was at about this time they began to manufacture pressed glass. When Bennett retired in 1867, William's sons, James and Frederick, joined the firm and the name was changed to Gillinder and Sons, Inc. After William's death in 1871, James took over as president and brought the company to national prominence when they constructed a very successful glass-making exhibit at the 1876 Centennial Exposition in Philadelphia. In 1888, the pressed glass operation was moved to Greensburg, Pennsylvania, and the Philadelphia plant concentrated on the manufacture of cut and blown glass. This lasted until 1891, when the Greensburg factory joined the United States Glass Company as factory G. The Philadelphia plant remained independent and signed an agreement with U.S. Glass not to produce any pressed tableware. They did produce some pressed glass after that agreement, however, including all but one of the candleholders seen in this chapter. In 1900, three of James Sr.'s sons joined the firm. Three years later, James Sr. died and his brother Edgar gained control of the factory. Then, in 1912, James Sr.'s sons withdrew from Gillinder & Sons and started their own glasshouse, incorporated as Gillinder Brothers, Inc., Port Jervis, New York. It is sometimes reported that Gillinder moved to Port Jervis in 1912, but this was clearly not the case. Instead, Gillinder & Sons and Gillinder Brothers were both in business at the same time, seemingly in direct competition with each other, since at the time of the split they both specialized in glass shades, oil fonts, vault lights, and other similar items. We have a 1919 catalog showing a picture of the Gillinder & Sons Philadelphia plant with the following caption: "The Modern Factory of the GILLINDER Products, Philadelphia. Erected 1902, Enlarged 1912, Again 1914, Covering Ten Acres." Several candleholders were still being shown in that catalog, but by the 1920s the catalogs were devoted to glass shades and electric lighting accessories, and showed no candleholders at all.

When Gillinder & Sons closed, some of their molds were purchased by the Mannington Art Glass Company of Mannington, West Virginia. Then, in the mid-1940s, the John E. Kemple Glass Works bought hundreds of molds from Mannington, including many that originally belonged to Gillinder. Those molds are currently in the possession of the Wheaton Village Museum of American Glass, Millville, New Jersey. Fifth-generation descendants of William T. Gillinder still operate Gillinder Glass on the site of the Gillinder Brothers factory in Port Jervis, New York. They primarily manufacture glass lenses for industry but also produce small collectibles, lamps and vases for sale through their gift shop and Web site. It is not clear if the Gillinder descendants are in possession of any of the original Gillinder & Sons molds.

It's likely that Gillinder & Sons made candleholders before the 1890s, but we have found no documentation confirming this. If such items were made, the molds were probably transferred to the Greensburg factory in 1888 and assimilated by U.S. Glass in 1891. Therefore, a few of the many candleholders known to have been made by U.S. Glass may have originally been early products of Gillinder & Sons.

COLORS

Several unusual or unique colors were manufactured by Gillinder and Sons. We know opal or milk glass was manufactured at the centennial exhibit in 1876. The first official mention of color that we could find was in a Feb. 1878 price list that read "Gillinder & Sons, manufacturers of flint and colored glassware." Ads from 1884 mention "colored ware" but don't elaborate. Opalescent glassware was described as "new" in 1891, as were three opaque colors (opal, ivory and blue) all advertised as bisque, which probably meant they had a satin finish. Pink (possibly another opaque color) was mentioned in 1892. Turquoise and Nile green were listed from 1896 to 1901. Both were opaque colors that must have been continued for several more years, even though the ads no longer mentioned them. Opal was made at least through 1919, and probably after that. Other known colors include a light amethyst and an opaque pale yellow or custard (we'll simply refer to it as custard from here on).

Gillinder had a very straightforward way of identifying its candleholders, numbering them consecutively starting with 1. The last number that we can confirm is 18, indicating that at least 18 different candleholders were manufactured. Even though we've been able to uncover numbers up to 18, not every number has been identified so there are still discoveries to be made. Of course, that's part of what makes this pursuit so interesting.

GI-1. TWO EXAMPLES OF THE NO.1 CRUCIFIX CANDLE-HOLDER IN OPAL. THE EARLIER VERSION IS ON THE LEFT. NOTE THE DIFFERENCE IN DETAIL AND COLOR

No. 1 crucifix. 9⅜" high with a 3⅞" hexagonal base and a 2⅝" cross arm. Known production dates are from 1896 to 1919, but it may have been manufactured earlier. Known in crystal and opal, this crucifix has an unusually small Christ figure in relation to its overall size. The opal versions exhibit a wide range of coloring, from milk white to clambroth. At some point the mold was slightly altered with the most noticeable change being an increase in the size of the "pseudo-wafer" beneath the candle cup. The 1919 catalog is the first we found to show this revised version. The early examples are distinctly more detailed and of considerably higher quality than the later ones. Crystal: $20.00 – 25.00. Opal: $30.00 – 35.00.

GI-2. NO. 2 CANDLE-STICK IN OPAL

No. 2 candlestick. This candlestick was originally advertised as being 6" high and later as being 7" high. Its actual dimensions are 6½" high with a 3⅜" base. This discrepancy is not unusual as published sizes were often approximations at best. Known production dates are from 1896 to 1919, but it may have been made earlier. When Gillinder started giving their candleholders names as well as numbers, this candlestick began showing up in advertisements as "Prism." Known in crystal and opal, it's very similar to candleholders made by Co-Operative Flint Glass, Phoenix Glass, and Kemple Glass. While those versions were from the same mold (slightly modified over the years), the Gillinder version is from its own mold. It has flatter hobs and a very narrow rim above the pattern on the candle cup. For a side-by side comparison of these candleholders see the chapter on Co-Operative Flint Glass on p. 121 of volume one of this series. Crystal: $16.00 – 20.00. Opal: $20.00 – 25.00.

GI-3. No. 3 CANDLESTICK IN OPAL WITH HAND PAINTED DECORATION

GI-3A. No. 3 CANDLE-STICK IN CRYSTAL

No. 3 candlestick. 6½" high with a 3¾" base. Circa 1898 – 1900. Known in opal and crystal, other colors are possible. Almost identical to McKee's "Manhattan" candleholder of the same period (which the John E. Kemple Glass Works later re-issued). The McKee is sometimes mold-marked inside the base, but unmarked examples can be easily confused with the Gillinder. Although the McKee tends to be of higher quality with bolder scrollwork, these differences are hard to spot if the examples are not side-by-side. The easiest way to tell them apart is illustrated in GI-3b. In order to make the comparison both candleholders must be facing so that the scrolls at the base of the candle cup look like those outlined in green on the photograph. This is important as each side has slightly different scrollwork. When viewing the candleholder from the indicated side, observe the two upper scrolls (outlined in red). These will face in the same direction on the McKee and in opposite directions on the Gillinder (as indicated by the red outlines). The Gillinder will also have a small rim inside the base, about 1½" up from the bottom. Crystal: $10.00 – 15.00. Opal: $20.00 – 30.00. Add 20 – 30% for a hand painted decoration in good condition.

GI-3B. COMPARISON OF THE GILLINDER No. 3 (LEFT) AND McKEE MANHATTAN (RIGHT)

No. 4 handled chamberstick. 4¼" high with a 4½" scalloped base. Circa 1898 – 1900. Known in opal, opaque turquoise, and custard. Also available decorated with hand painted floral designs. McKee, Dithridge, and others made very similar candleholders. A side-by-side comparison of these candleholders appears below. Opal: $15.00 – 20.00. Custard or opaque turquoise: $25.00 – 35.00. Add $5.00 for hand painted decoration in good condition.

GI-4. No. 4 HANDLED
CHAMBERSTICK IN CUSTARD

LOOKALIKES

The Gillinder candlestick is the most ornate, with well defined detail, but with the molded design appearing only on the rim of the base, the handle, and the candle cup.

McKee's Cinderella candlestick appears to be almost identical to the Gillinder. The only difference between them is that the center of the scroll on the rim of the base of the Gillinder candlestick curves to the right, whereas the McKee candlestick curves to the left. The McKee candlestick is 4½" high and 4½" wide at the base. The detail is also well defined on the McKee candlestick.

Dithridge made two similar candlesticks. The first one (pattern number unknown) has relatively little detail, with roses on the base that look like little more than lumps. It has the simplest rim on the candle cup, lightly scrolled, and the handle is also less ornate than any of the others, except the last unknown example. Although the quality of the Dithridge milk glass is only mediocre, it has more opalescence than any of the others. It is 4⅛" high with a 4½" base.

The second Dithridge candlestick (No. 40, known as Ray End to collectors) has distinctive fronds that appear on the points on the base. It is 4" high and 4½" wide at the base.

The final example shown is unknown. It is very similar to the McKee candlestick, but with a much taller neck. It is 4⅝" high and 4⅜" wide at the base. It even has the scroll on the rim curving to the left, as on the McKee candlestick. However, it does not have the medallion-like design on the candle cup. The quality of the milk glass, though with some opalescence, is mediocre.

All of the above candlesticks are likely to be found with hand painted floral decorations and/or gold trim, though often it becomes nearly worn off over the years.

A version of the candlestick with very detailed roses on the base has been attributed to Portieux and may have been the original that was copied by all of the others.

GI-4A, GI-4B, GI-4C & GI-4D. 1. GILLINDER No. 4 CANDLESTICK, FROM *CROCKERY AND GLASS JOURNAL*, JULY 26, 1900. 2. McKEE CINDERELLA CANDLESTICK, FROM *CHINA, GLASS AND LAMPS*, SEPTEMBER 7, 1899. 3. DITHRIDGE CANDLESTICK, FROM *CHINA, GLASS AND LAMPS*, AUGUST 3, 1899. 4. DITHRIDGE No. 40 CANDLESTICK IN OPAL WITH SATIN FINISH, UNKNOWN CANDLESTICK IN OPAL.

Handled maple leaf candlestick. 2⅞" high, 6½" long and 6" wide. This piece, described as an "extra large leaf shape candlestick," appears in a 1902 Butler Brothers catalog as part of an opal and satin etched crystal assortment. These assortments are known to be groupings from a single manufacturer and would often be "drop shipped" directly from the manufacturer to the retailer. This assortment included a pansy shaped pin tray that matches one advertised by Gillinder in 1902, as well as other items believed to be Gillinder, thus leading to our attribution to this company. Gillinder is also known to have made a maple leaf pattern in the 1800s, but it has a somewhat different appearance. Assuming that this is a Gillinder candleholder, the 1902 time period would make this either their No. 5, No. 6, or No. 8. Offered in opal and crystal with satin finish, decorated in "bright colors" with bronze gold trim. Also known in opal with the entire leaf decorated in dark brown. Other colors are possible. Opal: $25.00 – 35.00.

GI-5. HANDLED MAPLE LEAF CANDLESTICK, POSSIBLY No. 5, No. 6, OR No. 8

GI-6. No. 7 CRUCIFIX CANDLESTICKS IN CRYSTAL AND AMETHYST

No. 7 crucifix candlestick. 10" high with a 4½" round base and a 3⅜" cross arm. Circa 1902 – 1904. Probably the most ornate of all the Crucifix candleholders. Known in crystal, opal, and amethyst. The crystal versions were available "roughed" or frosted and all were offered with a gilded Christ figure. At some point the Mannington Art Glass Company purchased a large group of molds from Gillinder, with this crucifix being among them. It's not known if Mannington ever used the mold, but if they did they would have likely produced it in a grayish milk glass, something we have not seen to date. In the mid 1940s, the mold was part of a large grouping sold to the John E. Kemple Glass Works, who produced it in a shorter version with a cut-down socket and base as their No. 263. It isn't known if Kemple or Mannington was responsible for this modification to the mold.

GI-6A. No. 7 CRUCIFIX CANDLESTICKS IN OPAL (FRONT AND BACK VIEWS)

Crystal (plain or frosted): $50.00 – 60.00. Opal: $75.00 – 90.00. Amethyst: $160.00 – 200.00. (Add $10.00 for a gilded Christ figure in good condition.)

GI-7. No. 9 COLONIAL CANDLESTICK IN CRYSTAL

No. 9 Colonial candlestick. 7" high with a 3½" base. Circa 1904 – 1919. About the time this candlestick was introduced, Gillinder started to advertise their candleholders using names as well as numbers. The name would usually designate a style rather than a specific item, therefore several candleholders might share a name, with each size having it's own number. Known in crystal, but probably made in the same opaque colors as the larger sizes on the following page. It has a serrated rim on the candle cup. Crystal: $15.00 – 18.00.

No. 10 Colonial candlestick. 8" high with a 3¾" base. Circa 1904 – 1919. Known in crystal, and opaque turquoise, but probably made in the same colors as the larger size below. It has a serrated rim on the candle cup. Crystal: $16.00 – 20.00. Opaque colors: $25.00 – 30.00.

GI-8. No. 10
COLONIAL
CANDLESTICK
IN TURQUOISE

No. 12 Colonial candlestick. 9" high with a 4" base. Circa 1905 – 1919. Known in crystal, opaque turquoise, opaque Nile green, and custard. All colors can be found with a gold-encrusted decoration on the base. This member of the "Colonial" line seems to be a late addition, as we could not find any mention of it during 1904. This would also explain why this is number 12 instead of 11. Number eleven may have been assigned to another candleholder before it was decided to offer a third size in this line. Unlike the smaller sizes, which have a serrated rim on the candle cup, this one is plain. Crystal: $18.00 – 22.00. Opaque colors: $35.00 – 45.00. (Add 10% – 15% for gold-encrusted if gold is in good condition.)

GI-9. No. 12
COLONIAL
CANDLESTICK
IN NILE GREEN
WITH GOLD-
ENCRUSTED
DECORATION

No. 14 Grecian candlestick. 7" high with a 3¼" base. Circa 1905 – 1919. Known in crystal, but probably made in the same opaque colors as other Gillinder candleholders of this era. Crystal: $15.00 – 18.00.

GI-10. No. 14
GRECIAN
CANDLESTICK
IN CRYSTAL

No. 15 Grecian candlestick. 8" high with a 3⅜" base. Circa 1905 – 1919. Known in crystal and custard, but was probably made in other opaque colors. Crystal: $15.00 – 20.00. Opaque colors: $25.00 – 30.00.

GI-11. No. 15
GRECIAN
CANDLESTICK
IN CUSTARD

GI-12. No. 16 EGYPTIAN CANDLESTICK IN TURQUOISE

No. 16 Egyptian candlestick. 6⅞" high with a 3¼" base. Circa 1907 – 1919. Known in crystal and turquoise, but probably made in other opaque colors. Crystal: $15.00 – 20.00.

GI-13. No. 17 DUTCH CANDLESTICK IN NILE GREEN

No. 17 Dutch candlestick. 7" high with a 3½" base. Circa 1906 – 1919. Known in crystal, opaque Nile green, and opaque turquoise. Other opaque colors are likely. Crystal: $15.00 – 18.00. Opaque colors: $25.00 – 30.00.

GI-14. No. 18 DUTCH CANDLESTICK, FROM 1913 CATALOG

No. 18 Dutch candlestick. 8" high with a 3¾" base. Circa 1906 – 1919. Known only in crystal, but was probably also made in Gillinder's opaque colors. Crystal: $16.00 – 20.00.

GI-15. 9" DUTCH CANDLESTICK IN CRYSTAL

Dutch candlestick. Unknown pattern number. 9" high with a 4" base. Circa 1906. We initially purchased this candlestick because it had all the characteristics of being from Gillinder, but since we had no listing for a 9" Dutch candlestick, we couldn't be sure. Then, after owning it for over a year, we noticed a patent number on the beveled edge of the base that read "DESIGN PAT. 38293". Researching the patent showed that the inventor, Kraft Booth, assigned the patent to Gillinder & Sons, Inc. in 1906. (See GI-15b for the patent drawing.) This is the only Gillinder candlestick we've seen marked in this manner. Even the smaller versions of the Dutch candleholder don't have this mark. The logical pattern number would be No. 19, but this is only speculation. This size is not shown

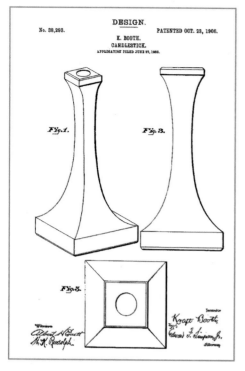

GI-15A. CLOSE-UP OF PATENT NUMBER LOCATION

in any catalog that we've seen. The inclusion of the patent number might indicate that it was only made briefly, soon after the patent was granted. Known only in crystal. Crystal: $18.00 – 22. 00.

GI-15B. US DESIGN PATENT DOCUMENT #38,293

No. 4005 candlestick. 3⅞" high with a 5" round base. Circa 1999. Made in black, crystal, and teal green. This candleholder is only available through the Gillinder Glass (formerly Gillinder Brothers) gift shop in Port Jervis, New York, where they sell for $20.00 each. A Gillinder employee did some research on this item and found that it was being made from an old mold that for as long as anyone could remember was referred to as No. 4005. She explained that the first digit (4) refers to the category and the last three (005) indicate the actual mold number. This could mean that this was originally the Gillinder and Sons No. 5 candleholder. If so, it would have originally been produced around the turn of the last century, but based on the style we believe that it's more likely to be a mold commissioned by Gillinder Brothers during the 1920's or 1930's. Either way, we have never seen a vintage example of this candlestick and assume them to be rare. Current price (new): $20.00.

GI-16. No. 4005 CANDLESTICK IN TEAL GREEN

HALEY (K. R.) GLASSWARE COMPANY, INC., Greensburg, Pennsylvania (1946 – 1973). This was a continuation of the General Glassware Company, founded in 1939 by Kenneth R. Haley, in partnership with Herman Lowerwitz, president of the American Glass Company in Carney, Kansas. Considering the length of time these two companies were in operation, it is surprising that so little information is available on them. General Glassware and the subsequent Haley company were glassware distributors only, with the actual glass produced by the American Glass Company and, in at least one case, the Phoenix Glass Company.

Kenneth Haley was the son of Reuben Haley, the well known designer who had worked for most of the major glass companies in the United States. Kenneth Haley himself was a master mold maker who did design work for many companies before going into partnership with Lowerwitz, including Consolidated, Morgantown, Phoenix (where he was design engineer from 1928 – 1934), Gillinder, McKee, and others.

HL-1. No. 188 DOLPHIN
CANDLESTICK IN MILK GLASS

No. 188 Dolphin candlestick. 9" high with a 4" square base. Made in 1948 in crystal and milk glass. The candlesticks were advertised as part of an assortment that was available both plain or with fired on hand painted flowers, so it is possible the candlesticks might be found decorated as well. This candlestick was originally designed by Kenneth Haley's father, Reuben Haley, as the No. 2562 Santa Maria dolphin candlestick, made around 1931 by Consolidated Lamp & Glass Company. (See CS-6 on p. 115 of volume one of this series.) This same candlestick was also made by the Imperial Glass Company from 1969 to 1980 in various colors, including milk glass. (See IM-119 on p. 212.) The Imperial versions are marked with the IG trademark and have stippling on the underside of the base. Although it is possible that Consolidated may have reissued this candlestick in milk glass in the 1950s, we have no documentation to support this and therefore believe that candlesticks found in milk glass that are not marked (such as the one seen in the accompanying photograph) are most likely those offered by Kenneth Haley. The bottom of this candlestick is ground smooth. $40.00 – 50.00.

Actual production of this candlestick was by the Phoenix Glass Company for Haley. According to Jack D. Wilson's *Phoenix & Consolidated Art Glass*, Kenneth Haley stated that he had a new mold made, with the Imperial reproductions made from yet a third mold. After comparing the Consolidated original with both the Imperial reproductions and the milk glass candlestick seen here, the authors were unable to detect any differences. If new molds were used, they were exceptionally close copies. Like the Consolidated original, the Haley dolphin candlesticks are very difficult to find today.

Note: A 1948 catalog page reprinted by Jack Wilson in the book cited above shows an additional candlestick also made at this time, the No. 179 lo [sic] candleholder. Unfortunately, the reproduction is not clear enough to make out any detail, but it may be Phoenix's No. 284 strawberry candleholder.

HAZEL-ATLAS GLASS COMPANY, Washington, Pennsylvania (1902 – 1977).

This company began in 1902 with the merger of the Atlas Glass and Metal Company with its neighbor, the Hazel Glass Company (founded 1885 as a manufacturer of fruit jars and bottles). The merger was a success from the beginning, and soon additional factories were set up in cities across the U.S. During the 1920s, the Clarksburg, West Virginia plant, which specialized in the production of tumblers and other house-wares, was one of the most fully automated factories in the country. From the 1930s through the 1950s, factories in Zanesville, Ohio, Washington, Pennsylvania, Blackwell, Oklahoma, Clarksburg, Grafton, and Wheeling, West Virginia, produced mold blown glassware, containers, and mold etched, machine-made patterns. In 1956, Hazel-Atlas was acquired by the Continental Can Company, who continued producing and selling glass under the Hazelware label. In 1964, the Brockway Glass Company acquired six of the old Hazel-Atlas plants in an anti-trust lawsuit settlement, but the Clarksburg factory, which produced the Hazelware line, remained with Continental Can until 1972 when it too was sold to Brockway. In 1977, the Clarksburg plant was sold to Anchor Hocking, who operated it until it was closed in 1987. The plant burned in 2000, and was demolished in 2001.

Some well known Hazel-Atlas patterns include New Century, Ribbon, Florentine No. 1 and No. 2 (AKA "Poppy"), Clover Leaf, Moderntone, Roxana, Royal Lace, Starlite, Newport (AKA "Hairpin"), and "Criss Cross" refrigerator dishes.

LOGOS, CA. 1924 – 1950S

LOGO, EARLY 1960S

LOGO, LATE 1960S

COLORS

The first patent ever granted for a glass color was received by Hazel–Atlas in 1936 for Platonite, a semi-opaque white glass. Originally, this color was opalescent around the edges; later, it became completely opaque. Early Platonite was often sold with fired-on pastel colors. Later, brighter colors were also used. Colors reported to have been offered by Hazel–Atlas include:

amber	1930s	Killarney green	1933+
avocado	Late 1960s – 1970s	milk glass	Late 1950s – 1960s
black	1930 – 1931	Moroccan amethyst	Late 1950s – 1960s
burgundy (dark amethyst)	1936+	Platonite	1934 – early 1950s
Capri blue (azure)	1962+	Ritz blue (cobalt)	1936+
gold (amber)	Late 1960s – 1970s	rose	Late 1930s
green	1929 – 1930s	ruby red	1930 – 1940
ice blue	1931 – 1935	sunset pink	1933
iridized	1920s – 1935	topaz yellow	1930 – 1935

Candlestick. Unknown pattern number. 3½" high with a 4½" round base. Late 1920s to the early 1930s. Known in black and crystal with an iridized finish or with fired-on green, red, or burnt orange. Attribution for this candleholder was made from a Hazel Atlas ad for gelatin molds, dated August 1928, that showed this candleholder in the background. It was made both with a plain base and with a design underneath the base similar to Imperial's Swirled Diamond pattern. Sears Roebuck and Butler Brothers both offered these candlesticks in their catalogs in sets of four, with a matching console bowl on a black base. All colors $6.00 – 8.00.

HA-1. CANDLESTICK,
UNKNOWN PATTERN NUMBER,
IRIDIZED

HA-1A. CANDLESTICKS,
UNKNOWN PATTERN NUMBER,
FIRED-ON GREEN DECORATION

Florentine No. 2 candleholder. 2½" high with a 4¼" round base. Circa 1932 – 1935. Made in crystal, green, and yellow. This pattern is also referred to as Poppy, No. 2 and was part of a complete dinnerware set. Crystal: $12.00 – 8.00. Green: $25.00 – 30.00. Yellow: $35.00 – 40.00.

HA-2.
FLORENTINE No. 2
CANDLEHOLDERS
IN GREEN AND
YELLOW

Royal Lace candleholder. 2¼" high with a 5" diameter. Circa 1934 – 1941. Made in amethyst, crystal, Ritz blue, green, and rose. Sold as part of a dinnerware set, this candlestick came in three versions: flared, rolled edge, and ruffled edge. Crystal, all styles: $25.00 – 35.00. Green, rose, flared: $50.00 – 60.00; crimped edge: $100.00 – 140.00; rolled edge: $120.00 – 160.00. Ritz blue, amethyst, flared: $80.00 – 110.00; crimped edge: $180.00 – 220.00; rolled edge: $220.00 – 270.00.

HA-3.
ROYAL LACE
CANDLE-
HOLDER
WITH
ROLLED
EDGE IN
RITZ BLUE

HA-4.
FLORAL
STERLING
CANDLESTICK
IN BLACK

Candlestick. Unknown pattern number. 2½" high with a 3¾" diameter base. Made in the early 1930s. Offered in black with a silver decoration called Floral Sterling Although marked "Sterling," these pieces are not silver overlay. The silver decoration seems to have been applied like an etching, so thinly that it cannot be felt. The example in the accompanying photograph is almost worn away. $10.00 – 12.00.

HA-5. No. K976
CANDLESTICK IN
RITZ BLUE

No. K976 candlestick. 7¼" high with a 3½" round base. Circa 1930s. A hollow, machine made, mold blown candleholder made in Ritz blue and crystal. At least some have a number on the bottom of the base. Made at Hazel-Atlas's Zanesville, Ohio factory. $10.00 – 15.00.

No. 929 Star, large well. 1¼" high. 4½" wide. Identical to the No. 930 Star below but with an oversized well for a large 1½" diameter candle. The design is based on a series of ashtrays introduced in December 1947. It isn't known when the candleholders were added to the line, but it could have been as early as the 1950s, with production continuing into the late 1960s. Made in crystal. $3.00 – 5.00.

HA-6A. No. 930 STAR, STANDARD WELL (ON LEFT) AND No. 929 STAR, LARGE WELL (ON RIGHT)

HA-6. No. 929 STAR, LARGE WELL

HA-7. No. 930 STAR, STANDARD WELL, IN MOROCCAN AMETHYST

No. 930 Star, standard well. 1¼" high, 4½" wide. Identical to the No. 929 Star above, but takes a standard ¾" taper. Also made in a larger size (dimensions unknown, but probably identical to the larger ashtray in this style). The design is based on a series of ashtrays introduced in December 1947. It isn't known when the candleholders were added to the line, but it could have been as early as the 1950s, with production continuing into the late 1970s (with production continued by the Brockway Glass Company). Made in crystal and Moroccan amethyst. It should be noted that there is some controversy about this candleholder. Local residents in Paden City believe that these were actually made by Paden City in that company's mulberry and that the mold was later sold to Hazel–Atlas in 1951. It is hard to reconcile this tradition with the candleholder's exact resemblance to the ashtrays advertised as new by Hazel–Atlas in 1947. (See HA-7a.) Note particularly, the distinct starburst on the bottom with rays of varying sizes surrounded by four hobnails. Libbey may have acquired this mold from Hazel–Atlas, since their No. 5017 Star candleholder (circa 1970s – 1990s) appears to be identical. Anchor Hocking (AH-21 on p. 16 of volume one of this series) and Indiana (IN-112 on p. 267) also made star candleholders, but with six rounded points. Crystal: $3.00 – 5.00. Moroccan amethyst: $50.00 – 75.00.

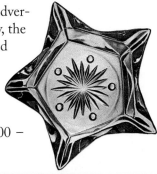

HA-7A. No. 1340 ASHTRAY, FROM *CROCKERY AND GLASS JOURNAL*, DECEMBER 1947

No. 487 Daisy. 1¼" with a 4⅜" round saucer base. Circa 1950s – 1970s (with production continued by Brockway Glass Company). Made in crystal and milk glass. The latter was advertised in July 1958 as part of the Early American Opaque line. $4.00 – 6.00.

HA-8. No. 487 DAISY

Candleholder. Unknown pattern number. 3½" high with a 4" diameter base. Circa 1960s. Known in milk glass only. Identical to the No. 507 Starlite and the No. A3242 candleholder below, but with no pattern on the underside. Advertised in September 1964 as one of the items shown at the recent Housewares Show, so this may have been the first of the three to be introduced. $6.00 – 8.00.

HA-9. CANDLEHOLDER, UNKNOWN PATTERN NUMBER, IN MILK GLASS

No. 507 Starlite candleholder. 3½" high with a 4" diameter base. Introduced 1965. Made in crystal, avocado, and gold (amber). This candleholder is the same as the plain version shown in HA-9 above and the No. A3242 candleholder below, but has a rayed pattern beneath the base. All colors $6.00 – $8.00.

HA-10. No. 507 STARLITE CANDLEHOLDER

No. A3242 candleholder. Known as Thumbprint. 3½" high with a 4" diameter base. Circa 1960s. Made in gold (amber) and avocado. This candleholder is identical to the plain version in HA-9 above and the No. 507 Starlite candleholder, but with a thumbprint pattern beneath the base. Hazel–Atlas made two patterns with a similar design, Skol (introduced in 1958 in crystal) and El Dorado (introduced in December 1968 in gold and avocado). It is possible this candlestick was created to complement one of these patterns. All colors $6.00 – 8.00.

HA-11. No. A3242 THUMBPRINT CANDLE-HOLDER IN AVOCADO

HA-12. NO. 4369 CONCORD CANDLEHOLDERS, FROM 1978 CATALOG

No. 4369 Concord candleholder. 3⅞" high. Made circa 1977 – 1978 in crystal and gold (as No. G4369). These candlesticks were produced by the Brockway Glass Company at one of the West Virginia factories acquired from Hazel-Atlas. They have a metal top and were made from the same mold as the salt and pepper in the pattern. They were sold in a gift-boxed set of three as a "candle holder cluster." $6.00 – 8.00.

HA-13. COMPOSITE FROM THE 1968 HAZELWARE CATALOG

HEISEY (A. H.) AND COMPANY, Newark, Ohio (1896 – 1957). By the time this

company began operations in 1896, Augustus H. Heisey was already a veteran in the field of glassware. After an early experience working for the King Glass Company, he joined the Ripley Glass Company, where he gained a reputation as one of the best salesmen on the road. In 1870, he married Susan Duncan, daughter of George Duncan, who eventually took control of the Ripley factory. It was renamed Geo. Duncan & Sons, with son-in-law Augustus Heisey as one of the partners. After the Duncan plant became part of the United States Glass Company in 1891, Augustus Heisey became general manager of the commercial department of the new combine. However, it appears that U.S. Glass was top-heavy with managers, or that Heisey was unhappy as a member of such a large conglomerate – quite possibly it was a combination of these two factors, since U.S. Glass let a number of other managers go within a few years of its formation — and, by 1893, Heisey seems to have been among those who had severed their connections with the company. He began looking for a site for a new factory of his own and settled on Newark, where construction began in 1895. After a number of delays, glass was made in the new factory for the first time in April 1896. Always an astute businessman, Heisey had made sure that his first two new patterns were on display at the annual trade show in Pittsburgh earlier that same year by taking the molds down the road to the Robinson Glass Company in Zanesville, Ohio, and having samples made there.

From the very beginning, Heisey concentrated on making high quality crystal, with many of the initial patterns being imitations of cut glass. The company's reputation was really established in 1899 when they brought out their No. 300 Peerless line — a colonial pattern that, as *Crockery and Glass Journal* stated, "only a metal maker capable of producing pure, fine crystal would be bold enough to adopt." Although at least one other company had produced a paneled pattern a year prior to Heisey, (the Riverside Glass Works' X Ray pattern), there is no doubt that the tremendous popularity of the No. 300 line was the beginning of what was to become a renaissance in colonial patterns. Within the next couple of years, virtually every other major glass manufacturer introduced similar lines — and Heisey was to continue offering one or more colonial patterns throughout the remainder of its history. The very first candlesticks made by Heisey were part of the No. 300 pattern.

Another innovation was the introduction of the Diamond H trademark in 1900. Heisey was one of the few companies to routinely impress its trademark in its glassware, a factor that has contributed greatly to making Heisey as collectible as it is today. Although the company was to later advertise that every piece was marked with the Diamond H, in some cases this referred to the use of a paper label. Nevertheless, a larger proportion of Heisey's ware was marked than is true of any other manufacturer.

Heisey also pioneered the use of advertisements in popular magazines like *House and Garden, The Woman's Home Companion*, and others, beginning as early as 1910. Prior to that, only one or two cut glass companies had explored this avenue for gaining name recognition. Once again, Heisey was in the vanguard, with most other pressed glass manufacturers soon following suit.

1914 brought the addition of blown ware, followed by an increase in the use of various decorating techniques, such as etching and cutting.

Augustus Heisey died in 1922, with the presidency of the factory passing to his son, E. Wilson Heisey. The bulk of color production occurred between 1925 and 1939 under his leadership. Some of the patterns most popular with collectors today also date from this period, including Empress, Old Colony, Ipswich, Saturn, Ridgeleigh, Crystolite, and Queen Ann – a mixture of traditional designs, Sandwich reproductions, and art deco.

E. Wilson Heisey died in 1942 and was replaced by his brother, T. Clarence Heisey. The forties saw the introduction of most of the animal figurines, many designed by Royal Hickman, that are so highly sought after today. Late patterns from the 1940s and 1950s included Lariat, Plantation, Old Williamsburg, and Cabochon. However, despite occasional successes, the 1950s were a time of struggle for the factory, with American handmade glassware in general vying against imported glassware, machine made domestic glass, and the growing plastics industry. Heisey investigated a number of schemes for revitalizing the factory, including moving to the manufacture of optical glassware, but none of them were realistic, probably due to the capital expense that would have been involved. So it was in December 1957 they closed for the traditional Christmas vacation – and never reopened.

In April 1958, the Imperial Glass Corporation bought all of the molds, etching plates, patents, trademarks, and batch formulas. By July, Imperial had begun advertising "Heisey by Imperial," with the slogan that "two good names are better than one." They continued to make pieces from the Heisey molds until their own closing in 1984. At that time, the Heisey Collectors of America, the national club located in Newark, Ohio, was successful in purchasing all of the molds except those belonging to the Old Williamsburg pattern, which were acquired by the Lancaster Colony Corporation. Most of the molds from the early years were destroyed long before Heisey went out of business (many of them during World War II, when scrap metal was in high demand). In the pages that follow, if specific mention of the mold is not made, it can be assumed to no longer be in existence.

COLORS

Emerald	A deep green, introduced in 1897 and only made for a few years.
Ivorina verde	An opaque, light yellow, sometimes with slight translucence, often referred to as custard. Introduced in 1897 and only in production for a few years.
Opal	Opaque milk glass, usually with fiery opalescence.
Canary	Also referred to as vaseline. Originally made around 1897, with very few pieces made. A slightly lighter shade of this color was reintroduced sometime in the 1920s, probably ca. 1923 – 1924.
Rose	Probably never a production color. Made experimentally in 1900 – 1901. Similar to Heisey's later flamingo, but a truer pink without the hint of orange found in that color.
Moongleam	Heisey's version of green, made from 1925 to 1935. Early pieces tend to be darker, very similar to the earlier emerald color; later pieces will be more pastel, with a hint of yellow. Greater variation will be found in moongleam than any of the other colors.
Flamingo	Pink, with a hint of orange. Made from 1925 to 1935. Variations in shade are also common with this color.
Amber	Some pieces may have been made as early as 1926, though most of Heisey's production in amber was for special orders and may have been made over a number of years. See Sultana on the following page for the reintroduction of amber as a production color.
Hawthorne	At its best, a delicate lavender color, made only from 1927 to 1928. Controlling the color was difficult, and it sometimes has a muddy, brownish tone.

Marigold	A strong, deep yellow-orange with green, vaseline-like highlights, made only from 1929 to 1930. The formula was unstable, and the surface of the glass had a tendency to craze, becoming cloudy.
Sahara	A pale transparent yellow, made from 1930 to 1937.
Alexandrite	A rich lavender color, made from 1930 to 1935. Actually dichroic, alexandrite changes shade depending on the light source: in sunlight, pink is predominant, while under fluorescent lighting, it turns greyish-blue. Under incandescent light, it is a true lavender.
Tangerine	A rich orange, sometimes shading to red, made from 1932 to 1935.
Stiegel blue	A deep blue, often referred to as cobalt. Made from 1933 to 1941.
Zircon	A pastel blue-green, made from 1936 to 1939. Reissued as Limelight in 1956.
Sultana	A deep amber, made around 1951. This is the only time that amber was offered by Heisey as a production color. Other amber items were made for special order only.
Dawn	Charcoal, or smoke. Made from 1955 to 1957.
Limelight	This is the same shade as the earlier zircon. Made from 1956 to 1957. Referred to as turquoise when offered with a satin finish.

In addition, a number of other experimental colors were made over the years, including at least two in which candlesticks are known: opalescent gold and light blue (possibly a Holophane color, since the latter company was Heisey's neighbor).

DECORATIONS

Although limited decorations were offered by Heisey in the early years, they were probably done for the company by other firms, such as the Oriental Glass Company. It wasn't until 1916 that a decorating department became an integral part of the factory. Many cuttings and etchings were offered over the years, with the golden age of cutting being from 1933 to the early 1940s, when Emil Krall, an engraver formerly associated with the royal court of Franz Josef of Austria, was hired. He was joined by his brother Willibald Krall and other master cutters, such as Max Seidel, who specialized in rock crystal engravings. Cuttings that can be attributed to any of these men are highly sought today. In addition, many production cuttings from later years are also highly popular, including Danish Princess (1939 – 1957), Narcissus (1941 – 1957), Moonglo (1942 – 1956), and Dolly Madison Rose (1949 – 1956).

Even more popular were some of the etchings made by Heisey: Empress (1928 – 1937), Old Colony (1930 – 1939), Chintz (1931 – 1942), Maytime (1937 – 1939), Rosalie (1937 – 1955), Minuet (1939 – before 1956), and Plantation Ivy (1950 – 1957). The two most sought after are Orchid (1940 – 1957) and Heisey Rose (1949 – 1957).

MARKS

TRADEMARK, 1900 – 1957

Heisey began using the Diamond H trademark in 1900 and, thanks to their persistence in advertising it as a mark that designated fine crystal, it became one of the best known trademarks in American glassware. Not only was the mark frequently used on the glass itself, but in around 1904 they began placing paper labels on every piece sold. The earliest design was simply an H in a diamond, larger on early pieces than on those made after the early 1920s. A trademark for a plain diamond without the H was also assigned to Heisey in 1909, but it isn't known if it was ever used in any form other than advertisements. The label was redesigned in 1947. Various other specialty labels were also used over the years, including ones specifically for flamingo and hawthorne. The Diamond H trademark is currently owned by the Heisey Collectors of America.

LOGO, CA. 1911 – 1920S

LABEL, 1932 – 1947

LABEL, 1947 – 1957

LABEL, 1930S

96

A note on the manufacturing process of Heisey candlesticks: One of the distinguishing characteristics of Heisey's colonial candlesticks, as well as of some of the later candlesticks issued in the 1930s and 1940s, is the pontil, or punty mark, on the bottom of the base. The mark left by the punty rod on the bottom of these candlesticks was almost always ground out and polished, leaving a smooth concave circle in the center, while the remaining portion of the base will either be fire polished only (to give it a smoother appearance) or full cut and polished. Only a few other companies — notably Fostoria and Jefferson — finished the bottoms of their candlesticks in this manner, because of the additional expense involved, and they often offered them both finished or unfinished. Heisey was one of the only companies that consistently ground the pontils on all of their candlesticks that had such marks.

No. 1 candlestick. Named Georgian by researchers. Originally released as part of the No. 300 pattern, known today as Peerless, and listed from 1900 to around 1905 as No. 1-300, after which time the "-300" suffix was dropped. Made in three sizes, with the 9" height (with a 4" hexagonal base) issued first from 1900 to ca.1931. A very rare 7" size was made from 1906 to 1909. The 11" height (with a 4¾" base) also came out in 1906, and remained in production until ca. 1931, but is also hard to find today. Production was in crystal only, with the exception of one trial run of the 9" candlesticks in rose, a color similar to flamingo that Heisey experimented with in the early years but never put into production. An inventory from 1900 lists 44 No. 1 candlesticks in rose. All three sizes were offered fire polished or full-cut (that is, with all surfaces cut and polished). In either case, the bottoms of these candlesticks will always have a ground pontil and will either be cut smooth or fire polished. The 9" size was also available with No. 1 and 2 gold decorations. This candlestick is only sometimes marked with the Diamond H in the constriction beneath the candle cup. 7": Unable to price. 9", crystal: $80.00 – 95.00. 9", rose: $500.00 – market. 11": $150.00 – 175.00.

HE-1. No. 1 GEORGIAN CANDLESTICKS, 9" AND 11"

HE-1A. No. 1 GEORGIAN CANDLESTICK, 9", IN ROSE (RARE)

HE-1B. J. D. BERGEN COMPANY'S COLONIAL CANDLE-STICK, FROM 1904 – 1905 CATALOG

HE-1C. C. F. MON-ROE COMPANY'S No. 3 CANDLESTICK, FROM 1906 – 1907 CATALOG

HE-1D. PITKIN & BROOK'S SIBOUR CANDLESTICKS, FROM CA. 1907 CATALOG

PROGRESSION OF A DESIGN

This is a copy of a candlestick originally made by various cut glass companies. The J. D. Bergen Company's No. 3 and 6 Colonial candlesticks (HE-1b) were made in two sizes (10" and 7½", respectively) and are shown here from their 1904 – 1905 catalog. C. F. Monroe Company's No. 3 candlestick, seen here from their 1906 – 1907 catalog (HE-1c) is very similar. Pitkin and Brooks of Chicago also sold an imported version as their No. 2, 4, and 6 Sibour candlesticks (HE-1d). These were made in three sizes, 10½", 9¼", and 7½", offered in a catalog dated circa 1907. These may be the candlesticks made by Val Saint-Lambert in Belgium (HE-1e), shown here from their 1908 catalog. The cut

HE-1E. VAL SAINT-
LAMBERT CANDLESTICK,
FROM 1908 CATALOG

HE-1F. VAL SAINT-
LAMBERT CANDLESTICK,
WITH OVERALL CUTTING,
FROM 1908 CATALOG

HE-1G. COMPARISON OF
HEISEY'S NO. 1 CANDLESTICK
AND PADEN CITY'S NO. 110
CANDLESTICK

glass originals often have hollow stems. A later pressed glass copy of this candlestick was made sometime after 1916 by the Paden City Glass Manufacturing Company in crystal and colors. The quality of the glass is not as good as Heisey's and it has a pressed star on the underside of the base. (See HE-1g.)

HE-2. NO. 2 OLD WILLIAMSBURG
CANDLESTICKS, 9" AND 11" IN CRYSTAL,
7" IN MOONGLEAM (RARE)

No. 2 Old Williamsburg candlestick. Originally issued as part of the No. 300 pattern, known today as Peerless, and listed as No. 2-300. As with the No. 1, the "-300" suffix was dropped. Today it is commonly referred to as the No. 2. Ultimately this candlestick became part of Heisey's No. 341 Old Williamsburg line, retaining its No. 2 designation. It was made in three sizes: The 9" height (with a 4" hexagonal base) came out first and was made from 1901 to 1935, then briefly reissued again in 1943. The 11" height (with a 4¾" base) was made from 1902 to 1931. And a 7" size (with a 3⅝" base) came out in 1903, becoming Heisey's longest lived candlestick and remaining in uninterrupted production until the factory closed in 1957 — and was then reissued by Imperial from 1958 to 1982, for a total production period of nearly 80 years! Heisey offered this candlestick in crystal only, with the exception of a turn of 259 candlesticks in moongleam, made in September 1925 (rarely seen today). From ca. 1908 – 1917, all three sizes were available either fire polished or full cut (that is, with all surfaces cut and polished). In any case, the bottoms of these candlesticks will either be cut smooth or fire polished and will always have a ground pontil. This candlestick is sometimes marked with the Diamond H at the top of the column. 7", crystal: $50.00 – 62.50. 7", moongleam: $325.00 – market. 9": $90.00 – 110.00. 11": $120.00 – 130.00.

The No. 2 candlestick was also the inspiration for the bases of several candelabra (pattern No. 300, 400, and 401) and a candlelamp (No. 300). As can be seen in HE-2a, the primary modification to the pattern required to do this was the increase in the size of the socket, making it possible to hold either a candelabra arm or hurricane shade. As of this writing, the design has come full circle, with the hurricane base currently being reproduced in Slovakia, but altered to become a candlestick (HE-2b). The reproduction is 10¼" high with a 5¼" hexagonal base and 2⅞" diameter socket. It is an almost exact copy of the Heisey original, but in 24% lead crystal with the base partially hollow (and a rim added inside the base) and the socket portion filled in so that it can accommodate either a standard taper candle or a 2¼" pillar candle. These reproductions have been seen etched "Neiman Marcus" and "Bombay" (for the Bombay Company) on the bottom.

HE-2A. NO. 300
OLD WILLIAMSBURG
CANDELABRA BASE

As mentioned on the preceding page, Imperial reissued this candlestick in several colors (see IM-137 on p. 217), but only in the 7" height. The earliest reissues from 1958 to 1969 are of excellent quality and may be marked with the Diamond H. (Imperial removed the mark from the mold after that date.) The bottoms will be ground smooth, but without the punty found on the Heisey originals. Later Imperial reissues are in colors that differ from those made by Heisey (with the possible exception of Imperial's emerald green); however, they are generally of poorer quality and have unfinished bottoms. When Imperial closed in 1984, the Old Williamsburg molds were the only ones not acquired by the Heisey Collectors of America, and therefore this became one of three candlestick molds acquired by the Lancaster Colony Corporation. At that time, the Fostoria Glass Company was one of their subsidiaries and, for a brief period before they discontinued making handmade glassware, Fostoria reissued this candlestick in crystal, nut brown, and ultra blue. (See FO-230 on p. 73.) Although the colors made by Fostoria are all ones that were originally offered by Imperial, the latter did not made this candlestick in ultra blue. Also, Imperial's reissues of the candlestick in nut brown had ground bottoms, whereas the Fostoria versions are probably unfinished on the bottoms. Early Imperial crystal candlesticks are also ground on the bottom, so it is only their later crystal candlesticks that probably cannot be distinguished from the Fostoria versions. Although the mold has not been used since, it is still owned by Lancaster Colony.

HE-2B. REPRODUCTION CANDLESTICK MADE IN SLOVENIA, MARKED "NEIMAN MARCUS"

HE-2C. CLOSE-UP OF ETCHED SIGNATURES ON REPRODUCTIONS MADE FOR BOMBAY COMPANY AND NEIMAN MARCUS

A number of other companies made candlesticks similar to the 7" size (HE-2d). All of these candlesticks have unfinished bottoms. The Jeannette Glass Company's No. 97 candlestick (see JE-13 on p. 274) has a round candle cup, as does the Westmoreland Glass Company's No. 1010 candlestick. The latter is the thinnest of the four and, in recent years, has been reissued by the Mosser Glass Company. The Lancaster Glass Company's candlestick has a slightly fatter stem and a candle cup that is very short in comparison with Heisey's. The Lancaster candlestick may be found both with an impressed star or a round knob on the bottom that could be confused with a pontil.

HE-2D. COMPARISON OF JEANNETTE NO. 97 CANDLESTICK IN AMBER, WESTMORELAND NO. 1010 CANDLESTICK, HEISEY NO. 2 CANDLESTICK, AND LANCASTER CANDLESTICK

In the same way that the No. 1 candlestick on page 97 was copied from a preexisting cut glass example, the No. 2 candlestick seems also to be a direct copy of the quadruple silverplated candlestick shown in HE-2e. It was made by the Forbes Silver Company of Meriden, Connecticut, ca. 1890 – 1896. At least three companies also offered cut versions of this candlestick in 9" and 11" heights. The Lackawanna Cut Glass Company's No. 2090 Colonial candlestick seen in HE-2f is shown in a catalog that dates between 1903 – 1905. T. B. Clark and Company's No. 315 Flute candlestick is from their 1905 catalog (HE-2g). Since both companies bought blanks from others, it is possible they bought them directly from Heisey and then simply cut all surfaces – however, Val St. Lambert also made their own version of this candlestick, as seen in HE-2h from their 1908 catalog, and definitely would have been the manufacturer.

HE-2E. FORBES SILVER COMPANY CANDLESTICK

HE-2F, HE-2G & HE-2H. 1. LACKAWANNA CUT GLASS COMPANY'S NO. 2090 COLONIAL CANDLESTICK, FROM CATALOG. 2. T. B. CLARK AND COMPANY'S NO. 315 FLUTE CANDLESTICK, FROM 1905 CATALOG. 3. VAL SAINT-LAMBERT CANDLESTICK, FROM 1908 CATALOG

HE-3. No. 3
MARLBORO
CANDLESTICK

No. 3 candlestick. Named Marlboro by researchers. Originally issued as part of the No. 300 pattern, known today as Peerless, and listed as No. 3-300. 9" high with a 4" hexagonal base. Made ca. 1902 – 1921 in crystal only. This was another imitation cut glass candlestick, with the serrated edges on the column actually molded. It was available either fire polished or, from ca. 1908 to 1917, full cut (that is, with all surfaces cut and polished). In any case, the bottoms of these candlesticks will either be cut smooth or fire polished, and will always have a ground pontil. We have not seen this candlestick marked with the Diamond H. $135.00 – 160.00.

HE-4. No. 4 ESSEX
CANDLESTICK

No. 4 candlestick. Named Essex by researchers. Originally issued as part of the No. 300 pattern, known today as Peerless, and listed as No. 4-300. 9" high with a 4" hexagonal base. Made ca. 1902 – 1921 in crystal only. This was another imitation of cut glass, as were most of the other early candlesticks. It was available either fire polished or, ca. 1908 – 1917, full cut (that is, with all surfaces cut and polished). In any case, the bottoms of these candlesticks will either be cut smooth or fire polished and will always have a ground pontil. We have not seen this candlestick marked with the Diamond H. Two other companies made similar candlesticks. The Union Stopper Company of Morgantown (which eventually became the Beaumont Company) advertised this candlestick in 1908; Union Stopper's quality may be comparable to Heisey's, if we can believe their advertising that stated they provided a "superior grade of glass." The Paden City Glass Mfg. Company's No. 111 candlestick also appears to be identical to Heisey's, but is not of comparable quality and has a pressed star on the underside of the base. (See HE-4a.) $140.00 – 165.00.

HE-4A. PADEN CITY
No. III CANDLESTICK

HE-5. No. 5 PATRICIAN CANDLESTICKS,
8", 11", AND 9", WITH TOY CANDLESTICK
IN FOREGROUND

No. 5 candlestick. Named Patrician by researchers. Made in six different sizes, with catalogue heights as follows: Toy (called 5" in the catalogues, but actually 4½" with a 2½" hexagonal base), ca 1905 – 1931; 5" (called "squat" in the catalogues, and actually 5¼" high) with a 3½" hexagonal base, ca. 1904 – 1931; 6" (actually 6¼" high) with a 3½" hexagonal base, ca. 1905 – 1931; 7" (actually 7½" high) with a 3¾" hexagonal base, ca. 1905 – 1933; 8" (actually 8¼" high) with a 4" hexagonal base, ca. 1906 – 1933; 9" with a 4¼" hexagonal base, ca. 1904 – 1933; 11" with a 5" hexagonal base, ca. 1904 – 1931. All sizes were made in crystal only. All sizes, except the toy, were available fire polished or, ca. 1908 – 1917, full cut (that is, with all surfaces cut and polished); the latter was also offered with the option of a cut star on the bottom. In any case, the bottoms of these candlesticks will either be cut smooth or fire polished, and will always have a ground pontil. Unlike the other sizes, the toy candlestick has a hollow base. Although early catalogs show the toy with a flat base, we have only seen it with this form of base. The toy candlestick is usually marked with the Diamond H on the bottom and the other sizes are often marked at the neck, just below the candle cup. There was also a series of No. 5 candelabra made in one-, two-, three- and four-light sizes. Toy and 5" squat: $55.00 – 65.00. 6", 7", 8": $50.00 – 60.00. 9": $70.00 – 85.00. 11": $110.00 – 145.00.

The 5" squat candlestick was reissued by Imperial from June 1980 to 1983 as No. 13791, included as part of the Old Williamsburg pattern. (See IM-176 on p. 228.) It was then reissued again in the late 1980s by the Indiana Glass Company as No. 1516. (See IN-97 on p. 264.) The reissues have unfinished bottoms and are much poorer quality glass. A toy candlestick in one of the authors' collections is also of rather poor quality, totally unlike that usually associated with Heisey; although Imperial is not known to have produced this size of the candlestick, it is possible they may have made a few as feasibility pieces.

A design patent was filed for the candlestick on October 8, 1904 and approved November 8, 1904 as D37,213. Augustus Heisey was listed as designer, though it is likely that he just signed the patent applica-

HE-5A. COMPARISON OF CO-OPERATIVE FLINT GLASS COMPANY'S NO. 344 CANDLESTICK WITH HEISEY'S NO. 5 5" SQUAT CANDLESTICK

tion as president. Despite this patent, a number of other companies made very similar candlesticks. The Co-operative Flint Glass Company's No. 344 candlestick may actually have predated the Heisey candlestick and bears a strong resemblance to the 5" squat No. 5 (see HE-5a), but with a pressed star in the base. (See CO-4 on p. 120 of volume one of this series for further information.) The H. C. Fry Glass Company also made a 5" cut candlestick that is very similar. (See FR-7 on p. 76.) Although we don't know if it preceded Heisey's candlestick, the possibility exists that it may have served as a model.

The Union Stopper Company of Morgantown (which eventually became the Beaumont Company) advertised what appears to be a candlestick identical to Heisey's No. 5 in 1908, which would have been during the period that Heisey's patent was still in effect. We don't know if Heisey took legal action for infringement or if the mold had been leased to Union Stopper. Sometime after 1916 (when Heisey's patent would have expired), the Paden City Glass Manufacturing Company's No. 109 candlestick was made; although we have not seen one, we can surmise that it would have been of poorer quality and would have had a pressed star in the base. Fenton's No. 249 candlestick (very similar to the 6" height) was made from 1921 to 1937 in several colors that are completely unlike any offered by Heisey. (See FN-7 on p. 181 of volume one of this series.) And finally, Westmoreland's No. 1036 candlestick was made in the early 1920s, but can be easily differentiated from Heisey's No. 5 because it has a round base.

Three other companies made similar candlesticks, but with bands at the top and bottom of the column: the New Martinsville Glass Mfg. Co., the United States Glass Company, and the Cambridge Glass Company. The original version of the Cambridge candlestick also had a band around its center (see CB-25 on p. 56 of volume one of this series), later removed (see CB-30 on p. 57 of volume one). This version was reissued by both the Imperial Glass Corporation and the Indiana Glass Company. (See IM-162 on p. 223 and IN-98 on p. 264.)

No. 1776 Kalonyal candlestick. 9" high. Introduced in January 1906 and only made until 1907 or 1908 at the latest. Crystal only. To the authors' knowledge, this candlestick has never been seen by collectors. Unable to price.

HE-6. NO. 1776 KALONYAL CANDLESTICK, FROM CA. 1906 CATALOG

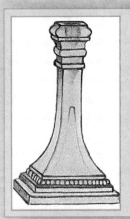

No. 6 candlestick. Named Doric by researchers. 9" high. To the authors' knowledge, this candlestick has never been seen by collectors, but appears in a price list that can be dated to ca. 1906 – 1907. The accompanying drawing is our best guess as to what it might look like, since it probably resembles the base of the No. 6 candelabra. (See HE-7a.) Unable to price.

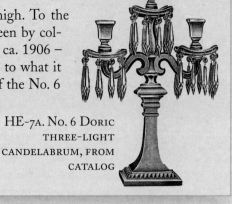

HE-7. No. 6 DORIC
CANDLESTICK. *(Artist's rendition)*

HE-7A. No. 6 DORIC
THREE-LIGHT
CANDELABRUM, FROM
CATALOG

HE-8. No. 8
JACOBEAN
CANDLESTICK

No. 8 candlestick. Named Jacobean by researchers. Made in two sizes: 7" and 8" (with a 4¼" hexagonal base). The 7" size has not been seen, but appears in a price list from ca. 1906. The 8" height was made from 1906 to 1923. Made in crystal only. The bottoms will either be cut smooth or fire polished, and will always have a ground pontil. Sometimes marked with the Diamond H in the constriction beneath the candle cup. $140.00 – 160.00.

HE-9. No. 11
CANTERBURY
CANDLESTICK,
FROM CA. 1906
CATALOG

No. 11 candlestick. Named Canterbury by researchers. 9" high. Made ca. 1906 – 1907 in crystal only. To the best of our knowledge, this candlestick has never been seen by collectors, but appears to be very similar to the No. 8 candlestick (see HE-7 above), except for the design of its candle cup, which imitates cut glass with cross-hatching between the "petals." It can be assumed that the bottom will either be cut smooth or fire polished, with a ground pontil. Unable to price.

Note: Price list 120, which dates to ca. 1906, lists several other candlesticks in crystal, all of which remain unknown:

No. 7. Handled, 4½" base.
No. 9. 9" high.
No. 10. 9" high.
No. 12. Handled, square base.
No. 13. Handled, puntied bottom.
No. 14. 5" (plain) and 6" (puntied bottom)
No. 15. 5" (plain) and 6" (plain)

No. 16 candlestick. Named Classic by researchers. Made in four sizes: 5" high with a 3½" hexagonal base; 7" with a 3⅝" base; 9" with a 4⅜" base; and 11" with a 5" base. Made ca. 1906 – 1931 in crystal only. Available either fire polished or, ca. 1908 – 1917, full cut (that is, with all surfaces cut and polished). In any case, the bottoms of these candlesticks will either be cut smooth or fire polished and will always have a ground pontil. The tops are also cut smooth. Sometimes marked with the Diamond H at the top of the column. This same shape was also used for the base of a series of 11 candelabra of different heights and configurations (patterns No. 17 – 19) as well as the No. 200 electroportable lamp.

Early catalogs show this candlestick with an optional removable bobeche. (See HE-10a.) Although the authors have not seen this bobeche, it apparently had a rim that fit into a shallow well around the opening of the candle cup (as seen in the close-up in HE-10b). 5", 7": $55.00 – 65.00. 9": $65.00 – 75.00. 11": $110.00 – 135.00.

HE-10. No. 16 CLASSIC CANDLE-STICKS, 9", 5", 11", AND 7"

HE-10A. No. 16 CANDLESTICK WITH REMOVABLE BOBECHE

HE-10B. CLOSE-UP OF CANDLE SOCKETS, SHOWING RIM ON LEFT FOR REMOVABLE BOBECHE

HE-11. No. 20 candlestick. Named Sheffield by researchers. A typed list dated October 22, 1907, describes this candlestick as a "plain standard" and includes prices for six sizes; the purpose of this list was to fix prices between Heisey, the Cambridge Glass Company, and the Fostoria Glass Company, so it isn't known if all these sizes went into production or if some of them were just speculative. At any rate, this list is the only source for the otherwise unknown 5", 6", and 8" heights. The sizes that actually appeared in catalogs were: 7" with a 5" diameter base; 9" with a 4½" base; and 11" with a 5⅛" base. Made ca. 1907 – 1931. Unique among Heisey's colonial candlesticks, this one was made in two pieces, with the candle cup molded separately. The tops are also sometimes cut smooth. The bottom of this candlestick will either be cut smooth or fire polished and will always have a ground pontil. Although production was primarily in crystal only, in September 1925 a single turn was made with crystal columns and the candle cups in moongleam. According to factory records, there were only 69 pairs produced, making them rare today. We have not seen this candlestick marked with the Diamond H. 7" $75.00 – 85.00. 9", all crystal: $85.00 – 95.00; with moongleam top: $525.00 – market. 11": $250.00 – market.

HE-11. No. 20 SHEFFIELD CANDLESTICKS, 7", 11", AND 9"

The No. 23 candlestick seen in HE-11a from a 1913 catalog, which has been named Sheffield (Standard) by researchers, appears to be identical, the only difference being that there is slightly less of a taper toward the top of the column. Factory records list four sizes: 9" (ca. 1907 – 1917), 11" (ca. 1907 – 1909), 15" (ca. 1907 – 1909), and 18" (ca. 1907). The 18" size does not appear in any catalogs, but only in the typed list noted above where it was among the other candlesticks priced out. This size has never been seen, but if it was put into production, it was the tallest candlestick made by Heisey.

HE-11A. No. 23 CANDLE-STICK, FROM 1913 CATALOG

HE-12. No. 21 ARISTOCRAT
CANDLESTICKS, 11", 7" (WITH No.
9005 CAIRO ETCHING), AND 9"

No. 21 candlestick. Named Aristocrat by researchers. Initially made in five sizes: 5" (unseen by the authors), ca. 1909 – 1910; 7" with a 3½" square base, ca. 1907 – 1935, reissued briefly in 1941; 9" with a 4½" square base, ca. 1907 – 1935, reissued briefly in 1941; 11" with a 5¼" square base, ca. 1907 – 1930; 15" with a 5¼" square base. Ca. 1913 – 1930. Made in crystal only. Although introduced in 1907, it wasn't until March 4, 1910, that a patent was filed for this candlestick. It was approved July 18, 1911, as D41,590. The designer was Andrew Sanford, who created most of Heisey's early patterns, probably including many that were patented under Augustus Heisey's name. Available either fire polished or, ca. 1908 – 1917, full cut (that is, with all surfaces cut and polished); the latter was also offered with the option of a cut star on the bottom. In all cases, the bottoms will either be cut smooth or fire polished, and will always have a ground pontil except when there is a cut star. The tops are also cut smooth. (One pair in the authors' collection has so much glass cut from the top that the beveled edge almost disappears.) Frequently marked with the Diamond H at the top of the column. Offered with Heisey's No. 693 Cloister cutting and 9005 Cairo plate etching. Also known with overall satin finish. Various decorating companies used this candlestick as a blank, including the Utopian Silver Deposit and Novelty Company, who advertised it with silver overlay in 1911, the Home Cut Glass Company in Carbondale, Pennsylvania, the Irving Cut Glass Company in Honesdale, and the Lewis and Neblett Company in Cincinnati, among others. 5": Unable to price. 7": $65.00 – 75.00. 9": $75.00 – 85.00. 11": $175.00 – 190.00. Add 50 – 75% for a Heisey etching or cutting, or intricate cuttings/silver overlay from other companies.

This candlestick was also used as the base for three different heights of electroportable lamp (made in crystal, flamingo, and moongleam), thirty different sizes and configurations of candelabra (with pattern numbers ranging from No. 34 through 45 and 61 through 62), and twenty different stand lamps, or kerosene lamps (pattern No. 53 through 60, 71 through 76, and 79 through 84). In 1922, a desk size version of the candlestick was introduced, which consisted of just the base and candle cup, with no intervening column. (See HE-34 on p. 112.)

In our previous book, *Heisey Candlesticks, Candelabra, and Lamps*, we noted that unmarked versions of the 7" size are sometimes seen with an unidentified floral etching and unfinished bottoms. At the time we hypothesized that they might have been specially ordered that way from Heisey by a decorating company. However we have since learned that what appears to be a candlestick identical to Heisey's was made by Josef Inwald, A.G., in Czechoslovakia, ca. 1925 – 1935, raising a distinct possibility that the candlesticks with unfinished bottoms are Bohemian. A satin finish candlestick in a bluish-green color similar to Heisey's zircon has also been reported with unfinished bottom and top, and is almost certainly Czechoslovakian as well.

No. 22 candlestick. Named Windsor by researchers. Made in three sizes: 7" with a 4" diameter round base with six panels; 9" with a 4½" diameter base (both ca. 1907 – 1933); and 11" with a 5⅛" diameter base (ca. 1907 – 1919). Made in crystal only. The bottoms will either be cut smooth or fire polished and will always have a ground pontil. The tops are also cut smooth. Often marked with the Diamond H on the bottom of the candle cup, just above the constriction. The same shape was also used for the base of the No. 201 electroportable lamp. The Libbey Glass Company made an almost identical 10" cut version of this candlestick ca. 1920. J. Hoare and Company also show a 9½" version of this candlestick in their 1911 catalog, both full cut or with an engraving. It is quite likely these decorations were done on Heisey blanks. 7": $55.00 – 70.00. 9": $75.00 – 85.00. 11": $115.00 – 135.00.

HE-13. No. 22 WINDSOR
CANDLESTICKS, 9", 11", AND 7"

No. 25 candlestick. Named Federal by researchers. Made in four sizes: 5" (unseen by the authors, ca. 1907 – 1909); 7" with a 3¾" hexagonal base; 9" with a 4¼" base; and 11" with a 5" base. The last three sizes were made ca. 1907 – 1929 in crystal only. From ca. 1908 to 1917, all three sizes were available either fire polished or full cut (that is, with all surfaces cut and polished). In any case, the bottoms of these candlesticks will either be cut smooth or fire polished and will always have a ground pontil. The tops are also cut smooth. Usually marked with the Diamond H on the candle cup, just above the column. Like most of Heisey's colonial candlesticks, the No. 25 was often decorated by other companies. The 7" one in the accompanying photograph is an example of a cutting by an unknown company. The 9" size was also used as the base for the No. 202 electroportable lamp. 5": Unable to price. 7": $75.00 – 95.00. 9": $85.00 – 110.00. 11": $130.00 – 155.00.

HE-14. No. 25 FEDERAL CANDLESTICKS, 7" (WITH UNKNOWN CUTTING), 11", AND 9"

No. 30 toy candlestick. Named Tom Thumb by researchers. 3" high with a 2⅛" hexagonal base. Made ca. 1907 – 1924 in crystal and crystal frosted. Although most of Heisey's early candlesticks were issued in numerical order, this one seems to have gone into production earlier than that sequence would suggest. Sometimes marked with the Diamond H on the candle cup and sometimes marked on the bottom of the base. Occasionally candlesticks are seen marked in both places. $80.00 – 90.00.

HE-15. No. 30 TOM THUMB toy CANDLESTICK IN CRYSTAL AND CRYSTAL SATIN

No. 150 handled chamberstick. Called Banded Flute by collectors. 4" high with 4⅜" diameter round, six-paneled base. Made ca. 1907 – 1930 in crystal only. Usually marked with the Diamond H at the neck, just beneath the candle cup. This was one of only a few pieces from the No. 150 pattern that does not have the distinctive bands that resulted in its popular name today. Available singly and as part of the No. 150-1 bedroom set, which consisted of the chamberstick, a 1¼ quart jug, and a tumbler, on a 13" tray. Duncan & Miller made a very similar candlestick (see DM-12 on p. 146 of volume one of this series), which predated the Heisey chamberstick and was probably copied by them. (The fact that Heisey was related to the Duncans by marriage made their rivalry friendly, but certainly didn't interfere with their competition with one another.) The most distinctive differences are in the shape of the candle cup and the distinctive thumb guard on the Duncan candleholder, as seen in the comparison in HE-16a. $40.00 – 55.00.

HE-16. No. 150 BANDED FLUTE HANDLED CHAMBERSTICK

HE-16a. COMPARISON OF HEISEY No. 150 HANDLED CHAMBERSTICK AND DUNCAN & MILLER No. 64 CHAMBER CANDLESTICK

HE-17. No. 150 BANDED FLUTE
SAUCER FOOT CANDLESTICK

No. 150 saucer foot candlestick. Called Banded Flute by collectors. 2" high with a 5" diameter saucer and a 3⅛" diameter foot. Made ca. 1908 – 1933 in crystal only. Has been seen with an iridized finish, probably applied by a decorating company. Unlike the handled chamberstick on the preceding page, this one has bands around the candle cup and the rim of the saucer. Usually marked with the Diamond H on the side of the candle cup. Available singly or as part of two bedroom sets: the No. 150-2 set consisted of the candlestick, a pint tankard with cover, a tumbler, and a covered match box, on a 10" tray. (See HE-17a.) The No. 150-3 set was identical, but with a match stand replacing the covered match box. A candlestick that is sometimes confused with Heisey's No. 150 saucer foot is Fostoria's No. 2063 candlestick, which can be found in crystal, green, and amber. The Fostoria candlestick is smaller in circumference (about 4½") and does not have the bands, among other variances. (See FO-39a on p. 21 for a comparison.) $55.00 – 60.00.

HE-17A. No. 150-2 BANDED
FLUTE BEDROOM SET

HE-18. No. 28
ELIZABETH
CANDLESTICKS,
11" AND 7"

No. 28 candlestick. Named Elizabeth by researchers. Made in three sizes: 7" with a 4" diameter, six-paneled round base; 9" with a 4½" base (both made ca. 1908 – 1921); and 11" with a 5¼" diameter base (ca. 1908 – 1917). Made in crystal only. The bottoms will either be cut smooth or fire polished and will always have a ground pontil. The tops are also cut smooth. Sometimes marked with the Diamond H at the top of the column, near the candle cup. 7": $110.00 – 120.00. 9": $120.00 – 130.00. 11": $160.00 – 180.00.

HE-19. No. 31 JACK-
BE-NIMBLE TOY CANDLESTICKS IN
SAHARA, CRYSTAL, AND MOONGLEAM

No. 31 toy candlestick. Named Jack-Be-Nimble by researchers. 2" high, 2⅜" hexagonal base. Made ca. 1908 – 1944 in crystal, moongleam, flamingo, and sahara, but considered rare in color. Usually marked on the bottom, though often the Diamond H is almost worn off. Reissued by Imperial from 1981 to 1982 in crystal, with a few sample pieces also made in emerald green. (See IM-184 on p. 230.) Because the mold was considered to be part of the Old Williamsburg line at the time that Imperial closed, it was among those that were sold to the Lancaster Colony Corporation. The Duncan & Miller Glass Company's No. 72 toy chamber candlestick (see DM-16 on p. 147 of volume one of this series) predates Heisey's toy and is very similar to it, the biggest difference being the loop handle on the No. 31. Westmoreland also made two very similar toys with loop handles (the No. 1039 handled birthday candlestick, which is hexagonal like the Heisey one, and the No. 1211 birthday candlestick, which is octagonal), but the handle on both of them touches the candle cup, whereas there is a space between the handle and candle cup on the Heisey toy. (The Westmoreland toys are being reproduced by Summit Art Glass today.) For a side by side comparison of all of these toys, see the appendix on p. 289. Heisey crystal: $35.00 – 40.00. Colors: $125.00 – 150.00.

No. 32 candlestick. Named Skirted Panel, with Handle by researchers. Made in two sizes: 5" with a 2¾" hexagonal base (ca. 1910 – 1929); and 7" with a 3¾" base (ca. 1910 – 1922). Made in crystal only. Sometimes marked with the Diamond H on the bottom of the candle cup just above the neck. The 5" size was used as part of two different bedroom sets: the No. 352 set, consisting of the candlestick, a No. 300 one pint decanter (without a stopper), a No. 150 covered match box, and a No. 393 eight ounce tumbler, on a No. 352 12" tray; and a "Colonial bedroom set," made up of the candlestick, a No. 391 one quart covered tankard, a No. 150 match stand, and a No. 341½ tumbler, on a No. 353 10" tray. The 5" candlestick was reissued by Imperial from 1980 – 1981 in crystal and emerald green, with a few pieces made for feasibility purposes in ruby. (See IM-177 on p. 228 and p. 293 of the appendix.) Because these reissues were considered part of the Old Williamsburg pattern at the time that Imperial's assets were sold, they were obtained along with the rest of the

HE-20. No. 32 SKIRTED PANEL, WITH HANDLE CANDLESTICKS, 7" AND 9"

molds for that pattern by the Lancaster Colony Corporation. The 5" size was briefly placed back into production by Fostoria (at that time a division of Lancaster Colony) from 1985 – 1986. (See FO-231 on p. 73.) The mold for the 7" size is no longer in existence. Heisey 5": $40.00 – 45.00. 7": $45.00 – 50.00.

A very similar candlestick was made by the Westmoreland Specialty Company around the same time (ca. 1912), in two sizes, 4½" and 5½", as No. 1011. The major differences are in the shapes of the candle cups and the fact that the Heisey candlestick only has a slight collar, whereas that on the Westmoreland candlestick extends down to touch the top of the handle. (See HE-20a.) More problematic is a Czechoslovakian copy made ca. 1925 – 1935 by Josef Inwald, A.G., of Prague, since in catalog reprints it appears to be identical to Heisey's candlestick.

HE-20A. COMPARISON OF WESTMORELAND'S NO. 1011 CANDLESTICK AND HEISEY'S NO. 32 CANDLESTICK

No. 33 candlestick. Named Skirted Panel by researchers. Made in five sizes: 3½" toy with a 2" hexagonal base; 5" with a 2⅞" base; 7" with a 3¾" base; 9" with a 4½" base; and 11" (base dimensions unknown). The three smaller sizes were made ca. 1910 – 1929, and the two taller ones from ca. 1910 to 1922. Sometimes marked with the Diamond H at the top of one of the skirted panels, just beneath the collar to the candle cup, and sometimes marked at the bottom of one of the panels. The skirted panel base was also used on four different one-light candelabra (No. 33/A, 33/B, 33/AA, and 33/BB). The toy size was reissued by Imperial from 1981 – 1982 in crystal (plain and iridized) and emerald green, with a few sample pieces made in ruby. Imperial also produced limited editions of the toy for the Heisey Collectors of America in sunshine yellow, ultra blue, pink, and light blue. (See IM-185 on p. 230.) Because these reissues were considered part of the Old Williamsburg pattern

HE-21. No. 33 SKIRTED PANEL CANDLESTICKS, 5", 9", 7", AND 3½" TOY IN FOREGROUND

at the time that Imperial's assets were sold, they were obtained along with the rest of the molds for that pattern by the Lancaster Colony Corporation. The molds for the remaining sizes are no longer in existence. 3" toy: $35.00 – 45.00. 5": $45.00 – 50.00. 7": $60.00 – 70.00. 9": 65.00 – 80.00. 11": $125.00 – 150.00.

Other companies made similar candlesticks, but as can be seen in HE-21a, there are distinct differences between them. Imperial's No. 700 candlestick is thicker at the neck and has a less defined rim on the candle cup. (See IM-8 on p. 180.) Tarentum's candlestick, made in 5" and 8" heights, has a wide rim on the candle cup and the base of the skirt flares dramatically, compared to the gradual taper of the Heisey candlestick. The Paden City Glass Manufacturing Company's No. 198 candlestick (not shown here) has a round candle cup and base, with eight panels, so isn't likely to be confused with the others.

HE-21A. COMPARISON OF HEISEY'S No. 33 CANDLESTICK, IMPERIAL'S No. 700 CANDLESTICK, AND TARENTUM'S CANDLESTICK (UNKNOWN PATTERN NUMBER)

HE-22. No. 27 Daisy
candlesticks, 7" and 9"
(with unknown cutting)

No. 27 candlestick. Named Daisy by researchers. Made in three sizes: 5" (base diameter unknown); 7" with a 4" diameter round, six-paneled base; and 9" with a 4½" diameter base. Produced ca. 1910 – 1922. This pattern number is earlier than some of the others that preceded it in the catalogs, indicating that it must have been designed a couple of years before it actually went into production. Made in crystal only. The bottoms will either be cut smooth or fire polished and will always have a ground pontil. Usually marked with the Diamond H on the candle cup, just above the knob at the top of the column. Like most of Heisey's colonial candlesticks, the No. 27 can be found decorated by other companies. The 9" one in the accompanying photograph is an example of a cutting by an unknown company. Inventory photographs from 1917 of cut glass manufactured by H. P. Sinclair & Company show an almost identical candlestick, but it isn't known which company copied the other in this instance. All sizes: $200.00 – market.

HE-23. No. 29 Sanford
candlesticks, 7", 11", and 9"

No. 29 candlestick. Named Sanford by researchers. Made in three sizes: 7" with a 4" diameter round, eight-paneled base; 9" with a 4⅝" diameter base; and 11" with a 5¼" diameter base. Note that although both the base and candle cup have eight panels, the shaft of the candlestick itself only has four. Made ca. 1912 – 1929, in crystal only. A design patent was filed September 13, 1912, and approved November 5, 1912 as D43,236. The designer was given as A. J. Sanford, the man who was responsible for the creation of most of Heisey's early colonial patterns. The bottoms will either be cut smooth or fire polished and will always have a ground pontil. The tops are also cut smooth. Sometimes marked with the Diamond H on the candle cup, just above the column. This was probably another copy of a cut glass design, since J. Hoare and Company made a very similar candlestick in 1910. 7": $65.00 – 70.00. 9": $110.00 – 115.00. 11": $150.00 – 165.00.

HE-24. No. 47 Regal candlesticks, 7" with No. 336
Rosette Band etching, 11",
and 9" with gold decoration
by Honesdale

No. 47 candlestick. Named Regal by researchers. Made in three sizes: 7" with a 3½" square base; 9" with a 4¼" base; and 11" with a 5" base. Produced 1912 – 1929, in crystal only. The bottoms will either be cut smooth or fire polished, and will always have a ground pontil. The tops are also cut smooth. Sometimes marked with the Diamond H at the top of the column, just beneath the candle cup. The 7" size was one of the few colonial candlesticks offered by Heisey with an etching, No. 336 Rosette Band (ca. 1916). The 11" size was also used as the base for the No. 209 electroportable lamp. A somewhat similar candlestick, with a stepped base, was made by Fostoria as No. 1639. (See FO-26 on p. 17.) 7": $75.00 – 95.00. 9": $125.00 – 135.00. 11": $175.00 – 195.00.

No. 68 candlestick. Named Hepplewhite by researchers. 9" high with a 4½" square base. Made ca. 1915 – 1924, in crystal only. The bottoms will either be cut smooth or fire polished and will always have a ground pontil. The tops are also cut smooth. Usually marked with the Diamond H on the candle cup. Has been seen with an etching similar to others done by Heisey during this period, but no documentation has been found, so it may have been applied by a decorating company. The example in the accompanying photograph also has a gold-filled etched band around the base and the top of the candle cup, applied by the Honesdale Decorating Company, who often used Heisey blanks. A somewhat similar candlestick was made by Fostoria as No. 1856. (See FO-33 on p. 19.) $135.00 – 145.00.

HE-25. No. 68 HEPPLEWHITE CANDLESTICK, WITH HONESDALE GOLD DECORATION

No. 69 candlestick. Named Sheraton by researchers. 9" high. Offered ca. 1915 – 1922, in crystal only, though factory records reveal that all production occurred prior to 1916, explaining why it is so rare today. Although the authors have not seen this candlestick, we can assume that the bottom will either be cut smooth or fire polished, with a ground pontil, and the top will also be cut smooth. Probably marked with the Diamond H on the candle cup. $175.00 – 190.00.

HE-26. No. 69 SHERATON CANDLESTICK, FROM CA. 1915 CATALOG

No. 70 candlestick. Named Octagon by researchers. Made in three sizes: 7" with a 3⅞" octagonal base; 9", and 11". Produced ca. 1917 – 1929. The bottoms will either be cut smooth or fire polished and will always have a ground pontil. The tops are also cut smooth. Usually marked with the Diamond H at the top of the column, just beneath the candle cup; sometimes double- marked on both sides of the candleholder. 7": $65.00 – 75.00. 9": $95.00 – 125.00. 11": $165.00 – 175.00.

HE-27. No. 70 OCTAGON 7" CANDLESTICK

No. 100 candlestick. Named Centennial by researchers. Made in three sizes: 6" with a 3¾" diameter round base (May 1921 – 1929); 8" (called 7" in the catalogs) with a 4¼" base (August 1922 – 1929); and 9" with a 4½" base (Feb. 1922 – 1929). A design patent was filed for this candlestick on March 17, 1923, almost two years after factory records indicate that it went into production. It was approved December 8, 1925. T. Clarence Heisey was given as the designer, though it is likely he merely signed the application as an officer of the company. Production was primarily in crystal, though the 9" size was also made in flamingo and moongleam. The 6" height has been seen in canary, probably on an experimental basis. All sizes are usually marked with the Diamond H in the constriction just above the

HE-28. No. 100 CENTENNIAL CANDLESTICKS, 6" IN CRYSTAL, 9" IN MOONGLEAM, AND 8" IN CRYSTAL

HE-28A. HAWKES THREE-LIGHT
CANDELABRA, MADE FROM HEISEY'S
No. 100 CANDLESTICK WITH
SILVER-PLATED FITTINGS

knob at the top of the column, with the Diamond H frequently appearing twice on both sides of the candleholder. At least two cuttings were offered on this candlestick, No. 741 Chantilly and 752 Camelot. This was also a popular blank for use by decorating companies. A most unusual example is the three-light candelabrum shown in HE-28a, which was created by T. G. Hawkes and Company around 1925 by cutting the candle cups from three candlesticks and then reattaching them with silver plated bands and a pair of silver plated arms. The candlestick is also cut with their Deauville satin engraving. Each of the candle cups is double marked with the Diamond H, the arms are marked Hawkes and the bottom is also signed Hawkes in acid script, making this one of the most heavily marked candlesticks we've ever seen! Hawkes also offered other decorations on this blank, and several other configurations, including a five-light candelabra similar to the three-light one shown. A version of this candlestick with a wide lip that held prisms was later made by Heisey as No. 105. (See HE-39 on p. 113.) 6", 7", crystal: $60.00 – 75.00. 6", canary: $300.00 – market. 9", crystal: $95.00 – 110.00; flamingo: $140.00 – 165.00; moongleam: $150.00 – 175.00. Add 50% for cutting.

HE-28B. HEISEY No. 100, McKEE No. 151 IN AMETHYST, CAMBRIDGE
No. 1273 IN EMERALD, TIFFIN No. 75 IN SKY BLUE, AND FOSTORIA No.
2324 IN AMBER

A number of companies made candlesticks that all bear a basic resemblance to one another. In most cases, the easiest way to tell them apart is the shape of the candle cup. The McKee Glass Company's No. 151 candlestick, which has a candle cup very similar to that on the Heisey candlestick, can be differentiated because it has two bands at the top and bottom of the column, unlike all of the others which only have single bands. Fostoria's No. 2324 candlestick is the most different from the others, since the "bands" are larger and more accurately described as knobs. (See FO-57b on p. 26.) Cambridge's 6¼" No. 1271 candlestick and 9" No. 1273 candlestick are most easily confused with Heisey, with the shape of the candle cup only differing slightly. (See CB-44 on p. 60 of volume one of this series.) Color may sometimes be a reliable differentiating factor, particularly in the case of some of Cambridge's very distinct opaque colors. Ebony is the exception to that rule, since Tiffin also made their candlestick in black, but the candle cup of Tiffin's No. 75 candlestick has a very different shape. The Heisey candlestick was probably the earliest. The McKee and Cambridge candlesticks came out a year later. The Tiffin and Fostoria candlesticks date to about 1924, with the latter also receiving a design patent.

HE-29. No. 71 OVAL
CANDLESTICK, WITH
No. 674 ADAMS
CUTTING

No. 71 candlestick. Named Oval by researchers. 10" high with a 4½" by 3⅞" oval base. Made from July 1921 to 1929, in crystal only. The bottom is cut smooth, with a polished punty. The top is also cut smooth. Usually marked with the Diamond H in the constriction of the neck. Offered with at least three cuttings: No. 674 Adams (seen in the accompanying photograph), 679 Windsor, and 741 Chantilly. Occasionally seen with gold etched bands on the base and candle cup, probably done by Honesdale Decorating Company. $200.00 – 215.00. Add 25 – 50% for cutting.

No. 101 candlestick. Named Simplicity by researchers. 9" high with a 4⅜" diameter round base. Made from March 1922 to 1929, in crystal only. Usually marked with the Diamond H at the top of the column. Offered with at least one cutting, No. 751 Avalon. Factory production records mention one turn having been made in a 7" size in December 1924. We suspect this was probably a typographical error, but it remains possible that a smaller version of this candlestick may have been made experimentally. $110.00 – 125.00.

HE-30. No. 101 SIMPLICITY CANDLESTICK

No. 102 candlestick. Named Ballstem by researchers. 9" with a 4⅞" diameter round base. Made from March 1922 to 1929, in crystal only. Usually marked with the Diamond H at the top of the column. Two other companies made the very similar pressed candlesticks seen in HE- 31a, but should cause no confusion. Cambridge's ball stem candlestick and New Martinsville's No. 10 candlestick are both usually found in color, have domed bases, and the rims on their candle cups are much wider. (For a detailed comparison of the two, see CB-46 on p. 62 of volume one of this series.) The Pairpoint Corporation also made a similar candlestick around 1922, the same year that Heisey's Ballstem was introduced, but it is blown with a hollow ball, made in various colors, and generally of higher quality than any of the other candlesticks of this style. $150.00 – 175.00.

HE-31A. CAMBRIDGE'S BALL STEM CANDLESTICK IN AZURITE AND NEW MARTINSVILLE'S No. 10 CANDLESTICK IN BLUE

HE-31. No. 102 BALL-STEM CANDLESTICK

No. 103 saucer foot candlestick. Named Cupped Saucer by researchers. 3" high with a base diameter of approximately 4⅜" (depending on how deeply the base was cupped). Made from April 1922 to 1929. Known in crystal and flamingo; moongleam is also a possibility, but has not been reported to date. Sometimes marked on the center of the bottom, or in the constriction at the bottom of the candle cup just above the knob. A few years after its introduction, this candlestick was also offered as No. 106, with the base turned down. (See HE-41 on p. 114.) Crystal: $22.50 – 25.00. Flamingo: $45.00 – 50.00.

HE-32. No. 103 CUPPED SAUCER CANDLESTICK

HE-33. No. 99 LITTLE SQUATTER CANDLE-BLOCKS IN FLAMINGO AND MOONGLEAM

No. 99 candleblock. Named Little Squatter by researchers. 1½" high with a 3¾" base. Made from June 1922 to 1944 in crystal, moongleam, and flamingo. Usually marked with the Diamond H on the center of the bottom, though sometimes the mark is so faint that it becomes invisible. Some catalogs describe this candleblock as a "toy." We don't have factory records for the entire period this candleblock was in production, but know that in just a two-year period, from 1924 to 1926, over 39,000 of them were made, indicating the popularity of this informal little candleholder, so very different from the more elegant candlesticks of Heisey's colonial period. Two other companies made similar candleblocks: Westmoreland's No. 1061 candlestick is the most likely to be confused with Heisey's, but has a pronounced lip around the opening of the candle cup that is basically square in shape with convex sides, aligned with and mirroring the sides of the candleblock. Heisey's Little Squatter does not have the lip, and has an indentation that runs from each corner of the candle cup to the bottom corner of the base. Less likely to be confused is Tiffin's No. 310 candleholder, which is larger (about 4⅛" wide) and has double ribs in place of the indentation. A similar candleblock was also made in pottery, by Rookwood – a fairly common occurrence, with both branches of manufacture often borrowing ideas from one another, though it isn't always easy to figure out who came up with the original design first. Crystal: $15.00 – 20.00. Flamingo: $22.50 – 25.00. Moongleam: $25.00 – 30.00.

HE-34. No. 21 ARISTO-CRAT DESK CANDLESTICK

No. 21 desk candlestick. Named Aristocrat by researchers. 3½" high with a 4⅛" square base. Made from December 1922 to ca. 1929 and then brought back into production from ca. 1939 to 1944. Known in crystal and flamingo (very rare). Usually marked with the Diamond H at the bottom of the candle cup. This was a short version of Heisey's earlier No. 21 candlestick (see HE-12 on p. 104), with the center column removed and the candle cup placed directly on the base. Like the earlier tall candlesticks, most of the desk candlesticks (or "square" candlesticks, as they were described in some catalogs) have ground bottoms with polished pontils, as well as tops ground smooth. However, during World War II, when labor shortages called for economy measures, this candlestick was made without the bottom being finished. At this period, the candlesticks were also offered as part of a console set with the No. 1489 Puritan oblong floral bowl. Crystal: $125.00 – 150.00. Flamingo: Unable to price.

HE-35. No. 72 BOX SWIRL CANDLESTICK

No. 72 candlestick. Named Box Swirl by researchers. 9" high with a 4" square base. Also made in a 10" height. Crystal only. Marked on the candle cup, just above the column. This was one of the last of Heisey's colonial-style candlesticks, with a pressed imitation of a deep cut design. The basic shape was based on the No. 21 candlestick. (See HE-12 on p. 104.) According to factory production records, there were only three turns of this candlestick made between December 1922 and April 1924, for a total of only 213 pairs. One additional turn was made in October 1924, with an indication that it was a "new" item, and the height given as 10", with only 32 pairs produced. This is one of the rarest of Heisey's early candlesticks. The bottom is ground, with a polished pontil, and the top is cut smooth. $1,000.00 – market.

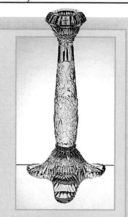

Candlestick. Named Egyptian by researchers. The original pattern number of this piece is unknown, so it has been assigned pattern No. 7075 by Clarence Vogel. 9½" high with a three-footed base that spans approximately 4½". Marked with the Diamond H on the candle cup, just beneath the rim. Crystal only. The top of the candle cup is ground smooth. Production dates are unknown, but it is possible that this is Heisey's No. 73 candlestick, mentioned in factory production records as having been made in December 1922. This is barely a month after the discovery of the tomb of Tutankhamun, which triggered a world-wide mania for all things Egyptian, and might be too soon for them to have created such a detailed mold. If it is the No. 73, there were only 112 made, which certainly would accord with the Egyptian candlestick's rarity today. Another good candidate, however, is the No. 3877 candlestick, described in production records as 9" high, with a single turn made in August 1924 of 343 candlesticks. $1,000.00 – market.

HE-36. EGYPTIAN CANDLESTICK

No. 104 candlestick. Named Bertha by researchers. 5" high with a 5⅜" diameter round base. Made from January 1924 to ca. 1929 in crystal, moongleam, and flamingo. Usually marked with the Diamond H at the top of the column. This is unique among Heisey's candlesticks in that it takes a 1½" candle, rather than the standard ¾" taper. A somewhat similar candlestick was also made by the Co-operative Flint Glass Company at around the same period as their No. 503. (See CO-12 on p. 123 of volume one of this series.) The Co-operative candlestick is hollow halfway up the stem, whereas the Heisey candlestick is solid. Crystal: $100.00 – 125.00. Flamingo: $140.00 – 165.00. Moongleam: $150.00 – 175.00.

HE-37. No. 104 BERTHA CANDLESTICK

No. 201 candlestick. Named Photo by researchers. 10" high. Made from April 1924 to February 1925, in crystal only. According to factory production records, there were only 171 of these candlesticks made, resulting in it's being one of the rarest of the early candlesticks. It is marked with the Diamond H at the top of the base, just beneath the "frame." The bottom is cut smooth, with a polished pontil. The frame in the center is intended to hold a photograph, possibly for use during closed casket funerals. The back of the candlestick has three cut notches into which metal spring clips could be placed to hold the photograph in place. This seems to have been the last of the colonial style candlesticks, with its hexagonal base and candle cup. $1,500.00 – market.

HE-38. No. 201 PHOTO CANDLE-STICK

No. 105 candlestick/candelabrum. Named Pembroke by researchers. Made in two sizes: 7" high, with a 5" diameter round base and a 3½" wide top rim (produced from March 1925 to ca. 1933); and 9" high, with a 5⅜" base and a 3⅞" top rim (May 1924 – ca. 1934). Offered in crystal, moongleam, and flamingo. Usually marked with the Diamond H in the construction, just above the knob at the top of the column. Offered with both a plain top rim (which we have never seen), or with pressed indentations around the edge of the rim to hold nine prisms. In addition to the standard faceted A prisms and flat C prisms, in 1926 both sizes were also available with crystal, amethyst, amber, or blue tear drop prisms. This candlestick was a modification of the No. 100 candlestick (see HE-28 on page 109) with the top rim added. 7", crystal: $75.00 – 85.00; flamingo, moongleam: $175.00 – 200.00. 9", crystal: $100.00 – 115.00; flamingo, moongleam: $200.00 – 225.00.

HE-39. No. 105 PEMBROKE CANDELABRA IN MOONGLEAM, 7" AND 9"

HE-40. No. 600 SQUARE-HANDLED
SAUCER FOOTED CANDLESTICK

No. 600 saucer footed candlestick. Named Square-Handled by researchers. 2¼" high with a 4⅝" diameter cupped base. Made from October 1924 to ca. 1936 and then reissued from May 1939 to ca. 1945; following this date, however, the candlestick continued to be made as a special order for the Harvey House restaurant chain (probably beginning as early as 1949) until the factory closed in 1957. Although it has been seen in crystal only, many of the items made for Fred Harvey were provided in amber, so this color is also a possibility. Usually marked with the Diamond H on the bottom of the candle cup, just above the saucer foot. The underside of the base is pressed with a narrow optic. $45.00 – 55.00.

HE-41. No. 106
INVERTED
SAUCER
CANDLESTICK
IN MOONGLEAM

No. 106 candlestick. Named Inverted Saucer by researchers. 3" high with a 4⅜" diameter round base. Made from January 1925 to ca. 1929 in crystal, moongleam, and flamingo. Sometimes marked with the Diamond H on the center of the bottom or in the constriction at the bottom of the candle cup, just above the knob. This is the No. 103 candlestick with the base turned down, instead of cupped. (See HE-32 on p. 111.) Crystal: $20.00 – 25.00. Flamingo: $40.00 – 45.00. Moongleam: $60.00 – 65.00.

HE-42. No. 107
WELLINGTON
CANDLESTICK IN
MOONGLEAM

No. 107 candlestick. Named Wellington by researchers. 10" high with a 5½" diameter round base. Made from January 1925 to ca. 1930 in crystal, moongleam, and flamingo. Usually marked with the Diamond H at the top of the column. Sometimes found decorated with cuttings. Crystal: $115.00 – 135.00. Flamingo: $135.00 – 155.00. Moongleam: $155.00 – 175.00.

HE-43. No. 108
THREE-RING
CANDLESTICK

No. 108 candlestick. Named Three-Ring by researchers. 7" high. Made from February 1925 to ca. 1929. Usually marked at the top of the column. This is another candlestick based on the design of the No. 100 (HE-28 on p. 109), with the three rings added, but was produced only in very limited quantities, making it rare today. $125.00 – 150.00. *(Photograph courtesy of the Heisey Collectors of America, Inc.)*

No. 109 candlestick. Named Petticoat Dolphin by researchers. Made in two styles, with a flared base (as seen in HE-44), 5¾" high with a 4¾" scalloped round base; or with a cupped base (as seen in HE-44a), 6½" high with a 3½" base. In production from August 1925 to ca. 1935. Offered in crystal, moongleam, flamingo, sahara, and Stiegel blue. None of the colors are easy to find, but flamingo is seen most often, generally with the flared base; crystal and moongleam (with the cupped base) are rare, and sahara and Stiegel blue have never been seen by the authors. This was a reproduction of a candlestick originally made by the Northwood Company in Indiana, Pennsylvania, around 1900. Heisey's own publicity attributed the original candlestick to the Boston and Sandwich Glass Company, a claim that has been repeated by other early researchers, but has since been found to be erroneous. At any rate, probably because this candlestick is a reproduction, it is not marked with the Diamond H. The differences between the Heisey version and the original are minute: the Heisey dolphin has much finer scales, whereas the design circling the scalloped edge is less detailed than on the original. In addition, the Northwood dolphins will be found in opalescent colors (crystal, blue, and canary). Heisey used this candlestick as the base for three different comports, sold with a pair of candlesticks to form a console set, by affixing either the No. 416 Herringbone soup plate, the No. 1185 Yeoman soup plate, or the No. 1225 8" plate. Often the comport features a colored base with a crystal top, or vice versa. The candlestick has also been seen with the candle cup removed and a fitting added to modify it for use as an electric lamp, but this was probably the work of a decorating company. Crystal: $110.00 – 125.00. Flamingo: $175.00 – 200.00. Moongleam: $225.00 – 250.00. Sahara, Stiegel blue: Unable to price.

HE-44. No. 109 PETTICOAT DOLPHIN CANDLESTICK IN FLAMINGO, FLARED BASE

HE-44A. HEISEY'S No. 109 PETTICOAT DOLPHIN CANDLESTICK IN MOONGLEAM, WITH CUPPED BASE, AND NORTHWOOD CANDLESTICK IN BLUE OPALESCENT

No. 110 candlestick. Named Sandwich Dolphin by researchers. 10" high with a 4¼" square base. Made from October 1925 to 1935, when it was discontinued, though factory records reveal that two final turns were made in December 1939. Offered in crystal, moongleam, flamingo, sahara, Stiegel blue, zircon, and amber. Crystal and flamingo are occasionally seen, moongleam less often, and the other colors are rare. Like the No. 109 Petticoat Dolphin above, this candlestick was advertised as a reproduction of a piece originally made by the Boston and Sandwich Glass Company. In this instance, the attribution of the original was correct. In fact, Heisey had obtained many of the original wooden models from the Sandwich company from an early salesman, James E. Johnson, including one for the dolphin candlestick. (This mahogany model, believed lost for many years, is now on display at the Heisey Glass Museum in Newark, Ohio.) Presumably because it was a reproduction, the Heisey dolphin is not marked with the Diamond H. The original Sandwich candlestick was made in two parts, with the candle cup attached to the tail of the dolphin using a wafer. (See BS-14 on p. 39 of volume one of this series.) The Heisey dolphin is molded as a single piece. Also, the original has only a slight bevel to the top edge of the base, whereas the beveling is much more pronounced on the Heisey version. Other companies have also reproduced this candlestick, including the Imperial Glass Corporation (made for the Metropolitan Museum of Art and marked MMA — see IM-172 on p. 226) and General Housewares Corporation (imported

HE-45. No. 110 SANDWICH DOLPHIN CANDLESTICKS IN CRYSTAL AND MOONGLEAM

HE-45A. NO. 110 SANDWICH DOLPHIN CANDLESTICK IN ZIRCON (RARE COLOR)

HE-45B. NO. 110 SANDWICH DOLPHIN CANDLESTICK IN STIEGEL BLUE

from Taiwan and marked GHC – see GH-1 on p. 81). For more information on all of these candlesticks, see the appendix to volume one of this series. An electric lamp made from the Heisey candlestick was sold by the Ideal Cut Glass Company of Canastota, New York, with a floral cutting on the base. Crystal: $175.00 – 225.00. Flamingo: $225.00 – 250.00. Moongleam: $275.00 – 300.00. Stiegel blue: $750.00 – market. Amber, sahara, zircon: Unable to price.

HE-46. NO. 112 MERCURY 3¾" CANDLESTICKS
IN HAWTHORNE, SAHARA, AND MOONGLEAM

No. 112 candlestick. Named Mercury by researchers. 3¾" high (listed in catalogs as 3") with a 4⅝" diameter round base. This candlestick was probably produced in the largest quantities of any candlestick ever made by Heisey, since it was in production from January 1926 until the factory closed in 1957, and was then reissued by the Imperial Glass Corporation from May 1958 to January 1964 and again from 1974 to 1976. (See IM-130 on p. 216.) A design patent was filed for this candlestick on March 23, 1926, and approved July 13, 1926, as D70,558, with T. Clarence Heisey given as the designer, though he probably just signed off on the application as an officer of the firm. Offered in crystal, moongleam, flamingo, hawthorne, and sahara. It has also been seen in experimental gold opalescent. Only occasionally marked with the Diamond H, in the constriction above the striated ball. This same design was used on three stemware patterns (No. 3355 Fairacre, 3357 King Arthur, and 3408 Jamestown).

This was a very popular blank for cuttings and etchings. Known cuttings include No. 326 Trinidad, 636 Clermont, 781 St. Anne, 789 Aberdeen, 802 Manchester, 803 Hialeah, 832 Continental, 835 Larkspur, 840 Briar Cliff, 844 Piccadilly, 845 Fontaine, 867 Chateau, 939 Festoon Wreath, 941 Barcelona, 942 Harvester, 947 Enchantress, 948 Boquet, 949 Evelyn, 965 Narcissus, 985 Sheffield, 1083 Jungle Flower, and 1803½ El Dorado. Known etchings include No. 454 Antarctic, 456 Titania, 457 Springtime, 458 Olympiad, 503 Minuet, 507 Orchid, 515 Heisey Rose, 516 Plantation Ivy, and 520B Leaf Etching.

The candle cups from this candlestick are sometimes found ground flat on the bottom as individual mini-candleholders. It is likely that these were made by factory workers from candlesticks that broke during the manufacturing process and were taken home in their lunch boxes. A 9" size of this candlestick was also made (see HE-47 on the following page), as well as a version modified to be used as an insert to a flower block (sold as No. 123 – see HE-59 on p. 120). The molds for this candlestick are currently owned by the Heisey Collectors of America. Crystal, flamingo: $25.00 – 30.00. Moongleam: $30.00 – 35.00. Sahara, hawthorne: $55.00 – 65.00. Add 50% for etching.

Note: According to factory production records, an unsuccessful attempt was made to produce an unknown No. 115 candlestick in June 1926. Price lists from 1927 to 1929 (a period for which production records are not available) list this candlestick, described as 3" high, in crystal, moongleam, and flamingo. The original mold drawing for this candlestick is in the archives of the Heisey Collectors of America and indicate that it is identical to the No. 112 candlestick (HE- 46 above), but with square handles on either side of the base like those used on the No. 1229 Octagon pattern. The drawing shows the base cupped, as it would come out of the mold, but presumably it would have been either flattened or turned up in a saucer shape. This candlestick has never been seen, but should be easy to recognize, because of its resemblance to the No. 112.

No. 112 candlestick. Named Mercury by researchers. 9" high with a 5⅛" diameter round base. Made ca. 1927 – 1930 in crystal, moongleam, and flamingo. Marked with the Diamond H at the top of the column. Unlike the 3" size of this candlestick (see HE-46 on the preceding page), which is one of Heisey's most common candlesticks, the 9" height is rarely seen. Crystal: $100.00 – 125.00. Flamingo, moongleam: $190.00 – 220.00.

HE-47. No. 112 MERCURY 9" CANDLESTICK IN MOONGLEAM (WITH 3¾" SIZE FOR COMPARISON)

No. 113 candlestick. Named Mars by researchers. 3½" high with a 4¾" diameter round base and a 3¾" round rim on the candle cup. Made from March 1926 to 1933. A design patent was filed for this candlestick on April 23, 1926, and approved August 24, 1926, as D70,879. T. Clarence Heisey was listed as designer, though he probably just signed the application as an officer of the company. Offered in crystal, moongleam, flamingo, hawthorne, marigold, and sahara. Sometimes marked with the Diamond H on the bottom of the candle cup, just above the top ring. Fostoria also made a candlestick with three rings on the stem, but with enough significant differences that there should be no problem distinguishing the two. (See FO-61 on p. 28.) Crystal, flamingo: $25.00 – 30.00. Moongleam: $35.00 – 40.00. Sahara, hawthorne, marigold: $75.00 – 85.00.

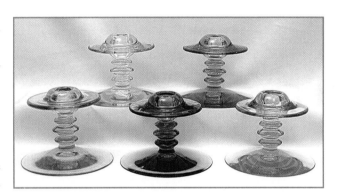

HE-48. No. 113 MARS CANDLESTICKS IN MARIGOLD, SAHARA, MOONGLEAM, HAWTHORNE, AND FLAMINGO

No. 114 candlestick. Named Pluto by researchers. 4" high (called 3½" in the catalogs) with a 4¾" diameter round base and a 3½" hexagonal rim on the candle cup. Made from May 1926 to 1931. Offered in crystal, moongleam, flamingo, hawthorne, and marigold. Sometimes marked with the Diamond H at the top of the column. In 1940, this mold was probably redesigned to become the No. 1521 Quilt candlestick (see HE-130 on p. 144) and then was redesigned again as the No. 1533 Wampum candlestick. A similar candlestick with a hexagonal rim around the candle cup, but with only one ball on the center column and a hollow base with a rim, was made by the Indiana Glass Company as part of their No. 603 Moderne Classic pattern. (See IN-19 on p. 242.) Crystal: $20.00 – 25.00. Flamingo: $25.00 – 30.00. Moongleam: $30.00 – 35.00. Hawthorne: $45.00 – 55.00. Marigold: $70.00 – 80.00.

HE-49. No. 114 PLUTO CANDLESTICKS IN HAWTHORNE, MOONGLEAM, AND FLAMINGO

HE-50. No. 116 OAK LEAF CANDLESTICKS IN CRYSTAL WITH MOONGLEAM FOOT, ALL HAWTHORNE, AND ALL CRYSTAL. (NOTE FROSTED OAK LEAF ON THE TWO CANDLESTICKS ON THE RIGHT)

No. 116 candlestick. Named Oak Leaf by researchers. 3" high with a 4⅛" diameter round base. Made from August 1926 to ca. 1929. A design patent was filed for this candlestick on January 7, 1927, and approved December 6, 1927, as D74,012. T. Clarence Heisey was named as designer, but probably just signed off on the patent application as an officer of the company. This candlestick was made in two parts, with an applied foot, making it one of the few to be offered in combinations of crystal and color. Known in all crystal, crystal top with a moongleam foot, all flamingo, flamingo top with a crystal foot, and hawthorne. The oak leaf is often frosted. Sometimes marked with the Diamond H in the constriction just above the base, but with the diamond turned on its side and so small that it can barely be discerned. This was one of the first candlesticks to have a bowl especially designed to accompany it as part of a console set. The candle cup portion was also sold as a toothpick holder, with the bottom ground. Crystal: $30.00 – 35.00. Crystal w/moongleam top: $45.00 – 50.00. Flamingo: $50.00 – 55.00. Hawthorne: $55.00 – 65.00.

HE-51. No. 118 MISS MUFFIT CANDLESTICKS IN FLAMINGO AND CRYSTAL. (NOTE DIAMOND OPTIC ON BASE OF CRYSTAL EXAMPLE)

No. 118 candlestick. Named Miss Muffit by researchers. 2¾" high (called 3" in the catalog) with a 4¼" diameter round base. Made from August 1926 to ca. 1930. Offered in crystal, moongleam, and flamingo. This candlestick has also been seen in Heisey's experimental opalescent gold. Sometimes marked on the bottom. Available with the foot plain or with diamond optic. Crystal: $17.50 – 20.00. Flamingo, moongleam: $35.00 – 40.00.

HE-52. No. 111 CHERUB CANDLESTICK IN MOONGLEAM

No. 111 candlestick. Named Cherub by researchers. 11½" high with a 5" diameter round base. Made from October 1926 to ca. 1929. The sequence of pattern numbers suggests that this candlestick was designed much earlier and, in fact, a former employee of the factory remembered that this was one of the most difficult molds the company had ever made, requiring nine months to complete. Made in crystal, moongleam, and flamingo, both plain and with satin finish. It isn't known if this was a reproduction of another candlestick, but it is very similar to earlier cherub candlesticks manufactured by the Central Glass Works (see CE-2 on p. 103 of volume one of this series) and later reissued by the U.S. Glass Company, which had themselves been inspired by French cherubs by Baccarat and others. The Heisey cherub is cut smooth on the bottom, with a ground pontil. Crystal satin: $250.00 – 275.00. Flamingo, moongleam: $650.00 – market.

HE-52A & 52B. No. 111 CHERUB CANDLESTICK IN CRYSTAL SATIN, FRONT AND REAR VIEWS

No. 1183 Revere vase candlestick. Made in two pieces. The vase portion is 7⅜" high with a 4¼" diameter round base and a width of 5¾" at the top. The candleholder insert is 3⅝" high with a 2½" base, with four circular openings allowing the piece to be used as both a candleholder and vase simultaneously. The insert sits on a rim inside the opening of the vase, giving the assembled set a total height of 10¼". Made from November 1926 to 1927 or 1928. (The vase by itself had been made as early as August 1924, and can be found without the insert.) The vase was available in crystal and moongleam, but the candle insert seems to have been made in crystal only. Usually marked with the Diamond H on the bottom, in the center of the base. The rim of the vase is drilled for 12 prisms, with

HE-53. No. 1183 Revere vase candlestick with No. 748 Tripoli cutting and blue prisms (some prisms removed to better show piece)

a choice of either "A" spear prisms or "C" flat prisms. Blue, amber, or amethyst prisms were also offered. Known with at least two cuttings: No. 679 Windsor and 758 Tripoli. The molds for the vase candlestick were modified in 1939 to create the No. 1511 Tourjours candlevase. (See HE-127 on p. 143.) Although the Revere pattern had been in existence as early as 1913 (with the punch cups in the pattern dating back to 1906), this was the first candleholder in the line. Two others were later added, the four-light base and candleholders (HE-87 on p. 130), and the epergne candleholder (HE-108 on p. 137). Crystal: $150.00 – 175.00. Moongleam: $175.00 – 210.00. Add 25 – 35% for cutting.

HE-53A. No. 1183 Revere vase candlestick in moongleam with crystal insert

No. 117 candlestick. Named Bamboo by researchers. 8" high with a 4¾" diameter round base. Made 1927 – ca. 1929. The candle cup was molded separately from the stem and foot. Offered with a crystal candle cup with moongleam or flamingo bottoms, moongleam top with a crystal foot, or flamingo top with a crystal foot. Very difficult to find in any color combination. Usually marked with the Diamond H at the top of the column. All colors: $500.00 – market.

HE-54. No. 117 Bamboo candlestick in moongleam, with crystal top

No. 119 candlestick. Named Jewel by researchers. 3" high. It was advertised in the November 1927 issue of *Heisey's Table Talk*, a newsletter distributed to their customers, in an advertisement that was repeated that month in both *National Geographic* and *House and Garden*. No other information available. To the authors' knowledge, only one of these candlesticks has ever been reported, in crystal. The advertisement cited above also mentions moongleam, flamingo, and hawthorne, so it is possible this candlestick may have been made in other colors. It is marked with the Diamond H in the constriction above the base. Unable to price.

HE-55. No. 119 Jewel candlestick, top view

HE-55A. No. 119 Jewel candlestick, side view

No. 120 candlestick. Named Overlapping Swirl by researchers. 3" high with a 4½" diameter round base. Made ca. 1927 – 1931. Known in crystal, moongleam, flamingo, and hawthorne. Sometimes marked with the Diamond H on the bottom. Crystal: $20.00 – 25.00. Flamingo: $30.00 – 35.00. Moongleam: $35.00 – 40.00. Hawthorne: $60.00 – 65.00.

HE-56. No. 120 OVERLAPPING SWIRL candle-sticks in MOONGLEAM, CRYSTAL, AND HAWTHORNE

No. 121 candlestick. Named Pinwheel by researchers. 1¾" high (called 2" in the catalogs) with a 4¼" diameter round base. (Depending on the treatment to the tops, which sometimes were left flat and sometime turned up at the end, the height may vary from 1¾" to 2⅛".) Made ca. 1927 to the early 1930s in crystal, moongleam, flamingo, and hawthorne. Generally marked with the Diamond H on the side, under the turned down edge of the candle cup. Crystal: $25.00 – 30.00. Flamingo, moongleam: $30.00 – 35.00. Hawthorne: $45.00 – 50.00.

HE-57. No. 121 PINWHEEL candlesticks in HAWTHORNE, flamingo, AND crystal. (NOTE VARYING TREATMENTS TO TOPS)

No. 122 candlestick. Named Zig Zag by researchers. 2" high with a 4⅛" diameter round base. Made ca. 1927 to the early 1930s in crystal, moongleam, flamingo, and hawthorne. Generally marked with the Diamond H on the side, under the turned down edge of the candle cup. Almost identical to the No. 121 candlestick (HE-57 above), but with a different pattern on the "mushroom" top. It has only been seen with the top turned down, but any of the other treatments to the top known on the No. 121 above are possible. Crystal: $25.00 – 30.00. Flamingo, moongleam: $30.00 – 35.00. Hawthorne: $45.00 – 50.00.

HE-58. No. 122 ZIG ZAG candlesticks in FLAMINGO AND CRYSTAL

HE-59. No. 123 MERCURY (INSERT) CANDLESTICK IN MOON-GLEAM

No. 123 candlestick. Named Mercury (Insert) by researchers. 5¼" high with a diameter of 2" at the base. This candlestick was intended to fit in the center of the No. 15 flower frog, which is 5¼" in diameter at the top with a 4⅜" diameter foot. Assembled, the two pieces are 6" high. Made from ca. 1927 – 1929 in crystal, moongleam, flamingo, and hawthorne, but scarce in all colors. Usually marked with the Diamond H in the middle, on the bottom. This is a modified version of the earlier No. 112 candlestick. (See HE-46 on p. 116.) Crystal: $60.00 – 75.00. Flamingo, moongleam: $75.00 – 95.00. Hawthorne: $100.00 – 125.00. (All prices are for candlestick with flower frog.)

No. 124 candlestick. Named Eva Mae by researchers. Before the Heisey Collectors of America acquired the original mold drawing for this piece and were thus able to determine the original pattern number, it was assigned No. 8040 by them. 6½" high with a 5½" diameter round foot. Probably made sometime around 1927 or 1928. Known in flamingo and moongleam, with crystal also likely. Marked with the Diamond H at the top of the column, just beneath the knob. The column on the candlestick is very similar to Heisey's No. 3360 Penn Charter stemware line, which went into production around 1926. The knob at the top of the stem is also very similar to that on the No. 112 candlestick and the modified version of it just above, the No. 123 candlestick. (See HE-46 on p. 116 and HE-59 on the preceding page.) Unable to price.

HE-60. No. 124 EVA MAE CANDLESTICK IN MOON-GLEAM

No. 125 Leaf Design candleblock. 1" high and approximately 5½" by 3" in size. Made ca. 1928 – 1929 in crystal, moongleam, and flamingo, and reissued briefly again ca. 1939 – 1941 in crystal only. To our knowledge, these candleblocks are not marked with the Diamond H. A very similar candleblock was also made in metal by an unidentified company, and was the subject of a design patent. Crystal: $75.00 – 85.00. Flamingo, moongleam: $100.00 – market.

HE-61. No. 125 LEAF DESIGN CANDLE-BLOCK

No. 126 candlestick. Named Trophy by researchers. 6" high with a 4⅞" diameter round base. Made ca. 1928 – 1929 in crystal, moongleam, and flamingo. Sometimes marked with the Diamond H at the bottom of the column. Crystal: $50.00 – 65.00. Flamingo, moongleam: $65.00 – 75.00.

HE-62. No. 126 TROPHY CANDLESTICKS IN CRYSTAL, MOONGLEAM, AND FLAMINGO

No. 520 candlelamp. Named Innovation by researchers. 4½" high. The bottom well is approximately 5" wide. Made ca. 1928 to the early 1930s in crystal only, with one brief final turn (possibly a special order) made in June 1941. A patent was filed for this very unusual item on January 30, 1928, and approved June 3, 1930, as No. 1,761,299. E. Wilson Heisey was given as the creator of the invention, but probably signed the application as president of the company. The candle lamp consists of two pieces, a bottle-like container, or well, which was meant to be "filled or partially filled with colored material of any type" (either colored water or sand), and a separate stopper with an "apron" (as described in the patent application) that "will have the effect of absorbing color rays, either from the colored material in the receptacle or from the candle light or from other sources." The stopper is generally marked with the Diamond H in the constriction beneath the candle cup. The candle lamp is known with at least one etching, No. 440 Frontenac, and other decorations from the period are likely. The example shown in the accompanying photograph has a light cutting on the bottom portion, and a gold filled etching on the stopper, done by the Honesdale Decorating Company. $110.00 – 125.00.

HE-63. No. 520 INNOVATION CANDLELAMP WITH LIGHT CUTTING AND GOLD FILLED ETCHING DONE BY THE HONESDALE DECORATING COMPANY

HE-64. No. 127
Twist Stem
candlestick
in moongleam

No. 127 candlestick. Named Twist Stem by researchers. 4¾" high with a 5⅜" diameter round base. (Because this candlestick was molded with two straight columns and then twisted to form the final piece, dimensions will vary even more than is customary.) Made ca. 1929 in crystal, moongleam, and flamingo. Rare in all colors. To our knowledge, this candlestick is not marked with the Diamond H. In catalog pictures, the rim around the candle cup appears to be circular, but is actually octagonal. Unable to price.

HE-65. No.
128 Liberty
candle-
sticks, 3½" in
moongleam,
6" in crystal

No. 128 candlestick. Named Liberty by researchers. Made in two sizes: 3½" high (called 3" in the catalogs) with a 4⅝" diameter round base; and 6" high with a 5¹⁄₁₆" base. Made ca. 1929 – 1936. The smaller size was offered in crystal, moongleam, flamingo, and marigold (very scarce); the 6" size, which is rare, was offered in the same colors, as well as in crystal with a moongleam foot. Sometimes marked with the Diamond H at the bottom of the column. 3½", crystal: $25.00 – 30.00; moongleam, flamingo: $35.00 – 50.00; marigold: $125.00 – 150.00. 6", all colors: add 100 – 125%.

HE-66. No. 129 Tricorn triplex
candlestick in flamingo

No. 129 triplex candlestick. Named Tricorn by researchers. 5" high with a 5¼" diameter round base and an arm spread of approximately 6⅛". Made from June 1929 to 1936 in crystal, moongleam, flamingo, and marigold (rare); also known with a crystal top and moongleam foot. Usually marked with the Diamond H just above the acorn, between two of the arms. Known with No. 503 Minuet etching. The acorn, which is the main design motif, matches that on the No. 130 candlestick below. Early advertisements suggest that this candlestick was intended to be used with pieces in the No. 1252 Twist pattern, often showing the candlesticks with the Twist nasturtium bowl as a console set. Crystal: $60.00 – 75.00; with moongleam foot: $90.00 – 110.00. Flamingo: $110.00 – 130.00. Moongleam: $150.00 – 175.00. Marigold: Unable to price.

HE-67. No.
130 Acorn
candle-
stick in
moongleam

No. 130 candlestick. Named Acorn by researchers. 4" high and with an irregularly shaped base approximately 5" long by 4" wide. Made ca. 1929 in crystal, moongleam, and flamingo. Rare in all colors. To the best of our knowledge, this candlestick is not marked with the Diamond H. The bottom is fire polished, with a ground pontil. The acorn that forms the main design motif on this candlestick matches that on the No. 129 triplex candlestick above. Crystal: $175.00 – 225.00. Flamingo, moongleam: $350.00 – market.

No. 132 candlestick. Named Sunburst by researchers. 2" high with a 3⅝" square base and a diameter on the top rim of approximately 3⅝". Made ca. 1929 – 1936 in crystal, moongleam, flamingo, and marigold (rare). Usually marked with the Diamond H under the rim of the candle cup, on the top portion of the thick center column. This candlestick was redesigned to become the No. 1469 Ridgeleigh square footed candlestick in 1936. (See HE-101 on p. 135.) Crystal: $22.50 – 25.00. Flamingo: $45.00 – 50.00. Moongleam: $50.00 – 55.00. Marigold: $95.00 – 100.00.

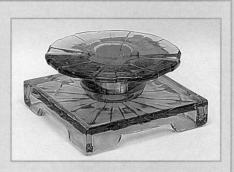

HE-68. No. 132 SUNBURST CANDLESTICK IN MOONGLEAM

No. 133 candlestick. Named Swan-Handled by researchers. 6½" high (called 6" in the catalogs) with a 4¾" diameter round base. Made ca. 1929 – 1936 in crystal, moongleam, flamingo, marigold, alexandrite, and sahara. Despite the relatively long production period, this candlestick is scarce in all colors, and rare in marigold and alexandrite. A mention of amber in the May 1930 issue of *House and Garden* may refer to either marigold or sahara, but could also indicate production in true amber. To the best of the authors' knowledge, this candlestick is not marked with the Diamond H. The design consists of a pair of finely detailed swans, back to back, with their beaks curving down towards their breasts to form handles. There was an accompanying floral bowl that also had swan handles – touted as "rather an innovation" by one of the trade journals when this console set was first released. Crystal: $150.00 – 175.00. Flamingo, sahara: $200.00 – 225.00. Moongleam: $300.00 – 325.00. Alexandrite, marigold: Unable to price.

HE-69. No. 133 SWAN-HANDLED CANDLESTICK IN MOONGLEAM

No. 134 two-light candlestick. Named Trident by researchers. 6" high (called 5" in the catalogs) with a 5½" diameter round base and an arm spread of 6½". Made from 1929 until the factory closed in 1957 and then reissued by Imperial from May 1958 to 1971. (See IM-131 on p. 216.) Known in crystal, all moongleam, moongleam foot with crystal arms, flamingo, marigold (very rare), alexandrite (rare), and sahara. Various other color combinations are also known, all of which can be considered rare: alexandrite arms with sahara foot, sahara arms with moongleam foot, tangerine arms with crystal foot, crystal arms with dawn foot. Most of these were probably experimental only. This candlestick is also known in experimental light blue (possibly a Holophane Glass Company color, since the two companies were adjacent to one another and are known to have exchanged molds on occasion). This candlestick is sometimes marked with the Diamond H just above the foot. Like many other candlesticks from this period, it has a matching floral bowl and was often sold as part of a console set. In later years, after this bowl had been discontinued, the candlesticks continued to be offered with floral bowls from other patterns, including No. 1401 Empress and 1519 Waverly. The mold is currently owned by the Heisey Collectors of America.

HE-70. No. 134 TRIDENT CANDLESTICK IN ALEXANDRITE

HE-70A. No. 134 TRIDENT CANDLESTICK IN SAHARA, WITH ALEXANDRITE FOOT (RARE COMBINATION)

This was by far Heisey's most popular blank for decorating, both by Heisey and other companies. Known cuttings offered by Heisey include No. 326

HE-70B. No. 134 TRIDENT CANDLE-
STICK IN MOONGLEAM

Trinidad, 602 Sprig, 636 Clermont, 781 St. Anne, 793 Monterey, 794 Riviere, 795 Will-o-the-Wisp, 797 Killarney, 799 Manhattan, 800 Greystone, 801 Wakiki, 802 Manchester, 803 Hialeah, 812 Sweet Briar, 816 Palmetto, 825 Sea Glade, 832 Continental, 834 Moulin Rouge, 835 Larkspur, 837 Cristobal, 838 St. Moritz, 839 Bonnie Briar, 840 Briar Cliff, 842 Singapore, 842½ Lucerne, 844 Piccadilly, 844½ Cromwell, 845 Fontaine, 847 Streamline, 848 Botticelli, 849 Nomad, 850 Del Monte, 851 Kalarama, 854 Lombardy, 855 Fuchsia, 861 Neopolitan, 865 Florentine, 866 Kent, 867 Chateau, 868 Minaret, 870 St. Albins, 871 Sophisto, 872 Mariemont, 873 Edwardian, 875 Sylvia, 876 Honolulu, 877 Pueblo, 885 Incognito, 896 Sungate, 900 Saratoga, 902 Orlando, 903 Zeuse, 908 Rondo, 913 Everglade, 916 Arlington, 919 Laurel Wreath, 920 Grey Laurel Wreath, 921 Danish Princess, 930 Narragansett, 933 Fan, 939 Festoon Wreath, 940 Westchester, 941 Barcelona, 942 Harvester, 943 Belfast, 944 Courtship, 947 Enchantress, 948 Boquet, 949 Evelyn, 957 Oriental, 958 Ping Pong, 965 Narcissus, 980 Moonglo, 984 Lancaster, 985 Sheffield, 1091 Wheat, 1092 Melody, 2503 Sussex, 2505, and A. A. #1 Dahlia. Emil Krall, Heisey's master engraver, is also known to have continued offering cuttings on this blank after his retirement from the factory, when he had his own studio in Newark.

Etchings offered on this candlestick included No. 448 Old Colony, 449 Pompeii, 450 Chintz, 450½ Formal Chintz, 454 Antarctic, 458 Olympiad, 480 Normandie, 497 Rosalie, 501 Belle-le-Rose, 502 Crinoline, 503 Minuet, 504 Tea Rose, 507 Orchid, 511 Gardenia, 512 Helen, 515 Heisey Rose, 602 Simplex, and 9014 Rose of Peace. Crystal: $25.00 – 35.00. Flamingo: $100.00 – 115.00. Moongleam: $115.00 – 130.00. Sahara: $80.00 – 100.00. Alexandrite: $275.00 – 325.00. Tangerine: $400.00 – market. Marigold, other color combinations: Unable to price. For Orchid, Heisey Rose, Old Colony etchings, add 75 – 100%; for other etchings, cuttings, add 50 – 75%.

HE-71. No. 135 EMPRESS
CANDLESTICK WITH No. 447
EMPRESS ETCHING

No. 135 Empress candlestick. 6½" high (called 6" in the catalogs) with a 5" diameter round base. Made from 1929 to 1937 in crystal, moongleam, flamingo, marigold (very rare), alexandrite (rare), sahara, and Stiegel blue (rare). May be marked with the Diamond H, possibly in the constriction beneath the candle cup. Although introduced as No. 135, with its own matching console bowl, the candlestick from the beginning was closely identified with the No. 1401 Empress pattern. Known cuttings include No. 781 St. Anne, 799 Manhattan, 803 Hialeah, and 816 Palmetto. Known etchings include No. 366 Peacock, 447 Empress, 448 Old Colony, 449 Pompeii, 450 Chintz, 450½ Formal Chintz, 451 Lafayette, 454 Antarctic, and 9009 Arctic. A very similar candlestick was also made by the Paden City Glass Manufacturing Company in the 1930s as part of their No. 890 Crow's Foot line. Where the Heisey candlestick has acanthus scrolls on the column, the Paden City candlestick has vertical rows of dart-shaped beads. (See HE-71a.) Crystal: $35.00 – 45.00. Flamingo: $75.00 – 95.00. Moongleam: $90.00 – 110.00. Sahara: $75.00 – 85.00. Alexandrite: $270.00 – 300.00. Marigold, Stiegel blue: Unable to price. Add 35 – 50% for etching.

HE-71A. COMPARISON OF
PADEN CITY No. 890 CROW'S
FOOT CANDLESTICK WITH
HEISEY No. 135

No. 1205 candleholder. Named Raindrop by researchers. 1¾" high (called 2" in the catalogs) with a 4¼" diameter round foot. Made ca. 1929 in crystal, moongleam, and flamingo. Generally marked with the Diamond H on the side, under the turned down edge of the candle cup. Very similar to the earlier No. 121 and 122 candlesticks (HE-57 and HE-58 on p. 120), but with elongated hobnails on the "mushroom" top. Paula Pendergrass and Sherry Riggs, in their *Elegant Glass Candleholders*, mention the availability of this candlestick in experimental gold opalescent. Crystal: $30.00 – 35.00. Flamingo, moongleam: $35.00 – 45.00.

HE-72. No. 1205 RAINDROP CANDLEHOLDER

No. 1231 candleholder. Named Ribbed Octagon by researchers. 2" high (called 3" in the catalogs) with a 4¼" diameter round foot. Made ca. 1929 – 1933 in crystal, moongleam, and flamingo. Part of a relatively small pattern group that includes some pieces in sahara; however, the candlestick has not been reported in this color. Generally marked with the Diamond H on the side, under the turned down edge of the candle cup. Also sometimes found with the rim turned down "mushroom" style, like the No. 121, 122, and 1205 candlesticks above (HE-57 and HE-58 on p. 120 and HE-72 immediately above). This candlestick features eight panels and is almost identical to the No. 1252 Twist candlestick below, except that its panels are straight and not twisted. Crystal: $20.00 – 25.00. Flamingo, moongleam: $25.00 – 30.00.

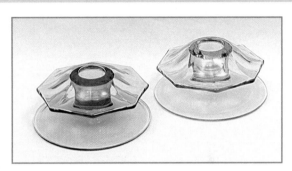

HE-73. No. 1231 RIBBED OCTAGON CANDLEHOLDERS IN MOONGLEAM AND FLAMINGO

No. 1252 Twist candleholder. 2" high with a 4¼" diameter round foot. Made ca. 1929 – 1933 in crystal, moongleam, flamingo, and marigold (rare). Generally marked with the Diamond H on the side, under the turned down edge of the candle cup. A patent for a plate in the Twist pattern was filed in 1928, but the actual introduction of the line seems to have been delayed until 1929. This candlestick is almost identical to the No. 1231 candleholder above, except that its eight panels are twisted, rather than straight. Crystal: $30.00 – 35.00. Flamingo, moongleam: $35.00 – 40.00. Marigold: $85.00 – 100.00.

HE-74. No. 1252 TWIST CANDLEHOLDER IN MOONGLEAM WITH UNKNOWN CUTTING

No. 1401 Empress toed candlestick. 6" high. Made from late 1929 to 1935 or 1936 in crystal, moongleam, flamingo, alexandrite, and sahara. Usually marked with the Diamond H on the back of one of the feet. The No. 135 candlestick (HE-71 on the preceding page) was also associated with the Empress pattern, but this was the first candleholder given the Empress pattern number. The prominent design elements are the fleur-de-lis motif and the feet (or "toes") in the form of dolphin heads. This candlestick was made in two parts, with the candle cup molded separately from the body. It was reissued by Imperial Glass Corporation in sunshine yellow for the Collectors Guild. (See IM-187 on p. 231.) Although this color might be

HE-75. No. 1401 EMPRESS TOED CANDLESTICKS IN FLAMINGO, MOONGLEAM, AND SAHARA

confused with Heisey's sahara, the quality of the glass is much poorer, and all but a few test pieces are marked with the letters CG in a circle on the side of the candlestick. This mold is currently owned by the Heisey Collectors of America. One additional candleholder was added to the Empress pattern in 1932. (See HE-80 on p. 127.) Crystal: $125.00 – 140.00. Flamingo: $175.00 – 200.00. Moongleam: $225.00 – 250.00. Sahara: $130.00 – 150.00. Alexandrite: $325.00 – market.

HE-76. No. 136 TRIPLEX THREE-LIGHT CANDLE-
STICKS IN CRYSTAL AND SAHARA

No. 136 three-light candlestick. Named Triplex by researchers. 6¼" high with an oval, scalloped base that is approximately 6⅛" by 4¼". Made from January 1931 to 1936 in crystal, moongleam, flamingo, sahara, and Stiegel blue. Scarce in all colors. To the best of our knowledge, this candlestick is not marked with the Diamond H. The bottom is ground smooth and has a polished pontil. Offered with at least one cutting, No. 797 Killarney. A ceramic copy of this candlestick is on display in the Heisey Glass Museum, maker unknown. Crystal: $50.00 – 75.00. Flamingo, sahara: $175.00 – 200.00. Moongleam: $275.00 – 300.00. Stiegel blue: Unable to price.

HE-77. No. 137
CONCAVE CIRCLE
CANDLESTICK IN SAHARA

No. 137 candlestick. Named Concave Circle by researchers. 5" high with a base that is approximately 4" by 2¾". Made from January 1931 to 1933 in crystal, moongleam, flamingo, and sahara. Very scarce in all colors. To the best of our knowledge, this candlestick is not marked with the Diamond H. The bottom is fire polished, with a ground pontil. This very unusual candlestick has concave cutouts on either side of its base. The May 1931 issue of the *Crockery and Glass Journal* described it as "a new arrangement for glass candlesticks that has infinite possibilities. By the simple expedience of cutting curves on opposite sides of the circular bases of candlesticks, the Heisey company makes possible the close grouping of any number. Thus by bringing close together the convex side of one of these candlesticks and the concave side of another, two are brought into close association while combinations of three and more may be made to form an infinite variety of designs and letters." Crystal: $150.00 – 175.00. All colors: $175.00 – 220.00.

HE-78. No. 1404 OLD SANDWICH
CANDLESTICKS IN CRYSTAL AND
SAHARA

No. 1404 Old Sandwich candlestick. 6" high with a 4¼" diameter round scalloped base. Made from September 1931 to 1937 in crystal, moongleam, flamingo, sahara, and Stiegel blue. Usually marked with the Diamond H in the center of the base underneath. The Old Sandwich pattern, which was fairly extensive, was inspired by a nineteenth century line known to collectors today as Pillar, attributed by Heisey to Sandwich. Heisey had obtained many of the original wooden models from the Sandwich company from an early salesman, James E. Johnson, including one for the goblet in this pattern. (The same pattern was also made by Bakewell, Pears & Company in Pittsburgh.) The candlestick, as was true of the rest of Heisey's pattern, was not an exact reproduction, but rather only loosely based on the Sandwich design. Many items, including candlesticks, were never made as part of the original pattern at all. The mold is currently owned by the Heisey Collectors of America. Crystal: $45.00 – 60.00. Flamingo: $115.00 – 130.00. Moongleam: $130.00 – 145.00. Sahara: $100.00 – 115.00. Stiegel blue: $250.00 – 275.00.

No. 138 Gascony candlestick. 6¼" high (called 5" in the catalogs) with a 3¾" octagonal base. Made from December 1931 to 1936 in crystal, moongleam, flamingo, sahara, and Stiegel blue. Difficult to find in all colors. Sometimes marked with the Diamond H on the base. Although given its own pattern number, this candlestick was intended for use with the No. 3397 Gascony line (which is blown, with pressed feet). Crystal: $75.00 – 80.00. Flamingo, moongleam: $175.00 – 185.00. Sahara: $150.00 – 160.00. Stiegel blue: $225.00 – 250.00.

HE-79. No. 138 GASCONY CANDLESTICK IN SAHARA

No. 1401 Empress footed, two-handled candlestick. 1⅝" high with four peg feet and a top diameter of 4³⁄₁₆". Made from March 1932 to 1936 in crystal, moongleam, flamingo, and sahara (scarce in color). Usually marked with the Diamond H on the bottom. This was the third candleholder in the Empress pattern, though only the second to share the No. 1401 pattern number. (See HE-71 on p. 124 and HE-75 on p. 125.) It has the fleur-de-lis typical of the pattern, but instead of dolphin feet, has plain peg feet. A number of other companies made very similar candleholders, but none of them are handled. When the Empress pattern was redesigned to become No. 1509 Queen Ann in 1938, this was one of the pieces that was modified, by flaring the rim and adding a wide optic to the inside of the bowl. (See HE-121 on p. 141.) Crystal: $30.00 – 35.00. Flamingo, moongleam, sahara: $65.00 – 85.00.

HE-80. No. 1401 EMPRESS FOOTED, TWO-HANDLED CANDLESTICK

No. 1405 Ipswich candlestick. 6" high with a 5" diameter round base. Offered from June 1932 to 1936 in crystal, moongleam, flamingo, and sahara. Rare in all colors. Usually marked with the Diamond H at the bottom of the column, just above the base. The Ipswich pattern (originally marketed as Early American Scroll Design), was a fairly extensive line, inspired by a pattern known to collectors today as Comet, originally made by Sandwich in the late 1850s or early 1860s. Heisey had obtained many of the original wooden models from the Sandwich company from an early salesman, James E. Johnson, including one for the goblet in this pattern. The candlestick, as was true of the rest of Heisey's pattern, was not an exact reproduction, but rather only loosely based on the Sandwich design. Many items, including candlesticks, were never made as part of the original pattern at all. The mold is currently owned by the Heisey Collectors of America. A limited edition of these candlesticks was made for them by Dalzell Viking in 1984 in light evergreen and ruby, marked "94 HCA" with a "D" underneath. (See DV-18 on p. 130 of volume one of this series.) Crystal: $175.00 – 200.00. Flamingo, moongleam: $350.00 – 400.00. Sahara: $350.00 – 375.00.

HE-81. No. 1405 IPSWICH CANDLESTICK

HE-82. No. 1405 IPSWICH FOOTED CENTERPIECES
AND VASES IN SAHARA, CRYSTAL, AND
STIEGEL BLUE

No. 1405 Ipswich footed centerpiece and vase. Made in two parts. The vase portion is 7½" high with a 3⅜" square base and a width of 5½" at the top. The candleholder insert is 3" high with a 2½" base. The insert sits on a rim inside the opening of the vase, giving the assembled set a total height of 9¾". Made from July 1932 to 1944 in crystal, moongleam, flamingo, sahara, and Stiegel blue. Moongleam and flamingo are rare, with the other colors (except crystal) very scarce. The vase is usually marked with the Diamond H on the bottom of the foot; the inserts are also sometimes marked. The Ipswich pattern (originally marketed as Early American Scroll Design), was a fairly extensive line, inspired by a pattern known to collectors today as Comet, originally made by Sandwich in the late 1850s or early 1860s. Heisey had obtained many of the original wooden models from the Sandwich company from an early salesman, James E. Johnson, including one for the goblet in this pattern. The candlestick, as was true of the rest of Heisey's pattern, was not an exact reproduction, but rather only loosely based on the Sandwich design. Many items, including candlesticks, were never made as part of the original pattern at all. The rim of the vase is drilled for 12 prisms, usually the standard "A" prisms (spear-shaped with a separate bead). During World War II, when imported prisms became unavailable, Heisey substituted their own single-piece "H" and "P" prisms, and even offered plastic "X" prisms for a brief period of time. The inserts were also sold by themselves as individual vases, which may explain why their bases are solid, unlike the similar inserts used on the No. 1183 Revere candle vase. (See HE-53 on p. 119.) Thus the Ipswich footed centerpiece could be used as either a vase or a candlestick, but not as both simultaneously. The molds for this set are currently owned by the Heisey Collectors of America. Crystal: $125.00 – 150.00. Flamingo, moongleam: $750.00 – market. Stiegel blue: $550.00 – 600.00. (All prices for complete centerpiece and vase.)

No. 402 two-light candlestick. Named Gothic by researchers. 11" high with a 6⅜" diameter round base and an arm spread of 9¾" (without bobeches) or 12" (with bobeches). Offered from December 1932 to 1936 in crystal, sahara, crystal with a Stiegel blue foot, and Stiegel blue with a crystal foot. Scarce in crystal and rare in colors. Sometimes marked with the Diamond H on the bottom of the center finial. Available both as a candlestick or a candelabrum, with bobeches added, each holding 10 prisms (either "A" spear prisms or "C" flat prisms). Also offered with a matte satin finish (No. 600 or 601), with only the base left clear. The example in one of the authors' collections has a cutting on the base that almost certainly was done by Heisey, though we haven't been able to identify it. Crystal: $275.00 – 300.00. Sahara: $500.00 – 575.00. Stiegel blue: Unable to price. (All prices for candelabra with bobeches and prisms.)

HE-83. No. 402 GOTHIC TWO-LIGHT
CANDLESTICK IN SAHARA

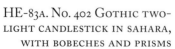

HE-83A. No. 402 GOTHIC TWO-
LIGHT CANDLESTICK IN SAHARA,
WITH BOBECHES AND PRISMS

No. 140 two-light candlestick. Named Crocus by researchers. 7½" high (called 7" in the catalogs) with a 5" diameter round base. Made 1933 – 1936 in crystal, moongleam, flamingo, sahara, and Stiegel blue. Rare in all colors. Usually marked with the Diamond H at the bottom of the column, just above the base. Crystal: $260.00 – market. Other colors: $625.00 – market.

HE-84. No. 140 CROCUS TWO-LIGHT CANDLESTICK IN SAHARA

No. 141 U-shaped candlestick. Named Edna by researchers. 6" high with an oval base, 5½" by 3", and an "arm" spread of 6¾". Offered from 1933 – 1936 in crystal, moongleam, flamingo, sahara, and Stiegel blue. All colors are in the rare to very rare range. Has been seen in crystal with satin finish and silver edges. Marked with the Diamond H just below the center of the curved candleholder, on the upper portion of the base. The bottom is ground smooth, with a polished pontil. This very unusual candleholder was intended to hold a U-shaped candle. It is marked inside the candleholder, "PAT. APPLIED

HE-85. No. 141 EDNA U-SHAPED CANDLESTICK IN SAHARA

FOR." However, it appears that Heisey's patent was not approved, possibly because another patent had been filed for a similar candlestick by Willard Morrison of Chicago in March 1931, and had been approved in May 1933. This was probably for the chromium candlestick with a Bakelite base advertised in 1931 – 1932 by the Can-Dle-Luxe Shop in New York City. Morrison's patent application cited the advantage that the "entire candle may be utilized and consumed," a practice that would have been very dangerous to the Heisey candlestick, since if the candles were allowed to burn too low, they would cause the glass to crack. Crystal: $300.00 – 350.00. Colors: $600 – market.

HE-85A. No. 141 EDNA U-SHAPED CANDLESTICK WITH CANDLE

No. 142 three-light candlestick. Named Cascade by researchers. 7¼" high with a 5⅜" diameter round base and an arm spread of approximately 7⅜". Made from 1933 until the factory closed in 1957. Offered in crystal, sahara (scarce), and Stiegel blue (rare). It was also reissued in crystal by the Imperial Glass Company from May 1958 to January 1968. (See IM-132 on p. 216.) The authors have not seen this candlestick marked with the Diamond H. This was a very popular blank for decorations, both by Heisey and other firms, including the Lotus Glass Company. The mold is currently owned by the Heisey Collectors of America.

Known Heisey cuttings include No. 602 Sprig, 636 Clermont, 781 St. Anne, 793 Monterey, 794 Riviere (seen on the sahara example pictured in HE-86), 796 Suffolk, 797 Killarney, 799 Manhattan, 801 Wakiki, 803 Hialeah, 812 Sweet Briar, 816 Palmetto, 832 Continental, 839 Bonnie Briar, 844 Piccadilly, 844½ Cromwell, 845 Fontaine, 850 Del Monte, 851 Kalarama, 865 Florentine, 866 Kent, 867 Chateau, 871 Sophisto, 872 Mariemont, 873 Edwardian, 874 Exotique, 875 Sylvia, 877 Pueblo, 895 Waterford, 900 Saratoga, 902 Orlando, 913

HE-86. No. 142 CASCADE TWO-LIGHT CANDLESTICK IN SAHARA WITH No. 794 RIVIERE CUTTING

HE-86A.
NO. 142
CASCADE
TWO-LIGHT
CANDLE-
STICK IN
STIEGEL
BLUE

Everglade, 919 Laurel Wreath, 921 Danish Princess, 924 Daisy, 933 Fan, 941 Barcelona, 942 Harvester, 943 Belfast, 944 Courtship, 945 Virginia, 947 Enchantress, 949 Evelyn, 965 Narcissus, 985 Sheffield, and 1015 Dolly Madison Rose.

Known etchings include No. 456 Titania, 458 Olympiad, 501 Belle-le-Rose, 502 Crinoline, 503 Minuet, 507 Orchid, 515 Heisey Rose, and 602 Simplex.

Crystal: $50.00 – 75.00. Sahara: $125.00 – 150.00. Stiegel blue: $500.00 – market. Add 50 – 75% for Heisey Rose or Orchid etchings; for other decorations, add 30 – 50%.

HE-87. No. 1183 REVERE FOUR-LIGHT BASE
AND CANDLEHOLDERS

No. 1183 Revere four-light base and candleholders. 8½" high with a 13¾" by 5" rectangular base. Offered from 1933 to ca. 1937 in crystal and sahara. Rare in crystal; to the best of the authors' knowledge, these candlesticks have never been seen in sahara. Has been seen in crystal entirely frosted except for the balls just beneath the candle cups. Marked with the Diamond H at the bottom of each column. Although the Revere pattern had been in existence as early as 1913 (with the punch cups in the pattern dating back to 1906), this was only the second candleholder in the line. Two others were made: the earlier vase candlestick (HE-53 on p. 119) and the epergne candleholder (HE-108 on p. 137) in 1937. The four-light base and candleholders are unique, not only for their art deco styling, but also because the set consists of four separate candleholders that screw into the base. Each one is individually threaded and ground to precisely fit. Each column is marked on the bottom (I, II, III, or IIII) and corresponding marks appear in the openings on the base so that the owner knows the appropriate one to screw the column into. It should be noted that the columns should never be screwed too tightly into the base, since that will cause irreparable damage to the threading. At least two cuttings were offered on this candleholder, No. 793 Monterey and 801 Wakiki. Other cuttings have also been seen, probably done by Heisey, but not among their production cuttings. Crystal: $1,500 – market. Sahara: Unable to price.

HE-88. No. 1425 VICTORIAN TWO-
LIGHT CANDLESTICK

No. 1425 Victorian two-light candlestick. 5¾" high with a 4¾" diameter round skirted base and an arm spread of 7⅛". Made from late 1933 to 1937 in crystal, sahara, and Stiegel blue, and then reissued again in crystal ca. 1949 – 1951. Sahara and Stiegel blue are rare. Generally marked with the Diamond H in the center of the underside of the skirted base. This was another one of Heisey's Early American patterns. It might have been inspired by a pattern known to collectors today as Waffle, originally made by the Boston and Sandwich Glass Company. Heisey had obtained many of the original wooden models from the Sandwich company from an early salesman, James E. Johnson, including several for goblets in this pattern. However, most early glass companies made versions of this pattern, so it is just as likely that it was actually based on the Block pattern made by Geo. Duncan and Sons in 1887, at a time when Augustus Heisey was a partner in the firm. At any rate, this candlestick, as was true of other pieces in the Victorian pattern, was not an exact reproduction, but rather only loosely based on the earlier designs. Many items in the line, including candlesticks, were not included in these original patterns at all. Crystal: $85.00 – 100.00. Sahara: $175.00 – 200.00. Stiegel blue: Unable to price.

No. 1428 Warwick two-light candlestick. 3⅜" high with a base that is approximately 5¼" by 3" and an arm spread of 7⅜". Made ca. 1933 – 1950 in crystal, moongleam, flamingo, sahara, and Stiegel blue, but difficult to find in most colors except sahara and crystal. One of these candlesticks is known in experimental light blue (possibly a Holophane Glass Company color, since the two companies were adjacent to one another and are known to have exchanged molds on occasion). Sometimes marked with the Diamond H on the top center of the base. The bottom is ground smooth. This candlestick was reissued by the Imperial Glass Company sometime before 1970 in verde and heather. (See IM-146 on p. 219.) The design consists of two cornucopias, tail to tail, on a scalloped base. The mold is currently owned by the Heisey Collectors of America. Crystal: $25.00 – 30.00. Flamingo, moongleam: $250.00 – 300.00. Sahara: $125.00 – 150.00. Stiegel blue: $175.00 – 195.00.

HE-89. No. 1428 WARWICK TWO-LIGHT CANDLESTICK

No. 1428 Warwick individual candlestick. 2½" high with a base that is approximately 3" by 2½". Made ca. 1935 – 1944 in crystal, moongleam, flamingo, sahara, and Stiegel blue. Rare in moongleam and flamingo. Frequently marked with the Diamond H in the center, on the bottom. Reissued by the Imperial Glass Company sometime before 1970 in verde and heather. (See IM-145 on p. 219.) There were three very similar items in the Warwick pattern: a cigarette holder (with a wide opening), the individual candlestick, and an individual vase. The latter is problematic, because the catalogs show the candlestick with a flat top, similar to the two-light candlestick above, while the vase is pictured with the top seen in HE-90. It seems likely that the catalogs were consistently in error, since only the item shown in the accompanying photograph will securely hold a standard taper. The cornucopia with the flat top has an opening too large for a candle. The mold is currently owned by the Heisey Collectors of America. Crystal: $20.00 – 25.00. Flamingo, moongleam: $175.00 – 200.00. Sahara: $55.00 – 75.00. Stiegel blue: $125.00 – 150.00.

The United States Glass Company's No. 104 candlestick, made in the 1930s, is almost identical to Heisey's individual candlestick. (See HE-90a.) The U.S. Glass candlestick has a slightly more ornate tail and its base is shaped differently.

HE-90. No. 1428 WARWICK INDIVIDUAL CANDLESTICK IN SAHARA

HE-90A. COMPARISON OF HEISEY NO. 1428 WARWICK INDIVIDUAL CANDLESTICK AND U.S. GLASS COMPANY NO. 104

No. 1447 Rococo two-light candlestick. 8¼" high with a 5¼" diameter round base and an arm spread of approximately 7⅜". Made ca. 1933 – 1938 in crystal and sahara (or sahara with a crystal foot). Difficult to find in crystal and rare in sahara. Usually marked with the Diamond H on the bottom, just above the base. Offered with at least four cuttings: No. 803 Hialeah, 816 Palmetto, 832 Continental, and 835 Larkspur. Offered with at least one etching (No. 477 Japanese Scene) and one carving (No. 5000 Bacchus), or with satin finish (No. 600 and 601). Crystal: $200.00 – 225.00. Sahara: 450.00 – market.

HE-91. No. 1447 Rococo TWO-LIGHT CANDLESTICK

No. 1433 two-light candlestick. Named Thumbprint and Panel by researchers. 5½" high with a 4½" skirted octagonal base and an arm spread of 6¼". Made ca. 1934 – 1937 in crystal, moongleam, flamingo, sahara, and Stiegel blue. (Flamingo and moongleam are the most difficult colors to find today.) Usually marked with the Diamond H in the constriction under the center finial. This was another design inspired by early American patterns made by the Boston and Sandwich Glass Company and others. As with all of Heisey's other early American lines, this candlestick was not an exact reproduction, but rather only loosely based on the earlier pieces. We have no record of this candlestick having been decorated by Heisey, but know that it was used as a blank by other decorating companies. The first mention of this candlestick in the trade journals featured a rock crystal cutting by the Phillips Glass Company. The crystal example in the accompanying photograph has a light cutting by an unknown firm. Crystal: $50.00 – 55.00. Flamingo, moongleam, sahara: $75.00 – 90.00. Stiegel blue: $165.00 – 175.00.

HE-92. No. 1433 TWO-LIGHT CANDLESTICKS IN CRYSTAL AND SAHARA

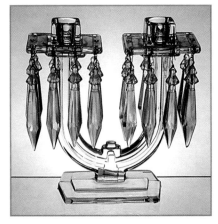

No. 4044 New Era two-light candlestick. 8" high with a rectangular base, approximately 4⅞" by 3", and an arm spread of 5¼" (without bobeches) or 7¼" (with bobeches). Made from 1934 to 1957, when the factory closed. Known in crystal and alexandrite (rare). It was also reissued by the Imperial Glass Company in crystal from May 1958 to January 1972. (See IM-135 on p. 217.) This candlestick is not marked with the Diamond H. It is ground smooth on the bottom. Also available with rectangular bobeches, turning it into a two-light candleabrum. Each bobeche holds 10 prisms, with a choice of either the standard "A" spear prisms (with beads) or flat "C" prisms. During World War II, when imported prisms were unavailable, this candelabrum was also offered with Heisey's own one-piece "H" and "P" prisms, with another American-made prism molded in one piece by the Keifer Company of Brooklyn (designated "R" and seen in the accompanying photograph), or with plastic "X" prisms. New Era is one of Heisey's most popular art deco lines, with a full line of stemware and other occasional pieces. It was designed by Rod Irwin, Heisey's sales manager, and was reportedly based on an earthenware line made by Jean Luce of Paris. The original name of the pattern was Modern Line. The mold for this candlestick is currently owned by the Heisey Collectors of America.

HE-93. No. 4044 NEW ERA TWO-LIGHT CANDLESTICK WITH BOBECHES AND WAR-TIME "R" PRISMS

This candlestick was a popular blank for cuttings, including No. 326 Trinidad, 636 Clermont, 795 Will-o-the-Wisp, 812 Sweet Briar, 825 Sea Glade, 826 Venus, 831 Valencia, 832 Continental, 843 Tahiti, 846 Neo-Classic, 867 Chateau, 871 Sophisto, 893 Carlton, 895 Waterford, 896 Sungate, 902 Orlando, 903 Zeuse, 913 Everglade, 919 Laurel Wreath, 926 George VI, 928 Legionnaire, 932 Coreopsis, 941 Barcelona, 943 Belfast, 944 Courtship, 945 Virginia, 960 Atlantic City, and 961 Versailles.

Also offered with at least one carving (No. 5010 Vanity Fair) or with satin finish (No. 600 or No. 601).

Crystal: $75.00 – 85.00. (Price is for candelabra with bobeches and prisms.) Alexandrite: Unable to price. Add 50% for decoration.

A very similar candlestick was sold by Sears Roebuck from 1937 to 1938, imported from Czechoslovakia. As can be seen in HE-93a, it is almost an exact duplicate, but with ridges on the arms and candle cups and with a serrated base. The glass quality is relatively poor, but it does have a ground bottom and the dimensions are identical.

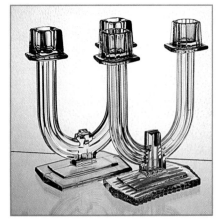

HE-93A. COMPARISON OF HEISEY No. 4044 NEW ERA TWO-LIGHT CANDLESTICK AND CZECHOSLOVAKIAN COPY

No. 4044 New Era candleblock. 2½" by 2½". Mentioned in a price list believed to be from 1935, marked discontinued, and then later written in price list 214-19, which came out April 15, 1939. Factory production records are incomplete for this period, with only one turn known of this candleblock in January 1940, when only 38 were produced. However, it apparently was also made in 1935 in alexandrite, as reported by Clarence Vogel in *The Heisey Glass Newscaster,* autumn 1980 issue. Ground and polished on all sides, with beveled edges. It is not marked with the Diamond H. Unable to price.

HE-94. No. 4044 NEW ERA CANDLE-BLOCK *(computer composite)*

No. 4044 New Era rectangle candleblock. 2½" by 4". Mentioned in a price list believed to be from 1935, marked discontinued, and then later written in price list 214-19, which came out April 15, 1939. At the time the authors' previous book, *Heisey Glass Candlesticks, Candelabra, and Lamps,* was published in 1984, this candleblock was presented as unknown, with an assigned pattern number and name (No. 8072 Plain Block). Thanks to the original mold drawings obtained by the Heisey Collectors of America when the Imperial Glass Company went out of business, it can now be verified that this is No. 4044 New Era. It is ground and polished on all sides, with beveled edges. It is not marked with the Diamond H. As noted in HE-94 above, the small New Era candleblock has been seen in alexandrite, so that is a possibility for the rectangle candleblock as well. Unable to price. *(Photograph courtesy of the Heisey Collectors of America, Inc.)*

HE-95. No. 4044 NEW ERA RECTANGLE CANDLE-BLOCK

No. 1445 one-light candlestick. Named Grape Cluster by researchers. 10" high with a 5½" diameter round base. Made 1935 – 1944 in crystal and Stiegel blue (rare); the two-light candlestick (HE-97 below) was also made in alexandrite and sahara, but the one-light has not been reported in these colors. The floral bowl from this pattern has been seen in zircon, so this color is also possible. Crystal examples have been seen with satin finish on the stem, with the candle cup and foot left clear. Usually marked with the Diamond H at the bottom, just above the base. With the addition of a No. 6 bobeche and 12 prisms, this candlestick was also sold as a candelabrum. The prisms used were ordinarily the standard "A" spear prisms with beads. During World War II, when imported prisms were unavailable, this candelabrum was also offered with Heisey's own one-piece "H" and "P" prisms, or with plastic "X" prisms. The candlestick was used as a blank for at least three cuttings: No. 799 Manhattan, 803 Hialeah, and 850 Del Monte. It was also offered with satin finish (No. 600 or No. 601). A hurricane lamp using this candlestick as the base was pictured in the November 1939 issue of *House Beautiful,* and again in that same magazine's winter 1939 – 40 *Guide for the Bride,* as being available from Reits in New York City. The holiday number for the 1935 – 36 *The Stylist* also showed this candlestick being used as an electric lamp. Crystal: $125.00 – 150.00; with bobeches and prisms: $150.00 – 175.00. Stiegel blue: Unable to price.

HE-96. No. 1445 GRAPE CLUSTER ONE-LIGHT CANDLESTICK

No. 1445 two-light candlestick. Named Grape Cluster by researchers. 9½" high with a 5½" diameter round foot and an arm spread of 8". Made 1935 – 1944 in crystal, alexandrite, sahara, and Stiegel blue (rare in colors other than crystal). The floral bowl from this pattern has been seen in zircon, so this color is also possible. Usually marked with the Diamond H at the bottom, just above the base. Used as a blank for a number of different cuttings, including: No. 326 Trinidad, 781 St. Anne, 793 Monterey, 794 Riviere, 795 Will-o-the-Wisp, 799 Manhattan, 801 Wakiki, 812 Sweet Briar, 832 Continental, 839 Bonnie Briar,

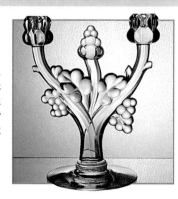

HE-97. No. 1145 GRAPE CLUSTER TWO-LIGHT CANDLESTICK

842 Singapore, and 851 Kalarama. Also offered with at least one etching (No. 458 Olympiad) or one carving (No. 5000 Bacchus), or with satin finish (No. 600 or No. 601). Crystal: $175.00 – 200.00. Alexandrite, Stiegel blue: Unable to price.

Note: There is a mold drawing in the archives of the Heisey Collectors of America for a three-light candlestick in this pattern, but no evidence that it was ever made.

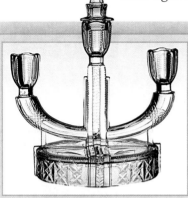

HE-98. No. 1471 Empire two-light candlestick (with center plug inserted). No. 859 Cohassett cutting on base

No. 1471 Empire three-light candlestick. 6⅞" high without the center plug and 9" high with the center plug, with an oval base that is 6" by 4¼" and an arm spread of 7¾". Made from June 1935 to ca. 1937, in crystal only. This candlestick was unique in that it came with a center plug used to convert it from a three-light candlestick to a two-light one. To the best of the authors' knowledge, this candlestick was never marked with the Diamond H. It was offered with at least five cuttings: No. 600 Mount Laurel, 849 Nomad, 859 Cohassett (seen in the accompanying photograph), 861 Neopolitan, and 862 Monaco. It was also available with one matte etching, No. 602 Simplex. Although very much in the art deco style, this candlestick and its accompanying floral bowl were advertised by Heisey as "produced ... after a design popularized during the reign of Napoleon." $250.00 – market.

HE-99. No. 1472 Parallel Quarter candlestick with No. 492 King House etching

No. 1472 candlestick. Named Parallel Quarter by researchers. 3½" high (called 3" in the catalogs) with a 4⅝" diameter round foot. Made from June 1935 to 1942, in crystal only. To the best of the authors' knowledge, this candlestick was not marked with the Diamond H. It was offered with at least one cutting, A.A. No. 1 Dahlia, and two etchings, No. 492 King House (seen in the accompanying photograph) and 604 Ruth (a matte etching appearing on the alternate panels of the candle cup). $30.00 – 35.00.

HE-100. No. 1469½ Ridgeleigh round candlestick

No. 1469½ Ridgeleigh round candlestick. 3" high with a diameter of 2⅛". Made 1935 – 1941 in crystal only. Not marked with the Diamond H. Ground smooth on the top and bottom. This may have been the first candleholder in Heisey's very popular Ridgeleigh pattern. A report in the April 1935 issue of the *House Furnishing Dealer* stated that Heisey had just brought out a "line of heavy mitred ashtrays, which are done in productions of fine French glass. This is primarily a smoker's line, and includes, also, a special cigarette box and candlesticks to match." (It is also possible that the first candlestick in the line is an unknown one, since the ½ designation on the 3" round candlestick could have been added to differentiate it from another candlestick already in production.) At any rate, these candlesticks were definitely being made by June 1935 when they were advertised as part of a console set in the *Crockery and Glass Journal*. Other candleblocks appear in trade journals around this same time, one that is shorter than the Heisey one and another that is square, both hand cut imports that may have been the inspiration for Heisey's Ridgeleigh. After this candleblock was discontinued, the Libbey Glass Company also made a shorter version as their No. 9740. $25.00 – 35.00.

Other American companies made somewhat similar pressed patterns. Fostoria's No. 2545 Flame low candleblock is of particular interest. (See FO-111 on p. 43.) In the archives of the Heisey Collectors of America is an original photograph showing a Heisey display in a department store from the 1930s. Mixed in with the Ridgeleigh is a pair of the Fostoria candleblocks, indicating that at least one enterprising salesperson saw their potential for being "mixed and matched" with Ridgeleigh.

No. 1469 Ridgeleigh square footed candlestick. 2" high with a 3⅝" square base and a diameter on the top rim of approximately 3⅝". Made January 1936 to 1942 in crystal and zircon (rare). Has also been seen in a darker shade of turquoise, probably an experimental color. Not marked with the Diamond H. The Ridgeleigh pattern was very popular, eventually growing to over 125 different pieces. Many of them were created by modifying older molds. In the case of the square footed candlestick, the earlier No. 132 candlestick (see HE-68 on p. 123) was redesigned by adding ridges to the top rim, the center column, and the underside of the base. This was the most popular of the Ridgeleigh candlesticks, with almost 30,000 made in just the first year alone. A ceramic copy has been seen, marked "Made in Japan." Crystal: $25.00 – 30.00. Zircon: Unable to price.

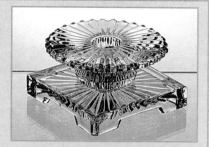

HE-101. No. 1469 RIDGELEIGH SQUARE FOOTED CANDLESTICK

No. 1469 Ridgeleigh candlevase. 4½" high with a 2¼" diameter round base and a 4⅞" wide top. Catalogs list this piece as 6" high, the size of the vase that was flared to create this item. Made from February 1936 to 1940 in crystal, sahara, and zircon. Sometimes marked with the Diamond H on the bottom of the foot. Crystal: $35.00 – 40.00. Sahara: $95.00 – 110.00. Zircon: $175.00 – 200.00.

HE-102. No. 1469 RIDGELEIGH CANDLEVASE

No. 1469 Ridgeleigh two-light candlestick. 6½" high with an oval base that is 5¼" by 3⅛" and an arm spread of 6". Made from February 1936 to ca. 1944, in crystal only. Not marked with the Diamond H. Many of Heisey's candlesticks were intended to double as candelabra by the addition of bobeches and prisms; this one is unique in that a single bobeche with six prisms was placed on the center column, rather than on the candle cups. The prisms used were ordinarily the standard "A" spear prisms with beads. During World War II, when imported prisms were unavailable, this candelabrum was also offered with Heisey's own one-piece "H" and "P" prisms, or with plastic "X" prisms. Two cuttings were offered on this candlestick, No. 883 Royal York and 884 Vincent. $110.00 – 125.00.

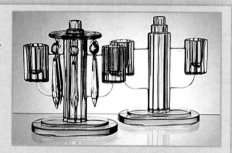

HE-103. No. 1469 RIDGELEIGH TWO-LIGHT CANDLESTICKS, SHOWN WITH AND WITHOUT CENTER BOBECHE AND PRISMS

Note: In addition to the candlesticks shown above, there were three candelabra in the Ridgeleigh pattern, two in one-light configurations and a two-light candelabrum. The latter was designed by Carl Cobel, who may have created some of the other Ridgeleigh pieces.

No. 1483 Stanhope two-light candelabra. 8" high with a lobe-shaped oval base that is 5" by approximately 3½" and an arm spread of 7½". Made from June 1936 to 1937 or 1938 in crystal. One of these candlesticks is known in experimental light blue (possibly a Holophane Glass Company color, since the two companies were adjacent to one another and are known to have exchanged molds on occasion). Stemware in the pattern was made in zircon, but the candlestick has not been reported in this color. Not marked with the Diamond H. The base is ground smooth, with a polished pontil. Also available as a two-light candelabrum, with square bobeches holding seven "A" spear-type prisms each. Cuttings

HE-104. No. 1483 STANHOPE TWO-LIGHT CANDELABRA

offered on this candlestick include No. 867 Chateau, 880 Salem, 881 Kashmir, 882 Yorkshire, 883 Royal York, and 888 Madeira. Etchings include No. 490 Maytime, 491 Frosty Dawn, 494 Swingtime, and 605 Frosted. The Stanhope pattern was created for Heisey by Walter Von Nessen, an internationally known industrial architect and designer, who had a studio in New York. Although not apparent from the candlestick, much was made of the fact that many of the other pieces in the pattern had interchangeable plastic inserts that fit into the handles and gave them a "spot of color." $125.00 – 140.00; with bobeches and prisms: $150.00 – 170.00.

HE-105. No. 1485 SATURN TWO-LIGHT CANDLE-BLOCK IN ZIRCON

No. 1485 Saturn two-light candleblock. 2½" high, 7⅜" long, and 3⅜" wide. Made January 1937 – 1938 in crystal and zircon. Rare in both colors. Not marked with the Diamond H. Ground smooth on the top. Offered with at least five cuttings, No. 888 Madeira, 890 Churchill, 891 Pembroke, 892 Berkeley Square, and 985 Sheffield. Saturn was another creation of Walter Von Nessen, an internationally known industrial architect and designer, who had a studio in New York. Crystal: $90.00 – 100.00. Zircon: $300.00 – 350.00.

HE-106. No. 1485 SATURN TWO-LIGHT CANDLESTICK

No. 1485 Saturn two-light candlestick. 6" high with a 4⅞" diameter round foot and an arm spread of 7¾". Initially made from 1937 to 1938 in crystal and zircon (rare), then reissued ca. 1947 – 1953 in crystal only. Not marked with the Diamond H. Offered with at least one cutting, No. 892 Berkeley Square, and one etching, No. 493 Coronation. Also available with a single "E" ball prism suspended from beneath each candle cup. Saturn was another creation of Walter Von Nessen, an internationally known industrial architect and designer, who had a studio in New York. When Saturn was put back into production in 1947, several new pieces were added to the line, including one new candlestick. (See HE-158 on p. 153.) Crystal: $125.00 – 150.00. Zircon: $750.00 – market.

HE-107 & 107A. PLASTIC MODEL FOR No. 1486 COLEPORT TWO-LIGHT CANDLEBLOCK, SIDE VIEW, AND TOP VIEW (RIGHT)

No. 1486 Coleport two-light candleblock. The only documentation we have for this candleblock is a typed page dated 6/18/37 inserted in price list 212, with the candleblock crossed out, and a pricing out worksheet dated July 16, 1937. It isn't known for certain whether this candleblock was actually made or not. Fortunately, the plastic model in the accompanying photographs has survived, giving us an idea of its general shape. Whether it would have been made with the cover shown is uncertain. The mold is also in the possession of the Heisey Collectors of America. Coleport was primarily a tumbler line, designed by Ray C. Cobel, foreman of Heisey's mold making department. Unable to price.

No. 1187 Yeoman epergne candleholder. Later reissued as No. 1183 Revere. 4" high with a 4⅞" diameter round foot and a bowl diameter of 10". Originally made as an epergne with the No. 4233 vase (as seen in HE-108) as part of the No. 1187 Yeoman pattern. It was then reissued from 1950 to 1952 as a "candlestick for epergne," with its pattern number changed to No. 1183 Revere. In addition to the base by itself, it was available with the 6" No. 4233 vase, the 5" No. 5013 vase, or the small No. 1519 Waverly epergnette. (See HE-168 on p. 157.) Made in crystal only. To the best of the authors' knowledge, this piece is not marked with the Diamond H. It was also offered with No. 507 Orchid etch. The mold is currently owned by the Heisey Collectors of America. When this item was added to the Revere line, it became the third candleholder in this pattern. The Revere pattern had been in existence as early as 1913 (with the punch cups in the pattern dating back to 1906). The two earlier candleholders were the vase candlestick (HE-53 on p. 119) and the four-light base and candleholders (HE-87 on p. 130). $115.00 – 125.00 (complete with insert vase). Add 100 – 150% for Orchid etching.

HE-108. No. 1187 Yeoman epergne candleholder (with vase insert)

No. 1488 Kohinoor two-light candlestick. 5¼" high with a multi-sided base approximately 5" by 3½" and an arm spread of 9" (without bobeches) or 10½" (with bobeches). Made 1937 – 1945 in crystal and zircon (rare). Not marked with the Diamond H. The bottom is ground smooth. Also available with square bobeches, each holding seven prisms (either the short "D" spear prisms with a bead or, during World War II, when imported prisms were not available, Heisey's own molded one-piece "J" prisms). This was a popular blank for cuttings, including No. 636 Clermont, 781 St. Anne, 832 Continental, 848 Botticelli, 866 Kent, 867 Chateau, 883 Royal York, 888 Madeira, 890 Churchill, 891 Pembroke, 892 Berkeley Square, 896 Sungate, 898 Trafalgar, 899 Norfolk, 901

HE-109. No. 1488 Kohinoor two-light candelabra

Delft Diamond, 902 Orlando, 921 Danish Princess, 2503 Sussex, and 2504. It was also offered with one etching, No. 493 Coronation (designed in 1937 for the coronation of King Edward VIII, who abdicated shortly after its introduction, making it scarce today). Kohinoor was one of the most popular patterns created by Walter Von Nessen, an internationally known industrial architect and designer, who had a studio in New York. The mold is currently owned by the Heisey Collectors of America. Crystal: $100.00 – 125.00. Zircon: $500.00 – market. (Price is for candelabra with bobeches and prisms.)

No. 1493 two-light candlestick. Named World by researchers. 6" high and approximately 10" long. The irregularly shaped base is 6⅜" by 3⅞". Offered 1937 – 1941, though production probably ceased as early as 1938. Crystal only. Rarely seen. Not marked with the Diamond H. The bottom is ground smooth. Offered with at least one cutting, No. 893 Carlton. There were no companion pieces in this pattern, but the candlesticks were advertised as a console set with the No. 1489 Puritan floral bowl. $400.00 – market.

HE-110. No. 1493 World two-light candlestick

HE-III. No. 1495 FERN TWO-LIGHT CANDLESTICK WITH No. 497 ROSALIE ETCHING

No. 1495 Fern two-light candlestick. 5½" high with a 5¼" diameter round foot and an arm spread of 7". Made from 1937 to 1955 or 1956. Known in crystal and zircon (rare). Not marked with the Diamond H. Available both as a two-light candlestick or as a two-light candelabrum, with circular bobeches holding five prisms each. The prisms used were ordinarily either the standard "A" spear prisms with beads or the shorter "F" spear prisms. During World War II, when imported prisms were unavailable, these candelabra were also offered with Heisey's own one-piece "H" or shorter "J" prisms. This was a popular blank for decorations. Known cuttings include No. 840 Briar Cliff, 893 Carlton, 894 Brambleberry, 895 Waterford, 896 Sungate, 902 Orlando, 908 Rondo, and 947 Enchantress. Known etchings include No. 497 Rosalie (shown in the accompanying photograph), 500 Belvidere, 507 Orchid, 508 Floral, 511 Gardenia, 607 Vicars, 9014 Rose of Peace, and 9016 Poppy. Fern was the last of the candlesticks created for Heisey by Walter Von Nessen, an internationally known industrial architect and designer, who had a studio in New York. Crystal: $50.00 – 75.00. Zircon: $500.00 – market. Add 100 – 125% for etching. Add $25.00 – 30.00 for bobeches and prisms.

Note: There is at least one other unknown candleholder, possibly two, in the Fern pattern. Factory production records from September 1939 indicate that 300 one-light candlesticks were made in the pattern. Similar records from November 1949 indicate that 313 candleblocks were made. Both turns were in crystal. These could be two completely unknown candleholders, a single one that was experimented with twice – or the pattern numbers given in the turn books might have been given in error.

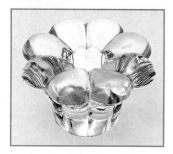

HE-112. No. 1503 CRYSTOLITE ROSETTE CANDLEBLOCK

No. 1503 Crystolite rosette candleblock. The pattern was originally issued in 1937 as No. 1496 Mahabar, then renamed No. 1503 Rajah, before finally becoming Crystolite in 1938. 2" high, 1⅝" wide at the base, and 3⅜" wide at the top. Made from 1937 to 1955. Known in crystal and amber (marketed as sultana around 1951 and very rare today). A design patent was filed for this candleblock on March 6, 1939, over a year after it went into production, and approved April 11, 1939, as D114,217. The designer was given as T. Clarence Heisey, but it is likely that he just signed the application as an officer of the company. Not marked with the Diamond H. The bottom is ground smooth. Crystolite was one of Heisey's largest and most popular patterns, and had more candleholders associated with it than any other. The rosette candleblock, in turn, was made in the largest numbers of any candleholder offered by Heisey. In just the first six years of production, over 300,000 were made, with probably well over half a million ultimately put on the market. Boxed sets of four (as seen in HE-112a) were sold as gift items. The candleblock was also reissued by the Imperial Glass Company from 1957 to 1976 in crystal and ruby. (See IM-125 on p. 214.) The candleblock was also utilized by Heisey (or by various decorating companies) as a lamp part, or as a "flower" finial on the metal lids often found on the Crystolite candy box. The mold is currently owned by the Heisey Collectors of America. A small version of the candleblock was also made by Heisey for use as a drawer pull. $12.50 – 15.00.

A very similar candleblock was made by the Beacon Glass Company in 1946. (See BE-1 on p. 19 of volume one of this series.) It was apparently modified just enough to avoid being an infringement of Heisey's patent by being given only six petals, instead of eight, with twelve overlapping ribs, as opposed to eight on the Heisey candleblock. Also, the Beacon candleblock is in lesser quality crystal and is not ground on the bottom. A somewhat thicker copy of the rosette candleblock is also sometimes seen used as the bottom of a cologne, probably made by Wheatoncraft in Millville, N.J.

HE-112A. No. 1503 CRYSTOLITE ROSETTE CANDLEBLOCKS, SET OF FOUR IN GIFT BOX

The small crystal version of this candleblock seen in HE-112b, about 1⅜" high and 2½" in diameter, was made in Taiwan in 1983 for Lillian Vernon of New York. The amethyst candleblock in the same picture, which is 1⅝" high and 2⅞" in diameter, is of somewhat better quality, but probably also of fairly recent manufacture by an unknown company.

HE-112B. COMPARISON OF SMALL UNKNOWN AMETHYST CANDLEBLOCK, HEISEY NO. 1503 CRYSTOLITE ROSETTE CANDLEBLOCK, AND SMALL VERSION MADE IN TAIWAN FOR LILLIAN VERNON

No. 1503 Crystolite one-light footed candlestick. The pattern was originally issued in 1937 as No. 1496 Mahabar, then renamed No. 1503 Rajah, before finally becoming Crystolite in 1938. 4" high with a 4¾" diameter foot. Made from 1937 to 1953, in crystal only. Not marked with the Diamond H. Occasionally seen with red stain on the "wings," probably done by a decorating company. Also offered with a No. 4233 5" insert vase. The mold is currently owned by the Heisey Collectors of America. $22.50 – 27.50.

HE-113. No. 1503 CRYSTOLITE ONE-LIGHT FOOTED CANDLESTICK

No. 1503 Crystolite two-light candlestick. The pattern was originally issued in 1937 as No. 1496 Mahabar, then renamed No. 1503 Rajah, before finally becoming Crystolite in 1938. 5¾" high with a 5" diameter scalloped base and an arm spread of 8⅝". Made from 1937 to 1953, in crystal only. Not marked with the Diamond H. The bottom is ground smooth. Available both as a two-light candlestick or as a two-light candelabrum, with rosette-shaped bobeches holding five prisms each. The prisms used were ordinarily either the standard "B" short spear prisms with beads or the even smaller "D" prisms. During World War II, when imported prisms were unavailable, Heisey's own one-piece "J" prisms were substituted. The mold is currently owned by the Heisey Collectors of America. $50.00 – 75.00. Add $25.00 – 30.00 for bobeches and prisms.

HE-114. No. 1503 CRYSTOLITE TWO-LIGHT CANDLESTICK

No. 1503 Crystolite three-light candlestick. The pattern was originally issued in 1937 as No. 1496 Mahabar, then renamed No. 1503 Rajah, before finally becoming Crystolite in 1938. 4⅛" high with a 4⅞" diameter round foot and an arm spread of 7". Made 1937 – 1957, in crystal only. A design patent was filed for this candlestick on March 20, 1939, well over a year after it went into production. It was approved June 27, 1939, as D115,400. The designer was given as E. Wilson Heisey, but he probably just signed the application as president of the company. Not marked with the Diamond H. The patent application referred to this piece as a "combined glass candlestick and vase holder," and it will sometimes be

HE-115 & 115A. No. 1503 CRYSTOLITE THREE-LIGHT CANDLESTICK (SHOWN AT LEFT WITH INSERT VASE)

found with the 5" No. 4233 insert vase, which was designed to fit exactly in the center candle cup so that its top flares out above the "wings." The mold is currently owned by the Heisey Collectors of America. $25.00 – 50.00. Add $20.00 – 25.00 for insert vase.

HE-116. No. 1503
CRYSTOLITE ONE-
LIGHT HURRICANE
LAMP

No. 1503 Crystolite one-light hurricane lamp. The pattern was originally issued in 1937 as No. 1496 Mahabar, then renamed No. 1503 Rajah, before finally becoming Crystolite in 1938. 3⅜" high with a base diameter of approximately 5¼". Three different size shades were offered on this base: the 6" No. 4060, 9" No. 300, and 12" No. 300. Made 1937 – 1953 in crystal only. Sometimes marked with the Diamond H in the center of the bottom. Cuttings offered on the shade include No. 913 Everglade, 915 Amarillo, 917 Sarasota, and 918 Winston. Emil Krall, Heisey's master engraver, is also known to have continued offering cuttings on this blank after his retirement from the factory, when he had his own studio in Newark. Other decorations offered by Heisey (again, on the shade only) include No. 450 Chintz etch and 5020 Lily carving. A curious advertisement from Reits Glassware in New York appeared in the March 1939 *House Beautiful*, offering these hurricane lamps with chimneys in "raspberry bubble glass, over fifty years old" (i.e. dating from the 1880s). This base was also used by Heisey for an electric lamp, from June 1939 to 1941. The Imperial Glass Company reissued this hurricane base in crystal (both plain and frosted) in 1966, but made considerable modifications to the mold. (See IM-158 on p. 222.) Among other changes, they replaced the metal ferrule used by Heisey to hold the candle with a molded candle cup and increased the hollow portion on the underside of the base. Although the result is still quite heavy, it is considerably lighter than the Heisey original. The mold is currently owned by the Heisey Collectors of America. $100.00 – 115.00 (complete with globe). Add 50 – 100% for cutting on globe.

HE-117. No. 1503 CRYSTO-
LITE ONE-LIGHT HURRICANE
BLOCK

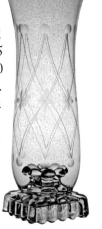

No. 1503 Crystolite one-light hurricane block. 2⅞" high with a 4" square base. Only one shade was offered on this lamp: the 10" No. 4061. Made from September 1938 to 1953, in crystal only. Not marked with the Diamond H. Cuttings offered on the shade include No. 915 Amarillo, 917 Sarasota, and 918 Winston. Etchings include No. 450 Chintz and 507 Orchid. One carving is also known on this shade, No. 5020 Lily. However, this hurricane block is found most often without a shade. The mold is currently owned by the Heisey Collectors of America. $30.00 – 35.00 (without globe). Add 100% to 150% for globe, 200 – 250% for decorated globe. With Orchid etching: $700 – market.

In addition to these initial six Crystolite candleholders, there were eventually four more added to the pattern. See HE-135 through HE-138 on p. 146-147.

HE-117A. No. 1503 CRYSTOLITE
ONE-LIGHT HURRICANE WITH No.
918 WINSTON CUTTING ON SHADE

HE-118.
No. 301 OLD
WILLIAMSBURG
ONE-LIGHT
HURRICANE
LAMP

No. 301 Old Williamsburg one-light hurricane lamp. 5⅝" high with a 5⅜" hexagonal base. Three different size shades were offered on this lamp: the 9" No. 300, 12" No. 300, and 12" No. 5080. Made 1938 – 1957 in crystal only. Sometimes marked with the Diamond H in the constriction above the base. Cuttings offered on the shade include No. 915 Amarillo, 917 Sarasota, and 918 Winston. Other engravings are also found on the shade. Etchings include No. 450 Chintz and 515 Heisey Rose. The base itself is sometimes found full cut by decorating companies. This base was also used for an electric lamp (from 1939 to 1941) and a series of candelabra (two-, three-, or four-light). A two-light hurricane lamp was also made. The mold is currently owned by the Heisey Collectors of America. $150.00 – 175.00 (complete with globe). Add 50 – 100% for cutting on globe.

No. 7000 Sunflower candlestick. Originally advertised under the pattern name Empress. 3½" high with a 4⁵⁄₁₆" diameter round foot. Made 1938 – 1942. Known in crystal and zircon (rare). Not marked with the Diamond H. A pair of these candlesticks were used with the gardenia bowl in the same pattern to form a traditional console set, with the candlestick also advertised as part of a "centerpiece set," which consisted of the bowl with a single candlestick fitted with a 7" No. 4233 insert vase. Other sizes and styles of insert vase were also offered with this set. The candlesticks were also decorated with silver overlay by the Silver City Glass Company of Meriden, Connecticut, who advertised them in a console set with a floral bowl from the New Martinsville Glass Manufacturing Company's Janice pattern. The mold is currently owned by the Heisey Collectors of America. Crystal: $25.00 – 35.00. Zircon: Unable to price.

HE-119. No. 7000 SUNFLOWER CANDLESTICK

No. 1509 Queen Ann one-light candelabra. Called 7½" in the catalogs (though the height will vary by as much as half an inch depending on how much the top rim is flattened), with a 4¾" diameter round foot. Made 1938 – 1957, in crystal only; reissued by the Imperial Glass Company from May 1958 to January 1971. (See IM-133 on p. 216.) Not marked with the Diamond H. The rim is drilled to hold eight prisms. The prisms used were ordinarily the standard "A" spear prisms with beads. During World War II, when imported prisms were unavailable, this candelabra was also offered with Heisey's own one-piece "H" and "P" prisms, with another American-made prism molded in one piece by the Keifer Company of Brooklyn (designated "R"), or with plastic "X" prisms. This was a popular blank for cuttings, including No. 839 Bonnie Briar, 913 Everglade, 916 Arlington, 933 Fan, 934 Olive, 941 Barcelona, 944 Courtship, 947 Enchantress, 965 Narcissus, 984 Lancaster, and 985 Sheffield. It was also used for at least four etchings: No. 497 Rosalie, 501 Belle-le-Rose, 503 Minuet, and 507 Orchid. Emil Krall, Heisey's master engraver, is also known to have continued offering cuttings on this blank after his retirement from the factory, when he had his own studio in Newark. Although many pieces in the Queen Ann pattern were redesigned from items previously offered as part of the No. 1401 Empress pattern, this candelabra was a brand new design. The mold is currently owned by the Heisey Collectors of America. $85.00 – 100.00. Add 300 – 400% for Orchid etching.

HE-120. No. 1509 QUEEN ANN ONE-LIGHT CANDELABRA

No. 1509 Queen Ann footed, two-handled candlestick. 1½" high with four peg feet and a top diameter of 4½". Made November 1938 – 1944, in crystal only. Usually marked with the Diamond H in the center, on the bottom. The second candleholder to be added to the "new" Queen Ann pattern was actually a redesigned version of the No. 1401 Empress footed, two-handled candlestick originally made 1932 – 1936 (see HE-80 on p. 127), modified by flaring the rim and adding a wide optic to the inside of the bowl. The mold is currently owned by the Heisey Collectors of America. $30.00 – 35.00.

HE-121. No. 1509 QUEEN ANN FOOTED, TWO-HANDLED CANDLESTICK

No. 1509 Queen Ann saucer candle base. 2¼" high (called 3" in the catalogs) with three "dolphin" feet and a top diameter of 5⅝". Originally made from March 1939 to 1944, then reissued from 1949 to 1951 and, briefly, for a final time in 1953. Crystal only. Usually marked with the Diamond H on the back of one of the feet. Although this candleholder was not originally made as part of the earlier No. 1401 Empress pattern, it was created by modifying the mold for the

HE-122. No. 1509 QUEEN ANN SAUCER CANDLE BASE

Empress 6" footed mint by adding the candleholder element and a wide optic to the inside of the bowl. The feet in the shape of dolphin heads and the fleur-de-lis designs around the side of the bowl are the primary design elements of the Empress/Queen Ann patterns. The mold is currently owned by the Heisey Collectors of America. $35.00 – 40.00.

HE-123. No. 1509 QUEEN ANN INDIVIDUAL CANDLEHOLDER

No. 1509 Queen Ann individual candleholder. 1½" high with three "dolphin" feet and a top diameter of 3⅛". Made from April 1939 to 1941, in crystal only. Sometimes marked with the Diamond H on the back of one of the feet. Although this candleholder was not originally made as part of the earlier No. 1401 Empress pattern, it was created by modifying the mold for the Empress individual nut dish by adding the candleholder element. It does not appear in any of the price lists or catalogs, but we know from original factory production records that there were only around 1300 produced, making them scarce today. The feet in the shape of dolphin heads and the fleur-de-lis designs around the side of the bowl are the primary design elements of the Empress/Queen Ann patterns. The mold is currently owned by the Heisey Collectors of America. $75.00 – 95.00.

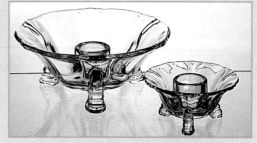

HE-123A. COMPARISON OF NO. 1509 QUEEN ANN SAUCER CANDLE BASE AND INDIVIDUAL CANDLEHOLDER (TO SHOW RELATIVE SIZES)

HE-124. No. 1506 WHIRLPOOL (PROVINCIAL) THREE-LIGHT CANDLESTICK, ORIGINAL VERSION

No. 1506 Whirlpool three-light candlestick. Later renamed Provincial. Made in two versions. The original is 6¼" high with a 5¼" diameter round foot and an arm spread of approximately 7". Made from December 1938 to 1947. The redesigned version is 5⅞" high with a 5⅛" diameter round foot and an arm spread of approximately 8". Made ca. 1948 – 1953. Both versions were made in crystal only. Neither version is marked with the Diamond H. This pattern is a fairly extensive one and was advertised as an "Early American thumbprint" design. The original pattern name was Cameo, soon changed to Whirlpool; however it is best known today as Provincial, the name that Heisey began using around 1950. The three-light candlestick was also sold with a 5" No. 4233 insert vase in the center candle cup, and consequently is sometimes referred to as a double candlestick in some trade journal reports. It was redesigned around 1948 by Horace King. The revised mold is currently owned by the Heisey Collectors of America. $45.00 – 50.00.

HE-124A. No. 1509 WHIRLPOOL (PROVINCIAL) THREE-LIGHT CANDLESTICK, REVISED VERSION

HE-125. No. 1506 WHIRLPOOL (PROVINCIAL) CANDLEBLOCK

No. 1506 Whirlpool candleblock. Later renamed Provincial. 2½" high (listed as 3" in catalogs) and approximately 3¼" in diameter. Made from March 1939 to 1944 and then reissued from January 1949 to 1957 when the factory closed. Known in crystal and limelight (very rare). Not marked with the Diamond H. Ground smooth on the bottom. Often advertised in sets of four with an accompanying floral bowl. Also made with a hole drilled through the bottom, probably for use as a lamp part. Reissued by the Imperial Glass Company from 1960 to 1968 in crystal, amber, heather, and verde. (See IM-144 on p. 219.) The mold is currently owned by the Heisey Collectors of America. Crystal: $35.00 – 40.00. Limelight: Unable to price.

No. 1506 Whirlpool two-light candlestick. 5½" high with a 4¼" diameter round, scalloped base and an arm spread of approximately 7⅜". Made from September 1939 to 1945, in crystal only. Marked with the Diamond H underneath, in the center of the base. According to factory production records, only about 700 pairs of these candlesticks were made, so it is rather scarce today. The mold is currently owned by the Heisey Collectors of America. $90.00 – 110.00.

Note: When the Imperial Glass Company reissued the Provincial pattern in the 1960s, they added an additional candleholder to the pattern, made from the nappy. (See IM-159 on p. 222.)

HE-126. No. 1506 WHIRLPOOL TWO-LIGHT CANDLESTICK

No. 1511 Tourjours candlevase (also referred to as a centerpiece and vase in some catalogs). Made in two pieces, consisting of a vase with a candleholder insert that sits on a rim inside its opening. Originally made in June 1939 and still being offered in 1941, factory production records reveal that only 246 vases and 729 of the inserts were made, making the complete sets rare today. Crystal only. Probably marked with the Diamond H on the bottom, in the center of the base. This was a redesigned version of Heisey's earlier No. 1183 Revere vase candlestick. (See HE-53 on p. 119.) A wide panel optic was added to the inside of the vase, and its lip was crimped. The candle insert was pinched in the middle, so that it would hold a standard candle more securely. As with the Revere original, the rim of the vase is drilled for 12 prisms. The prisms used were ordinarily the standard "A" spear prisms with beads. During World War II, when imported prisms were unavailable, the candlevase was also offered with Heisey's own one-piece "H" and "P" prisms, or with plastic "X" prisms. Offered with at least one cutting, No. 924 Daisy, and one etching, No. 503 Minuet. It has also been seen with a painted decoration applied by a decorating firm. The molds for this set are currently owned by the Heisey Collectors of America. $200.00 – 225.00. Add 20 – 25% for etching or cutting.

HE-127. No. 1511 TOUR-JOURS CANDLEVASE WITH MINUET ETCHING

No. 1511 Tourjours two-light candlestick. 8" high with a 5⅜" diameter round foot and an arm spread of approximately 6". Offered from June 1939 to January 1950, in crystal only. To the best of the authors' knowledge, these candlesticks are not marked with the Diamond H. Available both as a two-light candlestick or as a two-light candelabrum, with 3" diameter cupped octagonal bobeches holding eight prisms each. The prisms used were ordinarily the standard "A" spear prisms with beads. During World War II, when imported prisms were unavailable, these candelabra were also offered with Heisey's own one-piece "H" and "P" prisms, or with plastic "X" prisms. Available with five known cuttings: No. 924 Daisy, 925 Huguenot, 926 George VI, 932 Coreopsis, and 942 Harvester. Also offered with at least one etching, No. 503 Minuet. The mold is currently owned by the Heisey Collectors of America. $100.00 – 110.00. Add $30.00 – 40.00 for bobeches and prisms.

HE-128. No. 1511 TOURJOURS TWO-LIGHT CANDLESTICK

143

HE-129. No. 1513 BAROQUE THREE-LIGHT CANDELABRA EPERGNE WITH INSERT VASE

No. 1513 three-light candelabra epergne (also described in catalogs as a candelabra centerpiece or a three-light epergne). Named Baroque by researchers. 6⅛" high with an irregular base approximately 6½" by 4" and an arm spread of 8½" (without bobeches) or 10¼" (with bobeches). Made from May 1939 to 1957 when the factory closed, and then reissued by the Imperial Glass Company from May 1958 to 1973. (See IM-136 on p. 217.) Crystal only. Not marked with the Diamond H. The bottom is ground smooth. Available both with and without a pair of round bobeches holding six prisms each. The prisms used were ordinarily the standard "A" spear prisms with beads. During World War II, when imported prisms were unavailable, this candelabra was also offered with Heisey's own one-piece "H" and "P" prisms, with another American-made prism molded in one piece by the Keifer Company of Brooklyn (designated "R"), or with plastic "X" prisms. Although this candleholder could be used to hold three candles (and was uniformly described as a three-light in company literature), it was most often sold with a 5" No. 5013 vase in the center candle cup. The vase was offered plain, with a swirl optic, or with a narrow optic. The mold is currently owned by the Heisey Collectors of America. $75.00 – 85.00. Add $20.00 – 25.00 for insert vase.

HE-130. No. 1533 WAMPUM CANDLESTICKS, TWO VERSIONS

No. 1521 Quilt candlestick. Dimensions unknown. No. 1533 Wampum candlestick. Between 3¾" and 4" high with a 4½" diameter foot. Original factory records indicate that only 48 of the No. 1521 candlesticks were made in June 1940. A redesigned version was issued the following year as No. 1533 Wampum, with over 24,000 made between June 1941 and November 1942. Although there are two versions of this candlestick known, we do not think we have ever seen a Quilt example, which indicates that the Wampum version underwent a further redesign. Other pieces in the Quilt pattern have only a single bead at the intersections of the diamonds, so it seems likely that the candlestick would look something like the artist's conception in HE-130a. Of the two versions shown, the smaller one is more commonly found. Both, in their turn, are based on the earlier No. 114 candlestick. (See HE-49 on p. 117.) The mold is currently owned by the Heisey Collectors of America. $25.00 – 30.00.

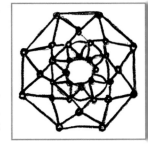

HE-130A. ARTIST'S CONCEPTION OF TOP DESIGN ON No. 1521 QUILT CANDLESTICK

HE-131. No. 1489 PURITAN CANDLEBLOCK

No. 1489 Puritan candleblock. Made in two sizes: 4⅜" square (called 4" in the catalogs) with a height of 1⅛" and a base that is 1½" square. Made July 1940 – 1943 in crystal only. In December 1940, a single turn of 343 6" candleblocks was also made. This size has never been seen by the authors. Neither size would be marked with the Diamond H. Available either fire polished all over or ground smooth on the top and bottom. Occasionally seen with all sides cut smooth. This candleblock is the same shape and size as the 4" ash tray in the pattern, but without the indentations in the corners for holding cigarettes. Advertisements offer the candleblocks in console sets with the Puritan gardenia bowl, sometimes as pairs and sometimes as sets of four. Two cuttings are known to have been offered on this blank, No. 941 Barcelona and 964 Maryland, as well as one carving, No. 5020 Lily. $65.00 – 75.00. Add 30 – 50% for decoration.

LOOKALIKES

An unknown company made an almost identical candleholder in two sizes, probably machine made, with a round, ribbed candleholder element instead of the square one seen on the Heisey candleblock. The small one is 3½" square while the larger is just over 4½". (See HE-131a.) The Federal Glass Company made almost identical ash trays in both these sizes, so is a possible candidate

HE-131A. COMPARISON OF UNKNOWN LOOKALIKE CANDLEHOLDERS, A 3½" VERSION SOLD BY SEARS (L) AND A 4½" VERSION (R), AND HEISEY NO. 1489 PURITAN CANDLEBLOCK (C)

for manufacturer. The copies can be dated to the 1940s, since the small candle candleholder appeared in the Sears Roebuck spring/summer 1942 catalog as part of a nine-piece console set for only $1.59.

Three other candleholders were added to the Puritan line in 1941 and 1942. See HE-134 on p. 146, and HE-150 and HE-151 on p. 151.

No. 1519 Oceanic two-light candlestick. Later named Waverly. 6¼" high with a 5⅜" diameter round foot and an arm spread of 6¾". Made from October 1940 to 1953, in crystal only. Not marked with the Diamond H. This was a popular blank for cuttings, including No. 866 Kent, 883 Royal York, 924 Daisy, 939 Festoon Wreath, 941 Barcelona, 942 Harvester, 944 Courtship, 947 Enchantress, 957 Oriental, and 965 Narcissus (seen in the accompanying photograph). At least one etching was also offered on this blank, No. 507 Orchid. In fact, the Oceanic pattern seems to have been designed primarily for use with this etching. The mold for this candlestick is currently owned by the Heisey Collectors of America. In 1949, the pattern name was changed to Waverly and a number of additional candleholders were added to the pattern at that time. (See HE-167 through HE-173 on p. 156-158.) $30.00 – 35.00. Add 100 – 125% for Orchid etch; 50 – 75% for cuttings.

HE-132. NO. 1519 OCEANIC (WAVERLY) TWO-LIGHT CANDLESTICK WITH NO. 965 NARCISSUS CUTTING

No. 5026 candlestick. Named Heirloom by researchers. 7½" high. Offered from December 1940 to 1944, in crystal only, with actual production ending in December 1941. According to factory records, there were only 787 of these candlesticks made. Considered very rare today. Because this candlestick is blown, it will not be marked with the Diamond H. It was offered with the No. 921 Danish Princess cutting (as seen in the accompanying photograph) and with the No. 507 Orchid etching. The mold into which this piece was blown is currently owned by the Heisey Collectors of America. Unable to price.

Another, unknown blown candlestick, listed as No. 5027, was made in July 1941, but appears to have never gone into full production, with only 66 made. Like the No. 5026 above, unless it were found with a known etching or cutting, it would probably never be recognized as Heisey. Although Heisey made much blownware, these two candlesticks (and the much later No. 6009A Roundelay candle centerpiece) are the only candleholders known to have been blown by them.

HE-133. NO. 5026 HEIRLOOM CANDLESTICK WITH NO. 921 DANISH PRINCESS CUTTING (VERY RARE)

HE-134. No. 1489½ PURITAN CANDLE-
BLOCKS. (NOTE VARIATIONS
IN HEIGHT AND SHAPE)

No. 1489½ Puritan candleblock. Listed as 2½" in the catalogs, but actual dimensions vary. Made from January 1941 to 1957 when the factory closed, in crystal only. Not marked with the Diamond H. This plain candleblock was one of Heisey's most popular, but is also one of the most difficult to identify today with any certainty. It was offered both fire polished all over or with the top and bottom ground. However, as can be seen in the accompanying photograph (HE-134), it was also offered full cut, and depending on how much glass was cut from each side, this could change the dimensions of the candleblock drastically. The candleblock on the left is cut on the top and bottom and can be confidently attributed to Heisey because it is part of a console set that includes a camellia bowl, which is distinctive in shape. The candleblock on the right has a provenance that traces it to ownership by a former Heisey employee in Newark, Ohio, so it can be reasonably assumed to be Heisey as well. In addition, note the shape of the recess for the candle, since this seems to be the one detail that can be used to tentatively tell the difference between a Heisey candleblock and one by another company. However, that said, there are marked differences between these two candleblocks. The full-cut example is actually the taller of the two, since less glass was cut from the top and bottom; but more glass was taken from the sides of the full cut candleblock, not only making it smaller in overall dimension but also changing the angle of its sides. The candleblock on the left is 1¾" high, 2½" square at the top and 1⅝" square at the base. The full-cut example is a full 2" high, but only 2¼" square at the top and 1½" square at the

HE-134A. COMPARISON OF HEISEY No.
1489½ PURITAN CANDLEBLOCK AND
UNKNOWN CUT CANDLEBLOCK
(PROBABLY EUROPEAN IN ORIGIN)

base. Heisey also offered this candleblock with their No. 925 Huguenot cutting and their No. 5020 Lily carving.

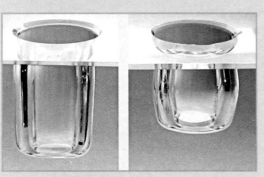

HE-134B. CLOSE-UP OF OPENING FOR CANDLE ON
HEISEY CANDLEBLOCK (L) AND
UNKNOWN LOOKALIKE (R)

Lacking a known decoration or a solid provenance, it is probably impossible to attribute these candleblocks with 100% certainty. Other similar candleblocks are frequently seen, most of them probably imported from Europe. This includes candleblocks that are found in green (similar to moongleam) or in alexandrite. HE-134a compares an imported candleblock with a rose cutting with one of the Heisey candleblocks. It is good quality and has been ground on all surfaces. Note in particular the difference in the opening for the candle. The No. 1489½ Puritan candleblock was the third of five candleholders in the Puritan pattern. (See HE-131 on p. 144 and HE- 150 and HE-151 on p. 151.) The mold is currently owned by the Heisey Collectors of America. $25.00 – 30.00.

HE-135. No. 1503¼ CRYSTOLITE
SQUARE CANDLEBLOCK

No. 1503¼ Crystolite square candleblock. 1⅞" high, 1½" square at the bottom, and 3" square at the top. Made from January 1941 to 1957 when the factory closed, and then reissued by the Imperial Glass Company from January 1970 to 1976. (See IM-126 on p. 215.) Crystal only. Not marked with the Diamond H. Ground smooth on the bottom. A design patent for this candleblock was filed on June 14, 1947, long after it had originally gone into production, and was approved on February 22, 1949, as D152,805. The designer was given as Horace King, who was obviously inspired by the earlier No. 1503 rosette candleblock. (See HE-112 on p. 138.) The mold is currently owned by the Heisey Collectors of America. Other earlier Crystolite candleholders include HE-112 through HE-117 on p. 138-140. $25.00 – 30.00.

No. 1503½ Crystolite melon candleblock. 2⅛" high and approximately 2¼" in diameter. Made from January 1941 to 1942, in crystal only (though it continued to be offered in catalogs up until 1944). Not marked with the Diamond H. The bottom is ground smooth. A design patent was filed for this candleblock on March 19, 1941, and approved July 22, 1941, as D128,373. The designer was given as T. Clarence Heisey, but he probably just signed the patent application as president of the company. The actual designer was almost certainly Horace King. The melon candleblocks were returned to production in later years, but drilled through to be used as lamp parts. The mold is currently owned by the Heisey Collectors of America. In addition to the other candleblocks issued in 1941, other Crystolite candleholders include HE-112 through HE-117 on p. 138-140 above. $35.00 – 45.00.

HE-136. No. 1503½ CRYSTOLITE MELON CANDLEBLOCK

No. 1503¾ Crystolite round candleblock. 2½" high with a diameter of 2½". Made from January 1941 to October 1943 (though it continued to be offered in catalogs up until 1944). According to original production records, less than 6400 of these candleblocks were made, making them the most difficult of the Crystolite candleholders to find today. Crystal only. Not marked with the Diamond H. Both the bottom and top are ground smooth. The mold is currently owned by the Heisey Collectors of America. In addition to the other candleblocks issued in 1941, other Crystolite candleholders include HE-112 through HE-117 on p. 138-140. $35.00 – 45.00.

HE-137. No. 1503¾ CRYSTOLITE ROUND CANDLEBLOCK

No. 1502 Crystolite swirl candleblock. 2¼" high with a bottom diameter of 1⅝" and a top diameter of 3⅜". Made from June 1941 to 1955 in crystal only. Not marked with the Diamond H. Ground smooth on the bottom. Designed by Horace King, who obviously was inspired by the earlier No. 1503 rosette candleblock. (See HE-112 on p. 138.) The Imperial Glass Corporation apparently made some feasibility samples of this candleblock, since the Heisey Glass Museum has one in nut brown that is still on the bust off. It was never placed in full production by Imperial. The mold is currently owned by the Heisey Collectors of America. In addition to the other candleblocks issued in 1941, other Crystolite candleholders include HE-112 through HE-117 on p. 138-140. $15.00 – 20.00.

HE-138. No. 1502 CRYSTOLITE SWIRL CANDLEBLOCK

LOOKALIKE

A very similar candleblock, with the swirls reversed in direction and a beaded foot, was made by Wheatoncraft in Millville, New Jersey, in the 1960s and 1970s in various colors. (See HE-138a.)

HE-138A. COMPARISON OF HEISEY NO. 1502 CRYSTOLITE SWIRL CANDLEBLOCK AND WHEATONCRAFT NO. 214 CANDLEHOLDER IN BLUE

HE-139.
No. 1504
Regency
candle-
block

No. 1504 Regency candleblock. 3" high with a diameter of 2½" at top and bottom. Made from January 1941 to 1944. Known in crystal and amber (very rare). Not marked with the Diamond H. Ground smooth on the top and bottom. Although Regency was a separate pattern, many pieces, including this candleblock, were often advertised with the No. 1503 Crystolite pattern. The mold is currently owned by the Heisey Collectors of America. A cologne that appears to be almost identical to the Regency candleblock is sometimes seen, but is of poorer quality glass. It was probably made by Wheatoncraft in Millville, New Jersey. Crystal: $50.00 – 60.00. Amber: Unable to price.

HE-140. No. 1504 Regency two-light
candlestick

No. 1504 Regency two-light candlestick. 3⅜" high with a 4½" by 2½" rectangular base and an arm spread of 8½". Made from August 1941 until 1957 when the factory closed, and then reissued by the Imperial Glass Company from January 1960 to 1965. (See IM-149 on p. 220.) Crystal only. Not marked with the Diamond H. The bottom is ground smooth. Although Regency was a separate pattern, many pieces, including this candlestick, were often advertised with the No. 1503 Crystolite pattern. In fact, after the regular two-light candlestick in the Crystolite pattern was discontinued, it was replaced in the catalogs with this one. The mold is currently owned by the Heisey Collectors of America. $40.00 – 45.00.

HE-141. No.
1543 Satellite
candleblock

No. 1543 Satellite (Lodestar) candleblock. 2⅝" high and approximately 4⅝" across from point to point on the base. Originally made from December 1941 to 1944 in crystal, with no pattern name assigned. Reissued from 1956 to 1957 in crystal as Satellite, and in dawn as Lodestar. Rare in both colors. Not marked with the Diamond H. Ground smooth on the bottom. The mold is currently owned by the Heisey Collectors of America. Crystal: $85.00 – 100.00. Dawn: $150.00 – 175.00.

HE-142.
No. 1540
Lariat
two-light
candle-
stick with
unknown
cutting

No. 1540 Lariat two-light candlestick. 5⅜" high with a 4¾" diameter round foot and an arm spread of 6¼". Made from December 1941 to 1957 when the factory closed, and then reissued by the Imperial Glass Company from May 1958 to January 1968. (See IM-134 on p. 217.) Crystal only. Not marked with the Diamond H. Cuttings offered on this candlestick included No. 980 Moonglo, 981 Moon Beam, 982 Moon Gleam, 984 Lancaster, and 985 Sheffield. The example in the accompanying photograph has a simple gravic cutting done by a decorating firm. The mold is currently owned by the Heisey Collectors of America. $25.00 – 30.00. Add 50% to 70% for Moonglo cutting.

No. 1540 Lariat three-light candlestick. 6¾" high with a 5⅛" diameter round foot and an arm spread of 6½". Made from February 1942 to 1953, in crystal only. Not marked with the Diamond H. Cuttings offered on this candlestick included No. 940 Westchester, 975 Bow Knot, 978 Bedford, 980 Moonglo, 981 Moon Beam, and 982 Moon Gleam. The mold is currently owned by the Heisey Collectors of America. $35.00 – 45.00. Add 50% to 70% for Moonglo cutting.

HE-143. No. 1540 LARIAT THREE-LIGHT CANDLESTICK

No. 1540 Lariat one-light candleblock. 1⅜" high with a 1½" diameter base and a 4¼" diameter top. Made from March 1942 to 1953, in crystal only. Not marked with the Diamond H. The bottom rim is ground smooth. Offered with at least one cutting, No. 980 Moonglo. Designed by Carl Cobel (who probably also designed many of the other early pieces in the pattern). The mold is currently owned by the Heisey Collectors of America. $20.00 – 25.00.

HE-144. No. 1540 LARIAT ONE-LIGHT CANDLEBLOCK

No. 1540½ Lariat three-light candleblock. 4½" high with a base that is approximately 2⅝" by 8⅛". Made from March 1942 to 1943, in crystal only. Not marked with the Diamond H. The bottom was available either ground smooth or just fire polished. This candleblock has been seen with a silver overlay decoration applied by an unknown company. Production was very limited, with only 725 pairs made, making them very scarce today. $175.00 – market.

HE-145. No. 1540½ LARIAT THREE-LIGHT CANDLEBLOCK

No. 1540 Lariat hurricane lamp. Referred to as a black out lamp in some wartime catalogs, intended for use during air raid drills, when all electric lights were supposed to be turned off. 1¾" high with a 2¾" diameter base and a 7¼" diameter top. Made from April 1942 to January 1950, in crystal only. Not marked with the Diamond H. The bottom rim is ground smooth. Available with a 7" No. 5040 shade. Catalog pictures show this hurricane lamp with an applied handle (as seen in the original company photograph in HE-146a), but it is seen most often today without a handle. Sometimes found with enamel flowers and leaves applied by decorating companies, ranging from the obviously inexpensive to the high quality of Charleton from Abels, Wasserburg and Company. The mold used for this hurricane base was that of the 7" cereal bowl from the pattern, with the candleholder element and prongs for holding the globe added. $35.00 – 40.00. Add 100% to 200% for globe.

HE-146. No. 1540 LARIAT HURRICANE LAMP BASE (WITHOUT HANDLE)

HE-146A. No. 1540 LARIAT HURRICANE LAMP (WITH HANDLE), ORIGINAL COMPANY PHOTOGRAPH

HE-147. No. 1540 LARIAT BLACK OUT LAMP

No. 1540 Lariat black out lamp. Height of the base: 2¼" with a 2¾" diameter round foot. Height of the assembled lamp: 6¾". Made from August 1942 to 1944 (though it continued to be offered in catalogs until 1946). Made in crystal only. Not marked with the Diamond H. The opening of the candleholder is smaller than normal, so a standard taper does not fit. Although we know from production records there were at least 1,800 of these made, they are not often seen today, and only rarely with the fragile No. 5041 5" shade intact. They were designed for wartime use during air raids, when all electric lights were supposed to be turned off. These lamps were advertised in the April 1943 issue of *House Beautiful* by Eunice Novelties in New York, with a choice of an engraved monogram or a lily-of-the-valley cutting on the globe. The mold is currently owned by the Heisey Collectors of America. $450.00 – market (with globe).

HE-148. No. 1540 LARIAT CANDLESTICK (NOT PRODUCTION – VERY RARE)

No. 1540 Lariat candlestick. Dimensions unknown. A single pair of these candlesticks has been reported to date. They were either an early design that never made it into the catalogs (in which case they probably date to early 1942), or a later addition from the period for which original factory production records are incomplete. What is immediately striking about the pair is their resemblance to Imperial's No. 400/80 Candlewick candleholder. (See IM-53 on p. 194.) According to a reminiscence by Fred Bosworth, one of Heisey's former employees, that appeared in the October 1983 issue of the *Heisey News*, "We salesmen complained bitterly to headquarters that we were hurting as Imperial hither-to had been a second class outfit, in our opinion, and through Candlewick, was now getting in 'our' stores for the first time. What to do?… Lariat was the answer — born of necessity, not art." If, indeed, Lariat was developed out of the need to compete with Imperial's highly popular pattern, the close similarity of this candlestick to one of Imperial's lead pieces is not surprising. It was probably made from the mold for the Lariat footed cheese, turned upside down and with the candle cup replacing its foot, which would explain why the loops on the stem turn downward – something that isn't seen on any of the other pieces in the pattern. The mold for the footed cheese is currently owned by the Heisey Collectors of America. Unable to price.

ORIGINS OF A PATTERN

As can be seen from the accompanying drawings, the unknown Lariat candlestick above was not the only design to be considered for the pattern that did not make it into the catalogues. It is probably unlikely that any of these others even made it to the feasibility stage (i.e., to the point of having sample pieces made), but we can't rule the possibility out. The drawings are all by Carl Cobel and are dated December 1941.

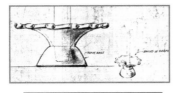

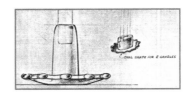
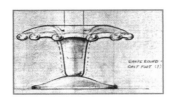

HE-148A-HE-148G. ORIGINAL DESIGNS BY CARL COBEL FOR LARIAT CANDLEHOLDERS THAT WERE NEVER PRODUCED

No. 1550 Dolphin (Fish) candlestick. 5" high with a 4" by 2¼" base. Made from January 1942 to 1948, in crystal only. Not marked with the Diamond H. Ground smooth on the bottom. Designed by Royal Hickman, who is best known for his work in ceramics, both for the Haeger Potteries and for his own company, Royal Hickman Industries. Perhaps not surprisingly, the same month these candlesticks went into production an advertisement appeared in *House and Garden* for a ceramic pair that is almost identical, except that they have a loop extending from the tail to the head, forming a handle. These were either the inspiration for Hickman's design or, more likely, they were also one of his own creations. Hickman went on to design a number of different animal figurines for Heisey very popular with collectors today, some of which were used in both the stage and movie versions of Tennessee Williams' *The Glass Menagerie*. The Dolphin (or Fish) candlesticks were actually the first of the animals. In addition to the candlesticks, there was also a matching 9" floral bowl and a 3" match holder. The candlesticks are sometimes found with rather garish painted decorations added by an unknown decorating firm. The mold is currently owned by the Heisey Collectors of America. In August 1982, a limited edition of these candlesticks was made by the Imperial Glass Corporation for the Heisey Collectors of America in sunshine yellow (465 plain and 170 with satin finish). These reissues are marked IG. (See IM-188 on p. 231.) In 1995, the mold was used again to produce these candlesticks as the souvenir for the Fourth Annual Percy Moore Memorial Dinner, sponsored by the HCA, in ice blue, with a few samples also made in cobalt. These were made by Dalzell Viking and are marked "94 HCA" with a "D" underneath. (See DV-19 on p. 130 of volume one of this series.) Heisey original: $150.00 – 200.00.

HE-149. No. 1550 DOLPHIN (FISH) CANDLESTICK

No. 1489 Puritan hexagon candleblock. Listed as 2" high. Made from May 1942 to 1943, with only about 1,500 candleblocks produced. Crystal only. Not marked with the Diamond H. Probably cut on the top and bottom (and possibly cut all over). This candleblock has never been seen by the authors. Like the No. 1489½ candleblock (HE-134 on p. 146), this would be a difficult candleblock to identify with 100% certainty, though its hexagonal shape is fairly distinctive. However, in recent years, a 2½" high hexagon candleblock has been sold by Lenox. It is drilled all the way through (possibly for use as a lamp part). The hexagon candleblock was the fourth of five candleholders in the Puritan pattern. (See HE-131 on p. 144, HE-134 on p. 146, and HE-151 below.) The mold is currently owned by the Heisey Collectors of America. $40.00 – 50.00.

HE-150. No. 1489 PURITAN HEXAGON CANDLEBLOCK
(Artist's rendition)

No. 1489 Puritan one-light hurricane block lamp base. 2" high, 4¾" square at the base, and approximately 3¼" square at the top. The height, assembled with a 10" No. 4061 globe, is 12½". Made from October 1942 until 1957 when the factory closed, in crystal only. Not marked with the Diamond H. Despite a long production period, it is rarely seen today. Offered with at least one cutting (on both the globe and the base), No. 964 Maryland, and one etching (on the globe only), No. 9012 Victory. This was the fifth candleholder added to the Puritan pattern. (See HE-131 on p. 144, HE-134 on p. 146, and HE-150 above.) The mold is currently owned by the Heisey Collectors of America. $250.00 – 275.00 (with globe).

HE-151. No. 1489 PURITAN ONE-LIGHT HURRICANE LAMP

HE-152. No. 1552 FOUR-LEAF CANDLEBLOCK

No. 1552 candleblock. Named Four-Leaf by researchers. 1½" high, with an oval base, approximately 2" by 1¾". The top is 4" by 4½". Made from April 1942 to January 1950, in crystal only. Not marked with the Diamond H. The base is ground smooth. Designed by Royal Hickman, who is best known for his work in ceramics, both for the Haeger Potteries and for his own company, Royal Hickman Industries. Heisey's No. 4 "table setting" included a single No. 1552 candleblock placed in the center of an 11" No. 1575 gardenia bowl, surrounded by three mallard figurines, which were also designed by Hickman. The mold is currently owned by the Heisey Collectors of America. $35.00 – 50.00.

Note: Price list 217-22, dated January 1944, also mentions a No. 1553 candleblock, which is unknown and does not appear in any of the extant factory production records (which only exist for alternate weeks during this period).

HE-153. No. 1559 COLUMBIA CANDLE-STICKS, CRIMPED FOOT (No. 1) AND SAUCER FOOT (No. 2)

No. 1559 Columbia candlestick. Listed in the catalog in two versions. The crimped foot, No. 1, is approximately 3⅛" high, with a 4⅝" diameter base. The saucer foot, No. 2, is 2¾" high, with a 4⅞" diameter base. A third version is also known, with a cupped base. (See HE-153a.) Made from January 1943 to 1944, in crystal only. Not marked with the Diamond H. The crimped foot candlesticks are relatively hard to find today (with only about 7,000 of them made), but are not as rare as the saucer-foot version (of which only 773 were produced). The mold is currently owned by the Heisey Collectors of America. $45.00 – 50.00.

HE-153A. No. 1559 COLUMBIA CANDLESTICK, CUPPED FOOT

HE-154. No. 1541 ATHENA TWO-LIGHT CANDLESTICK

No. 1541 Athena two-light candlestick. Sometimes referred to as Reverse Ess by collectors. 4¾" high with a 5⅞" diameter round foot and an arm spread of 7⅜". Made from November 1943 to December 1948, in crystal only. Not marked with the Diamond H. The Athena pattern was made exclusively for Montgomery Ward and Company. Originally introduced as a blown stemware line in 1942, the initial pieces were all designed by Roy Larsen, who worked for Montgomery Ward's Bureau of Design. By the time the line was expanded to include pressed pieces, like the two-light candlestick, it was being marketed under the pattern name Imperial. It wasn't until 1945 that it was renamed Athena. When Montgomery Ward discontinued selling the pattern in 1947, it was briefly put back into production between May and December 1948 for the Susquehanna Glass Company in Columbia, Pennsylvania, who offered the candlestick with various cuttings. The mold is currently owned by the Heisey Collectors of America.

Although not among the pieces sold by Montgomery Ward, two additional candleholders were added to the pattern in 1948. (See HE-164 and HE-165 on p. 155-156.) $40.00 – 50.00. Add 75 – 100% for cutting.

ATHENA BY HEISEY LABEL

No. 1565 Leaf candlestick. 1¼" high and approximately 6⅞" long by 3⅞" wide. Made ca. 1947 – 1949, in crystal only. Not marked with the Diamond H. Designed by Royal Hickman, who is best known for his work in ceramics, both for the Haeger Potteries and for his own company, Royal Hickman Industries. Heisey's No. 5 "table setting" included a pair of the Leaf candlesticks, along with a No. 1575 floral bowl with a gazelle figurine, also designed by Hickman. When the Imperial Glass Corporation made jade (1980 – 1982), this was one of the pieces they tested in the new color but did not put into production. (See IM-183 on p. 230.) The mold is currently owned by the Heisey Collectors of America. $30.00 – 35.00.

HE-155. No. 1565 LEAF CANDLESTICK

No. 1566 footed candleblock. Named Banded Crystolite by researchers. 3" high with a 2⅜" foot and a top diameter of approximately 3⅛". Made 1947 – January 1953. Known in crystal and amber (very rare). Not marked with the Diamond H. The bottom is ordinarily ground smooth, though it is occasionally seen with an unfinished bottom with a small pressed star. A design patent was filed for this candleblock on June 14, 1947, and approved February 22, 1949, as D152,804. The designer was Horace King. Although it has a different pattern number, this candleblock was intended for use with the No. 1503 Crystolite line. A very similar footed candleblock was also made by Wheatoncraft, but with swirled ribs. (See HE-138a on p. 147.) The mold is currently owned by the Heisey Collectors of America. Crystal: $50.00 – 60.00. Amber: Unable to price.

HE-156. No. 1566 BANDED CRYSTOLITE FOOTED CANDLEBLOCK

No. 1570 Lotus Leaf candleblock. About 2" high (listed as 1½" in the catalogs) with a base diameter of approximately 4". Made ca. 1947 – 1949, in crystal only. Sometimes marked with the Diamond H on the bottom. Designed by Royal Hickman, who is best known for his work in ceramics, both for the Haeger Potteries and for his own company, Royal Hickman Industries. Heisey's No. 7 "table setting" included a pair of the Lotus Leaf candlesticks, along with a No. 1575 gardenia bowl with a wood duck and four ducklings, all also designed by Hickman. The Imperial Glass Corporation reissued this candleblock, probably only making a few of them as feasibility items sometime in the 1970s, but with the base turned down so that it stands almost 3" high. (See IM-167 on p. 225.) The mold is currently owned by the Heisey Collectors of America. $35.00 – 40.00.

HE-157. No. 1570 LOTUS LEAF CANDLEBLOCK

No. 1485 Saturn one-light candlestick. 3½" high (called 3" in the catalogs) with a 4¾" diameter round foot. Made from late 1947 to 1953, in crystal. In 1956, when Heisey leased some of the Verlys molds from the Holophane Lighting Company, they reissued this candlestick as part of the Verlys line in crystal satin and turquoise (or limelight satin). Not marked with the Diamond H. Sometimes sold with the top cut smooth. The Saturn pattern had originally been brought out in 1937 – 1938, but was then discontinued for the duration of the war. When the pattern was brought back into production in 1947, several new pieces were designed, including this candlestick. The mold is currently owned by the Heisey Collectors of America. Crystal, clear or satin: $40.00 – 45.00. Turquoise: $130.00 – 150.00.

HE-158. No. 1485 SATURN ONE-LIGHT CANDLESTICK

HE-159. No. 1567
PLANTATION
HURRICANE
LAMP

No. 1567 Plantation hurricane lamp. 6" high with a base diameter of 4½" and a top diameter of approximately 4⅜". First made in January 1946 before going into full production from 1948 to January 1953. Crystal only. Marked with the Diamond H in the center underneath the base. Available with three different shades: the 9" No. 300, 12" No. 300, or 12" No. 5080. At least two etchings were offered on the globes, No. 515 Heisey Rose and 516 Plantation Ivy. Designed by Horace King. He actually began working on the pattern as early as 1944, with an initial turn of 118 of the hurricane lamp bases made in January 1946. It wasn't until July 1948, however, that the pattern was advertised as new. This base was also made with a hole allowing it to be electrified, with only 141 made. Since the electric lamps do not appear in any catalogs, they may have been made for another company. The mold is currently owned by the Heisey Collectors of America. $300.00 – 350.00 (with globe). Add 100% to 125% for etching on globe.

HE-160. No. 1567
PLANTATION
CANDLEBLOCK

No. 1567 Plantation candleblock. 3⅜" high (called 3" in the catalogues) with a 2⅜" diameter base. Made from 1948 to 1957, in crystal only. Not marked with the Diamond H. The bottom is ground smooth. Designed by Horace King. The mold is currently owned by the Heisey Collectors of America. $100.00 – 115.00.

HE-161. No. 1567 PLANTATION THREE-
LIGHT CANDLESTICK

No. 1567 Plantation three-light candlestick. 7" high with a 5⅞" diameter round foot and an arm spread of 10". Made from May 1948 to 1953, in crystal only. Not marked with the Diamond H. Designed by Horace King. Made in two versions, one with a lip to hold a bobeche and prisms. (See HE-161a.) The bobeches were the same ones used on the No. 1503 Crystolite two-light candelabra, holding five standard "A" spear-type prisms each. Far more of the candlesticks were made than the candelabra. Offered with at least one etching, No. 516 Plantation Ivy. The mold is currently owned by the Heisey Collectors of America. $135.00 – 145.00. Add $35.00 – 45.00 for bobeches and prisms.

Four additional candleholders were added to the Plantation line in 1949 and 1950. (See HE-174, HE-175, and HE-176 on p. 158-159.)

HE-161A. CLOSE-UP OF CANDLE CUPS ON No. 1567
PLANTATION THREE-LIGHT CANDELABRUM (WITH
LIP TO HOLD BOBECHE) AND CANDLESTICK

No. 341 Old Williamsburg epergnette. 2½" high and 5½" in diameter. Made from July 1948 to 1957 when the factory closed, and then reissued by Imperial from 1959 to 1966 and again from 1971 to 1980. (See IM-148 on p. 220.) Produced by Heisey in crystal and amber (very rare). The Heisey epergnettes are often marked with the Diamond H on the bottom of the peg. The idea for an "epergnette" (an insert that could be used with any candlestick or candelabra to allow it to be used for both candles and floral arrangements) was patented by Annie Lee Dillon and Mary G. Dillon on June 19, 1947, and approved August 9, 1949, as No. 2,478,864. The Dillons, who were prominent garden club members in Raleigh, North Carolina, formed a partnership with Heisey, who ultimately offered half a dozen different epergnettes, including the Old Williamsburg one. The Dillons also applied for a design patent for this version as an "epergne and candle-holder adapter for candlestick" on August 4, 1948, approved April 26, 1949, as D153,506. In 1949, this epergnette became the inspiration for a footed epergne candleholder in the pattern. (See HE-177 on p. 159 below.) Although most of the Old Williamsburg molds were purchased by the Lancaster Colony Corporation, this mold was not among them and is currently owned by the Heisey Collectors of America. $12.00 – 17.50.

HE-162. No. 341 Old Williamsburg epergnette

No. 342 Old Williamsberg epergnion. 3" high and 5½" in diameter. Made from August 1949 to 1953, in crystal only. Sometimes marked with the Diamond H on the bottom of the peg. The difference between an "epergnette" and an "epergnion" is that the latter is drilled to hold 10 prisms. It is also deeper than the No. 341 epergnette. Although most of the Old Williamsburg molds were purchased by the Lancaster Colony Corporation, this mold was not among them and is currently owned by the Heisey Collectors of America. $15.00 – 20.00.

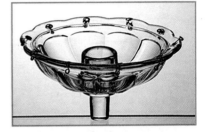

HE-163. No. 342 Old Williamsburg epergnion

Epergnettes were also made in the No. 1519 Waverly pattern (see HE-168, HE-169, and HE-170 on p. 157) and the No. 1619 Block Five line (see HE-185a on p. 162). It is interesting to note that one of the earliest designs for an epergnette was Horace King's drawing of a "Dillon candelabra bowl" in the Lariat pattern as seen in HE-163a. There is no evidence that the company ever attempted to make this epergnette.

HE-163A. Original design for No. 1540 Lariat epergnette (never made)

No. 1541 Athena hurricane block. Dimensions unknown. Made 1948, in crystal only. Not marked with the Diamond H. Although Athena was originally a pattern designed by and made exclusively for Montgomery Ward, and did include a two-light candlestick (see HE-154 on p. 152), the hurricane block was apparently a late addition to the line, after Montgomery Ward had discontinued offering it in their catalogs. Between May and December 1948, the pattern was apparently reissued exclusively for the Susquehanna Glass Company, a cutting company in Columbia, Pennsylvania. It appears that the hurricane block was newly designed for them at this time. It is very rare today. The example pictured is on display in the Heisey Glass Museum in Newark, Ohio. The mold is currently owned by the Heisey Collectors of America. $195.00 – 220.00. Add $45.00 – 50.00 for globe.

HE-164. No. 1541 Athena hurricane block with Susquehanna Glass Company cutting

HE-164A. Original design drawing for No. 1541 Athena hurricane block

HE-165. No. 1541
ATHENA ONE-LIGHT
CANDLEBLOCK

No. 1541 Athena one-light candleblock. 2⅞" high with a bottom diameter of approximately 2⅜" and a top diameter of 2⅝". Made in November 1948, in crystal only. Not marked with the Diamond H. Ground smooth on the bottom. According to factory production records, a single turn of 296 of these candleblocks was made. Although part of the Athena pattern, the production date for this candleblock is after Montgomery Ward discontinued their exclusive sales of the pattern in 1947. It was actually designed much earlier, but not put into production, according to a drawing by Horace King that is dated October 22, 1945. The candleblock bears a striking resemblance to Heisey's No. 1566 Banded Crystolite candleblock (see HE-156 on p. 153), another design by Horace King. Between May and December 1948, the Athena pattern was reissued exclusively for the Susquehanna Glass Company, a cutting company in Columbia, Pennsylvania, so it is conceivable the candleblock may have been requested by them, though obviously it wouldn't have been appropriate for use as a blank for decorating. Very rare today. The mold is currently owned by the Heisey Collectors of America. $125.00 – market.

HE-165A. ORIGINAL DESIGN DRAW-
ING FOR No. 1541 ATHENA ONE-
LIGHT CANDLEBLOCK

HE-166. No. 1590 ZODIAC TWO-
LIGHT CANDLESTICK

No. 1590 Zodiac two-light candlestick. 5¾" high with a 5½" diameter round foot and an arm spread of approximately 7". Offered from December 1948 to January 1950, in crystal only, with actual production ending in March 1949. Approximately 130 pairs were made in total. Marked with the Diamond H just above the foot. Designed by Horace King. The central figure portrays Jupiter on a rain cloud, with medallions on the candle cups featuring the more traditional symbols for four signs of the zodiac (Capricorn, Sagittarius, Taurus, and Leo). Reissued by the Imperial Glass Company in crystal, amberglo and verde from January 1969 to December 1970. (See IM-163 on p. 224.) The Imperial reissues are marked IG on the center medallion above the figure of Jupiter Pluvius. The mold is currently owned by the Heisey Collectors of America. $85.00 – 95.00.

HE-167. No. 1591 WAVERLY THREE-LIGHT
CANDLESTICK WITH No. 515 HEISEY ROSE
ETCHING

No. 1519 Waverly three-light candlestick. 7⅛" high with a 5⅜" diameter round foot and an arm spread of approximately 8¾". Made from January 1949 to 1957, in crystal only. Marked with the Diamond H just above the foot. Designed by Horace King. Offered with at least one cutting, No. 965 Narcissus, and two etchings, No. 507 Orchid and 515 Heisey Rose. The No. 1519 pattern had originally been introduced in 1940 as Oceanic, and included one candlestick (HE- 132 on p. 145); it wasn't until 1949 that the pattern was expanded and renamed Waverly, with several new candleholders added over the next year or so, including the three-light candlestick. The mold is currently owned by the Heisey Collectors of America. $60.00 – 75.00. Add 75 – 100% for etching.

No. 1519 Waverly epergnette. 2¾" high and 5" in diameter. Made from March 1949 to 1957 when the factory closed, and then reissued by Imperial from 1957 to 1977. Made in crystal only. The Heisey epergnettes are often marked with the Diamond H on the bottom of the peg. The idea for an "epergnette" (an insert that could be used with any candlestick or candelabra to allow it to be used for both candles and floral arrangements) was patented by Annie Lee Dillon and Mary G. Dillon on June 19, 1947, and approved August 9, 1949, as No. 2,478,864. The Dillons, who were prominent garden club members in Raleigh, North Carolina, formed a partnership with Heisey, who ultimately offered half a dozen different epergnettes, including three in the Waverly pattern. Imperial made this epergnette with three etchings, probably feasibility items only: Orchid, Heisey Rose, and Cambridge's Rose Point. (See IM-128 on p. 215.) The mold is currently owned by the Heisey Collectors of America. $12.00 – 18.00.

HE-168. No. 1519 WAVERLY EPERGNETTE

No. 1519 Waverly cupped epergnette. 3" high and 6½" in diameter. Made from March 1949 to 1957 when the factory closed, and then reissued by Imperial in 1975. (See IM-170 on p. 226.) Made in crystal only. The Heisey epergnettes are often marked with the Diamond H on the bottom of the peg. The idea for an "epergnette" (an insert that could be used with any candlestick or candelabra to allow it to be used for both candles and floral arrangements) was patented by Annie Lee Dillon and Mary G. Dillon on June 19, 1947, and approved August 9, 1949 as No. 2,478,864. The Dillons, who were prominent garden club members in Raleigh, North Carolina, formed a partnership with Heisey, who ultimately offered half a dozen different epergnettes, including three in the Waverly pattern. The mold is currently owned by the Heisey Collectors of America. $12.00 – 18.00.

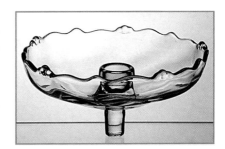

HE-169. No. 1519 WAVERLY CUPPED EPERGNETTE

No. 1519 Waverly deep epergnette. 3½" high and 6" in diameter. Made from November 1949 to 1957 when the factory closed, and then reissued by Imperial from 1957 to 1959 and 1973 to 1976. (See IM-128 on p. 215.) Made in crystal only. The Heisey epergnettes are often marked with the Diamond H on the bottom of the peg. The idea for an "epergnette" (an insert that could be used with any candlestick or candelabra to allow it to be used for both candles and floral arrangements) was patented by Annie Lee Dillon and Mary G. Dillon on June 19, 1947, and approved August 9, 1949 as No. 2,478,864. The Dillons, who were prominent garden club members in Raleigh, North Carolina, formed a partnership with Heisey, who ultimately offered half a dozen different epergnettes, including three in the Waverly pattern. The mold is currently owned by the Heisey Collectors of America. $12.00 – 18.00.

HE-170. No. 1519 WAVERLY DEEP EPERGNETTE

Epergnettes were also made in the No. 341 Old Williamsburg pattern (see HE-163 on p. 155) and the No. 1619 Block Five line (see HE-185a on p. 162). Heisey issued a brochure in 1949 showing some of the many arrangements possible using these devices. (See HE-170a.)

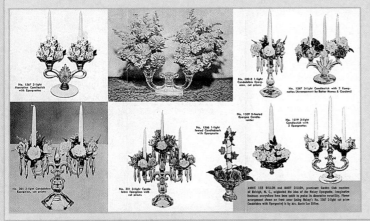

HE-170A. BROCHURE SHOWING VARIOUS USES FOR EPERGNETTES

HE-171. No. 1519 WAVERLY ONE-LIGHT CANDLEBLOCK

No. 1519 Waverly one-light candleblock. 4⅛" high with a 1" by 2" base. Made from January 1950 to 1952, in crystal only. Not marked with the Diamond H. The bottom is ground smooth. Designed by Jane Phillips, best known to collectors today as the creator of the No. 515 Heisey Rose plate etching and the No. 5072 Rose stemware line. HE-171a shows one of her drawings of an early version of this candleblock. The No. 1519 pattern had originally been introduced in 1940 as Oceanic, and included one candlestick (HE-132 on p. 145); it wasn't until 1949 that the pattern was expanded and renamed Waverly, with several new candleholders added over the next year or so, including the one-light candleblock. The mold is currently owned by the Heisey Collectors of America. $75.00 – 85.00.

HE-171A. DRAWING SHOWING ORIGINAL DESIGN FOR No. 1519 WAVERLY ONE-LIGHT CANDLEBLOCK (NEVER MADE)

HE-172. No. 1519 WAVERLY GARDENIA CENTERPIECE WITH No. 507 ORCHID ETCHING

No. 1519 Waverly gardenia centerpiece. 13" in diameter. Made from 1950 to 1952, in crystal only. Not marked with the Diamond H. The bottom rim is ground smooth. Offered with at least two etchings, No. 507 Orchid and 515 Heisey Rose. Also offered with the cupped epergnette, deep epergnette, 5" No. 5013 insert vase, or 6" No. 4233 insert vase. The No. 1519 pattern had originally been introduced in 1940 as Oceanic, and included one candlestick (HE-132 on p. 145); it wasn't until 1949 that the pattern was expanded and renamed Waverly, with several new candleholders added over the next year or so, including the gardenia centerpiece, which was adapted from the regular gardenia bowl in the pattern. The mold is currently owned by the Heisey Collectors of America. $60.00 – 65.00. Add 100% to 150% for etching.

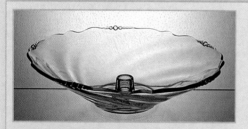

HE-173. No. 1519 WAVERLY FRUIT CENTERPIECE

No. 1519 Waverly fruit centerpiece. 13" in diameter and 3" high. Made from 1950 to 1952, in crystal only. Not marked with the Diamond H. The bottom rim is ground smooth. Offered with at least two etchings, No. 507 Orchid and 515 Heisey Rose. Also offered with the cupped epergnette, deep epergnette, 5" No. 5013 insert vase, or 6" No. 4233 insert vase. The No. 1519 pattern had originally been introduced in 1940 as Oceanic, and included one candlestick (HE-132 on p. 145); it wasn't until 1949 that the pattern was expanded and renamed Waverly, with several new candleholders added over the next year or so, including the fruit centerpiece, which was adapted from the regular fruit bowl in the pattern. The mold is currently owned by the Heisey Collectors of America. $60.00 – 65.00. Add 100% to 150% for etching.

HE-174. No. 1567 PLANTATION 5" FOOTED EPERGNE CANDLE-HOLDER

No. 1567 Plantation footed epergne candleholder. Made in two sizes: 5" high with a 4⅛" diameter round foot and a 5⅛" diameter top, made from June 1949 to 1953; 7" high, made from July 1949 to 1950. Only 700 of the taller epergne candleholders were made, and it has not been seen by the authors. The 5" size is marked with the Diamond H on the bottom. It was designed by Horace King and created by adding a candleholder element to the footed comport (or footed cheese, as it is also referred to in the catalogues). The mold is currently owned by the Heisey Collectors of America. The Plantation pattern was initially introduced in 1948, with three previous candleholders among the first pieces made. (See HE-159, HE-160, and HE-161 on p. 154.) 5": $120.00 – 125.00. 7": 125.00 – 135.00.

No. 1567 Plantation two-light candlestick. 5¾" high with a 5½" diameter round foot and an arm spread of approximately 8¾". Made from August 1949 to 1957, in crystal only. Not marked with the Diamond H. Available with at least one etching, No. 516 Plantation Ivy. Designed by Horace King. The mold is currently owned by the Heisey Collectors of America. The Plantation pattern was initially introduced in 1948, with three previous candleholders among the first pieces made. (See HE-159, HE-160, and HE-161 on p. 154.) $50.00 – 75.00. Add 75% to 100% for etching.

HE-175. No. 1567 PLANTATION TWO-LIGHT CANDLE-STICK

No. 1567 Plantation one-light footed candlestick. 5¼" high (called 5" in the catalogs) with a 4¾" diameter round foot. Made from August 1950 to 1955. Not marked with the Diamond H. Available with at least one etching, No. 516 Plantation Ivy. Designed by Horace King. The mold is currently owned by the Heisey Collectors of America. The Plantation pattern was initially introduced in 1948, with three previous candleholders among the first pieces made. (See HE-159, HE-160, and HE-161 on p. 154 above.) $100.00 – 125.00. Add 75% to 100% for etching.

HE-176. No 1567 PLANTATION ONE-LIGHT FOOTED CANDLESTICK

No. 341 Old Williamsburg footed epergne candleholder. 4½" high (called 5½" in the catalogs) with a 3½" diameter round foot and a diameter of 5¾" at the top. Made from 1949 to 1953, in crystal only. Marked with the Diamond H at the bottom of the column. A design patent was filed for this piece on May 25, 1949, and approved November 22, 1949, as D156,097. Although T. Clarence Heisey signed the patent application, the actual designer was Horace King, who referred to it as an "improvisation" based on the No. 341 epergnette (see HE-162 p. 155) combined with the stem of the No. 341 Old Williamsburg goblet, inverted. Rarely seen today. Although most of the Old Williamsburg molds were purchased by the Lancaster Colony Corporation, the disposition of this mold is not known. The inventory of molds owned by the Heisey Collectors of America includes a 5½" comport, which could be the mold used to create this candleholder. $150.00 – market.

HE-177. No. 341 OLD WILLIAMSBURG FOOTED EPERGNE CANDLEHOLDER

No. 1510 two-light candlestick. Named Square-on-Round by researchers. 5¾" high with a 5½" diameter round foot and an arm spread of approximately 8". Offered from January 1950 to January 1953, in crystal only. Marked with the Diamond H on one of the petals at the base of the candlestick, just above the foot. Designed by Horace King. Later reissued in dawn as No. 1632 Lodestar. (See HE-188 on p. 163.) Although the candlestick was new in 1950, an ash tray in the pattern had originally been made in 1939. It was this ash tray, with its square shape, ridged edges, and round base, that inspired the new items in the pattern, as well as the name by which the line is known today. The mold is currently owned by the Heisey Collectors of America. $75.00 – 85.00.

HE-178. No. 1510 SQUARE-ON-ROUND TWO-LIGHT CANDLESTICK

No. 1614 three-light candlestick. Named Plume by researchers. Dimensions unknown. Made from June 1950 to January 1953, in crystal only. Marked with the Diamond H at the bottom, just above the foot. Designed by Carl Cobel. His drawing of an early version of this candlestick, to the best of our knowledge never made, is seen in HE-179a. Rarely seen today. The mold is currently owned by the Heisey Collectors of America. $300.00 – market.

HE-179. No. 1614
PLUME THREE-LIGHT
CANDLESTICK

HE-179A. DRAWING
SHOWING ORIGINAL
DESIGN FOR NO. 1614
PLUME THREE-
LIGHT CANDLESTICK
(NEVER MADE)

HE-180. No. 1615 FLAME TWO-LIGHT
CANDLESTICK, WITH No. 1072
SOUTHWIND CUTTING

No. 1615 two-light candlestick. Named Flame by researchers. 10¼" high with a 5½" diameter round base and an arm spread of 9". Produced from December 1950 to 1957 when the factory closed, and then reissued by the Imperial Glass Company from September 1957 to January 1961. (See IM-127 on p. 215.) Made in crystal only. Marked with the Diamond H at the bottom, just above the foot. This was a popular blank for decorations. Cuttings available on it included No. 965 Narcissus, 1015 Dolly Madison Rose, 1034 Maytime, 1047 Autumn Rushes, 1070 Bel-Air, 1072 Southwind (seen in the accompanying photograph), and 1083½ El Dorado. Etchings included No. 507 Orchid, 515 Heisey Rose, and 516 Plantation Ivy. Designed by Carl Cobel. The design elements are very similar to those found on the No. 1519 Waverly pattern. (See HE-132 on p. 145 and HE-167 through HE-173 on p. 156-158.) It is likely this candlestick was intended to match the earlier pattern and, in fact, it was actually listed as Waverly in the 1953 and 1956 catalogs. The mold is currently owned by the Heisey Collectors of America. $110.00 – 125.00. Add 100% to 150% for Heisey Rose; 50% to 75% for other cuttings and etchings.

HE-181.
No. 1621
CYLINDER
CANDLE-
BLOCK
(computer composite)

No. 1621 candleblock. Named Cylinder by researchers. 3¾" high. Made ca. 1951 – 1953 in crystal and amber. This candleblock has not been seen by the authors, but is probably ground smooth on the top and bottom. It would not be marked with the Diamond H, which could account for its not being identifiable as Heisey, even if it were seen. Reports of the Cylinder candleblock in amber indicate that it was made with an air bubble. A Newark resident recalled that these candleblocks were sold at the factory retail outlet store as part of a set with the No. 1619 epergnette. (See HE-185a on p. 162.) Other sizes of the candleblock may have been made, since the inventory of molds currently owned by the Heisey Collectors of America includes four No. 1621 candleblocks: 1⅝", 2¼", 3", and 3¾". Unable to price.

No. 1951 Cabochon candelette. 1¾" high with a 1¹⁵⁄₁₆" "square" base and a 4⅜" diameter round top. Made from February 1951 to 1957. Marked with the Diamond H on the bottom. Offered with at least two cuttings, No. 980 Moonglo and 1025 Arcadia. The example seen in the accompanying photograph has cut polka dots and an applied silver rim, both done by a decorating company. This was the last major pattern to be brought out by Heisey. Designed by Horace King in response to a request from Rod Irwin, Heisey's sales manager, for "a modern back porch party line." The result was described in an advertisement in the November 1951 issue of *Living for Young Homemakers:* "The Circle and the Square are the two perfect shapes that are basic to all design. Cabochon is the ideal combination of these two perfect shapes… each piece so modern, so practical, so moderately priced!" The similarity to the Cambridge Square pattern brought out by the Cambridge Glass Company a year later is apparent. (See CB-163 on p. 94 of volume one of this series.) The mold for the Cabochon candelette is currently owned by the Heisey Collectors of America. $25.00 – 30.00.

HE-182. No. 1951 CABOCHON CAN-
DELETTE WITH UNKNOWN CUTTING
AND SILVER TRIM

No. 1951 Cabochon two-light candlestick. 5½" high with a 5½" by 2⅞" oblong base and an arm spread of 7⅝". Made from February 1951 to 1953, in crystal only. Marked with the Diamond H just above the base, in the center between the arms. The bottom is ground smooth. Designed by Horace King. Like other pieces in the Cabochon pattern, the design combines elements of the circle and the square. The center cabochon is very similar in shape to the advertising sign made in 1948 for use in store displays, which in turn was inspired by the paper label that had been used since 1932. The mold is currently owned by the Heisey Collectors of America. $85.00 – 95.00.

HE-183.
No. 1951
CABOCHON
TWO-LIGHT
CANDLE-
STICK

No. 1951 Cabochon hurricane. Dimensions unknown. Made ca. 1952 – 1953, in crystal only. To the authors' knowledge, this hurricane lamp has never been seen; however, it was pictured in the April 1953 issue of *American Home* as a suggested gift for new brides, so we know that it did go into production. It was designed by Jane Wilson Scott, whose original drawing of a "modern hurricane lamp," dated 1/28/52, can be seen in the accompanying picture. Her drawing indicates that the base was oblong or rectangular in shape; the photograph in *American Home* makes it appear to be more square, with rounded corners. The 12" No. 1951 shade was also designed by Scott specifically for use on this hurricane base. When Heisey introduced their Domesti-cater line in 1953, which consisted of glass pieces combined with metal and wood fittings, unit #6 was the hurricane lamp (seen in HE-184a), which used this globe on a wooden base with wire feet. The base was available either with a natural birch finish and black wire, or in black with polished wire feet. The Domesti-cater line was not successful, and these pieces are also quite rare today. The mold for the Cabochon hurricane base is currently owned by the Heisey Collectors of America. Crystal base with globe: $300.00 – market. Domesti-cater base with globe: $100.00 – 150.00.

HE-184A. DOMESTI-CATER
UNIT #6 (HURRICANE LAMP),
FROM 1953 CATALOG

HE-184. ORIGINAL
DESIGN DRAWING FOR
No. 1951 CABOCHON
HURRICANE

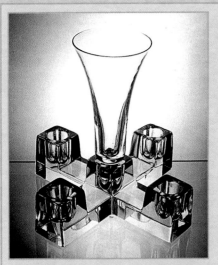

HE-185. No. 1619 Block Five five-light candle centerpiece

No. 1619 five-light candle centerpiece. Named Block Five by researchers. The arms are 7½" across. Made from July 1951 to 1955, in crystal only. Not marked with the Diamond H. The bottom is ground smooth. Rarely seen today. In the 1953 catalog, this candle centerpiece sold for $10.75 each, making it the most expensive candlestick in the catalog, which probably helps to explain its scarcity today. It could be purchased as a five-light candleholder or with a choice of the 6" No. 4233 insert vase (as seen in the accompanying photograph) or the 5" No. 5013 insert vase. There was also a No. 1619 epergnette designed to go with this candle centerpiece. The peg nappy seen in HE-185a is identical to the epergnette. It is 2⅝" high with a diameter of 4¾". It is marked with the Diamond H on the bottom of the peg and otherwise would be virtually impossible to distinguish from the similar peg nappy sold as part of the Cambridge Arms set that had been introduced by the Cambridge Glass Company in 1948. (See p. 96 in volume one of this series.) The Jeannette Glass Company also made a plain peg nappy. Neither Jeannette nor Cambridge made an epergnette with a candleholder element, however. The molds for both the candle centerpiece and the epergnette are currently owned by the Heisey Collectors of America. $375.00 – market.

HE-185A. No. 1619 PEG NAPPY

HE-186. No. 6009A Roundelay candle centerpiece in dawn
(original company photograph)

No. 6009A Roundelay candle centerpiece. 6" diameter. Made in 1954, in dawn only. This was a blown pattern, so it is not marked with the Diamond H. The bottom is probably ground. The pattern was designed by Eva Zeisel, internationally known for her work in modern ceramics for such companies as the Red Wing Potteries, Castleton, Western Stoneware, and the Hall China Company. She became Heisey's art director in 1953, a short-lived collaboration that resulted in awards and prestige for the company, but very little in the way of sales. Zeisel also designed an abstract fish cutting for use on blanks in the Roundelay pattern, possibly including the candle centerpiece. $175.00 – 195.00.

HE-187. No. 1632 Lodestar candle centerpiece in dawn

No. 1632 Lodestar candle centerpiece. 2" high with a star-shaped base and a top diameter of 4⅜". Made from January 1955 to 1957, in dawn only. Marked with the Diamond H on the bottom. The bottom is ground smooth. This was the last new candlestick to be offered by Heisey. The two other candleholders in the Lodestar pattern were reissues of earlier ones (HE- 141 on p. 148 and HE-188 on the following page, a reissue of HE-178 on p. 159). The mold is currently owned by the Heisey Collectors of America. $85.00 – 95.00.

No. 1632 Lodestar two-light candlestick. 5¾" high with a 5½" diameter round foot and an arm spread of approximately 8". Offered from January 1955 to 1957, in dawn only. Marked with the Diamond H on one of the petals at the base of the candlestick, just above the foot. This was a reissue of the earlier No. 1510 candlestick designed by Horace King. (See HE-178 on p. 159.) Difficult to find today. The mold is currently owned by the Heisey Collectors of America. $150.00 – 175.00.

HE-188. No. 1632 LODESTAR TWO-LIGHT CANDLE-STICK IN DAWN

HEISEY FAKE!

Diamond and Square chamberstick. 3⅛" high with a 5¼" diameter base. This candlestick is made in Taiwan and has been sold in a number of different colors by A.A. Importing Company, Inc., Castle Antiques and Reproductions, and possibly others, from 1982 to the present. Known colors include blue opaque, cobalt, green, milk glass, peach (transparent pink), pink milk glass, and teal. Most of these candlesticks are marked on the bottom, near the rim, with a crudely shaped Diamond H. This is not a Heisey pattern, the shape of the Diamond is wrong, and above all, the quality of the glass is extremely poor. Although a knowledgeable collector would never be fooled by these candlesticks, new collectors frequently are, and these candlesticks can be found daily on the Internet, being offered as Heisey by dealers who are either ignorant or unscrupulous. The Heisey Collectors of America obtained the rights to the Diamond H trademark in 1983. The HCA's attorney contacted the importers of these candlesticks (and other pieces, including a two-light candlestick and a covered hen, that are also marked with a Diamond H) and agreement was reportedly reached to have the mark removed from the mold. However, the fact that these candlesticks are once again readily available on the market indicates that this agreement has fallen into abeyance. Buyer beware! $5.00 – 10.00.

HE-189. HEISEY FAKE CHAMBER-STICK IN GREEN, MADE IN TAIWAN

HE-189A. CLOSE-UP OF FAKE DIAMOND H MARK

HIGBEE (JOHN B.) GLASS COMPANY, Bridgeville, Pennsylvania (1907 – 1918).

One of the founders of this company was John B. Higbee, who had previously been one of the founders of Bryce, Higbee and Company in 1879. However, he died before the new factory went into operation, and his son, Oliver Higbee, became its president when it opened. Production was largely tableware, including some patterns made from molds purchased from the now defunct Bryce, Higbee plant. During the brief eleven years they were in operation, they introduced 28 new patterns of their own. They also had great success with a sanitary vacuum bottle introduced in 1911. A precursor of the modern thermos, it was made entirely of glass and guaranteed to keep liquids hot for 24 hours or cold for 48 hours.

Despite this seeming success, the company declared bankruptcy for 60 days in 1913 and underwent a reorganization the following year. Following an apparent recovery, and under equally mysterious circumstances, the factory closed in 1918 amidst rumors that Oliver Higbee had departed and taken the company's cash with him. At any rate, the plant was sold in 1918 to the General Electric Company, who converted it to the manufacture of light bulbs (an activity that still goes on there today).

TRADEMARK

Higbee was one of the few companies to sometimes mark its pieces, beginning around 1908 and continuing until at least 1911. The mark used was the shape of a bee, with the letters H I G across its body. Versions of this mark were later used on reproductions by the L. G. Wright Glass Company and the Mosser Glass Company, but without the lettering.

BEE TRADEMARK

HI-1. No. C-169 COLONIAL CANDLESTICK, FROM CATALOG

No. C-169 Colonial candlestick. 7" high. Made sometime in the 1907 – 1917 period. Known in crystal only. Marked with the Higbee trademark on the corner of the base. This mold was obtained by the New Martinsville Glass Mfg. Company after Higbee closed and continued in production by them, but without the mark. Other companies also made very similar candlesticks, including the Indiana Glass Company (see IN-6 on p. 237), the United States Glass Company, and the Westmoreland Specialty Glass Company, but none of these have the beveled edge seen on the Higbee candlestick. $50.00 – 60.00 (with Higbee trademark).

HI-2. CANDLESTICK, UNKNOWN PATTERN NUMBER, FROM *POTTERY, GLASS & BRASS SALESMAN*, JULY 4, 1918

Candlestick. 8½" high. Introduced in June 1918, just months before the factory closed. Offered in crystal only. It is unknown if this candlestick was ever marked with the Higbee trademark. The mold was obtained by the New Martinsville Glass Mfg. Company after Higbee closed and continued in production by them. $25.00 – 30.00. (Double this value if marked with the Higbee trademark.)

REPRODUCTION

No. 64-35 Thistle candleholder. 1¾" high with a 5¼" diameter bowl. Although marked inside the candle cup with the figure of a bee (without the "H I G" lettering), this is not a Higbee piece. It is a reproduction of Higbee's Delta pattern (sometimes called Paneled Thistle), made for the L. G. Wright Glass Company in the 1970s. Wright sold a complete line of pieces in this pattern, all made from new molds. The original Delta pattern did not include a candleholder. It isn't clear if prices paid for these candleholders have been for Higbee or L. G. Wright, but they have sold in recent years for as much as $88.00. A more reasonable valuation would be in the $25.00 – 30.00 range.

HI-3. No. 64-35 THISTLE CANDLEHOLDER, REPRODUCTION MADE FOR L. G. WRIGHT GLASS COMPANY

Hobbs, Brockunier & Company, Wheeling, West Virginia (1845 – 1893).

Founded as Barnes, Hobbs & Company by James B. Barnes, his son James F. Barnes, and John L. Hobbs. Initially, their single furnace factory manufactured oil lamps, tumblers, and other household items under the name of the South Wheeling Glass Works. In 1849, James B. Barnes died. At that time John H. Hobbs (son of John L.) joined the partnership, and the name was changed to Hobbs, Barnes & Company. In 1856, the name reverted to Barnes, Hobbs & Company and the partnership was changed to include J. K. Dunham, but the following year the name was again returned to Hobbs, Barnes & Company (their sign painter must have been a very busy fellow). The company had also grown substantially over the decade and now included three furnaces, a mold shop, a cutting shop, a packing warehouse, their own fire company, and an on-site coal mine.

The prosperity continued until 1861, when a lack of manpower brought about by the Civil War caused them to shut down for six months. They eventually reopened, but the shortage of trained workers persisted throughout the war, and this may have contributed to Barnes' decision to sell his interest to the Hobbs family and withdraw from the company in 1863. That same year Charles W. Brockunier, the firm's bookkeeper, joined the partnership and the name was changed to J. H. Hobbs, Brockunier & Company.

In the fall of 1863, chemist and glass blower William Leighton, Sr. and his son, William, Jr., left the New England Glass Company to join the firm. This was a significant turning point in the fortunes of the company, for in 1864 a major breakthrough in glassmaking was made when William, Sr. developed a formula using lime to make crystal glass of similar quality to the heavier and more costly lead glass. The development of lime glass (a.k.a. soda glass) allowed the manufacture of quality tableware that was affordable to everyone.

By the 1870s, business was booming, with showrooms in several U.S. cities and Havana, Cuba. By 1876, the company was manufacturing massive chandeliers in addition to its many tableware lines, and had the capacity to produce sixty tons of glass a week. In 1881, shortly after the death of co-founder John. L. Hobbs, the company's name was shortened to Hobbs, Brockunier & Company.

On March 2nd, 1882, a major fire damaged a large part of the factory, but a massive rebuilding effort was begun immediately and the first furnace was back on-line in less than a week. By August the factory was operating at full capacity, and all repairs were completed by January of 1883.

In December of 1887, an industry-wide strike forced all of the glass companies to close down. During this time, Charles Brockunier retired as an active partner, the Leightons left to join Dalzell Brothers & Gilmore, and others left for positions with the newly formed Fostoria Glass Company. In August of 1888, the company was reorganized under a new charter as the Hobbs Glass Company, and the factory was restarted with Hanson E. Waddell as the new secretary and Nicolas Kopp taking William Leighton's place as chemist. With all old stock having been sold off during the strike and restructuring period, Kopp immediately started working on new lines, and soon the two larger furnaces were running at full capacity.

In 1891, Hobbs Glass Co. became a charter member of the newly formed U. S. Glass Company and was designated as Factory H, but the following years were difficult ones for the glass industry, and the high taxes and aging equipment of the Hobbs plant convinced the board of directors of U. S. Glass to close it permanently in the fall of 1893. The last of the inventory produced by Factory H was sold by May of 1894, and the building lay idle until it was purchased by Harry Northwood and Thomas Dugan in April of 1902.

Colors

An 1859 ad for Hobbs & Barnes mentions "fancy colored glass," but lists no specific colors. According to Neila & Tom Bredehoft in their book, *Hobbs, Brockunier & Co., Glass*, early Hobbs colors were thought to include purple, green, and olive. We suspect that opal glass was also made quite early. Colored glassware was officially introduced (or re-introduced) in 1881, when several new colors appeared. Many of the colors introduced at that time (or later) were probably made until the company became part of U.S. Glass in 1891, but there's little solid information available on how long many of these colors were in production.

Amberina	Amber with ruby edges. Circa 1884 – 1886 or later.
Burmese	See coral.
Canary	A yellow/green color often referred to by collectors as vaseline. 1878 – 1885 or later.
Coral	Amberina glass with an opal plating. Mentioned in late 1885, introduced in early 1886, and probably continued until the factory's closing.

Green opaque	Opaque pale green usually used for plated spangled ware. Circa 1883.
Indian	A red amber plated over spangled blue. Circa 1860s – 1887.
Lazuline	A medium blue plated over spangled blue. Circa 1860s – 1887.
Lemon yellow	A translucent color made plating canary with alabaster glass. Circa 1880's.
Marine green	A transparent apple green. Circa 1882 – 1885 or later.
Old gold	Amber. 1881 – 1885 or later.
Opal	White opaque or milk glass. Circa 1870s (or earlier) through the closing of the factory. Called porcelain in advertisements during the 1870s.
Peach Blow	Satin finished coral. Introduced in mid – 1886 and probably continued until the factory's closing.
Pink	Transparent pink. Circa 1887 – 1889.
Porcelain	Early (1870s) name used for opal or milk glass.
Rose	An opaque pink. Circa 1882.
Rubina	A partial ruby plating on crystal, producing an effect of ruby shading to crystal. Circa 1880s.
Rubina Verde	A partial ruby plating on canary glass, producing an effect of ruby shading to canary. 1881 – 1885 or later.
Ruby	A transparent cranberry color. Also available opalescent. Circa late 1881 – 1889 or later.
Ruby amber	A partial ruby plating on amber, giving an appearance similar to amberina. Circa 1885.
Ruby sapphire	A partial ruby plating on sapphire, producing an effect of ruby shading to sapphire. A rare color also known to collectors as bluerina. Circa 1885.
Sapphire	A deep, rich, transparent blue. Also available opalescent. Circa 1882 – 1889 or later.
Turquoise	Sapphire blue plated with opal, creating an opaque piece. Circa mid-to-late 1880s.

STAINS

Amber and ruby stains were used circa 1890 – 1891.

HB-1. LITTLE SAMUEL CANDLESTICK

Little Samuel or Infant Samuel candlestick. Unknown number. Dimensions unknown. Circa 1877. Known only in crystal, but other Little Samuel items are known in opal and crystal with a frosted figure. Published reports that this candlestick may also have been made by the Portland Glass Company can be discounted, since it is now known that Little Samuel was an original design for Hobbs, Brockunier. The confusion arises from the fact that Hobbs acquired some molds from Portland, including a bowl that they combined with the Little Samuel figure to form an epergne. Crystal: $250.00 – 325.00. *(Photograph courtesy of Walt Adams)*

HB-2. TREE OF LIFE WITH HAND FOOTED COMPOTE IN SAPPHIRE (PROBABLY NOT INTENDED AS A CANDLEHOLDER)

Tree of Life with Hand footed comport. 8¼" high with a 5¼" diameter base and a top diameter of 8". Patented April 20, 1875. Made in crystal, sapphire, and possibly other colors of the period. This is known to have been made with an epergne vase insert. Although purchased as a candleholder, it is not likely that Hobbs, Brockunier ever sold it for this purpose; however, the socket nicely holds a taper candle, so it may have been meant to serve a dual purpose. Crystal: $150.00 – 200.00. Sapphire: $275.00 – 350.00.

No. 1 Calvary candlestick. 9¾" high with a 3⅝" hexagonal base. Circa 1880 – 1885 (may have been made as early as the 1870s and/or as late as 1891). Advertised in crystal and opal. Made in two pieces, with the socket stuck to a platform on top of the cross (this type of construction did not use a wafer). Crystal: $18.00 – 22.50. Opal: $25.00 – 35.00.

HB-3. No. 1 CALVARY CANDLESTICKS IN OPAL (FRONT AND REAR VIEWS)

No. 2 Calvary candlestick. 12¾" high with a 5" diameter twelve-sided base. Made in crystal and opal. Circa 1880 – 1891 (may have been made as early as the 1870s). Production was continued until 1904 by U. S. Glass as their No. 10 candlestick. The Cape Cod Glass Company and the Boston & Sandwich Glass Company made very similar candlesticks. (See CC-1 on p. 100 – 101 and BS-13 on p. 38 of volume one of this series.) Like those, this has a hexagonal candle cup with a cross on each panel and is attached to the base with a wafer, but the candle cup on the Hobbs has a reinforcing ring around the rim (see HB-4a) that neither of the others have. The No. 2 also has a wider cross arm and less detail in the Christ figure than the other two. Crystal: $30.00 – 40.00. Opal: $50.00 – 65.00.

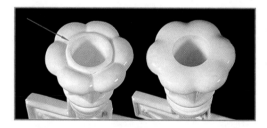

HB-4A. COMPARISON OF HOBBS No. 2 CALVARY candle cup (ON LEFT) WITH BOSTON & SAND-WICH/CAPE COD VERSION (ON RIGHT). NOTE THE REINFORCING RING AROUND THE CANDLE OPENING ON THE HOBBS

HB-4. No. 2 CALVARY CANDLESTICKS IN OPAL (FRONT AND REAR VIEWS)

No. 3 candlestick. 7¾" high with a 3⅞" base. Made in crystal and opal. Circa 1880 – 1891, with production continued through 1904 by U. S. Glass as their No. 18. The New England Glass Company made a very similar candlestick in three sizes, the largest of which is 8" high. The New England Glass Company version has more detail than the Hobbs and is made from flint (lead) glass, so it will "ring" when tapped. The Hobbs version is made from lime glass and will respond with a dull thud when tapped. Crystal: $25.00 – 30.00. Opal: $35.00 – 45.00.

HB-5. No. 3 CANDLESTICK

HOME INTERIORS & GIFTS, INC., Dallas, Texas (1957 to the present). Thi

company was founded by Mary C. Crowley and her son, Don Carter. They are not manufacturers, but rather a direct sale company with a network of over 70,000 independent home sales contractors who make their products available. As thei name suggests, they specialize in items for the house, such as mirrors, pictures, and objets d'art of all kinds, including can dlesticks. The company is often referred to as Homco.

HO-1.
CANDLESTICK,
MARKED HOMCO

Candleholder. 2⅛" high with a 3" diameter base. Production dates unknown. Crystal only. Marked on the bottom: "Homco®. Made in USA." $2.50 – 3.50.

HO-2.
CANDLESTICK,
MARKED HOMCO

Candlestick. 4" high with a 3¼" diameter base base. Production dates unknown. Crystal only. Marked inside the candle cup: "Homco®. USA." $3.00 – 4.00.

Candlestick. 5" high (with votive insert 9") with a 3¾" diameter base. Production dates unknown. Crystal only. The candlestick is not marked, but the insert is marked inside: "Homco." $6.50 – 7.50.

HO-3. CANDLESTICK,
WITH VOTIVE INSERT
MARKED HOMCO

HO-3A. CANDLESTICK, WITH
VOTIVE INSERT MARKED
HOMCO SHOWN SEPARATELY

HO-4.
CAMBRIDGE
CANDLESTICK,
MARKED HOME
INTERIORS

Cambridge candlestick. 6" high with a 3⅝" diameter base. Production dates unknown. Crystal only. Marked inside the candle cup: "Home Interiors. USA." $5.00 – 8.00.

Candlestick. 6¼" high with a 4¼" diameter hexagonal base. Production dates unknown. Crystal only. Marked on the underside of the base: "Homco®." $7.50 – 9.00.

HO-5. CANDLESTICK, MARKED HOMCO

Candlestick. 7⅝" high with a 3⅝" diameter base. Production dates unknown. Crystal only. Marked inside the candle cup: "Homco®. USA." $7.50 – 9.00.

HO-6. CANDLESTICK, MARKED HOMCO

Candleholder. Called Diamond Sawtooth. 1½" with a top diameter of 5¼". Production dates unknown. Made in crystal and amber. This candlestick has been attributed to the Indiana Glass Company. $5.00 – 6.50.

HO-7. DIAMOND SAWTOOTH CANDLEHOLDER IN AMBER

No. 11343 handled candleholder. 1⅛" high with a top diameter of 4⅝" and a total length of 6⅛". Production dates unknown. Crystal only. Marked inside the candle cup: "Homco®. USA." $4.50 – 6.00.

HO-8. No. 11343 HANDLED CANDLEHOLDER, MARKED HOMCO

No. 1171 (or No. 11710) cross candlestick. 7¼" high with a 3¾" diameter octagonal base. In current production. Crystal with satin finish on the figure of Christ. Marked inside the candle cup: "Home Interiors. USA." Also available with a votive insert. Earlier production of this candlestick has been attributed to Fostoria Glass Company, now out of business. The current manufacturer is unknown. A crucifix candlestick with a very similar base was made in the 1920s by the L. E. Smith Glass Company, but was only 5" high. Current price: $9.95.

HO-9. No. 1171 CROSS CANDLESTICK

HOUZE (L. J.) CONVEX GLASS COMPANY, Point Marion, Pennsylvania (1902 to the present).

This factory has a long and varied history. It was founded in 1902 as the Federated Glass Company, manufacturer of window glass by the hand-blown cylinder method. Its president and general manager was Leon J. Houze, a veteran of the glass industry known for his innovations in furnace design and as a pioneer in the manufacture of colored sheet glass. He received a number of patents in his life, but it was one approved in 1914 for a method of manufacturing and tempering convex glass articles that led to the company becoming the L. J. Houze Convex Glass Company. Convex glass was used not only for camera lenses, but also for goggles and other military uses — a line of manufacture that at one point led to the company being responsible for 75% of the goggle glass being made during World War I. In the 1920s and 1930s, the company expanded operations once again, offering MarbleX and Onxglas in 1928, under the brand name of HouzeX. These were formulas for marbleized glass (or slag glass, as it is often referred to today), with products ranging widely from ash trays and flower pots to gear shift balls. They also made large numbers of lamps in these colors, often confused today with products of the Akro Agate Company.

Sheet glass remained a mainstay, with Houze selected in the years 1949 through 1953, when the White House was renovated, as the only company able to duplicate the original windows in the same manner and quality as when they were originally made in 1792. By this time, they had also become the major manufacturer of sunglass lenses. Another major development in 1952 was the ability to transfer photographs to glassware by various processes using screen printing with permanently fired on ceramic colors. Over the next twenty years, pieces decorated in this manner proved equally popular for both direct sales and for advertising and souvenir purposes. In the late 1960s, the company began phasing out glass production and turned to decorating as their main business, using blanks from other sources. Today, as the Houze Glass Corporation, they are one of the largest specialty advertising firms, offering decorations on ceramic mugs as well as on glass.

HouzeX logo

COLORS

Colored sheet glass was an early specialty. By the time that Houze had expanded its production to household items in the 1920s, several transparent colors were being used, including amber, brown, green, amethyst, cobalt blue, and rose. Snowite (milk glass) was advertised in 1928, as were MarbleX and Onyxglas. The latter was advertised as "a beautiful cream color streaked with all the different color tones from a delicate tan to a rich brown." The base color for MarbleX (which is also marbleized, or slag glass, as it is often referred to today) is usually either white, pale yellow, or pale green, with contrasting colors that can range from dark browns and blues to bright turquoise and maroon. The possible combinations are endless. Other known opaque colors include coralex (pink), baby blue, Nile green, jet black, canary yellow, and lavender.

HZ-1. No. 851 candlesticks in MarbleX and Nile green (in center)

No. 851 candlestick. 1¾" high with a 3½" diameter base. Made ca. 1928 to the 1930s or later. Known in amber, green, amethyst, Nile green, and MarbleX. Other colors are possible. MarbleX examples have been seen with a number of color combinations, some with white as the base color (as in the two examples seen in the accompanying photograph), others with pale yellow or green as the base color. Two other companies made very similar candlesticks, Akro Agate and Westite. There are minute differences between the three as described on p. 8 of volume one of this series in the discussion devoted to the Akro Agate low plain candleblock. However, the Houze candlestick is the easiest of the three to identify, since it is usually marked "No. 851" on the bottom. Sometimes this mark is worn, and it is necessary to turn the candlestick to just the right angle to make it out. Marked pairs have been seen with a label saying "Guaranteed Hemill Product. Made in USA." (See HZ-1a.) We have been unable to find any information on Hemill, but assume that this was a trade name used by Houze at some point during their existence, perhaps similar to their Chateau Glasscraft division. (See HZ-3 on the following page.) Transparent colors: $10.00 – $15.00. MarbleX: $15.00 – 45.00. (Higher values depend on the number and vividness of the colors used.)

HZ-1a. CLOSE-UP OF HEMILL PRODUCT LABEL

Candlestick. 3¼" high with a 4½" diameter base. Production dates unknown, but probably 1930s. Known in MarbleX with white swirled with turquoise and beige, and light green swirled with brown. Other combinations are possible. $15.00 – 22.50.

HZ-2A. CANDLESTICK IN MARBLEX, PREDOMINANTLY LIGHT GREEN AND BROWN

HZ-2. CANDLESTICK IN MARBLEX, PREDOMINANTLY TURQUOISE AND BEIGE

Perfume lamp. 2¾" high (without the fixture), with a 4" octagonal base with eight feet. Introduced 1931. Made in rose, amber, and green (all satin finished), MarbleX (clam color with light marbleizing), and most of the opaque colors (milk glass, Nile green, baby blue, jet black, coralex, and canary yellow). Although sometimes shown as a candlestick, it is usually seen with various styles of metal fixture allowing it to be used as an electric lamp. It was marketed as a "perfume lamp," and sold with light bulbs that were coated with different scents. Sales of these lamps were through Chateau Glasscraft, Inc., apparently an independent division within the factory. L.E. Smith made a very similar candleholder as No. 230. Milk glass: $5.00 – 7.00. Colors: $10.00 – 12.00.

HZ-3. PERFUME LAMP IN MILK GLASS

Oriental Chrysanthemum candlesticks. Made in three sizes: 3", 5", and 7". Introduced in 1962 as part of a "group of hand-blown white opal glass accessories with ground and polished edges" (as described by *China, Glass & Tablewares* in the February 1962 issue). $10.00 – 20.00.

HZ-4. ORIENTAL CHRYSANTHEMUM CANDLESTICKS AND OTHER WHITE OPAL GLASS ACCESSORIES, FROM *CHINA, GLASS & TABLEWARES*, FEBRUARY 1962

HUNTINGTON TUMBLER COMPANY, Huntington, West Virginia (1901 – 1932).

In 1900, Anton Zihlman and others purchased the defunct factory of the Huntington Glass Company, which had only operated in the early 1890s. Zilhman had previously founded the Cumberland Glass Company in Maryland. When it joined the National Glass Company in 1900, he apparently began immediately to look for another opportunity to get back in the glass business, and found it in Huntington, West Virginia. As its name suggests, the new factory was devoted to blown tumblers, goblets, and barware, with an emphasis right from the beginning on decorations, including sand blastings, etchings, light cuttings, and enamelings. In the 1920s, the company expanded its output to include all types of stemware, vases, beverage sets, and other blown tableware, including candlesticks. The factory closed in 1932.

COLORS

Crystal only was made in the early years. By 1925, they had added gold iridescent lustres and other color treatments to their line of decorations. Amber was the first color made in 1925, with rose and green also in production by 1927. In the final years from 1929 to 1932, they offered combinations of crystal with green, amber, rose, ruby, topaz, black, amethyst, and Ritz blue.

No. 20 optic blown candlestick. 2¾" high with a 4¼" diameter. Introduced at the 1928 Pittsburgh trade show, as part of a console set, described as an "optic blown fourteen inch bowl and candlesticks, made in four colors in plain and decorated designs." The colors were crystal, amber, green, and rose. Curiously, the catalog page shown in HU-1a does not mention crystal. Neither of the accompanying illustrations clearly show the shape of the candlestick, the main portion of which is comprised of a series of bulbous rings, or ribs, topped by a wide lip that has a "waterfall" optic.

HU-1. No. 20 optic blown console set, from
Crockery and Glass Journal, January 25, 1928

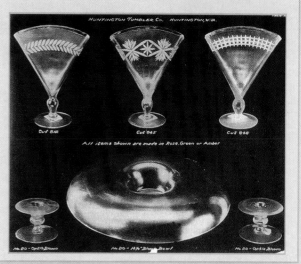

HU-1a. Undated catalog page showing
fan vases and No. 20 console set

Imperial Glass Company, Bellaire, Ohio (1901 – 1984).

The company was founded in 1901 by a group of investors from Wheeling, West Virginia, and Bellaire, Ohio. After spending several years constructing a building and making molds, glass making at the factory finally began in 1904. At this time, it was the largest glass factory under a single roof in the world. Initially, production consisted of clear pressed tableware for five and dime stores, with their first major sale being to F. W. Woolworth, but by the end of the decade they were beginning to expand their horizons. In 1909, they introduced their first iridescent glass in a marigold color they called rubigold. In 1911, they introduced pressed reproductions of "early English cut glass" under the NuCut label. The NuCut crystal line was popular, and the items were often given away as premiums. In 1912, they added Tiffany style lampshades under the NuArt label, and in 1916, they developed a beautiful line of iridescent glass with a unique onion-skin effect that collectors refer to today as "stretch glass." This is the glass that is sometimes called "Imperial Jewels" by collectors, although Imperial never used that name.

Loss of market share, due to competition from machine-made glass companies and the onset of the depression, forced Imperial into receivership in 1931. J. Ralph Boyd purchased the assets at a public auction in July of 1931, and the company was reorganized as the Imperial Glass Corporation in August of that same year. With the help of a new management team and two very popular new patterns (Cape Cod and Candlewick), they were able to get back on their feet and eventually return to prosperity.

In 1940, they purchased many molds from the Central Glass Works, and in 1958, they acquired the same from the A. H. Heisey Company, along with all rights to the name. Many Heisey patterns were reissued, some in Imperial's colors, under the name "Heisey by Imperial." In 1960, they acquired the assets of the Cambridge Glass Company. They reissued the Rose Point etching and other Cambridge patterns, including the "Cambridge Arms" candelabra, which became strong sellers in the Imperial lineup.

Through an exchange of stock in 1972, Imperial was acquired by Lenox, Incorporated. By the middle of 1981, a private investor, Arthur R. Lorch, purchased the company from Lenox. At the end of 1982, Lenox foreclosed on its note with Mr. Lorch, and the company was sold to Mr. Robert F. Stahl, Jr., who immediately filed for Chapter 11 bankruptcy in order to reorganize the company. A small amount of glass was made with an NI mark for "New Imperial," but production ceased for the last time on June 15, 1984. In August 1984, liquidation was ordered and the assets were sold to the Lancaster Colony Corporation, including many of the molds. The building was sold in 1985 and has since been razed.

Patterns

Imperial's two biggest successes were Candlewick and Cape Cod. Both were introduced in the 1930s, and remained in constant production until the factory closed roughly fifty years later. Because there were so many candleholders produced in both of these lines, we thought it would be helpful to present some broad–based information on each line here:

Cape Cod: Introduced in 1931. By the late 1930s, it was Imperial's best selling pattern, accounting for 17% of their total sales. Only Candlewick eventually surpassed it, making Cape Cod Imperial's second best seller. The line was initially offered in a few colors, but they were all discontinued before the early 1940s when the first Cape Cod candleholders appeared. We don't know why it took so long for candleholders to be added to the lineup, but we can find no evidence of any Cape Cod candleholder being made before 1942. During the 1940s, a few ruby stained pieces were made, but we have not seen any candleholders with this treatment. Color returned to the line during the 1970s and 1980s, and candleholders in production at that time can be found in the colors of the period. Colony Glassware's Park Lane and McKee's Plymouth Thumbprint patterns are often confused with Cape Cod. For candlesticks in this pattern, see IM-65, IM-66, IM-83, IM-84, IM-91, IM-96 through IM-101, and IM-107.

Candlewick: Officially introduced as a pattern name in 1937, but some pieces were known to have been manufactured as early as 1935. It went on to become one of the most recognized patterns in American pressed glass and remained in production until the factory closed. Unlike Cape Cod, candleholders seem to have been a part of the line-up from the beginning, with at least three dating back to the first year of production. Some colored Candlewick was made by Imperial, but many colored pieces are later reissues. When Imperial closed, the Candlewick molds were especially sought after, and several pieces in the pattern, including some candleholders, have been reissued in recent years by Boyd's Crystal Art Glass, the Summit Art Glass Company, and Dalzell Viking. Many other companies also made patterns resembling Candlewick, patterns that included many candlesticks. You will find a chart summarizing these in the addendum on p. 232 at the end of this chapter. For real Candlewick candlesticks, see IM-51 through IM-55, IM-57 through IM-59, IM-62, IM-63, IM-67, IM-75 through IM-81, IM-85 through IM-90, IM- 92 through IM-94, IM-110, and IM-150.

COLORS

Imperial often used prefixes to ascribe line designations, but sometimes the "line" was actually a color. This was the case when, beginning in 1950, they used 1950/ for regular milk glass and 1952/ for doeskin milk glass. This system lasted through most of the 1960s.

Amber	A transparent amber, circa 1929 – 1930s, 1951 – 1984.
Amber carnival	A warm iridescent amber, circa 1973 – 1975 and again in 1980.
Amberglo	A transparent amber, circa 1968 – 1973.
Amber ice	Amber with an onion skin, or satin iridescent finish, described as "crizzled on amber glass." Introduced in 1924 and continued until the late 1920s.
Amethyst	Iridescent purple, circa 1909 – 1910 and then continued as "azur" (see below).
Amethyst carnival	An iridescent amethyst, circa 1981. This was a short-lived reissue of the iridescent amethyst made in the early 1900s.
Amethyst ice	Amethyst with an onion-skin, or satin iridescent finish, described as "crizzled on mulberry glass." Introduced in 1924 and continued until the late 1920s.
Antique blue	A medium transparent blue, circa 1962 – 1974.
Aquamarine	A transparent light blue, circa late 1943. An advertisement also mentions this color in 1955. Used for some Candlewick, and for some pieces in the No. 11 and No. 176 (Continental) lines.
Aurora jewels	A sparkling iridescent finish on rich cobalt blue. Introduced in mid–1970 and discontinued in April of 1972.
Autumn amber	A dark transparent amber, circa 1962 – 1964, later called "amber."
Azalea	A deep rich transparent pink, circa 1964 – 1972.
Azur	A very dark amethyst glass with multicolored iridescence, circa 1910 – 1912. Initially called "amethyst," but the name was changed to azur by the end of 1910.
Azure blue carnival	An iridescent light blue, circa 1969 – 1971.
Bead green	A transparent, grayish light green, circa 1954 – 1962.
Black	An opaque black, early 1930s, circa 1960 – 1965, and 1980 – 1981.
Black and gold	Black glass with gold splatter decoration, circa 1953.
Black pearl	A transparent light black, circa 1960 – 1961. Used in the Bambu line.
Black suede	A satin black, circa early 1940s – 1943, and again circa 1954 and 1960.
Blue	A transparent blue, circa 1927 – 1928 and brought back in 1979.
Blue glow	An iridescent bluish gray on crystal glass, usually with a satin effect, very similar to sapphire. Circa 1920s.
Blue haze	A transparent blue, circa 1968 – 1974.

Blue ice	A smoky blue with an onion skin, or satin iridescent finish. Described as "blue crizzled on crystal glass." Introduced in late 1924 and produced until the late 1920s.
Blue satin	Light blue with a frosted finish, circa 1978 – 1981.
Blue slag	An opaque rich blue mixed with milk glass, circa 1965.
Bottle green	Mentioned in an advertisement from 1950.
Brown smoke	A light transparent brown, circa mid 1962 – 1966.
Burgundy	A darker transparent purple than heather, circa 1951, 1958 – 1961.
Burnt orange	A transparent orange, circa 1959 – 1960.
Canary	A transparent yellowish green, introduced 1925. This was also called "golden green" by Imperial and is also known to collectors as vaseline. Advertisements from 1955 and 1972 also mention canary, indicating that it was must have been periodically returned to production.
Canary iridescent	An iridescent canary yellow or vaseline color, circa 1925.
Caramel slag	Milk glass with shades of brown swirled in. Circa 1962 – 1976, and 1982.
Champagne	Unknown color. Listed in an advertisement from 1955.
Charcoal	A transparent dark gray that was used for the Elysian line, circa 1958 – 1962. Charcoal top (acquired from Houze Glass) were glued to crystal Heisey bases. Houze charcoal glass was also used for other pieces made by Imperial.
Charcoal brown	Dark brown, circa 1960 – 1961.
Chartreuse	A dark olive green, circa early 1951 – 1954. Also called smoky chartreuse, verde, or ripe olive.
Cobalt blue	A deep transparent blue, circa 1959, 1973, and 1980.
Cranberry	A deep transparent pink with a satin finish (satin version of azalea), 1964 – 1965.
Cranberry ruby	A deep transparent ruby, introduced mid-1962 – 1966.
Crystal	Produced throughout Imperial's history, was called olde flint in the 1950s.
Crystal satin or satin crystal	Circa 1979 – 1980. Was called satin crystal beginning in 1980. Sometimes referred to as camphor glass.
Dew Drop opalescent	Canary yellow with opalescent highlights, introduced in early 1965.
Doeskin	Imperial's term for an acid etched satin finish on opaque glass, created by sandblasting the item before dipping it in acid. Advertised as a "Lalique finish" in the 1940s, the terminology was changed to doeskin in the 1950s through the 1960s. The term "satin" was used during the 1970s.
Dresden blue	A transparent blue, circa late 1950's.
Drift wood brown	Circa 1952 – 1954.
Dynasty jade	An opaque green, introduced in 1960. Revived in 1980 as Imperial jade.
Emerald	A very deep transparent green, circa 1980 – 1981.
End o'day ruby (slag)	Milk glass with shades of ruby and orange swirled in. Circa 1969 – 1977.
Evergreen	A dark transparent green, circa late 1950.
Fern green	A transparent green, circa 1975 – 1976.
Flask brown	A deep, transparent amber, circa 1954 – 1955, 1960 – 1966.
Forest green	Circa 1952 – 1953.
Forget-me-not blue	Also called opaque blue. A pastel opaque blue, circa 1955 to the early 1960s.
Golden amber	A transparent honey amber, circa mid 1962.
Golden green	Also called canary or vaseline. Introduced in 1925.
Green	Transparent "depression" green, circa 1928 – 1930s.
Green ice	A teal or bluish green with an onion-skin finish. Described as "crizzled on green glass." Introduced in late 1924 and produced until the late 1920s.
Green slag	Milk glass with shades of green swirled in. Circa 1965 – 1966. Brought back into production in 1975 as jade slag.
Heather	A lighter transparent amethyst than burgundy, circa 1953 – 1980.
Helios carnival	A silvery iridescence on medium green carnival glass, originally made 1910 – 1911. Reissued 1967 – 1970.
Hemlock	Unknown color. Listed in an advertisement from 1951.
Hickory	Listed as a color for the Olde Jamestown single candle float bowl (see IM-118). We could not find any description of this color.
Honey	A light amber, circa 1957, 1968.
Horizon blue carnival	A light blue with an iridescent finish, introduced 1979 – 1980.

Ice colors	Included iris, rose, blue, amber, green, and amethyst. Introduced in late 1924 and produced until the late 1920s. All colors have a satin iridescent stretch or an onion-skin finish, and were described as "crizzled."
Imperial blue	A transparent blue, used for satin vases during 1982.
Imperial green	A light transparent green, circa 1930s.
Iris ice	White or pearl with an onion-skin, or satin iridescent finish. Described as "white crizzled on crystal glass." Introduced in late 1924 and produced until the late 1920s.
Ivory satin	An opaque creamy "off-white," similar to Midwest custard, circa 1978 – 1980.
Jade or Imperial jade	An opaque green, introduced as dynasty jade in 1960. Made again in 1980 – 1983.
Jade slag	Milk glass with shades of blue and green swirled in. Circa 1975 – 1977.
Jonquil	An opaque yellow, circa 1959 – 1960.
Larkspur blue	A transparent blue, circa late 1950s, used for the Provincial line.
Lemon frost	A dark yellow satin, introduced 1982 – 1983.
Lichen green	Opaque green, introduced in 1955. The color was withdrawn after a very short production time and not produced again.
Light blue	A transparent light blue, circa 1979 – 1980.
Madeira	A transparent dark amber, circa 1957 – 1960.
Mandarin gold	A transparent deep rich yellow, circa 1962 – 1965. This was a reissue of the Cambridge color.
Meadow green	Green with an iridescent finish, circa 1980 – early 1981.
Midwest custard	An opaque creamy "off-white," circa 1956 – 1959.
Milk glass	Opaque white. Advertised as "vintage milk glass," it was first made in the 1930s and then heavily produced and advertised from 1951 – 1970, and again from 1977 – 1979. Made glossy or with a doeskin finish.
Mint green satin	Introduced in 1981.
Mist blue	A light transparent grayish blue, circa mid-1962 – 1966. An advertisement from 1955 also mentions blue mist.
Moonlight blue	A light transparent blue that was produced from a Cambridge formula and used for Cambridge reissues, circa 1962 – 1965.
Moonstone blue	A deep rich transparent blue, circa 1978 – 1982.
Mulberry	A plain transparent amethyst, circa mid-1920s and again in 1961.
Murrhina	Crystal glass rolled into "frit," or finely crushed glass, then into crystal again to trap the tiny fragments, heated again, and stretched to form swirls in the glass, circa early 1959. Frit colors included cobalt blue, green, orange, ruby, or brown.
Mustard	A vivid transparent yellow, made only for a short time during 1960.
Nugreen (or "reef aqua")	A transparent bluish-green or teal, introduced in the 1920s.
Nuruby	An bright transparent red iridescent, circa 1911 – early 1920s. Also called red iridescent in early advertisements.
Nut brown	A transparent dark brown, circa 1968 – 1983.
Old gold	A rich gold iridescent on amber glass. Introduced mid-1911 and produced through late 1917.
Olde Flint	Crystal with a grainy look, circa 1960 – 1965.
Old lavender	A transparent medium amethyst, circa mid-1962 – 1966.
Olive	A transparent green similar to verde, circa 1968.
Opal	An opaque white, originally made in the 1930s and 1940s. Re-introduced 1949 – 1950 (see milk glass).
Opaque blue	Also called Forget-me-not blue. A light pastel blue. Produced from 1955 through the early 1960s.
Opaque custard	A creamy off-white, advertised as a "revival of ivory glass from the 1890s." Produced late 1950s – early 1960s.
Peach Blo	Cased glass with a milk glass interior and ruby shading to yellow on the exterior. Circa 1964. Advertised as "an imitation of Art Glass from the 1880s."
Peacock iridescent	Often referred to as smoke. Imperial described it as "very brilliant iridescence with every color of the rainbow, a golden yellow predominates." This was applied on crystal glass. Introduced in 1911, reintroduced in 1965, and again 1970 – 1971 and 1981.
Pearl colors	A group of iridescent colors introduced in July of 1916.
Pearl amethyst	A stretch iridescent medium amethyst. Introduced mid-1916 and discontinued about 1924.

Pearl green	A stretch gray-green iridescence on light green glass. Introduced mid-1916 and discontinued about 1924.
Pearl ruby	A heavy yellow/orange or deep marigold iridescence on crystal. Circa mid–1916 – 1920's. According to John Madeley and Dave Shetlar's *American Iridescent Stretch Glass*, this is probably the same color as nuruby iridescent.
Pearl silver	A dark purple glass with a silvery, stretch iridescence, circa 1916 – 1920s.
Pearl white	A white stretch iridescence on crystal glass. Added to the line in 1917 and discontinued in the early 1920s.
Pearl Venetian	Described as "a delicate iridescent on clear crystal," it was added to the pearl line of colors in late 1921 or early 1922 and was only listed in the one catalog.
Pink	A transparent pink, produced in the 1920s as Rose Marie. In 1926, the name was changed to rose pink, and the term "pink" was used again in 1955, 1961 – 1966, and 1978 – 1982.
Pink carnival	A transparent, iridescent pink, circa 1978 – 1982.
Pink satin	A light pink satin, circa 1980 – 1983.
Plum 1	A very dark purple. Produced in the early 1930s and again in 1973.
Plum 2	A deep rich transparent amethyst, circa 1981 – 1983.
Purple	Amethyst, circa 1906.
Purple glaze	A dark amethyst glass with a very dark blue iridescent finish, circa 1911.
Purple slag	Milk glass with various shades of purple swirled in. January 1959 – 1974.
Red glow	A yellow/orange iridescent on crystal glass, usually with a satin effect. Circa 1920s. Very similar to Nuruby.
Regal ruby	A deep transparent ruby, circa 1962 – 1963. Used for the No. 3797 Cambridge Square reissue.
Ritz blue	A transparent dark blue or cobalt, circa 1932 – 1943.
Rose ice	Pink with an onion-skin, or satin iridescent finish. Described as "pink crizzled on crystal glass." Circa 1924 – late 1920s.
Rose Marie	A transparent pink, circa 1926 – 1930s. Later called rose pink.
Rubigold	An iridescent deep marigold on crystal glass that was made circa 1909 – 1932 as Imperial's first iridescent color. It was reintroduced in 1965 – 1980. The color is commonly called marigold carnival or marigold iridescent.
Ruby	A transparent red, introduced in 1931 and continued to be made on and off throughout Imperial's history.
Ruby ice	Iridescent red with an onion-skin, or satin iridescent finish on crystal glass. Described as "crizzled," circa late 1924.
Sapphire	A dark bluish gray iridescent or smoke finish on crystal glass, introduced 1925.
Sea Foam colors	Imperial's first opalescent colors.
Sea foam blue	Also called Harding blue. A transparent blue with opalescent edges, circa 1931.
Sea foam green	Also called moss green. A transparent green with opalescent edges, circa 1931.
Sea foam pink	Also called burnt almond, with opalescent edges, circa 1931.
Smoke	A transparent gray, circa 1955 and again in 1966.
Stiegel green	A dark, transparent bluish green, originally circa mid-1930s. Reissued circa 1955 – 1962 and 1980 – 1981.
Sunburst carnival	An iridescent sunshine yellow, circa 1982 – 1983.
Sunset ruby	A golden iridescent ruby, introduced 1968 – 1973.
Sunshine yellow	A vivid, golden transparent yellow, circa 1974 – 1984.
Topaz	A transparent canary, or vaseline color. Circa 1930s. Previously referred to as golden green.
Turquoise	An opaque powder blue, circa 1955 – 1965.
Ultra blue	A transparent dark blue, circa 1975 – 1984.
Venetian	One of the "Pearl" colors. Described as a "delicate iridescent on clear crystal glass." Only listed in one catalog in late 1921, or early 1922.
Verde	A transparent olive green, made circa 1951 – 1985.
Viennese blue	A light transparent blue very similar to moonlight blue, circa 1937 – 1938. Also mentioned in an advertisement from 1955.
Vigna Vetro	Same as murrhina, but on a milk glass base. Circa early 1959.
White carnival	An iridescent finish over crystal, circa 1973 – 1976, and again in 1980 – 1981.

Amber ice	an iridescent amber satin, circa 1924. Produced until the late 1920s.
Amethyst ice	an iridescent amethyst satin, circa 1924. Produced until the late 1920s.
Blue ice	an iridescent blue satin, circa 1924. Produced until the late 1920s.
Green ice	an iridescent blue-green satin, circa 1924. Produced until the late 1920s.
Iris ice	an iridescent white satin or mother o' pearl, circa 1924. Produced until the late 1920s.
Rose ice	an iridescent pink satin, circa 1924. Produced until the late 1920s.
Ruby ice	an iridescent red satin, circa 1924. Produced until the late 1920s.

FINISHES

Although Imperial produced satin glassware throughout its history, the majority of it was manufactured during the second half of the company's existence. In 1950, they coined the term "doeskin" to describe a satin finish that was being applied to a number of items in milk glass and other opaque colors. In 1953, the same finish was used on black glass under the name "black suede." Black suede was actually first introduced during the early 1940s and was quite popular, but lack of materials during World War II caused Imperial to discontinue it in 1943 with relatively few pieces having been made. Since satinized items required additional finishing, they originally sold for more than their plain equivalents, but today's collectors seem split over which finish is more desirable and differences in value are usually slight. Therefore, our pricing will not usually differentiate between glossy and satin finished items. An exception is the black suede line, which still commands a premium price. Names used for later satin colors are listed below:

Blue satin, circa 1979.

Brown smoke, circa 1960s.

Cranberry or cranberry ruby, circa 1960s.

Crystal satin, circa 1979 (name changed to satin crystal in 1980).

Golden amber, circa 1960s.

Ivory satin, circa 1978.

Lemon frost satin, circa 1982 – 1983.

Mint green satin, circa 1981.

Mist blue, circa 1960s.

Old lavender, circa 1960s.

Pink satin, circa 1980.

MARKS

Imperial used a variety of marks in advertising, on their labels, and in many cases, on the glass itself. Their earliest trademarks, Nucut in 1911, followed by Nuart in 1912, were both used on glass, but not on any candlesticks. In 1913, they began using the mark referred to by collectors today as the "Iron Cross" or "Double I," sometimes by itself and sometimes with the letters "IMPERIAL" arranged on all four sides of the cross. (It is interesting to note that they applied for trademarks for the cross by itself and for the arrangement of letters by itself, so that when they combined them, they were actually using two trademarks simultaneously.) This mark will occasionally be found on pieces from the early years.

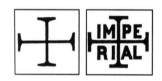

TRADEMARKS,
1913 – 1920s/1930s

In 1951, they began using the IG mark. Although they often did not use it on many of their most popular patterns, it does appear on many other pieces made between 1951 and 1972. When Lenox bought the company, the mark changed to LIG, and remained in use from 1973 to 1981. When Arthur Lorch acquired the factory, he added a slanted A to the mark, and ALIG was used from 1981 to 1982. During the final years of attempted reorganization (1983 – 1984), some items were sold marked NI for "New Imperial."

MARKS: IG (1951 – 1972),
LIG (1973 – 1981), ALIG
(1981 – 1982), NI (1983 – 1984)

A variety of labels were also used during these years. The Heisey by Imperial and Cambridge by Imperial labels were used in the 1960s, after Imperial bought out both of those companies. It should be noted that between 1959 and 1969, pieces made from Heisey molds often retained Heisey's Diamond H mark, which can be confusing to collectors today. This was perfectly legal, since Imperial had also purchased the rights to the trademark. However, after 1969, they voluntarily agreed to discontinue using it.

LABEL,
LATE 1930S – 1973

ADVERTISING SIGN

LABEL, 1970S – 1980S

HEISEY BY
IMPERIAL LABEL,
1959 – 1960S

CAMBRIDGE BY
IMPERIAL LABEL,
EARLY 1960S

IMPERIAL BY LENOX
LABEL, 1973 – 1981

IM-1: No. 9
CANDLESTICK
WITH SAUCER,
FROM 1909
CATALOG

No. 9 candlestick with saucer. 4¼" high with a 5¾" diameter base. Circa 1904 – 1916. Made in crystal. This candlestick was part of a pattern of about 30 pieces, and appeared in Imperial's very first catalog. $45.00 – 60.00.

IM-2. No. 119 CRUCIFIX CANDLESTICKS IN
AMETHYST AND MARIGOLD CARNIVAL.
NOTE STEPPED BASE ON
AMETHYST CANDLESTICK

No. 119 crucifix candlestick. 9½" high with a 4" or 4¼" octagonal base. Circa 1904 – 1924 in crystal, amethyst, and rubigold (marigold carnival), and reissued in milk glass in 1955. According to a catalog page in the materials from the Imperial archives microfilmed by the Corning Museum of Glass, the crucifix was "also furnished in purple colored glass." A typed date of 1906 has been added to this page, presumably years later by whoever arranged these materials in Imperial's files, but is probably reliable within a year or so. This would explain the scarcity of the amethyst crucifixes, since between 1909 and the late 1920s, it was advertised in crystal only. Another oddity regarding this candleholder is that there appears to have been two molds from the very beginning. The amethyst and milk glass versions have a stepped 4¼" base, whereas the crystal and rubigold versions usually have a 4" straight sided base. (The difference can be clearly seen in the accompanying photograph.) This seems to indicate that the stepped base mold was used at the very beginning, then not used again until the 1950s. All catalogs from 1909 until the introduction of the milk glass version show the straight sided base. Over the years, this candlestick has also been listed as No. 119½, No. 11/119, No. 30/119 (in amethyst), and No. 1950/119 (in milk glass). Crystal: $15.00 – 20.00. Milk glass: $40.00 – 50.00. Amethyst: $150.00 – 200.00. Rubigold (rare): $600.00 – market.

IM-3. No. 1
CANDLESTICK

No. 1 candlestick. 9¼" high with a 4⅞" diameter round base. Circa 1909 (or earlier) – 1924. Made in crystal. $30.00 – 45.00.

No. 246 candlestick. 9¼" high. Circa 1909 (or earlier) – 1924. Made in crystal. This is very similar in shape to a bitters bottle in the same line. The catalog picture makes it appear to be hollow inside, so it is possible that both were made from a single mold. $40.00 – 50.00.

IM-4. No. 246 CANDLESTICK, FROM 1909 CATALOG

No. 352 candlestick. Called Six-Sided by collectors. 7½" high with a 3⅞" base. Circa 1909 (or earlier) – 1920s. Made in crystal, crystal with a fired-on gold finish (as No. G352), and the scarce colors of azur (amethyst carnival), old gold (amber carnival), rubigold (marigold), and helio (green) carnival. It has also been reported in peacock iridescent (smoke). By the 1920s, this was also known as No. 352½. In the 1960s, the mold was modified to remove the patterning on the ridges of the stem and it was reissued as No. 43790. (See IM-161 on p. 223.) Westmoreland's No. 240 candlestick (seen in IM-5a) is a similar imitation cut glass design, but with a little study it is easy to tell them apart. Crystal: $20.00 – 25.00. Helio, rubigold: $125.00 – 175.00. Old gold, peacock iridescent: $200.00 – market. Azur: $300.00 – market.

IM-5A. WESTMORELAND No. 240 CANDLESTICK

IM-5. No. 352 CANDLESTICK IN AZUR

No. 41 candlestick. Also listed as No. 41½. Called Delta Base by collectors. 7" high with a 3½" base. Circa 1910 – 1929. Made in amber, crystal, golden green, milk glass, rubigold (marigold carnival), mulberry, nuruby (iridescent red), peacock (smoke iridescent), and possibly in old gold (amber carnival). Crystal, amber: $15.00 – 20.00. Mulberry: $20.00 – 25.00. Golden green, rubigold: $30.00 – 40.00. Old gold, peacock iridescent: $50.00 – 60.00. Nuruby: $75.00 – market.

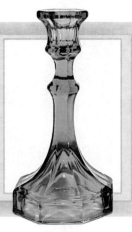

IM-6. No. 41 CANDLESTICK IN AMBER

No. 419 candlestick. Called Delta Base by collectors. 8⅞" high with a 4" base. Circa 1910 – 1929. Made in amber, crystal, mulberry, nuruby (iridescent red), peacock (smoke iridescent), old gold (amber carnival), and rubigold (marigold carnival). Crystal, amber: $20.00 – 25.00. Mulberry: $25.00 – 30.00. Rubigold: $50.00 – 75.00. Old gold, peacock iridescent: $65.00 – 90.00. Nuruby: $100.00 – market.

IM-7. No. 419 CANDLESTICK IN MULBERRY

IM-8. No. 700
CANDLESTICK IN
RUBIGOLD

No. 700 candlestick. 7¼" high with a 3¾" base. Circa 1910 – 1924 and 1937 – 1950. Made in crystal and rubigold (marigold carnival). Offered as part of the Etiquette line in 1943, it also can be found with six ball feet (making it 7½" high), or with a candle insert and prisms. Other companies made very similar candlesticks, most notably Heisey and Tarentum. The Imperial version is thicker at the neck. For a comparison of the three candlesticks, see HE-21a on p. 107. Crystal: $15.00 – 20.00. Rubigold: $25.00 – 30.00.

In 1923, Imperial introduced a line of "Free Hand Ware," or blown art glass, produced by a talented group of foreign-born glass artisans. The line included several candleholders and was heavily advertised, but it was expensive, failed to catch on, and was discontinued after just a few years. It took almost a decade for Imperial to sell off their inventory, and eventually the items were closed out at a fraction of their original prices. Reportedly, these were the same workers who produced a similar line of free hand ware for the Fenton Art Glass Company shortly after leaving Imperial. Unfortunately, Fenton had no better luck selling this merchandise than Imperial, and they also discontinued the line within a year. Ironically, these are currently among the most sought-after items Imperial and Fenton ever produced.

IM-9. FULL PAGE AD FOR FREE HAND WARE, FROM THE JULY 5, 1923 ISSUE OF *Crockery and Glass Journal*

FREE HAND
LABEL, CA. 1923

IM-9A. NO. 128
FREE HAND WARE
CANDLESTICK IN
ORANGE, WITH
COBALT SOCKET
AND BASE

No. 128 Free Hand Ware candlestick. 10¾" high with a 4" base. This is just one example of the extensive line of free hand ware, or blown art glass, manufactured by Imperial between 1923 and 1924. Most items were made in dominant colors of blue, green, and orange. Many styles similar to this were offered, some with applied handles, usually in contrasting colors. Designs included "hanging hearts" and "King Tut" (Egyptian-inspired) motifs. Colored threading and vivid iridescent finishes were also used. All colors in similar styles: $300.00 – market.

No. 319/30 Lead Lustre candlestick. 9⅛" high with a 3½" base. Circa 1924. The lead lustre line was blown into a paste mold (no seams), and was an attempt to offer an art glass line at a much lower cost than the pricey Free Hand Ware (see IM-9). Unfortunately, it was no more popular than its upscale cousin, and its manufacture was discontinued within a year. Remaining inventories persisted until the late 1920s, when they were closed out at bargain prices. Made in orange iridescent with a milky white interior, cobalt with an orange iridescent interior, and gray iridescent with an orange iridescent interior. All colors: $125.00 – market.

IM-10. No. 319/30 Lead Lustre candlestick in milk white cased in orange

No. 671 candlestick. 6⅞" high with a 3½" diameter round base. Named Amelia by Hazel Marie Weatherman and sometimes called Flute and Cane by collectors. Circa early 1920s – 1935 and 1982 – 1984. Made in crystal and rubigold (marigold carnival). Can be found with a plain base or with a molded "cane" pattern on the base rim. Early versions also had sunbursts pressed in each of the panels on the top of the base. Listed as No. 671½ in the mid–1920s, and later reissued as No. 43794. Colors at that time included caramel slag and milk glass. Crystal: $20.00 – 25.00. Caramel slag: $50.00 – 60.00. Rubigold: $80.00 – market.

IM-11. No. 671 candlesticks (two versions – note impressed sunbursts on the base on the right)

No. 635 candlestick. Called Premium by collectors. 8½" high with a 4⅛" base. Circa 1924 – 1930. Available in amber, green, Rose Marie, nugreen (teal), rubigold (marigold carnival), peacock iridescent, mulberry, golden green, and black. Plain crystal is also likely. Scarce or rare examples in azur (mulberry iridescent), old gold (amber iridescent), iris ice (white stretch), green ice (stretch), nuruby (iridescent red), and helio (green) carnival are said to exist, but we have not seen them. Sold with a plain base (No. 635) or a swirled pattern base (No. 635/3), called twisted optic by collectors. It was also offered with at least one cutting (No. 91). This design is similar to one from the Diamond Glass-ware Company (see DI-9 on p. 134 of volume one in this series). Tiffin's No. 300 candlestick is also similar, but is taller (10") and the arrangement of the rings at the top of the column is reversed, with the wider ring appearing below the narrow one. Amber, crystal: $12.00 – 15.00. Black, green, Rose Marie: $20.00 – 25.00. Nugreen, peacock iridescent, rubigold: $25.00 – 35.00. Golden green: $40.00 – 50.00.

IM-12. No. 635 Premium candlesticks in peacock iridescent, rubigold, and black

No. 677 candlestick. 7⅜" high with a 3½" square base. Circa 1924 – 1930. Known in black and crystal, both clear and with a satin finish. Offered with several cuttings, including No. 274½. This is very similar to Imperial's No. 6247 (see IM-17 p. 183), but the No. 677 has beveled corners and the glass quality is not as good, indicating that this candlestick was probably aimed at a lower priced market. That would also explain why two near-identical candleholders were being made at the same time. Crystal: $12.00 – 15.00. Black, cut crystal: $15.00 – 22.50.

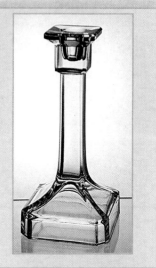

IM-13. No. 677
CANDLESTICK IN BLACK

IM-13A. No. 677
CANDLESTICK

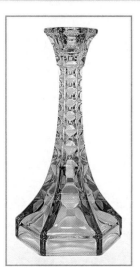

No. 765 candlestick. 9" high with a 4¼" base. Circa 1924 – 1940s. Made in crystal and green, with other colors possible. Designed by Phillip Ebeling, who was also responsible for Fostoria's American pattern. It was first introduced as Prism Crystal. Later the name was changed to Triangle, then to Lincoln. In the 1930s it was called Mount Vernon, but it was changed once again, this time to Washington, to avoid confusion with Cambridge's Mount Vernon line. During this long and complicated history, various other candleholders were added to the line. (See IM-33 on p. 188, IM-38 on p. 190, and IM-45 on p. 192.) Crystal: $25.00 – 30.00. Green: $35.00 – 45.00.

IM-14. No. 765 PRISM
(MOUNT VERNON)
CANDLESTICK IN GREEN

IM-14A. No. 765 PRISM
CRYSTAL candlestick,
FROM CA. 1924 CATALOG

No. 6007 candlestick. 6⅞" high with a 3⅜" base. Circa 1924 – 1943, but possibly made as late as the early 1950s. Made in nuruby iridescent, peacock iridescent (or smoke), pearl amethyst, sapphire iridescent, and nugreen (teal). Like most Imperial candleholders, these were often sold as part of a console set. Nugreen, rubigold: $20.00 – 30.00. Nuruby iridescent, peacock iridescent, pearl amethyst, sapphire iridescent: $50.00 – market.

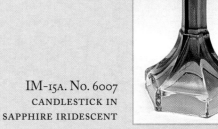

IM-15. No. 6007 CANDLESTICKS IN
RUBIGOLD AND NUGREEN. NUGREEN
EXAMPLE SHOWN WITH AN OPTIONAL
CANDELABRA INSERT

IM-15A. No. 6007
CANDLESTICK IN
SAPPHIRE IRIDESCENT

No. 6009 candlestick. 8⅞" high with a 4" base. Circa 1924 – 1930s. Known in blue, crystal, green ice (stretch finish), and nugreen (teal). Other colors from the era are probable. Advertised as "double polished." Crystal: $20.00 – 30.00. Blue, nugreen: $25.00 – 35.00. Green ice: $120.00 – market.

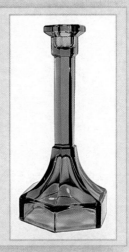

IM-16. No. 6009 CANDLESTICK IN NUGREEN

No. 6247 candlestick. 7" high. Circa 1924 – 1925, and possibly again in 1943 – 1950. Made in crystal, green, and Rose Marie. Can be found with No. 61, 63, 66, and 274½ cuttings, and others are possible. The Indiana Glass Company made a seemingly identical candlestick in the same size, circa 1925. (See IN-7 on p. 238.) The Indiana candlestick was probably made only in crystal. Another similar candlestick was also made by Imperial at about the same time as No. 677 (see IM-13 on the preceding page), but in lesser quality crystal with beveled edges. Crystal: $15.00 – 20.00. Green, Rose Marie: $25.00 – 35.00. Add 20 – 40% for cut.

No. 6249 candlestick. 9" high. Circa 1924 – 1925. Made in crystal, green, and Rose Marie. Offered with No. 61, 63, and 66 cuttings, and others are possible. Crystal: $18.00 – 25.00. Green, Rose Marie: $30.00 – 40.00. Add 20% – 40% for cut.

No. 62412 candlestick. 12" high with a 4" base. Circa 1924 – 1925. Made in crystal, green, and Rose Marie. Available with No. 61, 63, and 66 cuttings, advertised as "high grade hand cuttings on extra polished crystal." Others are possible. Crystal: $40.00 – 50.00. Green, Rose Marie: $60.00 – 75.00. Add 20 – 40% for cut.

IM-19A. No. 62412 CANDLESTICK IN CRYSTAL WITH No. 66 CUTTING

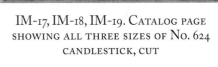

IM-17, IM-18, IM-19. CATALOG PAGE SHOWING ALL THREE SIZES OF No. 624 CANDLESTICK, CUT

No. 734 candlestick. 8½" high. Circa mid-1920s. Made in crystal and available with the No. 451 Monticello cutting, with others possible. Crystal: $20.00 – 25.00. Add 10 – 30% for cut.

IM-20. No. 734 CANDLESTICK WITH No. 451 MONTICELLO CUTTING, FROM UNDATED CATALOG

IM-21. No. 675 CANDLESTICKS IN GREEN, RUBIGOLD, AND GOLDEN GREEN

No. 675 candlestick. 3⅜" high with a 3⅜" base. Circa 1925 – 1930. Made in amber, blue, crystal, green, golden green, Rose Marie, and in the carnival colors of rubigold (marigold) and peacock. Known to collectors as Tree of Life, and in carnival as Soda Gold. The veining on this pattern is very pronounced, and raised from the stippled surface of the candleholder. Crystal, amber: $8.00 – 10.00. Green, blue, Rose Marie: $12.00 – 15.00. Rubigold, golden green: $20.00 – 25.00. Peacock: $25.00 – 35.00.

No. 715 candlestick. The plain base version was later listed as No. 320/1. Also available with a twisted optic base as No. 715/3. Named Packard by Hazel Marie Weatherman, but better known today by the name carnival glass collectors gave it, Double Scroll.

IM-22. No. 715 CANDLESTICKS IN RUBY AND GOLDEN GREEN

3⅜" high with a 3⅞" x 4¾" oval base. Circa 1925 – 1930s and 1982 – 1983. Made in amber, black, golden green, green, Rose Marie, and ruby. In 1982, it was reissued in lemon frost and pink carnival, both with a twisted optic base, as No. 51795SYS. Offered cut with Imperial's No. 200 and 451 Monticello cuttings, American Beauty Rose (offered by Larkin in 1934), an unknown laurel leaf cutting, and probably others. Amber, green, black, Rose Marie: $15.00 – 20.00. Lemon frost, pink carnival: $25.00 – 30.00. Golden green, ruby: $30.00 – 40.00. Add 10% for cut or for twisted optic base.

No. 320/2 candlestick. Also listed as No. 313/2 and as No. 3130 with a twisted optic base. Named Packard by Hazel Marie Weatherman, but better known today by the name carnival glass collectors gave it, Double Scroll. 8½" high with a 3⅞" x 4¾" base. Circa 1925 – 1935. Made in amber, green, golden green, Rose Marie, ruby, nugreen (teal), mulberry, rubigold (marigold carnival), peacock iridescent, red glow, and green ice (and possibly any of the other "ice" colors). Can be found with the following cuttings: No. 15, 200, 280, 451 Monticello, and probably others. Amber, green, Rose Marie: $25.00 – 30.00. Nugreen, rubigold: $35.00 – 40.00. Mulberry, peacock: $35.00 – 40.00. Golden green, ruby: $45.00 – 60.00. Red glow, green ice: $110.00 – market. Add 10 – 20% for cut or for twisted optic base.

IM-23. No. 320/2 CANDLESTICKS IN RED GLOW, GREEN ICE, AND GOLDEN GREEN

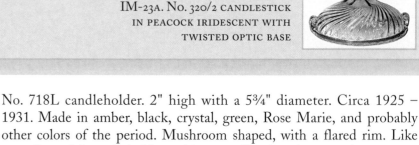

IM-23A. No. 320/2 CANDLESTICK IN PEACOCK IRIDESCENT WITH TWISTED OPTIC BASE

IM-24. No. 718L CANDLEHOLDER IN BLACK

No. 718L candleholder. 2" high with a 5¾" diameter. Circa 1925 – 1931. Made in amber, black, crystal, green, Rose Marie, and probably other colors of the period. Mushroom shaped, with a flared rim. Like most Imperial candleholders, this was offered with a matching center bowl. Available with gold or silver decoration, probably by an independent decorating firm. This mold was probably modified to be used for the No. 400/86 candlewick candleholder (see IM-55 on p. 195). Crystal: $8.00 – 10.00. Amber: $10.00 – 12.50. Green, Rose Marie: $15.00 – 20.00. Black, blue: $20.00 – 25.00.

No. 718R candleholder. Known as No. 414R when made with an impressed Diamond Quilted pattern (also known as Flat Diamond to collectors). 2" high and 4½" across. Circa 1925 – 1931. Made in amber, black, blue, crystal, green, and Rose Marie. Mushroom shaped, with a cupped rim. Offered as part of several console sets. The plain version was available with No. 19, 201, 202, and 204 cuttings. Other decorations were probably offered as well. At least two other companies offered rolled-edge candleholders, but both Cambridge's No. 632 (CB-62 on p. 67 of volume one of this series) and Fostoria's No. 2372 (FO-62 on p. 28) rest directly on their rolled-down rims, whereas the Imperial candleholder has a 2½" diameter foot. For another candlestick in the Diamond Quilted pattern, see IM-29 on the following page. Crystal: $8.00 – 10.00. Amber: $10.00 – 12.50. Green, Rose Marie: $15.00 – 20.00. Black, blue: $20.00 – 25.00. Add 10 – 20% for diamond optic. Add 20 – 40% for cut.

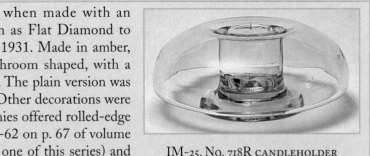

IM-25. No. 718R CANDLEHOLDER IN ROSE MARIE

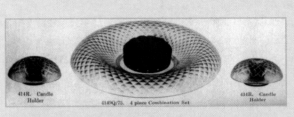

IM-25A. No. 414R DIAMOND QUILTED CONSOLE SET, FROM CATALOG

No. 727L candleholder. 2" high and 5½" diameter. Circa 1925 – 1931. Made in amber, crystal, green, and Rose Marie. Mushroom shaped, with a flared hexagonal edge. Offered as part of several console sets. In addition to the flared edge version and the rolled edge one discussed below, IM-26a shows a third style, with the edge turned up to form a cup. It is 3¼" high with a 3¾" diameter at the top and a 2⅛" diameter foot. Amber, crystal: $12.00 – 15.00. Green, Rose Marie: $15.00 – 20.00. Add 20 – 40% for cut.

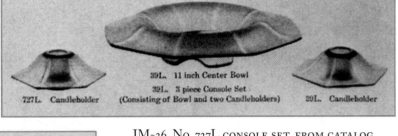

IM-26. No. 727L CONSOLE SET, FROM CATALOG

IM-26A. No. 727 CANDLESTICK IN ROSE MARIE, WITH VARIANT TREATMENT TO EDGE

No. 727R candleholder. 2" high and 4½" across. Circa 1925 – 1931. Made in amber, crystal, green, and Rose Marie. Mushroom shaped, with a rolled hexagonal edge. Offered as a part of several console sets. Available with several cuttings. We have seen a very similar candlestick attributed to the Beaumont Company, but have found no confirmation for this. McKee's No. 156 rolled edge candleholder is also somewhat similar, but has eight scallops rather than six. Amber, crystal: $12.00 – $15.00. Green, Rose Marie: $15.00 – $20.00. Add 20 – 40% for cut.

IM-27. No. 727R CANDLEHOLDER IN AMBER, WITH UNKNOWN CUTTING

IM-28. No. 637/3 candlesticks in amber and in rubigold with a crystal socket, both with a Twisted Optic domed base

No. 637 candlestick. 3⅜" high with a 4⅝" dome base. Circa 1925 – 1930. Made in amber, green, rubigold (marigold carnival) with a crystal socket, golden green, Ritz blue, black, ruby, Stiegel green, and Rose Marie. Offered as part of various console sets, it was also available with a Twisted Optic base (No. 637/3), a flat base (No. 637D, IM-28a), a plain domed base, and a diamond quilted base (IM-28b). The latter does not appear in any catalog that we have seen and is sometimes identified with the No. 414 pattern, known to collectors as Diamond Quilted (or Flat Diamond); however, the pattern of diamonds is very different on this candlestick, so we do not believe that it was intended to match. At least four cuttings were offered on the plain base (flat or domed version): No. 16, 91, 207, and No. 465 Viking. Others are possible. Also found with a blue and white, or a pink and white intaglio painted decoration on the underside of the base (IM-28c). For another candlestick in the Twisted Optic pattern, see IM-32 on the following page. Amber, rubigold: $10.00 – 15.00. Rose Marie, green, Stiegel green, painted: $15.00 – 20.00. Crystal with intaglio decoration, golden green, ruby, Ritz blue: $25.00 – 35.00. Add 10 – 20% for twisted optic or diamond quilted base. Add 20 – 40% for cut.

IM-28A. No. 637D candlestick with flat base, from catalog

IM-28B. No. 637 candlesticks in Rose Marie (with plain domed base) and green (with Diamond Quilted domed base)

IM-28c. No. 637 candlestick in crystal with pink and white intaglio decoration

IM-29. No. 39 candlestick with Pillar Flute base

No. 39 candlestick. Also sold with a Diamond Quilted base as No. 414/1 (also known to collectors today as Flat Diamond; IM-29a), and a ribbed base as No. 7796 Empire (IM-29b). 2⅝" high with a 4¼" base. Circa 1925 – 1943. Made in black, blue, crystal, green, Rose Marie, and ruby. The No. 39 candlesticks were shown on a catalog page featuring the No. 682 pattern, known as Pillar Flute. For an earlier candleholder in the Diamond Quilted pattern, see IM-25 on the preceding page. For another candleholder in the Empire pattern, see IM-39 on p. 190. Crystal: $6.00 – 8.00. Green, Rose Marie: $10.00 – 15.00. Black, blue (Diamond Quilted or Empire base), ruby: $22.00 – 27.50.

IM-29A. No. 414/1 Diamond Quilted candlestick in green

IM-29B. No. 7796 Empire candlestick

IS THIS IMPERIAL?

Candlestick. 2⅜" high with a 4⅜" diameter base. Probably made in the late 1920s or early 1930s. Known in green, pink, and marigold carnival. Is this Imperial? Probably not. Although this candleholder has sometimes been identified as Imperial's Twisted Optic pattern, we don't believe that it is. At this point, this is just an opinion since we can't say who did make it, but it appears to be machine made, which would point to the Federal Glass Company or the Jeannette Glass Company as likely candidates. U.S. Glass is also a possibility, and Imperial can't

IM-30. UNKNOWN CANDLESTICK IN GREEN, WITH REVERSE TWISTED OPTIC PATTERN ON BASE, OFTEN ATTRIBUTED TO IMPERIAL, BUT MORE LIKELY BY FEDERAL, JEANNETTE, OR SOMEONE ELSE

be ruled out, since all of these companies manufactured the colors this candleholder is known in, but we feel that Imperial is the least likely candidate of the four. The swirls go in the opposite direction from those on Twisted Optic pieces, there is a plain rim around the edge of the base that isn't seen on the Imperial pattern, and the quality just isn't that great. It is also made with no pattern on the base. Green, pink: $8.00 – 12.50. Marigold carnival: $15.00 – 20.00.

IM-30A. UNKNOWN CANDLESTICK IN GREEN (WITH PLAIN BASE) AND MARIGOLD CARNIVAL (WITH TWISTED OPTIC BASE)

No. 683/3 tray with candlestick. 8" high with a 9¾" diameter bowl. Sometimes referred to as Two Handled or Grecian. Appears in catalog 201, which dates to circa 1927 or 1928. Listed in amber, crystal, green, and Rose Marie. As can be seen in the accompanying reprint from that catalog, it was made with a swirled tray, and it was pictured on a page with pieces from the pattern known as Twisted Optic by collectors. Curiously, we have never seen it in any of these colors or with the swirl design. On the few occasions that this rather scarce item has turned up, it has always been iridized, and the bowl has been plain with a stretch treatment in blue ice or rubigold (marigold). The only non-iridized color we have seen it in is golden green. One source reports that these were originally sold as Christmas candlesticks. Crystal, amber, green, Rose Marie: $65.00 – $85.00. Rubigold: $85.00 – 100.00. Blue ice, golden green: $150.00 – market.

IM-31. No. 683/3 TRAY WITH CANDLE-STICK, FROM CA. 1927 – 1928 CATALOG

No. 708 candlestick. Known as Twisted Optic to collectors. 3⅜" high with a 3⅜" base. Circa 1927 – 1930. Made in amber, blue, golden green, green, and Rose Marie. Known to us only with the twisted optic base. For another candlestick in the Twisted Optic pattern, see IM-28 on the preceding page. Amber, green, Rose Marie: $10.00 – 15.00. Golden green, blue: $20.00 – 25.00.

IM-32. No. 708 CAN-DLESTICKS IN GREEN, GOLDEN GREEN, AND ROSE MARIE

IM-33. No. 134 Olive candleholders in Viennese blue and ruby

IM-33A. No. 6991 Washington candleholder

No. 73 candleholder (called Twisted Optic by collectors today), circa 1927 – 1930s in crystal and rubigold (marigold carnival); No. 134 Olive candleholder, circa 1930s in crystal, ruby, and Viennese blue; No. 6991 Washington candleholder, circa 1930s – 1940s, in crystal only; unknown pattern number candlestick, circa 1936 in ruby and probably crystal. All 2½" high with a 4" base. As can be seen from the above listings, this same basic shape served multiple duties over the years, with different designs impressed underneath the base. The earliest was the familiar twisted optic design on the No. 73 (not pictured, but similar to that seen on several of the candlesticks on preceding pages). The thumbprint design (No. 134, shown in IM-33) was part of the Olive pattern, but is often associated with the No. 166 Old English pattern, made at the same time. Catalog pages show Olive and Old English pieces intermixed, though the latter pieces tend to have more elongated thumbprints than Olive. The prism design on the No. 6991 (IM-33a) has an even more complicated history. When this candlestick was made, it was an addition to a pattern that had been around since the early 1920s as Prism Crystal and then Triangle. In the 1930s it was called Mount Vernon, but in 1942 was changed once again, this time to Washington, to avoid confusion with Cambridge's Mount Vernon line. During this long and complicated history, various other candleholders were added to the line. (See IM-14 on p. 182, IM-38 on p. 190, and IM-45 on p. 192.) A fourth version of this candlestick was advertised in a Butler Brothers catalog from 1936, in ruby, under the heading of "Imperial hand made gift glassware"

IM-33B. Candlestick, unknown pattern number, from Butler Brothers' 1936 catalog

(IM-33b). This candleholder was reissued from 1994 to 1998 by Dalzell Viking as No. 2157, featuring three of the aforementioned patterns (all but Olive). (See DV-16, p. 129 in volume one of this series.) Crystal: $6.00 – 10.00. Rubigold, ruby, Viennese blue: $15.00 – 20.00.

IM-34. No. 728 candleholder in Ritz blue

No. 728 candleholder. Also listed as No. 727. Called Munsell by Hazel Marie Weatherman. 3⅛" high with a 3" diameter round foot. Circa 1931 – 1933. Made in crystal, green, Ritz blue, rose pink, ruby, Stiegel green, and topaz. Available with the following cuttings: No. 451 Monticello, 600 (on ruby), and 2503 Noel. Other cuttings are possible. Crystal: $15.00 – 20.00. Green, rose pink: $30.00 – 35.00. Stiegel green, topaz: $35.00 – 40.00. Ritz blue, ruby: $40.00 – 50.00. Add 20 – 30% for cut.

IM-35. No. 169 twin candlestick with unknown cutting

No. 169 twin candlestick. 5¼" high with a 4½" x 3⅝" oval base. Circa early 1930s. Known in crystal and Ritz blue; other colors from the period are possible. Cuttings are likely; this candlestick has also been seen with an ornate decoration of silver and dark blue stain applied to portions of the body, probably done by another company. In later years, the mold was modified by adding balls to the outside of the circular stem to make the No. 782 candleholder, one of the earliest pieces that led to what became the Candlewick line. (See IM-51 on p. 194.) Crystal: $15.00 – 20.00. Ritz blue: $40.00 – 50.00. Add 10 – 30% for cuttings.

No. 153 twin candleholder. This pattern is sometimes referred to as Newbound, the name it was given by Hazel Marie Weatherman. 4⅜" high with a 3½" x 4¼" oval base. Circa 1933 – 1938. Reissued in milk glass as No. 1950/100 from 1950 through 1968. Some of the reissued milk glass candleholders have a rim around the top of the candle cup that was not present on the original version, apparently added sometime in the late 1950s or early 1960s. (See IM-36a for a comparison.) Although not officially part of the

IM-36. A GROUPING OF NO. 153 TWIN CANDLEHOLDERS. FRONT ROW: BLACK, RUBY, VIENNESE BLUE, GREEN. MIDDLE ROW: DARK AMBER, ROSE PINK, RITZ BLUE. BACK ROW: STIEGEL GREEN, CRYSTAL, LIGHT AMBER, MILK GLASS

pattern, these candleholders resemble (and were usually sold with) the Pillar Flute line. Made in amber (dark and light), black, crystal, Imperial green, Stiegel green, milk glass (glossy or doeskin), Ritz blue, rose pink, ruby, and Viennese blue. The example shown in IM-36b is in an opalescent moonstone, or clambroth, a color that we have not been able to document but that may be an early version of Imperial's opal (the precursor to their milk glass production in the 1930s). Crystal, late issue milk glass: $6.00 – $8.00. Amber, early issue milk glass: $8.00 – $10.00. Black, green, rose pink: $10.00 – $15.00. Stiegel green, Viennese blue: $20.00 – $25.00. Ruby, Ritz blue, moonstone: $25.00 – $35.00.

IM-36B. NO. 153 TWIN CANDLEHOLDER IN OPALESCENT MOONSTONE

IM-36A. NO. 153 TWIN CANDLEHOLDERS IN MILK GLASS, DOESKIN (SATIN) MILK GLASS, AND LATE ISSUE MILK GLASS (NOTE THE ADDITION OF A TOP RIM ON THE SOCKETS)

No. 760 square candleholder. 4¼" high with a 4" notched, square base. Circa early- to mid-1930s. Made in crystal, green, rose pink, ruby, and possibly black. We attribute this to Imperial because of its strong resemblance to the No. 760 line (named Hazen by Hazel Marie Weatherman), but we have not yet been able to confirm it through a catalog listing or ad. Available with at least one etching, as seen in the accompanying photograph, which we have also been unable to identify. Crystal: $15.00 – 20.00. Green, rose pink: $25.00 – 30.00. Ruby: $35.00 – 45.00. Add 20 – 40% for etched.

IM-37. SQUARE CANDLEHOLDER IN GREEN, BELIEVED TO BE NO. 760, WITH UNKNOWN ETCHING

IM-38. No. 749 LACED EDGE TWIN CANDLE-STICKS IN SEAFOAM GREEN AND SEAFOAM BLUE

No. 749 Laced Edge twin candlestick. Also known to collectors as Katy. 4½" high with a 4⅛" base. Circa 1935 – 1968. Made in amber, crystal, milk glass, Ritz blue, rose pink, ruby, seafoam blue, seafoam green, Stiegel green, and Viennese blue. In the 1960s it was available in burgundy, honey, and olive. Like many pieces in the line, this candleholder has an overall triangular pattern along with the lace edge detail. This pattern has an unusually complicated history. Although early catalog pages show this candlestick as part of the Laced Edge line, from 1935 – 1945 it was also sold by Montgomery Ward as Prism and then as Winthrop, the former name emphasizing its association with another pattern that had been around since the early 1920s (first as Prism Crystal and then as Triangle). When this candlestick joined that line in the 1930s, Imperial had begun marketing it as Mount Vernon, the name under which it was still being advertised in the fall 1942 Butler Brothers catalog. However, to complicate things further, Imperial's own January 1942 catalog had once again changed the name, this time to Washington, reportedly to avoid confusion with Cambridge's Mount Vernon line. (During this long and complicated history, various other candleholders were added to the line. See IM-14 on p. 182, IM-33 on p. 188, and IM-45 on p. 192.) But wait, the story isn't over. Between 1953 and 1964 this candlestick was offered in milk glass as No. 1950/279. In the 1960s, the pattern was sold through discount stores and offered as a premium by trading stamp companies as Belmont Crystal (a misleading name, since it was available in several colors). As if this weren't confusing enough, a 1939 Butler Bros. catalog offered this candlestick as handmade Fenton — a reference that we can only assume was an error. Another version of this candleholder was made with plain paneled sides in place of the triangular pattern as No. 780, replacing it in the Laced Edge line. (See IM-48 on p. 193.) For other Laced Edge candleholders, see IM-46 and IM-47 on p. 193. Crystal: $6.00 – 8.00. Amber, honey, olive: $10.00 – 15.00. Milk glass: $15.00 – 20.00. Rose pink, Viennese blue: $20.00 – 25.00. Stiegel green: $25.00 – 30.00. Burgundy, Ritz blue, ruby: $35.00 – 45.00. Seafoam blue, Seafoam green: $75.00 – 90.00.

IM-38A. No. 749 LACED EDGE TWIN CANDLESTICK IN MILK GLASS

IM-39. No. 779 EMPIRE DOLPHIN CANDLESTICKS IN VIENNESE BLUE AND CARAMEL SLAG

No. 779 Empire dolphin candlestick. 5" high. Early examples have a 3" square base, but later versions have an extra bead around the bottom that increases the base diameter to 3¼". Circa 1930s – 1968. Originally made in amber, crystal, green (rare color), and Viennese blue. Later made in black and gold (1953), black suede (1953), milk glass (as No. 1950/779, 1953 – 1960), caramel slag (1964 – 1968), and pink carnival (1981). Sears advertised this candlestick in 1938 as part of their Georgian pattern. The later versions are marked IG underneath the base. The Fenton Art Glass Company now owns this mold. For another candlestick in the Empire pattern, see IM-29b on p. 186. Crystal, amber: $15.00 – 20.00. Viennese blue, milk glass, pink carnival: $20.00 – 25.00. Caramel slag, black/gold flecked, green: $30.00 – 40.00. Black suede: $40.00 – $50.00.

No. 72 Tradition birthday cake plate. 13 – 14" in diameter. Originally made in the 1930s. Known in crystal and nut brown (believed to be rare). It holds 72 evenly spaced birthday candles around the plate rim. According to a letter to the editor written by Myrna Garrison to *The Daze*, this plate was made in three different versions. The diamonds that make up the central pattern, and the rays in the center of the plate, are swirled on the earliest version. Curiously, the same plate appears in the 1947 – 1949 Cape Cod catalog as No. 160/72, the same pattern number used for the birthday plate in the Cape Cod pattern. At some point, a second version was made, with the arrangement of the diamonds and center rays changed so that they radiate outward in straight lines. In 1954, the plate was modified for a third time, with the addition of three toes. This later version was made for a private mail order firm in 1983 and sold in their catalog, *Tapestry*. Since this is the correct time frame for nut brown, it was probably at this time that the rare colored examples were made,

IM-40. No. 72 Tradition birthday cake plate (early version)

possibly as feasibility items. Similar birthday plates were made in the Candlewick and Cape Cod patterns (see IM-77 on p. 201 and IM- 99 on p. 207, respectively). In 1977, a birthday cake plate was reissued as No. 51679, but it is impossible to tell from the catalog picture (IM-99a on p. 207) whether it is the Tradition or Cape Cod plate, both of which have similar rims. Crystal: $125.00 – market. Nut brown: cannot price.

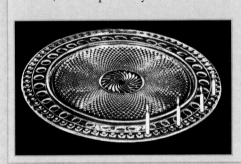

IM-40A. No. 72 Tradition birthday cake plate (early version), from catalog, showing placement of candles

No. 752 two-light candleholder. 5¼" high with a 4⅝" flat base or 5⅝" high with a 4¾" raised base. Circa 1930s – 1940s. Known only in crystal, though colors may be possible, since the similar three-light No. 753 below was made in various colors. Also available as a two-light candelabra with bobeches and prisms. Can be found with the No. 280 Danube cutting, with others possible. Crystal: $25.00 – 30.00. Add 20 – 30% for cut.

IM-41. No. 752 two-light candleholder, from catalog

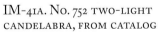

IM-41A. No. 752 two-light candelabra, from catalog

No. 753 three-light candleholder. 6½" high with a 4⅝" flat base or 6⅞" high with a 4¾" raised base. Circa 1932 – 1951. Made in crystal, crystal with a satin foot (Sunburst pattern), milk glass opalescent, Ritz blue, ruby, and Stiegel green. Also listed as No. 75, and advertised as "double fire polished by hand." Can be found cut with No. 261 Allard, 280 Danube, or 465 Viking. Decorated by Lotus with a gold filled etching. Crystal, crystal with satin: $35.00 – 40.00. Milk glass opalescent, Stiegel green: $50.00 – $55.00. Ruby, Ritz blue: $75.00 – 85.00. Add 20 – 30% for cut.

IM-42. No. 753 three-light candleholder in Stiegel green

IM-43. No. 550 BLOWN CONSOLE SET, FROM CATALOG

No. 550 blown candleholder. Dimensions unknown, but probably slightly taller than the No. 701 Reeded candleholder below, because of the addition of the foot. Circa 1935. Made in crystal, but probably also made in color, since this is essentially just the No. 701 candleholder without the reeding added. Advertised as part of a five-piece console set, with two of the pieces being the pressed crystal candle cups (1½" high with a top diameter of 1½") that sit in the opening of the blown ball, which is attached to a pressed foot. Crystal: $25.00 – 35.00.

IM-44. No. 701 REEDED BLOWN CANDLEHOLDERS
(ONE CANDLE CUP INSERT REMOVED)

No. 701 Reeded blown candleholder. Sometimes referred to as Spun, the name used by Hazel Marie Weatherman. 2¾" high. Circa 1935 – 1936. Made in crystal, amber, and Ritz blue. Other pieces of this pattern were also made in Stiegel green and ruby, so these colors are also likely. The pitcher and the tumbler in the line were patented in 1935 by Earl W. Newton, president of the corporation. Although the patents state that they are for the "ornamental design" of the items, it would seem that the actual claim was probably on the technique of blowing the items into a paste mold so that they take on the appearance of reeding. (Actual reeding is a process that requires laying thin threads of glass onto the blank by hand, and therefore is much more expensive to do.) Offered as part of a five-piece console set, with two of the pieces being the pressed crystal candle cups (1½" high with a top diameter of 1½") that sit in the opening of the blown ball. Made both without a foot, as seen in the accompanying photograph, or with a pressed foot like that on the No. 550 candleholder above. In the 1950s, a number of Reeded pieces were put back into production in various colors, some of them in crystal completely covered with bright gold, but there is no indication that the candleholders were reissued at this time. Crystal: $25.00 – $35.00. Amber: $30.00 – $40.00. Ritz blue: $50.00 – $60.00.

IM-45. No. 6992 MOUNT VERNON
SQUARE CANDLEHOLDER

No. 6992 Mount Vernon square candleholder. 2⅛" high and 3⅛" across. Circa 1935 – 1946. Made in crystal. This candleholder was also used as a base for a hurricane lamp. When it was first made, it was an addition to a pattern that had been around since the early 1920s as Prism Crystal (designed by Phillip Ebeling, who was also responsible for Fostoria's "American" pattern) and then Triangle. In the 1930s, when the square candleholder was introduced, it was called Mount Vernon, but in 1942 the name was changed once again, this time to Washington, to avoid confusion with Cambridge's Mount Vernon line. During this long and complicated history, various other candleholders were added to the line. (See IM-14 on p. 182, IM-33 on p. 188, and IM-38 on p. 190.) According to materials in the Imperial archives, the mold for the square candleholder was converted to become the No. 5020/2 Cathay Shen candlebase. (See IM-104 on p. 208.) Crystal: $20.00 – 30.00. Complete with hurricane globe: $40.00 – 50.00.

No. 78C Laced Edge crimped candleholder. 2½" high. 6" diameter. Made in crystal (circa 1935 – 1943) and milk glass (as No. 1950/78C, 1956 – 1960). In 1943, this item was sold exclusively to Sears as a hurricane lamp, No. 7802C. Sears marketed the line as Crocheted Crystal, part of their Harmony House line, but unlike other pieces in this very popular line, the hurricane lamp only remained in their catalog for a year. Crystal, milk glass: $10.00 – 15.00. Crystal with hurricane shade: $20.00 – 25.00.

IM-46. No. 1950/78C Laced Edge (Crocheted Crystal) crimped candleholder in milk glass

No. 78K Laced Edge candleholder. 3" high. Circa 1935 – early 1940s. Made in crystal and crystal with a red stained rim. Also known with a mirrored finish. It appears that No. 78K and No. 78C (IM-46 above) are from the same mold, and were formed to the desired shape after leaving it. This candleholder seems to have been discontinued before 1943 when Sears began selling the Laced Edge line as Crocheted Crystal, which would explain its scarcity compared to other items in the line. Crystal: $20.00 – 30.00. Crystal w/red stained rim: $30.00 – 40.00.

IM-47. No. 78K LACED EDGE console set, from catalog

No. 780 Laced Edge twin candleholder. 4½" high with a 4¼" base. Circa 1935 – 1950. Made in crystal, this candleholder is identical in shape to Imperial's No. 749, which was earlier included as part of the Laced Edge line (see IM-38 on p. 190). The difference is that the triangular pattern on the No. 749 is replaced with plain panels on the No. 780. Beginning in 1943, this candleholder was made exclusively for Sears as No. 1708. Sears marketed the Laced Edge line until 1950 as Crocheted Crystal, part of their Harmony House line. The twin candleholder was one of the few items that remained in their catalog during the entire period. Crystal: $6.00 – 8.00.

IM-48. No. 780 Laced Edge (Crocheted Crystal) twin candleholder

Twin candleholder. Unknown line number. 4½" high with a 4¼" base. Assumed to be from the 1930s, but could be as late as the 1960s. Known only in crystal. This is another candleholder that is identical in shape to Imperial's No. 749 (see IM-38 on p. 190) and No. 780 (IM-48 above), but with a different pattern on the dome base. We know of no catalog listing for this candleholder and have identified it as Imperial through its obvious resemblance to the aforementioned items. Crystal with unknown cutting: $15.00 – 20.00.

IM-49. Twin candleholder, unknown pattern number

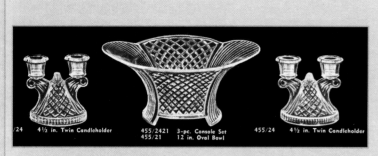

IM-50. No. 455/2421 CONSOLE SET, INCLUDING No. 455/24 TWIN CANDLEHOLDERS, FROM CATALOG

No. 455/24 twin candleholder. 4½" high. Circa 1936 – 1943. Known only in crystal. Shown in Butler Bros.' May – June 1936 catalog as Cristolbrite. A candlestick with a similar shape and identical arms was made by the Tiffin factory of the United States Glass Company as part of their No. 308-19 Williamsburg pattern. It was reissued in the late 1960s/1970s as Monticello by the Indiana Glass Company. (See IN-88 on p. 261.) A taller candlestick/hurricane lamp was also made in this pattern. (See IM-73 on p. 200.) Crystal: $12.00 – 17.50.

IM-51. No. 782 TWIN CANDLE-HOLDER, PRECURSOR TO CANDLEWICK, WITH No. 261 ALLARD CUTTING

No. 782 twin candleholder. 5¼" high with a 4½" x 3⅝" oval base. Circa 1936, possibly a year or so earlier. Made in crystal. This was made from the mold for the No. 169 candleholder, modified by adding the balls to the outside of the arms. (See IM-35 on p. 188.) It was available as part of a console set, with a bowl similarly modified from the No. 320 oval bowl. Materials in the Imperial archives, microfilmed by the Corning Museum of Glass, include a catalog page showing this bowl with the balls drawn in. There is also a Candlewick binder that includes a photograph showing this console set with six different cuttings (No. 261 Allard and others) sharing a page with another photograph of known Candlewick pieces, also cut. The inference seems to be that Imperial considered this candlestick to be part of the Candlewick pattern, even though it was never advertised as such, to our knowledge. Also, as purists will note, the balls on this piece are graduated in size, whereas other Candlewick items will generally have balls of a uniform size, except in the case of stemmed pieces or finials. Crystal: $30.00 – 40.00. Add 10 – 20% for cut.

IM-52. No. 400 CANDLEWICK CANDLEHOLDER, FROM 1936 BROCHURE (PROBABLY NEVER MADE)

No. 400 Candlewick candleholder. Unknown size. A drawing of this candleholder appeared in the back of a brochure introducing Candlewick in 1936, but there is no evidence to confirm that it is was ever produced.

IM-53. No. 400/80 CANDLEWICK CANDLE-HOLDER

No. 400/80 Candlewick candleholder. Listed in later catalogs as No. 14782. 3½" high with a 4¼" base. Circa 1937 – 1976. Made in crystal, crystal with gold or satin trim, and Viennese blue (1937 – 1938), plain or with frosted beads. A handled version was also made as No. 400/81 (on the following page). A reproduction with a flat base marked MI has been reported, apparently made in the early 1990s. This mark was used by Mirror Images, who owned many of the Candlewick molds and had various pieces made by Boyd's Crystal Art Glass, Mosser Glass Company, and Dalzell Viking. To the best of our knowledge, Mirror Images, like Dalzell Viking, is no longer in business. Crystal: $12.00 – 18.00. Crystal with gold or satin trim: $30.00 – 45.00. Viennese blue: $60.00 – 70.00. Add 30 – 40% for decorated.

No. 400/81 Candlewick candleholder. 3½" high. Circa 1937 – 1943. Made in crystal, crystal with satin trim, and Viennese blue. This is the same candlestick as No. 400/80, but with a handle added. Available with No. C108 Starlight cutting. Reportedly reissued in blue by Dalzell Viking. More recently, made by the Mosser Glass Co. for Mirror Images in vaseline and vaseline satin. Crystal: $50.00 – 60.00. Viennese blue: $80.00 – 90.00.

IM-54. No. 400/81 CANDLEWICK candleholder, from *HOUSE AND GARDEN*, DECEMBER 1943

No. 400/86 Candlewick candleholder. 2" high. 6" in diameter. Circa 1937 – 1941. Made in crystal, crystal with gold or colored beads, crystal with a satin trim, and Viennese blue (1937 – 1938). This may also have been made with a rolled edge as No. 400/86R, but seems to have been produced in this form only briefly. Available with No. C100 Dots and C108 Starlight cuttings. Crystal: $30.00 – 40.00. Viennese blue: $65.00 – 75.00. Add 30 – 40% for decorated.

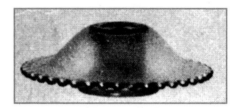

IM-55. No. 400/86 CANDLEWICK CANDLEHOLDER, FROM CATALOG

No. 1942 Athele three-way candleholder. Probably about 12" high. Circa 1939 – 1943. Made in crystal. This was a design by Wilbert C. Smith, of Washington, Pa., and was not assigned to Imperial at the time the patent was applied for on September 29, 1939. The patent was approved November 28, 1939, as D117,836. Unable to price.

IM-56. No. 1942 ATHELE THREE-WAY CANDLEHOLDER, FROM CATALOG

No. 400/79B Candlewick flat candleholder. 3¼" high. Circa 1939 – 1943. Made in crystal only. This is the same as the No. 400/79R below, but with the rim flat. It has been reported with the beads turned down, as well, so that the candleholder rests on them. Early versions have a plain candle cup as seen in the accompanying catalog reprint, but then a rim was added (as seen on the photograph of the No. 400/79R below). Crystal: $50.00 – 60.00.

IM-57. No. 400/79B CANDLEWICK FLAT CANDLEHOLDER, FROM CATALOG

No. 400/79R Candlewick rolled edge candleholder. 3¼" high with a 5¼" base. Circa 1939 – 1979. Made in crystal, crystal with a frosted base, and crystal with red stain (1943). This was the same as the No. 400/79B above, but with the rim turned up. Considerable variation will be found in the way the edge is rolled up. Early versions have a plain candle cup (as seen in the catalog reprint for the No. 400/79B above), but sometime before 1943 a rim was added, as seen in the accompanying photograph. Called a

IM-58. No. 400/79R CANDLEWICK ROLLED EDGE CANDLEHOLDER

IM-58A. No. 400/79R CANDLEWICK "OLD STYLE BOHEMIAN HURRICANE LAMP," FROM *INTERIORS*, OCTOBER 1942

Lafayette candleholder and listed as No. 14780 in later catalogs. Also offered as a hurricane lamp with shade. The ornately decorated hurricane lamp in IM-58a was featured in the October 1942 issue of the magazine *Interiors*, where it was described as an "Old style Bohemian hurricane lamp, 10" high, in cranberry decoration with tracings of gold on crystal. It is a reproduction of the original import." Presumably, it was the "Bohemian" decoration that was considered to be the reproduction. Crystal: $12.00 – 18.00. Frosted or stained: $50.00 – 60.00. Crystal w/hurricane shade: $100.00 – 120.00.

IM-59. No. 400/100 CANDLEWICK TWIN CANDLEHOLDER, WITH RED, YELLOW, AND BLUE STAIN ON BEADS

No. 400/100 Candlewick twin candleholder. 4½" high with a 5¼" base. Circa 1939 – 1968. Known in crystal, crystal with gold balls, crystal with red, blue, and yellow balls, amber, charcoal (smoke), pink (an experimental color), rubigold (marigold carnival), Viennese blue, and yellow. All of the colors were probably feasibility items or very limited production. A design patent was filed on May 24, 1941, and approved on July 8, 1941, as D128,113. The designer was given as Carl W. Gustkey, Imperial's president at the time of filing. The mold is currently owned by Mirror Images. Crystal: $15.00 – 20.00. Crystal with gold or multi-colored balls: $20.00 – 25.00. Colors: $65.00 – market.

IM-60. No. 280/100 CORINTHIAN TWIN CANDLEHOLDER, MARKED SI

No. 280/100 Corinthian twin candleholder. 4¼" high with a 5¼" base and a 6¾" spread. Circa 1940 – 1946, 1953 – 1954, and 1984. Made in crystal and crystal with a frosted base (1984). Originally introduced as Crystal Shell, but by late 1940 the name had been changed to Corinthian. After being phased out in the mid-1940s, the line reappeared in 1954 as Tiara. In 1984, it was reintroduced exclusively for sale through the Smithsonian Institution's gift shop and catalog, with the base and shell finial frosted and the arms clear. The reissues are marked with the initials SI beneath the base. This candleholder is often found with the bust-off (used to hold the item while it's being fire polished) still intact from the factory. This is because many pallets of these were still awaiting final finishing when Imperial went out of business, and their remaining inventory was sold as is. A design patent was filed February 19, 1940, and approved May 7, 1940, as D120,408. It was created by Onnie Mankki, an architect and industrial designer from Cleveland, Ohio. Available with at least one cutting, No. 613.
Marked SI: $30.00 – 40.00. Unmarked: $40.00 – 50.00. Add 20 – 30% for cut.

IM-60A. No. 280/100 CORINTHIAN TWIN CANDLEHOLDER, MARKED SI. NOTE THE BUST-OFF STILL ATTACHED TO THE BASE

No. 280/129R Corinthian urn candleholder. 4½" high. Circa 1941 – 1950 and 1953 – 1954. Made in crystal and black satin. Also offered (in crystal only) with six prisms attached to the rim as No. 280/129RP. The crystal Corinthian line was phased out in the mid–1940s, but a few items, including the No. 280/129R, were continued in black satin as part of Imperial's Black Suede line. In 1953, some crystal items were revived as Tiara. The No. 280/129R was among these but the No. 280/129RP was not. Although it does not have the Corinthian ribs on the urn, the patent drawing in IM-61a probably applies to this piece, since we are not aware of Imperial having produced a plain urn candleholder. It was filed June 19, 1941, and approved November 11, 1941, as D130,333. The designer was given as Carl J. Uhrmann, an official at the factory who later became its president. Crystal: $20.00 – 25.00. Crystal w/six prisms: $45.00 – 60.00. Black suede: $35.00 – 40.00.

IM-61A. PATENT DRAWING FOR BOWL CANDLEHOLDER, PROBABLY AN EARLY DESIGN FOR THE No. 280/129R CORINTHIAN URN CANDLEHOLDER

IM-61. No. 280/129R CORINTHIAN URN CANDLE-HOLDER, FROM CATALOG

No. 400/115 Candlewick three-way candleholder. 3" high. Circa 1941 – 1943. Made in crystal. Considered hard to find. The mold is in private hands. $140.00 – 170.00.

IM-62. No. 400/115 CANDLEWICK THREE-WAY CANDLEHOLDER, FROM CATALOG

No. 400/129R Candlewick urn candleholder. 6" high with a rolled edge. Circa 1941 – 1943. Made in crystal. Considered rare. Has been seen with a gold-filled etching on the rim. $150.00 – 175.00.

IM-63. No. 400/129R CANDLEWICK URN CANDLEHOLDER, FROM CATALOG

IM-63a shows a drawing dated August 20, 1941, for a three-light candleholder that was never put into production.

IM-63A. DRAWING DATED AUGUST 20, 1941, OF A CANDLEWICK CANDLEHOLDER THAT WAS NEVER PUT INTO PRODUCTION

IM-64. No. 165 TRADITION TWIN CANDLEHOLDER

No. 165 Tradition twin candleholder. 4½" high with a 4⅜" base. Circa 1942. Known only in crystal. This candleholder is a bit of a puzzler. It has long been considered part of the Tradition pattern, which dates back to the 1930s, when the line was offered in several colors. However, none of the known catalogs or price lists mention a candlestick. Our only reference for this candleholder comes from the fall-winter 1942 Sears catalog, where it was sold as part of a console set with an 11" footed bowl that is also otherwise unknown. Were these pieces late additions to the Tradition line? They certainly share design characteristics with the pattern (including a square foot on the floral bowl, which would match the stemware), but we have to conclude that there remains some doubt. We'll bow to tradition (pun intended) and leave it listed as Tradition, but have to acknowledge that there is presently no absolute proof that it is, or even that it is definitely Imperial. $12.00 – 17.50.

IM-65. No. 160/80 CAPE COD SINGLE CANDLEHOLDER

No. 160/80 Cape Cod single candleholder. Listed as No. 16790 in later catalogs. 5" high with a 4¾" base. Circa 1942 – 1976. Made in crystal. Although the tremendously successful Cape Cod line had been introduced in 1931, this seems to have been one of the first candleholders, along with the saucer candleholder below, to be made as part of the pattern. $25.00 – 30.00.

IM-66. No. 160/175 CAPE COD SAUCER CANDLEHOLDER

IM-66A. No. 160/175 CAPE COD SAUCER CANDLEHOLDER, FLARED

No. 160/175 Cape Cod saucer candleholder. 1½" high with a 4½" diameter (this size will vary according to how much the sides flare out). Circa 1942 – 1943, 1949, and again from 1953 to 1962. Made in crystal. Although the tremendously successful Cape Cod line had been introduced in 1931, this seems to have been one of the first candleholders, along with the single candleholder above, to be made as part of the pattern. It was also used as the base for a hurricane lamp from 1942 to 1943 and listed as No. 1609, then listed as No. 160/79 in 1949. (See IM-66b.) Note: The latter number was also used for a different hurricane lamp that was made from 1947 to 1953. Perhaps the earlier hurricane lamp was reissued using this number at a time when the other version had temporarily been discontinued from production. (See IM-91 on p. 205.) $25.00 – 35.00. With hurricane globe: $85.00 – 95.00.

IM-66B. No. 160/79 CAPE COD HURRICANE LAMP, FROM ADVERTISEMENT IN *Crockery and Glass Journal*, FEBRUARY 1949

No. 400/152 Candlewick hurricane lamp adapter. 4" in diameter. Circa 1942 – 1950. Made in crystal. Patented in 1942, this peg candleholder insert can be used to turn any candleholder into a hurricane lamp by providing a trough for the hurricane globe to rest in. During the 1940s, this was sold in conjunction with several Candlewick candleholders. It was available both plain or with seven prisms, and both with and without the peg that fits into the candle cup. The adapters without pegs fit the opening of a rose bowl, converting it to a candleholder. Design patent D133,955, filed May 28, 1942, and approved September 29, 1942. The designer was given as Carl J. Uhrmann, an official at the factory who later became its president. Insert alone: $60.00 – 80.00. Insert w/globe: $70.00 – 90.00.

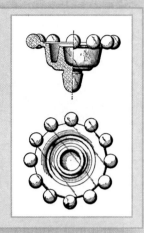

IM-67. Patent drawing for No. 400/152 Candlewick hurricane lamp adapter

No. 780 lace edge hurricane lamp adapter. Circa 1942 – 1950. Made in crystal. Patented in 1942, this peg candleholder insert can be used to turn any candleholder into a hurricane lamp by providing a trough for the hurricane globe to rest in. This was sold in conjunction with several Imperial candleholders throughout the 1940s. Design patent D133,956, filed May 28, 1942, approved September 29, 1942. The designer was given as Carl J. Uhrmann, an official at the factory who later became its president. Insert alone: $25.00 – 35.00. Insert w/globe: $35.00 – 45.00.

IM-68. Patent drawing for No. 780 lace edge hurricane lamp adapter

No. 777/1 eagle candlestick adapter. Unknown size. Circa 1942 – 1950. Made in crystal only. This is a peg insert that adds height and decoration to a candleholder. It has a socket for a candle but is otherwise very similar to the more common eagle ornament (No. 777/2). This was sold in conjunction with several Imperial candleholders throughout the 1940s. Design patent D134,312, filed June 24, 1942, approved November 10, 1942. The designer was given as Carl J. Uhrmann, an official at the factory who later became its president. These are considered rare. $100.00 – market.

IM-69. Patent drawing for No. 777/1 eagle candlestick adapter

No. 681 blackout bowl (candleholder bowl). 8" diameter. Circa 1943. The bowl was made in black suede and came with a crystal eagle ornament. Not pictured, but this was probably the same mold used for the No. 6024 flower float candle bowl introduced as part of the Olde Jamestown line in 1953. (See IM-118 on p. 212.) Black suede bowl with crystal eagle insert: $175.00 – market.

IM-71. No. 682-B PILLAR FLUTE
CANDLEHOLDER, FROM ORIGINAL
FACTORY PHOTOGRAPH

No. 682-B Pillar Flute candleholder. Approximately 8 – 9" in diameter. Circa 1943 – 1950. Probably only made in crystal, but other colors from the period are possible. The only information we have for this candleholder is the accompanying photograph from the Imperial archives, as microfilmed by the Corning Museum of Glass, which has typed dates of 1943 and 1950 on it. The Pillar Flute pattern was originally made in the 1920s. A catalog page from circa 1943 includes a salad set in the pattern, indicating that it must have been reissued around that time, and we suspect that this candleholder was probably made from the same mold as the 9½" No. 6828BG salad bowl, with the sides flared differently. Because the quality of the archival photograph is so poor, we are including a catalog reprint of the salad set, to give a clearer idea of the pattern. It is reminiscent of Heisey's Crystolite. Unable to price.

IM-71A. No. 6828BG PILLAR
FLUTE four-piece salad set,
FROM CA. 1943 CATALOG

IM-72. AD FOR No. 148
CANDLEHOLDER WITH
BELMONT HILLS CUTTING

No. 148 candleholder. 5" high. Circa 1943 – 1956. Made in crystal. This mold was acquired from the Central Glass Works in 1940 and was their No. 1480. (See CE-24 on p. 108 of volume one of this series.) This candlestick had also previously been included in one of Seneca's catalogs with their No. 834 cutting. Offered by Imperial with at least one etching (No. 436) and the following cuttings: No. C261 Belmont Hills (probably a special order for Bechtel, Lutz and Company of Reading, Pennsylvania, one of Imperial's largest accounts), 954 Valencia, 956 Vanessa, and 957 Valerie. Lotus also used this blank for decorating with etchings, both before and after it was acquired by Imperial. Used by Imperial as the base for the No. 148/780 hurricane lamp by including a lace edge adapter (see IM-68) and a globe. $25.00 – 30.00. Add 20 – 40% for cut or etched.

IM-73. No. 455/160
TWO-PC. HURRICANE
CANDLE, FROM CATALOG

No. 455 candleholder. 7" high. Circa 1939 – 1950. Made in crystal. This candleholder appeared in a photograph from the Imperial archives that showed it with a No. 777 eagle candleholder insert (see IM-70). It has an attached bobeche, and was listed as having "eight plastic prisms." It was also offered as a hurricane lamp base as No. 455/160. There was also a twin candleholder in this pattern. (No. 455/24, IM-50 on p. 194.) Crystal: $30.00 – 40.00.

No. 220 Swedish Pinched Crystal candleholder. 6" high. Circa 1943. Made in crystal. $25.00 – 35.00.

No. 400/32 Candlewick candleholder. Also listed as No. 400/155. 6½" high. Circa 1943. Made in crystal. Primarily sold as a base for a hurricane lamp and also available with the eagle candleholder insert. This base was produced for the Lightolier Lighting Company for use as a lamp part. The accompanying illustration is from the September 1943 issue of *China and Glass*. These are considered very rare. Crystal: $250.00 – market.

IM-75. No. 400/32 Candlewick candleholders with hurricane shades and comport, from *China and Glass*, September 1943

No. 400/147 Candlewick three-light candleholder. 5½" high with a 5" base. Circa 1943 – 1965. Made in crystal. This was based on the design for the twin candleholder (IM-59 on p. 196), patented by Carl W. Gustkey, Imperial's president. The mold is currently owned by Mirror Images. $40.00 – 50.00.

IM-76. No. 400/147 Candlewick three-light candleholder

No. 400/160 Candlewick birthday cake plate. 13 – 14" diameter. Circa 1943 – 1951. Made in crystal, it holds 72 evenly spaced birthday candles around the plate rim. Similar birthday plates were made in the Tradition and Cape Cod patterns (see IM-40 on p. 191 and IM-99 on p. 207, respectively). $450.00 – market.

IM-77. No. 400/160 Candlewick birthday cake plate, from catalog

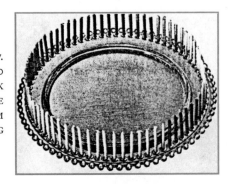

IM-78. No. 400/170 CANDLEWICK LOW CANDLE-HOLDER

No. 400/170 Candlewick low candleholder. In later years it was listed as No. 14997. 3¼" high with a 4¼" base. Circa 1943 – 1961 and 1978 – 1984. Made in crystal and also known in pink milk glass. Although the latter has been attributed to Imperial, we are not aware of the company ever having made such a color. Boyd's Crystal Art Glass currently owns the mold and has reissued it. (See BO-5, p. 43 in volume one of this series.) This piece has larger beads around the edge than most other Candlewick candleholders. Crystal: $12.00 – 15.00. Pink milk glass: $20.00 – 25.00.

IM-79. No. 400/1752 CANDLEWICK PRISM CANDLE-HOLDER, FROM CATALOG

No. 400/175 Candlewick tall candleholder. 6½" high. Circa 1943 – 1955. Made in crystal. Also offered as a three-piece hurricane lamp with a shade, candle adapter (IM-67), and prisms as No. 400/1753, or with just the candle adapter and prisms as No. 400/1752. Paden City's No. 444 is similar but has four balls on the stem. (See the addendum at the end of this chapter on p. 232-233.) Considered rare. $150.00 – 200.00. With bobeche/prisms: $375.00 – market.

IM-80. No. 400/178 CANDLEWICK BOWL CANDLE-HOLDER, FROM CATALOG

No. 400/178 Candlewick bowl candleholder. 1¾" high with a 7½" diameter. Circa 1943 – 1950. Made in crystal only. Beaded rim and shape similar to the No. 400/40F flower candleholder (IM-86 on p. 204.) Used as a hurricane lamp base, with three different styles made, one with a circle of beads inside the bowl that hold the chimney in place (probably the earliest version) and another with six risers instead of the row of beads. A third version, without beads or risers, is also known, presumably for use as a candleholder only, since it will not hold a hurricane shade securely. This is considered very rare. Unable to price.

IM-81. No. 400/680 CANDLEWICK TWIN CANDLE-HOLDER, FROM ORIGINAL FACTORY PHOTOGRAPH

No. 400/680 Candlewick twin candleholder. Unknown size. Circa 1943 – 1950. Made in crystal. This was also available as a candelabra with two bobeches and 16 prisms or as a hurricane lamp with two candlewick hurricane adapters (see IM-67 on p. 199) and two shades. Considered very rare. Unable to price.

No. 607 candle bowl. 4" high and 12" long. Circa 1942 – 1943, 1957 – 1966, 1975 – 1979, and 1982. Initially made in crystal only, with later production in milk glass (glossy or doeskin), as No. 1950/607. A 1942 Butler Bros. catalog offered it as a centerpiece bowl in an assortment of "Brilliant Nu-Cut Crystalware." A catalog page from around 1943 simply called it a console bowl. Finally, in 1975, when it was reissued in crystal once more as No. 41709, it became a candle bowl, listed as part of the Collectors Crystal Assortment. The pieces made during this period are marked with the IG trademark on the bottom.

IM-82. No. 1950/607 CANDLE BOWL
IN MILK GLASS

Although it was discontinued from Imperial's catalogs after 1979, it returned to production one last time in 1982 as a special order in lead crystal for the American Glassworks in New York. Crystal or milk glass: $25.00 – $35.00.

IM-82A. PACKAGE LABEL FOR AMERICAN GLASSWORKS'
No. 9207 CENTERPIECE CANDLELIGHT (REISSUE OF
IMPERIAL'S No. 41709 COLLECTORS CRYSTAL CANDLE BOWL)

No. 160/81 Cape Cod candleholder. 4" high with a 3½" square foot. Circa 1946 – 1947. Made in crystal. $30.00 – 35.00.

IM-83. No. 160/81 CAPE
COD CANDLEHOLDER

No. 160/100 Cape Cod two-light candleholder and ornament. 8½" long. Circa 1946 – 1947. Made in crystal. Imperial probably used the mold for the No. 160/192 partitioned peanut and mint with a different plunger to make this unique candleholder. The 1947 Imperial catalog states that the "Ornament is removable, for use as a three-light candleholder." In 1949, another candleholder in the Cape Cod line used the same number (see IM-101 on p. 209), which almost assuredly meant that this candleholder was in production for no more than a year or two. $125.00 – market.

IM-84. No. 160/100 CAPE COD TWO-LIGHT CANDLEHOLDER AND ORNAMENT, FROM CATALOG

No. 400/40C Candlewick flower candleholder. 5" diameter. Circa 1947 – 1967. Made in crystal, blue, and ruby. Also available with a miniature vase insert as No. 400/40CV. (The miniature vases are considered rare.) Crystal: $35.00 – 45.00. Colors: $250.00 – market. Crystal w/vase: $125.00 – market.

IM-85A. No. 400/40C
CANDLEWICK flower
CANDLEHOLDERS, FROM AD

IM-85. No. 400/40C CANDLEWICK
FLOWER CANDLEHOLDER

400/40F Candlewick low Flower Candle Holder, retails approximately $2.00 pair.

IM-86. No. 400/40F CANDLEWICK LOW FLOWER CANDLEHOLDER, FROM A JUNE 1949 AD IN *CROCKERY & GLASS JOURNAL*

No. 400/40F Candlewick low flower candleholder. 6" diameter. Circa 1947 – 1960. Made in crystal. Can be found with a sterling silver base. $40.00 – 50.00.

400/40 HC Candlewick, handled heart-shaped Flower Candle Holder, retails approximately $3.50 pair.

IM-87. No. 400/40HC CANDLEWICK HANDLED HEART-SHAPED CANDLEHOLDER, FROM A JUNE 1949 AD IN *CROCKERY & GLASS JOURNAL*

No. 400/40HC Candlewick handled heart-shaped flower candleholder. 5" diameter. Applied handle. Circa 1947 – 1951. Made in crystal. $90.00 – 120.00.

IM-88. No. 400/40S CANDLEWICK FLOWER CANDLEHOLDER, FROM CATALOG

No. 400/40S Candlewick flower candleholder. 5 – 6½" square (depending on how the sides of the bowl are turned up). Circa 1947 – 1951. Made in crystal and Viennese blue. Crystal: $60.00 – 80.00. Viennese blue: $95.00 – 105.00.

400/66 C Candlewick Crimped Flower Candle Holder, retails approximately $4.50 pair.

IM-89. No. 400/66C CANDLEWICK CRIMPED FLOWER CANDLEHOLDER, FROM A JUNE 1949 AD IN *CROCKERY & GLASS JOURNAL*

No. 400/66C Candlewick crimped flower candleholder. 4½" high. Circa 1947 – 1955. Made in crystal only. Footed, with two beads on the stem and a ruffled edge on the bowl. This is from the same mold as the No. 400/66F shown in IM-90 below. $100.00 – 125.00.

IM-90. No. 400/66F CANDLEWICK CANDLEHOLDER, FROM CATALOG

No. 400/66F Candlewick candleholder. 4" high. Circa 1947 – 1951. Made in crystal. Footed, with two beads on the stem and a plain rim on the bowl. This is from the same mold as the 400/66C shown in IM-89 above. $75.00 – $95.00.

No. 160/79 Cape Cod hurricane lamp. The base is 1⅝" high and 6" in diameter, with a top inside diameter of 3". Circa 1947 – 1953 and then reissued 1977 – 1980 as No. 16990. Made in crystal. Note: The No. 160/79 pattern number was used for a different hurricane lamp in the Cape Cod pattern in 1949. (See IM-66a on p. 198.) Using the same number for two different items would be contrary to Imperial's usual practice, so we assume that the "real" No. 169/79 hurricane lamp must have been temporarily discontinued from production for some unknown reason. $95.00 – 115.00.

IM-91. No. 160/79 (16990) CAPE COD HURRICANE LAMP BASE

No. 400/90 Candlewick handled candleholder. 5" high (cupped version); 4" high with a 5½" diameter (shallow version). Circa 1947 – 1967. Made in crystal only, sometimes with the base frosted, the earlier versions have a deep, cupped base, while the later examples are more shallow. The mold is in private hands and has been reproduced for Rosso Wholesale (by Mosser Glass Company) in cobalt, vaseline, and vaseline satin (in a limited issue of 107 pairs each). $50.00 – 70.00.

IM-92A. No. 400/90 CANDLEWICK HANDLED CANDLE-HOLDER, EARLY VERSION WITH CUPPED BASE, FROM CATALOG

IM-92. No. 400/90 CANDLEWICK HANDLED CANDLEHOLDER

No. 400/196FC Candlewick flower candle centerpiece. 9" high. Circa 1947 – 1955. Made in crystal and Viennese blue. Also used as the base for the No. 400/196 epergne set. $150.00 – 175.00

IM-93. No. 400/196FC CANDLEWICK FLOWER CANDLE CENTERPIECE, FROM CATALOG

No. 400/224 Candlewick candleholder. 5½" high with a 3¾" base. Circa 1947 – 1955. Made in crystal. Offered with several cuttings and as a base for a hurricane lamp (as No. 400/264). A variant pair of these candlesticks was reported on by Myrna Garrison in the October 1995 issue of *The Imperial Collectors Glasszette*. The tops were turned up in a cup-shape (or, more likely, this is the way they came from the mold and they were not flattened as they ordinarily would be). There is also a drawing in the Imperial archives (IM-94a) that shows another variation, with a standard candle cup in place of the beaded-rimmed top usually found. It isn't known if this version was ever actually produced. $150.00 – market.

IM-94A. DRAWING FROM IMPERIAL'S ARCHIVES OF VARIANT No. 400/224 CANDLEWICK CANDLEHOLDER (POSSIBLY NEVER MADE)

IM-94. No. 400/224 CANDLEWICK CANDLEHOLDER WITH FLORAL CUTTING

IM-95. No. 449 CANDLE AND FLOWER STICKUPS, WITH ORIGINAL CONTAINER AND INSTRUCTIONS

No. 449 candle and flower stickups. 2⅛" high. Circa 1948 – 1951. Made by attaching a suction cup to the bottom of a plain crystal candle cup. According to a 1949 advertisement from the Imperial archives, "STICKUPS make any smooth-surfaced article in the home adaptable to beautiful, exciting decorative arrangements." These originally retailed for $1.00 per set of three, complete with a pamphlet showing how and where to use them. Both the advertisement and carton say "Patent Pending," but if a patent was in fact granted, we have not been able to locate it. Complete set with box and instructions: $12.00 – 15.00.

IM-96. No. 160/45B CAPE COD FLOWER CANDLEHOLDER

No. 160/45B Cape Cod flower candleholder. 5" high with a flared bowl. Circa 1949. Made in crystal. A similar candleholder with a cupped bowl was available as No. 160/45N. (See IM-97 below.) $60.00 – 80.00.

IM-97. No. 160/45N CAPE COD FLOWER CANDLEHOLDER, FROM CATALOG

No. 160/45N Cape Cod flower candleholder. 5½" high with a cupped bowl. Circa 1949. Made in crystal. A similar candleholder with a flared bowl was available as No.160/45B. (See IM-96 above.) $90.00 – 120.00.

IM-98. No. 160/48BC CAPE COD FLOWER CANDLE CENTERPIECE

No. 160/48BC Cape Cod flower candle centerpiece. 6" high. Circa 1949. Made in crystal. $200.00 – market.

No. 160/72 Cape Cod birthday cake plate. 13" diameter. Circa late 1940s. Made in crystal, it holds 72 evenly spaced birthday candles around the plate rim. Similar birthday plates were made in the Tradition and Candlewick patterns (see IM-40 on p. 191 and IM-77 on p. 201, respectively). In 1977, a birthday cake plate was reissued as No. 51679, but it is impossible to tell from the catalog picture (IM-99a) whether it is the Cape Cod or Tradition plate, both of which have similar rims. $350.00 – market.

IM-99A. No. 51679 Cape Cod birthday cake plate (reissue of No. 160/72), from 1977 catalog

IM-99. No. 160/72 Cape Cod birthday cake plate

No. 160/90 Cape Cod handled Aladdin candleholder. 4" high. Circa 1949. Made in crystal. This appears to be made from a creamer with a candle adapter added, and was made for a very short time, making it quite scarce. $125.00 – market.

IM-100. No. 160/90 Cape Cod handled Aladdin candleholder, from catalog

No. 160/100 Cape Cod twin candleholder. 6" high with a 3½" square base and a 6¾" arm spread. Circa 1949 – 1962. Made in crystal. Note: In 1947, another short-lived candleholder in the Cape Cod line used the same number. (See IM-84 on p. 203.) $65.00 – 80.00.

IM-101. No. 160/100 Cape Cod twin candleholder

The Cathay line was created by Virginia B. Evans, an artist primarily known for her landscape paintings in oil, who also did freelance designs for a number of glass and pottery companies, including Fostoria, Viking, and Warwick China. Development of the Cathay pattern took nearly six years, beginning around 1943, and involved extensive research in museums and libraries. It wasn't introduced until April of 1949. The line, which has a Chinese theme, was then rolled out amid a heavy promotional campaign that included full page ads in national magazines and special packaging. Each item came in a jade-green velour gift box, with Evans' signature impressed in gold on the lid. An acid-etched version of this signature also appeared on many of the glass items themselves. But even with these promotional efforts, sales were sluggish. Production problems further hindered the sale of some items, including the No. 5009 dragon candleholder. The satin finish on these pieces was unusual, requiring that they be dipped twice in acid to give the rich highlights that make the line so distinctive. Originally, frosted crystal was the only color available, but some pieces were made in black and black suede (satin) during the 1950s, and jade was made for a short time in 1960. In 1964 – 1965, Imperial reissued some items in cranberry (a frosted version of azalea) and frosted verde. In the early 1980s, some items were again made in Imperial jade, black, and ruby. The Cathay molds were acquired by Tiara Exclusives; now that Tiara is out of business, they are presumably owned by Tiara's parent company, Lancaster Colony Corporation.

IM-102. No. 5009 CATHAY
DRAGON CANDLEHOLDER

No. 5009 Cathay dragon candleholder. Circa 1949. Made in crystal satin. Signed Virginia B. Evans. Imperial's promotional brochure for the Cathay pattern gave the following description: "While his coiled tail holds a tapered candle aflame, the story you can tell your dinner guests is this: he is another Lung, another dragon from the land of Cathay, where he long ruled the primitives who feared him. His countenance reveals his wisdom and his amused tolerance of men. He ruled through fear, through ignorance and because of human stupidity. The Far East fears him no longer these days; yet he continues to smile, for in the West appears a new, horrible dragon and all modern men are fearful! You see? Thus can ancient Dragon-lore be tied to current times! Your dinner conversation is off to an early successful tempo and Ch'ih Lung still smiles in his sagacious, knowing-way at the troubles of mortals." The dragon candleholder is not easily found as it was difficult to make. $200.00 – market.

No. 5013 Cathay pillow candlebase. 2½" high, 4" long x 2¼" wide. Circa 1949 – 1953. Made in crystal satin.

IM-103. No. 5013 CATHAY
PILLOW CANDLEBASE

Signed Virginia B. Evans on the bottom. The bottoms of the feet are ground and polished. Imperial's promotional brochure for the Cathay pattern gave the following description: "These candle bases were designed after intensive research and study of Chinese pillows. An especially lovely one, in porcelain, which we believe came from the household of the exotic Hsiang Fei, finally inspired us to do these crystal candleholders. The Fragrant One, Hsiang Fei, foreign sorceress who enraptured the mighty Sun of Heaven, Ch'ien Lung, had lavished upon her the finest of the Emperor's treasures and much of the best of available art works of those days. Grace, simplicity, pure design, once again entrusted to skilled crystal craftsmen, who have produced an appealing gift for those who appreciate fine things!" $125.00 – 150.00.

IM-104. No. 5020/2 CATHAY
SHEN CANDLEBASE

No. 5020/2 Cathay Shen candlebase. 2¼" high. 3¼" square. Circa 1949 – 1953 in crystal satin, sold as part of the Shen console set with a matching rectangular bowl. Although many of the original pieces in the Cathay pattern were signed Virginia B. Evans, the candle bases were not, because they were considered too small to have an appropriate space for the signature. Reissued in cranberry (satin azalea) and verde satin, 1964 – 1965, also not marked. Reissued in Imperial jade as No. 51785JA, 1981 – 1983, marked LIG on the underside of the base. Some black ones were also made at that time, marked ALIG and sold with 9" globes. The light blue example in the accompanying photograph is unmarked, and was probably a feasibility item circa 1979 – 1980. Imperial's promotional brochure for the Cathay pattern gave the following description for the Shen console set: "This modern-shaped flower box-bowl and its matching candle bases are the result of deliberate effort to present something new in table centre sets. You will discover waves and sea spray in the design devices and Chinese dragons of two types – P'an Lung, ruler of all the waters of the earth, and Shen Lung, schemer of the storms, winds and rains. Our complete design inspiration in this instance came from the early-dynasty carved Cathay jades and from the embroidery on the lower sections of ancient ceremonial robes of important members of the Imperial Court." Black, jade: $20.00 – 25.00. Light blue, verde, or cranberry satin: $30.00 – 35.00. Crystal satin: $75.00 – 100.00.

IM-104A. No. 5020/2 CATHAY SHEN
CANDLEBASES IN LIGHT BLUE (NOT
PRODUCTION) AND CRANBERRY

No. 5027 Cathay wedding lamp. 11½" high with a 4¾" hexagonal base. Originally made in crystal satin, circa 1949 – 1953. The clear crystal example in the accompanying photograph is a later reissue from 1961 – 1971 (marked IG on the underside of the base). Also reissued in milk glass (as No. 1950/79) in the 1950s; cranberry (satin azalea) and verde satin, circa 1964 – 1965; Imperial jade (as No. 51785JA, marked LIG on the underside of the base), 1981 – 1983; and ruby (probably a feasibility item). All came with a distinctively shaped, six-paneled crystal globe. Imperial's promotional brochure for the Cathay pattern gave the following description: "Ch'ien Lung (1736 – 1765 A.D.) had, as did many of China's rulers, real appreciation of fine art pieces. He once presented a very valuable pair of porcelain Wedding Lamps to the Buddhist Temple in Kiangsu. They were our inspiration for these CATHAY CRYSTAL candle lamps. The chimney bases are decorated with symbols originating in Tibet and the very, very old Chinese decorative device, 'the sleeping silk worm.' What a wonderful wedding gift! One of the interesting features of CATHAY CRYSTAL items is that they will harmonize with any decoration scheme and be at home in any setting." Clear crystal, milk glass: $75.00 – 100.00. Cranberry, verde satin: $125.00 – 150.00. Satin crystal, ruby: $200.00 – market.

IM-105. No. 5027 CATHAY WEDDING LAMP (REISSUE IN CLEAR CRYSTAL)

No. 5033/34 Cathay candle servants. 9" high. Circa 1949 – 1953. Made in crystal satin. Signed Virginia B. Evans on the back of the base. Both male and female figures were offered, and seem to have been sold in both mixed pairs and single-sex pairs. Imperial's promotional brochure for the Cathay pattern gave the following description: "More attractive crystal candleholders cannot be found! This pair of amiable servants will excite clever talk for long periods, contribute beauty and the unusual to your table and serve you well! Their unaffected, hearty willingness of manner distinguishes them as persons from those of the reserved nobility of old Cathay. We first found them, in different appearance of course, as little clay figures from Imperial tombs of the 618 – 907 A.D. years. They had been placed there (in substitution for living servants formerly buried with their masters) to serve the spirits of deceased royal lords. Note the carved, flowing, simple elegance of these figurines." $200.00 – market. (Photograph courtesty of Tom Bredehoft.)

IM-106. No. 5033/34 CATHAY CANDLE SERVANTS

No. 160/170 Cape Cod candleholder. 3" high. Circa 1950 – 1962. Made in crystal and verde. Crystal: $20.00 – 25.00. Verde: $25.00 – 30.00.

IM-107. No. 160/170 CAPE COD CANDLEHOLDER, FROM CATALOG

No. 1950/170 low candleholder. 1½" high with a 4½" diameter. Circa 1950 – 1960, 1978, and 1984. Made in milk glass (marked IG inside the candle cup), with limited runs of ultra blue carnival and white carnival. On page 109 of their *Encyclopedia of Glass Candlesticks*, Douglas and Margaret Archer show this candleholder in what they say was an experimental color. Unfortunately, they don't describe the color, but it looks like it might be rubigold (marigold). Whatever the color is, they say that only 24 of them were made. In 1978, about 300 were made in ultra blue carnival to be given as convention souvenirs for the Imperial Glass Collectors Society. In 1984, another 262 were

IM-108. No. 1950/170 LOW CANDLE-HOLDER IN MILK GLASS

made in white carnival for the same purpose. The souvenirs are marked on the bottom, "I.G.C.S." with the old-style Imperial cross and the date. This beaded edge design is similar to Candlewick but was not listed as part of that line. The Summit Art Glass Company currently owns the mold. Milk glass: $15.00 – 20.00. White carnival: $25.00 – 35.00. Ultra blue carnival: $35.00 – $45.00.

IM-109. No. 280 CANDLEHOLDER IN DOESKIN MILK GLASS

No. 280 candleholder. 4" high with a 3¾" base. Circa 1950. Made in milk glass and available with a glossy or doeskin finish. $15.00 – 22.50.

IM-110. No. 400/280 CANDLEWICK SINGLE CANDLEHOLDER, FROM CATALOG

No. 400/280 Candlewick single candleholder. 3½" high. Circa 1950 – 1955. Made in crystal only. This was an unusual addition to the line, since it only has one bead on the stem and does not immediately strike the viewer as Candlewick. $150.00 – market.

IM-111. No. 80 VINELF CANDLEHOLDERS IN MIDWEST CUSTARD WITH SATIN FINISH, DOESKIN MILK GLASS (NOTE OLDER BASE WITH NO RIM), AND ANTIQUE BLUE

No. 80 Vinelf candleholder. 7⅜" high with a 4½" base. Circa 1950 – 1965. Made in antique blue, black and gold (gold flecked), black suede, forget-me-not blue, lichen green (1955 only), Midwest custard, milk glass (as No. 1950/80), and verde. Also known in ultra blue, which may have been an experimental color. Most colors were available glossy or with doeskin finishes. Available as part of a console set with a matching Vinelf comport. Early milk glass examples will have a 4" base without the bead around the bottom. The L. E. Smith Glass Company currently owns this mold. Antique blue, milk glass, verde: $20.00 – 30.00. Midwest custard, forget-me-not blue: $30.00 – 40.00. Black and gold, black suede, lichen green, ultra blue: $35.00 – 55.00.

IM-112. No. 780 STAR HOLLY low CANDLEHOLDER IN MILK GLASS

No. 780 Star Holly low candleholder. 2¾" high with a 3½" base. 4½" across top. Circa 1951 – 1955. Made in amber (experimental color), crystal, and milk glass (glossy or doeskin). The crystal was sold exclusively by Sears as Leaf Fantasy, part of their Harmony House line in 1951. Sometimes marked IG on the underside of the base. The mold was acquired by Rastal, GmbH & Co., K.G., Germany. Crystal: $8.00 – 10.00. Amber, milk glass: $12.00 – 17.50.

No. 1950/766 Star Holly float bowl. 11" diameter. Circa 1952 – 1955 and 1956 – 1962 as No. 1950/840. The original version has the holly design in the center of the bowl and the leaves on the rim are closed; the leaf pattern on the rim is opened in the later version. Also known to collectors as Leaf and Leaf Open, respectively. Made in milk glass (glossy or doeskin finish), the bowl holds three candles. (Although some pieces in the Star Holly pattern were also made in crystal exclusively for Sears, the float bowl was not among them.) The mold was acquired by Rastal, GmbH & Co., K.G., Germany. $25.00 – 35.00.

IM-113. No. 1950/766 STAR HOLLY (LEAF) FLOAT BOWL IN MILK GLASS, FROM CATALOG

IM-113A. No. 1950/840 OPEN LEAF FLOAT BOWL IN MILK GLASS

No. 1950/81 handled candleholder. 1¾" high to top of handle (1¼" to rim of bowl). 5⅛" across. Circa 1952 – 1959 in milk glass (glossy or doeskin) and briefly (from July – December 1962) in glossy purple slag (as No. 81). This candleholder was also made in a footed version. (See IM-153 on p. 221.) Marked IG inside the socket. Milk glass: $15.00 – 20.00. Purple slag: $40.00 – $50.00.

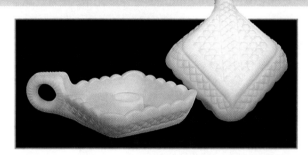

IM-114. No. 1950/81 HANDLED CANDLEHOLDERS IN DOESKIN MILK GLASS

No. 110/80 Imperial Twist footed candleholder. 3" high. Circa 1953. Made in crystal. $25.00 – 30.00.

IM-115. No. 110/80 IMPERIAL TWIST FOOTED CANDLEHOLDER, FROM CATALOG

No. 880 Grape candleholder. Listed as No. 42782 and No. 51784 in later catalogs. 3⅜" high with a 3⅞" base. Circa 1950 – 1981. Made in amber carnival (1973 – 1975), blue satin (1979 – 1980), crystal satin (1979 – 1981), end o' day ruby (glossy or satin, 1969 – 1973), ivory satin (1978 – 1980), milk glass (glossy or satin), milk glass with a brass foot (1956), peacock carnival, rubigold carnival (1966), and vintage ruby (1953). An identically shaped stick with a rose pattern was introduced as No. 160 in 1955. (See IM-120 p. 213.) Often marked IG on the bottom of the base. The mold is owned by the L. E. Smith Glass Company. Crystal, milk glass: $8.00 – 10.00. Amber carnival, blue or ivory satin: $10.00 – 15.00. Peacock carnival, ruby: $15.00 – 20.00. End o' day ruby, rubigold: $25.00 – 30.00.

IM-116. No. 880 GRAPE CANDLEHOLDER IN PEACOCK CARNIVAL

IM-116B. No. 880 GRAPE CANDLEHOLDER IN MILK GLASS, WITH BRASS FOOT

IM-116A. No. 880 GRAPE CANDLEHOLDER IN RUBY (NOTE FLAT BASE)

IM-117. No. 6021
OLDE JAMESTOWN
CANDLEHOLDER IN
FLASK BROWN

No. 6021 Olde Jamestown candleholder. 2¼" high with a 4" diameter. Circa 1950 – 1953. Made in bead green, chartreuse, flask brown, heather, and olde flint. An identically shaped item with an oversized hole was listed as a "cigarette or jumbo candleholder," offered as No. 6029 and later as No. 51782 (in nut brown, which would date it to sometime in the 1970s). (See IM-117a.) The genesis for this pattern, "inspired by Olde Jamestown," as the label and advertising stated, was the excavation of the site of the first glasshouse in America at Jamestown in 1948 – 1949. This, in turn, led to the building of a replica of the glasshouse, still a major tourist attraction today. Carl Gustkey, president of Imperial, spear-headed this effort. Olde flint (crystal): $6.00 – 8.00. All colors: $8.00 – 12.50.

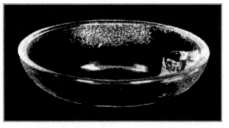

IM-117A. No. 6029 (51782) OLDE
JAMESTOWN CIGARETTE OR JUMBO CANDLE-
HOLDERS IN FLASK GREEN AND NUT BROWN

OLDE
JAMESTOWN
LABEL

No. 6024 Olde Jamestown candle float bowl. 8" diameter. Circa 1950 – 1953. Made in bead green, flask brown, heather, hickory, and olde flint. This is a flower float bowl and holds a single candle on the side of the bowl. It is probably from the same mold as the previously made blackout bowl (IM-70 on p. 199). Olde flint (crystal): $15.00 – 20.00. All colors: $20.00 – 30.00.

IM-118. No.
6024 OLDE
JAMESTOWN
CANDLE FLOAT
BOWL, FROM
CATALOG

IM-119. No. 51792 DOLPHIN CANDLEHOLDERS
IN FERN GREEN AND NUT BROWN

No. 1950/90 Dolphin candleholder. 9" high with a 4" square base. Made in milk glass circa 1954 – 1958 and again from 1976 to 1977 and in crystal (as No. 90) from 1969 to 1971 and again from 1974 to 1978. Listed in later catalogs as No. 51792, in fern green (1976 – 1977), nut brown, ultra blue (both 1976 and 1978), and horizon blue carnival (as No. 42792HB, 1979 – 1980). Also known in amber and pink carnival (1978). In 1978, 250 of these candlesticks were made for Levay Distributing Company in rubigold (marigold carnival). They are signed, dated, and numbered by Levay, as well as marked with the Imperial IG. This candlestick was a reissue of a candlestick that was originally made by the Consolidated Lamp & Glass Company and later by the Haley Glass Company. (See CS-6, p. 115, in volume one, and HL-1 p. 90, in this volume.) According to Kenneth Haley, as interviewed by Jack D. Wilson in *Phoenix & Consolidated Art Glass*, both Haley and Imperial had new molds made. However, after comparing a Consolidated original with the Imperial version and one that we believe to be Haley's, the authors were unable to detect any differences other than the fact that the Imperial version is stippled on the underside of the base and marked IG. The Imperial mold is currently owned by the Indiana Glass Company. Crystal, milk glass: $25.00 – 30.00. Fern green, nut brown, ultra blue: $30.00 – 35.00. Horizon blue carnival: $45.00 – 50.00. Rubigold: Unable to price.

No. 160 Rose candleholder. 3⅜" high with a 3⅞" base. Made in milk glass (as No. 1950/160, 1955 – 1971), milk glass with a brass base (as No. B160, 1956 – 1958), forget-me-not blue (glossy and satin, 1955 – 1958), Midwest custard (glossy and satin, 1955 – 1958), turquoise (glossy and satin, 1956 – 1959), peacock carnival (1966), rubigold (marigold carnival, 1966), and amber carnival (1973). Listed as No. 43784 in white carnival (1973 – 1975), caramel slag (glossy and satin, 1974 – 1976), end o' day ruby (glossy and satin, 1971 – 1976), purple slag (glossy and satin, 1974 – 1975), and jade slag (glossy and satin, 1975 – 1976). Listed as No. 42784 in pink carnival (1978) and horizon blue carnival (1979 – 1980). Reissued for a final time as No. 51791 in crystal satin and pink satin (both 1980 – 1981). Identical to the No. 880 Grape candleholder (see IM-116 p. 211) except for the pattern on the base. Often marked IG on the bottom of the base. The mold is currently owned by the L.E. Smith Glass Company. Their versions are marked "S." Crystal satin, milk glass: $8.00 – 10.00. Amber carnival, forget-me-not blue, Midwest custard, rubigold: $10.00 – 15.00. White carnival: $20.00 – 25.00. End o' day ruby slag, jade slag, peacock carnival, pink carnival, purple slag: $25.00 – 35.00.

IM-120. No. 160 ROSE CANDLEHOLDER IN PEACOCK CARNIVAL

IM-120A. No. 160 ROSE CANDLEHOLDERS IN FORGET-ME-NOT BLUE AND MIDWEST CUSTARD

No. 1950/325 candleholder. 3½" high with a 4" base. Circa 1955 – 1962. Available in milk glass with glossy or doeskin finish. Advertised as being a reproduction of a piece from the famous Belknap collection of early American milk glass. An advertising brochure stated, "These treasures are recognized by authorities as the largest and most renowned private collection of Early American Milk Glass. We at Imperial are indeed proud that we have been granted exclusive permission to reproduce authentic replicas." We have been unable to identify the original from which this candlestick was copied, however, since it was not included in Belknap's book on milk glass, nor have we been able to find it in any of the other literature on early milk glass. $10.00 – 15.00.

IM-121. No. 1950/325 CANDLEHOLDER IN MILK GLASS

No. 330 tall candleholder. Known as Atterbury. 7⅜" high with a 4⅝" base. Circa 1955 – 1978. Made in milk glass (1955 – 1960 and 1977 – 1978), amber (1964 – 1965), antique blue (1964 – 1965), cranberry (1964 – 1965), azalea (1966), nut brown (1977), purple slag (1960), ultra blue (1977), and verde (1964 – 1966). Milk glass was listed as No.1950/330 and was advertised in 1955 as being a reproduction of a piece in the famous Belknap collection of early American milk glass. An advertising brochure stated, "These treasures are recognized by authorities as the largest and most renowned private collection of Early American Milk Glass. We at Imperial are indeed proud that we have been granted exclusive permission to reproduce authentic replicas." We have been unable to identify the original from which this candlestick was copied, however (though certainly Atterbury is a good possibility). Listed as No. 51796 in later catalogs. Amber, verde, milk glass: $15.00 – 20.00. Nut brown, ultra blue, antique blue, cranberry, azalea: $25.00 – 30.00. Purple slag: $75.00 – 90.00.

IM-122. No. 1950/330 ATTERBURY TALL CANDLEHOLDER IN MILK GLASS

IM-122A. No. 330 ATTERBURY TALL CANDLEHOLDERS IN ULTRA BLUE AND VERDE

ATTERBURY LOOKALIKE

No. 4602 candlestick. 3⅞" high with a 4⅜" diameter base. When we first saw this candlestick, we were certain it had to be Imperial, based on its resemblance to the other Atterbury candlesticks. We now know, however, that it was actually made by the Nuutajarvi Glassworks in Finland, circa 1963. In addition to the ribbed-base version in milk glass seen here, it was also made in transparent colors without the ribs and with a cross-hatch pattern pressed on the underside of the base. $8.00 – 12.50.

IM-122B. NUUTAJARVI GLASSWORKS'
No. 4602 CANDLESTICK IN MILK GLASS

IM-123. No. 1950/366
LACE EDGE CUT
CANDLEHOLDER IN
MILK GLASS

No. 1950/366 Lace Edge Cut candleholder. 2½" high with a 6" diameter. Circa 1956 – 1960. Made in milk glass. $10.00 – 15.00.

IM-124. No. 1950/285 HOBNAIL
SQUARE CANDLEHOLDER
IN MILK GLASS

No. 1950/285 Hobnail square candleholder. 2½" high with a 4¼" base. Circa 1956 – 1960 in milk glass. Reissued 1965 – 1966 as part of the Stamm House line in Dew Drop opalescent (as No. 1886/285). The latter was also available with a hobnail globe as the No. 1886/2850 hurricane lamp. Marked IG on the underside of the base. Fenton currently owns the mold. Milk glass: $15.00 – 20.00. Dewdrop opalescent: $30.00 – 35.00.

1886/285
Square
Candleholder

1886/2850
2 Pc.
Hurricane
Lamp

IM-124A. No. 1886/285 STAMM HOUSE SQUARE CANDLEHOLDER AND No.
1886/2850 HURRICANE LAMP IN DEWDROP OPALESCENT, FROM 1966 CATALOG

IM-125. No. 1503/80 CRYSTOLITE ROSETTE CANDLE-
BLOCKS. RIGHT CANDLEHOLDER IS TURNED TO
SHOW IMPERIAL LABEL ON BOTTOM (HEISEY MOLD)

No. 1503/80 Crystolite rosette candleblock. 2¼" high with a 3⅜" diameter. Circa 1957 – 1976. Made in crystal (1957 – 1976) and in ruby (1969 – 1970). Later listed as No. 51780; this was a reissue of Heisey's No. 1503 Crystolite rosette candleblock. (See HE-112 on p. 138.) The mold is currently owned by the Heisey Collectors of America. Crystal: $12.50 – 15.00. Ruby: $40.00 – 45.00.

IM-125A. No. 1503/80
CRYSTOLITE ROSETTE CANDLE-
BLOCK IN RUBY (HEISEY MOLD)

No. 1503/81 Crystolite square candleblock. 1⅞" high and 3" across. Circa 1957 and 1970 – 1975. Made in crystal. Later listed as No. 51781, this was a reissue of Heisey's No. 1503¼ Crystolite square candleblock. (See HE-135 on p. 146.) The mold is currently owned by the Heisey Collectors of America. $25.00 – 30.00.

IM-126. No. 1503/81 CRYSTOLITE SQUARE CANDLEBLOCK (HEISEY MOLD)

No. 1615 Waverly two-light candleholder. Almost 10" high with a 5⅜" base and a 9" arm spread. Made from September 1957 to January 1961 in crystal. Reissue of Heisey's No. 1615 Flame candlestick. (See HE-180 on p. 160.) The mold is currently owned by the Heisey Collectors of America. $110.00 – 125.00.

IM-127. No. 1615 WAVERLY TWO-LIGHT CANDLEHOLDER (CATALOG DRAWING). FROM HEISEY MOLD

No. 1519 Waverly epergnette candleholders. Made in two sizes: 2¾" high with a 5" diameter (also sold as No. 1519/152 and No. 51812), circa 1957 – 1977; and 3½" high with a 6" diameter (also sold as No. 1519/153 and No. 51813), circa 1957 – 1959 and 1973 – 1976. Made in crystal, these were reissues of Heisey's No. 1519 Waverly epergnettes. (See HE-168 and HE-170 on p. 157.) A third style of epergnette was also reissued in 1975. (See IM-170 on p. 226.) Imperial made the smaller epergnette with three of the etchings most popular with today's collectors: Heisey Rose, Orchid, and Cambridge's Rose Point. These were probably feasibility items only and, to the best of our knowledge, the epergnette was not offered by Heisey with any of these etching. The mold is currently owned by the Heisey Collectors of America. $12.00 – 18.00. With etch: Unable to price.

IM-128. No. 1519 (51813 AND 51812) EPERGNETTES, FROM 1974 – 1975 CATALOG (HEISEY MOLD)

IM-128A. No. 1519 EPERGNETTE WITH ORCHID ETCHING (HEISEY MOLD)

HE-128B. No. 1519 EPERGNETTE WITH HEISEY ROSE ETCHING (HEISEY MOLD)

HE-128C. No. 1519 EPERGNETTE WITH ROSE POINT ETCHING (HEISEY MOLD)

No. 1950/236/1 Scroll candleholder. 1¾" high with a 5" diameter. Circa 1958 – 1960 in milk glass. Made in crystal in 1960 as Scroll Crystal (or Atterbury Scroll). $10.00 – 15.00.

IM-129. No. 1950/236/1 SCROLL CANDLEHOLDER IN MILK GLASS

IM-130. No. 112
CANDLEHOLDER
WITH No. DE507
ORCHID ETCHING
(HEISEY MOLD)

No. 112 candleholder. Known as Mercury to collectors today. Later listed as No. 11781, part of the Revere line. 3⅝" high with a 4¾" base. Circa 1958 – 1964 and 1971 – 1976. Made in crystal and available with two etchings, No. DE507 Orchid or DE515 Heisey Rose, both previously made by Heisey. This was a reissue of Heisey's very popular No. 112 candlestick, which had been originally made from 1926 to 1957. (See HE-46 on p. 116.) The mold is currently owned by the Heisey Collectors of America. $25.00 – 30.00. Etched: $35.00 – 45.00.

IM-131.
No. 134/100
WAVERLY
TWO-LIGHT
CANDLEHOLDER
(HEISEY MOLD)

No. 134/100 Waverly two-light candleholder. 5¾" high with a 5½" base. Made from 1958 to 1971. This was a reissue of Heisey's No. 134 Trident candleholder. (See HE-70 on p. 123.) Made in crystal and available with two etchings (No. DE507 Orchid and DE515 Heisey Rose) and one cutting (No. C980 Moonglo), all decorations originally made by Heisey. The mold is currently owned by the Heisey Collectors of America. Crystal: $25.00 – 35.00. Etched: $50.00 – 70.00.

IM-132.
No. 142/147
THREE-LIGHT
CANDLEHOLDER
(HEISEY MOLD)

No. 142/147 three-light candleholder. 7⅜" high with a 5½" base. Circa 1958 – 1968. Made in crystal and available with two etchings, No. DE507 Orchid and DE515 Heisey Rose, both previously made by Heisey. This was a reissue of Heisey's No. 142 Cascade candlestick. (See HE-86 on p. 129.) The mold is currently owned by the Heisey Collectors of America. Crystal: $50.00 – 75.00. Etched: $75.00 – 100.00.

IM-133. No.
1509 ONE-LIGHT
CANDELABRA
(HEISEY MOLD)

No. 1509 one-light candelabra. 8" high with a 5" base. Made from May 1958 to January 1971 in crystal. Reissue of Heisey's No. 1509 Queen Anne candelabra. (See HE-120 on p. 141.) The mold is currently owned by the Heisey Collectors of America. $75.00 – 85.00.

No. 1540 two-light candleholder. 5¼" high with a 5⅛" base. Made from May 1958 to January 1968 in crystal. Reissue of Heisey's No. 1540 Lariat two-light candlestick. (See HE-142 on p. 148.) The mold is currently owned by the Heisey Collectors of America. $25.00 – 30.00.

IM-134. No. 1540 TWO-LIGHT CANDLEHOLDER (HEISEY MOLD)

No. 4044 two-light candelabra. 7⅞" high with a 3" x 4⅞" base. Made from May 1958 to January 1972 in crystal. Reissue of Heisey's No. 4044 New Era two-light candlestick. (See HE-93 on p. 132.) The mold is currently owned by the Heisey Collectors of America. Complete with removable square bobeches/prisms: $75.00 – 85.00.

IM-135. No. 4044 TWO-LIGHT CANDELABRA (HEISEY MOLD)

No. 1513 three-light candelabra epergne. 6¼" high with a 6½" base and a 10½" arm spread, including the bobeches. Made from May 1958 to 1973 in crystal. Reissue of Heisey's No. 1513 Baroque three-light candelabra epergne. (See HE-129 on p. 144.) The mold is currently owned by the Heisey Collectors of America. Sold with a No. 5013 5" vase and two bobeches with six prisms each. Complete as described: $75.00 – 85.00.

IM-136. No. 1513 THREE-LIGHT CANDELABRA EPERGNE (HEISEY MOLD)

No. 341/2 Old Williamsburg candleholder. Later listed as No. 13790. 7½" high with a 4" hexagonal base. Made 1958 – 1984 in crystal; 1969 – 1970 in amber, antique blue, ruby, and verde; 1969 – 1971 in blue haze and nut brown; 1981 in emerald green. A reissue of Heisey's No. 2 Old Williamsburg candlestick. (See HE-2 on p. 98.) The candlesticks made before 1970 will have a ground bottom (as compared to the Heisey originals, which not only have ground bottoms but also a polished pontil); the later crystal and emerald green examples have unfinished bottoms and generally are far poorer quality than either the Heisey originals or the early Imperial reissues. Early crystal examples may be marked with Heisey's Diamond H, since this mark was not removed from the mold until 1968. After Imperial closed, this candlestick was briefly reissued by Fostoria. (See FO-230 on p. 73.) The mold is currently owned by the Lancaster Colony Corporation. Crystal: $15.00 – 20.00. Emerald green: $20.00 – 30.00. Amber, nut brown, verde: $30.00 – 40.00. Antique blue, blue haze, ruby: $35.00 – 45.00.

IM-137. No. 341/2 OLD WILLIAMSBURG CANDLE-HOLDERS IN BLUE HAZE, VERDE, EMERALD GREEN, RUBY, AND NUT BROWN. (HEISEY MOLD)

IM-138.
No. 300/0
ONE-LIGHT
CANDELABRA
(HEISEY MOLD)

No. 300/0 one-light candelabra. 10" high with a 4" base. Made from May 1958 to 1979 in crystal. This was originally made by Heisey as their No. 300-0 Old Williamsburg one-light candelabra from 1913 to 1957. The Imperial reissues will have a ground bottom (as compared to the Heisey originals, which not only have ground bottoms but also a polished pontil). Crystal: $55.00 – 65.00.

No. E-17 Elysian swirl candleholder. Dimensions unknown, but probably approximately 2" high. Circa 1958 – 1963. Made in crystal. This candleholder was also used as the foot for a 7½" crimped tray and an 11" cake stand seen in the accompanying advertisement. Both of those items came with charcoal tops made by the L. H. Houze Convex Glass Company glued to the Imperial bases. $15.00 – 20.00.

IM-139. ADVERTISEMENT FROM IMPERIAL'S
ARCHIVES FOR ELYSIAN. THE NO. E-17 ELYSIAN
SWIRL CANDLEHOLDER WAS USED AS THE BASE FOR
THE NO. E-1 CRIMPED TRAY AT THE TOP RIGHT

IM-140, IM-141, IM-142, IM-143. NO. E-19
ELYSIAN TAPER FLUTED CANDLEHOLDER (TURNED
ON ITS SIDE TO SHOW THE LABEL), E-18 PLAIN
ROUND CANDLEHOLDER, E-21 CANDLEWICK BASE
CANDLEHOLDER, AND E-20 PEAR SHAPE SWIRL
CANDLEHOLDER

No. E-18 Elysian plain round candleholder (IM-140). 2¼" high. Circa 1958 – 1963. Made in crystal. Very similar to Cambridge's No. 510 Pristine ball candlestick. (See CB-140 on p. 89 of volume one of this series.) The Cambridge candlestick is slightly taller (2⅜") and has a ⅝" indentation on the underside of the base, whereas the Elysian candleholder is flat. The rim around the candle cup is also flat on the Elysian candleholder, but indented on the Pristine candlestick. Orrefors also made a similar spherical candleblock, 2¾" in diameter and 2½" tall, ground flat on the bottom. $15.00 – 20.00

No. E-19 Elysian tapered fluted candleholder (IM-141). 2" high with a 2⅜" diameter at the bottom and a 1⅛" diameter at the top. Circa 1958 – 1963. Made in crystal. This candleholder was also used as the foot for a 6⅞" high, square shallow tray with a charcoal top. (See IM-139.) The top was made by the L.

H. Houze Convex Glass Company and glued to the Imperial base. The Akro Agate Company's inkwell style candleblock, type II, is very similar in shape, but with slightly larger dimensions (2" high and approximately 3" square.) See AK-2a on p. 6 of volume one of this series for a comparison. $15.00 – 20.00.

No. E-20 Elysian pear shape swirl candleholder (IM-142). 2¼" high and 2⅝" wide at the base. Circa 1958 – 1963. Made in crystal. This candleholder was also used as the foot for a 6½" comport with a charcoal top. (See IM-139.) The top was made by the L. H. Houze Convex Glass Company and glued to the Imperial base. $15.00 – 20.00.

No. E-21 Elysian candlewick base candleholder (IM-143). 1⅞" high with a diameter of approximately 4⅜". Circa 1958 – 1963. Made in crystal. Although described as a "candlewick base" in factory materials, the design is actually swirled and does not have traditional candlewick beads. This candleholder was also used as the foot for a 14" comport and a 12" crimped bowl. Both items came with charcoal tops, made by the L. H. Houze Convex Glass Company and glued to the Imperial bases. (See IM-139.) $18.00 – 22.00.

IM-141A. No. E-19 Elysian tapered fluted candleholder

No. 1506 Provincial one-light candleblock. 2½" high with a 3¼" diameter. Made 1959 – 1968 in crystal and 1960 – 1962 in amber, heather, and verde. This is a reissue of Heisey's No. 1506 Whirlpool/Provincial candleblock, which Heisey made only in crystal. (See HE-125 on p. 142.) Therefore, any example in color is by Imperial. The Heisey and Imperial crystal versions are most likely indistinguishable, since both are ground smooth on the bottoms. The mold is currently owned by the Heisey Collectors of America. Crystal: $12.00 – 17.50. Amber, heather, verde: $25.00 – 30.00.

IM-144. No. 1506 Provincial one-light candleblocks in verde, heather, and amber (Heisey mold)

No. 1428 Warwick cornucopia candleholder (not pictured). 2½" high with a base that is approximately 3" x 2½". Made in the late 1950s or early 1960s. Available in heather and verde. This was a reissue of Heisey's No. 1428 Warwick individual candlestick. (See HE-90 on p. 131.) The U. S. Glass Co. made a very similar candleholder, but the colors are different and the glass quality is not as good. (See HE-90a on p. 131.) The mold is currently owned by the Heisey Collectors of America. Verde: $25.00 – 35.00. Heather: $40.00 – 50.00.

No. 1428 Warwick two-light cornucopia. 3¼" high with a 5¼" base. Made in the late 1950s or early 1960s. Available in heather and verde. This was a reissue of Heisey's No. 1428 Warwick two-light candlestick. (See HE-89 on p. 131.) Like the Heisey originals, the bottom on the Imperial reissues is ground smooth. The mold is currently owned by the Heisey Collectors of America. Verde: $40.00 – 50.00. Heather: $65.00 – 75.00.

IM-146. No. 1428 Warwick two-light cornucopias in verde and heather (Heisey mold)

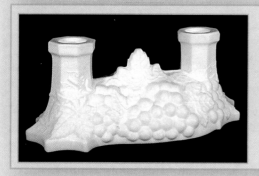

IM-147. No. 1950/137 GRAPE DOUBLE CANDLEHOLDER IN DOESKIN MILK GLASS

No. 1950/137 Grape double candleholder. 3⅜" high with an 8½" long base. Circa 1959 – 1961. Made in milk glass, in glossy or doeskin finish. Marked IG on the underside of the base. $40.00 – 50.00.

IM-148. No. 341/152 OLD WILLIAMSBURG EPERGNETTE CANDLEHOLDER (HEISEY MOLD)

No. 341/152 Old Williamsburg epergnette candleholder. 5½" diameter. Circa 1959 – 1966 and 1971 – 1980. Made in crystal as a reissue of Heisey's No. 341 Old Williamsburg epergnette. (See HE-162 on p. 155.) The mold is currently owned by the Heisey Collectors of America. $12.00 – 17.50.

IM-149. No. 1504 CRYSTOLITE TWO-LIGHT CANDLEHOLDER (HEISEY MOLD)

No. 1504 Crystolite two-light candleholder. Circa 1959 – 1965. Made in crystal as a reissue of Heisey's No. 1504 Regency candlestick. (See HE-140 on p. 148.) The mold is currently owned by the Heisey Collectors of America. $40.00 – 45.00.

IM-150. No. 400/207 CANDLEWICK THREE-TOED CANDLEHOLDER, FROM CATALOG

No. 400/207 Candlewick three-toed candleholder. 4½" high. Circa 1960 – 1967. Made in crystal. A report appeared in the February 1960 issue of *China, Glass & Tablewares* saying that Erwin Kalla, a designer "noted for his dinner and glass creations for a number of firms," had recently done seven pieces of Candlewick, so it seems likely this was one of them. Available with No. C108 Starlight cutting. $85.00 – 100.00.

IM-151. PAGE FROM 1966 CATALOG SHOWING CAMBRIDGE ARMS, INCLUDING No. 628 CANDLEHOLDER (CAMBRIDGE MOLD)

No. 628 candleholder. 4" high with a 4⅞" base. Circa 1961 – 1971. Made in crystal from Cambridge's mold of the same number (see CB-58 on p. 65 – 66 of volume one of this series) and sold as a part of the Cambridge Arms line. This could be purchased with several combinations of candle arm adapters, peg nappies, and/or candlevases. (See the accompanying page from catalog No. 66A.) Imperial also offered this candleholder with Cambridge's popular Rose Point etching. Plain: 10.00 – 15.00. Etched Rose Point: $30.00 – 35.00. Add for four-light candle arm: $20.00 – 25.00. Add for each nappy or vase: $8.00 – 12.50.

No. 37/67 Cambridge Square candleholder. Sometimes referred to as just Square. 2¼" high with a 2½" base and a 4½" diameter (across the top). Circa 1961 – 1964. Made in regal ruby. Reissued using Cambridge's No. 3797/67 mold. (See CB-163 on p. 94 of volume one of this series.) The mold is owned by the Summit Art Glass Company, who is currently making them in light green slag with a matte finish. Ruby: $25.00 – 30.00.

IM-152. Cambridge Square pattern in ruby, from 1962 catalog (including No. 37/67 candleholder). All from Cambridge molds

No. 81 Aladdin lamp handled candleholder. 3⅛" high to top of handle (2⅝" to rim of candleholder). 5" across with a footed base. Circa 1964 – 1969 in milk glass (glossy or doeskin, as No. 1950/81) and in crystal as part of the Collector's Crystal line. This candleholder was also made earlier without the foot. (See IM-114 on p. 211.) The Boyd's Art Glass Company currently owns the mold and has reproduced them in limited quantities. (See BO-3, p. 42, in volume one of this series.) $20.00 – 25.00.

IM-153. No. 81 Aladdin lamp handled candleholder, from 1966 catalog

No. 292 handled candlebowl. 3½" high. Made in crystal (1965 – 1966), as part of the Collectors Crystal line, and in ruby (1980). Also available with a hurricane globe as No. 2920, two-piece handled candlelamp. Crystal: $10.00 – 15.00. Ruby: $15.00 – 20.00. Add $10.00 for crystal hurricane globe.

IM-154. No. 292 Collectors Crystal handled candlebowl, from 1966 catalog

No. 505/90 handled candleholder. 5¼" diameter. Circa 1966 and 1974 – 1976 (as No. 41785). Made in crystal as part of the Collectors Crystal line. Other bowls in the Collectors Crystal pattern were adapted for use as candleholders for pillar-style candles, such as the No. 41802 handled candleholder and No. 41800 footed column candleholder. $12.00 – 15.00.

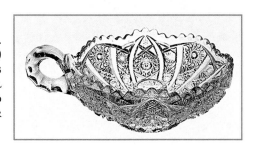

IM-155. No. 505/90 (41785) Collectors Crystal handled candleholder

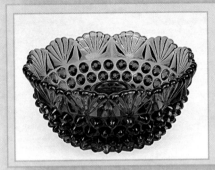

IM-156. No. 643 HOBNAIL CANDLE-HOLDER IN ULTRA BLUE

No. 643 Hobnail candleholder. 2" high and 4½" in diameter. Circa 1966 and 1977 – 79. Originally made in Dew Drop opalescent as part of the Stamm House line, it was later reissued in milk glass, nut brown, and ultra blue as No. 51783. The milk glass candleholders were also listed as No. 1950/643. Marked IG on the inside bottom of the dish. Milk glass, nut brown, ultra blue: $15.00 – 20.00. Dewdrop opalescent: $25.00 – 30.00.

IM-157. No. 46 HOFFMAN HOUSE CANDLE-HOLDERS IN ANTIQUE BLUE AND VERDE

No. 46 Hoffman House candleholder. 4¾" diameter. Circa 1966 – 1971. Made in amber, antique blue, heather, nut brown, ruby, and verde. The bottom rim is ground. Amber, nut brown, verde: $12.00 – 15.00. Antique blue, heather, ruby: $16.00 – 20.00.

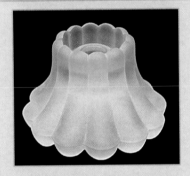

IM-158. No. 1503 CRYSTOLITE ONE-LIGHT ROUND HURRICANE BASE IN SATIN CRYSTAL (HEISEY MOLD)

No. 1503 Crystolite one-light round hurricane base. 3⅜" high with a base diameter of approximately 5¼". Made in 1966 in crystal, both plain and with satin finish. This was a reissue of Heisey's one-light hurricane lamp, originally made from 1937 to 1953. (See HE-116 on p. 140.) Imperial modified the mold, replacing the metal ferrule used by Heisey with a molded candle cup. They also increased the amount of hollow space on the underside of the base. Although the result is still quite heavy, it is considerably lighter than the Heisey original. The example shown was purchased at the Imperial factory with a pressed shade, rather than the usual blown one. The mold is currently owned by the Heisey Collectors of America. $50.00 – 65.00.

No. 1506 Provincial candleholder. 1¾" high with a 4½" diameter. Made January 1966 to January 1971 in amber, crystal, and verde, and January 1966 – 1968 in heather. Although this is from a Heisey mold, Heisey never made this candleholder. This mold was originally used for a nappy in Heisey's Whirlpool/Provincial pattern, then modified by Imperial to produce the candleholder. The bottom rim is ground. This mold is currently owned by the Heisey Collectors of America. Crystal: $10.00 – 15.00. Amber, verde: $12.00 – 17.50. Heather: $15.00 – 20.00.

IM-159. No. 1506 PROVINCIAL CANDLEHOLDER (HEISEY MOLD)

IM-159A. No. 1506 PROVINCIAL CANDLEHOLDERS IN HEATHER AND AMBER (HEISEY MOLD)

No. 207K Lace Edge flower arranger. 4" high and 5¾" across the top. Circa 1966 – 1967. Made in milk glass (as No. 1950/207K), antique blue, flask brown, heather, and verde. This is a two-piece candleholder/frog and vase combination. The candleholder/frog insert was made in crystal only. Marked IG on the bottom. Flask brown, milk glass, verde: $20.00 – 25.00. Antique blue, heather: $25.00 – 30.00.

IM-160. No. 207K LACE EDGE FLOWER ARRANGER IN FLASK BROWN

No. 43790 candleholder. 7½" high with a 4" base. Circa 1969 – 1982. Available in crystal, caramel slag (glossy or satin), and purple slag (glossy or satin). It was reissued as part of the Collectors Crystal line in 1969, and was listed in later catalogs as No. 41790 when it was also offered in a 5" size. (See IM-182 on p. 229.) In 1969 – 1973, it was made in crystal with fired gold decoration as No. G352. The Westmoreland Glass Company's No. 240 candleholder is similar but with the knob closer to the center of the stem. The history of this mold is somewhat convoluted. It began in the 1920s as Imperial's No. 352. The mold was modified slightly when it was reissued as No. 43790 by removing the simulated cuts running down the stem. (See IM-5 on p. 179 for the original version and a comparison with the Westmoreland candlestick.) Upon Imperial's demise the mold was acquired by the Indiana Glass Company, with the mold still owned today by Lancaster Colony Corporation, their parent company. Indiana reissued the candlestick circa 1986 – 1989 as their No. 1518 Collectors' Candleholder. (See IN-99 on p. 264.) In 1992 The Fenton Art Glass company produced it in dusty rose for Tiara Exclusives, a subsidiary of

IM-161. No. 43790 CANDLEHOLDERS IN CARAMEL SLAG AND PURPLE SLAG

Lancaster Colony. Although Lancaster Colony also owns the Indiana Glass Company, Indiana had stopped manufacturing hand-made glassware by that time. (See FN-98 on p. 205 of volume one of this series.) From 1991 – 1998, Dalzell Viking also offered this candleholder in crystal and several colors. (See DV-6, p. 127 in volume one of this series.) We assume they leased the mold from Indiana. Crystal: $10.00 – 15.00. Caramel slag, purple slag: $50.00 – 60.00.

No. 1440 tall candleholder. In later catalogs this was listed as No. 51794. 8½" high with a 4⅛" base. Circa 1969 – 1979. Made in crystal from a Cambridge Glass Company mold. Colored examples will be by Cambridge who also offered it as a one-light candelabra with locking bobeche and prisms. (See CB-30 on p. 57 of volume one of this series.) The U. S. Glass Company's No. 52 candlestick is very similar in shape and size, but will have a cut and polished top and bottom; the Imperial will not. Reissued by the Indiana Glass Company as their No. 1517 paneled candleholder. (See IN-98 on p. 264.) The mold is currently owned by the Lancaster Colony Corporation, Indiana's parent company. Crystal: $30.00 – 40.00.

IM-162. No. 1440 TALL CANDLEHOLDER (FROM A CAMBRIDGE MOLD)

No. 1590/100 Zodiac two-light candleholder. 6" high with a 5½" base and a 7" spread. Made from January 1969 to December 1970 in crystal, amberglo, and verde. This was a reissue of Heisey's No. 1590 two-light candlestick. (See HE-166 on p. 156.) Imperial examples will be marked with an IG on the center medallion above the figure of Jupiter Pluvius. All colors: $35.00 – 45.00.

IM-163. No. 1590/100 ZODIAC TWO-LIGHT CANDLEHOLDERS IN VERDE AND AMBERGLO (HEISEY MOLD)

IM-163A. CLOSE-UP OF CENTER MEDALLION. NOTE IG MARK IN THE UPPER RIGHT

IM-164. No. 282 CANDLEHOLDER IN RUBY

No. 282 candleholder. 2½" high with a 4⅝" diameter. Circa 1969 – 1971. Made in ruby. $20.00 – 25.00.

IM-165. No. 3800/72 CANDLEHOLDER IN SUNSET RUBY (CAMBRIDGE MOLD)

No. 3800/72 candleholder. 3½" high with a 4"base. Made in sunset ruby (1969 – 1973), meadow green carnival (1980), amethyst carnival (1981), and pink carnival (1982 – 1983). This was a reissue of the Cambridge Glass Company's No. 3800/72 Arcadia candlestick (see CB-148, p. 91 in volume one of this series) and can be found with a flat or raised base. Beginning in 1980, this was listed as No. 42788. Marked IG on the bottom. Amethyst carnival, pink carnival: $20.00 – 25.00. Meadow green carnival: $25.00 – 30.00. Sunset ruby: $35.00 – 40.00.

IM-166. No. 27/3531 RAM'S HEAD CANDLEHOLDER IN AURORA JEWELS (FROM A CAMBRIDGE MOLD)

No. 27/3531 Ram's Head candleholder. 6" high with a 4⅝" base. Produced from June 1, 1970, to April 1, 1972, in cobalt iridescent as part of the Aurora Jewels line. This was a reissue of the Cambridge Glass Company's No. 3500/31 Gadroon candlestick. (See CB-95, p. 77 in volume one of this series.) Marked IG on the base. The mold is currently owned by the Fenton Art Glass Company. $35.00 – 40.00.

No. 1570 Lotus Leaf candleblock. 2⅞" high with a 2¾" base. Made sometime between 1973 and 1980. Known only in crystal. This was a reissue of Heisey's No. 1570 Lotus Leaf candleblock. (See HE-157 on p. 153.) On the Heisey original, the base was flattened, making it considerably shorter at only about 2" high. The foot was left turned down by Imperial, which was probably the way it came from the mold (since items with flat bases are often molded with the flat surface cupped to ensure that they fill evenly with the molten glass). This was probably a feasibility item, with no indication that it ever went into production. Marked LIG on the underside of the base. The mold is currently owned by the Heisey Collectors of America. $30.00 – 40.00.

IM-167. No. 1570 LOTUS LEAF CANDLE-BLOCK (HEISEY MOLD)

No. 71762 Dolphin candleholder. 10¾" high with a 4" base. Circa 1972 – 1983. Made in crystal, crystal satin, crystal with a satin top, emerald green (1976 – 1983), dark blue, and sky blue (1980 – 1983). The latter color has also been seen with satin finish. The earliest trade journal reports also mention canary, though later MMA catalogs specifically state that only the version with the petal socket (IM-172 on the following page) was made in this color. These candlesticks were made for the Metropolitan Museum of Art (who owns the mold) as authentic replicas of a candlestick made in the mid-1800s by the Boston and Sandwich Glass Company. (See BS-16, p. 39, in volume one of this series.) The reproduction candleholder is made in two pieces like the original, but the socket is bonded to the base with modern adhesives rather than a wafer of semi-molten glass. They are marked on the bottom (sometimes very faintly) with the initials of the museum, MMA. In the early 1990s, the museum commissioned Dalzell Viking to make this same candleholder in crystal and sky blue. These are probably indistinguishable from the Imperial-made candlesticks. (See DV-8, p. 127, in volume one of this series.) Crystal, crystal satin: $30.00 – 40.00. Sky blue: $45.00 – 50.00. Emerald green: $60.00 – 80.00.

IM-168. No. 71762 DOLPHIN CANDLEHOLDERS IN EMERALD GREEN AND DARK BLUE (MADE FOR MMA)

No. 1155 candleholder. 3⅛" high and 4" in diameter. Made in aurora jewels (1970 – 1972) and white carnival (1973 – 1975). This three-footed candleholder was also listed as No. 42786 and was made using a mold originally produced by the Cambridge Glass Company as No. 1155 (originally not part of a pattern, but eventually incorporated into their Everglade line). (See CB-76, p. 71, in volume one of this series.) The Cambridge originals have their sides flared, while the Imperial reissues have their sides turned up, almost doubling their height. Marked IG or LIG on the bottom, depending on the year of issue. White carnival: $15.00 – 25.00. Aurora jewels: $20.00 – 30.00.

IM-169. No. 1155 CANDLEHOLDERS IN AURORA JEWELS AND WHITE CARNIVAL (FROM A CAMBRIDGE MOLD)

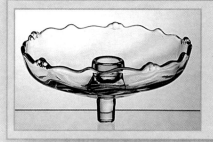

IM-170. No. 1519
Waverly deep
epergnette
(Heisey mold)

No 1519 Waverly deep epergnette. 3½" high and 6" in diameter. Circa 1975. Made in crystal as a reissue of Heisey's No. 1519 Waverly deep epergnette. (See HE-169 on p. 157.) The mold is currently owned by the Heisey Collectors of America. $12.00 – 18.00.

No. 71790 handled candleholder. 5⅜" high with a 3¾" square base. Made in crystal (1976 – 1982) and ultra blue (1980 – 1982) as part of a line of items copied from pieces in the collection of the Smithsonian Institution. Ad copy from a 1980 Imperial catalog reads, "Imperial is licensed to authentically reproduce pieces from the Smithsonian archives. Each piece so precisely duplicates the original that it carries a permanent mark (S.I.) to identify it as a Smithsonian reproduction." This particular candleholder is a copy of a very rare chamber candlestick, originally manufactured by the Boston and Sandwich Glass Company. (See BS-3, p. 36, volume one.) Made in two pieces, similar to the original candlestick except that the pieces are not connected with a true wafer, but instead are joined together using an adhesive. Upon Imperial's demise the mold was acquired by Dalzell Viking, who also produced them in crystal, crystal with a ruby top, and possibly other colors. (See DV-4, p. 126, volume one.) Marked with the initials SI worked into the design on the base, near the handle (see IM-171a). Crystal: $20.00 – 25.00. Ultra blue: $30.00 – 40.00.

IM-171. No. 71790 handled candleholders
in crystal and ultra blue, made for
the Smithsonian

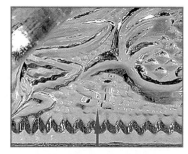

IM-171A. Close-up of a
No. 71790 base showing
the initials S.I.

IM-172. Dolphin candleholders
in alabaster with moonstone blue
socket and gold decoration and
canary (made for MMA)

Dolphin candlestick. 10⅝" high with a 3¾" square base. Circa 1978 – 1982. Available in canary yellow, moonstone blue, and alabaster with a moonstone blue socket (with or without a hand painted gold decoration). Made for the Metropolitan Museum of Art (who owns the mold) as authentic replicas of a candlestick made in the mid-1800s by the Boston and Sandwich Glass Company. (See BS-14, p. 39, volume one.) This candleholder is made in two pieces like the original, but the socket is bonded to the base with modern adhesives rather than a wafer of semi-molten glass. It is marked on the bottom (sometimes faintly) with the initials of the museum, MMA. Absent from the MMA catalogs for 1980 – 1981, it returned in 1982. Imperial also made a reproduction Dolphin candlestick for the MMA with a dolphin socket. (See IM-168 on p. 225.) The petal-socket version had been previously reproduced by Heisey in the 1920s as their No. 110 Sandwich Dolphin candlestick (see HE-45 on p. 115), and in the 1980s by General Housewares Corporation, whose reproductions were imported from Taiwan and marked GHC on the base (GH-1 on p. 81). For other differences between the various reproductions and originals, see the appendix to volume one. Crystal satin: $30.00 – 40.00. Moonstone blue: $40.00 – 50.00. Canary: $80.00 – 100.00. Alabaster/blue: $100.00 – 125.00. Alabaster/blue with h/p decoration: $130.00 – 150.00.

Hexagonal candlestick. 7½" high with a 3½" base. Circa late 1979 – early 1984. Made in canary yellow, crystal, and crystal satin for the Metropolitan Museum of Art and mold marked with the initials MMA on the underside of the base. This was a reproduction of a candlestick from the museum's collection dated 1850 – 1870 and attributed in the catalogs to Sandwich, but probably actually made by the New England Glass Company. These copies were later made for the museum by Dalzell Viking in crystal, amethyst, and cobalt and those examples will also be marked with the initials MMA; except for the crystal ones, they can be told apart by color. (See DV-1 on p. 125 of volume one of this series.) Another reproduction of this candlestick originates overseas, is of poorer quality, and is not marked. Crystal satin: $15.00 – 20.00. Canary: $25.00 – 35.00.

IM-173. PAGE FROM THE METROPOLITAN MUSEUM OF ART'S 1979 CHRISTMAS CATALOG, SHOWING THE HEXAGONAL CANDLESTICKS IN CANARY

No. 51221 Linear candleholder. 2¼" high. Circa 1979 – 1983. Made in crystal only. Reversible. As shown in the accompanying photograph, it takes a standard ¾" taper; reversed, it holds a 2", 2½", or 3" pillar candle. This candleholder was also used for the two-piece 9¾" No. 51224 hurricane lamp and as a base for the two-piece 6½" No. 51220 courting lamp (with the No. 51222 vase/candleholder placed on top). Reissued by the Indiana Glass Company in the late 1980s as their No. 1504 (or No. 1608) Reflections single light candleholder and also made from 1996 to 1998 for Tiara Exclusives as their No. 208 Reflections candleholder. (See IN-101 on p. 265.) The Libbey Glass Company's No. 80215 Concord hurricane also appears to be from the same mold. $8.00 – 10.00. Add $10.00 for shade.

IM-174. No. 51221 LINEAR CANDLEHOLDER

IM-174A. LINEAR CANDLEHOLDERS (ALL EITHER THE No. 51221 CANDLEHOLDER OR THE No. 51222 VASE/CANDLEHOLDER), FROM 1979 CATALOG

No. 51950 Linear hurricane lamp. 12" high. Circa 1979 – 1981. Made in crystal. Reissued by L.E. Smith in crystal and black as No. 26675 Linear in 1982 and by the Indiana Glass Company in the late 1980s as their No. 1507 Reflections hurricane lamp. (See IN-103 on p. 265.) $20.00 – 22.00.

IM-175. No. 51950 LINEAR HURRICANE LAMP, FROM 1982 –1983 CATALOG

No. 13791 Old Williamsburg candlestick. Listed as No. 13792 with a hurricane globe. 5" high with a 3½" hexagonal base. Made June 1980 – 1983 in crystal. This was a reissue of Heisey's No. 5 Patrician candlestick. (See HE-5 on p. 100.) It was then reissued by the Indiana Glass Company as their No. 1516 candlestick in the late 1980s. (See IN-97 on p. 264.) Both the Imperial and Indiana reissues are noticeably poorer quality and are unfinished on the bottoms, while the Heisey originals are ground smooth and have a polished punty. The mold is currently owned by the Lancaster Colony Corporation. $20.00 – 25.00.

IM-176. Selection of candlesticks from the 1982 – 1983 catalog, including the No. 13791 Old Williamsburg candlesticks (second and third from the right), all pieces from Heisey molds

IM-177. No. 13801 Old Williamsburg handled candlesticks in emerald green and ruby (not production), from the Heisey mold

No. 13801 Old Williamsburg handled candlestick . 5⅜" high with a 2⅞" base. Made in crystal (1980 – 1983), emerald green (fall of 1981), and ruby (1981 as a feasibility item). This is a reissue of Heisey's No. 32 Skirted Panel with Handle candlestick. (See HE-20 on p. 107.) Westmoreland made a similar candlestick (circa 1912) in crystal only. (For a comparison, see HE-20a on p. 107.) The Imperial examples will be marked with an ALIG on the outside rim of the base (see IM-178a). Because these reissues were considered part of the Old Williamsburg pattern at the time that Imperial's assets were sold, they were obtained along with the rest of the molds for that pattern by the Lancaster Colony Corporation and briefly placed back in production from 1986 to 1986 by Fostoria, at that time a division of Lancaster Colony. (See FO-231 on p. 73.) Crystal: $15.00 – 20.00. Emerald green: $20.00 – 30.00. Ruby: $40.00 – 50.00.

IM-177A. Close-up of ALIG mark on base of No. 13801

IM-178. No. 71794 candlestick (made for Smithsonian)

No. 71794 candlestick. 7½" high with a 3¾" base. Circa 1980 – 1982. Made in crystal as part of a line of items copied from pieces in the collection of the Smithsonian Institution. Ad copy from a 1980 Imperial catalog reads, "Imperial is licensed to authentically reproduce pieces from the Smithsonian archives. Each piece so precisely duplicates the original that it carries a permanent mark (S.I.) to identify it as a Smithsonian reproduction." The mark will be found on the outside rim of the base (see IM-178a). They were advertised in Smithsonian's catalogs as "Sandwich-type" candlesticks, and are similar to the ones made by the Boston and Sandwich Glass Company shown in BS-9 and BS-10 on p. 37 of volume one of this series. $25.00 – 30.00.

IM-178A. Close-up of SI mark on base of No. 71794

No. 51218 Linear stacking candleholder. 4¼" high. Circa 1980 – 1981. Made in crystal. Reversible. As shown in the accompanying catalog reprint, it holds a standard taper candle; turned the other way, it holds a votive candle. They could also be stacked upon one another or stacked on the No. 51221 candleholder (IM-174 page 227). Reissued by the Indiana Glass Company in the late 1980s as their No. 1513 Reflections candleholder. (See IN-105 on p. 266.) $8.00 – 10.00.

IM-179. Selection of Linear candleholders, from 1980 catalog, including No. 51218 stacking candleholder

IM-180. No. 51510 ("The Classic") and 51513 ("Fantasy Frost") hurricane lamps, from 1980 catalog

No. 51510 hurricane lamp, called "The Classic," and No. 51513F hurricane lamp, called "Fantasy Frost." Both 9" high. Made from 1980 to 1981, in crystal only. $12.00 – 15.00.

No. 51522 hurricane lamp. 11¾" high. Made from 1980 to 1981 in crystal satin, pink satin, and blue satin. $20.00 – 22.00.

IM-181. No. 51522 hurricane lamp in pink satin, from 1980 catalog

No. 41793 Collectors Crystal candleholder. Also sold as No. 41795 with a hurricane shade. 5" high. Circa 1980 – 1983. Made in crystal only. This was part of the Collectors Crystal assortment and was produced earlier in a 7½" size under various pattern numbers, beginning with No. 352. (See IM-5 on p. 179 and IM-161 on p. 223.) *The Collector's Encyclopedia of Glass Candlesticks* by Margaret and Douglas Archer indicates that this candlestick was originally issued in 1980 as No. 4190. The mold is owned by Indiana Glass and was reissued in the late 1980s as their No. 1519 Collectors candlestick. (See IN-99, p. 264.) From 1991 to 1993, this candlestick was made again, this time for Tiara Exclusives by Fenton, in dusty rose as the No. 754 Baroness candleholder. (See FN-98 on p. 205 of book one of this series.) $15.00 – 20.00.

IM-182. No. 41793 Collectors Crystal candleholders, from 1982 – 1983 catalog

IM-183. No. 1565 LEAF CANDLESTICK IN JADE (NOT PRODUCTION), FROM HEISEY MOLD

No. 1565 Leaf candlestick. 1¼" high and approximately 6⅞" long by 3⅞" wide. This was a feasibility item made in small quantities around 1980 when Imperial was developing its Imperial jade line. This was a reissue of Heisey's No. 1565 Leaf candlestick, originally made in crystal only, from 1947 to 1949. (See HE-155 on p. 153.) Marked LIG. $20.00 – 25.00.

IM-184. No. 13795 OLD WILLIAMSBURG MINIATURE HANDLED CHAMBERSTICK (HEISEY MOLD)

No. 13795 Old Williamsburg miniature handled chamberstick. 2" high with a 2⅜" hexagonal base. Circa 1981 – 1983. Made in crystal only. A reissue of Heisey's No. 31 Jack-Be-Nimble toy candlestick. (See HE-19 on p. 106.) Both Westmoreland and Duncan Miller made similar toy candlesticks. For a side by side comparison of all of these toys, see the appendix on p. 289. $12.00 – 15.00.

IM-185. No. 13794 OLD WILLIAMSBURG MINIATURE CANDLEHOLDERS IN EMERALD GREEN, CRYSTAL IRIDESCENT, AND RUBY (NOT PRODUCTION), FROM HEISEY MOLD

No. 13794 Old Williamsburg miniature candleholder. 3½" high with a 2" hexagonal base. Made in crystal (1981 – 1983), crystal iridescent (1983), emerald green (for a few months only in 1981 because of difficulties in producing the color), light blue (only 100 made in 1984), pink (only 100 made in 1984), ruby (approximately 20 made in 1981 as a feasibility item), sunshine yellow (only 100 made in 1984), and ultra blue (only 150 made in 1984). Light blue, pink, sunshine yellow, and ultra blue were made exclusively for the Heisey Collectors of America. This is a reissue of Heisey's No. 33 Skirted Panel toy candlestick. (See HE-21 on p. 107.) Marked either LIG or ALIG on the bottom rim, depending on the year of issue. Because these reissues were sold as part of the Old Williamsburg line at the time that Imperial's assets were sold, the mold was obtained along with the rest of that pattern by the Lancaster Colony Corporation. Crystal: $12.00 – 15.00. Crystal iridescent: $20.00 – 25.00. Emerald green, light blue, pink, sunshine yellow, ultra blue: $35.00 – 45.00. Ruby: $45.00 – 60.00.

IM-186. THREE-FACE CANDLESTICK IN CRYSTAL SATIN, MADE FOR MMA

Three-Face candlestick. 8¾" high with a 4½" base. Circa 1981 – 1984. Made for the Metropolitan Museum of Art with a clear crystal or crystal satin socket bonded to a crystal satin base. Although the base is an accurate reproduction of a pattern manufactured during the late 1800s by George Duncan and Sons (a pattern known as Three-Face to collectors), the original base is only found attached to comport bowls and oil lamp fonts. Duncan never made a Three-Face candleholder. Apparently this candlestick was manufactured to be a companion piece for the museum's Three-Face comport and was made by combining the Three-Face base with a petal socket from one of the museum's dolphin candlesticks (see IM-172 on p. 226). It's an attractive combination, but is not technically a reproduction, since you will not find a nineteenth century original of this candlestick. The museum's catalog told the romantic legend of the pattern's origins as follows:

"Elizabeth Miller sat reading by the light of an oil lamp in the parlor of her Pittsburgh home one wintry evening in 1875. Her husband, John Ernest Miller, then a young designer at the glass works of George Duncan & Company, was so moved by the beauty of his wife's profile silhouetted by the soft lamplight that he began immediately to sketch her. He then translated these sketches into molds for pressing glass." The candlestick is marked MMA on the underside of the base. This mold presumably belongs to the Metropolitan Museum, since they reissued the candlestick (made for them at that time in Portugal) after Imperial's closing. $45.00 – 65.00.

IM-186A. CLOSE-UP OF FACE DETAIL

No. 61790 SY toed candleholder. 6" high. Circa 1981 – 1982. Made in sunshine yellow only. This was a reissue of Heisey's No. 1401 Empress toed candleholder (see HE-75 on p. 125) made exclusively for the Collectors Guild as their No. 67546 Empress toed candlesticks. As part of a selection of six items announced as "a landmark re-issue of six famed Heisey glass designs," these were sold directly by Collectors Guild through their own catalog and also offered through three book clubs. However, it was at about this time that Imperial underwent the financial difficulties that led to its declaration of bankruptcy in late 1982 and, as a consequence, most of these candlesticks were never delivered to Collectors Guild and ended up being sold at the factory during its liquidation. There should be no confusion between this and the original, since Imperial's sunshine yellow is noticeably brighter than Heisey's sahara, the glass is of poorer quality than Heisey's, and all but the initial feasibility pieces are marked with a CG in a circle on the body. The mold is currently owned by the Heisey Collectors of America. $40.00 – 45.00.

IM-187A. COVER OF BOOK CLUB ASSOCIATES BROCHURE FOR COLLECTORS GUILD REISSUES

IM-187B. CLOSE-UP OF CG MARK ON No. 61790 SY

IM-187. No. 61790 SY TOED CANDLEHOLDER IN SUNSHINE YELLOW (MADE FOR COLLECTORS GUILD FROM THE HEISEY MOLD)

No. 1550 Dolphin (Fish) candlestick. Approximately 5" high with a 2⅜" x 3¾" base. Made in 1982 in sunshine yellow (465 glossy and 170 with satin finish). This was a limited edition made for the Heisey Collectors of America from a mold designed for Heisey by Royal Hickman in 1942. (See HE-149 on p. 151.) Marked with Imperial's IG on the tail. The bottoms are ground but not polished. The HCA owns the mold, and in 1995 there was another limited edition made by Dalzell Viking in ice blue, with a few samples also made in cobalt. (See DV-19, p. 130, of volume one in this series). Glossy or satin: $40.00 – 50.00.

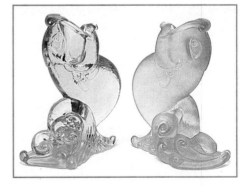

IM-188. No. 1550 DOLPHIN (FISH) CANDLESTICK IN SUNSHINE YELLOW, PLAIN AND SATIN FINISH (FROM HEISEY MOLD)

IMPERIAL ADDENDUM

THESE CANDLESTICKS ARE NOT IMPERIAL'S CANDLEWICK!

Imperial's Candlewick was such a popular pattern, both during the period of its original production and in the years since, among collectors, that there has grown up a tendency for any beaded-edge piece to be sold as Candlewick. It should be noted that many other companies did make similar patterns, sometimes in an attempt to compete with Imperial, though in other cases they actually predate Candlewick and/or simply reflect that fact that the motif is a classic one. The following candlesticks have all at one time or another been erroneously identified as Candlewick, but are *not*!

1. This is probably the candlestick most commonly advertised as Candlewick on eBay. Beware! It is actually the Anchor Hocking Glass Company's No. 984 candleholder (called Berwick or Hobnail by the company, but generally known as Boopie or Ball Edge by collectors today). It was made from the 1950s to the 1980s for the dime store trade and is frequently found today. See AH-11 on p. 13 of volume one of this series. Also made in crystal.

2. The ribs on the Peltier Glass Company's No. 224 candleholder appear from above to end in beads, making this another candleholder often confused with Candlewick. These are of recent vintage and are made in crystal and various colors.

3. This beaded design candlestick has a label indicating that it was made in Czechoslovakia by Avirunion. Of recent vintage, it has also been seen in pink.

4. Although less likely than some of the others on this page to be confused with Candlewick, this unusual candleholder by Altaglass in Canada has ribs that end in beads. Made in peach slag, as seen here, and in transparent colors in the 1960s.

5. This milk glass candleholder with small beads on the rim is currently unknown. Westmoreland made plates with a similar rim, but this style candleholder could just as easily be from Anchor Hocking or one of the other machine-made companies.

6. This milk glass hurricane lamp is another one with small beads that we have not been able to identify with certainty, though we believe it might be from the Rainbow Art Glass Company.

7. This attractive hand-painted candlestick is collectible in its own right. It is the Consolidated Lamp & Glass Company's No. 5460 Con-Cora hobnail candlestick, made only in milk glass from 1957 to 1962.

1. ANCHOR HOCKING NO. 984 BERWICK (BOOPIE) CANDLE-HOLDER – NOT CANDLEWICK!

2. PELTIER GLASS COMPANY'S NO. 224 CANDLEHOLDER

3. CANDLESTICK MADE IN THE CZECH REPUBLIC BY AVIRUNION

4. ALTAGLASS NO. 150 CANDLESTICK IN PEACH SLAG

5. UNKNOWN BEADED-EDGE MILK GLASS CANDLEHOLDER

6. HURRICANE LAMP WITH BEADED EDGE, POSSIBLY RAINBOW

7. CONSOLIDATED LAMP & GLASS COMPANY'S NO. 5460 CON-CORA HOBNAIL CANDLESTICK

See CS-15 on p. 119 of volume one of this series.

8. This is Duncan & Miller's very popular Tear Drop pattern, made from the mid-1940s to the 1950s, and later reissued by Tiffin. See DM-88 on p. 167 of volume one of this series.

9. This is the earlier two-light candlestick in Duncan's Tear Drop pattern, made circa 1937 – 1940. See DM-57 on p. 158 of volume one of this series.

10. This is a later two-light candlestick in Duncan's Tear Drop pattern, made from the mid-1940s to the 1950s and later reissued by Tiffin. See DM-89 on p. 167 of volume one of this series.

11. This one is particularly easy to confuse with Imperial's No. 400/175 Candlewick tall candleholder (IM-79 on p. 202), except that it has four balls on the stem rather than three. It is part of Paden City's No. 444 line, known as Alexander.

12. This is the two-light candlestick in Paden City's No. 444 pattern, known as Alexander to collector's today

13. The manufacturer of this three-light candlestick is unknown. (One sold on eBay with a Westmoreland label, but we have been unable to confirm this attribution — and Westmoreland labels have been readily available in recent years and are sometimes found on all manner of glass, leaving us a little suspicious in this instance.) In person, it is actually easily differentiated from Imperial's Candlewick pattern, since the "balls" on the arms are actually flat lozenges. It is 7¼" high with an arm spread of approximately 8¼".

14. This is Indiana Glass Company's No. 1016/1M1 Coronation candlestick, made in the early 1950s. (See IN-76 on p. 258.)

8. DUNCAN & MILLER'S No. 301-121 TEAR DROP CANDLESTICK

9. DUNCAN & MILLER'S No. 301 TEAR DROP TWO-LIGHT CANDLE-STICK

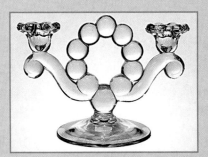

10. DUNCAN & MILLER'S No. 301-122 TEAR DROP TWO-LIGHT CANDLE-STICK

11. PADEN CITY'S No. 444 ALEXANDER ONE-LIGHT CANDLESTICK

12. PADEN CITY'S No. 444 ALEXANDER TWO-LIGHT CANDLESTICK

13. UNKNOWN THREE-LIGHT CANDLESTICK WITH FLAT "BALLS"

14. INDIANA'S No. 1016/1M1 CORONATION CANDLESTICK

INDIANA GLASS COMPANY, Dunkirk, Ind. (1904 – present). The origin of this facto-

ry began with the Beatty-Brady Glass Company, founded in 1895 and in operation in Dunkirk by 1897. In 1899, when the National Glass Company was formed, Beatty-Brady was one of the companies acquired by the combine. Frank W. Merry became superintendent and, in 1904, was involved in the formation of the Indiana Glass Company, which leased the plant from the National. After the failure of the National Glass Company, Merry and a group of associates purchased the factory, and Merry remained president until his death in 1930.

Early production ranged from jelly tumblers to imitation-cut tableware, both in original designs and from molds obtained from the Model Flint Glass Company of Albany, Ind., and the Indiana Tumbler and Goblet Company of Greentown, Ind. (both of which had also joined the National Glass Company). In the 1920s, they introduced a variety of old Sandwich reproductions, as well as a series of very modernistic designs strongly influenced by the Art Deco movement and including the very popular Tea Room pattern, while also producing large quantities of colonial style soda fountain and restaurant ware. Many of these patterns either remained staples for years or were periodically reissued to attract new generations of glass buyers. Production during these years was both handmade and machine-made. Simultaneously, the company also specialized in the production of automobile headlight lenses and other industrial glassware, at one time producing about 80% of the lenses used in the United States.

By the 1950s, the company had encountered financial difficulties, due in part to the acquisition of the Sneath Glass Company of Hartford City, Ind., in an unsuccessful attempt to transition to the manufacture of sealed-beam headlights, which had overtaken the old-style auto lenses in popularity. For a time, stockholders were forced to step in and take over management of the plant, but ultimately the company came back stronger than ever, beginning with a merger with the Lancaster Lens Company of Lancaster, Ohio, to become the Lancaster Glass Corporation and, ultimately, the Lancaster Colony Corporation in 1962. As the Indiana Glass Division of the new conglomerate, the Dunkirk factory continued to make glass under its own name, as well as under the Colony Glassware label for Pitman-Dreitzer & Company, Inc. (For further information on the overlap between these companies, see the chapter on Colony Glassware in volume one of this series.)

Throughout later years, Indiana not only continued to introduce new patterns, but also frequently reissued patterns originally brought out in the 1920s and 1930s. They also acquired and reworked molds from many other companies, including McKee, Paden City, Jenkins, U.S. Glass, Duncan and Miller, and Imperial.

This trend reached a climax in 1970, when Tiara Exclusives was formed as an offshoot of Indiana Glass. Tiara made no glass themselves, but offered sales through a home party plan where hostesses received premiums and bonuses for selling products to friends and invited guests. Jim Hoofstetter, one of the founders of Tiara Exclusives, was a former president of Indiana Glass. Between 1970 and 1998, a majority of Tiara's glassware was made from Indiana molds (or other molds acquired by Lancaster Colony, Indiana's parent company), and most of it was produced at the Dunkirk factory. The Sandwich pattern was Tiara's most successful line, continuing to be sold throughout the entire span of Tiara's existence. It consisted primarily of pieces originally made by Indiana from the 1920s on, supplemented by additional items from Duncan & Miller's Early American Sandwich pattern.

By the time Indiana discontinued handmade operations sometime in the mid-1980s, some Tiara pieces were also being produced by other companies, most notably the Fostoria Glass Company (which had also become a Lancaster Colony division around 1987), the Fenton Art Glass Company, and the L. E. Smith Glass Company. Both Fostoria and Fenton produced candlesticks for Tiara from Indiana molds as well as from their own molds, and other companies may have done so as well.

Indiana still operates today as a division of Lancaster Colony, although in late 2002 all glassware manufacture was discontinued at the Dunkirk factory and consolidated in Lancaster Colony's Sapulpa, Oklahoma, plant. As of this writing it was announced that the Indiana name will continue to be used, even though the glassware will no longer originate in that state. Candlesticks from Lancaster Colony are still in production and can even be found in some supermarkets today.

LABEL, 1940S/1950S

LABEL, 1951 – 1954

LABEL, 1954 – 1988

LABEL, 1954 – 1988

COLORS

Initially, Indiana made crystal only. By 1922, they were advertising "decorated ware, both fired and cold colors," treatments that are frequently found on Indiana's candlesticks from this period, often with black trim. Their first true colors were green and amber, introduced in 1925, followed by rose (pink) in 1926. Topaz (yellow) came out around 1930. According to Hazel Marie Weatherman, all of these colors except amber were relatively short-lived, and had been discontinued by the early 1930s. Dinnerware in an opaque ivory was issued in 1933. Transparent light blue was introduced around 1940. A rich blue-green (sometimes described as teal) was made in the 1950s and, like so many other companies, in 1957 Indiana began large-scale production of milk glass. Olive and gold were both advertised in 1963. Other 1960s colors include blue, lime green, lemon yellow, orange, amber, and red, many available with carnival or satin finishes. Crystal was also offered with ruby stain. Red carnival (called sunset, not to be confused with Tiara's amberina, also called sunset) was made in 1980. Late colors from the 1990s include ruby (stain on crystal), evergreen, and teal.

With the advent of Tiara Exclusives in 1969 – 1970, color became increasingly important. Colors made for Tiara (some by companies other than Indiana) include:

Ruby	1970; 1984 – 1990, called fiery ruby.
Gold	Sometimes called Sandwich gold, a version of amber, generally darker than the shade made in the 1920s, 1970 – 1991.
Sunset	Amberina, circa 1972 – 1978.
Lime	A medium shade of green, slightly on the yellow side, circa 1972 – 1977.
Blue	A medium shade of aquamarine, circa 1972 – 1980.
Rose pink	1973 – 1977; 1985 – 1987 (see also coral, dusty rose, and peach, below).
Smoke	Circa 1975 (see also platinum, below).
Black	In production by 1975 – 1994.
Amethyst	In production by 1975 (originally an Indiana color, and made by Fenton after 1986).
Green	A darker shade than lime, similar to the blue-green made in the 1950s, 1975 – 1977.
Bicentennial blue	A dark greenish blue, sometimes called midnight blue, 1976 – 1977.
Burnt honey	Amber shading to reddish brown, circa 1978 – 1982.
Teal	A deep greenish blue, 1980 – 1981; 1993.
Regal blue	Light cobalt, 1981.
Horizon blue	A deep aquamarine, 1981 – 1984.
Yellow mist	1981 – 1985.
Ruby stain	1981 – 1982.
Chantilly green	A light green, 1982 – 1991.
Ice blue	Light blue, 1982 – 1987.
Coral	Deep pink, 1983 – 1986 (see also dusty rose and peach, below).
Cobalt blue	1984 – 1986.
Emerald green	Dark green, 1985.
Hazel brown	1986.
Platinum	A soft grey/blue, 1986 – 1990.
Imperial blue	A medium dark shade of blue, 1986 – 1998.
White lace crystal	Opalescent crystal, a Fenton color, 1987 – 1991.
Dusty rose	A deep pink with lavender highlights, probably a Fenton color, 1986 – 1994.
Tea rose	Opalescent pink, probably a Fenton color, 1987 – 1989.
Wisteria	Violet, probably a Fenton color, July 1989 – Dec. 1991.
Provincial blue	Opalescent blue, a Fenton color, 1988 – Dec. 1991.
Peach	Light pink, July 1989 – 1998.
Green	A deep shade, close to teal, made by Fenton, 1990.
Sage mist	Opaque green, a Fenton color, 1990 – Dec. 1991.
Teal mist	Light opalescent green, a Fenton color, 1991 – 1993.
Aquamarine	Pastel greenish blue, 1991 – 1994; a darker shade of aquamarine was made by L. E. Smith, 1996 – 1997.
Azure blue	Medium bright blue, a Dalzell Viking color, 1991 – 1993.
Sea mist	A soft dark green, a Fenton color, 1992 – 1993.
Spruce	A bluish green, Dec. 1993 – 1998.
Plum	A dark amethyst, an L. E. Smith color, 1994.

Vintage blue	Pastel blue, darker than ice blue, an L. E. Smith color, 1992 – 1994.
Yellow	An L. E. Smith color, 1996 – 1998.
Green mist	A Dalzell Viking color, 1996 – 1997.
Spearmint	A light green, similar to Chantilly green, 1998.

IN-1. No. 300 TOY BIRTHDAY CANDLE-STICKS IN ICE BLUE, CRYSTAL, MILK GLASS, AND FROSTED CRYSTAL

No. 300 toy birthday candlestick. 3" high with a 2⅛" diameter hexagonal base. Introduced 1905, in crystal only. Reissued for Tiara Exclusives as colonial birthday candleholders, No. 10075 in frosted crystal (1978 – 1983) and No. 490 in ice blue (1983 – 1986). A companion footed tray (3½" high) was also offered, made by using the birthday candlestick as a base with a square ashtray attached. (This footed tray was offered in horizon blue as an appreciation gift for hostesses from 1983 to 1987, so the candlestick is also possible in this color.) The candlestick was also made in milk glass for Tiara, probably in the 1970s. The crystal example in the accompanying picture has a completely flat base, whereas the milk glass, ice blue, and frosted crystal examples have a raised circular rim around the edge of the opening on the underside. There is also a slight rim around the opening of the candle cups of the latter three that is missing on the crystal candlestick, both details probably indicating that the crystal example is from the original production period. Crystal, milk glass: $10.00 – 12.00. Ice blue: $20.00 – 30.00.

IN-2. No. 4 WEDGWOOD DESIGN CANDLESTICKS IN CRYSTAL WITH FIRED ON CANARY (YELLOW) AND HORIZON BLUE (FOSTORIA REISSUE FOR TIARA EXCLUSIVES)

No. 4 Wedgewood design candlestick. 8⅛" high with a 4⅛" diameter round base. Originally made from 1918 to 1929 in crystal with fired on colors: blue, canary (yellow), jade (green), and orange, all with black trim around the base and the top of the candle cup. Frequently offered as part of a console set. Reissued for Tiara Exclusives as the Duchess candlestick with a slightly thicker top rim, so that its height is 8⅜". The Tiara reissues were reportedly made by Fostoria, initially in horizon blue as No. 10009 and then as No. 009 (1982 – 1984), and as No. 292 in cobalt (1984 – 1985). (See FO-224 on p. 71.) Also known in pink and in crystal with amethyst stain; other colors are possible. Crystal: $12.00 – 15.00. Crystal w/fired-on color: $12.00 – 17.50. Horizon blue, cobalt: $17.00 – 25.00.

Candlestick. 7¾" high with a 3½" diameter round base. Made circa 1926 – 1928 in crystal with fired-on colors: blue, jade (green), orange, and, probably, canary (yellow), often with black trim. Has been attributed to Indiana, though we have found no catalog or other confirmation for this. However, the attribution seems likely, based on the colors (which are identical to those used on the preceding candlestick.) Almost identical to Cambridge's No. 437, 438, and 439 candlesticks, which were made from around 1922 to 1928. (See CB-49, p. 63, in book one of this series.) The main differences can be seen in the accompanying photograph (IN-3a); the rings on the Cambridge candlestick are more prominent and rounded and the foot is proportionately smaller. The mold seams on the Indiana candlestick are rough and unpolished. Crystal: $8.00 – 10.00. Crystal w/fired-on color: $10.00 – 15.00.

IN-3. CANDLESTICK, BELIEVED TO BE INDIANA, IN CRYSTAL WITH FIRED ON GREEN COLOR

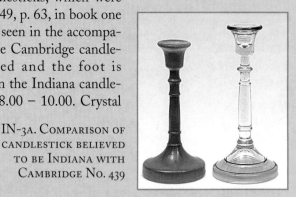

IN-3A. COMPARISON OF CANDLESTICK BELIEVED TO BE INDIANA WITH CAMBRIDGE No. 439

Candlestick. 8½" high with a 4½" diameter round base. Known in crystal with fired-on colors (blue with black trim, white with red trim, orange with black trim, jade with black trim, and ivory with blue or black trim); also made in amber, pink, green, and possibly other colors. Probably circa 1920s or early 1930s. Attribution to Indiana is based on the known colors and on the fact that this candlestick was reissued for Tiara Exclusives in 1992 in azure blue as Tiara's No. 606 Empress candlestick. However, by that time, Indiana was no longer pressing glass, so the Tiara reissue was actually made by Dalzell Viking. (See DV-7, p. 127, in volume one of this series.) The other pieces reissued for Tiara as part of the Empress pattern included items from molds originally belonging to McKee, so the source of the mold for the candlestick cannot be automatically assumed to be Indiana. Other refer-

IN-4. CANDLESTICKS, BELIEVED TO BE INDIANA, IN DARK GREEN, PINK, LIGHT GREEN, AND CRYSTAL WITH FIRED ON IVORY AND BLACK DECORATION

ence works have tentatively attributed this candlestick to the U.S. Glass Company because of its stylistic resemblance to that company's No. 87 one-light candelabrum. The Tiara reissue has ribbed swirls extending to the bottom of the base, whereas the original has ribs on the column only. Crystal: $12.00 – 15.00. Amber, crystal w/fired-on color: $12.00 – 20.00. Green, pink: $15.00 – 20.00.

Handled candlestick. 4¼" high with a 3½" diameter octagonal base. This candlestick has been attributed to Indiana by James Measell and Berry Wiggins in their *Great American Glass of the Roaring 20s*. It is known in crystal, amber, jade, and black. Probably circa 1920s. It has been seen with fired-on blue color with a hand painted parrot decoration very similar to that offered by the United States Glass Company in 1926. Very similar to L. E. Smith Glass Company's No. 221 candlestick (circa 1954), as can be seen in the accompanying photograph (IN-5a), the Smith candlestick being the one on the left. Crystal: $6.00 – 8.00. Amber, black: $10.00 – 12.50.

IN-5. HANDLED CANDLE-STICK IN BLACK, ATTRIBUTED TO INDIANA

IN-5A. COMPARISON OF HANDLED CANDLESTICK, ATTRIBUTED TO INDIANA (ON RIGHT) AND L. E. SMITH'S No. 221 CANDLESTICK (ON LEFT)

Candlestick, unknown pattern number. 7¼" high with a 3¼" square base. Known in crystal only. Appears in an Indiana catalog circa 1925. Other companies made similar style candlesticks, but with different proportions, including the J. R. Higbee Glass Company (see HI-1 on p. 164) and the Westmoreland Glass Specialty Company. Tiffin's No. 63 candlestick, made in black satin, is also very similar. $10.00 – 15.00.

IN-6. CANDLE-STICK, UNKNOWN PATTERN NUMBER

IN-7. CANDLE-
STICK, UNKNOWN
PATTERN NUMBER,
FROM CA. 1925
CATALOG

Candlestick, unknown pattern number and dimensions. Appears in the same Indiana catalog, circa 1925, as the candlestick on the preceding page (IN-6). Two very similar candlesticks were made by the Imperial Glass Company. Imperial's No. 6247 appears to be identical (see IM-17 on p. 183), whereas their No. 677 has beveled edges. (See IM-13 on p. 182.) $10.00 – 15.00.

IN-8.
CANDLESTICK,
UNKNOWN
PATTERN
NUMBER

Candlestick, unknown pattern number. 8½" high with a 3¾" hexagonal base. Known in crystal only. Appears in an Indiana catalog circa 1925. The example shown has a simple cutting. Several other companies made similar candlesticks, notably Westmoreland's No. 1034, Northwood's No. 695, and Fenton's No. 449 (FN-1 on p. 179 of volume one of this series), but without the step-up base seen on the Indiana candlestick. Lancaster Glass Company also made an almost identical candlestick, but its base is 15⁄16" high, compared to only 5⁄8" on the candlestick in the accompanying photograph. $15.00 – 20.00.

Unknown candlestick. 8½" high with a 3⅞" hexagonal base. Attribution of this candlestick to Indiana is tentative, but based on a number of factors, most notably its similarity to the preceding candlestick, IN-8. Virtually all of the dimensions of these two candlesticks are identical, the most noticeable difference (other than the impressed design) being the addition of a rim on the top of the candle cup, presumably to hold a bobeche and prisms in place. (It might be noted that this was standard with most of Indiana's candlesticks of the 1930s and 1940s, which might be the era to which this candlestick belongs.) The quality of the glass is also very similar to that of most Indiana, i.e., good, but with a slight film. Also, the impressed design is similar to other known Indiana lines, with the flowers and scrolling foliage reminiscent of a pattern advertised in 1911 (that did not include a candlestick, to the best of our knowledge), as well as to the later No. 371 line. (See IN-36 on p. 248.) The use of horizontal ribs also appears on other patterns. Is it Indiana? We don't know, but present it as a possibility. If not Indiana, an English origin is also a possibility. $15.00 – 20.00.

IN-9. UNKNOWN
CANDLESTICK

No. 170 Sandwich low candlestick. This pattern is also known as Early American. 3½ to 3¾" high with a 4 to 4⅛" diameter round base. The Sandwich pattern was originally brought out in January 1926, probably including the low candlestick. Production continued until at least the 1930s, and probably a full decade longer, since the low candlestick appears in a 1940 Blackwell Wielandy Company catalog. It also appears in a catalog that has been dated to around 1950, but it isn't known if production was continuous for this entire period. It was later reissued for Tiara Exclusives from 1971 to 1993. Original colors for the pattern included crystal, amber, green, and pink. The Tiara reissues were offered in amber (as No. 10216 and, later, No. 216, 1971 – 1982), bicentennial blue (as No. 10250, 1976 only, with reportedly less than 15,000 made), peach (as No. 897, 1992 – 1994, probably made by Fenton), and sea mist green (as No. 552, 1993 only). It is possible that some candlesticks may also have been made in Chantilly green in 1984, since a footed cake plate was offered that year made from the wine tray in the pattern with the low candleholder used as a foot, but if so, they were never part of Tiara's regular production. The Tiara amber may have been a deeper shade than the early amber; in addition, at some point prior to the Tiara reissues the mold was reworked and, as can be seen from the accompanying photograph and the range of dimensions given above, it is fairly easy to differentiate between early production and the later reissues because of the distinct difference in the proportions of the earlier candlestick, which is only 3" in diameter at the constriction, compared to 4" for the Tiara low candlestick. There is also a ⅛" difference in the diameter of the base, and the heights are slightly different, primarily because the Tiara low candlestick has a more pronounced rim. Some pieces in this pattern were reissued in the 1950s in blue-green (or teal) and in milk glass, so it is possible the candlesticks were made in these colors as well. Tiara production of the pattern included pieces in ruby in 1969 and spruce green from 1994 to 1998, but the low candlesticks are not listed in factory literature in these colors. The candlestick shown in IN-10a might be teal, sea mist green, or spruce green. The candlesticks have been seen in crystal, with red stain on the flower at the center of the base and the remainder of the piece silvered, a decoration applied by Cape Cod Glass. Other decorations and colors are possible. Tiara also used this candlestick in amber as the base for their No. 219 candle lamp (1988 – 1991) by adding a clear glass globe, giving it an overall height of 9¾". Crystal: $8.00 – 10.00. Amber: $10.00 – 12.50. Bicentennial blue, green, peach, pink: $12.50 – 15.00.

IN-10. No. 170 SANDWICH LOW CANDLESTICKS IN AMBER, CRYSTAL, AND BICENTENNIAL BLUE

IN-10A. No. 170 SANDWICH LOW CANDLESTICK IN GREEN (POSSIBLY TEAL, SEA MIST GREEN, OR SPRUCE GREEN)

Other companies made versions of the Sandwich pattern, including Duncan and Miller, Tiffin (using the Duncan molds), and Anchor Hocking, but none of them made this style of candlestick. The molds for Duncan's Early American Sandwich pattern were ultimately acquired by Indiana, including the No. 41 candlestick (DM-68, p. 161, in volume one of this series), which was reissued by Indiana for Colony Glassware (CL-12, p. 112, in volume one of this series.)

No. 170 Sandwich handled candlestick. This pattern is also known as Early American. 3½" high with a 4" diameter round base. Production dates unknown. Although the pattern was originally made from 1926 until at least 1940, and was then returned to production intermittently in the 1950s, before its becoming a best selling line for Tiara Exclusives from 1971 to the 1990s, we have not found this style candlestick in any of the catalogs. Known in crystal, amber, and green. Although the theory has been proposed that these may have been hostess gifts or special promotional items made during the Tiara era, they do not appear in any Tiara literature and demonstrate the same difference in proportions that can be seen in the comparison of the early issue candlestick shown in IN-10 above with the Tiara reissues. The color of the handled candlestick is also a lighter amber that is more on the yellow-gold side

IN-11. No. 170 SANDWICH HANDLED CANDLESTICKS IN CRYSTAL AND AMBER

than the deeper amber used for the Tiara pieces. (Though it should be noted that Tiara amber is not a uniform shade, but ranges from only slightly darker than the early amber to the much darker shade seen in IN-10 and IN-13.) Finally, the detail of the pattern in the handled candlestick is much sharper. It also bears a strong resemblance to the unknown candlestick that is shown below (see IN-12), with both sharing the same slender proportions, which might suggest an earlier production period (possibly either in the 1920s or in the 1960s, when the color gold was in production). Crystal: 12.50 – 15.00. Amber: 15.00 – 25.00. Green: $20.00 – 30.00.

IN-12. LOW CANDLESTICK, PATTERN NUMBER UNKNOWN

Low candlestick. 3½" high with a 4" diameter round base. No information available, but it appears to be the same general shape as the early version of the No. 170 Sandwich low candlestick (IN-10 on the preceding page), but without the Sandwich pattern impressed in the base and with the same general proportions as the No. 170 Sandwich handled candlestick (IN-11 on the preceding page). Production dates unknown. The authors have seen this candlestick in crystal only, but colors are possible. $8.00 – 10.00.

IN-13. No. 170 SANDWICH TALL CANDLESTICKS IN AMBER, CRYSTAL, AND CHANTILLY GREEN

No. 170 Sandwich tall candlestick. This pattern is also known as Early American. 8½" high with a 5" diameter round base. The Sandwich pattern was originally brought out in January 1926, probably including the tall candlestick. (Reports that the mold for this candlestick originally belonged to Duncan & Miller are erroneous, since it appears in original Indiana catalogs from the 1920s and 1930s; also, the only candlestick made by Duncan & Miller as part of their Early American Sandwich line was a low one, only 4" high — see DM-68 on p. 161 of volume one of this series.) Production continued until at least the 1930s, and possibly a full decade longer, since the Sears catalog offered this candlestick as part of a console set as late as 1939 and the low candlestick (IN-10 on the preceding page) appears in a 1940 Blackwell Wielandy Company catalog. Both candlesticks appear in a catalog that has been dated to around 1950, but it isn't known if production of the pattern was continuous for this entire period. The candlestick was later reissued for Tiara Exclusives from 1971 to 1995. Original colors for the pattern included crystal, amber, green, and pink. The Tiara reissues were offered in amber (as No. 10258 and, later, No. 258, 1978 – 1986), Chantilly green (as No. 10345 and, later, No. 345, 1982 – 1986), peach (as No. 679, 1993 – 1995, probably made by Fenton), and spruce (as No. 471, 1995 only, made by Fenton). Some candlesticks were also made in crystal, both plain and with satin finish, as special promotions. The green candlesticks dating from the 1920s are a slightly brighter shade than Chantilly green. Differentiating between the early pink and later peach may be more difficult through color alone. However, it is actually quite easy to identify the early candlesticks from this pattern because the molds were modified at some point prior to being reissued by Tiara. As can be seen from the accompanying photograph, the Tiara reissues differ in three ways: 1) The original version has additional leaves appearing on the bottom half of the column, below the stippled area, a design element removed from the later mold; 2) The proportions of the two candlesticks are noticeably different, with the circumference at the bottom of the column of the early version being only 2⅜", in comparison with 2¾" for the Tiara reissue; and, 3) the rim of the base on the original version is only ⅛" high, whereas the rim on the Tiara reissue is ½". Some pieces in this pattern were reissued in the 1950s in blue-green (or teal) and in milk glass, so it is possible the candlesticks were made in these colors as well. Tiara's production of the pattern included pieces in ruby in 1969, but the tall candlesticks were not among the items made at that time. The candlesticks have been seen with a floral decoration on the base and the remainder of the piece in fired-on white. Other decorations and colors are possible. Crystal: $10.00 – 15.00. Amber: $12.50 – 17.50. Chantilly green, green, peach, pink, spruce: $15.00 – 25.00.

IN-13A. TIARA REISSUE (LEFT) AND OLD SANDWICH CANDLESTICK (RIGHT)

No. 10245 Sandwich footed candleholder. Later listed as No. 245. Also known as Early American. 3¼" high with a 3" diameter round footed base. Although the Sandwich pattern was originally made from 1926 until at least 1940 and was then returned to production intermittently in the 1950s and later, this item was not included as part of the original pattern. It was introduced after the Sandwich line was reissued by Tiara Exclusives. Its design was probably based on the footed sherbet, with a ribbed, scalloped rim added and the well for a candle inserted. It is listed in factory literature in amber only (1980 – 1983). Tiara also made a fairy lamp (or "glo lamp") using the sherbet with a plain rim and a domed lid, in amber (as No. 10237, and later, No. 237, 1975 – 1989), regal blue (as No. 492, 1981 only), pine green (as No. 422, 1983 only), Chantilly green (as No. 364, 1985 – 1991), hazel brown (as No. 413, 1986 only), and peach (as No. 910 or No. 998, originally made in limited quantity in 1991 and added to the regular line from 1993 to 1997). Unlike the other candlesticks in the Sandwich pattern, which were hand made, the footed candleholder and glo lamp were both machine made. $10.00 – 12.50.

IN-14. No. 10245 SANDWICH FOOTED CANDLEHOLDER IN AMBER (TIARA EXCLUSIVES)

No. 172 Old English candlestick. Pattern is also known as Threading. 4" high with a 4⅛" diameter round base. Circa 1926 – 1929. Made in crystal, amber, green, and pink (rare). Other pieces in the pattern were made with fired-on colors (red with black trim) or with lavender stain; it is possible the candlesticks may be found with these or other decorations. An identical candlestick without the "threading" on the underside of the base was also made as No. 12. (See IN-43 on p. 249.) Amber, crystal: $10.00 – 15.00. Green: $15.00 – 20.00. Pink: $30.00 – 40.00.

IN-15. No. 172 OLD ENGLISH CANDLESTICK IN GREEN

No. 7 candlestick. 2" high with a 4⅛" diameter round base. Advertised as early as 1927, when it appeared in the spring Sears catalog as part of a five-piece console set (consisting of two pairs of candlesticks and a bowl, in either amber or green, for only 98 cents). Also known in crystal and with a lavender stain, with other colors/decorations possible. Although not in a catalog that can be dated to the 1930s, this candlestick must have been returned to production at a later time, since Hazel Marie Weatherman shows it in a reprint from a 1950 catalog. Amber, crystal: $6.00 – 7.50. Crystal w/stain, green: $10.00 – 12.50.

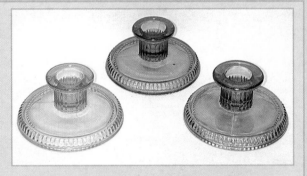

IN-16. No. 7 CANDLESTICKS IN GREEN, AMBER, AND CRYSTAL WITH LAVENDER STAIN

No. 600 low candlestick. Known as Tea Room to collectors today, this pattern was originally advertised as Centennial. 3" high with a 4¾" base. Made 1928 – 1931. (Although some sources indicate this pattern was made beginning in 1926, the earliest advertisement for it was in December 1927, announcing that the complete line would be shown at the glass show in January 1928.) Made in crystal, green, and pink; there was limited production of the pattern in amber, so this color is also possible for the candlestick. The pattern was covered by design patent D76,986, filed September 24, 1928, and approved November 27, 1928. The designer was given as Jeddia B. Clark. The candlestick was among

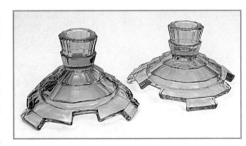

IN-17. No. 600 TEA ROOM LOW CANDLESTICKS IN GREEN AND PINK

IN-17A. No.
600 TEA ROOM
LOW CANDLE-
STICK IN
CRYSTAL, WITH
FROSTED
HIGHLIGHTS

an assortment of pieces offered in the fall 1930 Sears catalog as Art Moderne, with a three piece console set selling for 98 cents. Because the sharp edges on this pattern were so prone to damage, perfect pieces today will sell for considerably higher prices! Crystal: $20.00 – 25.00. Green, pink: $30.00 – 40.00.

IN-18. CANDLESTICK, POSSIBLY INDIANA, IN TWO
SHADES OF AMBER AND CRYSTAL WITH HAND PAINTED
AZALEA DECORATION

IN-18A. LARKIN
COMPANY CATALOG,
FEATURING HAND
PAINTED AZALEA
GLASSWARE

IS THIS INDIANA?

Candlestick. 3¾" high with a base diameter that varies from 4⅝" to 5". Circa 1928 – 1932. Known in crystal, amber, black, green, and pink. There has been some uncertainty involving attribution of this candlestick. William Heacock, James Measell, and Berry Wiggins' *Diamond/Dugan* identifies it as Diamond's No. 625 candlestick. (See DI-2 on p. 132 of volume one of this series.) However, it appears as part of an assortment in a Larkin Company catalog with a hand painted decoration to match Noritake's Azalea pattern (see IN-18a) and all of the other items in the assortment match shapes found in Indiana's Moderne Classic line (see IN-19 below). Either both companies made identical candlesticks, a third company bought pieces from both and combined them to create the Azalea assortment – or this candlestick was, in fact, made only by Indiana. The candlesticks with the Azalea decoration were offered circa 1929 – 1932 as Larkin Brothers' No. 114. Amber, crystal: $8.00 – 10.00. Black, green, pink: $12.50 – 15.00. Crystal with Azalea decoration: $80.00 – 110.00.

IN-18B. CANDLE-
STICK WITH HAND
PAINTED AZALEA
DECORATION (TO
MATCH NORITAKE
CHINA). NOTE
DIFFERENCE IN THE
DECORATION FROM
EXAMPLE IN IN-18

IN-19. No. 603 MODERNE
CLASSIC CANDLESTICK IN
CRYSTAL WITH FIRED-ON
COLOR AND HAND PAINTED
DECORATION

No. 603 Moderne Classic candlestick. 3¾" high with a 4½" diameter round base. Circa 1928 – 1940 or later. Known in crystal, green, pink, and yellow; amber and black are also possible, considering the time period this candlestick was in production. Most often seen in crystal with fired-on colors, hand–painted decorations, or a combination of both, sometimes with platinum trim. Also available etched or cut. Very similar in general shape, especially the octagonal rim around the candle cup, to Heisey's No. 114 candlestick (1926 – 1931, see HE-49 on p. 117). Crystal: $8.00 – 10.00. Crystal w/decoration, green, pink, yellow: $15.00 – 20.00.

No. 300 Intaglio triangular candlestick. Later known as Constellation. 5" high, with a base that measures 4" from point to point. The pattern originally came out in 1935, but it isn't known when the triangular candlestick was added. It does not appear on a catalog page that probably dates from that year, but does appear in a catalog that has been estimated to be around 1950. Original production was probably in crystal only, though colors are possible. The candlesticks were reissued by Tiara Exclusives in sunset (as No. 10087, 1977 – 1980), teal (as No. 10153, 1980 – 1981), and yellow mist (as No. 10185, 1982 – 1983). Other known colors include amber (possibly early production), horizon blue (circa 1981), and horizon blue with satin finish; other colors are possible. The pattern was originally called Intaglio because of the grape design appearing in the center of some pieces. (See IN-21 below.) Crystal: $10.00 – 12.00. All Tiara colors: $12.50 – 15.00.

IN-20. CONSTELLATION TRIANGULAR CANDLESTICKS IN HORIZON BLUE AND TEAL (TIARA EXCLUSIVES REISSUES OF No. 300 INTAGLIO)

No. 300 Intaglio two-light candlestick. (Some pieces in the pattern were reissued by Tiara as Constellation, though this candlestick was not among them.) 5⅜" high with a 5⅛" diameter round base and an arm spread of 6". The pattern originally came out in 1935, but it isn't known when the two-light candlestick was added. It does not appear on a catalog page that probably dates from that year, but does appear in a catalog from around 1950. It is shown in three styles, but is actually found in even more combinations: both with and without the "intaglio" grape design in the center medallion, with and without a figured base (with the star-like design that inspired the later name of Constellation for this pattern when some pieces were reissued by Tiara Exclusive), and with or without a satin finish on the base. Other decorations are also possible, since Indiana often offered candlesticks from this period with various combinations of clear and satin finish, as well as with a variety of colored stains. It has also been seen in all satin with a silver overlay decoration applied by the Silver City Glass

IN-21. No. 300 INTAGLIO TWO-LIGHT CANDLESTICKS – NOTE VARIANCES TO CENTER MEDALLION AND BASE

Company. Known in crystal only. Three design patents were applied for with this pattern: D98,052 for a plate (filed October 29, 1935 and approved January 7, 1936), D98,236 for a goblet (filed October 16, 1935, and approved January 21, 1936), and D98,453 for a bowl (filed November 21, 1935, and approved February 4, 1936). The designer on all three was Jeddia B. Clark. Plain panel: $15.00 – 20.00. Intaglio panel: $20.00 – 30.00.

THE "INDIANA PONTIL MARK" – A POSSIBLE CLUE TO MANUFACTURER?

The No. 300 Intaglio two-light candlestick also has a distinctive mark on the underside of its base that will be referred to frequently in the following pages. It is an irregular mark (see the close-up in IN-21a) that appears to have resulted from the manufacturing process. For want of a better term, we have referred to this as a "pontil mark," since it was probably caused by attaching the candlestick to a pontil rod or other similar tool. When the candlestick was removed from this tool, the removal left a mark which appears on virtually every candlestick with a similarly flattened base that was made by this company. Taking this a step further, we have encountered this same mark on a number of "unknown" candlesticks that bear both stylistic resemblance to Indiana and also are similar in glass quality, but have not found this mark on any candle-

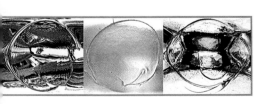

IN-21A. CLOSE-UP OF PONTIL MARKS APPEARING ON THE BOTTOM OF INDIANA CANDLESTICKS

sticks that we can attribute to any other known company. (Some Paden City Glass Mfg. Company candlesticks have "straw marks" on the bottom that in rare instances might be confused with this mark, but that usually are not circular in shape, as the Indiana marks generally are.) In the pages that follow, we will include a number of these candlesticks, emphasizing that our attribution is tentative by enclosing them in purple boxes, but also feeling confident that, after taking all of these factors into consideration, the probability is that they are products of the Indiana Glass Company.

Two-light candlestick. 5½" high with a 5" diameter round base and an arm spread of 5¾". Known in crystal only, with satin finish or colored stain on the intaglio design in the center medallion. No other information available. The fruit design is very similar to that used on the No. 300 Intaglio two-light candlestick on the preceding page (IN-21), as is the general design. Also, this candlestick has the pontil mark described on that candlestick. $20.00 – 30.00.

IN-22. UNKNOWN TWO-LIGHT CANDLESTICK, PROBABLY INDIANA

IN-23. No. 301 GARLAND TWO-LIGHT CANDLESTICK WITH MULTI-COLORED STAIN

No. 301 two-light candlestick. Called Garland by collectors. 5½" high with a 5⅛" diameter round base. Originally advertised in crystal in 1935, it appears in a catalog that has been dated to circa 1950, so production appears to have been extensive. Reissued in milk glass circa 1957 – 1964 or later. The crystal versions were available plain, with a satin-finish base, with satin finish on the fruit only, with ruby stain on the base, with ruby or amber stain on the fruit, and with various multi-colored stains; other combinations and decorations are possible. Has been seen with silver overlay done by the Rockwell Silver Company. This pattern is often confused with Westmoreland's Della Robbia line, which dates to roughly the same years and also employs a fruit motif. This candlestick has the irregular shaped pontil mark described on p. 243. The 12½" oval bowl in the pattern was reissued in blue carnival in the late 1960s as part of a console set including the No. 2970 Harvest footed candleholders. (See IN-86 on p. 261.) Crystal: $12.00 – 17.50. Crystal w/stain, milk glass: $20.00 – 25.00.

IN-23A. No. 301 GARLAND TWO-LIGHT CANDLESTICK IN MILK GLASS

IN-24. UNKNOWN TWO-LIGHT CANDLESTICK, POSSIBLY INDIANA GARLAND

Two-light candlestick. 4½" high with a 4⅝" diameter round base. Known in crystal only. Is this No. 301 Garland? We aren't sure, but believe that it probably is, based on the fruit design. The oversized grapes are very similar to those on IN-23 above, as is the general shape and pattern of the veining on the leaves. Other pieces in the pattern also have peaches and bananas in pairs, arranged in a similar fashion to those found on this candlestick. The quality of the glass is also comparable to other pieces of Indiana. If this is Garland, it probably dates to the 1930s or 1940s. The other well known fruit pattern from this period, Westmoreland's Della Robbia, does not have bananas and has grapes that are much smaller in proportion to the rest of the fruit. $15.00 – 20.00.

Three-light candlestick. 5¼" high, with a 5⅛" diameter round base and an arm spread of 7⅜". Known in crystal only, but has been seen decorated with green stain on the arms and a white and silver base; other decorations are likely. This candlestick has the irregular pontil mark described on p. 243. It was offered by Montgomery Ward from 1936 to 1938 as part of a console set with a grey floral cutting on the base. The bowl that accompanied the set bears some resemblance to Paden City's Largo pattern, raising the possibility that Paden City was the manufacturer; however, the preponderance of evidence leads us to believe this is another Indiana candlestick. $15.00 – 22.50.

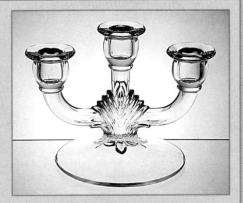

IN-25. UNKNOWN THREE-LIGHT CANDLESTICK, PROBABLY INDIANA

Candlestick. 8½" high with a 4½" diameter removable bobeche. The base is square with rounded corners (4¾" x 5⅜"). Known in crystal only. Like the three-light candlestick above (IN-25), this one was also offered by Montgomery Ward, in their fall/winter 1936 – 1937 catalog, but can be confidently attributed to Indiana because the bobeche is one that was used on other known Indiana candlesticks and can be verified through catalogs. The egg and dart design on the bobeche also appears on the border on the bottom rim of this candlestick. $12.00 – 17.50. Add $5.00 – 7.50 for bobeche and prisms.

IN-26. CANDLESTICK, UNKNOWN PATTERN NUMBER

Two-light candlestick. Dimensions unavailable. Known in crystal only. This candlestick has been seen with the same bobeches known to have been used on IN-26 above and appears to be from the same pattern, so probably also dates to the mid-1930s. $15.00 – 22.50. Add $10.00 – 12.00 for bobeches and prisms.

IN-27. TWO-LIGHT CANDLESTICK, UNKNOWN PATTERN NUMBER

IN-27A. TWO-LIGHT CANDELABRA, UNKNOWN PATTERN NUMBER

IN-27B. CLOSE-UP OF BOBECHE, USED ON MANY INDIANA CANDELABRA

IN-28. No. 303 TWO-LIGHT
CANDLESTICK

No. 303 two-light candlestick. Also offered as part of the No. 1000 pattern. 5⅜" high with a 5" diameter round base. Introduced in 1936 and in production until at least 1940. Made in crystal only, but known with blue stain on the base, cut to clear, and probably available with other decorations or stains, including ruby and amber. Other pieces in the pattern were offered with gold encrusted decoration. Offered as part of a console set. Also available with bobeches and prisms. The candlesticks with these bobeches were sold by Montgomery Ward from 1937 to 1940; however, in their last appearance in a Montgomery Ward catalog, they were offered with a different bobeche than the standard one. This candlestick has the irregular pontil mark described on p. 243. $15.00 – 20.00. Add $10.00 – 12.00 for bobeches and prisms.

IN-29. No. 303
ONE-LIGHT
CANDLESTICK
WITH SILVER
DECORATION ON
BASE

No. 303 one-light candlestick. Also offered as part of the No. 1000 pattern. 6½" high with a 5⅛" diameter round base. Made circa 1936 – 1940. Made in crystal only, but also offered with ruby and amber stain or with gold encrusted decoration. The example pictured has alternating rings of silver and satin finish on the foot. Also sold with a bobeche and prisms. $15.00 – 20.00. Add $5.00 – 7.50 for bobeche and prisms.

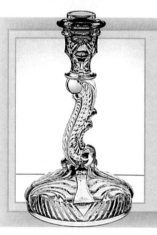

IN-30. No. 303
ONE-LIGHT
CANDLESTICK

No. 303 one-light candlestick. 8½" high with a 4⅝" diameter base. Originally made in crystal, circa 1936 – 1938; later reissued in black, probably in the 1970s or after. Other pieces in the pattern are known with amber, ruby, and blue stain or with gold encrusted decoration, so any of these are possible. The third candlestick in the No. 303 pattern, this one has the ridges found on the other pieces, but is otherwise atypical of the pattern, appearing more baroque in design than art deco. Also available with bobeche and prisms, using the same bobeche seen in IN-27b on the preceding page. $12.00 – 17.50. Add $5.00 – 7.50 for bobeche and prisms.

IN-31. No. 303 CANDLEBOWL
OR EPERGNE BASE

No. 303 candlebowl (?). Approximately 4½" high, with a diameter of 9" x 13". Production dates unknown, but probably circa 1936 – 1940, in crystal only. This piece does not appear in any of the catalogs we have had access to and we are not even certain that it is intended to be a candleholder. The element in the center of the bowl would take a 1" diameter candle and is almost 1¾" deep; however, it is possible that it is meant to hold a vase instead. There is a No. 303½ comport shown in one of the catalogs, but shaped differently; although it looks like a floral bowl with its sides turned upward, the terminology "comport" suggests that it might be a differently tooled version of this piece. However, the catalog picture gives no indication of its having the center element. Two of the baskets in the line are identical to the shape of this piece, but with handles added. $20.00 – 25.00.

No. 305 two-light candlestick. 5⅜" high with a 5⅛" diameter round base and an arm spread of 8". Production dates unknown, but probably originally made in crystal in the late 1930s and reissued in milk glass in the late 1950s. A very ornate design of fruit and leaves; the crystal versions are likely to have been decorated both with satin finish and colored stains. Although not visible on the milk glass example shown in the accompanying photograph, the underside of the base has an impressed diamond pattern. Crystal: $20.00 – 25.00. Milk glass: $25.00 – 30.00.

IN-32. No. 305 TWO-LIGHT CANDLESTICK IN MILK GLASS

No. 370 two-light candlestick. 5¼" high with a 5¼" diameter round base and an arm spread of 7¾". Available both with a plain foot and a figured foot, though it is the figured version with its checkerboard pattern that resembles the other pieces in the pattern. Made circa 1939 – 1945 or later. The version with the plain foot may be found lightly etched with leaves or with decorations and it is likely that both versions were offered with colored stains or satin finish. Also offered with bobeches and prisms. This candlestick has the irregular pontil mark described on p. 243. $15.00 – 20.00. Add $10.00 – 12.00 for bobeches and prisms.

IN-33. No. 370 TWO-LIGHT CANDLESTICKS (NOTE BASE WITH PRESSED DESIGN ON THE LEFT AND ETCHED LEAVES ON THE RIGHT)

No. 370 one-light candlestick, figured foot. 8½" high, with a 5" diameter round, paneled base. Made circa 1939 – 1945. Known in crystal only. Decorations such as stains or satin finish are possible. Also available with a bobeche and prisms. $15.00 – 20.00. Add $5.00 – 7.50 for bobeche and prisms.

IN-34. No. 370 ONE-LIGHT CANDLESTICK

Candleholder. 5⅛" high with a 4½" by 3⅜" oval base. Known in crystal only. Is this Indiana? We don't know, but believe it might be because of the similarity of its design to the No. 370 pattern with its alternating patchwork squares. The ribbed blocks on No. 370 are diagonal, while the ribbed blocks on this candlestick are horizontal. The quality of the crystal is also typical of Indiana. The candle cup is supported by two wave-like plumes, with the center between them hollow. $12.00 – 15.00.

IN-35. UNKNOWN CANDLESTICK, POSSIBLY INDIANA

IN-36. No. 371 TWO-LIGHT CANDLESTICK

No. 371 two-light candlestick. 5¼" high with a 4⅜" diamond-shaped base and a 7¼" arm spread. Probably introduced in the late 1930s or 1940. Known in crystal only, but probably also offered decorated with stain or satin finish. The Blackwell Wielandy Company's 1940 – 1941 catalog shows this candlestick decorated by Cape Cod Art Glass with sterling silver deposit on the flowers, and the base, the candle cups, and the background of the floral panel covered with ruby stain. This candlestick has rims on the candle cup and was probably also offered with bobeches and prisms. This candlestick has the irregular pontil mark described on p. 243. $20.00 – $30.00. Add $10.00 – 12.00 for bobeches and prisms.

IN-37. No. 372 TWO-LIGHT CANDLESTICK

No. 372 two-light candlestick. 5½" high with a 5" diameter round base and a 7½" arm spread. Probably introduced in the late 1930s or in 1940. Known in crystal only, but probably also offered decorated with stain or satin finish. Also offered with bobeches and prisms. This candlestick has the irregular pontil mark described on p. 243. $20.00 – 30.00. Add $10.00 – 12.00 for bobeches and prisms.

IN-38. No. 373 ONE-LIGHT CANDLESTICK, FROM CATALOG

No. 373 one-light candlestick. 5¼" high. Probably made in the 1930s or early 1940s. Known in crystal only, plain or with satin highlights. Because of its similarity to Duncan & Miller's No. 112 Caribbean pattern, this candlestick has been erroneously attributed to that company. $20.00 – 25.00.

IN-39. No. 373 TWO-LIGHT CANDLESTICK WITH SATIN HIGHLIGHTS

No. 373 two-light candlestick. 5¼" high. The base is rectangular in shape, with one end curved, approximately 5" by 3". Probably made in the 1930s or early 1940s. Known in crystal, plain or with satin highlights, as seen in the accompanying photograph. This candlestick has the irregular pontil mark described on p. 243. $25.00 – 30.00.

No. 607 two-light candlestick. 5¼" at its highest point, with a 5" diameter round base and an arm spread of 7¼". Probably made in the late 1930s or in the 1940s. Known in crystal only. The example shown has a simple cutting on the base. Other decorations are likely. The arms have a leaf design that does not appear on the floral bowl that seems to have been the only other item in the pattern. The candlestick has rims on the candle cup and was probably also offered with bobeches and prisms. This candlestick has the irregular pontil mark described on p. 243. $15.00 – 20.00. Add $10.00 – 12.00 for bobeches and prisms.

IN-40. No. 607 TWO-LIGHT CANDLE-STICK

No. 10 low candlestick. 2¾" high with a 4⅛" diameter round base. Made circa 1940 – 1942. Known in crystal only. Advertised in October 1942 by Winia M. Harriman of New York City as part of an assortment with silver overlay decoration. Very similar to L. E. Smith's No. 408 candleholder. (See IN-41a.) The Smith candleholder is ½" wider, has less detail than the Indiana candlestick, has a domed base with a pattern on its underside (and is consequently taller as well, being about 3¼" high), and differs in various other ways. The Indiana candlestick has the irregular pontil mark described on p. 243. $10.00 – 12.50.

IN-41. No. 10 LOW CANDLESTICK

IN-41A. L. E. SMITH's No. 408 CANDLEHOLDER IN BLACK WITH WHITE SPATTER DECORATION

No. 11 low candlestick. 3½" high with a 4" diameter round, paneled base. Appears in Blackwell Wielandy Company's 1940 – 1941 catalog, described as a "Colonial design." Still in production in the early 1960s. Known in crystal, plain and with ruby or amber stain. $4.00 – 6.00.

IN-42. No. 11 LOW CANDLESTICK

No. 12 low candlestick. 4" high with a 4⅛" diameter round base. In production by the early 1940s and known in crystal, plain or with fired-on colors and/or hand-painted decorations. However, the example in the accompanying photograph is in topaz, which could indicate an initial introduction date from the early 1930s. If so, other colors are possible. This seems to be a reissue of the candlestick earlier produced as No. 172 Old English (or Threading), circa 1926 – 1929. (See IN-15 on p. 241.) Crystal: $6.00 – 8.00. Crystal w/decoration: $10.00 – 15.00. Topaz: $15.00 – 20.00.

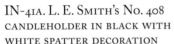

IN-43A. COMPARISON OF No. 172 OLD ENGLISH CANDLESTICK IN GREEN WITH No. 12 LOW CANDLESTICK IN HAND PAINTED CRYSTAL

IN-43. No. 12 LOW CANDLESTICK IN TOPAZ

249

IN-44. MAYFLOWER TWO-LIGHT
CANDLESTICK WITH YELLOW STAIN

Two-light candlestick. 5½" high with a 5" diameter round base and an arm spread of 7½". Tiara Exclusives reissued a basket and candy box in this pattern, stating that they were from original Indiana molds designed in the 1930s. The pattern name used by Tiara was Dewdrop. The Blackwell Wielandy Company's 1940 – 41 catalog offered the candlestick and several other pieces under the name of Mayflower. The candlestick is known in crystal, plain and with yellow stain. Other stains and satin highlights are also likely. This candlestick has the irregular pontil mark described on p. 243. Crystal: $20.00 – 25.00. Crystal w/stain: $25.00 – 30.00.

IN-45. No. 1004
ONE-LIGHT
CANDLESTICK
WITH SATIN
HIGHLIGHTS

No. 1004 one-light candlestick. 2⅞" high with a 3¾" diameter round base. Probably introduced around 1940 and in production only for a few years. Known in crystal only, plain or with satin highlights; ruby stain is also possible. $10.00 – 12.50.

IN-46. No. 1004
TWO-LIGHT
CANDLESTICK

No. 1004 two-light candlestick. 5⅜" high with a 5" diameter round base and an arm spread of 7⅜". Probably introduced around 1940 and in production only for a few years. Known in crystal only, plain or with satin highlights or ruby stain. This candlestick has the irregular pontil mark described on p. 243. $15.00 – 20.00.

IN-47. No. 1005 LOW CANDLESTICK

No. 1005 low candlestick. 2⅛" high with a 3" x 3" base. The pattern was in production by 1940, but it isn't known if this candlestick was part of the original line. It appears in a catalog that has been dated to around 1950 and may only have been made for a short time, since it is not seen as often as either of the other two candlesticks in the same line. However, it was reissued in 1957, when it was advertised with a vase insert as the "newest idea at the Pittsburgh show." The advertisement in the December issue of *China, Glass & Tablewares* goes on to state, "The set is 'Candlelight and Flowers,' with nine possible combinations of base, vase and peg compotes. Bases are candleholders alone, and slender stem compotes or graceful vases fit nicely into each candleholder." The peg compotes are known to have been made in milk glass, so it is possible that the low candlesticks were also produced in this color. $8.00 – 10.00.

No. 1005 one-light candlestick. 5¼" high with a 4⅝" diameter base. The pattern was in production by 1940, but it isn't known if this candlestick was part of the original line. It was offered by Montgomery Ward in their fall 1945 – winter 1946 catalog and is in an Indiana catalog that has been dated to around 1950, so probably continued in production into the early 1950s. Known only in crystal, but probably also available with ruby stain or satin highlights. $15.00 – 20.00.

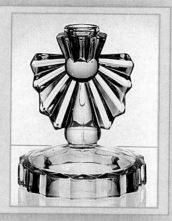

IN-48. No. 1005 ONE-LIGHT CANDLESTICK

No. 1005 two-light candlestick. 5¼" high with a 5¼" x 3½" oval base and an arm spread of 6¾". In production by 1940 when it appeared in Blackwell Wielandy Company's catalog as part of an assortment of "hand-made Swedish-style" glassware. Originally made in crystal only, plain or with ruby stain or frosted highlights, it continued to be made until the 1950s. In 1958, it was reissued in milk glass as part of a five-piece set that included an oblong center bowl and a pair of peg compotes, all with gold trim. This candlestick has the irregular pontil mark described on p. 243. Crystal: $25.00 – 30.00. Crystal w/stain, milk glass: $30.00 – 35.00.

IN-49. No. 1005 TWO-LIGHT CANDLE-STICK

No. 1006 two-light candlestick. 5" high with a 5⅛" diameter round base. Made around 1940, in crystal only. The example shown has silver overlay applied by a decorating company. Other decorations are possible, including ruby stain or frosted highlights. This candlestick has the irregular pontil mark described on p. 243. Crystal: $25.00 – 35.00. Crystal w/silver overlay: $30.00 – 35.00.

IN-50. No. 1006 TWO-LIGHT CANDLESTICK WITH SILVER OVERLAY

No. 1007 one-light candlestick. 7" high with a 4" diameter round base. Produced circa 1942 to the early 1950s. Originally made in crystal only, though probably available with ruby stain or frosted highlights. Uniquely, this candlestick was also offered with the "bobeche" seen in IN-51a – a single piece that fit over the top of the candlestick, with a rim that was designed to mimic prisms. Some pieces in the pattern were made in milk glass in the late 1950s, so that color is a possibility for this candleholder as well. $15.00 – 20.00. Add $10.00 – 12.00 for bobeche.

IN-51A. No. 1007 ONE-LIGHT CANDLESTICK WITH BOBECHE, FROM CATALOG

IN-51. No. 1007 ONE-LIGHT CANDLESTICK

IN-52. No. 1007 TWO-LIGHT
CANDLESTICK WITH SATIN FINISH
AND PASTEL STAIN

No. 1007 two-light candlestick. 6" high with a 5⅛" x 4¼" base and an arm spread of approximately 6". Produced circa 1942 – 1954. Known in crystal, both plain and satin finished. The example shown has faint remains of pastel stain. Other decorations are possible. Sears Roebuck offered this candlestick in 1942 with bobeches and prisms – real ones, though it is also possible that the "bobeches" seen in IN-51a on the preceding page were also available on this candlestick. This pattern, including the two-light candlesticks, took on a new popularity when it was sold by Montgomery Ward from 1947 to 1954 as part of their Oleander pattern (though the rest of the pieces in the pattern were actually from Indiana's No. 1008 Willow pattern). Some pieces in the pattern were made in milk glass in the late 1950s, so that color is a possibility for this candleholder as well. This candlestick has the irregular pontil mark described on p. 243. $10.00 – 12.50.

IN-53. No. 1007 VASE CANDLESTICKS
IN BLUE, OLIVE, AND SUNSET

No. 1007 vase candlestick. Made in two styles: flared (3¾" high) and deep (4½" high), both with 3" diameter round bases. Originally made circa 1942 to the early 1950s in crystal, with ruby stain or satin finish possible. Some pieces in the pattern were made in milk glass in the late 1950s, so that color is a possibility for this candleholder as well. Reissued in the 1960s in blue, olive, and sunset (amberina) as part of the Canterbury Collection. The scallops on the top rim of the flared version are much less prominent than on the deep ones. (See the green candlestick in the accompanying photograph.) Crystal: $10.00 – 12.50. Olive: 12.50 – 15.00. Blue, sunset: $15.00 – 17.50.

IN-54. No. 1008 WILLOW ONE-LIGHT
CANDLESTICKS IN GREEN AND CRYSTAL

No. 1008 Willow one-light candlestick. 4¼" high with a 4" diameter round base. According to a letter that Arthur L. Harshman, assistant to the president of Indiana Glass, wrote to the *Depression Glass Daze* in 1979, this pattern was introduced in the late 1930s in crystal only; however, the earliest documentation we have found for the pattern is its appearance in Montgomery Ward's catalogs from 1947 to 1954 as their Oleander pattern (but with the No. 1007 two-light candlestick substituted for the candlesticks from the Willow line). It should be noted that during this same time period, Indiana continued to advertise the pattern as Willow. In addition to clear crystal, this candlestick is also known with satin finish (the example shown in IN-54a has green highlights) and ruby stain. Other decorations are possible. It was also made in green, probably in the 1950s. This candlestick has the irregular pontil mark described on p. 243. Crystal: $15.00 – 20.00. Green: $20.00 – 25.00.

IN-54A. No. 1008
WILLOW ONE-LIGHT
CANDLESTICK IN
CRYSTAL SATIN WITH
GREEN HIGHLIGHTS

IN-54B. No. 1008 WILLOW
ONE-LIGHT CANDLESTICK IN
CRYSTAL, WITH SATIN WINGS.
(NOTE LABEL SHAPED LIKE
THE STATE OF INDIANA)

No. 1008 Willow two-light candlestick. 5½" high with a 4¾" x 2¾" oval base. See IN- 54 on the preceding page for a discussion of the probable production dates for this pattern. The two-light candlestick is known in plain crystal and has also been seen with blue, yellow, and ruby stain, as well as with frosted highlights. It was also made in green, probably in the 1950s. This candlestick has the irregular pontil mark described on p. 243. Crystal: $15.00 – 20.00. Green: $20.00 – 30.00.

IN-55A. No. 1008 WILLOW TWO-LIGHT CANDLESTICK IN GREEN

IN-55. No. 1008 WILLOW TWO-LIGHT CANDLESTICK

No. 1008 Willow vase candlestick. Sold by Butler Brothers as Magnolia Leaf. 4" high with a 3" x 3" diamond-shaped base. See IN-54 on the preceding page for a discussion of the probable production dates for this pattern. The vase candlestick is known in crystal and green (the latter probably made in the 1950s), but is likely to have also been decorated with various colored stains and/or satin finish. Crystal: $15.00 – 20.00. Green: $20.00 – 30.00.

IN-56. No. 1008 WILLOW VASE CANDLE-STICK IN GREEN

No. 1009 Leaf one-light low candlestick. 1½" high with a 6" x 3¾" oval base. Exact production dates unknown. The *Tiara Exclusives Product Information Manual*, issued in 1995, estimated that the original molds were from 1930 to 1945. Judging from the scarcity of pieces in the pattern, we suspect that it was probably only made for a few years in the 1940s. The one-light low candlestick is known in crystal only, both plain or satin finish, but may have also been decorated with colored stains. The two-light low candlestick was reissued in milk glass in the late 1950s, but there is no evidence that the one-light was reissued at the same time. Crystal: $10.00 – 12.50.

IN-57. No. 1009 LEAF ONE-LIGHT LOW CANDLESTICKS IN CRYSTAL SATIN AND CLEAR

No. 1009 Leaf two-light low candlestick. 1¾" high and 8½" long. Exact production dates unknown. The *Tiara Exclusives Product Information Manual*, issued in 1995, estimated that the original molds were from 1930 to 1945. Judging from the scarcity of pieces in the pattern, we suspect that it was probably only made for a few years in the 1940s. The two-light low candlestick was originally made in crystal only, probably both plain and frosted, and possibly decorated with colored stain. It was reissued in milk glass in 1957. The mold was apparently modified at this time, since the original catalog pictures show it with ridges between the leaves on the base (similar to those seen on the one-light candlestick in IN-57 above). It was reissued again in 1991 by Tiara Exclusives in sage mist (opaque green) as No. 556 Desert Blossoms; however, by this time the Indiana Glass Company had discontinued its handmade glass operation and these pieces were made by Fenton. (See FN-95 on p. 204 of book one of this series.) Crystal: $12.00 – 15.00. Milk glass: $20.00 – 25.00.

IN-58. No. 1009 LEAF TWO-LIGHT LOW CANDLESTICK IN MILK GLASS

IN-59. No. 1009 LEAF TWO-LIGHT CANDLE-STICK

No. 1009 Leaf two-light candlestick. 6¼" with a 5" diameter round base. The only catalog page we have seen for this pattern, reproduced in the November 1981 *Depression Glass Daze*, did not include this candlestick, so production dates are even more difficult to pin down for it than for the rest of the pattern. It probably dates to the mid-1940s. The attribution to Indiana is certain, not only because the candlestick has the leaf motif on its arms, but also because it was purchased as part of a console set with a No. 1009 Leaf floral bowl. It is known in crystal only, but could have been made with any of the decorations known on other pieces in this scarce pattern (satin finish or stains). It has the irregular pontil mark described on p. 243. $20.00 – 25.00.

IN-60. No. 1009 LEAF FOOTED CANDLEHOLDERS IN BLACK AND SUNSET (MADE FOR TIARA EXCLUSIVES)

No. 1009 Leaf footed candleholder. 3¾" high with a 3¼" diameter round base and a top diameter of 4⅛". This is another candleholder that does not appear in the catalog page reprinted in the November 1981 *Depression Glass Daze*, so we don't know if this was original to the pattern or if it was only made for Tiara Exclusives. (The mold for the sherbet was used to produce this candleholder; however, the sherbet does not appear in the catalog reprint either.) The only colors we have seen are those made for Tiara: sunset (amberina, as No. 10011 Sunset Leaf, 1974 – 1977), burnt honey (production dates unknown, but sometime between 1978 and 1982), and black (production dates unknown, but possibly 1988 – 1989). From 1990 to 1991, it was reissued one final time as No. 559 Desert Blossoms in sage mist (opaque green); however, by this time Indiana had discontinued its handmade glass operation and these pieces were made by Fenton. (See FN-96 on p. 204 of book one of this series.) All colors: $12.00 – 15.00.

The next few pages show candlesticks for which we have not found documentation but believe to be Indiana Glass because they all have the irregular pontil mark described on p. 243, as well as other characteristics of Indiana such as glass quality, known decorations, colors, etc. Continued research will ultimately prove or disprove these attributions.

IN-61. TWO-LIGHT CANDLE-STICK, PROBABLY INDIANA

Two-light candlestick. 5¼" high with a 4¾" diameter round base and an arm spread of 8½". Known in crystal only, plain or with satin highlights. Very similar in style to Heisey's No. 1488 Kohinoor two-light candlestick (1937 – 1945), which could indicate a possible production period. (See HE-109 on p. 137.) This candlestick has the irregular pontil mark described on p. 243. $25.00 – 30.00.

Two-light candlestick. 8¼" high with a 5⅛" diameter decagon base and an arm spread of 9". Montgomery Ward offered this candlestick in their spring – summer 1943 catalog, with bobeches and prisms. It has also been seen with globes added to make it a hurricane lamp. Known in crystal only. This candlestick has the irregular pontil mark described on p. 243. $25.00 – 30.00. Add $10.00 – 12.00 for bobeches and prisms.

IN-62. TWO-LIGHT CANDLE-STICK, PROBABLY INDIANA

Two-light candlestick. 8¼" high with a 5¼" diameter round base and an arm spread of 9". Available both with a plain base (the example pictured has a light cutting on the base) or with a figured base with ribs and scallops. The latter is also sometimes seen with matching bobeches and prisms. Known in crystal only. This candlestick has the irregular pontil mark described on p. 243. Very similar to Fostoria's No. 2484 Baroque two-light candelabra and probably dates from around the same period (circa 1932 – 1940). Another very similar candlestick that has been attributed to Paden City is also sometimes seen. (See FO-94 on p. 37 for a comparison of the three.) $25.00 – 30.00. Add $10.00 – 12.00 for bobeches and prisms.

IN-63. TWO-LIGHT CANDLE-STICK, PROBABLY INDIANA

Two-light candlestick. 5½" high with a 5" diameter round base and an arm spread of 7½". Since the candle cups have rims, it is likely this candlestick was also offered with bobeches and prisms. Known in crystal and milk glass. This candlestick has the irregular pontil mark described on p. 243. $15.00 – 20.00. Add $10.00 – 12.00 for bobeches and prisms.

IN-64. TWO-LIGHT CANDLE-STICK, PROBABLY INDIANA

Three-light candlestick. 5¼" high with a 5¼" diameter round base and an arm spread of 11". Known in crystal only. Has been seen with a peg nappy in the center candleholder. This candlestick has the irregular pontil mark described on p. 243. $20.00 – 25.00.

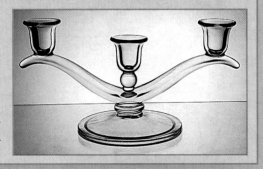

IN-65. THREE-LIGHT CANDLE-STICK, PROBABLY INDIANA

One-light candlestick. 6½" high with a 4" diameter round base. Known in crystal only. This candlestick has the irregular pontil mark described on p. 243. $15.00 – 20.00.

IN-66. ONE-LIGHT CANDLESTICK, PROBABLY INDIANA

Two-light candlestick. 4" high with an arm spread of 8". Known in crystal only. This candlestick has the irregular pontil mark described on p. 243. $15.00 – 20.00.

IN-67. TWO-LIGHT CANDLESTICK, PROBABLY INDIANA

Two-light candlestick. 5½" high with a 5⅛" diameter round base and an arm spread of 7". The underside of the base has an impressed pattern of punties and diamonds. Of this group of unknown candlesticks, this is the one that can perhaps be most confidently attributed to Indiana, since it is known in crystal, milk glass, and the same distinctive shade of green that was used for the No. 1008 Willow candlesticks. (See IN-54, IN-55, and IN-56 on p. 252-253.) In addition, this candlestick also has the irregular pontil mark described on p. 243. Crystal, milk glass: $20.00 – 25.00. Green: 25.00 – 30.00.

IN-68. TWO-LIGHT CANDLESTICK IN MILK GLASS, PROBABLY INDIANA

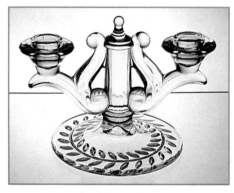

IN-69. NO. 1010 LAUREL TWO-LIGHT CANDLESTICK

No. 1010 Laurel two-light candlestick. (Note: Laurel does not appear to have been an original factory name, but was used by Sears for the pattern in their fall 1948 catalog.) 5" high with a 5⅜" diameter round base and an arm spread of 7½". Introduced 1948 and made until at least the mid-1950s. Known in crystal only, plain or "colored with thin gold rim or acid etched" (*Crockery and Glass Journal*, February 1948). The underside of the base has an impressed laurel leaf pattern. This candlestick has the irregular pontil mark described on p. 243. $20.00 – 25.00.

No. 1010 low one-light candlestick. 1½" high and 5½" at its widest point. The design is that of a 12-pointed star, making it the only item in the No. 1010 pattern that does not have the Laurel motif that resulted in the line being given that name in the 1948 Sears catalog. (Note: this candlestick does not appear in the Sears catalog, but is shown in Indiana's catalogs as No. 1010.) Production circa 1948 – 1954. Known in crystal and amethyst. An advertisement in the October 1954 issue of *Giftwares* introduced a new group of pieces "attractively packaged for gift giving" in boxes of "canary yellow with a smart all over design in silver." This group included the star candlesticks boxed as a pair. Crystal: $10.00 – 12.50. Amethyst: $12.50 – 15.00.

IN-70. No. 1010 LOW ONE-LIGHT CANDLESTICK

IN-70A. No. 1010 LOW ONE-LIGHT CANDLESTICK IN AMETHYST

No. 1010 Laurel vase candlestick. 4¼" high with a 2¾" diameter round foot. Appears in a catalog that has been dated to around 1950; production dates are probably circa 1948 to the early 1950s. Offered in crystal only. $12.50 – 15.00.

IN-71A. No. 1010 LAUREL VASE CANDLESTICK, FROM CA. 1950 CATALOG (NOTE DIFFERENCE IN FLARING OF RIM)

IN-71. No. 1010 LAUREL VASE CANDLESTICK

Norse candleholder. Dimensions unknown. Advertised as part of the Norse line in the April 1949 issue of *Crockery and Glass Journal*. Although the line remained a popular one through at least the mid-1950s, this candleholder was apparently only made for about a year, since it does not appear in a catalog that can be dated to around 1950 – 1951. Advertised in crystal only. A second candleholder that may also have been part of this line was issued in 1955 (see IN-80 on p. 259), though shortly after that Indiana began producing a pattern called Yankee Swedish that is very similar in style. $12.50 – 15.00.

IN-72. ADVERTISEMENT FOR THE NORSE LINE, FROM *Crockery and Glass Journal*, APRIL 1949

No. 1011 Teardrop low one-light candlestick. 3¼" high; other dimensions unknown. In production by circa 1950; the pattern continued to be made on into the 1960s, but with this candlestick discontinued before 1959. Offered in crystal, plain and probably also with ruby stain on the teardrops. Other pieces in the pattern were made in the late 1950s in milk glass, but this candlestick has not been reported in that color. Crystal: $15.00 – 20.00. Crystal w/ruby stain: $20.00 – 25.00.

IN-73. No. 1011 TEARDROP LOW ONE-LIGHT CANDLESTICK, FROM CA. 1950 CATALOG

257

IN-74. No. 1011
TEARDROP
ONE LIGHT
CANDLESTICK

No. 1011 Teardrop one-light candlestick. Listed as 5" high (but actually 5½") with a 3¼" diameter scalloped round base, hollow inside, like a goblet turned upside down. In production by circa 1950; the pattern continued to be made on into the 1960s, but with this candlestick discontinued before 1959. Offered in crystal, plain or with ruby stain on the teardrops. Other pieces in the pattern were made in the late 1950s in milk glass, but this candlestick has not been reported in that color. Crystal: $20.00 – 25.00. Crystal w/ruby stain: $25.00 – 30.00.

IN-75. No. 1011
TEARDROP
TWO LIGHT
CANDLESTICK

No. 1011 Teardrop two-light candlestick. 6" high with a 5⅛" diameter round base. In production by circa 1950; the pattern continued to be made on into the 1960s, but with this candlestick discontinued before 1959. Offered in crystal, plain and probably also with ruby stain on the teardrops. Other pieces in the pattern were made in the late 1950s in milk glass, but this candlestick has not been reported in that color. This candlestick has the irregular pontil mark described on p. 243. $20.00 – 25.00.

IN-76. No.
1016/1M1
CORONATION
CANDLESTICK

No. 1016/1M1 Coronation candlestick. 4½" high with a 3½" diameter round base. Made in the early 1950s. Known in crystal only. Available with silver overlay applied by an unknown decorating company. This was one of many companies' candlesticks that were inspired by Imperial's hugely popular Candlewick. This candlestick has the irregular pontil mark described on p. 243. Crystal: $15.00 – 20.00. Crystal w/silver overlay: $20.00 – 25.00.

IN-77. No. 6
CANDLESTICK

No. 6 candlestick. 2¾" high with a 4¼" diameter octagonal base. Made in the 1950s, though it is possible that production began earlier. Known in crystal only. It is basically identical to the No. 14 candlestick (IN-78 on the following page), except that the No. 6 candlestick takes a large, 1½" candle, whereas the No. 14 takes a standard ¾" taper. $8.00 – 10.00.

No. 14 low candlestick. 2½" high with a 4¼" diameter octagonal base. Made in the 1950s, though it is possible that production began earlier. Known in crystal and cobalt (possibly a later reissue?). It is basically identical to the No. 6 candlestick (IN-77 on the preceding page), except that the No. 14 takes a standard ¾" candle, whereas the No. 6 take a large 1½" taper. Crystal: $8.00 – 10.00. Cobalt: $12.50 – 15.00.

IN-78. No. 14 LOW CANDLE-STICKS IN CRYSTAL AND COBALT

Console set. Dimensions of the candleholders are unknown. (The bowl is 10½" in diameter.) Introduced 1955. Crystal only, with removable Dirilyte bases. This very unusual set is in the same style as the earlier Norse pattern, which imitated Swedish modern, as well as the set shown below as IN-80. $10.00 – 12.50.

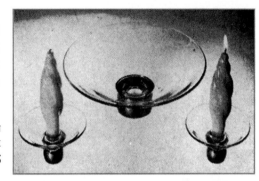

IN-79. TRADE JOURNAL PHOTOGRAPH OF UNKNOWN CONSOLE SET WITH DIRILYTE BASES, FROM *CROCKERY AND GLASS JOURNAL*, FEBRUARY 1955

Console set. Dimensions of the candleholders are unknown. (The bowl is 10" in diameter.) This set was described in the October 1955 *Crockery and Glass Journal* as "Swedish type" glassware. The pieces are very similar to Indiana's Norse pattern (see IN-72 on p. 257), which was probably still in production, but also resemble another line that was released in 1957 called Yankee Swedish, so it isn't known if these candleholders were intended to be part of a specific pattern. Probably made in crystal only. $8.00 – 10.00.

IN-80. TRADE JOURNAL PHOTOGRAPH OF UNKNOWN CONSOLE SET, FROM *CROCKERY AND GLASS JOURNAL*, OCTOBER 1955

No. 7290 Crown low candlestick. Also known as Crown Thumbprint. 3⅛" high with a 2⅞" diameter base and a 3¾" diameter bowl. Made circa 1958 to the early 1960s in crystal (with ruby, cranberry, or blue stain on the rims) and milk glass. Indiana then reissued this candleholder in 1966 for Colony Glassware in cobalt, gold (amber), and olive green. (See CL-11 on p. 112 of volume one of this series.) By this time, both Indiana and Colony were divisions of Lancaster Colony. In 1986, the pattern was reissued a final time by Indiana, this time for Tiara Exclusives, but the footed candleholder was not included. There is considerable confusion about this pattern and it has an unusually complicated history. It was originally introduced by Adams and Company of Pittsburgh in December 1890 as XLCR (or Excelsior), and continued to be made by the United States Glass Company after Adams joined that combine in 1891. U.S. Glass reissued the pattern as Dubonnet in 1943 and again from 1952 to 1962 as, variously, Thumbprint, Old Thumbprint, and King's Crown (the name by which it is best known to collectors today). It has often been reported that Indiana bought the molds from U.S. Glass, modifying some of them; however, as can be seen from the overlapping dates of production (with Indiana first advertising the pattern in 1958 and U.S. Glass including it in catalogs up to 1962), this clearly cannot have been the case. And in fact, Ruth Hemminger, Ed Goshe, and Leslie Pina report in their

IN-81. No. 7290 CROWN LOW CANDLESTICK WITH CRANBERRY STAIN

Tiffin Glass, 1940 – 1980, that interoffice correspondence exists from 1959 in which officers of the U.S. Glass Company complain about Indiana's having "pirated" the pattern. In this context, it is interesting to note that Indiana's advertising from 1958 offers "Traditional Crown pattern ... at a new low price!" — that is, at a price lower than U.S. Glass was selling it. Although "borrowing" one another's patterns was not unusual in the glass industry, in Indiana's defense it should be noted that many other companies made the same pattern, including the D. C. Jenkins Glass Company, the Imperial Glass Company, L. G. Wright, and the Rainbow Art Company (the latter decorating blanks purchased from U.S. Glass) — and Indiana, itself, who claimed that two of the stemware pieces in the pattern could be traced back to a catalog of their own that predated 1910. All these complications aside, it does not appear that any of these other companies, including U.S. Glass, ever made a sherbet-style footed candleholder. Gold, olive: $8.00 – 10.00. Cobalt, milk glass: 12.00 – 15.00. Crystal w/stain: $20.00 – 25.00.

IN-82. No. 7291 CROWN TALL CANDLESTICK WITH RUBY STAIN, FROM 1962 CATALOG

No. 7291 Crown tall candlestick. This pattern was later also known as Crown Thumbprint, but not until after this candlestick was discontinued. 8½" high with a 4" top diameter. Made circa 1958 – 1963. Offered in crystal with ruby or cranberry stain on the bottom rim. Like IN-81 one the preceding page, this is a unique candleholder made only by Indiana in a pattern that was probably copied from the United States Glass Company's King's Crown line. (See preceding candleholder for the full and complicated history of this pattern.) $25.00 – 35.00. *(Catalog reprint courtesy of the West Virginia Museum of American Glass.)*

IN-83. No. 7 WILD ROSE AND LEAVES CANDLECUP IN MILK GLASS

No. 7 candlecup (also listed as No. 7139, when sold with candles included). Known as Wild Rose and Leaves to collectors and called Gloria Anne by Hazel Marie Weatherman. 2¼" high with a 4½" top diameter. Advertised in milk glass in 1959, though the pattern in crystal may have been introduced earlier. Production probably continued until the 1960s or later, with this candleholder also known in marigold carnival. Other decorations, including fired-on colors, are possible. It appears to be from the same mold as the fruit cup in the pattern. Milk glass: $4.00 – 6.00. Marigold carnival: $6.00 – 8.00.

IN-84. No. 7135 URNS IN MILK GLASS, FROM 1962 CATALOG

No. 7135 urn. Dimensions unknown. Offered in catalog circa 1959 – 1963 in milk glass with candles. The same catalog also shows the urn in smoke or gold, but does not indicate whether it was intended to double as a candleholder in these colors. Crystal or other colors/finishes are possible. $10.00 – 20.00. *(Catalog reprint courtesy of the West Virginia Museum of American Glass.)*

No. 301 Pineapple vase candlestick. 4" high with a 1½" diameter round base and 3⅜" diameter top opening. Original production, circa 1959 to the early 1960s, seems to have been in milk glass only, though it is possible they were also made in crystal earlier when other pieces in the No. 301 pattern were issued. In 1960, this candlestick was advertised by Gay Fad Studios, a decorating company, in milk glass mounted on square walnut bases. Also offered in the 1960s in blue, lemon yellow, lime green, and orange (both clear or with satin finish) as part of the Della-Robbia pattern. From 1993 to 1994, the pineapple candleholders were reissued for Tiara Exclusives by L. E. Smith in teal (as No. 423) and ruby (as No. 871). Milk glass: $10.00 – 12.50. Blue, green, sunset, yellow: $12.00 – 15.00.

IN-85A. No. 301 PINEAPPLE VASE CANDLESTICK IN BLUE

IN-85. No. 301 PINEAPPLE VASE CANDLESTICK IN MILK GLASS

No. 2970 Harvest candlestick. 4" high with a 3" diameter base and 4½" diameter bowl. Originally made by Indiana circa 1962 for Colony Glassware in milk glass only (see CL-10 on p. 111 in volume one of this series) and reissued in 1967 under Indiana's own name in blue iridescent, lime iridescent, and amber iridescent. The Harvest pattern, with its grape and leaf motif, was an extensive one and remained popular for many years. Milk glass: $8.00 – 10.00. Amber iridescent: $12.00 – 15.00. Blue iridescent, green iridescent: $15.00 – 20.00.

IN-86. No. 2970 HARVEST CANDLESTICK IN BLUE IRIDESCENT

Sandwich Glass candlestick. 4" high with a 4⅜" diameter base. Advertised in October 1967 as "Authentic Sandwich Glass, since 1825, a Colony exclusive." Also referred to as Star and Scroll pattern in the same advertisement. In fact, this was a reissue of Duncan & Miller's No. 41-121 Early American Sandwich candlestick, which had initially been made in crystal and milk glass from 1940 to 1953 (first by Duncan and later by Tiffin — see DM-68 on p. 161 of book one of this series). The mold was obtained by the Indiana Glass Company in the 1960s, who reissued the candlestick for Colony in crystal and possibly other colors. In 1972, Colony once again made this candlestick in blue, green, and sunset (amberina), exclusively for Montgomery Ward for one year only as part of their 100th anniversary. (See CL-12 on p. 112 of volume one of this series.) The 1925 date mentioned in the advertisement above refers to Indiana's own Early American Sandwich pattern (IN-10 through IN-14 on p. 239-241 above), many pieces of which were later reissued in various colors for Tiara Exclusives; however, this candlestick was not among them. $15.00 – $20.00.

IN-87. SANDWICH GLASS CANDLESTICK (FROM DUNCAN & MILLER MOLD)

Monticello two-light candlestick. 4¼" high with a 4¼" diameter round base and an arm spread of 4½". This was a reissue of the United States Glass Company/Tiffin No. 308-19 Williamsburg candlestick, which had been made on and off from 1942 to 1962 in various colors. Indiana acquired the molds in the 1960s after U.S. Glass closed. The candlesticks were produced in blue (as No. 7266), lemon yellow (as No. 1951), lime green (as No. 2520), and orange (as No. 7107), with other colors known for the pattern possible, including milk glass and teal. Indiana's green might be confused with Tiffin's empire

IN-88. MONTICELLO TWO-LIGHT CANDLESTICKS IN LIME GREEN AND ORANGE (FROM TIFFIN MOLD)

green, which was used for some Williamsburg pieces; however, the Tiffin color is a somewhat darker, richer emerald and the Tiffin candlesticks are finished better and do not have the slightly mottled surface that is typical of Indiana. A candlestick with a similar shape and identical arms was also made by Imperial as No. 455/24. (See IM-50 on p. 194.) All colors: $15.00 – 20.00.

IN-89. Diamond Point candleholder in black

Diamond Point candleholder. 3¼" high. Made in black for Tiara Exclusives as part of their Cameo line from 1977 to 1981. Also known in crystal with cranberry stain around the rim and in plain crystal, appearing in an Indiana catalog as late as 1999. Made both with the rim straight or flared (or crimped). The Diamond Point line was a popular one for many years, offered in several different colors, so it is possible the candleholder was made in other colors as well. Crystal: $6.00 – 8.00. Black, crystal w/stain: $10.00 – 12.50.

IN-90. Diamond Point tall footed candleholder

Diamond Point tall footed candleholder. 7½" high with a 3¾" round foot and a top diameter of approximately 7". Known in crystal, with other colors or decorations possible. Production dates unknown, but probably 1980s. This appears to be made from the same mold as the No. 4529 tall footed compote, with the candleholder element added and the lip flared. $15.00 – 20.00.

IN-91. No. 10426 Monarch candleholders in sunset carnival (cupped, part of the Heirloom Series) and black (flared, made for Tiara Exclusives)

No. 10426 Monarch candleholder (flared), 1¾" high with a 4¾" top diameter and a 2¼" foot, made 1977 – 1978 for Tiara Exclusives in black; and Heirloom Series candleholder (cupped), 2" high with a 3¾" top diameter and a 2¼" foot, made circa 1980 in sunset (red carnival) and possibly other carnival colors. Both of these candleholders are from the same mold, which was created by adding a candle cup to the mold for a nappy from one of Indiana's early imitation cut glass patterns (possibly No. 123, circa 1910 — though, if so, the pattern itself was also slightly modified — or another closely related line). In any case, these pieces were very similar to candleholders also made from old imitation cut glass patterns offered by L. E. Smith (in crystal, milk glass, and carnival colors) and Imperial Glass Corporation (as part of the Collector's Crystal line). Black: $8.00 – 10.00. Ruby carnival: $12.50 – 15.00.

IN-92. Crystal Ice candleholder, from *Housewares*, March 7, 1990 (Federal mold)

Crystal Ice candleholder. Listed as 4". This was a reissue of the Federal Glass Company's No. 2658 Glacier Ice candleholder (see FD-9 on p. 174 of book one of this series), originally made from 1977 to 1979, and reissued by Indiana in 1980. It was still in production in 1990. Known in crystal only. $5.00 – 10.00.

No. 378 Recollection candleholder. 2½" high with a 3¾" diameter base. This pattern was originally made by Federal as Madrid in the 1930s and then reproduced by them from new molds from 1976 to 1979 as Recollection, with each piece marked "76." (See FD-1 on p. 172 of book one of this series.) Indiana purchased the molds when Federal went out of business, and reissued this candleholder in crystal (1982 – 1990), pink (1985 – 1990), light blue (as No. 4776, 1986 – 1990), and black amethyst. Other colors and iridescent finishes are possible. The Indiana candleholders can easily be distinguished from the original Madrid candleholders and the later Federal reissues, since ribs were added to the interior of the candle cup and the "76" was moved from the mold. Indiana also added some new pieces to the line, including a hurricane lamp (seen IN-94 below) and a footed butter, both of which used the candleholder as a base. Crystal: $5.00 – 7.50. Pink, light blue: $6.00 – 10.00.

IN-93. No. 378 Recollection candleholder in pink (from Federal mold)

Recollection hurricane lamp/vase. 8⅜" high with a 3¾" diameter base. This pattern was originally made by Federal as Madrid in the 1930s and then reproduced by them from new molds from 1976 to 1979 as Recollection, but did not include a hurricane lamp. When Indiana purchased the molds after Federal went out of business, they reissued the pattern with new pieces added. This one was created by combining the candleholder (IN-93 above) with a 15 ounce tumbler. Made in crystal, pink, and light blue in the 1980s. Crystal: $8.00 – 10.00. Pink, light blue: $10.00 – 12.50.

IN-94. Recollection hurricane lamp/vase (from Federal mold)

American Whitehall three-toed candleholder. 2¼" high, with a diameter of 6⅛". Indiana's Whitehall pattern dates back many years earlier to the late 1960s or early 1970s and was an inexpensive copy of Fostoria's very popular American pattern. Ultimately Lancaster Colony became the parent company of both Indiana and Fostoria and, when Fostoria was closed in 1986, the American molds were transferred to Indiana's factory, where machine-made production began using molds from both patterns, now renamed American Whitehall. Although we don't know the date of introduction for the three-toed candleholder, we suspect it was probably after 1986, with manufacture continuing to recent years. Crystal only.

IN-95. American Whitehall three-toed candleholder

Although Fostoria's American pattern included many candlesticks, none of them have been reissued under the American Whitehall name, nor does the American line include a candleholder that might be confused with this one. Indiana also made a domed two-piece candlelamp for Home Interiors. $8.00 – 10.00.

No. 0853 American Whitehall taper/pillar holder. 1¾" high with a 3½" top diameter. The base is in the shape of a 10-pointed star. This is another piece that does not directly copy any of the candleholders in Fostoria's American pattern and that was probably introduced in the late 1980s, after Indiana's Whitehall pattern was combined with Fostoria's American to become American Whitehall. (See IN-95 above for more information on these patterns.) Reissued circa 1996 – 1998 for Tiara Exclusives as No. 219 and probably still in current production. Known in crystal, pink, and black. Designed to take either a standard ¾" taper candle or a 2½" pillar candle. $4.00 – 6.00. Black, pink: $6.00 – 8.00.

IN-96. No. 0853 American Whitehall taper/pillar holder

IN-97. No. 1516 CAN-DLESTICK, FROM 1988/1989 CATALOG

No. 1516 candlestick. 5" high with a 3½" hexagonal base. Made in the late 1980s. This is a reissue of a candlestick originally made by Heisey (as No. 5, 1904 – 1931) and then reissued by Imperial (as No. 13791, 1980 – 1983). When the Heisey Collectors of America purchased the original Heisey molds after Imperial's closing, the only ones they did not obtain were those for the Old Williamsburg line, which were bought by Lancaster Colony. Even though Heisey did not consider this candlestick to be part of the Old Williamsburg pattern, Imperial did, so this was one of the molds that thus became part of the Indiana family. It is easy to differentiate the reissues from the original Heisey candlesticks, which are usually marked with the Diamond H, are of very high quality, and have a ground and polished pontil on the bottom. Determining the difference between the Imperial and Indiana reissues may be more difficult, since both are much poorer in quality and have unfinished bottoms. (See HE-5 on p. 100 and IM-176 on p. 228.) $10.00 – 15.00.

IN-98. No. 1517 CANDLESTICK, FROM 1988/1989 CATALOG

No. 1517 paneled candleholder. 8½" high with a 4⅛" hexagonal base. Made in the late 1980s. This is a reissue of a candlestick originally made by Cambridge from circa 1940 to 1958 as their No. 1440 (see CB-30 on p. 57 in book one of this series) and then reissued by Imperial, initially under the same number (later changed to No. 51794), from 1969 to 1979. Known in crystal only from Indiana. (See IM-162 on p. 223.) $15.00 – 20.00.

IN-99. No. 1518 CANDLE-STICK, FROM 1988/1989 CATALOG

No. 1518 Collectors candlestick. 7⅛" high with a 3¾" diameter base. Made in the late 1980s. This is a reissue of a candlestick originally made by Imperial in the 1920s and then reissued by them from 1969 to 1982 as their No. 352 (or No. 41790) Collector's Crystal candlestick. (See IM-161 on p. 223.) Indiana's production was in crystal only. Reportedly the LIG mark (standing for "Lenox Imperial Glass") was left in the mold. From 1990 to 1993, this candlestick was made again for Tiara Exclusives by Fenton in dusty rose as No. 754 and as the base for the No. 727 Baroness candle lamp. (See FN-98 on p. 205 of book one of this series.) From 1991 to 1998, Dalzell Viking also offered this candleholder in crystal and several colors. (See DV- 6, p. 127 in volume one of this series.) We assume they leased the mold from Indiana. $10.00 – 12.50.

IN-100. No. 1519 CANDLESTICK, FROM 1988/1989 CATALOG

No. 1519 Collectors candlestick. 5" high. Made in the late 1980s. This is a reissue of a candlestick originally made by Imperial from 1982 to 1983 as the No. 41793 Collector's Crystal candlestick. (See IM-182 on p. 229.) Indiana's production was in crystal only. From 1991 to 1993, this candlestick was made again for Tiara Exclusives by Fenton in dusty rose as the No. 754 Baroness candleholder. (See FN-98 on p. 205 of book one of this series.) $8.00 – 10.00.

No. 1504 Reflections single light candleholder; also listed as No. 1608. 2¼" high with 2¼" and 4⅜" diameter bases (depending on which way the candleholder is turned). Made by Indiana in the late 1980s and offered in Tiara Exclusive's catalogs as the No. 208 Reflections candleholder from 1996 to 1998. Made in crystal and possibly pink and light blue. This was a reissue of a candleholder originally made by Imperial as No. 51221 Linear from 1979 to 1983. (See IM-174 on p. 227.) Reversible. As shown in the accompanying photograph, it takes a standard ¾" taper; reversed, it holds a 2", 2½", or 3" pillar candle. $5.00 – 7.50.

IN-101. No. 1504 REFLECTIONS SINGLE LIGHT CANDLEHOLDER (IMPERIAL MOLD)

No. 1496 Reflections candlevase; also listed as No. 1514. 4¼" high. Made by Indiana in the late 1980s in crystal. Pink and light blue are also possible. This candlevase could be inverted and placed on top of a No. 1504 candleholder (IN-101 above) to form the No. 1497 candlelamp seen in IN-102a. This was a reissue of a vase/candleholder originally made by Imperial as No. 51222 Linear from 1979 to 1983. (See IM-174 on p. 227.) $5.00 – 7.50.

IN-102A. No. 1497 REFLECTIONS CANDLELAMP, FROM 1988/1989 CATALOG (IMPERIAL MOLD)

IN-102. No. 1496 REFLECTIONS CANDLEVASE, FROM 1988/1989 CATALOG (IMPERIAL MOLD)

No. 1507 Reflections hurricane lamp. 12" high. Made by Indiana in the late 1980s in crystal and pink. Light blue is also possible. This was a reissue of a hurricane lamp originally made by Imperial as No. 51950 Linear from 1979 to 1983. (See IM-175 on p. 227.) $14.00 – 17.50.

IN-103. No. 1507 REFLECTIONS HURRICANE LAMP, FROM 1988/1989 CATALOG (IMPERIAL MOLD)

No. 1508 Reflections hurricane lamp. 9" high. Made by Indiana in the late 1980s in crystal. This was a reissue of a hurricane lamp originally made by Imperial as No. 51224 Linear from 1979 to 1983. (See IM-174 on p. 227.) $12.00 – 15.00.

IN-104. No. 1508 REFLECTIONS HURRICANE LAMP, FROM 1988/1989 CATALOG (IMPERIAL MOLD)

IN-105. No. 1513
REFLECTIONS
CANDLEHOLDER,
FROM 1988/1989
CATALOG
(IMPERIAL MOLD)

No. 1513 Reflections candleholder; also listed as No. 1539. Made by Indiana in the late 1980s in crystal. Reversible; turned the other way, it holds a votive candle. This was a reissue of a piece originally made by Imperial as their No. 51218 Linear stacking candleholder from 1980 to 1983. (See IM-179 on p. 229.) $8.00 – 10.00.

IN-106.
CANDLEHOLDER
IN BLACK,
UNKNOWN
PATTERN NUMBER

Candleholder. 2¼" high with a 3" diameter round base. Made from circa 1990 in crystal and black. Other colors are possible, especially green or crystal with ruby stain. Crystal: $3.00 – 5.00. Black: $4.00 – 6.00.

IN-107. No. 7512
CANDLEHOLDER IN
CRYSTAL WITH
RUBY STAIN

No. 7512 candleholder. 2" high with a 3" diameter ribbed base. Made in the 1990s in crystal (clear), with cranberry stain, with ruby stain, and in teal. Other colors are possible. Crystal: $2.50 – 3.00. Crystal w/ruby stain, teal: $3.50 – 5.00.

IN-108.
No. 1139 (1340)
CANDLESTICKS
IN CRYSTAL AND
BLACK

No. 1139 (1340) candlestick. 6" high with a 4¼" diameter round base. Made from circa 1990 in crystal and black. From 1990 to 1991, the black candlestick was also used as the base for Tiara Exclusive's No. 405 Gentry candlelamp (or hurricane lamp), with a globe added. Crystal: $7.50 – 10.00. Black: $10.00 – 12.50.

IN-109. No. 1141
(1341) CANDLESTICK

No. 1141 (1341) candlestick. 6⅛" high with a 4¼" diameter skirted base. Made from circa 1990 in crystal (and possibly black). $8.00 – 10.00.

No. 017 Venetian candleholder. 7¼" high with a 4½" diameter skirted base. Originally designed by Fostoria Glass Company and made as No. 079 for Tiara Exclusives from 1984 to 1986 in 24% lead crystal (see FO-229 on p. 72); the molds were then moved to the Indiana Glass Company who continued production in non-lead crystal from 1987 to 1998. Also offered with satin highlights (as No. 032, 1993 – 1994), cranberry stain on the base (as No. 254, Easter 1996 only), and ruby stain all over (as No. 364, Christmas 1996 and 1997 only). Used as the base for a candlelamp (or hurricane lamp — No. 046 in Fostoria's lead crystal, 1986 – 1990, and No. 018 in Indiana's non-lead crystal, 1990 – 1995). A smaller version of this candlestick was also made. (See IN-111 below.)
Crystal: $12.50 – 17.50. Crystal w/ruby stain (full or partial): $15.00 – 20.00.

IN-110. No. 017 VENETIAN CANDLE-HOLDERS IN CRYSTAL AND WITH RUBY STAIN (MADE FOR TIARA)

No. 018 Venetian candleholder. 5½" high with a 4" diameter skirted base. Originally designed by Fostoria Glass Company and made as No. 078 for Tiara Exclusives from 1984 to 1986 in 24% lead crystal (see FO-229 on p. 72); the molds were then moved to Indiana Glass Company, who reissued this candlestick in black only from 1993 to 1995. A taller version of this candlestick was also made. (See IN-110 above.) Black: $10.00 – 15.00.

IN-111. No. 018 VENETIAN CANDLEHOLDERS IN BLACK, FROM TIARA'S 1994 CATALOG

No. 2535 star taper holder. 1⅛" high and 4½" wide. Made in the 1990s in crystal, ruby stain, and evergreen (as No. 3884). Very similar to Anchor Hocking's No. 986 Star Design candleholder (see AH-21 on p. 16 of book one of this series), except that the latter has small beads at the base of each point of the star and spikes between each point. Hazel-Atlas (HA-7 on p. 92), Libbey, and possibly Paden City also made similar shape star candleholders, but with only five points (that are much sharper than the Indiana or Anchor Hocking candleholders). All colors (prices for current production as of this writing): $1.50 – 2.00.

IN-112. No. 2535 STAR TAPER HOLDER IN GREEN

IN-112A. CLOSE-UP OF LABEL

No. 2245 candlestick, 4½" high with a 3¼" diameter round base; No. 2246 candlestick, 6" high with a 3½" diameter round base; No. 2247, 7¾" high. These three candlesticks were made in the 1990s in plain crystal with cranberry or ruby stain, black, and evergreen. The small size is easily confused with Libbey's frequently seen candlestick, which was made in 24% lead crystal and various colors from 1994 to the present. (See IN-113a for a comparison of the two.) These candlesticks have been seen with round red, white, and blue Fostoria labels, presumably sold under that name after the Fostoria Glass Company (a sister company of Indiana's, both owned by Lancaster Colony) stopped making glass in 1986. All colors (prices for current production as of this writing), 4½" high: 2.50 – 3.50; 6" high: $3.00 – 4.00; 7¾" high: $3.50 – 4.50.

IN-113A. COMPARISON OF INDIANA No. 2245 WITH RUBY STAIN (ON LEFT) AND LIBBEY'S FREQUENTLY SEEN CANDLE-STICK (ON RIGHT)

IN-113. No. 2246 CANDLESTICK IN CRYSTAL WITH RUBY STAIN

IN-114.
No. 12011
CELESTIAL
CANDLELAMP
(FEDERAL
MOLD)

No. 12011 three-piece Celestial candlelamp. Base is 1⅛" high and 5¼" in diameter; with the globe, the height is 9¼" high. Made beginning in 1997, in crystal, as part of the Home Harmonies collection. Also known in satin finished orange, with other colors/treatments possible. The candleholder was originally made by Federal Glass Company without a globe as their No. S-500 Celestial pattern from circa 1972 to 1979 in Gem-Tone (crystal with purple and iridescent edges), limelight (avocado green), and probably other colors; Fostoria then reissued it in 1985 as their No. 318 candleholder in crystal, blue, and sun gold with iridescent finish. (See FD-8 on p. 174 of volume one of this series and FO-233 on p. 73 of this volume.) The Indiana reissue has three equidistant nubs added around the well of the candleholder to hold the globe in place. $12.50 – 15.00.

No. 6222 candlestick/bud vase. 7" high with a 3" diameter round base. Made circa 1997 to the present in crystal, cobalt, green, and other colors. All colors (prices for current production as of this writing): $2.50 – 3.50.

IN-115. CANDLESTICK/
BUD VASE IN COBALT

IN-115B.
CLOSE UP
OF LABEL

IN-115A. CANDLESTICK/
BUD VASE IN CRYSTAL
WITH RUBY STAIN

JAMESTOWN GLASSHOUSE, Jamestown, Virginia (1957 to the present). Glassmaking

began in Jamestown, Virginia, in 1608, just a year after the English colonists arrived in the Americas. Although this initial effort only lasted a few months, with a second attempt from 1621 to 1624 scarcely more successful, it is significant because this was America's first industry. The glasshouse site was excavated in 1948 – 1949. Interested in preserving this heritage, and spearheaded by Carl Gustkey of the Imperial Glass Company, a coalition of American glass manufacturers formed. As the Jamestown Glasshouse Foundation, with Gustkey as president, they decided to build a replica of the original glasshouse, to be operated for two summers, 1957 and 1958, to commemorate the 350th anniversary of the original factory. Carl Erickson of the Erickson Glass Works was chosen to blow the first glass, and Gerald Vann Dermark, from the same company, was named supervisor. These demonstrations were so popular with tourists that the glasshouse was turned over to the National Park Service in 1959. A fire in 1974 destroyed the Glasshouse, but it was rebuilt in 1976 and is still in operation today, run by the Eastern National Park and Monument Association.

All glassware is blown freehand using seventeenth century techniques and tools. The only concession to modern times is the use of natural gas as fuel for the furnace rather than wood. According to a brochure put out by the Park Service, "Fragments of the original green glass have provided a key to proper color and composition, so that the glass has the same appearance as the original." It goes on to mention "the clearly visible pontil mark" on each piece. "This is the distinctive mark of a hand blown product. No two pieces are identical." The glassware will frequently also have many bubbles. Some crackle ware was produced, but was discontinued in 1968 because it wasn't considered authentic for the seventeenth century. During the first two years, when only bottles seem to have been made, a seal was embedded in the glass while it was still hot, marking the pieces as reproductions. Since then, only paper labels have been used.

Various items have been made over the years, including bottles, tumblers, pitchers, vases, and the two candlesticks seen below. During the early years, the Glasshouse offered some of these products through mail order. At the present time, glass can be bought at the Glasshouse only, with paperweights among the most popular souvenir items being offered.

Handled candlestick. 2¼" high with a base diameter of approximately 4¼". Made in green only. Production could be any time from 1959 to the present. The base of this candlestick is hollow and it has a rough pontil on the bottom.

JA-1. HANDLED CANDLESTICK IN GREEN

Candlestick. 6¼" to 6½" high with a 2⅜" diameter foot. Made in green only. Production could be any time from 1959 to the present. There is a rough pontil on the bottom of the foot.

JA-2. CANDLESTICK IN GREEN

Reproduction candlestick. 6⅝" high with a 2¾" diameter base. The origin of this candlestick is unknown, but it was purchased with another candlestick believed to be from the Jamestown Glasshouse. Probably made in green only. The center stem is hollow and there is a rough pontil on the bottom of the base.

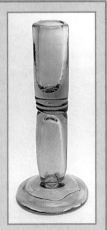

JA-3. REPRODUCTION CANDLESTICK IN GREEN, POSSIBLY JAMESTOWN

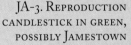

JEANNETTE GLASS COMPANY, Jeannette, Pa. (1898 – 1983). Originally founded to

produce bottles, by 1906 the Jeannette Glass Company had expanded its production to include salts, peppers, and a number of specialties. Significantly, by this time they had already installed at least one machine for the manufacture of milk bottles. By 1922, they were making full lines of pressed ware and various decorative pieces (including some with light cuttings), but with an increased reliance on automation. In 1927, they discontinued all handmade production and in subsequent years produced machine-made glassware only. In 1930, they were reported to be the first company to produce a full line of tableware in three colors simultaneously — crystal, pink, and green — completely by machine. As a pioneer in what we now refer to as Depression Glass, they were responsible for many of the patterns popular with collectors today, such as Adam, Cherry Blossom, Doric, Windsor, and others. They also produced large amounts of kitchen ware and items for the hotel and restaurant trade.

By 1947, the factory had doubled in size. In 1961, they expanded further when they purchased the McKee Glass Company and moved their entire facility to the newly acquired property, which was nearly three times the size of their previous location. After renovation, they boasted the largest electric glass furnace ever built. Their catalog for 1962 featured 5,220 items, including "Glasbake ovenware, tumblers, bar sets, gift items, glassware accessories for every room in the house." In 1971, they were renamed the Jeannette Corporation, having by this time purchased the Harker China Company, the Royal China Company, and Brookpark-Royalon, a manufacturer of melamine dinnerware. The combined revenues of all these subsidiaries for that year were in excess of $30,000,000. Candles were added to their product line in 1975, with the purchase of Old Harbor, Inc. A year later, the Walker China Company joined the Jeannette empire. While glass continued to be advertised, some of it was now imported. It seems probable that all of this capital expansion contributed to Jeannette's closing just a few years later, in 1983.

COLORS

Known early colors include aquamarine blue and canary. In 1925, Jeannette Green and topaz were introduced. Jeannette green was described as "delicate, somewhat like a brilliant apple green," while topaz was a "warm, rich amber." Rose pink, sometimes referred to as Wild Rose, came out in 1927. After Jeannette went to all machine-made ware, pink and green were the two primary colors produced through most of the 1930s. Jadite (opaque green) was added in 1932 and Delfite (opaque blue) in 1936. Although mostly used for kitchen wares, both of these colors will sometimes be found in other pieces, including candlesticks. Other known colors from this period include yellow and light blue. Ultra marine (a deep, almost green shade of aqua, with considerable variation) was made from 1937 to 1949. Transparent pink was revived briefly from 1947 to 1949. A decade later, opaque shell pink was introduced. In the early 1960s, like many other companies, Jeannette also offered giftware in milk glass.

Beginning in the 1920s, and periodically throughout their history, the company offered iridescent finishes, including marigold carnival. Some pieces thus decorated were molded to appear crackled. Fired-on colors may also be found, sometimes with one color shading into another (such as white with blue edges). From the late 1960s on, these were the prevalent "colors" offered by Jeannette. Some of these treatments included amberina and emerald-glo (a green-amber combination) in 1975, frosty peach and frosty mint in 1979, sapphire blue and walnut brown in 1980 and 1981.

MARKS

Jeannette used a number of trademarks over the years, such as the ones seen here. Only the early J-in-a-triangle mark will occasionally be found impressed in some glass pieces, though we do not know of any candlesticks with this mark.

JEANNETTE TRADEMARKS,
1950s – 1960s

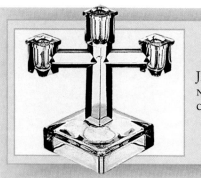

JE-1. No. 5133
NOVELTY
CANDELABRUM

No. 5133 novelty candelabrum. 4⅛" high with a 2¼" square base. Appears in a catalog that can be dated ca. 1920 – 1925. Known in crystal only. This size would be considered a child's or toy candlestick by collectors today, but is unusual for being multiple-light and for its art deco styling. $50.00 – 75.00.

No. 5055 small octagon style candlestick. 4½" high. This size would be considered a child's or toy candlestick by collectors today. Appears in a catalog that can be dated ca. 1920 – 1925. Known in crystal only. $25.00 – 30.00.

JE-2. No. 5055 SMALL OCTAGON STYLE CANDLE-STICK, FROM CATALOG, CA. 1920 – 1925

No. 5058 large octagon style candlestick. 8½" high. This is a full-size version of the toy candlestick in the preceding entry. It appears in a catalog that can be dated ca. 1920 – 1925. $12.50 – 15.00.

JE-3. No. 5058 LARGE OCTAGON STYLE CANDLE-STICK, FROM CATALOG, CA. 1920 – 1925

No. 5119 square style candlestick. 7¼" high with a 3½" square base. Appears in a catalog that can be dated ca. 1920 – 1925. Known in crystal and blue, both clear and with the inside of the base satin-finished. Other colors are possible. According to the catalogue, available plain or cut. Crystal: $10.00 – 15.00. Blue: $15.00 – 20.00. Blue satin: $20.00 – 25.00.

JE-4. No. 5119 SQUARE STYLE CANDLESTICK IN BLUE SATIN

Is This Jeannette?

Candlestick. 6⅜" high, with a 3⅜" square base. Known in crystal and blue. The combination of color and general quality of the finish, which is rather wavy and mottled, lead us to suspect this might be a Jeannette product. Very similar to candlesticks made first by Higbee (see HI-1 on p. 164) and later reissued by New Martinsville, and Westmoreland, except that the Higbee/New Martinsville version has a beveled edge and is taller, (7") and the Westmoreland versions are also different sizes (6" and 7"). Crystal: $10.00 – 15.00. Blue: $12.00 – 17.50.

JE-5. CANDLESTICK IN BLUE, POSSIBLY JEANNETTE

No. 5132 hexagon style candlestick. 7" high with a 4" diameter base. Made ca. 1920 – 1925. Known in crystal, marigold carnival, and other iridescent colors, and with various fired-on colors; other colors and finishes are likely. A 1923 advertisement offered this candlestick as part of the X-28 cut glass assortment, with a light cutting; a catalog, ca. 1920 – 1925, also shows it as part of the No. X-11 cut buffet set. The same catalog offers two other buffet (or console) sets, No. X-11 and X-24, in "amber," this being the name used by the company for marigold carnival. The candlestick also appears in Butler Brothers' 1925 catalogue as part of an assortment "in allover gold iridescent, some in sunset and satin effects." The accompanying bowl in the assortment has a stretch finish. At least one other company made a very similar candlestick. Westmoreland's No. 1021 candlestick is 7⅜" high, with the biggest difference between the two candlesticks being that the base of Jeannette's is hollow only about halfway up, whereas Westmoreland's is hollow all the way up to within one half inch of the candle cup.

JE-6. No. 5132 HEXAGON STYLE CANDLESTICK IN MARIGOLD CARNIVAL

Crystal (clear or w/fired-on colors): $10.00 – 15.00. All iridescent colors: $35.00 – 50.00.

JE-7. HEXAGON STYLE CANDLESTICK, KNOWN AS CRACKLE, IN MARIGOLD CARNIVAL

Hexagon style candlestick. Known as Crackle to collectors. A water set in a Jeannette catalog with this pattern was described as being "Crackled Effect." 7" high with a 4" diameter base. Made ca. 1925. Known in marigold carnival, with other colors or finishes likely. It features a Tree of Life motif with a stippled background. Because of a slight resemblance to the Imperial Glass Company's Tree of Life or Soda Gold pattern, it has been identified in some sources as Imperial Crackle, though the latter's Tree of Life pattern is actually very different. The bright golden iridescence is identical to the finish used on other pieces by Jeannette and is quite different from Imperial's marigold carnival. The pattern matches that on the candlestick in JE-8 below. $15.00 – 17.50.

JE-8. Low CANDLESTICK, KNOWN AS CRACKLE, IN GREEN

Low candlestick. Known as Crackle to collectors. A water set in a Jeannette catalog with this pattern was described as being "Crackled Effect." 3½" high with a 3¾" round six-paneled base. Known in marigold carnival and Jeannette green, with other colors and finishes likely. It features a Tree of Life motif with a stippled background, identical to that on the candlestick in JE-7 above. All colors: $8.00 – 12.50.

JE-9. No. 5179 TWELVE RINGS CANDLESTICK IN MARIGOLD CARNIVAL

No. 5179 candlestick. Known as Twelve Rings to collectors today. 9" high with a 4⅜" diameter base. Appears in a catalog that can be dated ca. 1920 – 1925 as part of the X-23 amber console set, "amber" being marigold carnival, the color most often seen. Also known in blue, with other colors (including plain crystal) possible. All colors: $35.00 – 50.00.

No. 5198 candlestick. Known as Spiral to collectors. 8" high. Appears in a catalog that can be dated ca. 1920 – 1925 as part of the X-30 amber console set, "amber" being marigold carnival, the color most often seen. Also known in Jeannette green, smoke carnival, and green carnival, with other colors (including plain crystal) possible. Prior to positive identification of this candlestick as Jeannette, it was tentatively attributed to Imperial. Amber (marigold): $50.00 – 60.00. Green, smoke carnival: $60.00 – 75.00. Green carnival: $80.00 – 90.00.

JE-10. No. 5198 Spiral candlestick in marigold carnival

No. 5201 candlestick. 6½" high with a 3¾" diameter round base. Appears in a catalog that can be dated ca. 1920 – 1925 as part of two different amber console sets, "amber" being the name used by the company for marigold carnival; Butler Brothers was still selling this candlestick as late as 1931. Known in crystal, amber, black, blue, green, rose, and with various fired-on colors. What appears to be a very similar candlestick at first glance was made by U.S. Glass, ca. 1919, as their No. 56. However, these candlesticks are actually easy to tell apart, because the U.S. Glass candlestick has an oval skirt, whereas the Jeannette one is round. The Jeannette candlestick has been seen with an electrical fitting added, to take a light bulb, and a matching gold carnival shade. Crystal: $7.50 – 10.00. All colors: $17.00 – 20.00.

JE-11. No. 5201 CANDLESTICKS IN BLUE AND MARIGOLD CARNIVAL

Candlestick, apparently a variation of No. 5201 above. Called Tree Bark by collectors, but described in an Indiana catalog as "Crepe Design." 6½" high with a 3⅞" diameter round base. Shown here in Jeannette green. A console set was offered in Butler Brothers' August 1931 catalog with "allover rainbow iridescent coloring." Other colors and finishes are possible. The basic shape of this candlestick is identical to the one above, but slightly thicker all around, which could be attributable to having reworked the mold to add the "tree bark" finish. Another difference is that the hollow portion of the base on the No. 5201 above extends upward approximately 3", whereas the hollow portion of the base on the green candlestick is only about 2". All colors: $20.00 – 25.00.

JE-12. Tree Bark (Crepe Design) candlestick in green

No. 97 candlestick. 7⅛" high with a 3¼" diameter hexagonal base and a 1¾" diameter round candle cup. Advertised in 1926 in Jeannette green and amber as part of the No. 26-97 console set; crystal has also been seen. Various other companies made a similarly-shaped candlestick. Heisey's No. 2 candlestick and Lancaster's candlestick both have hexagonal candle cups, as well as being generally thicker; the most difficult candlestick to differentiate from Jeannette's is Westmoreland's No. 1010 candlestick (which has been reissued in recent years by Mosser Glass). It also has a round candle cup, but with slightly different overall dimensions. It is 7⅜" in height with a 3⅛" diameter base. The Westmoreland candlestick also has a thinner stem. The most significant difference between the two, however, is the tapered area between the base and the bottom knob on each candlestick. As can be seen from the accompanying photograph (JE-13a), the knob on the Jeannette candlestick sits almost directly on its base, whereas there is a half-inch taper below the knob on the Westmoreland candlestick. For a detailed comparison of all four look-alike candlesticks, see HE-2d on p. 99 of the Heisey section. Crystal: $10.00 – 12.50. Amber, green: $15.00 – 20.00.

JE-13. No. 97 CANDLESTICK IN AMBER

JE-13A. CLOSE-UP COMPARISON OF JEANNETTE No. 97 CANDLESTICK (ON LEFT) AND WEST-MORELAND No. 1010 CANDLESTICK (ON RIGHT)

JE-14. LOW CANDLESTICK IN AMBER, WITH LIGHT CUTTING

Low candlestick. 2⅝" high, with a 4⅞" diameter round base. Advertised in 1926 in Jeannette green and amber; also known in canary, with crystal and other colors possible. This distinctively shaped candleholder was offered as part of at least three console sets: No. X-67, consisting of a pair of candlesticks with a rolled-edge bowl on a black stand; No. X-68, consisting of 4 candlesticks and the same bowl and stand; and No. X-69, consisting of a pair of the candlesticks and the same bowl without the stand, but with a light floral cutting (actually a rather crudely executed gravic cutting, seen in the accompanying photograph). Amber, crystal: $10.00 – 12.50. Green: $12.50 – 15.00. Canary: $15.00 – 20.00.

JE-15. LOW CANDLESTICK IN JEANNETTE GREEN, WITH LIGHT CUTTING

Low candlestick. 2½" high with a 3½" x 4½" rectangular base. Advertised in 1926 as part of the No. 127-137 console set, with a light cutting, available in amber and green; probably also made in crystal and possibly in other colors. A short version of the tall square-based candlestick that follows. Amber, crystal: $12.00 – 17.50. Green: $15.00 – 22.50. Add 10 – 20% for cutting.

JE-16. TALL, SQUARE-BASED CANDLESTICKS IN GREEN AND AMBER, WITH LIGHT CUTTINGS

Tall, square-based candlestick. Advertised in 1926 as part of the No. 127-99 console set, with a light cutting, available in amber and green; probably also made in crystal and possibly in other colors. A taller version of the preceding low square-based candlestick. This was one of a group of pieces advertised in 1929 by Thayer and Chandler, Chicago, as a suitable blank for hand-painting by the home hobbyist. Amber, crystal: $20.00 – 25.00. Green: $25.00 – 35.00. Add 10 – 20% for cutting.

Floral candlestick. Also known as Poinsettia to collectors, although the actual flower in the pattern is reportedly a passion flower. 4" high with a 4" diameter round base. Made ca. 1931 – 1935. Known in green and rose pink; some pieces in the pattern were also made experimentally in crystal, yellow, amber, jadite, and delfite. This was the first of the patterns that included a candlestick made by Jeannette after they converted entirely to machine-made glassware. A version of this candlestick with a swirl design was also made (JE-18) and it is very similar in style to the Adam candlestick in JE-19. Green: $40.00 – 50.00. Pink: $55.00 – 65.00.

JE-17. FLORAL CANDLESTICK IN GREEN

Swirl design candlestick. 4" high with a 4" diameter base. Unknown production period, but probably early 1930s. Known in delfite. Considered rare. Other colors are possible. This is a redesigned version of the Floral candlestick above. $100.00 – 110.00.

JE-18. SWIRL DESIGN CANDLESTICK IN DELFITE

Adam candlestick. 3¾" high with a 3¾" square base. Made ca. 1932 – 1934. Known in rose pink, green, and delfite, but quite rare in the latter color; a few pieces in the pattern were also made in crystal and yellow. Similar in style to the Floral candlestick shown above. Pink: $40.00 – 45.00. Green: $50.00 – 55.00. Delfite: $100.00 – 110.00.

JE-19. ADAM CANDLESTICKS IN GREEN AND PINK

No. 387 Iris two-light candlestick. Also called Iris and Herringbone. 5¼" high with a 4½" diameter round base; the spread of the arms is 6⅛". Made from 1928 to 1932 in crystal, both clear and with a satin finish. The candlesticks were returned to production by 1946, when they were advertised as part of a No. F-1934 console set by Century Metalcraft Corporation in "Satintone enhanced with delicate, two-toned pastel shading in rose and green or orchid and gold." Century also offered pieces in the pattern in their Corsage decoration (ruby stain and coin gold) at around the same time. They may also have been responsible for the candlesticks occasionally seen with an all-over ruby stain. The pattern was once again reissued in 1951, in golden iridescent (marigold carnival) and including the candlesticks. Although some pieces continued to be made as late as the early 1970s, the candlestick does not seem to be among them. Some items in the Iris pattern have been reported in transparent pink and green (or light blue), as well as with fired-on white trimmed with various colors and other two-toned combinations, so it is possible that the candlesticks may be found in these colors as well. Crystal: $18.00 – 22.50. Marigold: $20.00 – 25.00.

JE-20. NO. 387 IRIS TWO-LIGHT CANDLESTICKS IN GOLDEN IRIDESCENT AND CRYSTAL

JE-20A. NO. 387 IRIS TWO-LIGHT CANDLESTICK IN CRYSTAL SATIN

This was the first of a series of candlesticks made by Jeannette with very similar shapes but different design motifs. The Swirl candlestick (JE-24 below) has an almost identical outline, while three others (JE-25 and JE-26 on p. 277, and JE-41 on p. 281) are clearly all from the same designer.

JE-21. TWO-LIGHT VASE CANDLESTICK

Two-light vase candlestick. 7⅜" high with a 4" diameter 12-paneled base; the spread of the arms is approximately 8½". Made ca. 1935 – 1940. Known in crystal or with an over-all fired-on white decoration trimmed in blue (with other color trims likely). Although other companies made combination items intended both for flowers and candles, this one is unique in being molded in a single piece with arms on either side of a traditional vase. Crystal: $25.00 – 35.00. Fired-on white w/blue trim: $40.00 – 45.00.

JE-22. WINDSOR CANDLE-HOLDER

Windsor candleholder. Also known as Windsor Diamond. 3" high with a 3¾" diameter base. Made ca. 1936 – 1946. Known in crystal and pink; other items in the pattern were made in green with some experimental pieces known in Delfite, light blue, amberina, and yellow, though the candlesticks have not been reported in any of these colors. Crystal with ruby stained edges is also possible. The pattern consists of rows of large diamonds. A very similar candleholder was made by Jeannette as part of their Holiday pattern (also known as Button and Bows) from 1947 to 1949, with the diamonds broken up into smaller facets by rows of buttons. (See JE-32 on p. 279.) Crystal: $10.00 – 15.00. Pink: $45.00 – 50.00.

JE-23. WINDSOR HANDLED CANDLEHOLDER

Windsor handled candleholder. Also known as Windsor Diamond. 1⅛" high with a 3⅜" diameter base; 4⅞" wide, excluding the handle. The Windsor pattern was made ca. 1933 – 1946 in pink and green, but this candleholder is known only in crystal and marigold carnival and has been dated ca. 1947 – 1972 by Sherry Riggs and Paula Pendergrass in their *20th Century Glass Candle Holder*, indicating that it may be a look-alike and not an actual part of the pattern. The candle cup is unusually shallow, barely ¼" in depth. Crystal: $10.00 – 15.00. Marigold: $12.00 – 17.50.

JE-24. SWIRL TWO-LIGHT CANDLESTICKS IN PINK AND ULTRA MARINE

Swirl two-light candlestick. Also known as Petal Swirl. Sold as part of the No. 1500/3 console set. 5½" high with a 4⅛" diameter round scalloped base; the spread of the arms is 6⅛". Made ca. 1937 – 1938. Known in ultra marine (sometimes shading almost to green) and pink. Gene Florence, in his *Collector's Encyclopedia of Depression Glass*, reports a single branch candleholder in this pattern in Delfite, otherwise unknown. A few pieces in the pattern are also known in amber. The outline of this candlestick is virtually identical to that of the No. 387 Iris candlestick (JE-20 on the preceding page), with the same swirled panels on the candle cups and center fan, but with the Iris motif removed; the biggest difference is in the foot, which is paneled and scalloped, in place of the iris and herringbone pattern found on the earlier candlestick. The two candlesticks following (JE-25 and JE-26) and the No. 387P shell pink candlestick (JE-41 on p. 281) are also very similar in design. Ultra marine: $20.00 – 25.00. Pink: $25.00 – 35.00.

JE-24A. SWIRL TWO-LIGHT CANDLESTICKS IN ULTRA MARINE (NOTE VARIATION IN COLOR)

No. 1774 two-light candlestick. Known variously as Laurel, Sunburst, or Herringbone. 5¼" high with a 4⅞" diameter round scalloped base; the spread of the arms is 6⅛". Made in the late 1930s, early 1940s. Advertised by the Blackwell Wielandy Company as part of their No. 214/7238 console set in 1940. Known in crystal only. This is the same general shape as the No. 387 Iris candlestick (JE-20 on p. 275) and Swirl candlestick (JE-24 on the preceding page), but with straight panels on the candle cups instead of swirls, and a plain fan between the arms, decorated only by a sunburst effect. The base is also plain, with a laurel border. Almost identical to the candlestick immediately following (JE-26), which has no impressed design at all, and very similar also to the No. 387P shell pink candlestick (JE-41 on p. 281). $15.00 – 20.00.

JE-25. No. 1774 SUNBURST TWO-LIGHT CANDLESTICK

Two-light candlestick. 5¼" high with a 4⅞" diameter round scalloped base; the spread of the arms is 6⅛". Probably made in the 1940s or later. Known in crystal only. Identical to the No. 1774 two-light candlestick (JE-25 above), but with a completely plain center fan and base, sometimes decorated with a light etching showing a flowering vine. This etching was most likely machine-applied and is unusual in that the designs on the pair are complementary but not identical. Also known with satin finish on the fans and base. This candlestick belongs to the same family of shapes already discussed above (JE-20 on p. 275 and JE-24 on the preceding page), as well as the No. 387P shell pink candlestick (JE-41 on p. 281). $15.00 – 20.00.

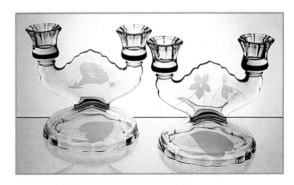

JE-26. TWO-LIGHT CANDLESTICKS WITH LIGHT ETCHING

No. 464 handled candlestick. 2⅛" high, with a 5⅛" diameter ridged base. Made ca. 1940 – 1945 in crystal only. It is probable that this candlestick was also meant to be used with a hurricane globe, since they are sometimes found with a spring fitting around the top of the candle cup. $6.00 – 10.00.

JE-27. No. 464 HANDLED CANDLEHOLDER

JE-28. No. 2200 NATIONAL CANDLEHOLDER

No. 2200 National candleholder. 3" high, three-footed. Made ca. 1945 to the mid-1950s. Known in crystal only, sometimes with ruby stain (on alternate panels or on the feet only). A ribbed panel design very similar to Heisey's Crystolite, with pieces offered in various sets as "National gift ware." The candlesticks appear in the fall 1945 catalog as part of the No. 2200/1 console set. $8.00 – 12.50.

JE-29. TWO-LIGHT COSMOS CANDLESTICK

Two-light candlestick. Known as Cosmos. 4½" high with a 5⅛" diameter round scalloped base; the spread of the arms is 7¾". Probably ca. 1945 to the early 1950s. Crystal only. Similar to the three-light candlestick in the pattern (JE-30 below), but with impressed fruit and leaves on the underside of the base. $12.00 – 15.00.

Three-light candlestick. Known as Cosmos. 4½" high with a 5⅛" diameter round scalloped base; the spread of the arms is 7¾". Made ca. 1945 to 1956. Crystal only. Similar to the two-light candlestick in the pattern shown above (JE-29), but with a ribbed pattern impressed on the underside of the base, instead of the two-light's fruit motif. A number of different accessories were available with these candlesticks, including peg nappies, 4½" peg vases, and shorter, wider vases that could be used for votive candles or converted to candy jars by the addition of a cover. These various insert pieces were offered both plain and with fired-on white floral decorations. The candlesticks shown below (JE-31) could also be fit over the outer arms of these candlesticks, converting them into "candelabra." $15.00 – 18.00. Add $5.00 – 7.50 for each insert.

JE-30. THREE-LIGHT COSMOS CANDLESTICK WITH INSERT VASES

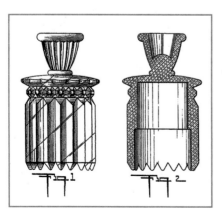

JE-31. COMBINATION CANDLEHOLDER, BOBECHE, AND PRISMS, FROM PATENT DRAWING

Candlestick (combination candleholder, bobeche, and prisms). 4½" high and 3" in diameter. Patent applied for April 7, 1951, and approved April 8, 1952, as D166,428. Designed by Kirkland W. Todd. Crystal only. Described in the patent simply as a candlestick, it could be used alone or fit over the candle cups of another candlestick (such as the Cosmos three-light candlestick, No. JE-30 above) to create the appearance of being a candelabrum, with bobeches and prisms. The entire piece, including the "prisms," is molded as a single unit, hollow inside with a ledge that rests on the rim of the host candle cups. $10.00 – 15.00.

Holiday candleholder. Also known as Buttons and Bows. 3" high with a 3¾" diameter base. Made from 1947 to 1949 in pink. A very few pieces in the pattern were made in crystal, iridized crystal, and shell pink, but the candleholder has not been reported in any of these colors. Modified from the earlier Windsor candleholder (JE-22 on p. 276), made ca. 1936 – 1946, but with the diamonds on that pattern broken up into smaller facets by rows of buttons. Crystal: $15.00 – 20.00. Pink: $25.00 – 35.00.

JE-32. HOLIDAY CANDLEHOLDER IN PINK

Anniversary candleholder. 2½" high with a 4⅞" top diameter. The pattern was made from 1947 to 1949 in crystal, and reissued in the late 1960s to the mid-1970s in crystal and marigold iridescent. Other pieces in the pattern were made in the early years in pink, but the candleholder has not been reported in this color, suggesting that it might have been a late addition not introduced until the 1960s. Crystal: $8.00 – 12.00. Marigold iridescent: $12.00 – 15.00.

JE-33. ANNIVERSARY CANDLEHOLDER. *(Artist's rendition)*

Camellia candlestick. 2⅝" high with a 5" diameter round base. Made ca. 1947 – 1951. Crystal only; also known with gold painted decoration on the underside of the base. The camellias are impressed on the bottom of the base, one on each side. The same candlestick was later reissued with no pattern on the base (see JE-35 below). $10.00 – 12.50.

JE-34. CAMELLIA CANDLESTICK

Candlestick. 2⅝" high with a 5" diameter round base. This candlestick, a plain version of the Camellia candlestick above (JE-34), appears in the 1956 catalog and probably remained in production until the 1960s. Crystal only. Offered plain or with a 22 karat gold rim, with a delicately figured etched band around the bottom rim. A version of this candlestick with a modified candle cup was also made (see JE-36 below). A somewhat similar candlestick was made by the Paden City Glass Mfg. Co. as part of its No. 1503 line; the Paden City candlestick is taller (2⅞"), has a flat base without a rim, and the candle cup is more rounded. $8.00 – 10.00.

IN-35. CANDLESTICK WITH PLAIN BASE AND GOLD RIM

Candlestick. 2½" high with a 5" diameter round base. This is a modified version of the candlestick above (JE-35), probably also made ca. 1955 until the 1960s, in crystal only. Offered plain or with a 22 karat gold rim around the base. Also known with the inside bottom of the base inside the rim satin finished, and with an overall fired-on green decoration. Other treatments are possible. The modification to the candlestick above was the addition of a 2½" flat lip on the candle cup, which could be used to hold a 9" hurricane shade (available plain or with a fired-on white floral decoration) that could also be used as a vase. This candlestick was featured without the shade in the November 1955 issue of the *Crockery and Glass Journal*. $8.00 – 10.00. Add. $8.00 – 10.00 for shade.

JE-36. CANDLESTICK, WITH SATIN FINISH ON BASE

JE-37. TWO-LIGHT CANDLESTICK

Two-light candlestick. 5⅛" high with a 5⅛" diameter round, scalloped base. Probably made in the 1950s. Known in crystal; marigold iridescence is a possibility, but has not been reported. A modified version of the No. 3375 Floragold candlestick (JE-38 below), with ribs added to the arms, candle cups, and base. A completely plain version of this candlestick is also known, used for light etchings (like the ones seen on JE-26, p. 277) and ruby stain. This may have been the earliest version of the candlestick, since it was sold by Montgomery Ward in 1943 with a "silvery-gray" cutting. $20.00 – 25.00.

JE-38. No. 3375 FLORAGOLD TWO-LIGHT CANDLESTICK IN MARIGOLD IRIDESCENT

No. 3375 Floragold two-light candlestick. 5⅛" high with a 5⅛" diameter round base. Made in the 1950s in marigold iridescent. Sometimes called Louisa because of the pattern's resemblance to the older Westmoreland carnival glass pattern by that name. The design on the base is an intricate floral motif. The same shape, minus the floral design, was used for two other candlesticks, one with a ribbed design (JE-37 above) and one that is completely plain. The latter can be found in crystal with the same light etching of a flowering vine seen on JE-26 (p. 277) and with ruby stain overall. $25.00 – 30.00.

JE-39. No. 3475 PHEASANT CANDLEHOLDER

No. 3475 Pheasant candleholder. 2½" high with a 4⅞" diameter round base. Produced ca. 1956 in crystal (plain and with gold trim around the edge of the base and candle cup) and in shell pink (considered rare). The crystal version has only a few reeds impressed on opposite sides beneath the base; for the shell pink version, a row of reeds was added encircling the top of the base. Pairs of the candlestick were available in gift boxes or as part of the No. 3624/3/501 dinette set, also gift boxed. The bowl to this set is known in amber, so it is possible that the candleholders were made in this color as well. Crystal: $30.00 – 35.00. Shell pink: $200.00 – market.

JE-40. No. 3423 EAGLE CANDLEHOLDERS IN BLUE IRIDESCENT AND SHELL PINK

No. 3423 Eagle candleholder. 3" high, with three feet. Made ca. 1957 – 1959. Known in crystal, plain, with a fired-on blue iridescence, with an over-all matte silver finish, and in shell pink. The pattern consists of three eagles with their wings outspread, almost touching. The interior has three ledges in addition to the usual candleholder at the bottom, making it possible to use any candle from ¾" to 2½" in diameter. A gift boxed set was advertised in the September 1957 *China, Glass & Tablewares*, consisting of one candlestick with a 12½" hurricane shade (which sits on the table, surrounding the entire candleholder), and a 9" ivory rope candle. Crystal: $12.00 – 17.50. Blue iridescent, shell pink: $25.00 – 35.00.

No. 387/P two-light candlestick. 5¼" high with a 4" diameter round base; the spread of the arms is 6". Made ca. 1958 – 1959, in shell pink only. A matching bowl was offered as the No. 3435/P four-toed Lombardi bowl. The candlestick exhibits a marked similarity in outline to the earlier No. 387 Iris candlestick (JE-20 on p. 275) and Swirl candlestick (JE-24 on p. 276), as well as the No. 1774 two-light candlestick (JE-25 on p. 277) and the plain candlestick shown as JE-26 on p. 277, but with a completely different molded floral design on the fan and the exterior of the base. $22.00 – 30.00.

JE-41. No. 387/P
TWO-LIGHT
CANDLESTICK IN
SHELL PINK

JEFFERSON GLASS COMPANY, Steubenville, Ohio (1900 – 1906); Follansbee, West Virginia (1907 – circa 1935).

In 1900, Harry Bastow, who had been superintendent of the Northwood Glass Works of the National Glass Company, leased the idle Sumner Glass Company plant in Steubenville, Ohio, forming the Jefferson Glass Company. Their earliest products were fancy vases, lemonade sets, and novelties in opalescent and decorated effects, that were intended to compete with foreign imports. Their success led them to purchase and expand the Steubenville plant in 1903. In 1905, a second factory was leased in Toronto, Canada. It isn't known how long this Canadian branch operated, but it set the stage for the eventual purchase of a Canadian factory in 1912 that continued to operate until 1925.

In 1906, citing an inability to further expand the Steubenville plant, the company began construction of a new factory across the Ohio River in Follansbee, West Virginia, where they moved the following year. A trade journal reported around this time that the "tendency to exclusive manufacture of fancy glassware of the Bohemian order seems to have reached the limit, and a swing back towards regular tableware and crystal is noted" (*Crockery and Glass Journal*, June 14, 1906). In addition to expanded capacity in the production of opalescent lemonade sets and novelties, the move also allowed the company to introduce a new colonial line and go into the production of tableware on a larger scale. By 1908, this became the company's primary focus with the acquisition of the molds, patents, and trademarks for the Ohio Flint Glass Company's very popular Krys-Tol line, which included the Chippendale pattern that had been introduced the previous year. This occurred when Benjamin W. Jacobs, president of Ohio Flint and the designer of Chippendale, resigned his position to become Jefferson's general manager. Jefferson advertised this line heavily until 1918, offering to pay freight charges both ways for any pieces returned if they did not "outsell any and all other high grade Colonial glassware." Claiming they had not received a single return order, in 1910 they issued a $2,000.00 challenge to any manufacturer who could claim a better quality of glass, more artistic merit, or higher sales, "to be decided by a competent and disinterested board of judges composed of manufacturers, jobbers and retail dealers." Though the results of this challenge are not known, there can be no doubt that the Chippendale pattern was one of the most popular colonial lines ever issued. It was eventually sold to the Central Glass Works in 1919, who continued to offer Chippendale until 1933. Pieces marked Krys-Tol may be from any of the three companies who produced this pattern.

In 1910, the company was purchased by Harry Schnellbaugh, general manager of the Macbeth Evans Glass Company, and at this time lighting glassware was introduced to Jefferson's line. A further expansion occurred in 1915 when Jefferson purchased the bankrupt Radium Glass Company in Millersburg, Ohio, which they put back into operation producing lenses until 1919.

By 1920, the company had turned exclusively to the manufacture of lighting goods, which they continued to manufacture until the early 1930s. In 1933, the factory was sold at auction, victim to the Depression as so many other glass companies were during the same years. Although purchased by a consortium of stockholders, it isn't known if an attempt was made to reopen the plant.

COLORS

In competition with Bohemian imports, Jefferson's earliest production featured many different colors, including wine-ruby, green (both clear and opalescent), royal blue, blue opalescent, canary opalescent, amber opalescent, rose, and others. All of these were offered with gold trim and enamel decorations. No candlesticks are known from this period. After the move to Follansbee, the company concentrated on the production of high quality crystal. The only colors known to have come out during this period were Corona, milk glass with a matte finish described as "a distinctive glass composition… which so closely resembles Italian Marble as to puzzle any layman," and antique green. Some pieces in the Chippendale pattern are also known in blue and canary, although it isn't known for certain if these pieces were made by Jefferson or Central.

JF-1. No. 2 CHIPPENDALE CANDLESTICKS, 7½", 4½", AND 9½" SIZES

No. 2 Chippendale candlestick. Offered in four sizes: 4½" with a 3" diameter hexagonal base (also listed as No. T314); 6½" high; 7½" high with a 4⅝" diameter hexagonal base; and 9½" high (also listed as No. T317). The Canadian branch of the factory offered these same sizes as No. 1601, 1602, 1603, and 1604, respectively. Made by Jefferson from 1908 to 1918. This was the earliest candlestick in the Chippendale pattern and the only one also made by the Ohio Flint Glass Company. It was patented by Benjamin W. Jacobs, president of Ohio Flint, on June 18, 1907, as No. D38,626. Made in crystal. The tall size is also known in canary, but it is unknown whether this was a Jefferson or Central color. Sometimes marked Krys-Tol or "PAT June 11 1907 Krys-Tol." This patent also applied to a later candlestick that was nearly identical, but without arms. (See JF-7 p. 284.) The 7½" size and the 4½" toy continued to be made by Central from 1919 to the mid-1920s (CE-6 on p. 103 of volume one of this series). An almost identical candlestick, listed as 4" high, was advertised by Westmoreland in 1910 as No. 1015S and remained in production through the end of the 1920s. (See the appendix, p. 297, for a comparison of the two.) Toy: $35.00 – 40.00. Middle sizes: $30.00 – 40.00. Large, crystal: $40.00 – 60.00. Canary: $70.00 – 100.00.

JF-2. No. T305 CHIPPENDALE CHILD'S COLONIAL CANDLESTICK

Chippendale child's colonial candlestick. Original pattern number unknown, but later listed as No. T305. 4¼" high with a 2½" hexagonal base. Made from 1910 to 1918 by Jefferson and 1919 to the mid-1920s by Central, in crystal only (CE-3 on p. 103 of volume one of this series). Sometimes marked Krys-Tol on the top of the base. $25.00 – 30.00.

JF-3. No. T310 CHIPPENDALE CANDLESTICK

Chippendale candlestick. Original pattern number unknown, but later listed as No. T310. 6½" high with a 3¼" diameter hexagonal base. Made from 1910 to 1918 by Jefferson and from 1919 to the mid-1920s by Central in crystal (CE-4 on p. 103 of volume one of this series). $20.00 – 25.00.

Chippendale candlestick. Original pattern unknown, but later listed as No. T332; sold by the Canadian branch of the company as No. 1606. 9" high. Made by Jefferson from 1910 to 1918 and by Central from 1919 to the mid-1920s (CE-7 on p. 104 of volume one of this series). Known in crystal only. A close copy of this candlestick was also made by Josef Inwald, A.G., of Czechoslovakia, circa 1925 – 1935. $30.00 – 35.00.

JF-4. No. T332 CANDLESTICK, FROM EARLY CATALOGUE

Chippendale candlestick. Original pattern unknown, but later listed as No. T335. 8½" with a five-sided scalloped base approximately 4⅜" wide and a ribbed column. Made by Jefferson from 1910 to 1918 and by Central from 1919 to the mid-1920s (CE-8 on p. 104 of volume one of this series). Known in crystal only. $35.00 – 40.00.

JF-5. No. T335 CHIPPENDALE CANDLESTICK

No. 6 Chippendale candlestick (later listed as No. T340 and offered by the Canadian branch of the company as No. 1607). 8" high with a 4" square base. Made by Jefferson in crystal from 1910 to 1918 and in Corona (a matte-finished milk glass resembling Italian marble) beginning in 1910. Central continued to make this candlestick from 1919 to the mid-1920s in crystal and moonstone (CE-9 on p. 104 of volume one of this series). Very similar candlesticks were made by the New Martinsville Glass Mfg. Company and the Paden City Glass Mfg. Company (as No. 113) in a series of heights: 3½", 5½", 7", and 8½", but will have a rayed pattern in the base, whereas the Chippendale candlesticks either have a puntied bottom or a plain, unfinished bottom. What appears to be the same candlestick was advertised as part of a Colonial buffet set with a fruit bowl in 1922 by the Japana Specialty Company of Grand Haven, Michigan, in a matte-white similar to Corona, as "another 'Japana' specialty." The example shown in JF-6a is 7" high. It has a rayed bottom, slightly different from that on the New Martinsville or Paden City candlesticks, so its actual manufacturer remains unknown. It is tempting to speculate that Japana acquired unsold stock in Corona from Jefferson, but this could also be Central's moonstone with a matte finish or from some completely unknown company. Crystal: $25.00 – 30.00. Opaque white: $20.00 – 25.00.

JF-6. No. 6 CHIPPENDALE CANDLESTICK

JF-6A. MATTE-WHITE CANDLESTICK WITH HAND PAINTED DECORATION, POSSIBLY JAPANA SPECIALTY COMPANY OR SOME OTHER MANUFACTURER

JF-7. No. T355
CHIPPENDALE
CANDLESTICK

Chippendale candlestick. Original pattern unknown, but later listed as No. T355. Made in two sizes, 7" and 9" high. Produced 1910 – 1918 by Jefferson. Known in crystal and canary. May be found marked Krys-Tol and "PAT June 11 1907 Krys-Tol." This refers to the patent for the earlier No. 2 candlestick (JF-1 p. 282), with this candlestick being nearly identical in shape, but with the arms removed. Both sizes were reissued by Central from 1919 to the mid-1920s as No. T325 and T328; the 9" size was also made as No. T325, with the mold modified to make the rim on the candle cup much thicker than on the Jefferson original. (See CE-11 on p. 105 of volume one of this series.) Also available with cutting. Crystal: $25.00 – 30.00. Canary: $40.00 – 55.00.

JF-8. No. 3820
HEPPLEWHITE
CANDLESTICK

No. 3820 Hepplewhite candlestick. (Later listed as No. T370.) 8"-12" high with a 4¼" diameter hexagonal base. Made by Jefferson from 1910 to 1918. Reissued by Central from 1919 to the mid-1920s as part of the Chippendale pattern (CE-13 on p. 105 of volume one of this series). Known in crystal only. The bottom of the candle cup and the column feature a prescut flower design. $35.00 – 40.00.

JF-9. No. T345 CHIP-
PENDALE CANDLESTICK
IN CRYSTAL SATIN

No. T345 Chippendale candlestick. 9½" high with a 4" square base. Known in crystal, green, and canary. Made by Jefferson circa 1915 – 1918 as No. T345 (and No. T346 with puntied bottom and cut top). Reissued by Central from 1919 to the mid-1920s. (See CE-10 on p. 104 of volume one of this series.) Seen here in crystal with an unusual satin finish, almost appearing sand-blasted, with a silvery-gray luminescence. We don't know if this was done by Jefferson or by Central. Also available with cutting. Crystal: $35.00 – 40.00. Colors: $50.00 – 65.00.

Appendix — Toy Candlesticks

Toy candlesticks come in many varieties, and were made for many different purposes. Some of them are truly toys, intended to be played with by children. Some of these will hold small candles, but others won't, making them much safer for this purpose. Others were marketed as birthday candlesticks, and would have been lit only on special occasions. Many others might more accurately be described as miniatures, sold as novelty items rather than toys. These include the many figural candleholders made in Taiwan and imported in recent years. What all of these candlesticks have in common is their small size and the fact that they take candles that are only ½" in diameter or smaller.

Early Toys

Nineteenth century glass companies known to have made toys include the Boston and Sandwich Glass Company, the New England Glass Company, the Cape Cod Glass Company, McKee and Brothers, and others. Due to a lack of documentation and past errors in identification, this is a particularly confusing area of study. The accompanying photograph shows three nineteenth or early twentieth century candlesticks. The larger cobalt one, which is 3" high, we believe to be McKee. The drawings in McKee's catalogs are often inaccurate and do not give dimensions, but we believe this to be the toy candlestick seen in the accompanying catalog page from 1859. Items on the page are not in proportion. However, if the toy candlestick is the same size as the adjacent bar tumbler, it would be about 3" high. This toy candlestick continued to be shown in McKee's catalogs for many years.

MCKEE COBALT TOY ON LEFT, SANDWICH COBALT TOY IN CENTER, AND U. S. GLASS COMPANY'S NO.87 TOY CANDLESTICK IN ELECTRIC BLUE ON RIGHT

MCKEE & BROTHERS' CATALOG FROM 1859, INCLUDING TOY CANDLESTICK

The smaller cobalt toy (1⅝" high) can be documented as Sandwich from fragments recovered from the factory site. Because its shape is so similar to that shown in the McKee catalog, it has often been assumed that both companies made identical candlesticks. However, as pointed out above, we believe the McKee toy was substantially larger. The Sandwich toy was in production from circa 1850 to 1870. The rival Cape Cod Glass Company, founded by Deming Jarves after his withdrawal from the Boston and Sandwich Glass Company, is also known to have made a toy candlestick. As was the case with so many of the items made by both companies, it is likely that the Cape Cod toy is identical to the Sandwich one. According to Raymond E. Barlow and Joan E. Kaiser's *The Glass Industry in Sandwich*, volume three, these toys were pressed using a wheel mold, with the bases "attached to a center 'hub' from which the hot metal was forced into each candlestick mold." They also mention that the hole for the candle will be approximately the size of a modern pencil eraser and warn that if it is small enough to hold a contemporary birthday candle, it is not Sandwich.

The third candlestick, in electric blue (2" high), is often attributed to Sandwich or, more frequently, to the New England Glass Company. This toy, along with the smaller, handled toy (also usually misattributed) can be seen in the accompanying catalog reprint from the United States Glass Company. It dates to circa 1918 – 1925 and, to the best of our knowledge, was not made earlier, since it does not appear in any catalogs prior to 1919. Although highly collectible in its own right, this toy often commands higher prices than it should.

U.S. Glass did make one earlier toy candlestick, with handles, seen in the photograph on p. 288. It is 2¾" high and was offered in the early 1890s, possibly continuing production from one of the combine's member companies. The King Glass Company's No. 143 toy candlestick (seen here in a catalog reprint from circa 1890 – 1891) is 1¾" high. These are the only toys that we can attribute with certainty to the nineteenth century, though some of the others shown in the following cabinet shot on page 287 are probably also early.

No. 88 AND 87 TOY CANDLESTICKS, FROM U.S. GLASS CATALOG, CA. 1918 – 1919

KING GLASS COMPANY'S NO. 143 TOY CANDLESTICK, FROM CA. 1890 – 1891 CATALOG

The photographs that follow, with their accompanying charts, identify many of the known toy candlesticks, though by no means all. We have made a special effort to show reissues and reproductions. The popularity of these little items has meant that some molds have had a long life, while others have obviously been copied, leading sometimes to bewildering variations. Readers who would like more comprehensive information, including a number of candlesticks we were not able to include here, are encouraged to seek out the books of Doris Anderson Lechler, referenced in the bibliography. She assigned "standard" numbers to the candlesticks; for the sake of convenience, these are cited in the accompanying chart when appropriate.

Page 287, Shelf 1:

Manufacturer	Dimensions	Date	Colors	#
1 & 2. McKee & Brothers	3" high	Ca. 1859 – 1880s	Cobalt, crystal	N/A
Notes: See the catalog reprint on p. 285 with our explanation as to why we believe these to be the McKee toys.				
3 & 11. Unknown	2" high	Unknown, but probably 1900s	Light green, cobalt	C-43
Notes: Lacy pattern chambersticks. See close-up on p. 288 for detail of design. Also known in dark amethyst.				
4. Unknown	4⅛" high	Unknown, but probably 1900s	Dark green	N/A
Notes: Intricate pattern of grape vines on the column. See close-up on p. 288 for detail of design.				
5. United States Glass Company	2¾" high	Ca. 1891 – 1898	Crystal	N/A
Notes: No. 1 small candle. See close-up on p. 288. Also made in opal.				
6. Boston & Sandwich Glass Company	1⅝" high	Ca. 1850 – 1870	Cobalt	C-34
Notes: See p. 285 for a discussion of this candlestick. Also made in crystal, fiery opalescent, canary, amethyst, and green.				
7. United States Glass Company	1" high	Ca. 1918 – 1919	Crystal	C-32
Notes: No. 88 toy candlestick. Often misattributed to New England Glass Company or Sandwich. See p. 285 for a catalog reprint from 1919 and further discussion. Also available with cased colors on the bottom (blue, orange, yellow).				
8 & 9. United States Glass Company	2⅛" high	Ca. 1918 – 1926	Crystal, blue	C-24
Notes: No. 87 toy candlestick. Often misattributed to New England Glass Company or Sandwich. See p. 285 for a catalog reprint from 1919 and further discussion. Offered in Butler Brothers' April 1918 catalog as a "midget" birthday candlestick. Also available in canary and light green.				
10. Unknown	3¾" high	Unknown	Crystal cased in ruby	N/A
Notes: Ruby cased, cut to clear. This is probably Bohemian. Blown and hollow all the way through the stem to the base.				
12. Unknown	2¼" high	Unknown	Crystal with satin finish	N/A
Notes: This is a very finely detailed piece, with the bottom ground smooth and polished. See close-up photo on p. 288.				

Shelf 2:

Manufacturer	Dimensions	Date	Colors	#
1, 3, & 4. Portieux-Vallerysthal	3½" high	Ca. 1890s – 1930s	Opal, amber	C-5
Notes: Called Swirl or Ribbed Swirl by collectors. No. 1 and 3 are impressed "Portieux" on the underside of the base. No. 1 has more opalescence and slightly sharper detail, probably an indication that it is an earlier piece. No. 4 in amber is not marked, but is from the same mold. Portieux catalogs list this candlestick both as No. 4075 and No. 2117. Since they also made a shorter version of this toy, one of these numbers may be for the latter. Also made in opaque green and turquoise.				
2, 7, & 10. Portieux-Vallerysthal	3¼" high	Ca. 1890s – 1930s	Light amber, opaque green, turquoise	C-5
Notes: Called Swirl or Ribbed Swirl by collectors, but from a different mold than the toy candlestick described above. This one is ¼" shorter and has a straight stem, whereas the other toy has a slightly tapered stem. The amber one has a paper label on the bottom that says "PV France."				
5 & 9. Unknown, made in Taiwan	3" high	Ca. 1970s – 1980s	Crystal	N/A
Notes: The quality of the glass on both of these is poor. No. 5 is impressed "Taiwan" on the bottom and is slightly better quality than no. 9, which is marked "Made in Taiwan" around the top of the candle cup. Note that these candlesticks seem to be copied from the Portieux toys, but are not made from either of the Portieux molds. They are shorter and the shape of the base is different. Also known in pink and amethyst with satin finish.				
6. Unknown	2⅛" high	Unknown	Crystal	N/A
Notes: This two-third size version of the Swirl toy is probably made in Taiwan.				

Manufacturer	Dimensions	Date	Colors	#
8. Unknown, but probably French	3½" high	Unknown	Opaque green	C-58

Notes: Impressed "SV" on the underside of the base. The similarity of this toy and other marked pieces to items made by Portieux-Vallerysthal is evident, but we have not been able to establish a connection. It is possible this mark was used by a contemporaneous nineteenth century company who copied Portieux designs. Also known in turquoise.

| 11. Unknown | 3½" high | Probably 1980s or later | Crystal | N/A |

Notes: Probably made in Taiwan. Has a thinner stem than the other Swirl toys and differently shaped candle cup.

Shelf 3:

| 1, 2, 4, & 6. Probably Portieux-Vallerysthal | 1¾ – 1⅞" high | Ca. 1890s – 1930s | Opal, turquoise, amber | C-6 |

Notes: Known as Swirl to collectors, the design in the base being similar to that on the taller toys in the shelf above. Catalogs from Portieux-Vallerysthal show this style toy as both No. 4074 and No. 2118. All four of these are likely to be Portieux-Vallerysthal, but are not identical, with the most noticeable differences being in the shape of the candle cups. Note that the swirl pattern is on the underside of the base and is therefore invisible on the opaque toys. Also known in cobalt (possibly the reproduction mentioned below).

| 3, 5, & 7. Unknown, made in Taiwan | 2" high | Ca. 1980s and later | Pink, satin, crystal | |

Notes: From a different mold than the ones believed to be Portieux-Vallerysthal. The satin example has a sticker, "Made in Taiwan." Although there are minor variances between it and the other two, we believe all three are of the same origin. The main difference from the Portieux toys is the almost complete lack of scallops around the rim of the candle cup.

CLOSE-UP OF PAGE 287, SHELF 1, #3 & 11: UNKNOWN lacy pattern toy CHAMBERSTICKS IN LIGHT GREEN AND COBALT

CLOSE-UP OF PAGE 287, SHELF 1, #4: UNKNOWN TOY CANDLE-STICK IN DARK GREEN WITH GRAPE VINE PATTERN

CLOSE-UP OF PAGE 287, SHELF 1, #5: U.S. GLASS NO. 1 SMALL CANDLE

CLOSE-UP OF PAGE 287, SHELF 1, #12: UNKNOWN EARLY TOY CUPID CANDLE-STICK WITH SATIN FINISH

Page 289, Shelf 1:

Manufacturer	Dimensions	Date	Colors	#
1-5, 7 & 8. Summit Art Glass Company	1⅞" high	1985 – present	Milk glass, cobalt, opalescent crystal, tangerine, azurite, light blue, amethyst	N/A

Notes: Reissue of Westmoreland's No. 1211 birthday candlestick. Most of the colors shown were made by Summit in 1985 for Phil Rosso, but this toy has also appeared in Summit's own catalog. Other colors are possible. Cobalt examples are sometimes seen with decals of Shirley Temple.

6. Westmoreland Glass Company	1⅞" high	ca. 1924 – 1929, 1984	Crystal	N/A

Notes: No. 1211 birthday candlestick. Reissued briefly in 1984 in crystal just before Westmoreland's closing and in various colors (as mentioned above) by Summit Art Glass. Note that this toy has an octagonal base, in comparison with the very similar Westmoreland No. 1039 birthday candlestick and the Heisey No. 31 toy candlestick seen on shelf 2 below.

Shelf 2:

1. Westmoreland Glass Company	2" high	ca. 1924 – 1932	Crystal	C-26

Notes: No. 1039 handled birthday candlestick. Very similar to the No. 1211 birthday candlestick above, but with a hexagonal base, rather than an octagonal one. Also easily confused with Heisey's No. 31 toy candlestick; the main difference is that the handle on the Westmoreland toy touches the candle cup, whereas the Heisey one does not. Daniel Low & Company, of Salem, MA, advertised this candlestick in 1925 with red stain on the base and a hand painted candle in the shape of Santa Claus.

2. Unknown	2" high	ca. 1986	Crystal	N/A

Notes: Has a label saying "Made in Taiwan." Very poor quality glass. This appears to be from the Westmoreland mold, which is currently owned by Summit. (See below.)

3 & 4. Summit Art Glass Company	2" high	ca. 2001 – present	Cobalt iridescent, canary iridescent	N/A

Notes: Reissued from the Westmoreland No. 1039 handled birthday candlestick mold

5. Unknown	1" high	ca. 1990s	Crystal	N/A
6. Unknown	⅞" high	ca. 1990s	Crystal	N/A

Notes: These two "miniature miniatures" are probably of recent vintage and made in Taiwan, but are unmarked, so we cannot be certain.

7. R. Wetzel Glass Company	2" high	ca. 1976	Amber	N/A

Notes: Reissue of Westmoreland's No. 1039 handled birthday candlestick. We have been able to obtain little information on this company, which was located in Zanesville, Ohio, from 1975 until sometime in the 1980s. Wetzel was both a glass maker and a mold maker, so it is possible that they made a new mold, leased the mold from Westmoreland, or had these candlesticks made as a special order by Westmoreland. They may also have acquired the mold after 1984, when Westmoreland went out of business, though this would disagree with the date given above for the candlesticks, which is based on the previous owners' recollection of when they obtained the pair. They are marked on the bottom, "Merry Christmas from the Wetzels."

8 – 10. A. H. Heisey & Company	2" high	ca. 1908 – 1944	Sahara, moongleam, crystal	C-25

Notes: No. 31 toy candlestick. Also made in flamingo. Rare in all colors. Sometimes marked with the Diamond H on the bottom. Very similar to Westmoreland's No. 1039 handled birthday candlestick, but with a space between the handle and the candle cup, unlike the Westmoreland toy, whose handle touches the candle cup. For more information, see HE-19 on p. 106.

Manufacturer	Dimensions	Date	Colors	#
11. Imperial Glass Corporation	2" high	1981 – 1982	Crystal	N/A
Notes: No. 13795. Reissue of Heisey's No. 31 toy candlestick. A few sample pieces were also made in emerald green. The example shown has a paper label, but is otherwise unmarked. The quality of the glass is not as good as the Heisey original. For more information, see IM-184 on p. 230.				
Shelf 3:				
1. Duncan & Miller Glass Company	2" high ca.	1900 – 1923	Crystal	C-42
Notes: No. 72 toy chamber candlestick. Easy to differentiate from the Heisey and Westmoreland toys above because of the distinctive shape of its handle. For further information, see DM-16 on p. 147 of volume one of this series.				
2-4. Tiffin Glass Company	2" high	ca. 1922 – 1936	Green, crystal, blue	N/A
Notes: No. 17 small, handled candleholder.				
5-7. Akro Agate Company	1⅞" high	ca. 1940s	Crystal (plain and w/overall gold paint), white opaque	N/A
Notes: Called Banded Swirl by collectors. Available both with the plain handle seen here and with a notched handle and additional swirls on the top of the base. Some of these were made for the Lander Company of New York, a cosmetic retailer, and sold with small perfume bottles in the shape of candles. For further information see AK-10 on p. 9 of volume one of this series.				

Page 291, Shelf 1:

Manufacturer	Dimensions	Date	Colors	#
1, 2, 7. Unknown, Bohemian	2½" high	Unknown	Crystal, pink, light blue	N/A
3-6. Unknown	2½" high	Late 1940s, early 1950s (possibly later)	Crystal with ruby stain, green opaline, azure blue, yellow opaline	N/A
8 & 9. L. E. Smith Glass Company	2½" high	Early 1980s	Crystal, plain & satin	N/A

Notes: Smith No. 6660 petite angel candlesticks. This group of toys is particularly difficult to pin down. Although at first glance, they all appear identical, in fact there are many differences between them. There are at least three molds involved here. Things to note are the shape of the wings and the detail of the features, the amount of detail on the hair and the sharpness of the facial features, the relative size of the candle cup, and the detail of the hands.

The first angel on the left has a label saying "Bohemia glass. Made in Czechoslovakia." There is a definite pattern on the wings, but it isn't symmetrical on both sides. Strands of hair are visible, and so are the fingers on the hands. The candle cup is proportionately larger than any of the others. The inside of the base is flat. The pink and light blue angels are from the same mold.

The crystal angel with the ruby stain was advertised in 1949 in two sizes, 2½" and 4½". It has been attributed as French, but we don't know the basis for this. It has well-patterned wings and the most detailed facial features. Both of the opaline angels are from the same mold. The azure blue angel may also be from this mold, but if so, it must be a more recent production, because the detail is considerably less, which might be due to the mold being worn. The wing is also shorter and more rounded at the top – possibly due to the mold not being completely filled. Other details seem to match, including three folds appearing at the back of the angel's robe (as compared to only a single fold on the Bohemian angels). Also, on all four of these candlesticks, the insides of the bases are partially hollow up into the body of the angel.

The Smith petite angels were purchased at the factory in 1982. There is almost no detail to the wings, hair, or faces. They have the three folds at the back of the robe and also the hollow extending into the bodies of the angels, and this suggests that Smith may have acquired the worn molds from whoever produced the four preceding examples – especially since Smith also made a 4½" size. (We can't rule out the possibility that Smith may have introduced this candlestick in 1948, reissuing it in the 1980s.) However, if this is the case, they must have modified the molds, since the candle cup is slightly taller (⅛") and the star bases have a distinct bevel on their bottom edges.

Shelf 2:

1-10. Weishar Enterprises	1" (flat) & 1⅜" (cupped)	ca. 1988 – 1993	Cobalt, crystal, pink (plain & carnival)	N/A

Notes: Part of a series of half scale miniatures of the Moon and Star pattern produced by Weishar (who is associated with the Island Mould & Machine Company). Made in two styles, "nappies" and "plates." There is an impressed signature ("Weishar") on the bottom of each piece.

Shelf 3:

1 & 10. Mosser Glass, Inc.	1¼" high	1991 to the present	Moonlight blue, cobalt	N/A

Notes: No. 225 Lindsey candlestick. Available as part of a set with two candlesticks and a fruit bowl. Also made in crystal. This is a miniature version of Cambridge's No. 67 Caprice candlestick, originally made 1936 – 1950s. (See CB-106 on p. 80 of volume one of this series.) Cambridge did not make a small size of this candlestick.

2 & 9. Mosser Glass, Inc.	3¾" high	1992 – 2001	Moonlight blue, cobalt	N/A

Notes: No. 225 Lindsey candlestick with prism. Also made in crystal. This is a miniature version of Cambridge's No. 70 Caprice candlestick with prism, originally made 1936 – 1954. (See CB-109 on p. 81 of volume one of this series.) Cambridge did not make a small size of this candlestick.

3, 5, 7. Mosser Glass, Inc.	3" high	1980s – 1990s	Red, blue milk, amber	C-54

Notes: No. 213 miniature candlestick. Red was discontinued sometime in the 1980s. Marked with an "M" inside the base. This is a reproduction of a toy candlestick known as "Dutch Boudoir" or "Dutch Kinder" that has been attributed to the United States Glass Company, ca. 1910. The originals are known in milk glass and transparent green. The design features a boy on one side of the candlestick, and a dog on the other.

4, 6, 8. Mosser Glass, Inc.	2" high	1985 to the present	Gold krystol, apple green, pink	N/A

Notes: No. 140 Jennifer candlestick. Available as part of a set with two candlesticks and a fruit bowl. This is a miniature version of the Hocking Glass Company's Cameo candlestick (also known as Ballerina or Dancing Girl), 1930 – 1934. (See AH-2 on p. 10 of volume one of this series.) Hocking did not make a small size of this candlestick.

Shelf 4:

1. Westmoreland Glass Company	4¼" high	ca. 1917 – 1930s	Crystal	C-15

Notes: No. 1014 birthday candlestick. Very similar to a candlestick currently in production by Mosser Glass, but with a round socket on the candle cup, compared to the Mosser toy, which is octagonal. Both candlesticks have hexagonal bases. Sometimes found with the base ground and polished. The pink and crystal toys to the far right of the photograph are either reproductions or made from the original mold with modifications.

Manufacturer	Dimensions	Date	Colors	#
2-4. Mosser Glass, Inc.	4⅛" high	1988 – 2001	Cobalt, crystal, red	N/A

Notes: No. 154 mini candlestick. Very similar to Westmoreland's No. 1014 birthday candlestick above, but with an octagonal rim on the candle cup, rather than a round one. Also available in crystal satin. Other colors reported for this style candlestick are aquamarine, black, and vaseline, but these colors were not made by Mosser, so are probably the reproductions discussed below.

5 & 6. Unknown	4¼" high	Unknown	Pink, crystal	N/A

Notes: These candlesticks have a round rim like the Westmoreland No. 1014 birthday candlestick above. The pink example is probably from the Westmoreland mold, in rather poor quality glass with lots of bubbles, possibly made in Taiwan. The crystal example is also very similar, but if it was made from the Westmoreland mold, it must have been modified, since the base is hollow up to the beginning of the stem, unlike the pink version and the Westmoreland original, which are both flat. The quality of the glass is poor, with bubbles, suggesting Taiwan as its place of manufacture.

Page 293, Shelf 1 & 2:

Manufacturer	Dimensions	Date	Colors	#
Westmoreland Glass Company	4½" high	1910 – 1930s, 1970s	Green mist, apricot mist, light blue mist, cobalt, mother of pearl, ruby, canary, light blue, crystal	C-1

Notes: No. 1013 candelabra (listed as 5"). Early crystal examples are marked "Pat. Applied For" around the top rim of the middle candle cup. The patent was filed Oct. 6, 1910, and approved Mar. 21, 1911, as D41,256. Designer: George R. West. Originally made primarily in crystal, with some color production by the 1930s; reissued in the 1970s in various colors. Other reported colors include dark blue mist and lavender; pink was made in a limited edition for the Levay Distributing Company in the late 1970s (with satin finish and possibly clear as well), as were ruby and light blue. Cobalt, mother of pearl (iridized milk glass), and canary have been reported to be reproductions; however, the ones pictured here were all purchased between 1980 and 1984 when Westmoreland was still in business, so it seems more likely they were made by the company as special orders. The Colonial Candle Company of Cape Cod offered these candlesticks in the 1920s decorated in yellow, rose, or old blue, and also with just the candle cups painted red; the first three colors were also advertised by the Eastern Specialty Manufacturing Company in 1922.

The Cambridge Glass Company made an almost identical candlestick as their No. 2750 three-prong candlestick (ca. 1910 – 1915), as seen in the accompanying catalog reprint. Although one of the authors expressed the opinion in volume one of this series that this might be the Cambridge toy, we are now in agreement that this is not the case. A more likely possibility for the variant is that it was made by Jeannette, but this is just a guess. There is also a rarely-seen version of this candlestick with a diamond-shaped base (actually square-shaped, with the point of the square facing forward). (See CB-15 on p. 53 of volume one of this series.)

Shelf 3:

1. A. H. Heisey & Company	3½" high	ca. 1910 – 1929	Crystal	N/A

Notes: No. 33 candlestick. Known as Skirted Panel. Usually marked with the Diamond H at the top of the skirt, just beneath the candle cup. (See HE-21 on p. 107.) Also made in 5", 7", 9", and 11" sizes.

2-9. Imperial Glass Corporation	3½" high	1981 – 1982	Crystal iridized, ultra blue, sunshine yellow, ruby, light blue, emerald green, pink, crystal	N/A

Notes: No. 13794. Reissue of Heisey's No. 33 toy candlestick. Iridized crystal and ruby were sample pieces that did not go into full production; ultra blue, sunshine yellow, light blue, and pink were made in limited editions for the Heisey Collectors of America. The plain crystal examples are not marked, but are not as good crystal as the originals. The ruby ones are marked LIG on the bottom rim and the other colors are all marked ALIG in the same location. (See IM-185 on p. 230.)

Shelf 4:

1-4. Indiana Glass Company	3" high	ca. 1905, 1978 – 1986	Crystal, ice blue, frosted crystal, milk glass	C-23

Notes: No. 300 toy birthday candlestick. First made in crystal only, and later reissued for Tiara Exclusives as No. 10075 in frosted crystal and No. 490 in ice blue. Milk glass production probably dates to the 1970s. (See IN-1 on p. 236.)

5-6. Unknown	⅝" high	Recent production	Crystal, ruby	N/A

Notes: No. HJ-103 heart shaped glass candleholder, sold by Wicks 'n' Sticks.

7. Unknown	3½" diameter	Unknown	Milk glass	N/A

Notes: Has a border of open hearts. Westmoreland made a full size heart plate with a similar border, but it isn't known who made the small, round version.

8-9. Unknown	1½" & 1¼" high	Unknown	Crystal	N/A

Notes: Miniature versions of the Cambridge No. 2798 birthday candlestick below. Probably made in Taiwan.

10-11. Unknown	3" high	Unknown	Crystal, pink satin	N/A
12. Cambridge Glass Company	3" high	ca. 1912 – 1920s	Crystal	C-22

Note: No. 2798 birthday candlestick. The close-up in the accompanying photograph shows this toy in opal, previously unreported. Also known in pink, probably Cambridge's peach-blo (but see information about reissues below). For further information, see CB-19 on p. 54 of volume one of this series.

13. Biedermann	3" high	Late 1980s	Crystal	N/A

Note: Appears to be made from the same mold as the Cambridge No. 2798 birthday candlestick above. The label says "Biedermann. Made in Taiwan." Otherwise unmarked, but the glass quality is very poor, so there should be no problem differentiating the reproductions from the originals.

14. Unknown	3" high	Unknown	Blue slag	C-34

Notes: May be made from the same mold as the Cambridge No. 2798 birthday candlestick above, but if so, the proportions are a little different, with the panels and depth of the candle cup a fraction larger than the original. Also known in peach slag.

CAMBRIDGE NO. 2750
THREE-PRONG CANDLE-
STICK, FROM CATALOG, CA.
1910 – 1915

UNKNOWN 3-LIGHT TOY
CANDLESTICK WITH
SQUARE BASE

CLOSE-UP OF SHELF 4,
#12: CAMBRIDGE NO.
2798 BIRTHDAY
CANDLESTICK IN OPAL

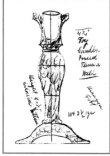

This sketch of a 4¼" toy candlestick was reproduced in William Heacock, James Measell, and Berry Wiggins' *Dugan/Diamond*. It is labeled "Diamond Glass Ware Co.," and was done by Charles E. Voitle, the executive secretary of the National Association of Manufacturers of Pressed and Blown Glassware. It is dated March 15, 1930. Another candlestick from the same drawing is known to have been produced by the company, but we have never seen this in person. According to the notes that accompany the sketch, it has a hexagonal foot.

Page 295, Shelf 1:

Manufacturer	Dimensions	Date	Colors	#
1. Unknown	4⅜" high	Unknown	Crystal	C-18

Notes: The similarity of this candlestick to the No. T310 Chippendale candlestick made by the Jefferson Glass Company (ca. 1910 – 1918), and then by the Central Glass Company (1919 to the mid-1920s), leads us to suspect this might also be part of the Chippendale pattern. (See CE- 5 on p. 103 of volume one of this series.)

Manufacturer	Dimensions	Date	Colors	#
2. Duncan & Miller Glass Company	4" high	ca. 1900+	Crystal	C-8

Notes: No. 66 candlestick. (See DM-13 on p. 147 of volume one of this series.) Also made in 6" and 7½" sizes.

3. Westmoreland Glass Company	3¾" high	ca. 1912 – 1932	Crystal	C-37

Notes: No. 1005 birthday candlestick.

4. Brockwitz, Glasfabrik, AG (Meissen, Germany)	4" high	ca. 1931	Crystal	N/A

Notes: No. 8177 candlestick. Also made in two taller sizes (10 cm. and 12 cm.)

5. McKee Glass Company	4¾" high	ca. 1910 – 1927	Crystal	N/A

Notes: No. 20 Colonial Design candlestick. One of McKee's Prescut lines. Also made in a 7" size.

6. United States Glass Company	4⅛" high	ca. 1912 – 1919	Crystal	N/A

Notes: No. 15140 Athenia candlestick. Known as Panelled 44 and Reverse 44 by collectors. Also made in a 7" size.

Shelf 2:

1. A. H. Heisey & Company	4½" high	ca. 1904 – 1931	Crystal	C-17

Notes: No. 5 candlestick. Known as Patrician. Usually marked with the Diamond H on the bottom. Heisey made six other sizes of this style candlestick, but with flat, puntied bottoms. Although early catalogs show the toy with a flat bottom as well, we have only seen it with the hollow base shown here.

2. New Martinsville Glass Manufacturing Company & Paden City Glass Manufacturing Company	3¾" high	ca. 1917 – 1920s	Crystal	N/A

Notes: New Martinsville No. 12 or Paden City No. 113 candlestick. To the best of our knowledge, the candlesticks made by both companies are identical, with a pressed star on the base. Also offered in 5½", 7", and 8½" sizes. Sometimes found with silver overlay decoration. Other companies made similar candlesticks, but not in a toy size.

3. Jeannette Glass Company	4⅛" high	ca. 1920 – 1925	Crystal	C-19

Notes: No. 5133 novelty candelabrum. (See JE-1 on p. 270.)

4. New Martinsville Glass Manufacturing Company & Paden City Glass Manufacturing Company	3½" high	ca. 1917 – 1920s	Crystal	C-12

Notes: New Martinsville No. 14 or Paden City No. 112 candlestick. To the best of our knowledge, the candlesticks made by both companies are identical, with a pressed star on the base. Also offered in 5½", 7", and 8½" sizes. Sometimes found with silver overlay decoration. The example shown is slightly sun-purpled.

5. Unknown	4" high	Late 19th, early 20th century	Crystal, with gold trim	C-10

Shelf 3:

1 & 3. A. H. Heisey & Company	3" high	ca. 1907 – 1924	Crystal, plain & satin finish	C-21

Notes: No. 30 toy candlestick. Known as Tom Thumb. Sometimes marked with the Diamond H on the candle cup, and sometimes on the bottom of the base. Unusual in satin finish. (See HE-15 on p. 105.)

2. Cambridge Glass Company	2½" diameter	1939 – 1958	Crystal	N/A

Notes: No. 1 Star candlestick. Known in amethyst and moonlight blue, with other colors possible. Cambridge also made a 4" No. 2 Star, a 5" No. 3 Star, and a huge 11" No. 4 Star. (See CB-150 on p. 91 of volume 1 of this series.)

4. Unknown	3" high	Unknown	Crystal	N/A

5. Jefferson Glass Company & Central Glass Works	2¼" high	1910 to the mid 1920s	Crystal	C-28

Notes: No. T305 Chippendale child's colonial candlestick. Sometimes marked Krys-Tol on the top of the base. Originally made by Jefferson from 1910 to 1918, and then by Central. (See JF-2 on p. 282 & CE-3 on p. 103 of volume one of this series.)

6. Irving W. Rice & Company	1¼" high	Unknown	Crystal	N/A

Notes: Full cut all over. One has a label saying "An Irice product. Made in Czechoslovakia. Irving W. Rice & Co., New York City."

7. Franklin Mint	3" high	1984	Crystal	N/A

Notes: "English glass candlestick," part of the Curio Cabinet Glass Miniatures collection. Made in Japan. The bottom is ground smooth.

Manufacturer	Dimensions	Date	Colors	#
Shelf 4:				
1. Unknown	4" high	Unknown	Crystal	N/A
2. Federal Glass Company	5¼" high	1940 – 1950s	Crystal	N/A
Notes: No. 2809 Petal hurricane lamp. A design patent was filed for this piece on August 14, 1940, and approved October 1, 1940, as D122,877. Designer: Albert H. Nicholson. Sometimes found with amethyst or yellow stain. (See FD-4 on p. 173 of volume one of this series.)				
3. Unknown	3⅝" high	Unknown	Crystal	C-36

This is a lacy style toy chamber stick in opal, probably nineteenth century. The drape pattern on the candle cup also appears on the underside of the base, but is not visible due to the opaque color — this suggests that it was probably also made in transparent colors. It is 2" high with a 2¾" diameter base. It was purchased in Australia, which could indicate an English origin.

This is a Baccarat toy, probably late nineteenth or early twentieth century. It is 4⅜" high with a 2¼" hexagonal base. It is marked Baccarat underneath the base. The rim on the candle cup and bottom are cut and polished.

Jeannette No. 5055 small octagon candlestick. (Lechler C-14.) 4½" high. From a catalog dating to ca. 1920 – 1924. (See JE-2 on p. 271.)

Page 297, Shelf 1:

Manufacturer	Dimensions	Date	Colors	#
1 & 3. Unknown (boy & girl angels)	3 to 3¼"	Unknown	Crystal	N/A
2. Unknown (locomotive)	1¾" long	Unknown	Crystal	N/A
4. Unknown (rocking horse)	3" long	ca. 1983	Crystal	N/A
5. Biedermann (angel). Made in Taiwan	2½" high	ca. 1988	Crystal	N/A
6. Biedermann (unicorn). Made in Taiwan	3⅜" long	ca. 1993	Crystal	N/A
7. Biedermann (butterfly). Made in Taiwan	2⅝" wingspread	Unknown	Crystal	N/A
Shelf 2:				
1. Unknown (bear)	2" high	Unknown	Crystal	N/A
2. Unknown (bear)	3¼" high	Unknown	Crystal satin	N/A
3. Biedermann (Teddy bear). Made in Taiwan	2¼" high	ca. 1988	Crystal	N/A
4. Unknown (cat). Made in Taiwan	2¼" high	ca. 1985	Crystal	N/A
5. Unknown (cat)	1¾" high	Unknown	Crystal	N/A
6. Unknown (frog). Made in Taiwan	1¾" high	ca. 1986	Crystal	N/A
7. Biedermann (deer). Made in Taiwan	2⅜" long	ca. 1987	Crystal	N/A
Shelf 3:				
1. Biedermann (bunny). Made in Taiwan	2½" high	ca. 1988	Crystal	N/A
2 & 3. Biedermann (rabbits). Made in Taiwan	2" high	ca. 1993	Pink, crystal	N/A
4. Unknown (rabbit)	2¾" long	Unknown	Crystal	N/A
5. Biedermann (swan). Made in Taiwan	2½" long	ca. 1993	Crystal	N/A
6. Biedermann (elephant). Made in Taiwan	3½" long	ca. 1993	Crystal	N/A
7. Biedermann (duck). Made in Taiwan	2¼" long	ca. 1988	Crystal	N/A
Shelf 4:				
1-3. Biedermann (sparrows). Made in Taiwan	2½" – 2¾" long	ca. 1984 – 1988	Crystal	N/A
4. Biedermann (dinosaur). Made in Taiwan	3¾" long	ca. 1993	Crystal	N/A

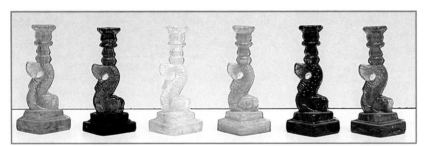

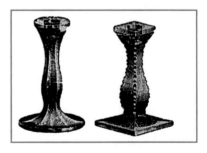

Miniature dolphin candlesticks in tourmaline green, emerald green, fiery opalescent, powder blue, midnight blue, and cranberry opalescent. 2¾" high. These scale reproductions of the Sandwich dolphin candlestick with double step base and petal candle cup (BS-15 on p. 39 of volume one of this series) were made by Kirk Nelson, former curator of the Sandwich Glass Museum in 1991. Advertised as "hand crafted with a press designed in 1831," they were manufactured using authentic techniques. The five opalescent examples have hollow bases and are mold marked "KN" inside. The base on the emerald example has been ground flat, with the result that it is a little smaller than the others. "KN 193" is scratched on the bottom.

This catalog reprint features toy candlesticks from the Canton Glass Company. The one on the left was called the Florence junior candlestick and the one on the right is the No. 2038½ imitation cut candlestick. (Lechler C-11.) Both were listed as 3½" high and made ca. 1919 – 1924. (See CN-4 and CN-5 on p. 98 of volume one of this series.) The New Martinsville Glass Manufacturing Company also made a very similar imitation cut toy as their No. 15.

These two candlesticks, if they were not side by side, might appear to be identical. As can be seen when they are together, there is a difference in the size. The taller one (4½" high with a 3" diameter hexagonal base) was originally made by the Ohio Flint Glass Company as part of the Chippendale pattern. It was patented in 1907 by Benjamin W. Jacobs. The Jefferson Glass Company acquired the Chippendale pattern and continued to make this candlestick as No. T314 from 1908 to 1918 (see JF-1 on p. 282) and then it was made by the Central Glass Works from 1919 to the mid-1920s (see CE-6 on p. 103 of volume one of this series). Early examples may be marked "PAT JUNE 11 1907 Krys-Tol," while later ones will only say "Krys-Tol" or will be unmarked. The shorter candlestick is 3⅞" high with a 2⅜" base. It was advertised in 1910 by the Westmoreland Specialty Company as No. 1015S, part of "the largest and best line of novelties in glass to retail at 5c and 10c each in the market." The Ohio Flint Glass patent, which presumably would have also been acquired by Jefferson when they obtained the rights to produce the Chippendale pattern, was still in effect in 1910, but we have found no indication of legal action taken against Westmoreland, who continued to offer this toy until the early 1930s. Both companies made larger versions of this candlestick, as well: 7½" and 9½" by Jefferson/Central, and 6" by Westmoreland.

Believe it or not, these are 1" scale hand-blown candlesticks made by contemporary craftsmen for dollhouse use. The tallest is 1³⁄₁₆" high and the shortest only ¾".

This black candlestick is a little taller than most toys, but obviously is not a full-size candlestick, either, though it does take a ½" taper. It is 4⅞" high with a 3⅛" diameter base. It was purchased in Scotland and may be English in origin.

GLOSSARY

Amberina. Coloring that shades from a light yellow to red or fuchsia. Created by adding gold powders to a batch of amber glass and then reheating portions of the finished product.

Applied foot. As related to candlestick production, this term refers to the technique of adding the foot or base to the body of the candlestick after it has been removed from the mold. Distinguished from a molded foot or base where the foot is produced in the mold. Mold marks will normally be visible on a molded foot, whereas an applied foot will not have any. An applied foot was shaped by hand, which can result in slight irregularities and/or differences in size between the candlesticks in a pair.

Art deco. A style popularized in the 1920s and 1930s. The name is a shortened from the Exposition Internationales des Arts Decoratifs et Industriels Modernes, the exhibition in Paris that first introduced the style in 1925, though it has roots dating back earlier. Sometimes called Art Moderne. Design elements tend to be geometric, almost architectural at times, with simple lines and restrained decoration.

Bedroom set. Normally consists of a tray, a tumbler, a water pitcher or tankard, and a candlestick, sometimes with a match holder.

Blank. A completed piece of glassware with no decoration (other than that produced in the mold).

Bobeche. A disk or saucer affixed beneath the candle socket of a candlestick or candelabrum to catch wax drippings. Often has prisms suspended from it. May be either permanently attached or removable. A peg bobeche has a fitting on the bottom that inserts into a candle cup.

Brocade etching. Among the more popular forms of decoration offered by Fostoria, brocade etchings differed from normal etchings by covering almost the entire piece, with very little of the surface left clear. See also Etching.

Bust off. That portion of an item which when extracted from the mold is excess and is broken away. Although not part of the completed item, it is nevertheless a necessary element in the molding process of many articles, including certain candlesticks. It is, in effect, an overflow of molten glass in the mold which ensures that the plunger forces the glass into every portion of the mold. Unfinished candlesticks are occasionally found with the bust off still attached.

Carnival glass. See Iridescent.

Carving. A method of decorating glass by sand blasting those portions not covered by a rubbery coating. The result is a roughened surface that appears to be frosted, deeper than the designs created by the etching process. During the process, portions of the resist could be progressively removed, so that the final decoration can have considerable depth and almost sculptural highlights.

Cased glass. Two or more layers of different colored glass, sometimes with the outer layer cut back to reveal the color underneath. Crystal or another transparent color may also be cased over an opaque color or used to "sandwich" another decorating technique between the layers.

Clambroth. A semi-opaque glass with a slightly smoky look. See also Opaline.

Console set. A combination of candlesticks and a floral bowl, usually in the same pattern, used as a centerpiece for a table setting. This practice became popular in the latter half of the 1920s, with most companies producing these combinations well into the 1950s or 1960s. Many decorating companies bought bowls and candlesticks from various sources, putting them together with their own decorations added, so that it is possible to find "matching" sets with pieces originally made by different glass factories.

Controlled bubbles. A decorative technique where bubbles in the glass are created intentionally by rolling the molten glass over a spiked form, then applying a second layer of glass to trap the resulting air cavities.

Convex glass. Flat glass curved to form decorative or utilitarian items. Also known as bent glass.

Copper wheel engraving. See Engraving.

Crackle glass. Decorative treatment that resembles cracked ice. Creating by plunging the article while still in a molten state into cold water. The resulting thermal shock creates fine cracks on the surface. The glass is then reheated and final shaping takes places.

Crystal. Clear, colorless glass. In general usage, "crystal" denotes any colorless glass, though technically it must contain a minimum of 24% lead to be officially labeled as such. Crystal is also made with potash-lime. Our use in this book simply reflects a lack of color.

Crystal print. A form of etching offered by Fostoria that was more delicate than normal plate etchings. See also Etching.

Cutting. A method of decorating glass by use of rapidly turning iron, stone, and wooden wheels (for roughing, smoothing, and polishing, respectively). Usually a three-stage process in which an abrasive agent such as sand, pumice powder, or putty powder is used along with the grinding and polishing wheels to effect the cutting. Cutting often involves deep lines and curved miter designs. See also Engraving.

Depression glass. Refers to machine-made glass produced in the late 1920s and 1930s. Collectors today often refer to "Depression-era" glass, which also includes the handmade glassware from the same period.

Doeskin. Term used by Imperial to designate satin-finished milk glass.

End of day glass. See Slag glass.

Engraving. A method of decorating glass by use of rapidly turning copper wheels of many sizes, some as small as an eighth of an inch. An abrasive agent of emery or pumice mixed with water and oil is used. In engraving, the glass blank is held under the wheel so that the view of it is cut off by the wheel itself, unlike cutting, where the blank is held over or on top of the wheel. Engraving involves much shallower cuts and results in much more detailed, intricate designs. Engravings may be left "grey" or may be polished with acid to return them to a state of clearness. The term "rock crystal" is often used to refer to acid polished engravings. See also Cutting.

Epergnette. A small saucer fitted with a peg that could be inserted into any candelabra or candlestick and filled with candy, pine cones, nuts, flowers, or fruit. They were available with or without a candleholding element molded into the center. Originated by Heisey, but later made by various companies, who generally referred to them as "peg nappies."

Epergnion. An epergnette with the rim drilled to hold prisms.

Etching. A method of decorating glass by applying designs created by hydrofluoric acid eating into the surface of the glass, leaving a frosted finish. There are several techniques for applying etchings, with plate etching being one of the more common forms. This involves the transfer of a design from a metal plate covered with acid resistant beeswax to a piece of special tissue paper. The tissue coated with beeswax is then applied to the blank to be decorated so that the wax transfers onto the glass. The portions of the glass that remain uncovered with the acid resist or beeswax are the portions that make up the design. The item is immersed in hydrofluoric acid for fifteen to twenty minutes. When the wax is removed, the etched design appears on those surfaces that were not protected by the acid resist. See also Satin finish.

Feasibility item. A test piece made to determine the potential for manufacture and marketability of an item. Generally made in only small quantities, ranging anywhere from half a dozen pieces to no more than a couple of dozen. These may be tests conducted to try out a brand new mold, pieces made in an old mold but in different colors, or samples of a new color. Many of these pieces, for a variety of reasons, never go into regular production.

Ferrule. A threaded metal spool used as a connector part on a candelabra to connect the arms to the base and the candle cups to the arms, holding them firmly in place.

Fire polishing. Refers to the process whereby a glass article (which has already been shaped or molded into its final form) is held to the open flame of the glory hole for a few minutes to restore its brightness and obliterate tool or mold marks, producing a polished surface.

Fired-on color. A solid color, usually applied to all surfaces of a blank. Often found both in crystal and milk glass. The coated piece is then fired in a kiln. Sometimes referred to as "baked-on."

Flint glass. Originally referred to 19th century glass made with fine silica produced from quartz (or "flint") that had been pulverized. Some early companies also began using oxide of lead in their glass batch, which resulted in flint glass being used synonymously for lead glass. In the later 19th century and early 20th century, after it had been discovered that crystal could be produced using lime, "flint glass" remained in common usage to describe this less expensive glass, as well.

Free hand. Glassware created entirely by hand, without the use of molds to impart the final shape of the piece.

Frosted. See Satin finish.

Gravic cutting. A form of cutting where multiple cuts could be made simultaneously. Characterized by simple floral designs made up of several parallel cuts, close together, generally left gray without polishing, this was a less expensive form of decoration than full cutting or engraving. Also known as "gang cutting."

Hobnail. A popular pressed pattern made by many companies, featuring evenly distributed small knobs, so named because they resemble the heads of the hobnails used for studding shoe soles. Sometimes called Dewdrop.

Hurricane lamp. A candleholder fitted with a globe to protect the flame from being snuffed out by the wind. Most hurricane lamps have removable globes, but some are formed as a single unit.

Iridescent. A rainbow-like colored finish with a metallic appearance, often referred to as carnival glass. Some lustres (a form of staining) also have an iridescent finish. Iridescence is created by spraying metallic salts on the glass while it is still hot. See also Stretch glass.

Jadite. A light green opaque glass, made in large quantities by McKee, Jeannette and Anchor Hocking. Opaque green shades produced by other companies are often referred to as jadite, as well.

Lustre. The term used by Fostoria to refer to a one-light candelabrum. In other contexts, this is a form of iridescence (see above).

Marbleized glass. See Slag glass.

Matte finish. See Satin finish.

Milk glass. Popular name for opaque white glass. Most early companies referred to this color as opal and some milk glass will have opalescent highlights. Today's collectors use milk glass to refer to all opaque glass, including blue opaque, green opaque (jadite), and even black. See also Slag glass.

Mosaic glass. See Slag glass.

Novelties. A term used by glass companies to refer to individual items that were not part of larger patterns, including some utilitarian pieces. Most novelties were occasional pieces, often in unusual or imaginative shapes or with brightly colored hand painted decorations. Opal novelties included smoking items, toothpick holders, candlesticks, and other small items.

Offhand glassware. Blown pieces created without the use of molds. Most "blown" glassware is made by blowing the glass into a mold that gives it its basic shape. Offhand glassware, also known as freehand glassware, was made using only a blowpipe and could be decorated with a variety of techniques while still in a malleable state.

Opal. See Milk glass.

Opalescent. Transparent glass with milky white edges, with a fiery appearance resembling opals. Created by adding calcium phosphate (or bone ash) to the glass batch. When the pieces are reheated, the edges (and often raised portions of the pattern) turn opalescent.

Opaline. Partly translucent glass, less dense then milk glass, but with a generally even distribution of color, unlike opal or opalescent glass. Sometimes has a slightly smoky look, referred to as clambroth.

Optic. A decorative technique used mostly in blown items consisting of faint lines in the glass that catch the light. Popular optics include diamond, panel, festoon (or drape). Created by inserting the partially blown item into a mold to pick up the optic pattern and then blowing it to its full shape and size, which causes the optic pattern to become less distinct.

Paste mold. Used for producing blown-mold glass. The inside of the mold is coated with a carbon paste, which allows rotation of the object being blown, removing mold marks in the process.

Peg nappy. A small bowl with a fitting on the bottom that allows it to be inserted into the socket of a candlestick, converting it into a comport or container for a floral arrangement. Called an epergnette by Heisey.

Plate etching. See Etching.

Plated glass. See Cased glass.

Plunger. As it relates to the manufacture of pressed glass, that part of a pressing machine which fits into the opening of a mold in order to force the molten glass into all portions or crevices of the mold. By using different plungers, pieces could be produced from a single mold with varying designs, such as different pressed patterns on the underside of the base.

Pontil. Also called a pontil rod or punty rod. The iron tool used to hold a piece of pressed glass while it is still hot enough to be shaped into its final form. When the item is removed from the rod, it leaves a rough scar, referred to as a pontil mark or punty mark. Some manufacturers ground and polished this mark away, sometimes leaving a smooth, circular, concave impression, also referred to as a punted bottom.

Prescut. A molded design that could be augmented by simple cutting to give the impression of being a full-cut piece. The cut portions were often left gray, or might be polished. Cambridge's Nearcut patterns are examples of Prescut designs.

Puntied or Punty. See Pontil.

Reissue. A piece made in the original mold years after the initial production dates, by either the same company or a subsequent owner of the mold.

Reproduction. A piece made in a newly created mold in imitation of an earlier issued item or pattern. This includes items added to a reproduced line that were not initially made by the original company.

Rock crystal cutting. See Engraving.

Ruby stain. See Stain.

Satin finish. A form of etching where the entire piece is dipped in acid to give it a frosted or matte finish. Some companies added the satin finish to portions of an item, leaving the remainder clear. The finish can range from dull gray to lustrous.

Silver deposit/overlay. A decorative technique where a thin layer of silver is deposited permanently on the glass in various designs. There are several different techniques used in applying the silver, resulting in a technical distinction between overlay and deposit, though the final product in both cases presents a similar appearance. An inexpensive means of decorating with silver involved brushing the liquid silver on, but this did not have the permanence of either silver deposit or overlay.

Slag glass. Two or more colors combined to give the appearance of natural, variegated marble. Also known as marble glass or mosaic glass. Frequently referred to as "end of day" glass, implying that pieces were made using leftover batches of glass mixed together. In fact, slag glass is produced using carefully controlled formulas heated to very precise temperatures. Most slag glass is a mixture of milk glass with one or more transparent colors.

Spangled glass. Gold or silver mica flecks applied over a gather of colored glass with a layer of crystal on top.

Stain. A form of decoration achieved by spraying or painting a part or whole of an item and then reheating it so that a transparent color becomes a permanent part of the glass. When metallic oxides were used, the result was a lustre stain, with iridescent qualities. Ruby and amber are the most common colors used for staining, though other colors have been popular at various times. Often referred to as "flashing," which is an erroneous term. Some companies, such as Consolidated, used similar techniques to apply semi-opaque colors, which they referred to as "washes."

Stretch. A form of iridescent glass that is reheated in the furnace after it has been sprayed with the metallic salts, then reworked by hand until it has been formed into the desired shape. This causes the iridescent finish to develop a web-like network of overall "stretch marks."

Trindle. Term used by Fostoria to refer to their three-light candlesticks.

Turn. Most glass factories that had sizeable operations worked in four hour shifts called turns. Usually the team of workers, or "shop," which could consist of anywhere between three to six men (depending on the type and complexity of the item being made) would work together for the four hours producing a large quantity of the same item. Therefore, "turn" refers not only to a period of time, but also to the number of items being produced during the turn.

Wafer. Many early pressed glass pieces (or combination pressed and blown items) were formed in two or more parts. In the case of candlesticks, this often meant that the candle cup, the stem, and sometimes the foot were all pressed separately. The individual pieces were joined together, while still hot, by using a small glob of molten glass pressed flat between them, so that it takes on a rough wafer shape. (Some pieces may have multiple wafers.) A true wafer can be identified by tracing the mold marks on the rest of the finished item. A mold mark will not appear on the wafer and often the marks on the top and bottom pieces will not even line up with one another. As companies got away from this manufacturing technique and began making entire candlesticks in one molded piece, they often continued to produce popular styles with a "pseudo-wafer" – a molded wafer that mimicked the real thing. Pseudo-wafers will also be found on many twentieth century reproductions.

Whimsey. A one-of-a-kind item, created by changing the shape of a production piece (or making an entirely new piece freehand), usually during a workman's off time. It is sometimes difficult to know whether a previously-unreported shape in a pattern is a whimsey or a short-lived production piece (or feasibility item) that never made it into a catalog.

In compiling the terms related to decorated glass above, the authors are particularly indebted to the series of articles by Helen and Robert Jones in "Glass, the Many Ways It's Decorated," in *Glass Collector's Digest.*

BIBLIOGRAPHY AND RESOURCES

FACTORIES, COLLECTORS CLUBS, AND MUSEUMS

Baystate Heisey Collectors Club. www.ziplink.net/users/daberg

Corning Museum of Glass, One Museum Way, Corning, NY 14830-2253. www.cmog.org

Dixieland Heisey Club. www.dixielandheisey.org/sys-tmpl/door

Fostoria Glass Collectors, Inc., P.O. Box 1625, Orange, CA 92856. www.fostoriacollectors.org/. Newsletter: *Glass Works*

Fostoria Glass Society of America, P.O. Box 826, Moundsville, WV 26041. www.fostoriaglass.org/index.htm. Newsletter *Facets of Fostoria*

Fostoria, Ohio Glass Association, 109 N. Main St., Fostoria, Ohio 44830. www.fostoriaglass.com/main.htm

Fry (H. C.) Glass Society, P.O. Box 41, Beaver, PA 15009. rochesterpenn.com/fryglass/index.htm. Newsletter: *The Shards*

Gibson Glass, Amos St., Milton, WV 25541.

Gillinder Glass, Erie and Liberty Streets, Port Jervis, NJ 12771. www.gillinderglass.com

Heisey Club of California. www.heiseyclubca.org. Newsletter: *Pony express.*

Home Interiors and Gifts, Inc., 4550 Spring Valley Rd., Dallas, TX 75244. www.homeinteriors.com

Houze Glass Corporation, 902 S. Main St., Point Marion, PA 15474. www.houze.com/houze.html

Jamestown Glasshouse, Jamestown, VA. www.nps.gov/colo/TEACHERS/SG_Act/Glasshouse.htm

National Capital Heisey Collectors Club and the National Capital Heisey Study Club. www.capitalheiseyclub.org Newsletter: *The Heisey Herald*

National Heisey Glass Museum, 169 W. Church St., Newark, OH 43055. www.heiseymuseum.org. Newsletter: *Heisey News.*

National Imperial Glass Collectors Society, Inc., P.O. Box 534, Bellaire, OH 43908. www.imperialglass.org. Newsletter: *The Imperial Collectors Glasszette.*

National Milk Glass Collectors Society. www.nmgcs.org. Newsletter: *Opaque News.*

West Virginia Museum of American Glass, P.O. Box 574, Weston, WV 26452. members.aol.com/wvmuseumofglass. Newsletter: *The Glory Hole.*

BOOKS AND PERIODICALS

Adams, Walt. "Figural Novelties." (In *Glass Collector's Digest*, Aug./Sept. 1996, p. 82 – 86)

Archer, Margaret & Douglas. *Glass Candlesticks.* Paducah, KY: Collector Books, 1975.

_____. *Glass Candlesticks: Book II.* Paducah, KY: Collector Books, 1977.

_____. *Imperial Glass.* Paducah, KY: Collector Books, 1978.

_____. *The Collector's Encyclopedia of Glass Candlesticks.* Paducah, KY: Collector Books, 1983.

Barlow, Raymond E. & Joan E. Kaiser. *The Glass Industry in Sandwich, Vol. 3.* Windham, NH: Barlow-Kaiser Pub. Co., 1987.

Birkinbine, Mandi. "Amber Sandwich Glass by Tiara." www.enclopedia.netnz.com/ glass/ambertiara.htm

_____. *Collecting Tiara Amber Sandwich Glass.* Meridian, ID: Birkinbine, 2001.

_____. *Collecting Tiara Bicentennial Blue Sandwich Glass.* Meridian, ID: Birkinbine, 2001.

_____. *Collecting Tiara Chantilly Green Sandwich Glass.* Meridian, ID: Birkinbine, 2001.

Bond, Marcelle. *The Beauty of Albany Glass (1893 to 1902)* Berne, Ind.: Publishers Print. House, 1972.

Bones, Frances. *Fostoria Glassware, 1887 – 1982.* Paducah, KY: Collector Books, 1999.

Bredehoft, Neila & Tom. *Fifty Years of Collectible Glass, 1920 – 1970, Vol. 1.* Dubuque, IA: Antique Trader Books, 1997.

_____. *Handbook of Heisey Production Cuttings.* St. Louisville, OH: Cherry Hill Publications, 1991.

_____. *Heisey Glass, 1896 – 1957.* Paducah, KY: Collector Books, 2001.

_____. *Hobbs, Brockunier & Co., Glass.* Paducah, KY: Collector Books, 1997.

Bredehoft, Neila. *The Collector's Encyclopedia of Heisey Glass, 1925 – 1938.* Paducah, KY: Collector Books, 1986.

Brenner, Robert. *Depression Glass for Collectors.* Atglen, PA: Schiffer Pub., 1998.

Burkholder, John R. & D. Thomas O'Connor. *Kemple Glass, 1945 – 1970.* Marietta, OH: Glass Press, 1997.

Burns, Carl O. *Imperial Carnival Glass.* Paducah, KY: Collector Books, 1996.

Chiarenza, Frank & James Slater. *The Milk Glass Book.* Atglen, PA: Schiffer Pub., 1998.

Coward, Mary. *Altaglass: a Guide for Collectors.* Edmonton, Can.: Coward, 1999.

DeAngelo, Constance. "Recollection by Indiana." (In *The National Journal*, Feb. 1982, p. 22)

Doty, David. *David Doty's A Field Guide to Carnival Glass.* Marietta, OH: Glass Press, 1998.

Doub, Kathy. "Shirley Temple and Candlewick??" (In *The Imperial Collectors Glasszette*, Jan. 2000, p. 14 – 15.)

Edwards, Bill & Mike Carwile. *Standard Encyclopedia of Carnival Glass, 6th Ed.* Paducah, KY: Collector Books, 1998.

Eige, Eason. *A Century of Glassmaking in West Virginia: Exhibition, June 8 – September 1, 1980*. Huntington, WV: Huntington Galleries, 1980.

Farrar, Estelle Sinclaire. *H. P. Sinclair, Jr., Glassmaker, Vol. 1*. Garden City, N.Y.: Farrar Books, 1974.

Felt, Tom & Bob O'Grady. *Heisey Candlesticks, Candelabra and Lamps*. Newark, OH: Heisey Collectors of America, 1984.

Felt, Tom. "Heisey Candlesticks: #1540 Lariat, a Previously Unknown Candlestick." (In *Heisey News*, October 1990, p. 12 – 13)

_____. *A. H. Heisey & Company: a Brief History*. Newark, OH: Heisey Collectors of America, 1996.

_____. *Heisey's Lariat & Athena Patterns*. Newark, OH: Heisey Collectors of America, 1986.

Florence, Gene. *Collectible Glassware from the 40s, 50s, 60s, 4th Ed*. Paducah, KY: Collector Books, 1998.

_____. *Collectors Encyclopedia of Depression Glass, 14th Ed*. Paducah, KY: Collector Books, 2000.

_____. *Glass Candlesticks of the Depression Era*. Paducah, KY: Collector Books, 2000.

Fry (H. C.) Glass Society. *The Collector's Encyclopedia of Fry Glassware*. Paducah, KY: Collector Books, 1990.

Garmon, Lee & Dick Spencer. *Glass Animals of the Depression Era*. Paducah, KY: Collector Books, 1993.

Garmon, Lee. "Cathay Crystal: a Jewel for Imperial's Crown." (In *Glass Collector's Digest*, Apr./May 1990, p. 58 – 62.)

Garrison, Myrna & Bob. *Imperial Cape Cod: Tradition to Treasure*. Arlington, TX: Collector's Loot, 1982.

_____. *Imperial's Candlewick: Little Known Facts*. Arlington, TX: Garrison, 1999.

_____. *Imperial's Vintage Milk Glass, 1st Ed*. Arlington, TX: Collector's Loot, 1992.

_____. *Milk Glass: Imperial Glass Corporation, plus Opaque, Slag, and More*. Atglen, PA: Schiffer Pub., 2001.

Glass Factory Year Book Directory, 1944 ed. Pittsburgh: American Glass Review, 1944.

Grizel, Ruth Ann. *A Pocket Guide to Imperial Slag*. Iowa City, IA: FSJ Pub. Co., 1991.

_____. *The Collector's Guide to Lesser Known Modern Milk Glass*. Iowa City, IA: FSJ Pub. Co., 1996.

_____. *Westmoreland Glass: Our Children's Heirlooms*. Iowa City, IA: FSJ Pub. Co., 1993.

Heacock, William, James Measell & Berry Wiggins. *Dugan/Diamond*. Marietta, OH: Antique Publications, 1993.

_____. "Czechoslovakian Glass by Josef Inwald A.G., Prague, Czechoslovakia, circa 1925 – 1935," pt. 1. (In *Collecting Glass*, vol. 2, p. 83 – 95.)

_____. "Religious Figures in Glass." (In *Glass Collector's Digest*, June/July 1987, p. 80 – 91.)

Hemminger, Ruth, Ed Goshe, Leslie Pina. *Tiffin Glass, 1940 – 1980: Figurals, Paperweights, Pressed Ware*. Atglen, PA: Schiffer Pub., 2001.

Higby, Lola & Wayne. *Bryce, Higbee and J. B. Higbee Glass*. Marietta, OH: Glass Press, 1998.

Innes, Lowell. *Pittsburgh Glass, 1797 – 1891: a History and Guide for Collectors*. Boston: Houghton Mifflin Co., 1976.

Iwen, Marg. "Indiana Glass." (In *Glass Collector's Digest*, Dec./Jan. 1995, p. 42 – 54.)

Jones, Helen & Bob. "Glass: the Many Ways it's Decorated." (In *Glass Collector's Digest*, Dec. – Jan. 2000, p. 38 – 47; Feb. – Mar. 2000, p. 63 – 70; Apr. – May 2000, p. 42 – 47; June – July 2000, p. 34 – 42.)

Jones, Jim & Vince Sparacio. *Heisey's Classic "Ridgeleigh" Glassware*. Newark, OH: Heisey Collectors of America, 1987.

Kerr, Ann. *Fostoria: an Identification and Value Guide of Pressed, Blown & Hand Molded Shapes*. Paducah, KY: Collector Books, 1994.

_____. *Fostoria: Vol. II, Identification and Value Guide to Etched, Carved & Cut Designs*. Paducah, KY: Collector Books, 1997.

Koch, Nora. "Jeannette Glass Company." (In *The Daze*, Nov. 1985, p. 60.)

Kolb, Willard. "The 'New' Imperial Candlewick Line Introduced at the 1936 Wheeling Centennial." (In *The Imperial Collectors Glasszette*, Oct. 1993, p. 6 – 9.)

Kovar, Lorraine. *Westmoreland Glass, 1950 – 1984*. Marietta, OH: Antique Publications, 1991.

Lafferty, James R. *Peart Art Glass: Foval*. [S.l.]: Lafferty, 1967.

Lechler, Doris Anderson. *Children's Glass Dishes, China, and Furniture, Vol. II*. Paducah, KY: Collector Books, 1986.

_____. *Children's Glass Dishes, China, and Furniture*. Paducah, KY: Collector Books, 1983. 1967.

_____. *Toy Glass*. Marietta, OH: Antique Publications, 1989.

Lehner, Lois. *Ohio Pottery and Glass Marks and Manufacturers*. Des Moines, IA: Wallace-Homestead Books, 1978.

Long, Milbra & Emily Seate. *Fostoria Tableware, 1924 – 1943: the Crystal for America*. Paducah, KY: Collector Books, 1999.

_____. *Fostoria Tableware, 1944 – 1986: the Crystal for America*. Paducah, KY: Collector Books, 1999.

_____. *Fostoria, Useful and Ornamental: the Crystal for America*. Paducah, KY: Collector Books, 2000.

Long, Milbra. "Fostoria Colors after 1950." (In *The Daze*, March 1993, p. 5.)

_____. "Fostoria Hurricane and Candle Lamps." (In *Glass Collectors' Digest*, Feb./Mar. 1996, p. 75 – 78)

_____. "Fostoria Remembered at Christmas." (In *Glass Collector's Digest*, Dec./Jan. 1990, p. 56 – 58.)

Madeley, John & Dave Shetlar. *American Iridescent Stretch Glass*. Paducah, KY: Collector Books, 1998.

Mauzy, Barbara & Jim. *Mauzy's Depression Glass, 2nd Ed*. Atglen, PA: Schiffer Pub., 2001.

McGrain, Patrick. *Fostoria – the Popular Years*. Frederick, MD: McGrain Publications, n.d.

McKearin, George S. & Helen. *American Glass*. New York: Crown Publishers, 1948.

Measell, James & Berry Wiggins. *Great American Glass of the Roaring 20s & Depression Era, Book 2*. Mariett, OH: Glass Press, 2000.

_____. *Great American Glass of the Roaring 20s & Depression Era*. Marietta, OH: Glass Press, 1998.

Measell, James & W. C. "Red" Roetteis. *The L. G. Wright Glass Company*. Marietta, OH: Glass Press, 1997.

Measell, James, editor. *Imperial Glass Encyclopedia*, vol. I. Marietta, OH: Glass Press, 1995.

_____. *Imperial Glass Encyclopedia*, vol. II. Marietta, OH: Glass Press, 1997.

_____. *Imperial Glass Encyclopedia*, vol. III. Marietta, OH: Glass Press, 1999.

Miller, C. L. *Depression Era Dime Store Glass*. Atglen, PA: Schiffer Pub., 1999.

Newark Heisey Collectors Club. *Heisey by Imperial, 2nd Ed*. Newark, OH: Heisey Collectors of America, 1982.

Newbound, Betty & Bill. *Collector's Encyclopedia of Milk Glass*. Paducah, KY: Collector Books, 1995.

Newbound, Betty. "Children's Dishes by Westmoreland." (In *Glass Collector's Digest*, June/July 1997, p. 30 – 36)

Newman, Harold. *An Illustrated Dictionary of Glass*. London: Thames and Hudson, 1977.

Page, Bob, Dale Frederiksen & Dean Six. *Noritake, Jewel of the Orient*. Greensboro, NC: Replacements, 2001.

Pendergrass, Paula & Sherry Riggs. *Glass Candleholders: Art Nouveau, Art Deco, Depression Era, Modern*. Atglen, PA: Schiffer Pub., 2000.

Peterson, Arthur G. *400 Trademarks on Glass*. DeBary, FL: Peterson, 1971.

Pina, Leslie. *Crackle Glass Too: 1950s – 2000*. Atglen, PA: Schiffer Pub., 2001.

_____. *Crackle Glass in Color: Depression to '70s*. Atglen, PA: Schiffer Pub., 2000.

_____. *Fostoria American: Line 2056*. Atglen, PA: Schiffer Pub., 1999.

_____. *Fostoria Designer George Sakier*. Atglen, PA: Schiffer Pub., 1996.

_____. *Fostoria: Serving the American Table, 1887 – 1986*. Atglen, PA: Schiffer Pub., 1995.

Racheter, Richard G. "Imperial's Tradition: the Colorful Third in the Trio." (In *Glass Collector's Digest*, Apr./May 2001, p 57 – 64.)

Ream, Louise, Neila M. Bredehoft & Thomas H. Bredehoft. *Encyclopedia of Heisey Glassware, Vol. 1, Etchings and Carvings*. Newark, OH: Heisey Collectors of America, 1977.

Revi, Albert Christian. "Fostoria's Opal Glass Dresser Sets." (In *Facets of Fostoria*, Mar. 1988, p. 7, reprinted from *Spinning Wheel*, Jan. – Feb. 1971.)

_____. *American Art Nouveau Glass*. Exton, PA: Schiffer Pub., 1968.

_____. *American Pressed Glass and Figure Bottles*. Nashville: T. Nelson, 1964.

Riggs, Sherry & Paula Pendergrass. *Twentieth Century Glass Candle Holders: Roaring 20s, Depression Era & Modern Collectible Candle Holders*. Atglen, PA: Schiffer Pub., 1999.

Roller, Dick, compiler. *Indiana Glass Factories Notes*. Paris, IL: Acorn Press, 1994.

Schroy, Ellen T. *Warman's Depression Glass*. Iola, WI: Krause Publications, 1997.

Seligson, Sidney P. *Fostoria American, a Complete Guide, 3rd Ed*. Wichita Falls, TX: Seligson, 1997.

Six, Dean. *West Virginia Glass Between the World Wars*. Atglen, PA: Schiffer Pub., 2002.

Smith, Shirley. *Glass Hens on Nest: Covered Animal Dishes*. Published online: home.ntelos.net/~smithsa/.

Snyder, Jeffrey B. *Morgantown Glass: from Depression Glass through the 1960s*. Atglen, PA: Schiffer Pub., 1998.

Stillwagner, Pat. "Paden City: Hidden Lines and Rare Pieces." (In *Glass Collector's Digest*, Apr. – May 2000, p. 31 – 36 & editor's note, June – July 2000, p. 4 – 5.)

Stinson, Ronald & Sunny. *Coin Glass: Handcrafted by Fostoria, 1958 – 1982*. San Angelo, TX: Stinson, 1988.

Stout, Sandra McPhee. *Depression Glass III*. Des Moines: Wallace-Homestead Book Co., 1976.

_____. *The Complete book of McKee Glass*. North Kansas City: Trojan Press, 1972.

Taylor, Dorothy. *Encore by Dorothy, Book I*. Kansas City, MO: Taylor, 1979.

_____. *Encore by Dorothy, Book II*. Kansas City, MO: Taylor, 1979.

Teal, Ron, Sr. *Tiara Exclusives: Company Catalog Reprints*. Marietta, OH: Glass Press, 2000.

Thompson, Donald C. *Houze Glass*. CD-ROM. [S.l.]: Thompson, 2001.

Tiara Exclusives. *Tiara Exclusives Product Information Manual*, revision 1/95. Dunkirk, IN: Tiara Exclusives, 1995.

Vizvarie, Chris. "Fry Threaded Glass." (In *Glass Collector's Digest*, Feb. – Mar. 1998, p. 83 – 86.)

Vogel, Clarence. "Whimsey Cube." (In *The Heisey Glass Newscaster*, autumn 1980, p. 10.)

Ward, Jessie Moser. "Who is Houze?" (In *Glass Collector's Digest*, Feb. – Mar. 1995, p. 40 – 46.)

Weatherman, Hazel Marie. *Colored Glassware of the Depression Era 2*. Springfield, MO: Weatherman Glassbooks, 1974.

_____. *Fostoria, Its First Fifty Years*. Springfield, MO: The Weathermans, 1972.

Weitman, Stan & Arlene. *Crackle Glass, Book II*. Paducah, KY: Collector Books, 1998.

Wetzel, Mary M. *Candlewick, the Jewel of Imperial*. Marceline, MO: Walsworth Pub. Co., 1990.

Wetzel-Tomalka, Mary M. *Candlewick, the Jewel of Imperial*. Bk. 2. Marceline, MO: Walsworth Pub. Co., 1995.

_____. *Candlewick, the Jewel of Imperial*. Notre Dame, IN: Wetzel-Tomalka, 1998.

Whitmyer, Margaret & Kenn. *Children's Dishes*. Paducah, KY: Collector Books, 1984.

Wilson, Jack D. *Phoenix & Consolidated Art Glass, 1926 – 1980*. Marietta, OH: Antique Publications, 1989.

Wilson, Mary Lee. "Imperial's Olde Jamestown." (In *The Imperial Collectors Glasszette*, Oct. 2002, p. 12.)

_____. "The Jamestown Glasshouse Project." (In *The Imperial Collectors Glasszette*, Oct. 2002, p. 10 – 11.)

"WVMAG Seeks Jefferson Glass." (In *The Glory Hole*, fall/winter 2001 – 02, p. 1, etc.)

INDEX

FOSTORIA

FO-1

FO-1A

FO-2

FO-3

No. 6 RIBBONED CANDLE.
Ribbons Assorted Colors.

FO-4

No. 140 HANDLED CANDLE.

FO-5

FO-5A

FO-6

No. 41 Candle.

FO-7

No. 19 Saucer Candle.

FO-8

FO-9

FO-10

FO-11

FO-12

FO-13

FO-14

FO-15

FO-16

FO-17

FO-18

FO-19

No. 1095. 11 inch
Cut top and bottom
$1.26 each

FO-20

FO-21

FO-22

FO-22A

FO-23

FO-24

No. 1612. 5-inch Christmas Candle

FO-25

No. 1029. 6-inch
Deep Etched "D"

FO-26

FO-27

No. 1652. 8-inch

FO-28

No. 969 9 inch
Cut top and bottom
15 cents each

FO-29

FO-30

No. 31 Lustre Candlestick
With Prismatical Prisms
Height 6½ in. Diameter of Bar 4¾ in.
Pair on Illustrated $2.80

FO-31

FO-32

FO-32B

FO-33

FO-33A

FO-34

No. 1963. 8-inch
Deep Etched

FO-35

FO-36

327

FO-37

FO-38

FO-39

FO-40

FO-41

FO-42

FO-44

FO-45

FO-46

FO-47

FO-48

FO-49

FO-50

FO-51

FO-52

FO-53

FO-54

FO-55

FO-56

FO-57A

FO-57B

FO-57C

FO-58

FO-59

FO-60

FO-61

FO-61A

FO-62

FO-63

FO-64

FO-65

FO-66

FO-67

FO-68

FO-69A

FO-70

FO-71

FO-72

FO-73

FO-74

FO-75

FO-76

FO-77   FO-78   FO-79   FO-80   FO-81   FO-82

FO-83   FO-84   FO-85   FO-86   FO-87   FO-88

FO-89   FO-90   FO-91   FO-92   FO-93   FO-94A

FO-94B   FO-94C   FO-95   FO-96   FO-97   FO-98

FO-99   FO-100   FO-101   FO-102   FO-103   FO-104

2510—5½ in. Candlestick

FO-105   FO-106   FO-107   FO-108   FO-109   FO-109A

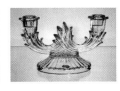

FO-110   FO-110A   FO-111   FO-112   FO-113   FO-114

FO-115

FO-116

FO-117

FO-118

FO-119

FO-120

FO-121

FO-122

FO-123

FO-124

FO-125

FO-126

FO-127

FO-128

FO-129

FO-130

FO-131

FO-132

FO-133

FO-134

FO-135

FO-136

FO-137

FO-138

FO-139

FO-140

FO-141

FO-142

FO-143

FO-144

FO-145

FO-146

FO-147

FO-147A

FO-148

FO-149

FO-150

FO-151

FO-152

FO-153

FO-154

FO-155

FO-156

FO-157

FO-158

FO-159

FO-160

FO-161

FO-162

FO-163

FO-164

FO-165

FO-166

FO-167

FO-168

FO-169

FO-170

FO-171

FO-172

FO-173

FO-174

FO-175

FO-176

FO-177

FO-179

FO-180

FO-181

FO-182

FO-183

FO-184

FO-185

FO-186

FO-187

FO-188

FO-189

FO-190

FO-191

FO-192

FO-193

FO-194

FO-195

FO-196

FO-197

FO-197A

FO-198

FO-199

FO-200

FO-201

318

FO-202

325

FO-203

FO-204

FO-205

FO-206

FO-207

FO-208

2521/327

FO-209

2864/327

FO-210

2883/319

FO-211

317

FO-212

FO-213

FO-214

FO-215

FO-216

FO-217

FO-218

FO-219

FO-220

FO-221

FO-222

FO-223

FO-224

FO-225

FO-226

FO-227

FO-228

FO-229

FO-230

FO-231

FO-232

FO-233

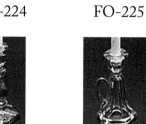

FO-234

FRY

FR-1

FR-2

FR-3

FR-4

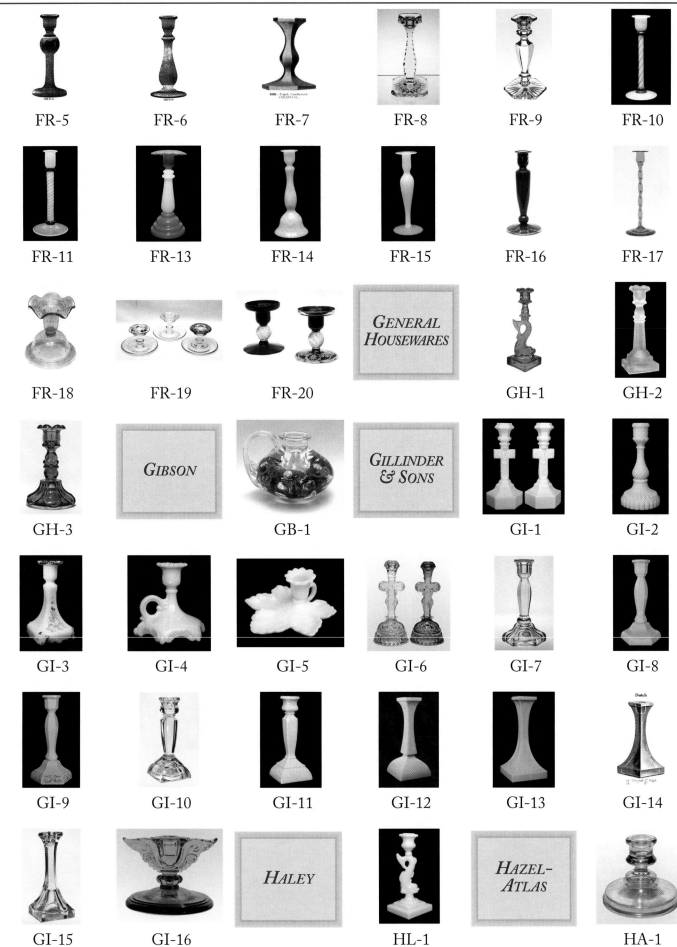

FR-5

FR-6

FR-7

FR-8

FR-9

FR-10

FR-11

FR-13

FR-14

FR-15

FR-16

FR-17

FR-18

FR-19

FR-20

GENERAL HOUSEWARES

GH-1

GH-2

GH-3

GIBSON

GB-1

GILLINDER & SONS

GI-1

GI-2

GI-3

GI-4

GI-5

GI-6

GI-7

GI-8

GI-9

GI-10

GI-11

GI-12

GI-13

GI-14

GI-15

GI-16

HALEY

HL-1

HAZEL-ATLAS

HA-1

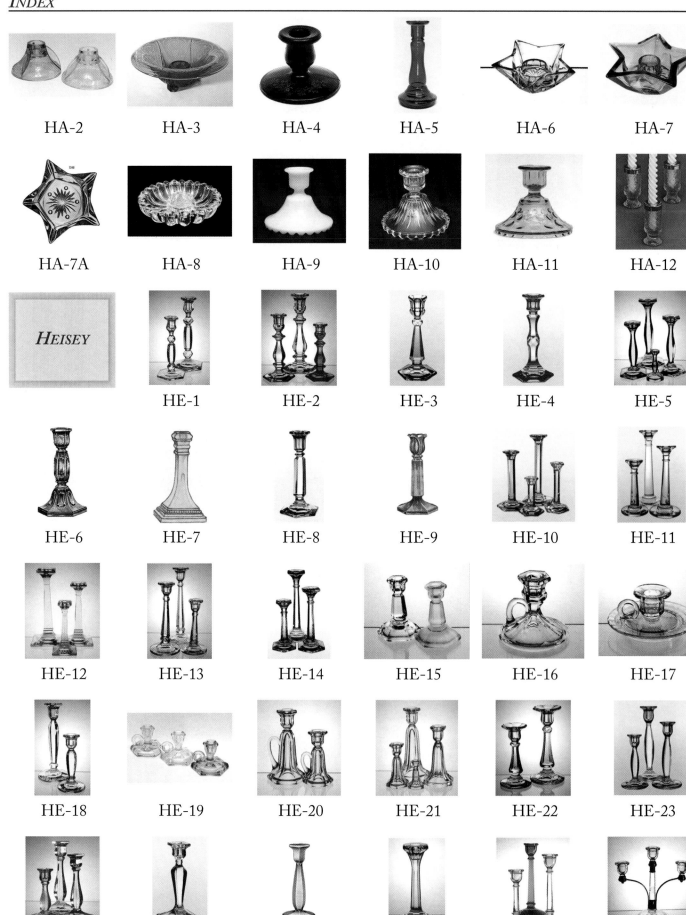

HA-2

HA-3

HA-4

HA-5

HA-6

HA-7

HA-7A

HA-8

HA-9

HA-10

HA-11

HA-12

HEISEY

HE-1

HE-2

HE-3

HE-4

HE-5

HE-6

HE-7

HE-8

HE-9

HE-10

HE-11

HE-12

HE-13

HE-14

HE-15

HE-16

HE-17

HE-18

HE-19

HE-20

HE-21

HE-22

HE-23

HE-24

HE-25

HE-26

HE-27

HE-28

HE-28A

HE-28B HE-29 HE-30 HE-31 HE-32 HE-33

HE-34 HE-35 HE-36 HE-37 HE-38 HE-39

HE-40 HE-41 HE-42 HE-43 HE-44 HE-45

HE-46 HE-47 HE-48 HE-49 HE-50 HE-51

HE-52 HE-53 HE-54 HE-55 HE-56 HE-57

HE-58 HE-59 HE-60 HE-61 HE-62 HE-63

HE-64 HE-65 HE-66 HE-67 HE-68 HE-69

HE-70

HE-71

HE-72

HE-73

HE-74

HE-75

HE-76

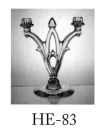

HE-77

HE-78

HE-79

HE-80

HE-81

HE-82

HE-83

HE-84

HE-85

HE-86

HE-87

HE-88

HE-89

HE-90

HE-91

HE-92

HE-93

HE-94

HE-95

HE-96

HE-97

HE-98

HE-99

HE-100

HE-101

HE-102

HE-103

HE-104

HE-105

HE-106

HE-107

HE-108

HE-109

HE-110

HE-111

HE-112

HE-113

HE-114

HE-115

HE-116

HE-117

HE-118

HE-119

HE-120

HE-121

HE-122

HE-123

HE-124

HE-124A

HE-125

HE-126

HE-127

HE-128

HE-129

HE-130

HE-131

HE-132

HE-133

HE-134

HE-135

HE-136

HE-137

HE-138

HE-139

HE-140

HE-141

HE-142

HE-143

HE-144

HE-145

HE-146

HE-147

HE-148

HE-149

HE-150

HE-151

HE-152

337

HE-153

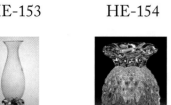

HE-154

HE-155

HE-156

HE-157

HE-158

HE-159

HE-160

HE-161

HE-162

HE-163

HE-164

HE-165

HE-166

HE-167

HE-168

HE-169

HE-170

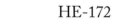

HE-171

HE-172

HE-173

HE-174

HE-175

HE-176

HE-177

HE-178

HE-179

HE-180

HE-181

HE-182

HE-183

HE-184A

HE-185

HE-186

HE-187

HE-188

HE-189

HIGBEE

HI-1

Our New Candlestick—A Corker

HI-2

HI-3

338

HOBBS

HB-1

HB-2

HB-3

HB-4

HB-5

HOME INTERIORS

HO-1

HO-2

HO-3

HO-4

HO-5

HO-6

HO-7

HO-8

HO-9

HOUZE

HZ-1

HZ-2A

HZ-3

HZ-4

HUNTING-TON

HU-1

IMPERIAL

IM-1

IM-2

IM-3

IM-4

IM-5

IM-6

IM-7

IM-8

IM-9A

IM-10

IM-11

IM-12

IM-13

IM-14

IM-15A

IM-16

IM-19

IM-20

IM-21

IM-22

IM-23A

IM-24

IM-25

IM-26

IM-26A

IM-27

IM-28

IM-29

IM-30

IM-31

IM-32

IM-33

IM-34

IM-35

IM-36B

IM-37

IM-38A

IM-39

IM-40

IM-41

IM-42

IM-43

IM-44

IM-45

IM-46

IM-47

IM-48

IM-49

IM-50

IM-51

IM-52

IM-53

IM-54

IM-55

IM-56

IM-57

IM-58

IM-58A

IM-59

IM-60

IM-60A

IM-61

IM-62

IM-63

IM-63A

IM-64

IM-65

IM-66

IM-66A

IM-71

IM-72

IM-73

IM-74

IM-75

IM-76

IM-77

IM-78

IM-79

IM-80

IM-81

IM-82

IM-83

IM-84

IM-85

IM-86

IM-87

IM-88

IM-89

IM-90

IM-91

IM-92

IM-93

IM-94

IM-95

IM-96

IM-97

IM-98

IM-99

IM-100

IM-101

IM-102

IM-103

IM-104

IM-105

IM-106

IM-107

IM-108

IM-109

IM-110

IM-111

IM-112

IM-113

IM-113B

IM-114

IM-115

IM-116

IM-117

IM-118

IM-119

IM-120

IM-121

IM-122

IM-122B

IM-123

IM-124

IM-125A

IM-126

IM-127

IM-128

IM-129

IM-130

IM-131

IM-132-

IM-133

IM-134

IM-135

IM-136

IM-137

IM-138

IM-140

IM-141

IM-144

IM-146

IM-147   IM-148   IM-149   IM-150   IM-151   IM-152

IM-153   IM-154   IM-155   IM-156   IM-157   IM-158

IM-159   IM-160   IM-161   IM-162   IM-163   IM-164

IM-165   IM-166   IM-167   IM-168   IM-169   IM-170

IM-171   IM-172   IM-173   IM-174   IM-175   IM-176

IM-177   IM-178   IM-179   IM-180   IM-181   IM-182

IM-183   IM-184   IM-185   IM-186   IM-187   IM-188

IM-189A

IM-189B

IM-189C

IM-189D

IM-189E

IM-189F

IM-189G

IM-189H

IM-189I

IM-189J

IM-189K

IM-189L

IM-189M

INDIANA

IN-1

IN-2

IN-3

IN-4

IN-5

IN-6

IN-7

IN-8

IN-9

IN-10A

IN-11

IN-12

IN-13

IN-14

IN-15

IN-16

IN-17

IN-17A

IN-18

IN-19

IN-20

IN-21

IN-22

IN-23

IN-24

IN-25

IN-26

IN-27

IN-28 IN-29 IN-30 IN-31 IN-32 IN-33

IN-34 IN-35 IN-36 IN-37 IN-38 IN-39

IN-40 IN-41 IN-42 IN-43 IN-44 IN-45

IN-46 IN-47 IN-48 IN-49 IN-50 IN-51

IN-52 IN-53 IN-54 IN-55 IN-56 IN-57

IN-58 IN-59 IN-60 IN-61 IN-62 IN-63

IN-64 IN-65 IN-66 IN-67 IN-68 IN-69

IN-70

IN-71

IN-72

IN-73

IN-74

IN-75

IN-76

IN-77

IN-78

IN-79

IN-80

IN-81

IN-82

IN-83

IN-84

IN-85

IN-86

IN-87

IN-88

IN-89

IN-90

IN-91

IN-92

IN-93

IN-94

IN-95

IN-96

IN-97

IN-98

IN-99

IN-100

IN-101

IN-102

IN-103

IN-104

IN-105

IN-106

IN-107

IN-108

IN-109

IN-110

IN-111

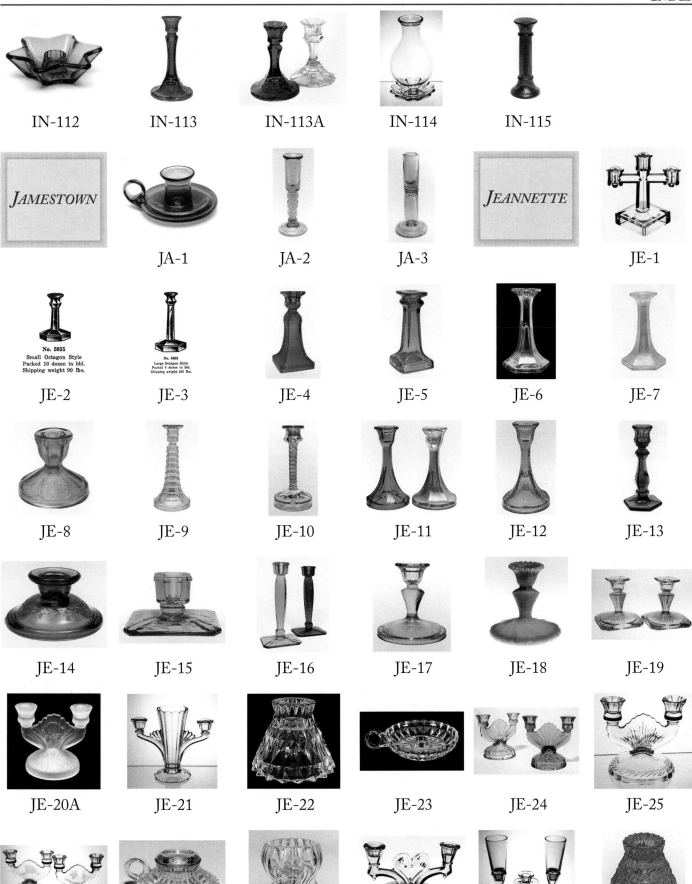

IN-112 IN-113 IN-113A IN-114 IN-115

JAMESTOWN JA-1 JA-2 JA-3 *JEANNETTE* JE-1

JE-2 JE-3 JE-4 JE-5 JE-6 JE-7

JE-8 JE-9 JE-10 JE-11 JE-12 JE-13

JE-14 JE-15 JE-16 JE-17 JE-18 JE-19

JE-20A JE-21 JE-22 JE-23 JE-24 JE-25

JE-026 JE-27 JE-28 JE-29 JE-30 JE-32

JE-33   JE-34   JE-35   JE-36   JE-37   JE-38

JE-39   JE-40   JE-41   *JEFFERSON*   JF-1   JF-2

JF-3   JF-4   JF-5   JF-6   JF-6A   JF-7

JF-8   JF-9

Other volumes of THE GLASS CANDLESTICK BOOK

avaliable from COLLECTOR BOOKS

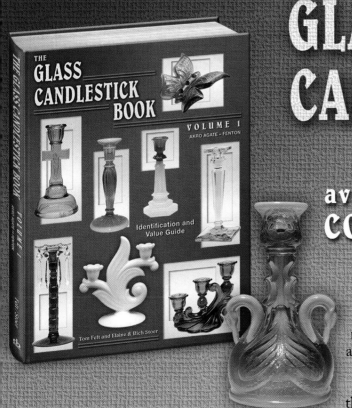

Volume 1 of this series highlights candlesticks made by 33 different American companies, arranged alphabetically from the Akro Agate Company to the Fenton Art Glass Company, including Cambridge, Duncan, and many more. The book features more than 620 candlesticks with over 500 color photographs and over 220 reprints from old trade journals and advertisements. A well-illustrated appendix on identifying dolphin candlesticks is included in this volume.

Volume 3 begins with the Kanawha Glass Company and ends with Wright Glass. Over 40 companies are represented in this final volume, including Morgantown, New Martinsville, Northwood, Paden City, U.S. Glass, and Westmoreland. Once again, a plethora of photographs appears, this time exceeding 900, as well as more catalog reprints and trade advertisments that collectors are sure to enjoy. Detailed information on identifying crucifix candlesticks is included in the appendix.

Each chapter of both volumes includes a history of the factory and information about production colors and trademarks used. Every candlestick is described with dimensions, production dates, known colors, information on reissues and reproductions, the current location of the mold, as well as current values. A glossary and an extensive bibliography round out both books. Each features an illustrated index which includes thumbnail photographs of all the candlesticks in the book.

With this three-volume set, collectors will own the most complete reference work ever done on the subject. Other books on the subject don't hold a candle to this series!

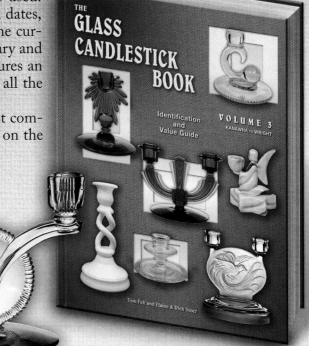

COLLECTOR BOOKS
P.O. Box 3009
Paducah, KY 42002–3009
www.collectorbooks.com

COLLECTOR BOOKS
informing today's collector

www.collectorbooks.com

For over two decades we have been keeping collectors informed on trends and values in all fields of antiques and collectibles.

DOLLS, FIGURES & TEDDY BEARS

4631	**Barbie Doll** Boom, 1986–1995, Augustyniak	$18.95
2079	**Barbie Doll** Fashion, Volume I, Eames	$24.95
4846	**Barbie Doll** Fashion, Volume II, Eames	$24.95
3957	**Barbie** Exclusives, Rana	$18.95
4632	**Barbie** Exclusives, Book II, Rana	$18.95
6022	The **Barbie Doll** Years, 5th Ed., Olds	$19.95
3810	**Chatty Cathy** Dolls, Lewis	$15.95
5352	Collector's Ency. of **Barbie** Doll Exclusives & More, 2nd Ed., Augustyniak	$24.95
4863	Collector's Encyclopedia of **Vogue Dolls**, Izen/Stover	$29.95
5904	Collector's Guide to **Celebrity Dolls**, Spurgeon	$24.95
5599	Collector's Guide to **Dolls of the 1960s and 1970s**, Sabulis	$24.95
6030	Collector's Guide to **Horsman Dolls**, Jensen	$29.95
6025	**Doll Values**, Antique to Modern, 6th Ed., Moyer	$12.95
6033	**Modern Collectible Dolls**, Volume VI, Moyer	$24.95
5689	**Nippon Dolls** & Playthings, Van Patten/Lau	$29.95
5365	**Peanuts Collectibles**, Podley/Bang	$24.95
6026	**Small Dolls of the 40s & 50s**, Stover	$29.95
5253	Story of **Barbie**, 2nd Ed., Westenhouser	$24.95
5277	**Talking Toys** of the 20th Century, Lewis	$15.95
2084	**Teddy Bears, Annalee's & Steiff** Animals, 3rd Series, Mandel	$19.95
1808	Wonder of **Barbie**, Manos	$9.95
1430	World of **Barbie** Dolls, Manos	$9.95
4880	World of **Raggedy Ann** Collectibles, Avery	$24.95

TOYS & MARBLES

2333	Antique & Collectible **Marbles**, 3rd Ed., Grist	$9.95
4559	Collectible **Action Figures**, 2nd Ed., Manos	$17.95
5900	Collector's Guide to **Battery Toys**, 2nd Edition, Hultzman	$24.95
4566	Collector's Guide to **Tootsietoys**, 2nd Ed., Richter	$19.95
5169	Collector's Guide to **TV Toys** & Memorabilia, 2nd Ed., Davis/Morgan	$24.95
5593	Grist's Big Book of **Marbles**, 2nd Ed.	$24.95
3970	Grist's Machine-Made & Contemporary **Marbles**, 2nd Ed.	$9.95
5267	**Matchbox Toys**, 1947 to 1998, 3rd Ed., Johnson	$19.95
5830	**McDonald's** Collectibles, 2nd Edition, Henriques/DuVall	$24.95
5673	Modern **Candy Containers** & Novelties, Brush/Miller	$19.95
1540	Modern **Toys** 1930–1980, Baker	$19.95
5920	**Schroeder's Collectible Toys**, Antique to Modern Price Guide, 8th Ed.	$17.95
5908	**Toy Car** Collector's Guide, Johnson	$19.95

FURNITURE

3716	American **Oak** Furniture, Book II, McNerney	$12.95
1118	Antique **Oak** Furniture, Hill	$7.95
3720	Collector's Encyclopedia of **American** Furniture, Vol. III, Swedberg	$24.95
5359	Early **American** Furniture, Obbard	$12.95
3906	**Heywood-Wakefield** Modern Furniture, Rouland	$18.95
1885	**Victorian** Furniture, Our American Heritage, McNerney	$9.95
3829	**Victorian** Furniture, Our American Heritage, Book II, McNerney	$9.95

JEWELRY, HATPINS, WATCHES & PURSES

4704	Antique & Collectible **Buttons**, Wisniewski	$19.95
1748	Antique **Purses**, Revised Second Ed., Holiner	$19.95
4850	Collectible **Costume Jewelry**, Simonds	$24.95
5675	Collectible **Silver Jewelry**, Rezazadeh	$24.95
3722	Collector's Ency. of **Compacts**, Carryalls & Face Powder Boxes, Mueller	$24.95
4940	**Costume Jewelry**, A Practical Handbook & Value Guide, Rezazadeh	$24.95
5812	Fifty Years of Collectible **Fashion Jewelry**, 1925–1975, Baker	$24.95
1424	**Hatpins** & Hatpin Holders, Baker	$9.95
5695	**Ladies' Vintage Accessories**, Bruton	$24.95
1181	100 Years of Collectible **Jewelry**, 1850–1950, Baker	$9.95
4729	**Sewing Tools** & Trinkets, Thompson	$24.95
6038	**Sewing Tools** & Trinkets, Volume 2, Thompson	$24.95
6039	Signed Beauties of **Costume Jewelry**, Brown	$24.95
5620	Unsigned Beauties of **Costume Jewelry**, Brown	$24.95
4878	Vintage & Contemporary **Purse Accessories**, Gerson	$24.95
5696	Vintage & Vogue Ladies' **Compacts**, 2nd Edition, Gerson	$29.95
5923	**Vintage Jewelry** for Investment & Casual Wear, Edeen	$24.95

INDIANS, GUNS, KNIVES, TOOLS, PRIMITIVES

6021	**Arrowheads** of the Central Great Plains, Fox	$19.95
1868	Antique **Tools**, Our American Heritage, McNerney	$9.95
5616	Big Book of **Pocket Knives**, Stewart	$19.95
4943	Field Guide to Flint **Arrowheads** & Knives of the North American Indian	$9.95
3885	**Indian Artifacts** of the Midwest, Book II, Hothem	$16.95
4870	**Indian Artifacts** of the Midwest, Book III, Hothem	$18.95
5685	**Indian Artifacts** of the Midwest, Book IV, Hothem	$19.95
6132	**Modern Guns**, Identification & Values, 14th Ed., Quertermous	$14.95
2164	**Primitives**, Our American Heritage, McNerney	$9.95
1759	**Primitives**, Our American Heritage, 2nd Series, McNerney	$14.95
6031	Standard **Knife** Collector's Guide, 4th Ed., Ritchie & Stewart	$14.95
5999	**Wilderness** Survivor's Guide, Hamper	$12.95

PAPER COLLECTIBLES & BOOKS

4633	**Big Little Books**, Jacobs	$18.95
5902	**Boys' & Girls' Book** Series	$19.95
4710	Collector's Guide to **Children's Books**, 1850 to 1950, Volume I, Jones	$18.95
5153	Collector's Guide to **Chldren's Books**, 1850 to 1950, Volume II, Jones	$19.95
1441	Collector's Guide to **Post Cards**, Wood	$9.95
5926	**Duck Stamps**, Chappell	$9.95
2081	Guide to Collecting **Cookbooks**, Allen	$14.95
2080	Price Guide to **Cookbooks** & Recipe Leaflets, Dickinson	$9.95
3973	**Sheet Music** Reference & Price Guide, 2nd Ed., Pafik & Guiheen	$19.95
6041	Vintage **Postcards for the Holidays**, Reed	$24.95
4733	**Whitman Juvenile Books**, Brown	$17.95

GLASSWARE

5602	Anchor Hocking's **Fire-King** & More, 2nd Ed.	$24.95
5823	Collectible **Glass Shoes**, 2nd Edition, Wheatley	$24.95
5897	Coll. **Glassware** from the 40s, 50s & 60s, 6th Ed., Florence	$19.95
1810	Collector's Encyclopedia of **American Art Glass**, Shuman	$29.95
5907	Collector's Encyclopedia of **Depression Glass**, 15th Ed., Florence	$19.95
1961	Collector's Encyclopedia of **Fry Glassware**, Fry Glass Society	$24.95
1664	Collector's Encyclopedia of **Heisey Glass**, 1925–1938, Bredehoft	$24.95
3905	Collector's Encyclopedia of **Milk Glass**, Newbound	$24.95
4936	Collector's Guide to **Candy Containers**, Dezso/Poirier	$19.95
5820	Collector's Guide to **Glass Banks**, Reynolds	$24.95
4564	**Crackle Glass**, Weitman	$19.95
4941	**Crackle Glass**, Book II, Weitman	$19.95
4714	**Czechoslovakian Glass** and Collectibles, Book II, Barta/Rose	$16.95
5528	Early American **Pattern Glass**, Metz	$17.95
6125	**Elegant Glassware** of the Depression Era, 10th Ed., Florence	$24.95
3981	Evers' Standard **Cut Glass** Value Guide	$12.95
5614	Field Guide to **Pattern Glass**, McCain	$17.95
5615	Florence's **Glassware Pattern Identification** Guide, Vol. II	$19.95

19	**Fostoria**, Etched, Carved & Cut Designs, Vol. II, Kerr	$24.95
61	**Fostoria Tableware**, 1924 – 1943, Long/Seate	$24.95
61	**Fostoria Tableware**, 1944 – 1986, Long/Seate	$24.95
04	**Fostoria**, Useful & Ornamental, Long/Seate	$29.95
99	**Glass & Ceramic Baskets**, White	$19.95
44	**Imperial Carnival Glass**, Burns	$18.95
27	**Kitchen Glassware** of the Depression Years, 6th Ed., Florence	$24.95
00	Much More Early American **Pattern Glass**, Metz	$17.95
15	**Northwood Carnival Glass**, 1908 – 1925, Burns	$19.95
36	Pocket Guide to **Depression Glass**, 13th Ed., Florence	$12.95
23	Standard Encyclopedia of **Carnival Glass**, 8th Ed., Edwards/Carwile	$29.95
24	Standard **Carnival Glass** Price Guide, 13th Ed., Edwards/Carwile	$9.95
35	Standard Encyclopedia of **Opalescent Glass**, 4th Ed., Edwards/Carwile	$24.95
32	**Very Rare Glassware** of the Depression Years, 5th Series, Florence	$24.95

POTTERY

27	**ABC Plates & Mugs**, Lindsay	$24.95
29	**American Art Pottery**, Sigafoose	$24.95
30	**American Limoges**, Limoges	$24.95
12	**Blue & White Stoneware**, McNerney	$9.95
59	**Blue Willow**, 2nd Ed., Gaston	$14.95
51	Collectible **Cups & Saucers**, Harran	$18.95
73	Collector's Encyclopedia of **American Dinnerware**, Cunningham	$24.95
31	Collector's Encyclopedia of **Bauer Pottery**, Chipman	$24.95
34	Collector's Encyclopedia of **California Pottery**, 2nd Ed., Chipman	$24.95
23	Collector's Encyclopedia of **Cookie Jars**, Book I, Roerig	$24.95
39	Collector's Encyclopedia of **Cookie Jars**, Book III, Roerig	$24.95
48	Collector's Encyclopedia of **Fiesta**, 9th Ed., Huxford	$24.95
61	Collector's Encyclopedia of **Early Noritake**, Alden	$24.95
12	Collector's Encyclopedia of **Flow Blue China**, 2nd Ed., Gaston	$24.95
31	Collector's Encyclopedia of **Homer Laughlin China**, Jasper	$24.95
76	Collector's Encyclopedia of **Hull Pottery**, Roberts	$19.95
62	Collector's Encyclopedia of **Lefton China**, DeLozier	$19.95
55	Collector's Encyclopedia of **Lefton China**, Book II, DeLozier	$19.95
09	Collector's Encyclopedia of **Limoges Porcelain**, 3rd Ed., Gaston	$29.95
34	Collector's Encyclopedia of **Majolica Pottery**, Katz-Marks	$19.95
58	Collector's Encyclopedia of **McCoy Pottery**, Huxford	$19.95
77	Collector's Encyclopedia of **Niloak**, 2nd Edition, Gifford	$29.95
37	Collector's Encyclopedia of **Nippon Porcelain**, Van Patten	$24.95
65	Collector's Ency. of **Nippon Porcelain**, 3rd Series, Van Patten	$24.95
53	Collector's Ency. of **Nippon Porcelain**, 5th Series, Van Patten	$24.95
78	Collector's Ency. of **Nippon Porcelain**, 6th Series, Van Patten	$29.95
47	Collector's Encyclopedia of **Noritake**, Van Patten	$19.95
64	Collector's Encyclopedia of **Pickard China**, Reed	$29.95
79	Collector's Encyclopedia of **Red Wing Art Pottery**, Dollen	$24.95
18	Collector's Encyclopedia of **Rosemeade Pottery**, Dommel	$24.95
41	Collector's Encyclopedia of **Roseville Pottery**, Revised, Huxford/Nickel	$24.95
42	Collector's Encyclopedia of **Roseville Pottery**, 2nd Series, Huxford/Nickel	$24.95
17	Collector's Encyclopedia of **Russel Wright**, 3rd Editon, Kerr	$29.95
70	Collector's Encyclopedia of **Stangl Dinnerware**, Runge	$24.95
21	Collector's Encyclopedia of **Stangl Artware**, Lamps, and Birds, Runge	$29.95
14	Collector's Encyclopedia of **Van Briggle Art Pottery**, Sasicki	$24.95
80	Collector's Guide to **Feather Edge Ware**, McAllister	$19.95
76	Collector's Guide to **Lu-Ray Pastels**, Meehan	$18.95
14	Collector's Guide to **Made in Japan Ceramics**, White	$18.95
46	Collector's Guide to **Made in Japan Ceramics**, Book II, White	$18.95
25	**Cookie Jars**, Westfall	$9.95
40	**Cookie Jars**, Book II, Westfall	$19.95
09	**Dresden Porcelain** Studios, Harran	$29.95
18	Florence's Big Book of **Salt & Pepper Shakers**	$24.95

2379	Lehner's Ency. of **U.S. Marks** on Pottery, Porcelain & China	$24.95
4722	**McCoy Pottery**, Collector's Reference & Value Guide, Hanson/Nissen	$19.95
5913	**McCoy Pottery**, Volume III, Hanson & Nissen	$24.95
5691	**Post86 Fiesta**, Identification & Value Guide, Racheter	$19.95
1670	**Red Wing Collectibles**, DePasquale	$9.95
1440	**Red Wing Stoneware**, DePasquale	$9.95
6037	**Rookwood Pottery,** Nicholson & Thomas	$24.95
1632	**Salt & Pepper Shakers**, Guarnaccia	$9.95
5091	**Salt & Pepper Shakers** II, Guarnaccia	$18.95
3443	**Salt & Pepper Shakers** IV, Guarnaccia	$18.95
3738	**Shawnee Pottery**, Mangus	$24.95
4629	Turn of the Century **American Dinnerware**, 1880s–1920s, Jasper	$24.95
3327	**Watt Pottery** – Identification & Value Guide, Morris	$19.95
5924	**Zanesville Stoneware** Company, Rans, Ralston & Russell	$24.95

OTHER COLLECTIBLES

5916	Advertising **Paperweights**, Holiner & Kammerman	$24.95
5838	Advertising **Thermometers**, Merritt	$16.95
5898	Antique & Contemporary **Advertising Memorabilia**, Summers	$24.95
5814	Antique **Brass & Copper** Collectibles, Gaston	$24.95
1880	Antique **Iron**, McNerney	$9.95
3872	Antique **Tins**, Dodge	$24.95
4845	Antique **Typewriters & Office Collectibles**, Rehr	$19.95
5607	Antiquing and Collecting on the **Internet**, Parry	$12.95
1128	**Bottle** Pricing Guide, 3rd Ed., Cleveland	$7.95
3718	Collectible **Aluminum**, Grist	$16.95
5060	Collectible **Souvenir Spoons**, Bednersh	$19.95
5676	Collectible **Souvenir Spoons**, Book II, Bednersh	$29.95
5666	Collector's Encyclopedia of **Granite Ware**, Book 2, Greguire	$29.95
5836	Collector's Guide to **Antique Radios**, 5th Ed., Bunis	$19.95
3966	Collector's Guide to **Inkwells**, Identification & Values, Badders	$18.95
4947	Collector's Guide to **Inkwells**, Book II, Badders	$19.95
5681	Collector's Guide to **Lunchboxes**, White	$19.95
5621	Collector's Guide to **Online Auctions**, Hix	$12.95
4864	Collector's Guide to **Wallace Nutting Pictures**, Ivankovich	$18.95
5683	**Fishing Lure** Collectibles, Vol. 1, Murphy/Edmisten	$29.95
5911	**Flea Market Trader**, 13th Ed., Huxford	$9.95
6227	**Garage Sale** & Flea Market Annual, 11th Edition, Huxford	$19.95
4945	**G-Men and FBI Toys** and Collectibles, Whitworth	$18.95
3819	**General Store** Collectibles, Wilson	$24.95
5912	The **Heddon** Legacy, A Century of Classic **Lures**, Roberts & Pavey	$29.95
2216	**Kitchen Antiques**, 1790–1940, McNerney	$14.95
5991	**Lighting Devices** & Accessories of the 17th – 19th Centuries, Hamper	$9.95
5686	**Lighting Fixtures** of the Depression Era, Book I, Thomas	$24.95
4950	The **Lone Ranger**, Collector's Reference & Value Guide, Felbinger	$18.95
6028	Modern **Fishing Lure** Collectibles, Vol. 1, Lewis	$24.95
6131	Modern **Fishing Lure** Collectibles, Vol. 2, Lewis	$24.95
2026	**Railroad** Collectibles, 4th Ed., Baker	$14.95
5619	**Roy Rogers and Dale Evans** Toys & Memorabilia, Coyle	$24.95
6137	**Schroeder's Antiques** Price Guide, 21st Edition	$14.95
5007	**Silverplated Flatware**, Revised 4th Edition, Hagan	$18.95
6239	**Star Wars** Super Collector's Wish Book, 2nd Ed., Carlton	$29.95
6139	Summers' Guide to **Coca-Cola**, 4th Ed.	$24.95
5905	Summers' Pocket Guide to **Coca-Cola**, 3rd Ed.	$12.95
3977	Value Guide to **Gas Station Memorabilia**, Summers & Priddy	$24.95
4877	Vintage **Bar Ware**, Visakay	$24.95
5925	The Vintage Era of **Golf Club Collectibles**, John	$29.95
6010	The Vintage Era of **Golf Club Collectibles** Collector's Log, John	$9.95
6036	Vintage **Quilts**, Aug, Newman & Roy	$24.95
4935	The W.F. Cody **Buffalo Bill** Collector's Guide with Values	$24.95

This is only a partial listing of the books on antiques that are available from Collector Books. All books are well illustrated and contain current values. Most of these books are available from your local bookseller, antique dealer, or public library. If you are unable to locate certain titles in your area, you may order by mail from **COLLECTOR BOOKS**, P.O. Box 3009, Paducah, KY 42002-3009. Customers with Visa, Master Card, or Discover may phone in orders from 00–5:00 CT, Monday–Friday, Toll Free **1-800-626-5420**, or online at **www.collectorbooks.com**. Add $3.00 for postage for the first book ordered and 50¢ for each additional book. Include item number, title, and price when ordering. Allow 14 to 21 days for delivery.

1-800-626-5420   Fax: 1-270-898-8890

www.collectorbooks.com

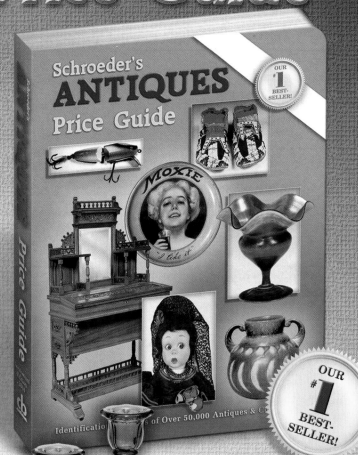